MAKING SENSE OF AN HISTORIC LANDSCAPE

Making Sense of an Historic Landscape

STEPHEN RIPPON

OXFORD
UNIVERSITY PRESS

OXFORD
UNIVERSITY PRESS

Great Clarendon Street, Oxford, OX2 6DP,
United Kingdom

Oxford University Press is a department of the University of Oxford.
It furthers the University's objective of excellence in research, scholarship,
and education by publishing worldwide. Oxford is a registered trade mark of
Oxford University Press in the UK and in certain other countries

© Stephen Rippon 2012

The moral rights of the author have been asserted

First Edition published in 2012

Impression: 1

All rights reserved. No part of this publication may be reproduced, stored in
a retrieval system, or transmitted, in any form or by any means, without the
prior permission in writing of Oxford University Press, or as expressly permitted
by law, by licence or under terms agreed with the appropriate reprographics
rights organization. Enquiries concerning reproduction outside the scope of the
above should be sent to the Rights Department, Oxford University Press, at the
address above

You must not circulate this work in any other form
and you must impose this same condition on any acquirer

British Library Cataloguing in Publication Data

Data available

Library of Congress Cataloging in Publication Data

Library of Congress Control Number: 2012930497

ISBN 978–0–19–953378–7

Printed in Great Britain by
MPG Books Group, Bodmin and King's Lynn

Links to third party websites are provided by Oxford in good faith and
for information only. Oxford disclaims any responsibility for the materials
contained in any third party website referenced in this work.

Preface and Acknowledgements

This book reflects ideas that have been slowly gestating for many years. My work in this region began in 2001–2 with a major Leverhulme Trust-funded project to examine palaeoenvironmental sequences that covered the Roman period through to the present day in South West Britain (Rippon, Fyfe, and Brown 2006). This interdisciplinary project involved myself and two physical geographers—Tony Brown and Ralph Fyfe—both of whom have a strong archaeological background and which opened my eyes to the opportunities for integrating palaeoenvironmental evidence with the study of the historic landscape. At around this time, the landscape research group at Exeter was bolstered by a growing community of postgraduates whose theses shared in common a quest to understand the history of our countryside, and in particular where the historic landscape of today originated (Gillard 2002; Cannell 2005; Ryder 2007; Lambourne 2008). Researching a paper, 'Landscapes of Pre-Medieval Occupation' that was to appear in Roger Kain's *England's Landscape, volume 3: The South West* (Rippon 2006b) allowed me to explore pre-history for the first time in many years. That research fell during the period of my involvement with the Whittlewood Project, an interdisciplinary investigation into the origins and development of medieval landscapes on the Buckinghamshire–Northamptonshire border. This was a countryside of classic villages and open fields which really brought home just how different these landscapes were to those in the South West, and indeed the south-east of England where I was born and brought up. The discussions between members of the team—Chris Dyer and Mark Page, both historians, Mark Gardiner and Richard Jones, both archaeologists, and myself—after a number of the project meetings proved a fruitful testing ground for some of the ideas that eventually gained maturity in this study.

My interest in historic landscape characterization began in the 1990s when the Gwent Levels Historic Landscape Study (Rippon 1996) contributed to the development of the technique in Wales. I was able to revisit this methodology when the Blackdown Hills Rural Partnership funded a study of the historic landscape in the Blackdown Hills AONB (*The Living Past: Understanding the Historic Environment of the Blackdown Hills*: Rippon, Smart and Wainwright 2006), and through another Leverhulme Trust-funded project, this time looking at the history and landscape of the medieval royal silver mines at Bere Ferrers on the Devon/Cornwall border (Rippon *et al.* 2009). This was another interdisciplinary project, using the archaeological skills of Chris Smart and the historical expertise of Peter Claughton, and it again highlighted the importance of integrating archaeological and documentary evidence with information contained within the physical fabric of the historic landscape.

All this work in the South West served to reinforce in my mind just how different landscapes were, and are, in this region compared to the central part of England. It was also clear, however, that there was a very real bias in recent scholarship towards understanding the origins and development of landscapes characterized by villages and open fields, with more 'peripheral' areas—the two-thirds of England in the south-east and the west—sadly neglected, and my book *Beyond the Medieval Village* was an explicit attempt to redress this Midland-centric imbalance. Like so many pieces of research, this older book raised as many questions as it answered, and so I embarked on the project that has come to fruition here. *The Living Past* project had somewhat fortuitously looked in detail at one of the crucial boundaries in landscape character that *Beyond the Medieval Village* had identified, and the aim of this book is to expand this earlier unpublished work, comparing the contrasting landscapes either side of the Blackdowns in order to investigate why such marked local and regional variations in the nature of the countryside have emerged.

I must thank the many friends and colleagues who helped with particular aspects of the research in this book, and in particular Jeremy Lake and Pete Herring of English Heritage, and Sue Shaw of the Somerset Vernacular Architecture Research Group, for discussing the standing buildings of the study area. John Allan, Stuart Blaylock, Chris Gerrard, and Alejandra Gutierrez kindly supplied information on the distribution of medieval material culture, and Richard Bradley, Andy Jones, and Henrietta Quinnell helped cast some light on pre-history. Neil Holbrook and staff at Cotswold Archaeology supplied information on various sites including the early medieval settlement at Hayes Barn in South Petherton. I would also like to thank Olaf Bayer (University of Central Lancashire) for sharing the results of his fieldwork at Latchmoor Green in Rewe. A large number of students on the MA Landscape Archaeology at the University of Exeter, along with Phil Knibb, Lucy Ryder, Chris Smart, and Adam Wainwright carried out Tithe map digitization, and these are acknowledged in Table 7.1.

A major piece of research for this book was a review of palaeoenvironmental data, and this was only possible because so many specialists and field units were prepared to pass on copies of their unpublished research. For this I must thank Mary Alexander (Cotswold Archaeology), Wendy Carruthers, Simon Davis, Jessica Grimm (Wessex Archaeology), Andy Jones (Cornwall County Council), Jayne Lawes and Dawn Hodgson (Bath and Camerton Archaeological Society), Sheila Hamilton-Dyer, Annette Hancocks, and Neil Holbrook (Cotswold Archaeology), Loraine Higbee, Ann Reynolds (Cornwall County Council), Julie Jones, Kelly Powell (Oxford Archaeology), Clare Randal and Richard Tabor (South Cadbury Environs Project), Wendy Smith and

Chris Stevens (Wessex Archaeology), Vanessa Straker (English Heritage), Naomi Sykes (University of Nottingham), Bruce Williams (Bristol and Region Archaeological Services), and Faye Worley (English Heritage).

The historic landscape characterization undertaken for this book (Plate 2) was carried out by Adam Wainwright and entered into the GIS by Chris Smart, Bryn Morris, and Penny Cunningham. Richard Sandover subsequently maintained the GIS, and added data on Tithe survey land-holding. Although most of the photography and illustrations in this book were prepared by the author, several are the work of others, and for this I wish to thank Tristan Billing (Fig. 4.9), Rachel Oakes (Plate 5), Mike Rouillard (Figs. 6.4–6.6), Lucy Ryder (Plate 7), Richard Sandover (Figs. 4.4 bottom, and Plate 3), Adam Wainwright (Figs. 3.1 and 4.1–4.6), Aaron Watson (Fig. 14.8), and Adam Worth (Plate 8). For permission to reproduce illustrations I thank Richard Bradley (Fig. 14.8), Jeremy Lake and English Heritage (Fig. 5.11 right), Edward Martin and Suffolk County Council (Plate 1B), Mark Overton (Fig. 15.6), and the Somerset Records Office (Fig. 4.1). The pilot when Figure 1.1 and Plate 9 were taken was Philip Pearce. Finally, I must also thank Wendy Carruthers, Pete Herring, Jeremy Lake, Richard Jones, Naomi Sykes, and the anonymous reader for commenting on various draft chapters of this book.

Rewe, Devon

June 2011

Contents

List of figures	x
List of plates	xv
List of tables	xvi
List of abbreviations	xviii

1. Introduction — 1
2. The physical character of landscape — 15
3. 'The most beautiful landskip in the world'? The perceived character of landscape — 35
4. Characterizing the cultural landscape: the pattern and language of settlement — 53
5. Houses in the landscape — 87
6. The character of the fieldscape — 111
7. Beyond the morphology of fieldscapes — 131
8. Reconstructing early medieval territorial arrangements — 151
9. Early folk territories on and around the Blackdown Hills — 165
10. People in the landscape: the development of territorial structures in early Medieval western Wessex and beyond — 185
11. Patterns of land use: documentary evidence and palaeoenvironmental sequences — 205
12. Arable cultivation and animal husbandry in the medieval period — 241
13. Arable cultivation and animal husbandry in the Roman period — 263
14. Regional variation in landscape character during the late prehistoric and Roman periods — 287
15. Discussion and conclusions: communities and their landscapes — 315

Bibliography — 345
Index — 393

List of figures

CHAPTER 1

Fig. 1.1. The northern edge of the Blackdown Hills, looking east from Wellington Hill. — 2
Fig. 1.2. The major areas of nucleated settlement in Britain, with the local and regional study areas used in this book. — 6
Fig. 1.3. The series of nested study areas used in this book, and the parishes that make up the local study area. — 9

CHAPTER 2

Fig. 2.1. Mappings of regional variation in landscape character across southern Britain. — 16
Fig. 2.2. The superimposition of a medieval county boundary on earlier territorial arrangements in East Anglia. — 17
Fig. 2.3. Solid geology of the regional study area, and Holocene deposits of the Somerset Levels. — 21
Fig. 2.4. Ham Stone buildings in Barrington, central Somerset. — 22
Fig. 2.5. Cob-built Buddle Cottage, Cheriton Fitzpaine, Devon. — 23
Fig. 2.6. Topography of the regional study area, with places referred to in the text. — 24
Fig. 2.7. Drainage patterns within the regional study area. — 25
Fig. 2.8. Simplified mapping of the soils within the regional study area. — 26
Fig. 2.9. Measures of current agricultural potential (Agricultural Land Classification and Land Use Capability). — 28
Fig. 2.10. The major *pays* within the regional study area. — 30

CHAPTER 3

Fig. 3.1. An interpretation of references made within John Leland's mid-16th century itineraries to 'enclosed' and 'champion' countryside. — 36
Fig. 3.2. The eight 'districts' in Vancouver's (1808) *General View of the Agriculture of the County of Devon*. — 42
Fig. 3.3. The view south from Molland Common, on the southern fringes of Exmoor. — 44
Fig. 3.4. The 'corn ditch' at Luckworthy, on the southern fringes of Molland Common. — 45
Fig. 3.5. The classic Devon 'finger post' road sign at Elworthy Cross in Witheridge. — 45
Fig. 3.6. Gently rolling countryside in Stockleigh Pomeroy, just north of the Raddon Hills. — 46

List of figures   xi

Fig. 3.7. The broad lowland plain of the Exe and Culm valleys, looking
          south east from Raddon Hill.   46
Fig. 3.8. The Culm valley, looking south west from Paddleford Bridge
          towards Rewe.   47

CHAPTER 4

Fig. 4.1.   Type A1 settlement pattern: Lopen.   57
Fig. 4.2.   Type A2 settlement pattern: South Petherton.   58
Fig. 4.3.   Type B1 settlement pattern: Misterton.   59
Fig. 4.4.   Type C1 settlement pattern: Broadhembury.   60
Fig. 4.5.   Type D1 settlement pattern: Clayhidon.   61
Fig. 4.6.   Type D2 settlement pattern: Bradninch.   62
Fig. 4.7.   The distribution of parishes with settlement patterns Type A–E
           across the local study area.   64
Fig. 4.8.   The distribution of late medieval (sixteenth-century and earlier)
           houses in South Petherton, Broadhembury, and Clayhidon.   65
Fig. 4.9.   The location of medieval parish churches in relation to their local
           topography.   68
Fig. 4.10. Place-names of the 'personal name + Farm' type, and river- and
           woodland-indicative names.   71
Fig. 4.11. 'field' and '-ton' place-names.   73
Fig. 4.12. '-cott' and '-worthy' place-names.   75
Fig. 4.13. '-hayes'/'-hayne' and 'Barton' place-names.   77
Fig. 4.14. 'Park' and 'Gratton' field-names.   82
Fig. 4.15. 'Arrish' and 'Furlong' field-names.   83
Fig. 4.16. 'Breach' and 'Close' field-names.   84

CHAPTER 5

Fig. 5.1.   Fieldwork carried out on the vernacular architecture of the local
           study area, and dominant building materials across eastern Devon,
           southern Somerset, and western Dorset.   90
Fig. 5.2.   Divergent development of house plans in Devon and Somerset
           during the sixteenth and seventeenth centuries.   91
Fig. 5.3.   Barton Cottages and Rewe Barton model farm.   94
Fig. 5.4.   Road sign for Chapelhaies, Northdown, and Tedbridge in Bradninch. 96
Fig. 5.5.   Great Aunk, in Clyst Hydon.   97
Fig. 5.6.   Town Farm, in Clyst St Lawrence.   97
Fig. 5.7.   Fairby, in Tiverton.   100
Fig. 5.8.   Cottage immediately east of Kingstone church.   100
Fig. 5.9.   Somerville, in Hinton St George.   101
Fig. 5.10. Density of listed buildings with lateral stacks, and percentage
           of sixteenth-century and earlier listed buildings with lateral as
           opposed to axial stacks.   104

CHAPTER 6

Fig. 5.11.	Different rates of growth in lay wealth between 1334 and 1515, and the distribution of pre-1550 listed buildings.	107
Fig. 5.12.	Distribution of model farms in the local study area.	109

CHAPTER 6

Fig. 6.1.	The former extent of open field as mapped by Gonner (1912).	112
Fig. 6.2.	Regional variation in the character of field systems.	114
Fig. 6.3.	Suggested extents of former open field in the local study area.	116
Fig. 6.4.	Ordnance Survey First Edition Six Inch map of the northern part of Clayhidon.	122
Fig. 6.5.	Transcribed Tithe map of the northern part of Clayhidon.	123
Fig. 6.6.	Transcription of the estate map of Clayhidon manor of 1739.	124
Fig. 6.7.	Extract from the Devon HLC for the northern part of Clayhidon.	125
Fig. 6.8.	Results of the historic landscape characterization carried out for this project of the northern part of Clayhidon.	126

CHAPTER 7

Fig. 7.1.	Ordnance Survey First Edition Six Inch map of Chard.	133
Fig. 7.2.	The location of fieldwork to determine the character of field boundaries.	139
Fig. 7.3.	Documentary evidence for common field in Somerset and the extent of ridge and furrow.	141
Fig. 7.4.	Example of an area in Upottery that the Devon HLC identified as being 'medieval enclosures based on strip fields'.	143
Fig. 7.5.	Example of an area in Upottery and the historic landscape characterization used in this study.	144
Fig. 7.6.	Interpretation of the historic landscape characterization carried out for this project.	147

CHAPTER 8

Fig. 8.1.	The former minster church at Branscombe in east Devon.	154
Fig. 8.2.	Domesday hundreds across the regional study area.	155
Fig. 8.3.	Minster churches across the regional study area.	157
Fig. 8.4.	Evidence for the Curry/Isle 'early folk territory'.	158–9
Fig. 8.5.	Ordnance Survey First Edition Six Inch map of Misterton.	161

CHAPTER 9

Fig. 9.1.	Early folk territories and great estates in the regional study area.	166
Fig. 9.2.	Early folk territories and great estates in the local study area.	167
Fig. 9.3.	Western boundary of the Culm/Clyst early folk territory as it crosses Raddon Hill, west of Thorverton.	170

List of figures xiii

CHAPTER 10

Fig. 10.1. A comparison of early territorial arrangements from across early medieval England with those reconstructed on and around the Blackdown Hills. 187
Fig. 10.2. The Exe/Lowman and Culm/Clyst early folk territories. 192
Fig. 10.3. The impact of the Blackdown Hills on the movement of people: the trading influence of Saint White Down fair 1637–49, and importers of goods into Exeter 1350–99 and their debtors. 202

CHAPTER 11

Fig. 11.1. The regions used in the study of palaeoeconomic data (animal bones and charred cereals). 208
Fig. 11.2. Thirsk's 16th and early 17th century 'farming regions' in South West England. 208
Fig. 11.3. Places with documentary records used by Campbell to study medieval demesne agriculture. 209
Fig. 11.4. Cattle and pigs as a percentage of the demesne livestock recorded in Domesday. 212
Fig. 11.5. Sheep and goats as a percentage of the demesne livestock recorded in Domesday. 213
Fig. 11.6. Location of palaeoenvironmental sequences. 220

CHAPTER 14

Fig. 14.1. Reconstructions of *civitas* boundaries in the south west of Britain and their relationship to topographic zones and pre-1974 county boundaries. 288
Fig. 14.2. The distribution of South Devon Ware. 291
Fig. 14.3. Distribution of Romano-British towns, roads, temples, and villas. 293
Fig. 14.4. The relationship of the Fosse Way to the historic landscape in central Somerset. 298
Fig. 14.5. Distribution of 'Early Anglo-Saxon' burials and fifth- to sixth-century Mediterranean imports. 304
Fig. 14.6. The distribution of Durotrigian coins across the regional study area. 306
Fig. 14.7. The distribution and size of Iron Age hillforts across the regional study area. 308
Fig. 14.8. A characterization of Iron Age settlement in Britain and the near continent. 309

CHAPTER 15

Fig. 15.1. Interpretation of the historic landscape characterization carried out for this project and seven *pays* identified from this. 319
Fig. 15.2. Domesday population density and percentage of slaves. 324

Fig. 15.3. The number of acres per Domesday ploughteam, and % of ploughteams that were on the demesne.	325
Fig. 15.4. Domesday population density across South West England.	326
Fig. 15.5. Manors held by Algar in 1066.	329
Fig. 15.6. Settlement character and the natural environment across England and Wales.	332
Fig. 15.7. A model for the spread of villages and open fields.	334
Fig. 15.8. The development of open field, Model A: indigenous development from small ovoid enclosures spread right across the landscape.	336
Fig. 15.9. The development of open field, Model B: indigenous development from small open fields in the lowlands, followed by their spread up onto the Blackdown Hills.	337
Fig. 15.10. The development of open field, Model C: spread south-westwards from the East Midlands.	338

List of plates

Plate 1 The extent of former open field mapped in the Somerset and Devon HLCs, and HLCs for Hertfordshire, Essex, and Suffolk.

Plate 2 The historic landscape characterization carried out as part of this study, and the historic landscape character type 'Enclosed Strip Fields'.

Plate 3 Transcription of the Tithe map for Chard.

Plate 4 Parishes in the local study area for which data on land ownership and land occupancy have been mapped based on the Tithe surveys of *c.*1840.

Plate 5 Transcription of the Tithe map for Burlescombe.

Plate 6 The ovoid enclosure north of Westcott Dairy in Sheldon.

Plate 7 Transcription of the Tithe map for Clayhidon.

Plate 8 Transcription of the Tithe map for Churchstanton.

Plate 9 Aerial photograph of Combe St Nicholas from the west.

Plate 10 Cross-section through a typical Devon hedgebank at West Raddon in Shobrooke.

List of tables

Table 2.1	Sources used in studying the physical background.	31
Table 2.2	Soils and the geology from which they are derived.	33
Table 3.1	Rapid field assessment of landscape character in the west of our study area.	47
Table 4.1	A typology of settlement patterns.	63
Table 4.2	The portfolios of place-names in Bradninch and South Petherton.	79
Table 5.1	Summary of the initial date of construction for listed houses in the study area, and from other work in Somerset.	101
Table 5.2	Distribution of lateral stacks.	105
Table 7.1	Research into patterns of land holding based on the Tithe maps and apportionments.	134
Table 7.2	Small ovoid-shaped enclosures with strip-based fields and fragmented land holding, and selected open fields for comparison.	137
Table 10.1	Early folk territories and 'great estates' reconstructed in this study.	189
Table 10.2	The fragmentation of the Culm/Clyst folk territory.	196
Table 11.1	Demesne livestock listed in the *Liber Exoniensis* for Devon, Dorset, and Somerset.	211
Table 11.2	The relative proportions of Domesday demesne livestock on the Blackdown Hills and adjacent areas.	214
Table 11.3	Domesday stocking densities of demesne livestock on the Blackdown Hills and adjacent areas.	215
Table 11.4	Domesday herd/flock sizes of demesne livestock on the Blackdown Hills and adjacent areas.	216
Table 11.5	Changing patterns of population density and predominant land use across the regional study area.	221
Table 11.6	Summary of the results from palaeoenvironmental analyses from off-site sequences and major concentrations of on-site assemblages.	234
Table 12.1	Statistical analysis of the percentages of cattle, sheep/goat, and pig from different categories of site in medieval Britain.	249
Table 12.2A	Summary of middle medieval bones from sites of different social status from each of the *pays* within the study area.	250
Table 12.2B	Summary of middle medieval bones from sites of different social status from each of the *pays* within the study area grouped by sites of different social status.	252

Table 12.3	Summary of the middle medieval cereal grains from sites of different social status from each of the *pays* within the study area.	259
Table 13.1	A statistical analysis of the percentages of cattle, sheep/goat, and pig from sites of different status in Roman Britain.	264
Table 13.2	Summary of Romano-British bones from sites of different social status from each of the *pays* within the study area.	265
Table 13.3	Summary of the Romano-British cereal grains from non-corn-drier contexts on sites of different social status from each of the *pays* within the study area.	273
Table 13.4	Percentages of grain identified as emmer, spelt, and bread wheat.	276
Table 13.5	Changing patterns of population density and land use across the regional study area.	282
Table 14.1	Non-ceramic Romano-British finds reported through the Portable Antiquities Scheme 2003–8.	292

List of abbreviations

CAT	Cotswold Archaeological Trust
DB	Domesday Book
HLC	Historic Landscape Characterisation
MMG	Mercian Mudstone Group (Triassic mudstones)
MNI	Minimum Number of Individuals
NRS	New Red Sandstone
OS 1st Edn 6"	Ordnance Survey First Edition Six Inch to the Mile maps
SVBRG	Somerset Vernacular Buildings Research Group

1

Introduction

LANDSCAPE AND A SENSE OF IDENTITY

The landscape around us provides a remarkable record of human achievement in exploiting, modifying, and transforming the natural environment over many millennia. It is both the context within which human lives were enacted, and a product of this human endeavour. From the earliest woodland clearances to intensive farming regimes that characterized the twentieth century, each generation of our ancestors has done something to shape the landscape we live in today. What is particular striking, however, is that even within a relatively small island such as Britain, the character of our landscape varies so much from one location to another. If one leaves the city of Exeter in Devon, for example, and heads east into the surrounding countryside, it soon becomes apparent that the landscape in these gently undulating lowlands is characterized by small hamlets and isolated farmsteads dotted along winding lanes. Further the east there is higher ground—the Blackdown Hills—whose densely wooded scarp slope forms a prominent local landmark (Fig. 1.1). The settlement pattern in the Blackdowns is also dispersed, but just a few kilometres further east, in the lowlands of central Somerset, the character of the landscape suddenly changes to one dominated by large, nucleated villages often linked by long, straight roads. These lowlands around Exeter and in central Somerset both have gentle relief and fertile soils, and there is nothing immediately apparent in their topography that explains why the settlement patterns are so different. If one looks back in time, however, it is noticeable that the people living either side of the Blackdown Hills had discrete and distinctive identities for at least the last two millennia, and the differences in today's settlement patterns are just one manifestation of this.

Marked differences in landscape character such as those seen on the Blackdown Hills can be found right across Britain. Further down the South West Peninsula, the landscape of Cornwall has its own distinctive identity portrayed, for example, through its predominantly Celtic place-names (Padel 1999), while in the West Midlands differences in landscape character between the Felden and the Arden can be traced back to the Roman period at least

Fig. 1.1. The northern edge of the Blackdown Hills, looking east from Wellington Hill, with Clayhidon on the right (show in Plate 2). This well-wooded scarp slope is a prominent local landmark, and from a distance gives the Blackdown Hills a dark and forbidding appeareance.

(Roberts and Wrathmell 2000b). Across in East Anglia a boundary in landscape character runs diagonally through the modern county of Suffolk that can be traced back as far as the Iron Age (*see* Chapter 2), and quite possibly further. Understanding the origins and development of local and regional variation in landscape character such as these is important for not just landscape archaeologists, historical geographers, and local historians—whose specific interests are in the history of the countryside—but are central to our appreciation of human society's relationship with the natural environment. French geographers refer to regions with a distinctive character as *pays*, and assert that their nature is independent of environmental control as it was the effect of human activity over time that produced particular countrysides with their own personalities and distinctive ways of life (Muir 1999, 8). *Pays* is, however, a term that in Britain has not achieved widespread currency. While it has been used by historians and historical geographers for several decades, there has been a tendency to use the term for generic types of landscape strongly influenced by the natural environment, rather than unique locales in the French sense. This British approach is seen most clearly in the work of the Leicester School of local historians (e.g. Everitt 1986), and also underlies Thirsk's (1967; 1987) identification of generic 'farming regions', types of countryside which in the sixteenth and seventeenth centuries had common patterns of agricultural husbandry. Dyer, however, has quite rightly recognized that a close analysis of these farming regions usually reveals that no one area is ever quite like another, and although there are broad regions that over a long period have been primarily oriented towards a particular type of agriculture, within these are the smaller districts which were 'infinitely varied in their use of land and methods of farming' (Dyer 1988, 12). In this book, the term *pays* is similarly used in the sense of unique locales, with one particular district—the Blackdown Hills—and the lowlands either side forming the focus of our attention.

It is understanding subtle but important variations in landscape character that lies at the heart of this book, and in doing so it is important to focus on the districts with which past communities themselves would have had an affinity. A central concern here is therefore to expand on the traditional academic preoccupation of characterizing landscapes in terms of the their settlement patterns and field systems, and to try and understand the ways that people in the past have expressed their identities through standing buildings, the language of landscape (field- and place-names), agricultural practices, and the territorial structures within which they lived. All too often the study of these aspects of landscape character has been the domain of groups of specialists with their own conferences and their own journals—such as *Agricultural History Review* and *Vernacular Architecture*—and one of the aims of this current study is to try to break down these disciplinary barriers.

A crucial issue in how we perceive *pays* is the role of the natural environment. In recent decades it has become fashionable to play down the significance of physical geography in shaping human behaviour—so-called 'environmental determinism'—with emphasis placed on the freedom of communities to shape their own world. In the early twenty-first century we are, however, at an interesting point in the history of landscape studies (e.g. Fleming 2006; 2007; Johnson 2007; Rippon 2009). The phrase 'social agency' is now common in the literature, and to describe someone as an 'environmental determinist' is a damning criticism. Academic ideas, however, tend to go in and out of fashion and in recent years a number of scholars have once again argued that the natural environment did have a significant effect on human behaviour. Williamson (2003; 2010), for example, has argued that particular characteristics of different soils were important in shaping medieval agricultural practices, while Draper (2006) shows how chalk downland in Wiltshire had a very different economy and landscape to lowland clay vales. In the late seventeenth century John Aubrey described how 'on the downs...where 'tis all upon tillage, and where the shepherds labour hard, their flesh is hard, their bodies strong', in contrast to the 'dirty clayey country', where the people 'speak drawling: they are phlegmatic, skins pale and livid, slow and dull, heavy of spirit; hereabout is but little tillage or hard labour, they only milk the cows and make cheese' (Ponting 1969, 11). Whilst Thirsk's (1987, 14) argument that 'an exceptional region in the south east was the Weald of Kent where the heavy clay soils *imposed* pasture framing' (emphasis added) is too simplistic, and the crude constraints of environmental determinism must be avoided, we cannot deny that landscape character is in part influenced by geology, soils, topography, and drainage patterns. Markedly different landscapes such as the chalk downland and heavy clayland of Wiltshire, for example, will clearly have encouraged the communities living there to adopt different patterns of land-use because, as any farmer or gardener will tell you, different plants thrive on different soils. There are, however, other examples of landscapes where the natural environment is completely uniform yet the settlement patterns and field systems are very different, and here human agency certainly was the driving force behind landscape character (e.g. wetlands reclaimed in the medieval period, *see* Rippon 2006a; 2008a). What seems clear is that we should keep an open mind about the relative significance of environmental factors and social agency in explaining regional variation in landscape character.

AN AGENDA FOR STUDYING LANDSCAPE

The success of landscape-based research relies on several factors including the identification of clear research aims and objectives, the selection of a suitable case study area, and the application of appropriate methodologies. In this book, the aim is to understand the origins and development of long-standing boundaries in landscape character such as those marked by the Blackdown Hills, to which end there are three specific objectives:

- to go beyond the traditional focus of landscape archaeologists and historical geographers on morphological differences in settlement patterns and field systems and explore other facets of landscape character such as how the landscape was perceived in the past, and how social identity was expressed through phenomena like vernacular architecture, the language of landscape (field- and place-names), and patterns of land use;
- to understand the origins and development of local and regional variation in landscape character in the context of the social and territorial structures within which people lived;
- to illustrate, explain, and discuss the research process, rather than simply presenting the results of this work as a *fait accompli*.

These themes are explored here within a study area that focuses on the frontier between two of the major regions of England: the highly Romanized central zone that in the medieval period saw the development of villages and open fields, and the west of Britain that was relatively un-Romanized and in the medieval period had more dispersed settlement patterns. The concept, or concepts, of frontiers in medieval Europe has seen considerable discussion in recent decades, although most attention has focused on the cultural significance of often unstable political boundaries and the interaction between peoples on either side of them. Within historical studies it is striking how little use is made of physical evidence contained within the landscape (e.g. Bartlett and MacKay 1989; Power and Standen 1999; Ainsworth and Scott 2000). Archaeologists, in contrast, are well used to dealing with physical evidence and they have long been interested in frontiers both in the sense of 'marginal' areas within the landscape (e.g. Roberts and Glasscock 1983; Bailey 1989; Klápště and Sommer 2009), and discrete monuments that marked political boundaries such as Offa's Dyke (Hill and Worthington 2003). These various studies reveal that the term 'frontier' means different things to different people, ranging from the edges of a political entity to the fluctuating limit of cultivation within the territory of a farming community. Frontiers could be between two human populations and their different ideologies, or between humans and nature (e.g. Corbin 1994).

In recent years there has been much debate about the origins and development of regional variations in landscape character across Britain (Fig. 1.2), but far less attention paid to the nature of the boundaries between them. In a broad 'Central Zone' (Lambourne 2010, 16) stretching from the south coast in Dorset, up through the East Midlands, and across to the North East, most medieval settlement within a parish or township was condensed, or 'nucleated', into a single village, with the surrounding agricultural land arranged in a small number of vast open fields, subdivided into unenclosed strips that were managed by the whole community. On either side of this central zone, settlement patterns were more dispersed, characterized by small hamlets and isolated farmsteads, and the field systems comprised a mixture of small open fields and large areas of closes held 'in severalty' (i.e. small fields enclosed by a hedge or bank, and which were held a single tenant). The origins of this broad tripartite division of the English landscape have been much debated, with a series of important books presenting very different views. In *Village, Hamlet and Field*, Lewis, Mitchell-Fox, and Dyer (1997) focused on why the central zone was different to rest of England, arguing that it was socially and economically the most progressive region, which saw the replacement of scattered farmsteads and hamlets with nucleated settlements during a 'village moment' around the tenth century. In *Region and Place*, Roberts and Wrathmell (2002) studied landscape character across the whole of England. They also concluded that villages and open fields originated in the East Midlands and spread out across a 'Central Province' which they argue was that part of early medieval England most extensively cleared of woodland (Fig. 1.2). In arguing that this 'antecedent landscape character' was a major factor in determining which areas saw the development of villages and open fields, the emphasis once again was on seeing the central zone as one of positive development, while the areas beyond were peripheral and less well-developed. In *Shaping Medieval Landscapes*, Williamson (2003) also considered why villages and open fields only

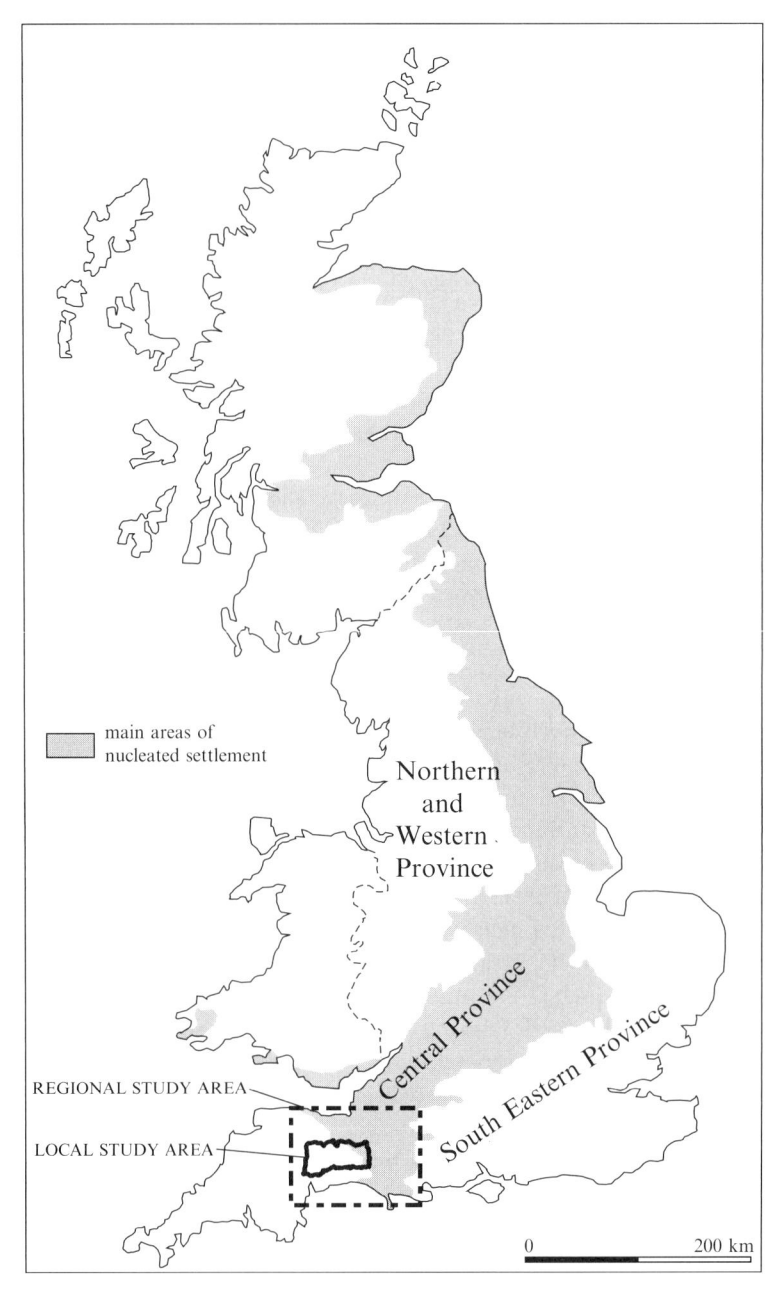

Fig. 1.2. The major areas of nucleated settlement in Britain and the three main 'settlement provinces' of England, with the local and regional study areas used in this book. (After Roberts 1987, fig. 1.1, and Roberts and Wrathmell 2002, fig. 1.4.)

developed in the central zone suggesting that its agricultural practices were determined by the nature of its heavy soils. Williamson agreed with Brown and Foard (1998) that rather than a short 'village moment' in the tenth century, the nucleation of settlement had a longer chronology, starting perhaps as early as the eighth century. This longer chronology was supported by this author's contribution to the debate—*Beyond the Medieval Village* (Rippon 2008a)—that argued for a significant period of landscape change across much of southern England that started during what historians have referred to as the 'long eighth century' (Hanson and Wickham 2000; Wickham 2005; Rippon 2010), and which continued for several centuries.

In addition to Lewis *et al.*'s (1997) study of the four East Midland counties of Bedfordshire, Buckinghamshire, Leicestershire, and Northamptonshire, there have been a large number of other major projects focusing on the origins of villages in England's central zone. This trend began with the long-term programme of survey and excavation at Wharram Percy in Yorkshire (Beresford and Hurst 1990), and has continued in more recent work at Raunds and Higham Ferrers in Northamptonshire (e.g. Chapman 2010), Whittlewood on the Northants/Buckinghamshire border (Jones and Pages 2006), Milton Keynes in Buckinghamshire (e.g. Mynard 1994), Yarnton and nearby sites on the Thames gravels in Oxfordshire and Berkshire (e.g. Hey 2004), and Shapwick in Somerset (Gerrard, with Aston 2007). The most complete reconstruction of what a medieval landscape looked like is also in Northamptonshire (Foard *et al.* 2005; 2009). It was in the context of all this Midland-focused work that first, *Beyond the Medieval Village,* and now this study try to redress this 'Midland-centric' bias by examining areas at the margins of, and beyond, England's central zone.

Although the topic at the heart of this book is one of general significance—the origins and development of regional variation in landscape character and how we study it—it is based upon a specific case study area that straddles the south-western boundary of England's central zone. This boundary runs through a semi-upland area, the Blackdown Hills, and as such may be an example of Phythian Adams's (1993; 1999) argument that the British landscape can be divided into a series of 'cultural provinces' that broadly correspond to drainage basins that were separated by sparsely populated areas of high ground, largely used for pasture, where folklore suggested bad things lived, and across which cultural contacts were limited. As we shall see, the long-term significance of the Blackdown Hills as one of these watersheds can be seen in the way that they marked the westerly limit of medieval landscapes characterized by villages and open fields, of Early Saxon burials furnished with grave goods, of the highly Romanized countryside characterized by villas, temples, and small towns, and of Iron Age landscapes dominated by large, developed, multivalate hillforts full of grain-storage facilities.

A distinctive feature of this study area is its size, which marks a deliberate attempt to propose an alternative scale for landscape research compared to those traditionally adopted in both history and archaeology. Phythian Adams (1993) and Fox (2009, 1) have both observed that too many historical studies of past society have examined very small study areas, which is matched by the long-established tradition within landscape archaeology of studying individual parishes (e.g. Wharram Percy: Hayfield 1987; Raunds: Parry 2006; Shapwick: Gerrard with Aston 2007). Parish-scale analysis is ideal for detailed fieldwork or documentary research, but it does have the disadvantage that the chosen parish may not be typical of the local area, and in recent years a number of studies have chosen a somewhat larger scale for their research, such as Fleming's (1998a) twenty townships in Swaledale, and the eleven-parish Whittlewood Project (Jones and Page 2006). What is common to all these projects, however, is the philosophy of taking a single study area all of which was researched in roughly equal detail, whereas in this book a different approach is followed with a series of 'nested' study areas. The 'local study area' taken here extends across the Blackdown Hills and into the adjacent lowlands and saw the most intensive research (covering 14,223 km^2 in 104 parishes and parts of three others), while a larger 'regional study area' of 8,800 km^2 extends from the English Channel to the Severn Estuary, and from the Culm Measures of central Devon across to the chalk downland of Wessex, across which less intensive work was conducted. Some research was even carried out across the five counties of Cornwall, Devon, Dorset, Somerset, and Wiltshire where a broader view was required (Fig. 1.3).

This approach of using 'nested' study areas was first used by the author on the North Somerset Levels (Rippon 2006a), and was also adopted by Fox (2009) albeit with an extremely tight time frame (from the seventeenth to the nineteenth century). Phythian Adams (1993) and Fox (2009) have both commented on a tendency in the past to identify 'regions' based on single characteristics—e.g. Schürer's (2004) 'Surnames and the search for regions'—and in contrast this study has a very long time frame, from prehistory through to the present day, and a very wide range of archaeological, architectural, cartographic, documentary, and place-name evidence. The starting point was the physical form of the natural environment and the 'historic landscape'—the patterns of settlements, fields, roads, land uses, and the like—as recorded on the Ordnance Survey First Edition Six Inch to the Mile (OS 1st Edn 6") maps that in the south-west of England were surveyed in the 1880s. Other physical facets of the cultural landscape were examined using a variety of sources including domestic architecture and the form taken by individual field boundaries. The OS 1st Edn 6" maps also record large numbers of place-names, while Tithe maps and apportionments of the 1840s were used to study field-names and patterns of land ownership and occupancy. Although no large-scale field surveys or excavations were undertaken as part of this study, a wide variety of

Fig. 1.3. The series of nested study areas used in various stages of data collection and analysis, and the parishes that comprise the local study area. (Parish boundaries after Kane and Oliver 2001, drawing by Stephen Rippon.)

archaeological data have been used; for example, in mapping selected pottery styles and coin distributions, and tabulating data from the Portable Antiquities Scheme as a way of quantifying Romanization and engagement in the market economy. Past archaeological excavations have also provided assemblages of animal bones and charred cereals that have been used to study regional variation in the farming economy. Palaeoenvironmental sequences tell us about changing patterns of land use, and for the medieval and post-medieval periods we have a series of documentary sources that enable patterns of farming to be reconstructed. From the sixteenth century there is also a wide range of evidence that reflects the ways that people in the past have perceived the landscape, including folklore, and its inclusion is an example of how this book consciously tries to move beyond the traditional archaeological approach of simply mapping morphology. Overall, it is hoped that this study of a specific landscape can provide inspiration for similar work elsewhere through its strongly interdisciplinary approach and the illustration of the source material being used.

THE STRUCTURE OF THIS BOOK

Rather than presenting the results of research as a *fait accompli*, this book tries to reflect the research process by often adopting a retrogressive approach that starts with the known and then works back towards the unknown. As this is a strongly interdisciplinary study, care will also be taken to describe and illustrate the source material used: the various maps and tables are the landscape equivalent of the specialist reports found in excavation monographs. In **Chapter 2** our journey begins by introducing the study area in terms of its physical characteristics. The geology, topography, drainage patterns, soils, and climate are described, along with two measures of current agricultural potential. These show how our study area comprises a series of distinctive *pays* with very different physical characteristics, and in **Chapter 3** the ways that these were perceived in the past are explored, starting with the sixteenth-century topographers, John Leland and William Camden. For the seventeenth century we have the views of both national travellers, such as Celia Fiennes and Daniel Defoe, as well as a number of local writers. For the eighteenth century we again have the qualitative accounts of local topographers, along with reports to the Board of Agriculture by the likes of Charles Vancouver that provide a national perspective. We finish this chapter by exploring how local communities may have perceived their landscape as reflected in folklore. A key question in this chapter is to explore whether the *pays* that we can identify based on our modern cartographic sources have had any reality in the past. The very clear answer is that they did.

In **Chapter 4** we turn to the physical character of the historic landscape and, in particular, the patterns of settlements depicted on the OS 1st Edn 6" maps of the 1880s. A typology of settlement patterns is proposed that ranges from almost wholly nucleated in the lowlands of central Somerset to almost wholly dispersed in some Blackdown Hills parishes. The location of parish churches in relation to topography is then considered, again with very marked regional variation being identified. We then move on to consider a series of place- and field-name elements that form a distinctive part of landscape character in many areas. In **Chapter 5** we consider another aspect of the landscape of settlement: regional variation in vernacular architecture. Whilst the use of locally available building materials is an obvious aspect of this, differences in the design of houses, and the periods when they were built or rebuilt, are equally significant.

In **Chapter 6** we leave the settlements and move out into the wider countryside using a characterization of the field systems based on the OS 1st Edn 6" maps. In **Chapter 7** we add depth to this morphological analysis by looking at patterns of land ownership and land occupancy. The nature of the field boundaries themselves is also considered, with the extent of the South West's distinctive hedgebanks also mapped. A particular aim here is to reconstruct the extent of open-field farming, although a consideration of why Midland-style common fields (the classic two- and three-field system) never spread to the west of the Blackdown Hills is reserved for the Conclusion (Chapter 15).

In Chapters 8 to 10 we look at the territorial structures within which communities managed the landscape. **Chapter 8** begins with a discussion of the sources and methods we can use to reconstruct early estate centres and their associated territorial structures, and this is followed in **Chapter 9** by a series of case studies on and around the Blackdown Hills. It is argued that what are referred to here as 'early folk territories' fragmented into a series of smaller 'great estates' and that the latter were often used when other secular and ecclesiastical administrative units were created (hundreds and *parochiae*). Rather than the Blackdown Hills simply being the upland, peripheral, part of social territories based in the adjacent lowland areas, it appears that they were occupied by their own 'early folk territory'. In **Chapter 10** the postulated evolution of early medieval territorial structures within our study area is compared with the rest of western Wessex and beyond.

In Chapters 11 to 13 our attention turns to regional variation in farming practice across the different *pays* of South West England. A broadly retrogressive approach is followed, starting with the well-documented post-medieval period, working back through the medieval period, and ending up in the Roman period for which we have far less evidence. In **Chapter 11** we focus on the documentary sources that are excellent for the post-medieval period but more fragmentary for the medieval period, and the palaeoenvironmental sequences that allow us to study broad changes in land use from the present day back into prehistory. In **Chapter 12** we look at the preserved cereal remains and animal bones from medieval sites, which in **Chapter 13** are compared to those dated to the Roman period. The key research question in these chapters is whether the distinctive farming regions identified by historians in the post-medieval periods were simply the product of changes to society and the economy in the late-medieval period, or whether they are more deeply rooted in regional variations in landscape and society.

Having started to explore the Romano-British landscape in Chapters 12 and 13 we continue in **Chapter 14**. Our study area lay within two Iron Age tribal areas and Roman *civitates*: those of the Dumnonii to the west of the Blackdown Hills and the Durotriges to the east. In both the Iron Age and Roman periods, very clear differences in material culture are observed alongside variations in the physical character of the landscape, most visibly the degree of Romanization. In the Iron Age there are also clear differences either side of the Blackdowns reflected in material culture, burial practices, and the nature of settlements (with heavily defended hillforts containing large-scale grain storage facilities to the east, and far more modest enclosed settlements to the west that lacked comparable grain storage capacity). The Late Bronze Age is poorly understood in the South West, but we can tentatively suggest that this regional variation in landscape character may have originated in the Middle Bronze Age or even earlier.

Our exploration concludes in **Chapter 15** with a discussion of how the marked regional variation in landscape character described in the preceding chapters came to be perpetuated throughout the historic period. It is shown that for several millennia, the Blackdown Hills divided communities that chose to structure their landscape very differently, and while variations in the natural environment certainly played a part, they are not the whole explanation. Instead, it appears that there were deep-rooted differences in the nature of society either side of the Blackdown Hills that includes how social stratification was displayed, and the propensity for embracing change.

A NOTE ON TERMINOLOGY AND REFERENCING OF SOURCE MATERIAL

- **Counties** are referred to as they relate to the pre-1974 situation.
- **Open field** is used for any agricultural system in which units of landholding consisted of strips of land not marked by a bank, ditch, or hedge, with the term '**common field**' reserved for one specific type of open-field farming—the 'Midland' two- and three-field system.
- **Period terminology** follows that laid out by the Society for Medieval Archaeology (2003) with the term '**medieval**' used for AD 410 to about 1540. The early medieval period is the early fifth to the mid-eleventh century (410 to 1066), the high medieval period the mid-eleventh century to the mid-fourteenth century (1066 to 1348), and the late medieval period the mid-fourteenth century to the mid-sixteenth century (1348 to about 1540). **Anglo-Saxon** is not used as a period term unless it is repeating its usage by others, as from the early fifth to the mid-seventh century, the

area west of the Blackdown Hills was a British kingdom and as such the term 'Anglo-Saxon period' is inappropriate. 'Anglo-Saxon' is, however, used as a collective term for immigrants from mainland Europe who arrived in Britain during the fifth and sixth centuries AD, and 'Early Anglo-Saxon' is used when referring to burials, building styles, and the material culture of this period that has been attributed to these settlers (although it should be recognized that some of the individuals buried in this fashion may in fact be native Britons: e.g. Hills 2009).

2

The physical character of landscape

There are various reasons why a particular landscape may be selected for research. Many people choose the parish or county in which they live, and local studies of this type can be both rewarding for the individual and of wider academic significance if a good-quality publication results. This approach to deciding where to research is essentially 'bottom up': you choose your study area and then make what you can of it. Another approach can be thought of as 'top-down': you begin with a research question and then decide the best place to study it. This book takes a 'top-down' approach to selecting its study area because its focus is a broad topic—how regional variation in landscape character came about—and the Blackdown Hills are simply one of many places that could have been researched.

The significance of the Blackdown Hills has been noted in passing in a number of earlier studies (Fig. 2.1). Fox's (1932) *The Personality of Britain* identified them as marking the edge of the 'highland zone', and a number of his distributions maps of prehistoric material culture provide hints that by the Iron Age, communities with different identities were emerging on either side (Fox 1932, figs. 11, 12, and 37). This is something that has become even clearer since (Cunliffe 2005). Most scholars place the boundary between the *civitates* of the Durotriges and the Dumnonii in this area, which also marked the western limit of extensive Romanization as reflected in the distribution of villas, small towns, pottery kilns, and mosaic pavements (Jones and Mattingly 1990; Millett 1990). In the medieval period, Gray (1915) identifies the Blackdowns as marking the western limit of the medieval two- and three-field systems, and even as late as the eighteenth and nineteenth centuries there remained significant amounts of common field agriculture to the east of the Hills but not to the west (Gonner 1912). The south-western edge of Roberts and Wrathmell's (2000a) 'Central Province'—based upon nineteenth-century settlement patterns—was along a very similar line.

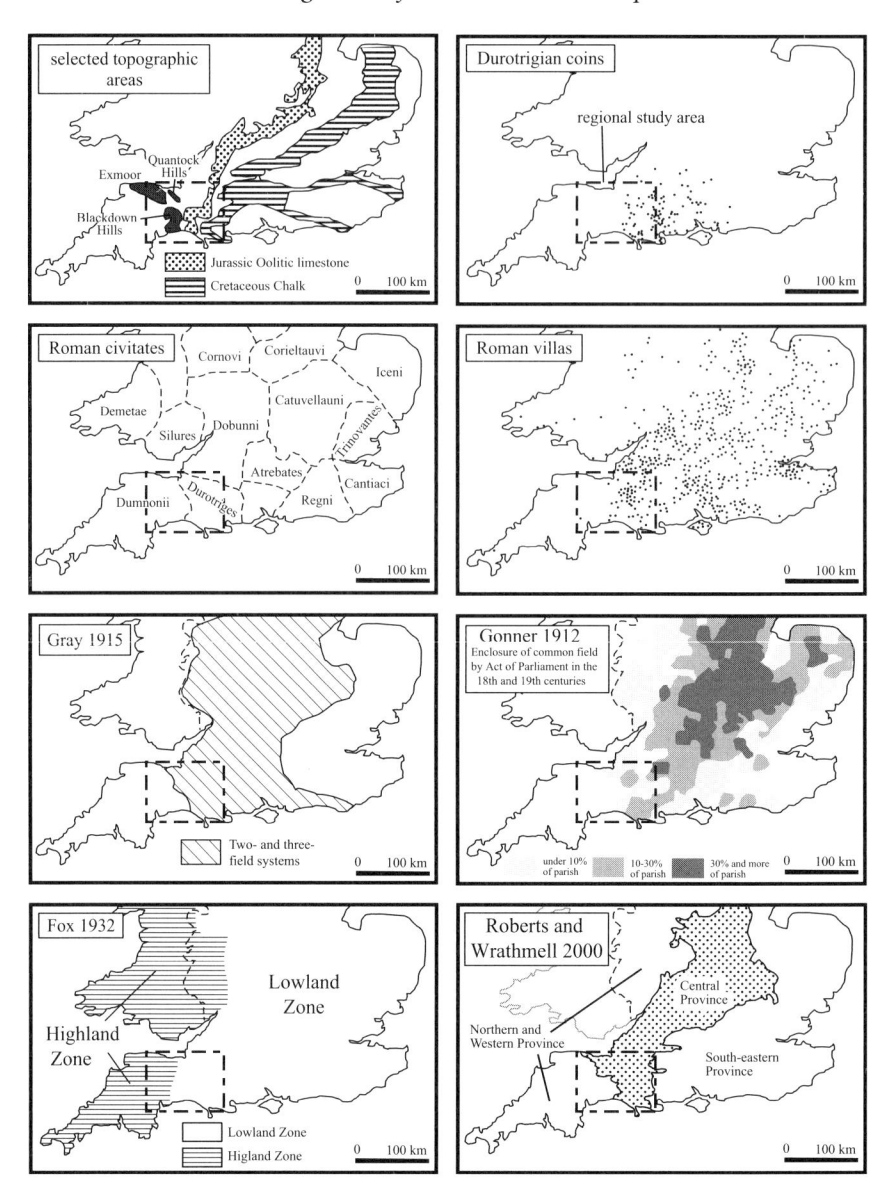

Fig. 2.1. Mappings of regional variation in landscape character across southern Britain. (Durotrigian coins: Cunliffe 2005, fig. 8.3; *civitates*: after Jones and Mattingly 1990, map 5.11; Roman villas: Jones and Mattingly 1990, map 7.6.)

DETERMINING THE BOUNDARIES OF A STUDY AREA

Once a research question has been identified, and a place where it can be studied has been selected, the boundary of that study area must be determined. There is a long history in Britain of using counties as the spatial unit for archaeological and historical research, although this can be problematic when it comes to studying the landscape. Our pre-1974 counties were certainly in

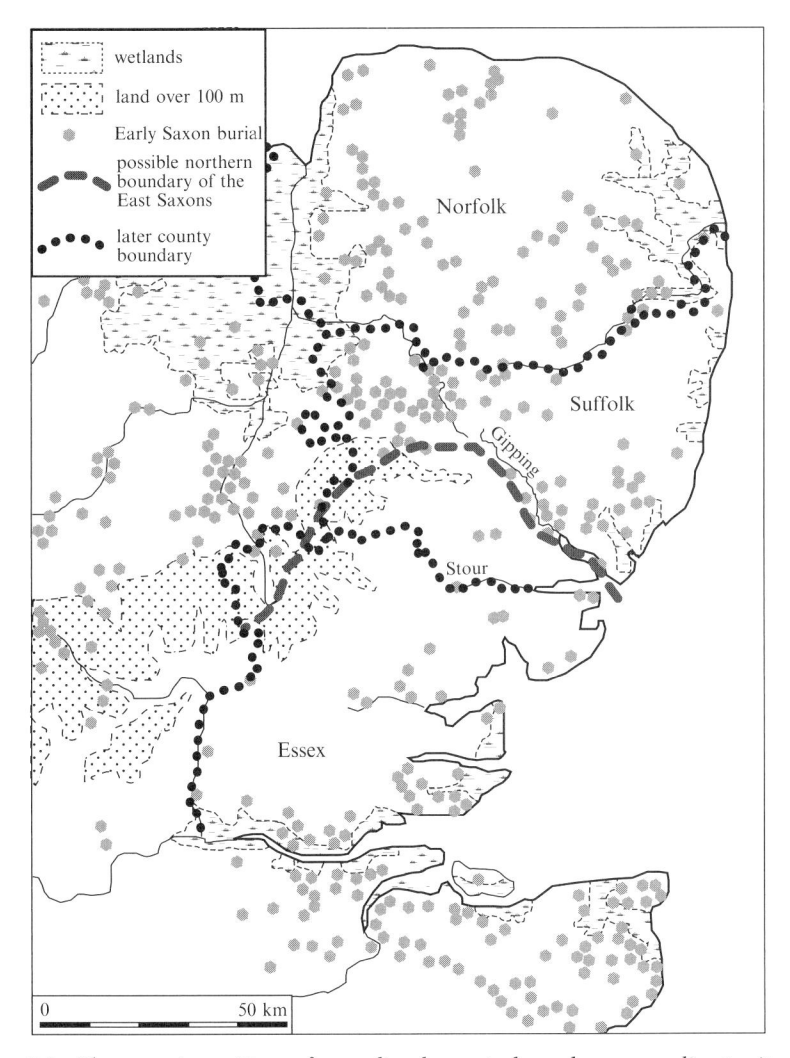

Fig. 2.2. The superimposition of a medieval county boundary on earlier territorial arrangements in East Anglia: the distribution of Early Saxon cemeteries (shown here) and a variety of other material culture, suggests that the northern boundary of the East Saxons, and the Roman *civitas* of the Trinovantes that preceded them, embraced a large part of what is now southern Suffolk. (After Rippon 2008a, figs. 5.1 and 5.2.)

existence at the time of the Domesday Book, but many have a very arbitrary feel, being bureaucratic constructions imposed upon the landscape to aid local administration within the emerging English state during the tenth century. A good example of this is East Anglia (Fig. 2.2). The boundary between the early medieval kingdom of the East Angles—which appears to correspond quite closely to the Romano-British *civitas* and pre-Roman tribal grouping of the Iceni—and the early medieval kingdom of the East Saxons—which appears to have occupied a very similar area to the Romano-British *civitas* and pre-Roman tribal grouping of the Trinovantes—runs diagonally through the modern county of Suffolk, roughly along the line of the Gipping valley or its watershed to the south. What is particularly interesting about this boundary is that it also marks a significant division in landscape character, with relatively nucleated settlement and greater areas of open field to the north, and more dispersed settlement and very little open field to the south. When the three shires of Essex, Suffolk, and Norfolk were created around the tenth century, however, this long-standing cultural boundary was ignored, and the division between Essex and the 'south-folk' of East Anglia (Suffolk) was moved south to the river Stour (Williamson 2006a, b; Rippon 2007a; 2008a). While the modern-day counties in that area form convenient areas for research, they clearly do not correspond to what were meaningful territorial units in the past.

Another factor that will determine the design of a study area is whether the aim is to research a single landscape/community, or to compare the history of two different areas. If the latter is the case, then the study area should take the form of a transect straddling these different countrysides, running from the heart of one *pays*, across the boundary, and to the middle of the next. The question then becomes where the precise boundaries of the study area should lie. Initially, some basic research needs to be carried out across a wide area into the natural environment (geology, topography, drainage, and soils) and the cultural landscape (the settlement patterns, field systems, and land uses) in order to identify the extent of the *pays*, and then to position a study area so that it is representative. There are a number of useful sources for such a rapid assessment of landscape character including the *Domesday Geography* series that give simplified maps of relief, geology, and the distribution of certain Domesday resources (e.g. Darby and Welldon Finn 1967). Reports of the 1930s *Land Utilisation Survey* (e.g. Stuart-Monteath 1938), and the *Atlas of Rural Settlement in England* (Roberts and Wrathmell 2000a; 2000b; 2002) also map various aspects of the physical and the cultural landscape. The 1:625,000 Ordnance Survey *Map of Roman Britain*, now in its fifth edition, plots the distribution of major sites against a background of the modern roads and settlements, while the fourth edition is also very useful as it maps the archaeology of Roman Britain against a simple background of relief (Ordnance Survey 1978; 2001). Jones and Mattingly's (1990) *Atlas of Roman Britain* is another invaluable source of distribution maps for that period.

Having rapidly assessed the physical and cultural landscape of South West England, and established that the limit of landscapes characterized by both greater Romanization and medieval villages and open fields ran through the Blackdown and Quantock Hills, a **'regional study area'** was identified. This ran from the English Channel in the south to the Mendip Hills and Bristol Channel in the north, and from the chalk downland of Wessex in the east across to the moorlands of the central Devon Culm Measures in the west (Figs. 1.3 and 2.3). This regional study area of 8,800 km^2 was the subject of research into its geology, topography, drainage, soils, Agricultural Land Classification, Land Use Capability, and early medieval territorial structures. The sources used for this research are summarized in Table 2.1. The regional study area was also used to map data that only survive infrequently, or can only be understood when mapped on a large scale, in order to place the local study area in context, such as the distribution of Roman villas and 'Early Anglo-Saxon' burials. For one piece of analysis—the archaeological and documentary evidence for past patterns of land use—it was found that an even larger study area was required, covering all of Cornwall, Devon, Dorset, Somerset, and Wiltshire.

Following the establishment of this regional picture, a smaller **'local study area'** was identified across which it was practical to carry out more detailed analysis. This comprised a block of 104 parishes and parts of three others[1] in eastern Devon, southern Somerset, and north-west Dorset (covering in total 14,223 km^2),[2] extending from the river Exe in eastern Devon, across the Blackdown Hills, and as far east as the River Parrett in the lowlands of central Somerset. This local study area embraced the eastern fringes of the Culm Measures (that dominate central and western Devon), the fertile lowlands

---

[1] **Devon**: Awliscombe, Bickleigh, Blackborough, Bradninch, Broadclyst, Broadhembury, Buckerell, Burlescombe, Butterleigh, Churchstanton, Clayhidon, Clyst Hydon, Clyst St Lawrence, Cullompton, Combe Raleigh, Cotleigh, Culmstock, Dunkeswell, Feniton, Halberton, Hemyock, Hockworthy, Holcombe Rogus, Huntsham, Huxham, Kentisbeare, Luppitt, Membury, Monkton, part of Thorverton (Nether Exe), Payhembury, Plymtree, Poltimore, Rewe, Sampford Peverell, Sheldon, Silverton, Stoke Canon, Talaton, Thorncombe (a detached part of Devon in Dorset), part of Tiverton, Uffculme, Uplowman, Upottery, Whimple, Willand, Yarcombe. **Dorset**: Broadwindsor, Burstock, Chardstock, Mosterton, Stockland (a detached part of Dorset in Devon), and Wambrook. **Somerset**: Ashill, Barrington, Beer Crocombe, Bickenhall, Broadway, Buckland St Mary, Capland, Chaffcombe, Chard Chillington, Combe St Nicholas, Corfe, Crewkerne, Cricket Malherbie, Cricket St Thomas, Cudworth, Curland, Curry Mallet, part of Curry Rivel (Earnshill), Dinnington, Donyatt, Dowlish Wake, Hatch Beauchamp, Hinton St George, Ilminster, Ilton, Isle Abbots, Isle Brewers, Kingstone, Kingsbury Episcopi, Knowle St Giles, Lopen, Merriott, Misterton, Orchard Portman, Otterford, Pitminster, Puckington, Sampford Arundell, Seaborough, Seavington St Mary, Seavington St Michael, Shepton Beauchamp, South Petherton, Staple Fitzpaine, Stocklinch, Thurlbear, Wayford, Wellington, West Dowlish, West Hatch, White Lackington, Whites Staurton and Winsham.

[2] Based on Tithe survey acreages in Kain and Oliver (1995), or http://www.visionofbritain.org.uk where there was no Tithe survey. The local study area only includes those parts of Tiverton and Thorverton to the east of the river Exe, and that part of Curry Rivel (i.e. Earnshill) south of the Isle.

of eastern Devon, the northern parts of the Blackdown Hills, the lowlands of central Somerset, and the hills and valleys of southern Somerset and northwest Dorset. This smaller study area was used to examine aspects of historic landscape character that were particularly time-consuming to research including settlement patterns, place- and field-names, vernacular architecture, field systems, and the distribution of resources recorded in Domesday.

THE GEOLOGICAL FOUNDATIONS OF THE LANDSCAPE (FIG. 2.3)

The rocks that lie beneath the surface of the landscape influence relief, drainage, and soils, that together have a profound effect upon the character of the countryside. One of the fundamental reasons why the British landscape is so rich and varied in its character is that its geology is so complex, and our study area straddles one of the most complex areas of all. A key division in the geology of Britain is the 'Jurassic Ridge' that runs from the coast of North Yorkshire, down through the East Midlands to the coast of Dorset. Immediately to the east lies an area of softer clay (the Oxford Clays and Kellaway Beds) which then give way to the Cretaceous greensands and chalk downland of the Yorkshire Wolds, the Chiltern Hills, Berkshire Downs, Salisbury Plain, and Cranbourne Chase. To the west of the Jurassic Ridge there are also extensive areas of softer rocks (Triassic mudstones and the Lower Lias) that underlie the relatively flat plain of Midland England, with the older, harder, rocks that characterize the uplands of the south-west of England and Wales to the west.

The local and regional study areas of this project straddle this Jurassic 'backbone' of the British landscape, and in order to understand the geology of this area as it is exposed on the surface, we must first consider the sequence of rocks in chronological order.

The oldest formations in our region that form the uplands of Exmoor and the Quantock Hills to the west comprise a complex sequence of interbedded slates, mudstones, sandstones, and limestones laid down during the Devonian period. To the east these are succeeded by a sequence of rocks laid down in the Carboniferous period, with a basal shale overlain by limestone, the main outcrop of which is the Mendip Hills in northern Somerset. The Carboniferous limestone is overlain by a complex deposit of sandstones, siltstones, and shales that dominate central and western Devon, where they are known as the Culm Measures. The term 'Culm' has nothing to do with the East Devon river of the same name, but refers to thin layers of coal that in Devon is known as 'culm' (Edmonds *et al.* 1975, 34).

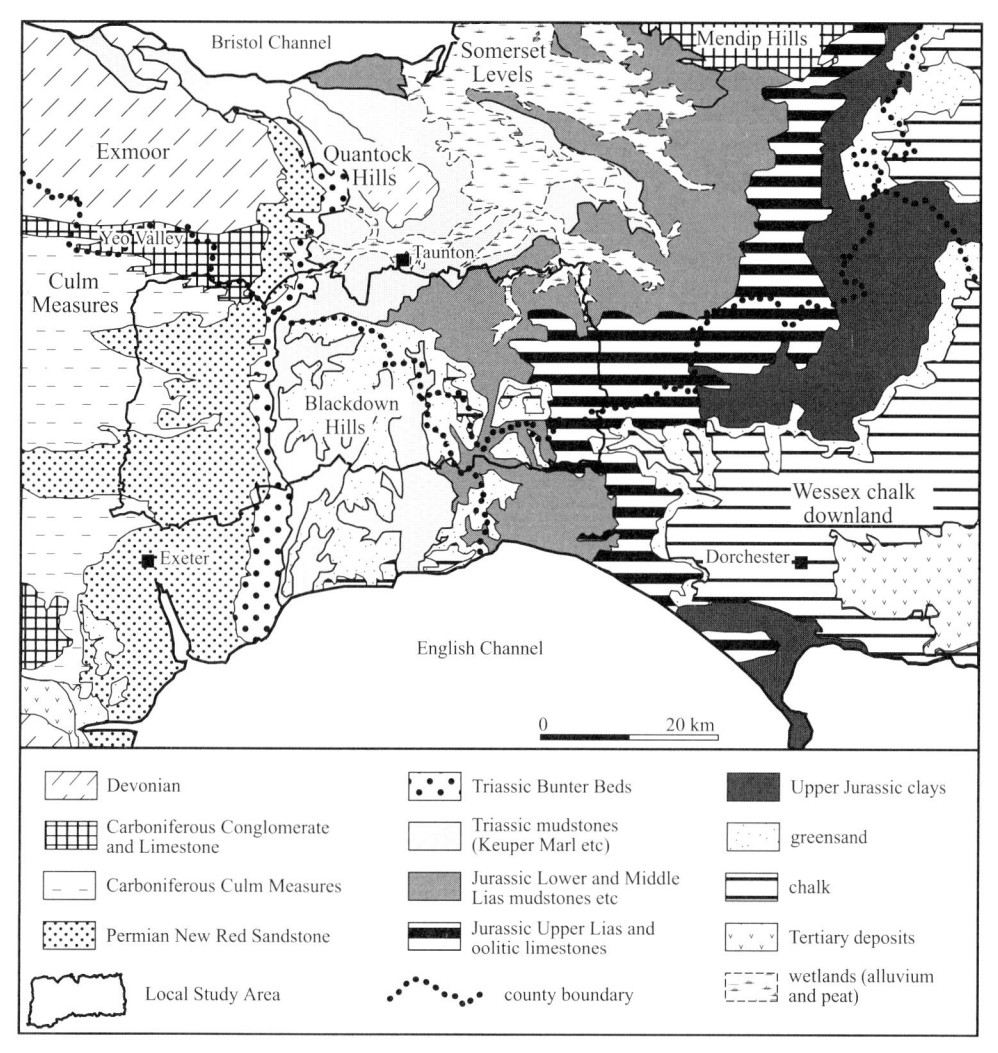

Fig. 2.3. Solid geology of the regional study area, and Holocene deposits of the Somerset Levels. (After Institute of Geological Sciences 1979.)

East of the Culm Measures lie a series of distinctive red breccias, conglomerates, sandstones, and marls of the 'New Red Sandstone' laid down during the Permian era that are exposed in the Creedy and lower Exe valleys in an area that is sometimes called 'Red Devon' (Dudley Stamp 1941, fig. 23). These were succeeded by Triassic sandstones (the Bunter Beds) that outcrop in a narrow zone from Budleigh Salterton on the east Devon coast to Williton in west Somerset. These are overlain by red silty mudstones of the 'Mercian Mudstone Group' (formerly called the 'Keuper Marls') that underlie many low-lying parts of our study area including the Vale of Taunton Deane, and the foothills of the Blackdown and Quantock Hills.

During the Jurassic the Lower Lias limestone (Blue Lias) and clays were deposited. These were succeeded by the Pennard Sands, along with marls and siltstones of the Middle Lias, and then the Upper Lias that underlie large areas around South Petherton and which include the Yeovil Sandstone. In places, these are capped by a distinctive orange, shelly limestone known as Ham Stone that is used extensively in local buildings (Fig. 2.4). Along with other distinctive building materials used elsewhere, this is an example of how geology contributes to local landscape character (e.g. Fig. 2.5). In parts of southern Somerset and western Dorset this Lower Jurassic Lias sequence is capped by oolitic limestones of the Middle Jurassic that further north forms the Jurassic Ridge that runs through the heart of Midland England, and which includes the Cotswold Hills. In the east of our study area, the limestone is overlain by a series of Upper Jurassic clays that form a broad lowland vale in north-east Dorset and south-west Wiltshire. During the Cretaceous period, a thick deposit of greensand was laid down that forms the Blackdown Hills, followed by the distinctive white chalk that now forms the Wessex downland. In the far south-east of our regional study area, these Cretaceous deposits are overlain by Tertiary sands and gravels that form the extensive heathlands of southern

Fig. 2.4. The distinctive Ham Stone forms a key character defining feature of the landscape in and around Barrington in central Somerset.

Fig. 2.5. Buddle Cottage and Bowdel, Cheriton Fitzpaine, Devon. A seventeenth-century, three-roomed cross-passage house, extended to the east (right) in the eighteenth century. The walls are plastered cob on rubble footings. The hipped roof is a common feature of cob buildings in the South West as this building material was not suitable for vertical gable-end walls. The prominent chimneystack, placed laterally on the outside wall, is also characteristic of Devon.

Dorset. Both the greensand and chalk are in places capped by more recent deposits known as 'clay-with-flints'. The only other significant drift deposits within our regional study area are alluvium and peat in the Somerset Levels, and terrace deposits in the floodplains and river valleys.

THE TOPOGRAPHY OF THE STUDY AREA (FIG. 2.6)

Our study area is dominated by the Blackdown Hills: a flat-topped plateau around 250 metres above sea level, that is bounded to the south by the English Channel, and to the east, north, and west by an extensively wooded steep scarp slope (Fig. 1.1). The Blackdowns are first named in the thirteenth century (Gover *et al*. 1931, 18), and labelled in this way on Saxton's 1575 map of Somerset (Ravenhill 1992, 40–1). Although Moore (1829, 10) suggested they were 'so called from their dreariness', the name probably reflects the dark and foreboding nature of their steep, well-wooded slopes (the Black Downs). To the east of the Blackdown Hills the land falls away into the low-lying plain of

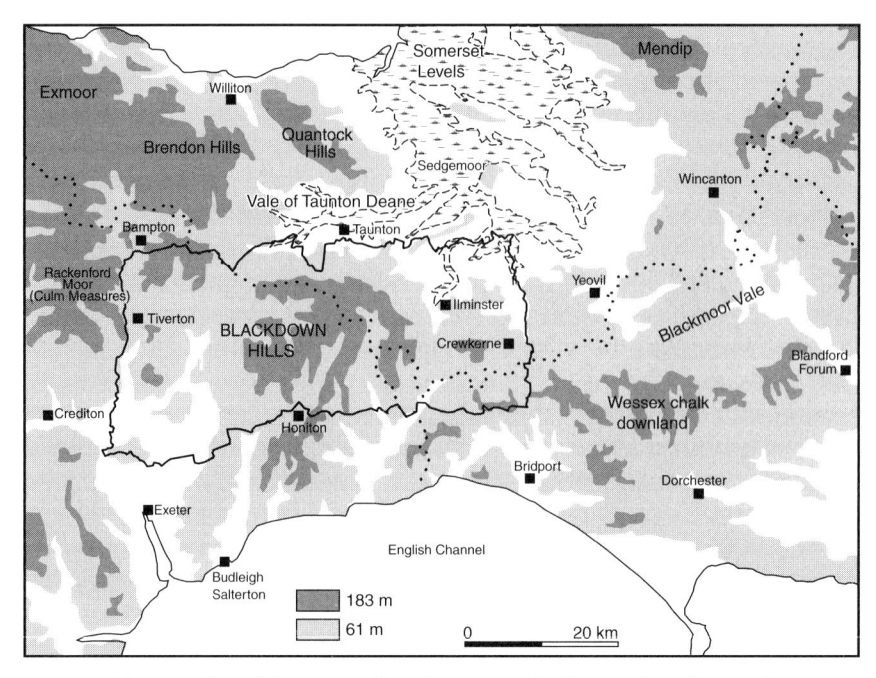

Fig. 2.6. Topography of the regional study area, with places referred to in the text.

central-southern Somerset at around 30–60 m above sea level, but which includes a series of often steep-sided and flat-topped hills formed from the Jurassic Upper Lias (including Ham Stone) which rise to over 100 m in places. Further east lies the broad low-lying plain of the Vale of Blackmoor (formed from the soft Upper Jurassic Oxford Clays), beyond which is the steep scarp slope of the chalk downland of Wessex. To the north of the Blackdown Hills lie the flat Triassic claylands of central Somerset at just 15–30 m above sea level. Within this area a series of very gently sided valleys—including the rivers Isle, Parrett, and Yeo—are separated by long promontories that extend into the Somerset Levels. The highest of these ridges, between the river Isle and the West Hatch Brook, has a steep scarp slope on its western side, between Curry Rivel and Hatch Beauchamp, which divides these central Somerset lowlands from the Vale of Taunton Deane to the west. To the west of the Blackdown Hills lie the gently undulating lowlands of eastern Devon, fringed on their western side by rolling hills of Permian breccia that reach over 200 m in places. Finally, in the far west of our region lie the Culm Measures with topography characterized by gently undulating plateaus and dissected by steep-sided valleys.

WETLANDS AND WATERSHEDS: THE DRAINAGE SYSTEM (FIG. 2.7)

Close to their sources, in the upland parts of our regional study area, rivers flow through quite steep-sided valleys, but downstream these develop broader floodplains that provide areas of rich pasture and meadow (e.g. Fig. 3.8). In upland areas, the watersheds between drainage systems are often quite well-defined, although in lowlands the areas between rivers can have more muted relief and the 'interfluvial' areas can suffer from poor drainage. Our region is dominated by two major drainage systems radiating off the Blackdown Hills. To the north there are a series of river basins—notably the Tone, Isle, Parrett, and Yeo—that flow into the southern part of the Somerset Levels (the area known as Sedgemoor), while the western side of the Blackdown Hills is drained by the River Exe and its tributaries, the Clyst, Culm, and Lowman. The southern parts of the Blackdown and Jurassic Hills are drained by a series of minor rivers that flow into the English Channel. To the east, the landscape is drained by the catchments of the rivers Frome and Stour.

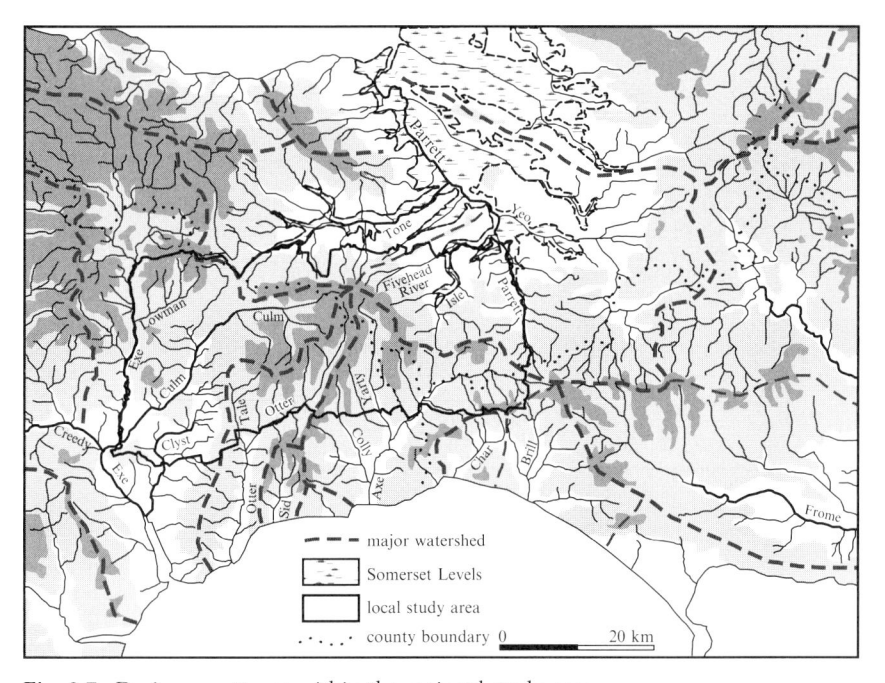

Fig. 2.7. Drainage patterns within the regional study area.

SOILS (FIG. 2.8)

The geology that forms the foundations of our landscape has been subject to a variety of natural processes (weathering) and cultural activities (notably ploughing) that have produced the surface soils of today. This is a region with a particularly complex range of soils, summarized in Table 2.2. The flat plateaus of the Blackdown Hills are covered in fine silty/loamy soils over slowly permeable clay (the clay-with-flints) that suffer from slight seasonal waterlogging. Where the underlying Cretaceous greensand is not capped with clay-with-flints, there are coarse, loamy soils with some surface peat caused by the flat topography of the plateaus and resultant poor drainage. The slopes of

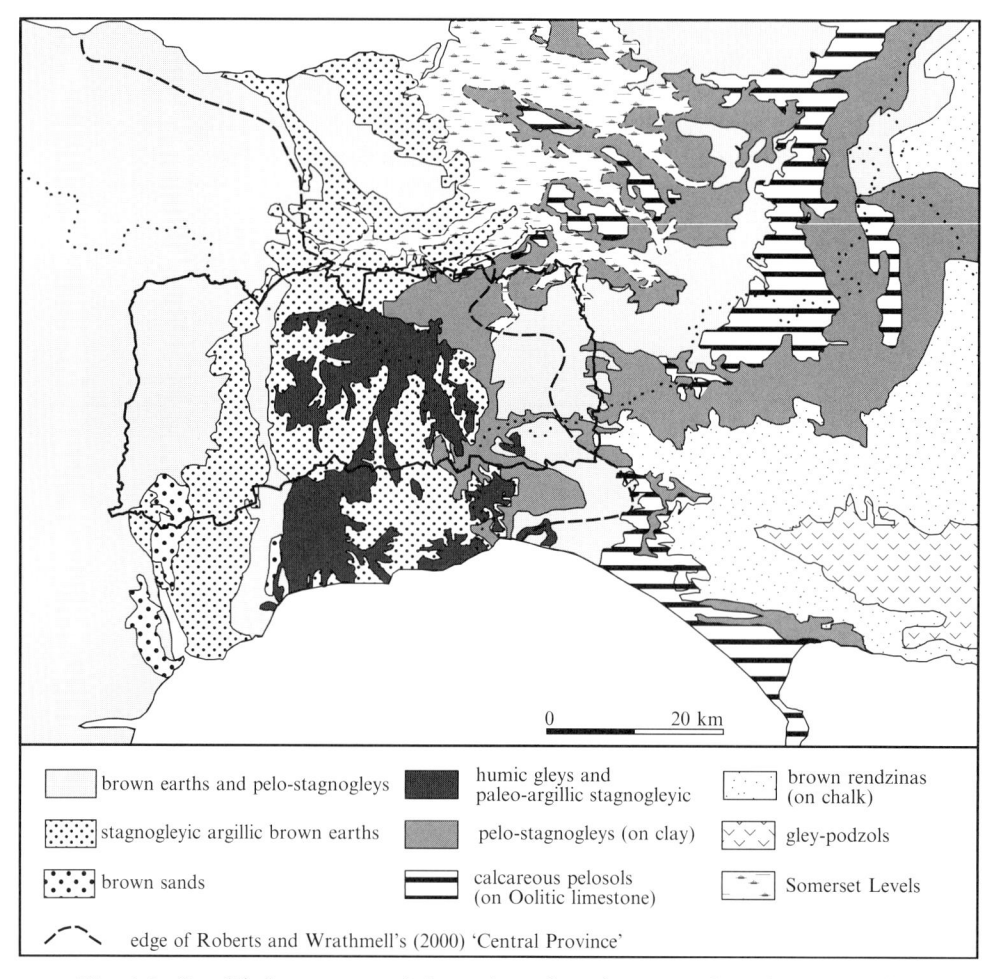

Fig. 2.8. Simplified mapping of the soils within the regional study area. (After Mackney *et al.* 1983.)

the valleys within the Blackdown Hills are covered in better drained fine loamy soils over slowly permeable clay (the Triassic mudstones) that suffer from slight seasonal waterlogging. The alluvial floodplains of the major rivers are covered in stoneless clayey soils.

To the east of the Blackdown Hills, in southern Somerset, there are predominantly well-drained loamy and silty soils that overlie the Middle Lias sandstones and siltstones. Further east lie areas of heavier, clayey soils on the Upper Jurassic clays of the Blackmoor Vale, beyond which there are various mostly shallow, well-drained, calcareous soils on the chalk downlands. The lowlands of central Somerset, between the Blackdown Hills and the Somerset Levels, are covered in slowly permeable clayey soils overlying the Lower Lias. To the west of the Curry Rivel to Hatch Beauchamp ridge, in the Vale of Taunton Deane, there are slowly permeable, fine, loamy soils overlying the Triassic mudstones (Keuper Marls, etc.). Immediately west of the Blackdown Hills, in the gently undulating lowlands of the Otter and Tale valleys, well-drained loamy sands overlie Triassic sandstone. The hills to the west of the Tale have the same reddish, fine, loamy soils that are found in the valleys of the Blackdown Hills and in the Vale of Taunton Deane, with areas of slightly heavier, slowly permeable, and seasonally waterlogged fine loamy soils in the flatter interfluvial areas. West of the Culm, on the hills around the Exe Valley, soils are predominantly well-drained brown earths with a deep red colour that forms an important part of the character of this landscape. Further west, overlying the Culm Measures and Devonian rocks of Exmoor, the Brendon Hills, and the Quantocks are a complex series of mostly slowly permeable, seasonally waterlogged clayey and silty soils (greatly simplified on Fig. 2.8).

CLIMATE

In terms of rainfall, the uplands of Exmoor and Dartmoor have around 160 cm a year, with Mendip, the Blackdown Hills, and the Culm Measures receiving c.100 cm, and the lowlands of Devon, Dorset, and Somerset having around 80 cm (i.e. half that of the uplands, a variation that occurs over just 20 km in places). On the uplands, the mean daily maximum temperature is 10° Celsius compared to 14° C in the lowlands, while snow lies of the uplands on average fifteen mornings a year, but just five in the lowlands. The growing season is around 225 days on Dartmoor and Exmoor, 275 days on the Blackdown Hills and higher areas of the Culm Measures, but around 300 days in the lowlands (Stuart-Menteath 1938, 31–41; Tavener 1940, 259; Dudley Stamp 1941, 476–84; Perry 1997; Caseldine 1999).

We should not, however, assume that these patterns have always been the same, as there have been significant changes in the climate over the past two

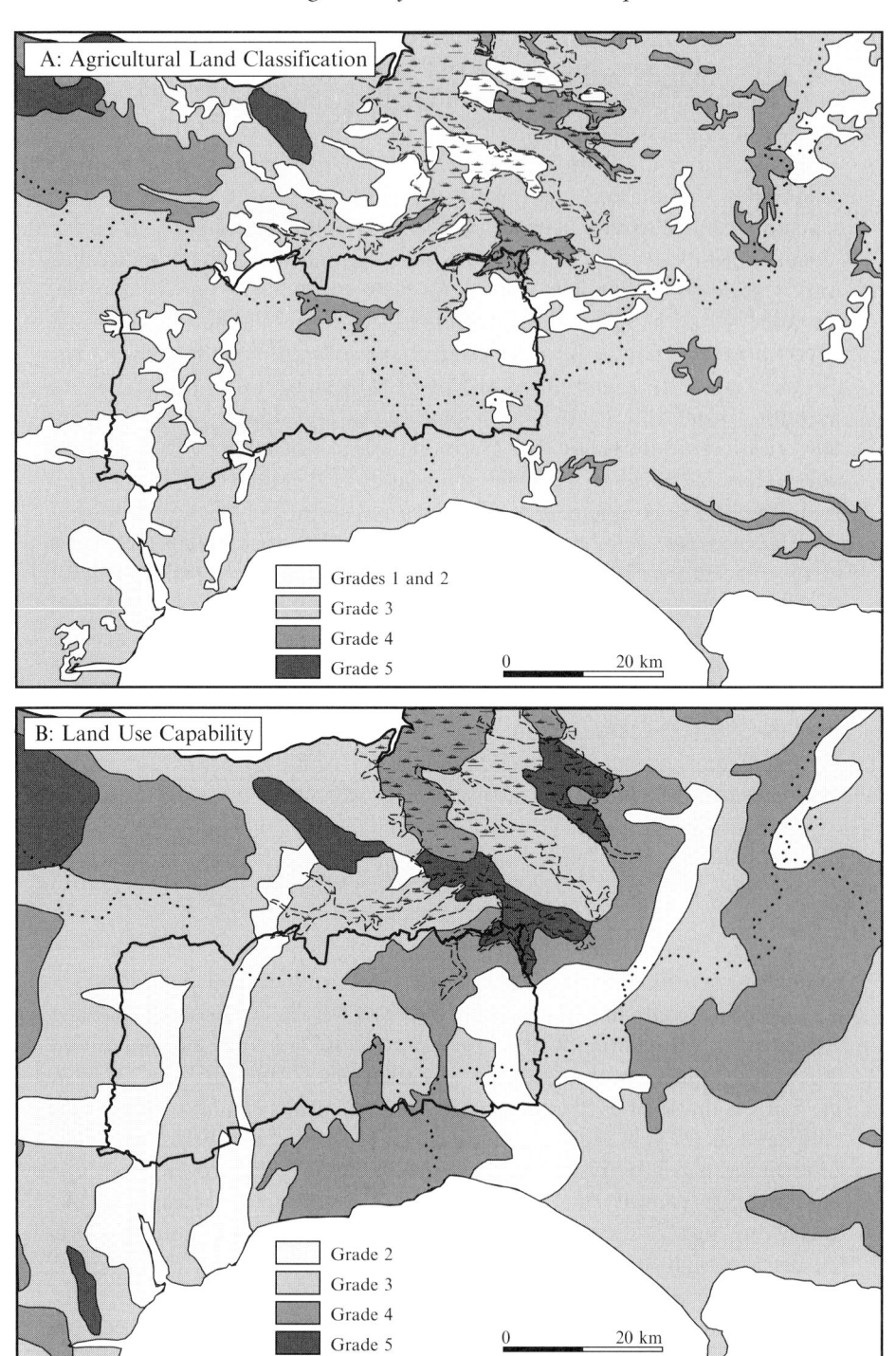

Fig. 2.9. Measures of current agricultural potential. (A) Agricultural Land Classification (Ministry of Agriculture, Fisheries and Food 1979); (B) Land Use Capability (Mackney 1979).

millennia (Lamb 1982; Mayes and Wheeler 1997; Dark 2000, 19–33; Baillie and Brown 2003). It appears that the first millennium BC was relatively cold and wet, although from around the second century BC the climate became milder, and by the early Roman period was probably very similar to or even warmer than today. Warming continued into the late Roman period, although in the fifth and sixth centuries there was a return to cooler, wetter conditions. Around the seventh and eighth centuries the climate improved with drier, warmer summers but colder winters, which was followed by a brief return to cooler and wetter conditions in the ninth century. From around the tenth century there was a more prolonged period of warmer, drier weather that lasted until the fourteenth century when conditions started to deteriorate in what has become known as the 'Little Ice Age' that lasted until the eighteenth century. Against these long-term climatic changes, there were also shorter-term events, such as around AD 540 when a narrowing of the growth rings in trees reflects an environmental downturn and which was followed by plague: the cause of this downturn is unclear, with a volcanic eruption and a close encounter with a comet being recent suggestions (Baillie 2001). The impact of climate change on human communities in the past has been much debated, with traditional views that climatic deterioration forced people to abandon physically 'marginal' environments—such as uplands or very heavy soils—having largely been rejected. Falling summer temperatures will have reduced the growing season at higher altitudes to the point at which growing crops became increasing difficult, but no part of our local study area lies this close to the climatic 'margins': whilst we should be aware that the climate did change during the period we are studying, no areas are likely to have experienced significant difficulties because of it.

CURRENT AGRICULTURAL POTENTIAL (FIG. 2.9)

The Ministry of Agriculture, Fisheries and Food's (1979) system of 'Agricultural Land Classification', and the Soil Survey of England and Wales's mapping of 'Land Use Capability' (Mackney 1979) combine the physical properties of topography, soils, and climate with the demands of modern agriculture and the technologies currently available, to determine the potential of different areas for farming. In terms of **Agricultural Land Classification**, the best quality land (Grades 1 and 2) in our regional study area is restricted to a small number of lowland areas, notably the lower Exe and Culm valleys, the Vale of Taunton Deane, and the central Somerset lowlands. Grade 3 land, that presents some limitation on land use, is by far the most common grade right across our study area and is particularly characteristic of the Culm Measures, the hills north of Tiverton, and the valleys and foothills of the Blackdown

Hills. Grade 4 land, with severe limitations, is found in small patches right across our study area including the higher plateaus of the Blackdown Hills, while the poorest quality Grade 5 land is restricted to the high uplands of Exmoor and the Quantock Hills. Four of the seven grades of **Land-use Capability** are found in our study area. Grade 2 land, with minor limitations, found in the Creedy, Exe and Tale valleys and parts of the lowlands of central Somerset, while Grade 3 land, with moderate limitations, forms the most common type covering the remaining lowland areas, the Blackdown Hills, and the fringes of the Culm Measures. Grade 4 land with moderately severe limitations, are found in the Yarty valley on the Blackdown Hills, and in the lowlands to the north that are underlain by Lower and Middle Lias clays. Grade 5 land, with severe limitations, is only found on the high uplands of Exmoor and the low-lying backfens of the Somerset Levels.

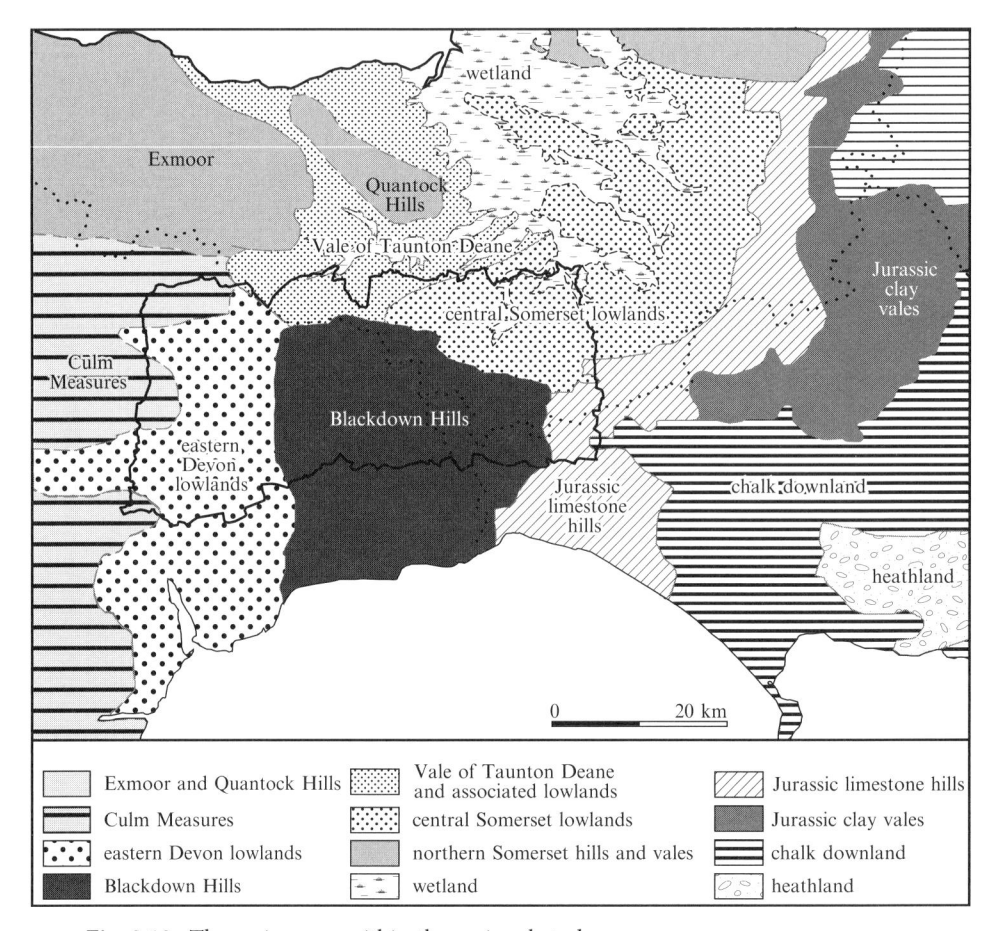

Fig. 2.10. The major *pays* within the regional study area.

The physical character of landscape 31

Table 2.1. Sources used in studying the physical background.

Geology	The British Geological Survey (formerly known as the Institute of Geological Sciences) has produced mapping at a variety of scales (http://www.bgs.ac.uk/catalogue/home.html). A good starting point is the 1:625,000 (about 1 inch to 10 miles) mapping that covers the whole of mainland Britain in two sheets (north and south), with separate versions for the 'solid' (i.e. underlying bedrock) and 'drift' (i.e. later, superficial deposits such as alluvium). The larger scale 1:250,000 series covers mainland Britain in 33 sheets, with separate maps for 'solid' and 'quaternary' (i.e. drift) available for many areas. The most detailed mapping available for the whole country is at a scale of 1:50,000 which covers mainland Britain in 360 sheets, each covering 30 km by 20 km. There is an accompanying memoir for each map describing the geological sequence (e.g. Ussher 1902; Edwards 2000), while a series of regional guides provide a more general overview (e.g. Edmonds *et al.* 1975).
Topography	Information on topography is readily available from modern Ordnance Survey mapping at scales of 1:250,000 ('Travel Map' series), 1:50,000 ('Landranger' series), and 1:25,000 ('Explorer' series) (http://www.ordnancesurvey.co.uk/oswebsite/). On modern editions of Ordnance Survey maps, data on relief take the form of contours, although some older series used much clearer cartography, with differently coloured tints between the contours giving an instant impression of the topography of a region. The early nineteenth-century One Inch to One Mile series (1:63,360) presents topography in an altogether different way with hashers used to denote steeper slope. This is a more schematic and subjective way of representing significant topographical features but one that is very effective, particularly for a newcomer to an area who wants a simple introduction to the overall lie of the land. It is now possible to undertake a 'virtual' flight across a landscape using the website Google Earth (http://earth.google.com/).
Drainage	Drainage systems are depicted on all Ordnance Survey mapping, and the 1:25,000 Explorer series maps are particularly useful in that they show field boundaries in wetland areas as blue, reflecting their permanently high water-table. The 1:50,000 Landranger series maps do not show individual field boundaries but, like the Explorer series maps, they do depict streams and rivers. Finding the names of minor rivers and streams can be a challenge as they often do not appear on modern maps, though searching a variety of older Ordnance Survey map series, particularly the larger scales, usually locates a name.
Soils	Soils have been mapped by the National Soil Resources Institute based at Cranfield University (formerly the Soil Survey of England and Wales), that has published a simplified map showing the soils of England and Wales at a scale of 1:100,000 (Avery *et al.* 1975). This provides a very useful summary of the main characteristics of the different soil types, while the most detailed mapping which covers the whole of England and Wales is published in five sheets at a scale of 1:250,000 (Mackney *et al.* 1983). Selected areas have been surveyed at 1:25,000, 1:50,000, or 1:63,360 (http://www.silsoe.cranfield.ac.uk/nsri/services/pdf/publicationslist.pdf). These detailed maps have an accompanying memoir that describes the soils in that area, as well as providing a useful summary of the underlying geology (e.g. Clayden 1971).

(*continued*)

Table 2.1. Continued

Climate	Information on climate is available in a wide range of sources, including useful summaries in Dudley Stamp's *The Land of Britain* volumes, and Mayes and Wheeler (1997).
Agricultural Land Classification	For England and Wales, the Ministry of Agriculture, Fisheries and Food (1979) have identified five grades of agricultural land that have been mapped at a scale of 1:625,000 (http://www.magic.gov.uk/staticmaps/regional.html): • Grade 1: land with very minor or no physical limitations. Typically consists of deep, well-drained loams on level or gently sloping ground. Retains good reserves of water and is either well supplied with nutrients or is highly responsive to fertilizers. No climatic problems. • Grade 2: land with some minor soil or climatic limitations that may hinder cultivation or harvesting leading to slightly lower yields and some restrictions on what can be grown. • Grade 3: land with moderate limitations due to soils, relief, or climate that restrict the choice of crops, timing of cultivation, or level of yield. Soil problems include structure, texture, drainage, depth, stoniness, or water-holding capacity. • Grade 4: land with severe limitations due to adverse soils, relief, or climate. Today, such land will generally be under grass although there may be occasional fields of oats, barley, or forage crops. • Grade 5: land with severe limitations due to adverse soils, relief, or climate such as very steep slopes, very poor drainage, shallow depth of soil, or excessive stoniness. Today, such land will generally be under grass or rough pasture.
Land Use Capability	The Soil Survey of England and Wales has identified seven types of land-use capability that have been mapped at a scale of 1:1,000,000 (Mackney 1979), of which four are found in our study area: • Grade 2: land with minor limitations that reduce the choice of crops and interfere with cultivation. • Grade 3: land with moderate limitations that restrict the choice of crops and/or demand careful management. • Grade 4: land with moderately severe limitations that restrict the choice of crops and/or require very careful management practices. • Grade 5: land with severe limitations that restrict use to pasture, forestry, and recreation.

These two schemes present a very similar picture, with the best quality agricultural land (in terms of modern farming) being in the lowlands of the eastern Devon, the Vale of Taunton Deane, and central Somerset. The Blackdown Hills and the Culm Measures have moderate potential, and land with the greatest limitations is restricted to the lowest-lying wetlands of the Somerset Levels and the high uplands of Exmoor. Along with the other data mapped in this chapter, this suggests that our regional study area consisted of all or parts of twelve distinctive districts (*pays*) (Fig. 2.10). The high uplands of Exmoor and the Quantock Hills lie to the north and the moderately high plateaus of the Culm Measures to the west. These are separated from the

Table 2.2. Soils and the geology from which they are derived (from Mackney *et al.* 1983).

Blackdown Hills

plateaus	Batcombe	582a	stagnogleyic paleo-argillic brown earths	clay-with-flints
	Dunkeswell	714a	paleo-argillic stagnogley soils	clay-with-flints
	Hense	871b	humic gley soil	Cretaceous greensand
valley sides	Bearsted 2	541b	typical brown earth	Triassic mudstones (MMG)
	Brockhurst 1	711b	typical stagnogley soils	Triassic mudstones (MMG)
	Whimple 3	572f	stagnogleyic argillic brown earths	Triassic mudstones (MMG)
	Worcester	431	typical argillic pelosols	Triassic mudstones (MMG)

Jurassic hills of southern Somerset

valleys and plains	Curtisden	572i	stagnogleyic argillic brown earth	Upper and Middle Lias
	South Petherton	541m	typical brown earth	Upper Lias
hilltops	Elmton 2	343b	gleyic brown earths	lower oolitic limestone
	Sherborne	343d	gleyic brown earths	upper oolitic limestone

Blackmoor Vale

	Denchworth	712b	pelo-stagnogley soils	Upper Jurassic clays
	Wickham 2	711f	typical stagnogley soils	drift over Upper Jurassic clays

Wessex downland

	Andover 1	343h	brown rendzinas	Cretaceous chalk

central Somerset claylands

plain	Evesham 1	411a	typical calcareous pelosols	Jurassic clay (Lower Lias)
	Evesham 3	411c	typical calcareous pelosols	Jurassic clay (Lower Lias)
	Denchworth	712b	pelo-stagnogley soils	Upper Jurassic clays
	Wickham 2	711f	typical stagnogley soils	drift over Upper Jurassic clays
limestone hills	Sherborne	343d	gleyic brown earths	upper oolitic limestone

Vale of Taunton Deane

	Whimple 3	572f	stagnogleyic argillic brown earths	Triassic mudstones (MMG)
	Worcester	431	typical argillic pelosols	Triassic mudstone (MMG)

Otter valley and northwards

	Bromsgrove	541b	typical brown earth	Triassic sandstone
	Newnham	541w	typical brown earth	Triassic sandstone

(*continued*)

Table 2.2. Continued

Otter–Culm interfluve				
	Whimple 3	572f	stagnogleyic argillic brown earths	Triassic mudstones (MMG)
	Brockhurst 1	711b	typical stagnogley soils	Triassic mudstones (MMG)
	Goldstone	631e	humo-ferric podzols	Budleigh Salterton Pebble Bed
Culm–Exe–Creedy valleys				
	Crediton	541e	typical brown earths	Permian basal breccia of the NRS
Culm Measures				
	Neath	541h	typical brown earths	Carboniferous sandstone and shale
	Hallsworth 2	712e	pelo-stagnogley soils	Carboniferous sandstone and shale
	Manod	611c	typical brown podzolic soil	Carboniferous sandstone and shale

Key to nomenclature
Brown Earths
   typical brown earths: non-alluvial loamy soils with a non-calcareous subsoil without significant clay enrichment
   brown sands: non-calcareous sandy soils
   brown earths: brownish or reddish loamy soils
   argillic brown earths: brown or reddish loamy or loamy-over-clayey soils with a subsurface horizon with significant clay enrichment
   paleo-argillic brown earths: loamy or clayey soils with a reddish clay-enriched subsoil
   stagnogleyic argillic brown earths: brown or reddish loamy or loamy-over-clayey soils with a slowly permeable subsurface horizon with significant clay enrichment
   Groundwater gley soils: soils with predominantly mottled or uniformly grey subsoils resulting from periodic waterlogging by a fluctuating groundwater-table
   pelo-alluvial gleys: loamy or clayey soils overlying recent alluvium, affected by fluctuating but often high groundwater levels
   humic gley soils: loamy or clayey soils with an organic-rich or peaty topsoil
Surface-water gleys: seasonally waterlogged, slowly permeable soils
   typical stagnogley: seasonally waterlogged, slowly permeable soils with a clay-enriched subsoil
   pelo-stagnogley: clayey, seasonally waterlogged, slowly permeable soils
Lithomorphic: shallow soils in which the only significant pedogenic process has been the formation of an organic-enriched mineral surface horizon
   rendzinas: thin calcareous soils over chalk
Pelosols: slowly permeable clayey soils
   typical argillic pelosols: slowly permeable clayey soils with a clay-enriched subsoil
Podzolic: normally acidic soils with a black or dark brown subsurface horizon resulting from the accumulation or iron, aluminium, or organic material.
MMG: Mercian Mudstone Group
NRS: New Red Sandstone

Blackdown Hills by the fertile lowlands of eastern Devon and the Vale of Taunton Deane, with the central Somerset lowlands and Somerset Levels to the north. Further east lie the Jurassic limestone hills, the lowlands of the Jurassic clay vales, the chalk downland, and finally the heathlands of south-east Dorset.

3

'The most beautiful landskip in the world'? The perceived character of landscape

In Chapter 2, we characterized the landscape based on relatively objective criteria and our modern understanding of the natural environment. In the past, however, people did not have the benefit of this scientific knowledge and so we will now examine how writers in the past perceived the different *pays* of our regional study area. Unfortunately, we have little indication of what illiterate local communities thought about their environment, though we can get some insights from looking at the folklore that was written down. Finally, we will look at how the landscape appears today. The overall aim is to try and understand if the distinctive *pays* that we can identify based on our modern mapping of topography, geology, soils, and land use are simply the scholarly creations of an academic mind, or whether they had a reality in the consciousness of people in the past.

JOHN LELAND, 1538–1546

Although there are some written sources from before the sixteenth century that describe aspects of the landscape, such as the travels of Giraldus Cambrensis through late twelfth-century Wales (Wright 1968; Richter 1976), and William of Worcester who journeyed across parts of southern England in the late fifteenth century (Harvey 1969), the topographical detail they contain is very limited. The earliest detailed account we have of the English landscape is the itinerary of John Leland, written between 1538 and 1546. Several editions have been published, and although the most accurate transcription is that of Lucy Toulmin Smith (1906–10), John Chandler's (1993) edition is the most user-friendly, as the text is written in modern English and there are maps of each county showing the routes that Leland appears to have taken. Although Leland himself never mapped the different types of landscape that he observed, his various references to enclosed and 'champion' countryside (i.e. characterized by open field) can be mapped (Fig. 3.1).

South of Honiton, he describes the landscape as having good arable land and pasture with some woodland, while areas towards the coast are described as 'fairly good ground' with 'not much woodland' (Chandler 1993, 123, 131–2). He viewed the area we now call the Jurassic Hills (between Bridport and Beaminster) as having soils that were 'exceptionally good all the way, and

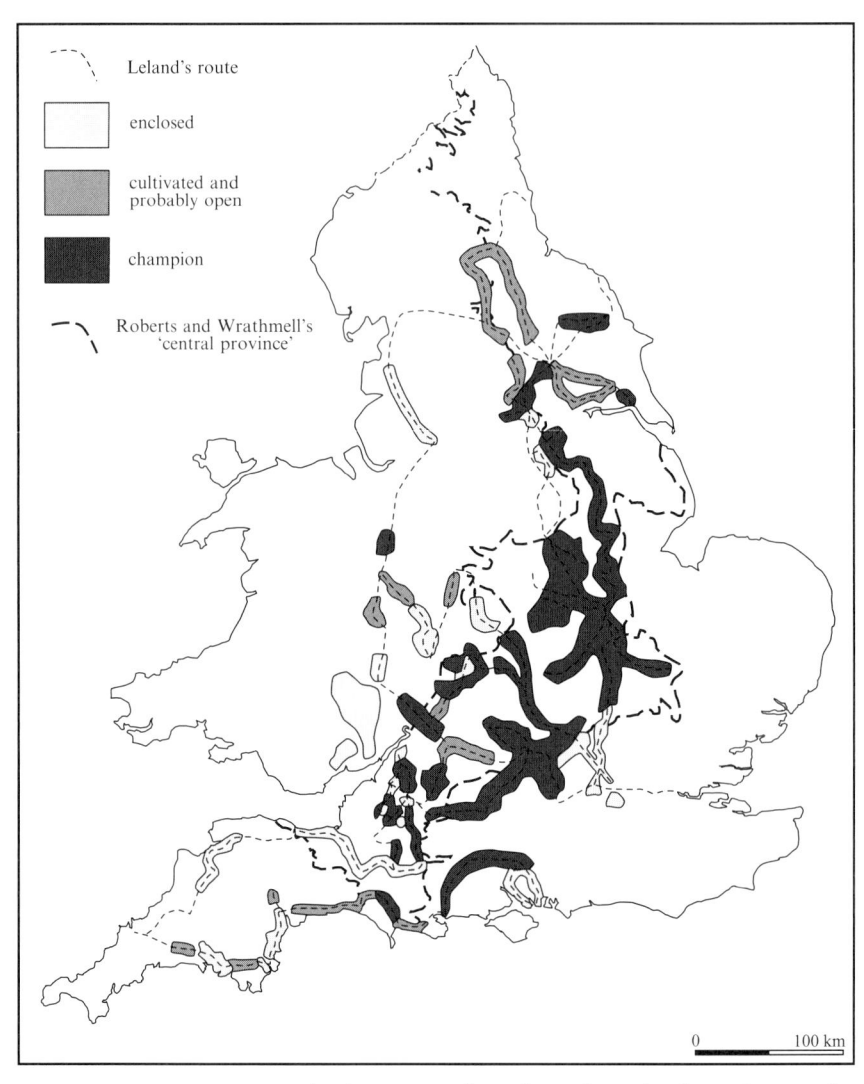

Fig. 3.1. An interpretation of references made within John Leland's mid-sixteenth-century itineraries to 'enclosed' and 'champion' countryside (after Slater 1907, 47). The divisions between the two broadly correspond with other attempts to map the extent of former common fields based on later sources (e.g. Fig. 2.1). (Drawing by Adam Wainwright.)

this stretch of country is almost the best in the whole of Dorset for arable, pasture and wood'. He described the hills in south Somerset as 'hilly country, which nevertheless produces good corn and grass crops, as well as the elms which make up the hedgerows of enclosures', and with 'good pasture and arable land, which was enclosed and reasonably supplied with woods' (note the references to enclosed fields; Chandler 1993, 419, 421). Returning to Dorset, Leland then travelled north-east from Beaminster to Evershot, across a landscape of very different character which he described as 'largely waste, which was nevertheless good pasture for breeding cattle' (Chandler 1993, 133): we can identify this dramatic change as corresponding to the greensand. Leland then travelled 'uphill for about a mile past fertile and well-wooded land' and then 'six miles along a high ridge across open country' from which he saw 'little arable and no woodland, but everywhere were large flocks of sheep' (Chandler 1993, 134): plot this on a map and we see that he had travelled up onto the chalk downland. Further west, Leland describes the landscape of central Somerset around Ilchester as 'low-lying ground as far as the eye could see . . . all along my route the pasture grounds and fields were largely enclosed with hedgerows of elm trees'. He also notes the use of a distinctive blue-grey stone in local buildings, that we can now identify as Blue Lias (*see* Chapter 2), and describes how the 'area has often been ploughed, and has produced very good yields' (Chandler 1993, 416–17). Leland's account of the Devon landscape is less detailed, although he describes the country between Exeter and Crediton as producing exceptionally fine corn, grass, and woodland, while the Culm Measures to the west were characterized by enclosed fields and an abundance of moorland that was nonetheless a very good breeding ground for cattle (Chandler 1993, 107, 122).

WILLIAM CAMDEN, 1586

Another great sixteenth-century traveller was William Camden, who published his description of *Britannia*, in Latin in 1586, and which is available in various later translations (e.g. Gibson 1695). It does not contain as much topographical detail as Leland's Itinerary, but we hear that he viewed the Vale of Taunton Deane as 'beautified with green meadows [and] abounds in delightful orchards', the Exe Valley as 'pretty rich grounds', and Exmoor as 'a filthy barren' place (Gibson 1695, 30).

LOCAL WRITERS: TRISTRAM RISDON, *c*.1630

Britain has a long tradition of local, often county-based topographies of which a fine example from our study area is Tristram Risdon's *Chorographical Description or Survey of the County of Devon* (finished in *c*.1630). Risdon was clearly well-acquainted with the various districts within the Devon landscape describing, for example, how in the far east of the county, on the high ground he referred to as the Downs [the Blackdown Hills] 'mould [soil] standeth most upon white chalk, which is passing good for sheep and corn'. His description of the 'red marl' of the Triassic mudstones (Keuper Marl) is particularly evocative: 'this soil is most natural for pasturing of beasts, though it be plentifully stored with corn . . . nevertheless, this soil is a great enemy to sheep, whose fat it melteth', a reference to foot rot and liver fluke, diseases to which we now know sheep are particularly prone on heavy clay soils (Risdon *c*.1630, 4). By contrast, in the north and west, in what we now refer to as the Culm Measures, 'the land is more lean and barren, except about towns where the husbandman, by improvement, hath inforced fertility; and near the sea from whose shore sand is carried to between their grounds, both for grain and grass; otherwise, so churlish and unthankful to the husbandman's labour that it hardly affords rye and oats for moors and hills are untractable to tillage' (Risdon *c*.1630, 5–6).

SAMUEL COLEPRESSE AND THE ROYAL SOCIETY 'ENQUIRIES', 1660s

Two years after it was founded in 1662, the Royal Society set up a 'Georgical Committee' that established a series of enquiries into the state of agriculture in the shires though unfortunately only those for Cornwall, Devon, and parts of Dorset, Gloucestershire, Kent, and Yorkshire were received (Leonard 1932). That for Devon and Cornwall was written by Samuel Colepresse, vicar of Plympton St Mary (Stanes 1964) who described the Culm Measures as 'a cold, weepeing, clayie ground'.

CELIA FIENNES, 1682–98

Another great travel-writer was Celia Fiennes (Morris 1984). She describes the chalk downland of Wiltshire as 'most champion and open . . . its husbandry is mostly corn and sheep' and where the short grass feed was 'sweet' and 'produces the finest wool and sweet meat' (Morris 1984, 42, 214). Somerset, in contrast, was regarded as full of orchards, 'generally a good fruitful country' for corn, much of which was enclosed which made the tracks very narrow. The area around Chard, for example, in the eastern fringes of the Blackdown Hills, was described as 'such an enclosed country and narrow lanes you cannot see a bow shot before you' (Morris 1984, 41–2, 214). Having travelled through Somerset, she then passed into Devonshire on the road between Wellington and Cullompton and over 'a high ridge of hills which discovers a vast prospect on each side full of enclosures and lesser hills . . . you could see vast tracts of ground full of enclosures, good grass and corn beset with quicksets and hedge rows' (Morris 1984, 196). This was presumably Maiden Down that marks the watershed between the Vale of Taunton Deane to the north (in which Wellington lay) and the Culm Valley to the south.

DANIEL DEFOE, 1724–7

Between 1722 and 1727 Daniel Defoe wrote an itinerary that describes some parts of our region in great detail. He considered the soils of the Blackdown Hills as 'a rich marl, in some parts, and a fertile, sandy soil in others', also commenting on the 'richness of the soil' south of Honiton which he said stood 'in the best and pleasantest part of the whole county' with the view as one approached Honiton from Yeovil in the east 'the most beautiful landskip in the world' (Defoe 1742a, 305, 309, 313). In eastern Somerset and western Wiltshire, the clay vales are described as 'low and flat, being a rich, inclosed country, full of rivers and towns, and infinitely populous', while eastern and southern Wiltshire—the chalk downland—were 'all hilly, spreading themselves far and wide in plains and grassy downs, for breeding and feeding vast flocks of sheep' (Defoe 1742b, 35). The area around Taunton is described as 'that rich track of ground vulgarly [locally] called taunton-dean' (Defoe 1742b, 18). He describes the lowlands of eastern Devon as having 'a fat, strong soil, of a deep-red colour, intermixed with veins of different kinds of loam, [that] produce very great crops of corn, and peas of the best kind, not to be excelled in the whole island. Neither doth it fall behind in meadow around, and pasturage, and turnips; as is evident to a person who goes through any of the markets, and beholds the fine, well fed beef and mutton, with which they are plentifully stored' (Defoe 1742a, 305). Of the area to the west that we now call the Culm Measures, he was pointedly less complimentary, describing it as having:

'very coarse, moory or fenny soil, very barren in its nature; in some places productive of nothing but a dwarf kind of furze[1] of little or no value. In other places, grow nothing but rushes, or a course, sour[2] kind of pasture, which the cattle will not feed upon and therefore it dries up and withers into a sedge. The soil here is generally a stiff clay, through which the waters cannot soak away: this renders it very unhealthy especially to sheep, which in those parts are a small kind, and very subject to the rot which (in wet seasons especially) destroys them in great numbers; and what adds to the malady is that neither industry of the husbandsman (for which this county is deservedly famous) no any compost that has yet been found out, will to any purpose cure this sterility' (Defoe 1742b, 305a).

EIGHTEENTH- AND NINETEENTH-CENTURY COUNTY HISTORIES

The eighteenth and nineteenth centuries saw a fashion for writing county histories and these also contain valuable descriptions of how the landscape was perceived (*see* Currie and Lewis (1994) for a general guide to these histories). Richard Polwhele (1797, 2, 45–6), for example, describes how Devon was bounded to the east by the Blackdown Hills, 'a name to which the dreariness of their aspect may justly entitle them'. Their soils consisted of a 'blackish mould' (reflecting the high organic content of what are now classified as soils of the Hense Association: *see above*, Table 2.2). 'White-down, between Columbton [Cullompton] and Tiverton', which corresponds to the easternmost outcrop of the Culm Measures, was described as a 'rough and barren tract', while the area between Tiverton and South Molton (also corresponding to what we now call the Culm Measures), was described as 'hill country, by no means agreeable to the eye', with 'coarse moory soil' that in places 'is so cold in nature, that on many of the higher grounds it bears little else but sour grass, moss and heath': it was regarded as 'the worse sort of soil in Devon' (Polwhele 1797, 2, 46–7). The lowlands north of Exeter were viewed altogether more positively, having 'a red loam of a closer texture, and consequently retains most of the rain, the salts it receives from higher ground . . . and the richness of manures'. These soils were regarded as 'prolific' in nature and the 'best tillage ground' in Devon (Polwhele 1797, 46–7). Writing some three decades later, Thomas Moore agreed, noting how the 'fine land' with 'deep red soils' in the lowlands of eastern Devon were used chiefly for arable cultivation, and with a climate more 'favourable' than elsewhere in Devon; in contrast, the Culm Measures

---

[1] Gorse, *Ulex europaeus*: see Riley *et al.* (2005, 20) for how poorly valued 'furze' was.
[2] Land was regarded as 'sour' if it had acidic soil and was in need of marling (Williamson 2002, 67).

had a climate that he regarded as 'less favourable' and commons that were 'highly improvable', i.e. not yet enclosed (Moore 1829, 435–7, 440–2).

THE BOARD OF AGRICULTURE REPORTS, c.1800

In the late eighteenth century, Britain was no longer self-sufficient in grain, and a series of poor harvests, along with war with France and the threat of invasion, led to growing concerns over the nation's food supply. In 1793, The Board of Agriculture and Internal Improvement was set up, and almost immediately arranged for a series of county-based surveys to be prepared. These were qualitative accounts, presenting the views, and prejudices, of their authors, but they do provide a detailed and systematic impression of how the agricultural potential of the landscape was perceived. They were published in a series of individual county-based reports such as A *General View of the Agriculture of the County of Devon* (Vancouver 1808), with a complete set of summaries brought together by Marshall (1808; 1809; 1811; 1815; 1817). These accounts have been studied by Kerridge (1967), who used them to map a series of 'farming countries' that he thought were largely determined by the underlying geology.

The format of the county reports is broadly similar, describing the buildings, rural occupations, arable regimes, livestock, and so on. In Devon, for example, Charles Vancouver (1808) divides the county into eight districts, which are shown on an accompanying map (Fig. 3.2). The Blackdown Hills, his District VII, was an area of 'strong brown loam' and 'tough red flinty clay', with uncultivated moorland on the 'high table tops' and 'red loamy marl' in the valleys. While prone to winds that were injurious to crops, this district was not regarded as liable to the same 'local disadvantages' that afflicted the west of the county (i.e. the Culm Measures of District III) with its strong winds, high rainfall, coarse wetlands, and steep hillsides cloaked in woodland. In contrast, the eastern lowlands of Devon, around Exeter and Crediton (District VI), were characterized by a mild climate, rich, red, loamy soils, and large and valuable tracts of meadow ground in the river valleys whose fertility was enriched through annual flooding.

In Somerset, John Billingsley (1797) describes how what are now called the Jurassic Hills were high sheep-walks with corn the main forms of husbandry, and where folding was unremittingly pursued with wheat seldom sown without two foldings and fallowing every four or five years. The area of the central Somerset lowlands that corresponds to the Lower Lias claylands was described as exceedingly fertile both in corn and pasture, abounding in good orchards and fine luxuriant meadows and was 'altogether as well cultivated and as productive as most parts of the kingdom'. In the Vale of Taunton Deane the

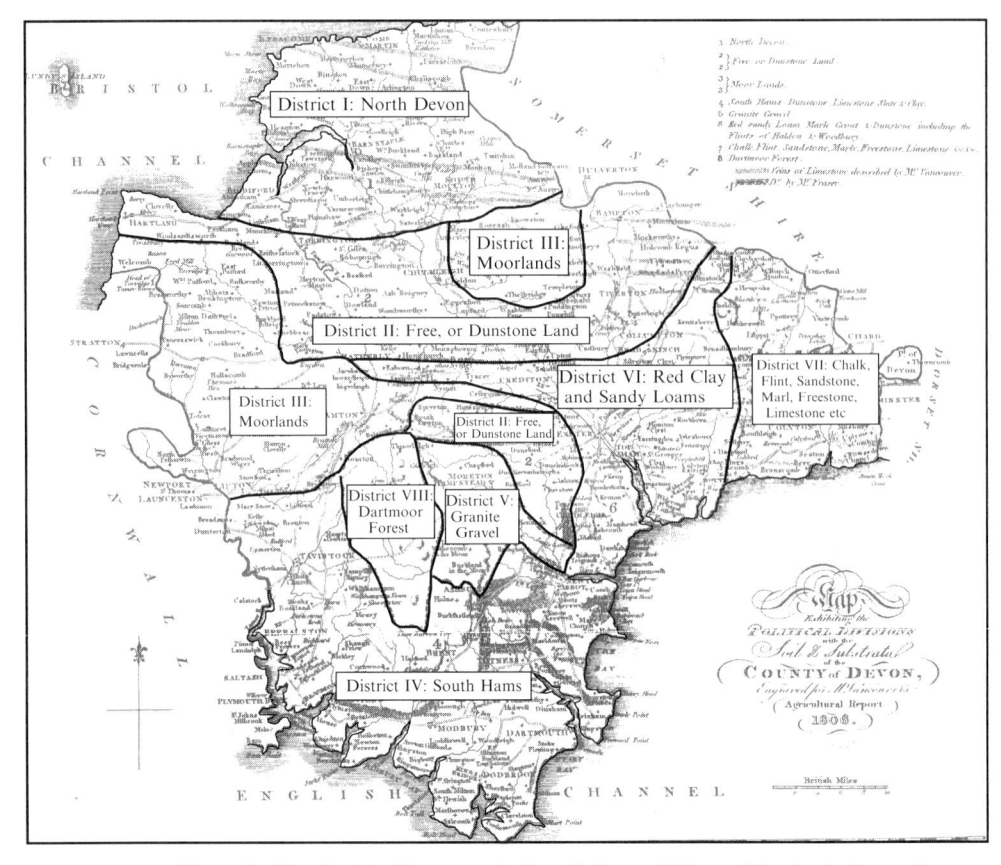

Fig. 3.2. The eight 'districts' in Vancouver's (1808) *General View of the Agriculture of the County of Devon*, which are a mixture of specific localities (e.g. District I: North Devon) and generic types of landscapes (e.g. District III: Moorlands) of which there are several examples.

climate was particularly mild, the soils highly productive, and 'the eye is agreeably relieved by a judicious mixture of arable and pasture' (Billingsley 1797, 165).

THE 'MYTHICAL LANDSCAPE': FOLKLORE AND THE LANDSCAPE

In addition to the relatively rational ways in which these travel writers and agriculturalists described the landscape, we can also get an insight into how local communities perceived their environment through looking at folklore.

Of particular importance here is the notion of a dangerous wilderness beyond the settled and enclosed land of a community. Not surprisingly, Dartmoor is the area of Devon claimed to have the highest concentration of supernatural beings (Franklin 2006, 152). On the Blackdown Hills, several roads had sinister reputations as being haunted, and bandits used such superstitions and fears of unenclosed areas to move through the landscape unchallenged (Coxhead 1954, 147–8; Tongue 1965, 97). One of the ghosts was said to be attributed to the Monmouth Rebellion of 1685, as it was known that men from local communities joined the uprising and were hanged on Black Down (Coxhead 1954, 144–7; Dudridge 1984, 26).

Other mythical phenomena that worried local inhabitants were 'Spunkies', or spirits believed to be the souls of unbaptized children that were doomed to wander until Judgement Day (Tongue 1965, 93–4; Webber 1976, 176–7). As with stories about witches and black dogs, however, such phenomena are found right across the landscape and it is not clear whether they were perceived as being a greater problem on the Blackdown Hills than in adjacent areas (Coxhead 1954, 103; Brown 1961, 396; Tongue 1965, 65–84, 107–10; Palmer 1976, 86–7; Whitlock 1977, 41–51, 60–2; Dudridge 1984, 11; Franklin 2006, 156). The same is true of devilish activity, an example of which is the 'Devil's Lapful', a prehistoric cairn on the Blackdown Hills,[3] as there are legends about the devil being present in adjacent lowland areas too (Coxhead 1954, 79; Tongue 1965, 123–31; Whitlock 1977, 16–27). The neighbouring uplands of the Quantock Hills were also said to have been home to various bad things, including three dragons (Whistler 1908), and when Phythian Adams (1999, 134–8) mapped the 'topography of superstition' in western Somerset, he noted how the Quantocks also divided networks of places linked by narrative events, illustrating how high ground acted as a barrier in how communities perceived the landscape.

Pixies and fairies appear to have had a particularly strong affinity with remote places such as the Blackdown Hills (Whitlock 1977, 28–40). In 1684, for example, Bovet described a 'Fairy Fair' on Blagdon Hill, near Churchstanton (Palmer 1976, 20), and Poole (1878, 35–6), reports that 'the place near which they [fairies] most ordinarily showed themselves was on the side of a hill, named Black Down, between the parishes of Pitminster and Chestonford [Churchingford in Churchstanton], not many miles from Taunton'. Combe St Nicholas and Buckland St Mary, also on the flanks of the Blackdowns, seem to have a particular concentration of fairy stories (Tongue 1965, 111–12). Stories of pixies and fairies are found elsewhere, but it does seem that these myths were greatest in number in remote, unenclosed places. Considering the dark,

---

[3] It was said that the devil wanted to stop the construction of the nearby church at Wellington and so he carried away the building stone in his apron; when the strings of his apron snapped the stones were left in a pile (Palmer 1976, 28; Dudridge 1984, 8; Franklin 2006, 157).

foreboding nature of the densely wooded, steep scarp slope around the edge of the Blackdown Hills (Fig. 1.1), it is not surprising that the area was regarded with some suspicion by local communities.

MODERN REALITY: GETTING OUT INTO THE FIELD

Having characterized the landscape of our regional study area based upon its physical properties and how it was perceived in the past, the next stage is to consider what it looks like today and this was achieved through a series of drive-through surveys. A sample 'itinerary' is described in Table 3.1 and illustrated in Figures 3.3–3.8, which was undertaken on Friday 10 August 2007, on a warm, bright, sunny day, with the aim of assessing landscape character in the area between Exeter and Exmoor along the western side of the regional study area. In Table 3.1, initial observations made in the field have been written up in the left-hand column, and on the right what subsequent examination of geology and soil maps revealed.

Fig. 3.3. The view south from Molland Common, on the southern fringes of Exmoor, looking out from unenclosed rough ground, across the Culm Measures, towards Dartmoor in the far distance.

Fig. 3.4. Luckworthy, on the southern fringes of Molland Common, looking east along the edge of the currently enclosed land. The moor edge is marked by a substantial 'corn ditch': a bank and ditch designed to keep deer living on the open moor to the north (on the left) from getting into agricultural fields to the south (on the right). This division between the open and enclosed landscape can also be seen on the far hillside.

Fig. 3.5. The classic Devon 'finger post' roadsign at Elworthy Cross in Witheridge. The place-name 'Nomansland' relates to a small settlement that formed around a road junction and inn on the high ground that marks the boundary between Witheridge and Cruwys Morchard. The place-name reflects the bleakness of the higher plateaus on the Culm Measures.

Fig. 3.6. Gently rolling countryside in Stockleigh Pomeroy, just north of the Raddon Hills.

Fig. 3.7. The broad lowland plain of the Exe and Culm valleys, looking south-east from Raddon Hill, with the Blackdown Hills in the distance. Raddon Court lies bottom right.

Fig. 3.8. The Culm valley, looking south-west from Paddleford Bridge towards Rewe (whose church is visible top right).

Table 3.1. Rapid field assessment of landscape character in the west of our study area.

Field observation	Explanation from background research
University of Exeter north, over Stoke Hill, down into the Exe valley. Fine views of steep-sided rolling hills to the west of the Exe Valley.	Stoke Hill is the most south-westerly outcrop of the Culm Measures (south of the Crediton Tough).
Across the Culm floodplain at Stoke Canon, and up onto a low ridge between the Culm and the Exe; through Rewe to Silverton. Low-lying, very gently undulating land, overlooked by the Raddon Hills to the west, the hills above Silverton to the north, and the hill of Killerton Clump to the east. Much arable cultivation but very little woodland in the lowlands.	The geology of these lowlands is Permian sandstone, in place capped with terrace deposits and head. The Raddon Hills are Permian breccia.
North of Silverton village the land rises steeply before flattening out to a gently undulating plateau, with a series of steep-sided, partly wooded valleys around its edges. The ploughed fields have a distinctive red colour. Large numbers of 'combe' and '-ley' place-names. To the east, the ground falls away sharply into the Culm Valley which is a broad, low-lying, very gently undulating plain all the	The hills immediately north of Silverton, Bradninch, and Cullompton, rising to 232 m OD, and on the western side of the Exe Valley (north of Thorverton), are Permian breccias that fringe the easternmost extensions of the Culm Measures.

(continued)

Table 3.1. Continued

Field observation	Explanation from background research
way across to the Blackdown Hills, whose dark, wooded, scarp slope looms up in the far distance. The concave northern scarp slope of the Blackdown Hills is a particularly distinctive feature of the skyline.	
North across these hills towards the valley of the Lowman. Down the steep Newte's Hill into Tiverton and the confluence of the Exe and Lowman rivers. East to Halberton and Sampford Peverell across a low, very gently undulating plain of the Lowman valley. Distinctive red soils, red mud on the roads, red building stone, and where the render has fallen off older agricultural buildings, red cob walls. Steep-sided hills rise to the north and south, partly wooded, with road signs to a series of 'combe' and '-ley/-leigh' place-names. Soils on the hillside at Warnicombe are brown.	The distinctive redness of the valley results from the underlying Permian sandstone and breccia; the brown soils at Warnicombe are derived from the Culm Measures.
North from Uplowman, up the Lowman valley which is now narrow, steep-sided, and wooded in places. Through Huntsham and up onto the relatively flat plateau of Bampton Down to the west. Across to the Exe and up the Barle valley to Dulverton. Steep-sided, rolling hills that are not dissimilar to the fringes of the Culm Measures further south but lacking in the extensive plateaus.	The Lowman valley is cut into the Culm Measures, whereas the area between Bampton and Dulverton has a different geology: shales and limestone of the Lower Carboniferous.
From Dulverton west up onto the Anstey Ridge and the open moorland of Molland Common. Looking south one can see right across mid-Devon as far as Dartmoor (Fig. 3.3). In the foreground (immediately south of the Anstey Ridge) lies the broad valley of the river Yeo. To the south rise the Culm Measures that form a relatively flat plateau intermediate in height between the lowlands of the Yeo Valley and the uplands of Exmoor and Dartmoor. Several of the higher areas are recognizable, including the partly wooded Witheridge Moor, and Bradleigh Down west of Tiverton.	These uplands, rising to 350 m OD, are the southern edge of the Devonian rocks that underlie Exmoor. The Yeo valley is carved out of Lower Carboniferous shales and limestone. On the Culm Measures, the higher areas are recognizable as those having relatively heavy soils of the Hallsworth 2 Association, in contrast to better-drained soils of the Neath Association on the sloping valley sides.
Down from the Anstey Ridge, through the corn ditch that marks the moor edge (Fig. 3.4), and into a landscape of steep-sided valleys and 'combe' place-names in East Anstey, and then across the gently undulating lowlands of the Yeo Valley to Oldway Cross; no extensive floodplain.	This valley corresponds to the Lower Carboniferous shales and limestone.

South of Oldway Cross the ground rises slowly but steadily up onto the plateau of the Culm Measures. Although appreciably lower than Exmoor to the north, and Dartmoor to the south, this area has an upland feel, with areas of open common and bracken in the roadside banks. The place-name Nomansland captures the monotonous bleakness to this landscape, broken by occasional valleys, often with areas of woodland. Dark grey/brown building stone, and light brown cob (Fig 3.5).

The Culm Measures in this area typically lie between 200 and 250 m OD.

From Poughill south, around Cheriton Fitzpaine and Stockleigh Pomeroy, the plateau starts to change into a landscape of hills and valleys (Fig. 3.6).

This area corresponds to the southern fringes of the Culm Measures, where they are dissected by a series of relatively gentle-sided river valleys.

South of Stockleigh Pomeroy the ground rises up steeply to an east–west-oriented range of hills (the Raddon Hills). Red soils again dominate the landscape. Looking south, the gently undulating Creedy, Culm, and Exe valleys are in sharp contrast to the steep, well-wooded hills in the distance (Fig. 3.7). Across the Exe and the Culm, the flatness of the landscape, and the lushness of the vegetation, is in stark contrast to the hills further north.

The Raddon Hills, rising to 235 m OD, mark the western continuation of the outcrop of Permian breccia seen north of Silverton. The Creedy valley is underlain by Permian breccias and sandstones, while the hills to the south are Culm Measures.

DISCUSSION: THE PHYSICAL *PAYS* OF THE STUDY AREA (FIG. 2.10)

The mapping of geology, topography, drainage systems, and soils, the more subjective evidence of how past travellers and writers perceived the landscape, and a programme of fieldwork, led to the identification of a series of discrete districts or *pays*, each with a distinctive set of characteristics:

- **Exmoor** (Figs. 3.3 and 3.4) and the Brendon Hills: distinctive upland districts (but peripheral to our study).
- **The Culm Measures** of central and western Devon (Figs. 3.3 and 3.5): a bleak landscape of gently rolling plateaus formed from Carboniferous slates, shales, and mudstones giving rise to often poorly drained soils on the extensive interfluvial areas, but dissected by valleys with better-drained soils which offer some shelter. Higher rainfall (by around 20 cm), and shorter growing season (by around 25 days) compared to the adjacent lowlands. Traditionally seen as very poor agricultural land,

and an area with relatively low population and a predominantly pastoral economy, with oats tending to dominate cropping regimes. Used for rearing livestock rather than dairying.

- **The eastern Devon lowlands** (between the Culm Measures and the Blackdown Hills, including the Creedy, Culm, Clyst, and Otter Valleys): beyond the rolling hills south of the Culm Measures (Fig. 3.6) lies gently undulating lowland with well-drained loamy soils (Figs. 3.7 and 3.8). Several distinctive subdivisions. Immediately west of the Otter, at the western foot of the Blackdown Hills, the north–south-oriented outcrop of Triassic sandstone give rise to lighter soils. The most distinctive area was 'Red Devon' (the Creedy, Exe, and Lowman valleys): low-lying, gently undulating plains fringed by rolling hills, with distinctive red soils of the Permian breccias and sandstones. The redness of the soils when the fields are ploughed is matched by the red stone and cob (mud and straw) walling that was used in older buildings. Overshadowed by uplands in almost all directions (the Blackdown Hills to the east, the Culm Measures to the west, and Exmoor to the north). Traditionally seen as exceptionally fertile agricultural land with extensive arable land and good pasture/meadow used for dairy production.

- **The Blackdown Hills**: dominate the Dorset, Devon, and Somerset borders, with flat-topped hills and steep scarp slopes rising above the surrounding countryside (Fig. 1.1 and far horizon of Fig. 3.7). Extensive woodland on these slopes adds to the dark and mysterious external appearance of these hills. Soils on the plateau tops are heavy clay-with-flints, while the valleys have generally fine, loamy soils. These valleys are more welcoming landscapes and have a sense of seclusion and are somewhat isolated from the outside world. The Blackdown Hills have a higher rainfall (by around 20 cm), and shorter growing season (by around 25 days) compared to the adjacent lowlands, although this would not have seriously affected the practice of agriculture. The plateaus were seen as dreary wasteland, but the valleys as picturesque. An area with relatively low population, and a predominantly pastoral economy with some arable land.

- **The Vale of Taunton Deane**: gently undulating lowlands in the shadow of Exmoor, and the Blackdown and Quantock Hills. Bounded by the extensive wetlands of the Somerset Levels to the east. Covered in fine, loamy soils with some risk of waterlogging. Seen as fertile agricultural land by early writers; densely populated with extensive arable land used to grow a variety of crops, and good quality pasture/meadow.

- **The central Somerset lowlands**: a flat, low-lying landscape to the north of the Blackdown Hills, with slowly permeable clayey soils, interrupted by occasional steep-sided hills of harder rock. A distinctive band of Blue Lias

limestone is used extensively in local buildings. Traditionally seen as fertile agricultural land.
- **The Somerset Levels**: a highly distinctive district characterized by its permanently high water-table.
- **The Jurassic hills** of southern/eastern Somerset and western/north-west Dorset: steep-sided, flat-topped hills formed of Jurassic limestones and sandstones, separated by broad gently undulating valleys, with well-drained, loamy soils. The rich orange-coloured limestone from Ham Hill forms a distinctive local building material (Fig. 2.4). Traditionally seen as sheep and corn country in which the soils need abundant manure.
- **The clay vales** of eastern Somerset and north Dorset (including Blackmoor Vale): broad lowland plain of Upper Jurassic clays giving rise to slowly permeable clayey soils and a largely pastoral economy.
- **The chalk downland of Wessex**: rolling downland with shallow, calcareous, brown earths overlying the chalk, whose steep scarp rises dramatically above the clay vales to the west. Traditionally seen as sheep and corn country in which the soils needed abundant manure.
- **The heathlands of south-east Dorset**: a highly distinctive district characterized by its acidic, sandy soils.

The overall aim of this chapter was to try and understand if the distinctive *pays* that we can identify based on our modern mapping of topography, geology, soils, and land use described in Chapter 2 are simply the scholarly creations of an academic mind, or whether they had a reality in the consciousness of people in the past. What clearly emerges is that perceptions of these *pays* have remained remarkably constant over many centuries: the lowlands of eastern Devon, for example, are always seen as having had rich, fertile soils in contrast to the poorly drained Culm Measures, and travellers and writers both from Devon and outside have consistently recognized this. The development of scientific research in the nineteenth century helps us to understand the link between geology, soils, topography, and drainage, but what has been striking is that although writers of the sixteenth, seventeenth, and eighteenth centuries did not have this knowledge, they did appreciate how the agricultural potential of different districts varied, and that these differences were remarkably stable over time: *pays* do appear to possess certain inherent, unchanging, characteristics.

4

Characterizing the cultural landscape: the pattern and language of settlement

In Chapters 2 and 3 we have seen how our study area embraces a wide range of physically different landscapes that in the past have been perceived by agriculturalists and travel writers in very different ways. These different districts can be mapped because we have empirical data on geology, topography, soils, and drainage. In this chapter, we begin to do the same for aspects of the cultural landscape. After an introduction to the concept of the 'historic landscape', variation in the regions in which people lived will be examined both in terms of differences in settlement patterns (i.e. the spatial configuration of settlement within parishes), and the position of parish churches in relation to topography. Consideration will then be given to differences across our study area in what people called those places (i.e. place-names), and to complete the discussion of the language of landscape, the nature of field-names will then be discussed. In Chapter 5, we return to the settlements and examine regional variation in domestic vernacular architecture which contributes so much to landscape character, while in Chapter 6 we will move beyond the settlements into the wider landscape and explore the character of fields systems, including the much-disputed question of the extent of 'open fields' in South West England. Overall, the aim of these chapters is to see whether differences in settlement pattern are also reflected in other facets of landscape character.

CHARACTERIZING THE 'HISTORIC LANDSCAPE'

The term 'historic landscape' refers to the physical fabric of our current landscape—both urban and rural—and includes individual buildings, settlement patterns, field systems, communication networks, and land uses such as agriculture, forestry, industry, recreation, and defence. Other facets of historic landscape character are conceptual in nature rather than physical or visible, such as patterns of land ownership and land occupancy, and cultural associations that influence how a locale is perceived. An important part of historic landscape character in some areas is also provided by features which have gone out of use, but that although no longer serving their original function, are still visible and form part of the present landscape's appearance—what we can refer to as 'relict landscapes', such as derelict mine workings, or the ridge-and-furrow of former medieval open fields (e.g. Fig. 7.3B).

The term 'historic landscape' first came into use as recently as the early 1990s as a concept developed by archaeologists to advise planners and countryside managers of the historical depths present in the modern landscape (e.g. Rippon and Turner 1993). Interest in studying the historic landscape began with somewhat different responses in England, Scotland, and Wales to a Government White Paper *This Common Inheritance*, inviting English Heritage to consider preparing a list of landscapes of historic importance to complement the *Register of Parks and Gardens of Special Historic Interest*. In Wales, Cadw and the Countryside Council for Wales embarked upon the creation of a register of the most important cultural landscapes (Cadw 1998; 2001), alongside a detailed study of one particular area—an extensive reclaimed wetland in south-east Wales known as the Gwent Levels—which served as a pilot project for subsequent work in each of the landscapes included in the *Register* (Rippon 1996). In England, a different approach was adopted with English Heritage sponsoring a series of county-wide 'Historic Landscape Characterisations', the earliest of which was in Cornwall (Cornwall County Council 1994; Herring 1998; 1999; Aldred and Fairclough 2003). Historic Scotland developed their own version known as 'Historic Land-Use Assessment' (Stevenson and Dyson-Bruce 2002).

In essence, 'Historic Landscape Characterisation' (HLC) of the type carried out in Cornwall, Devon, and Somerset involved attributing each parcel of land (e.g. a field) to one of a series of predetermined historic landscape 'types': 'enclosed land', 'woodland', 'unenclosed land', and so on. These types could be subdivided: 'enclosed land', for example, can be broken down into 'ancient (pre-AD 1600) enclosure', 'post-medieval (1600–1850) enclosure', and 'modern (post-1850) enclosure'. Other 'attributes' can be added to each parcel, such whether an area of 'post-medieval enclosure' appears to be derived from the enclosure by agreement of former open field or Parliamentary Enclosure. HLC has now been carried out for most of England,[1] but is not without its critics. A paper by Williamson (2006b) and an editorial in the journal *Landscapes* (Austin and Stamper 2006) highlighted some of these concerns, such as different methodologies being used in adjacent counties. A session organized by the author and David Austin at the 2006 *Theoretical Archaeology Group* Conference held at Exeter in 2006 led to lively debate, and the publication of those conference contributions in the journal *Landscapes* the following year

---

[1] Progress to October 2008 is mapped at <http://www.english-heritage.org.uk/server/show/nav.1293>

highlighted both support for and criticism of HLC (Austin *et al.* 2007; and *see* Belcher 2008). It must be stressed, however, that 'Historic Landscape Characterisation' is not the same as historic landscape characterization, and criticism of the English Heritage-sponsored programme of work should not detract from the research value of studying historic landscape character. One aim of this study is, therefore, to show how we can add depth to traditional characterization by looking at other facets of the landscape.

One feature of an English Heritage-sponsored HLC is that it represents a rapid assessment, having to cover a very large area—usually an entire county—with finite resources. In contrast, research for academic purposes, while still constrained by time and resources, can be applied to smaller study areas allowing them to be examined in greater depth. Another criticism of HLC is that it has sometimes based the historic landscape of today on modern mapping, rather than using historical sources such as the nineteenth-century OS 1st Edn 6" maps that pre-date the ravages of modern farming that have led to the removal of so many field boundaries and other historic features. The reason for this is simple: HLC is a 'future-oriented' research technique (Bloemers 2002), developed to inform planners and countryside managers of the historic character of the present-day countryside. As such, it is the landscape as it exists today that must be characterized, even if large areas are now vast arable prairies in which most of the historic character has been swept away. In contrast, what landscape archaeologists and historians are interested in is 'past-oriented' research whose focus is on understanding the history of our countryside, and which must therefore use the earliest cartographic sources available. We should not, therefore, criticize HLC for using modern mapping if its sole purpose is to inform planners and countryside managers of the historic character of the landscape as it exists today, although one ought to bear in mind that if an HLC claims to write the history of that landscape and it has not used earlier cartographic sources, then it is likely to be seriously flawed.

Another issue with the English Heritage-sponsored HLCs is that different methodologies were permitted in each of the counties where they were undertaken. For example, HLCs have been completed for both Somerset (with Exmoor National Park: Aldred 2001)[2] and Devon (Turner 2005; 2007)[3] although because different methodologies were used in each case, the results cannot easily be combined, there being a sharp discontinuity in historic landscape character either side of the county boundary (e.g. Plate 1.A; this is discussed further in Chapters 6 and 7). The impact of different HLC methodologies being adopted in adjacent counties is not seen only in the southwest. It has recently also been illustrated graphically in East Anglia (Plate 1.B).

---

[2] <http://www.somerset.gov.uk/somerset/cultureheritage/heritage/>
[3] <http://www.devon.gov.uk/index/environment/historic_environment/landscapes/landscape-characterisation.html>

Having outlined some of the problems with HLC, it should come as no surprise that the approach adopted in this study is somewhat different. The characterization work presented here began when the Blackdown Hills Rural Partnership approached the author to undertake a study of the historic landscape in their Area of Outstanding Natural Beauty (AONB) in a project titled *The Living Past: The Origins and Development of the Historic Landscape of the Blackdown Hills* (Rippon, Smart, and Wainwright 2006). When designing that project, it was assumed that the existing county-wide HLCs for Somerset and Devon could be used, although this soon proved impractical, such are the differences in methodology that had been used in the two counties. The result was a bespoke characterization carried out across the AONB, which was subsequently extended across the considerably larger 'local study area' that is the subject of this book.

ADDING DEPTH TO CHARACTERIZATION: A TYPOLOGY OF SETTLEMENT PATTERNS (FIGS. 4.1–4.7)

HLC has traditionally focused on the morphology of field systems. The work presented here represents a significant departure from this as it includes many other facets of landscape character including the nature of settlement patterns, the location of parish churches within the landscape, place-names, field-names, and vernacular architecture. The most comprehensive mapping of settlement patterns in England is Roberts and Wrathmell's (2000a) *Atlas of Rural Settlement in England*. This Atlas mapped settlement in a simple, morphological way: a dot for each nucleation, and a form of shading for different densities of dispersed settlement based on the number of settlements within four-square-kilometre boxes. In this study, however, a different approach was adopted that tried to see settlement in the context of the territorial framework within which the landscape was managed in the past (i.e. parishes), and the nature of the field systems that surrounded these settlements. Four types (each divided into two subtypes) of settlement pattern can be identified ranging from nucleated (A) through to dispersed (D), with a fifth category (E) of parish where the pre-eighteenth-century settlement pattern has been destroyed by later development (Table 4.1).

The application of this scheme to our local study area is shown in Fig. 4.7 and reveals very clear spatial patterning. Village-based landscapes associated with former open fields—settlement patterns Types A and B—are concentrated within the central lowlands of Somerset, with an outlier of this group on the eastern flanks of the Blackdown Hills (in Chard and Combe St Nicholas).

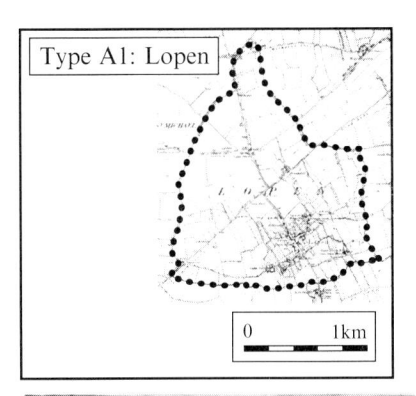

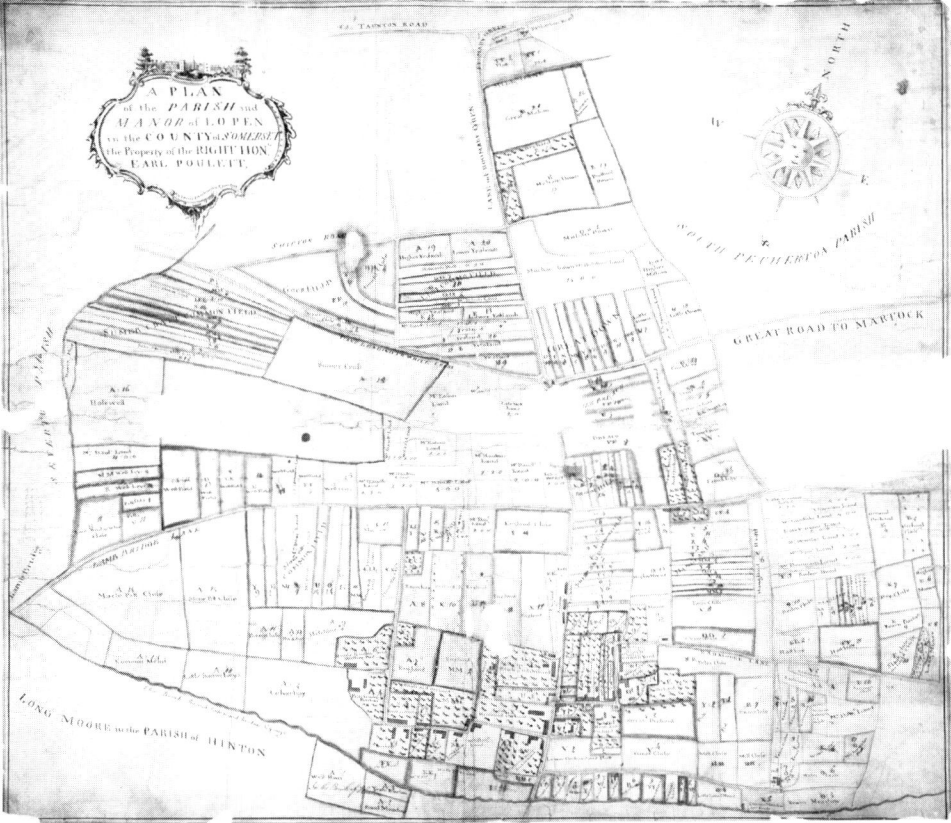

Fig. 4.1. Type A1 settlement pattern: Ordnance Survey First Edition Six Inch map of Lopen (1886), and the estate map of 1774 (SRO DD/PT/MAP1 11) that covers most of the parish. (Photograph by Richard Sainsbury; original held at the Somerset Heritage Centre. Used with permission.) The estate map shows a still functioning open field, complete with strips and furlongs, while clear evidence of this can be seen in the post-enclosure landscape on the Ordnance Survey map. The eleven adjacent closes all called 'Broadmead', that were held by nine separate tenements, along with another large close called 'Common Mead', were presumably once common meadows, while the name of 'Little Summer Leys' points to the seasonal use of these wetland environments.

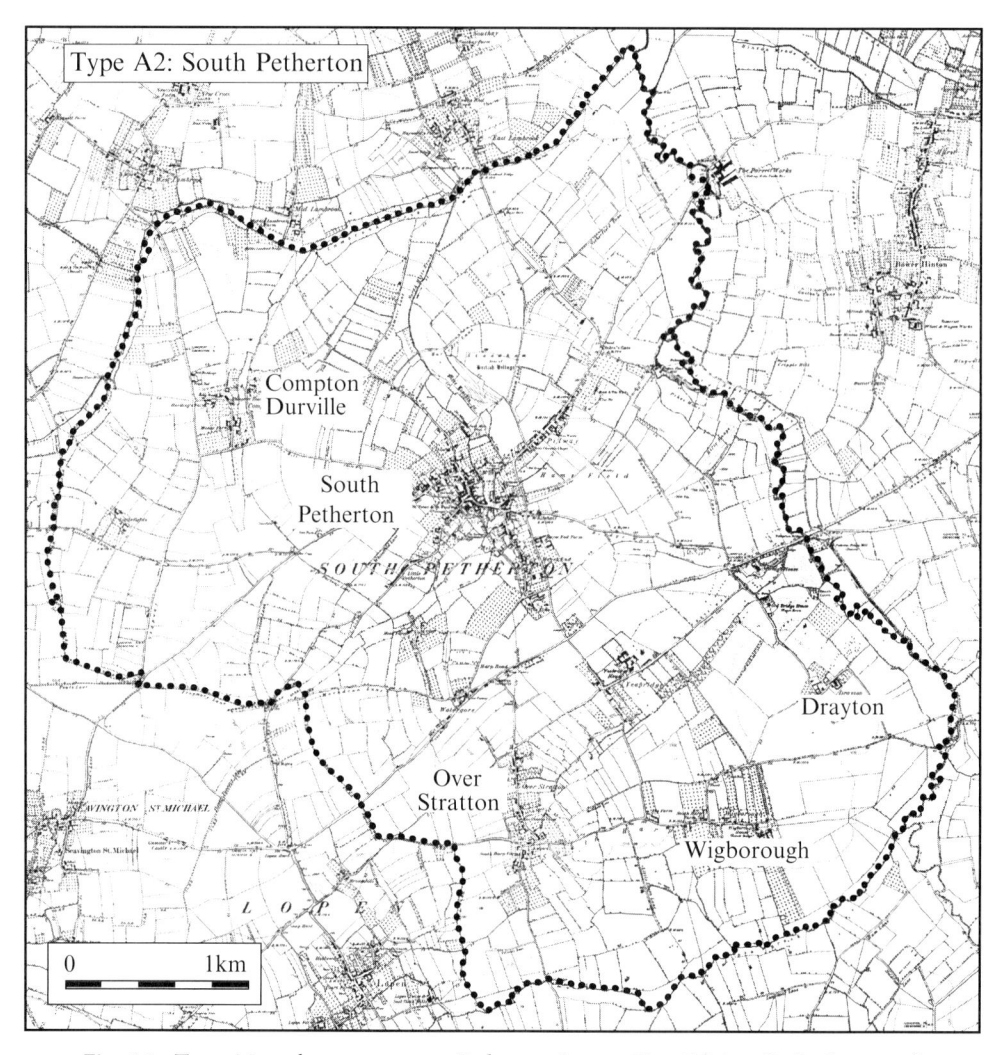

Fig. 4.2. Type A2 settlement pattern: Ordnance Survey First Edition Six Inch map of South Petherton (1886). In the fourteenth century it is documented that in addition to those of the main village, the hamlets of Compton Durville, Stratton, Wigborough, and Drayton also had three- or four-field common field systems. (Dunning 1978, 171–2.)

The remaining lowland areas have more dispersed settlement patterns, although they contain some hamlet-based landscapes, most notably on the lighter soils immediately west of the Blackdown Hills (Figs. 2.8 and 4.7). The Blackdown Hills are characterized by an extremely dispersed settlement pattern, as was the case on the fringes of the Culm Measures.

Characterizing the cultural landscape 59

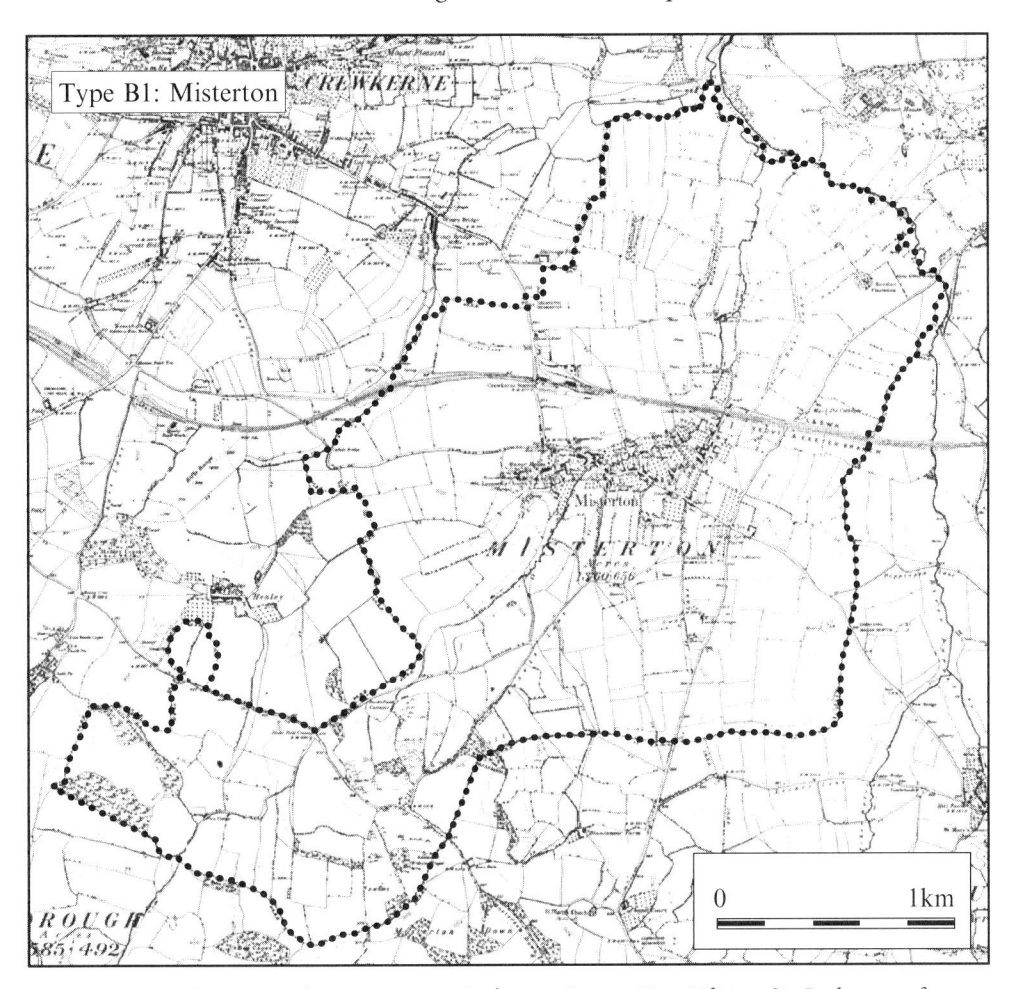

Fig. 4.3. Type B1 settlement pattern: Ordnance Survey First Edition Six Inch map of Misterton (1886). The relationship of Misterton's parish boundary to the historic landscape is analysed in Figure 8.5.

THE ORIGINS OF VILLAGE-BASED SETTLEMENT PATTERNS

The village-based Type A and B settlement patterns are typical of those seen across a broad swathe of central England (Fig. 1.2). In recent years, a broad consensus has emerged that in the southern part of this central zone, villages and their associated open fields replaced earlier landscapes characterized by dispersed settlements in the late first millennium AD. Some scholars prefer to date this around the tenth century (e.g. Lewis *et al.* 1997; Dyer 2003), and

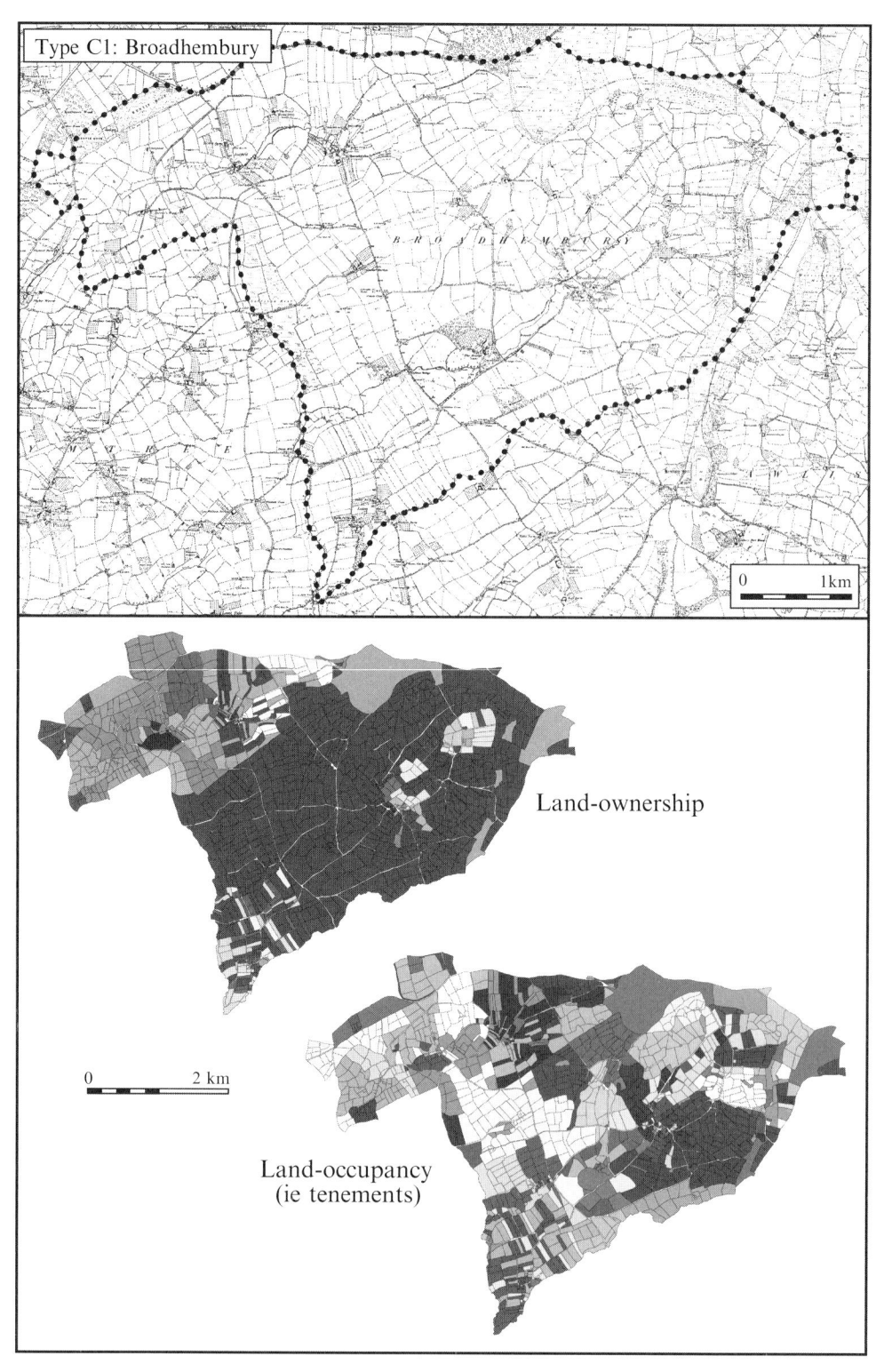

Fig. 4.4. Type C1 settlement pattern: Ordnance Survey First Edition Six Inch map of Broadhembury, and mapping of land-ownership and land-occupancy recorded in the tithe survey (drawn by Richard Sandover). In addition to the main village (centre right), that is surrounded by a fieldscape suggestive of a former open field, there were small hamlets also associated with former open fields at Luton (bottom left) and Kerswell (top left).

Characterizing the cultural landscape 61

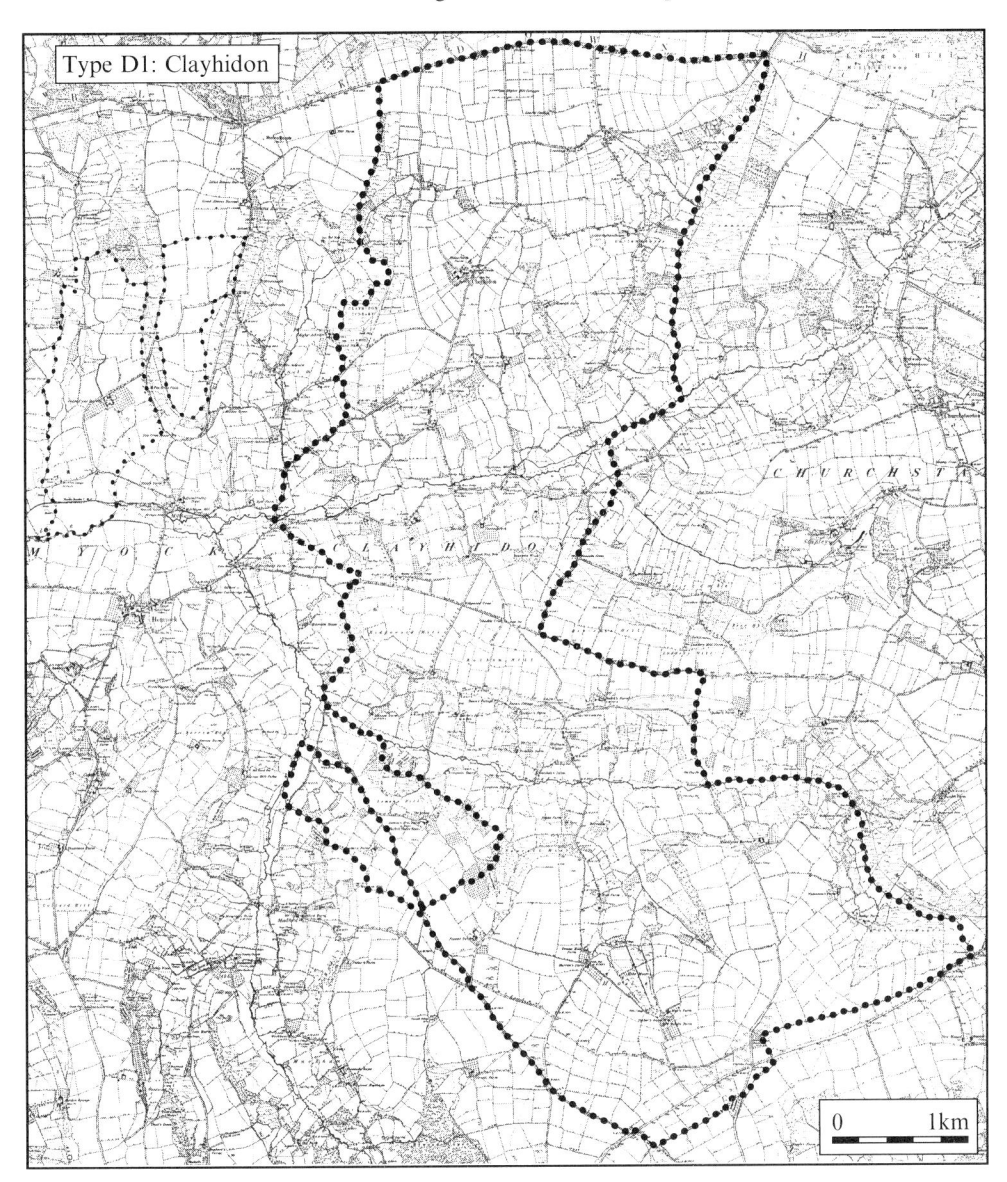

Fig. 4.5. Type D1 settlement pattern: Ordnance Survey First Edition Six Inch map of Clayhidon (1886–7) showing a wholly dispersed settlement pattern of isolated farmsteads and just a few small hamlets. The northern part of this parish is studied in depth in Figures 6.4–6.8.

others suggesting that nucleation may have begun around the eighth century, with subsequent reorganizations of these settlements around the tenth century giving rise to the village plans of today (Brown and Foard 1998; Rippon 2008a). A major problem in studying the origins of medieval settlement within Somerset and the South West is that the fifth to ninth centuries are aceramic

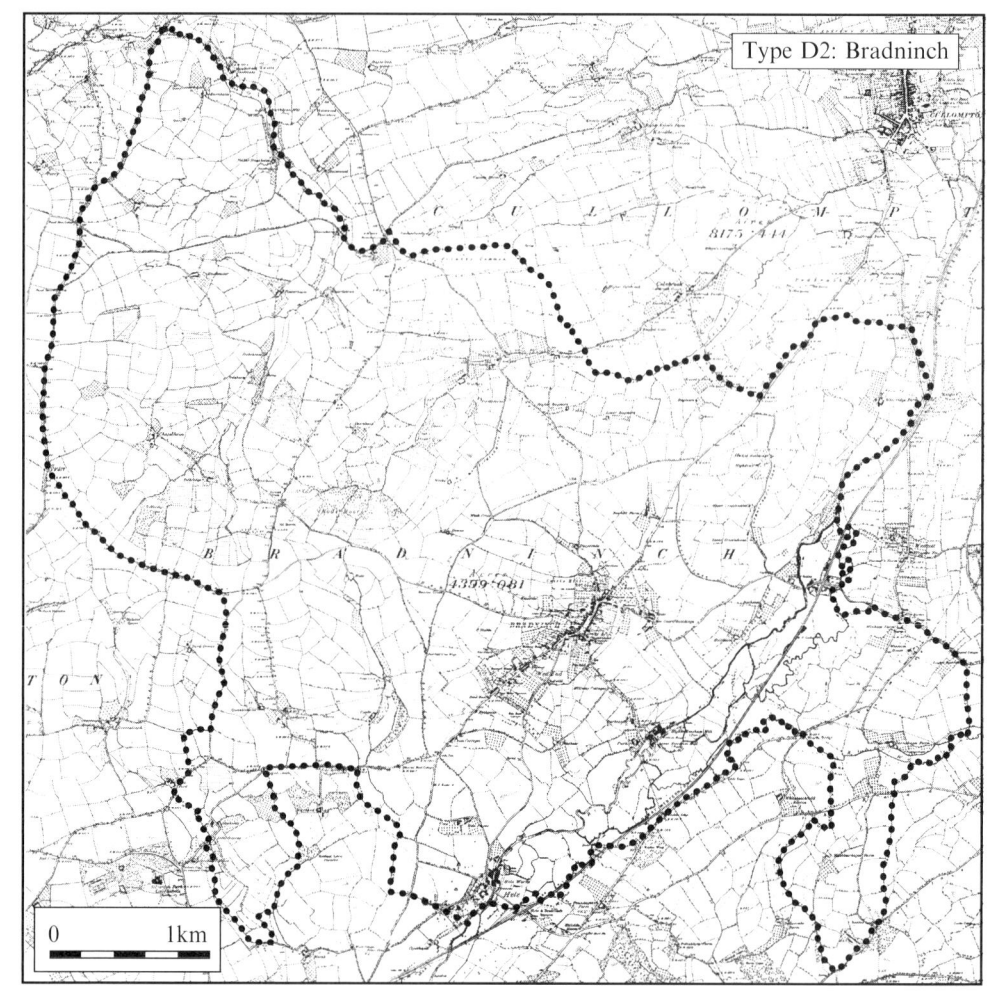

Fig. 4.6. Type D2 settlement pattern: Ordnance Survey First Edition Six Inch map of Bradninch (1886–7): apart from the one substantial nucleation (a former medieval small town), the settlement pattern is wholly dispersed.

(apart from a small amount of fifth- and sixth-century pottery imported from the Mediterranean found on a few high-status sites: *see* Chapter 14), and with just very small amounts of pottery in circulation in the tenth century. This is illustrated in an important excavation next to the church in the parish of Brent Knoll (Young 2009). Two aceramic phases of occupation were revealed, the first (which yielded a radiocarbon date of cal. AD 692–942) with features on a different orientation to the later village plan, and the second on the same orientation as a series of later, ceramically dated eleventh-century ditches that are aligned with the present village layout. This suggests occupation on the site

Characterizing the cultural landscape

Table 4.1 A typology of settlement patterns.

Type A	Village-based settlement patterns, where any isolated farmsteads appear to post-date the enclosure of former open fields.
Type A1	• small parishes with a single village whose open fields embraces most of the land (found in many of the central Somerset parishes such as Lopen, Fig. 4.1).
Type A2	• large parishes with a central village and a number of smaller hamlets, each associated with open fields, that together embrace most of the land in the parish (found in a small number of parishes in central Somerset such as South Petherton, Fig. 4.2).
Type B	Largely village-based settlement patterns, but with some dispersed settlement in peripheral areas.
Type B1	• where the village is clearly associated with a former open field (found intermingled with Type A settlement patterns in the lowlands of central Somerset, such as Misterton (Fig. 4.3), and on the eastern foothills of the Blackdown Hills in Chard (Figs. 7.1 and Plate 2) and Combe St Nicholas).
Type B2	• where there is little evidence in the morphology of the nineteenth-century historic landscape for the village having been surrounded by open field (found in a small number of parishes in the lowlands of central Somerset).
Type C	More dispersed settlement pattern characterized by small nucleations (hamlets) and some isolated farmsteads.
Type C1	• parishes with several small hamlets, one or more of which was associated with small open fields (e.g. Broadhembury, Fig. 4.4). Settlements around the parish churches show some of the characteristics of villages, notably the inclusion of service provision (church, school, shop, inn, etc.) and cottages that could have housed non-agricultural workers, alongside working farms. Unlike true villages, however, these were one of many settlements in the parish, and the land farmed from them covered only a small proportion of the parish. An analogy for these settlements is the 'church towns' of Cornwall (e.g. Herring 2006a, Fig. 33) and there is good place-name evidence that the larger settlements were indeed called 'town' (e.g. 'Town Farm' next to the church in Clyst St Lawrence, Fig. 5.6). Polwhele (1797, 367) also uses the term 'town' for small settlement nucleations around the churches in this area (e.g. Burlescombe).
Type C2	• parishes with several hamlets but little evidence in the morphology of the nineteenth-century historic landscape for associated open fields.
Type D	Strongly dispersed settlement patterns (small hamlets and isolated farmsteads) and closes that do not appear to have been former open fields.
Type D1	• wholly dispersed settlement patterns with no significant nucleations (e.g. Clayhidon, Fig. 4.5).
Type D2	• parishes with a wholly dispersed rural settlement pattern but also a substantial nucleated settlement that originated as a small medieval town (e.g. Bradninch, Cullompton, Sampford Peverell, Silverton, Tiverton, and Wellington: Beresford and Finberg 1973; Letters 2004). The physical form of Halberton is so similar that, although lacking a borough charter, it can be added to this category.
Type E	• Parishes that are unclassified due to the loss of the medieval landscape; for example, through urban expansion or the creation of landscape parks and gardens.

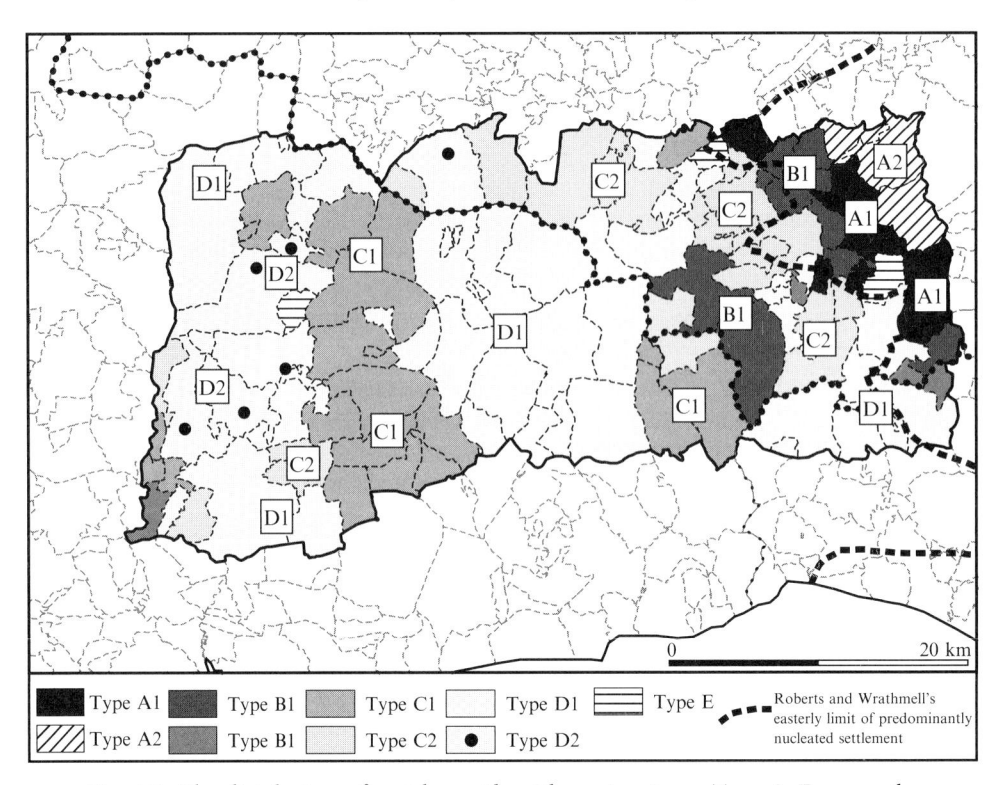

Fig. 4.7. The distribution of parishes with settlement patterns Type A–E across the local study area.

from the eighth or ninth centuries, with a subsequent reorganization of the landscape sometime between then and the eleventh century.

Within the villages in the north-eastern part of our local study area, a range of evidence supports this established model of a dispersed settlement pattern being replaced by villages and open fields around the eighth to tenth centuries. At Hayes Barn, in South Petherton, two aceramic features (two hearths and a pit) yielded radiocarbon dates from the sixth and seventh centuries, although at some stage after this the settlement was abandoned and overlain by open fields.[4] Small-scale excavations within nearby Kingsbury Episcopi revealed aceramic features radiocarbon-dated to around the ninth century.[5] There is far less evidence from the lowlands west of the Blackdown Hills for when the

---

[4] The Somerset HER refers to this site as East Lambrook which is misleading as that hamlet is in the neighbouring parish of Kingsbury Episcopi; the name Hayes Barn is used here as it is the nearest settlement to the site in South Petherton. The radiocarbon dates are 500–640 cal. AD and 540–650 cal. AD (Joyce et al. 2009).

[5] 1183±40 BP (710–970 cal. AD; Som. HER 18458).

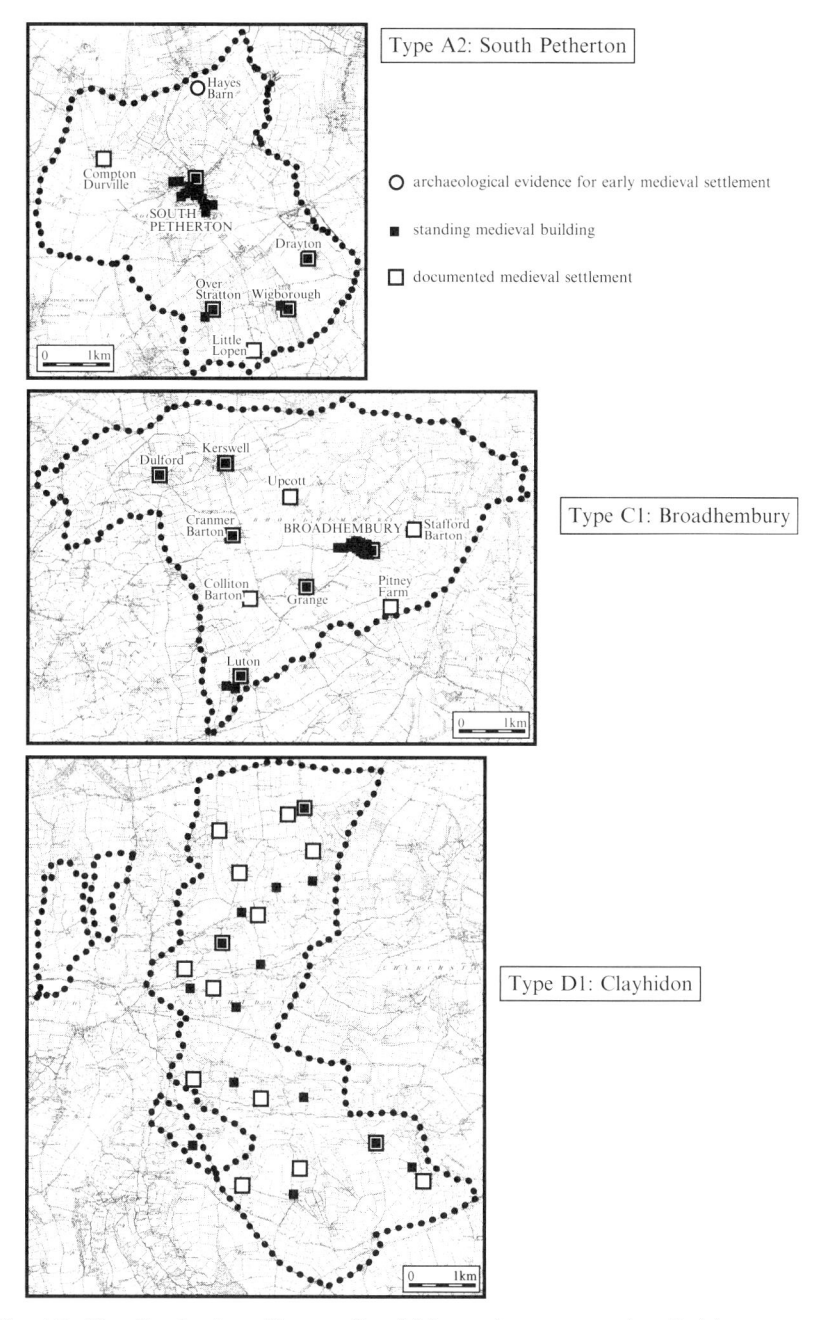

Fig. 4.8. The distribution of late medieval (sixteenth century and earlier) houses, and documented medieval settlements (Gover *et al.* 1932) in South Petherton, Broadhembury, and Clayhidon. This confirms that the broad patterns of nucleated and dispersed settlement seen in the nineteenth century can be traced back at least as far as the sixteenth century.

hamlet-based settlement patterns emerged, although two seventh-century wells have been excavated about 700 m east of the present village of Burlescombe (Reed *et al.* 2006; Best and Gent 2007), which hint at a more dispersed early medieval settlement pattern some elements of which were abandoned in the late first millennium AD.

Other strands of evidence confirm that the basic regional differences in settlement pattern seen on nineteenth-century maps existed from at least the late-medieval period. This can be seen through plotting the location of standing medieval houses, and comparing examples from the village-based landscape of central Somerset (exemplified by South Petherton), the highly dispersed settlement pattern of the Blackdown Hills (Clayhidon), and the hamlets of Broadhembury in the lowlands further west (Fig. 4.8). In South Petherton, all of the standing late-medieval houses are located in the main village or one of its subsidiary hamlets. In Clayhidon, in contrast, the standing medieval houses are scattered across most of the parish with no nucleations at all. In Broadhembury the pattern is confirmed as one of small hamlets. Overall, a characterization of the settlement patterns across our study area shows some very marked variations, and a combination of the available archaeological and architectural evidence points to the differences identified on nineteenth-century maps as existing by the late-medieval period.

THE LOCATION OF SETTLEMENT, WORSHIP, AND BURIAL IN THE LANDSCAPE

This analysis of settlement patterns is a departure from traditional HLCs which have paid little or no attention to this facet of landscape character. In another departure from traditional HLC, we will shortly examine the place-names that form such an important part of landscape character in many areas, but first we must consider one other aspect of the physical disposition of settlement: the location of parish churches. The focal point of any community is where it worshipped and buried its dead, and another facet of regional variation in landscape character across our study area is where these rituals took place. It is very noticeable that the Romano-Celtic temples in our study area—all of which are to the east of the Blackdown Hills—are mostly found on hilltop locations away from known areas of settlement (ApSimon 1965; Leech 1986; Watts and Leach 1996; Rippon 1997, 76; Rahtz *et al.* 2000), although some small towns are known to have contained shrines and temples (Burnham and Wacher 1990, 296; Leach 2001b, 257, 260). Relatively few Romano-British cemeteries have been excavated in our study area, although those that we know about tend to be immediately adjacent to settlement and temples (e.g. Leach 2001b).

In the early medieval period, there are a number of cemeteries in Dorset and Somerset that have been categorized as 'sub-Roman' (i.e. dating from the fifth to the seventh centuries, with east–west oriented graves lacking in grave goods) along with a small number of burials that have produced sixth- and seventh-century 'Anglo-Saxon' artefacts (Rahtz 1977; Webster and Brunning 2004; Webster 2008, 182–3). All of these are found well away from later parish churches. What has not been previously recognized is just how recent the use of these sub-Roman cemeteries appears to have been, making them contemporary with the 'open-ground cemeteries' or 'field cemeteries' that have been identified across southern England and are thought to have been in use between the abandonment of Early Anglo-Saxon cemeteries characterized by the deposition of grave goods in the fifth to the seventh centuries, and the onset of churchyard burial around the tenth century (Astill 2009, 223). One of the two radiocarbon dates from Lamyatt Beacon, for example, is published AD 782±90 (Leech 1986), while Winthill in Banwell has recently produced a date of AD 660–810 (Aston et al. 2011). At Cannington, radiocarbon dates suggest the use of this cemetery well into the ninth century.[6] The latest of a sequence of dates from a small cemetery within the Roman small town of Shepton Mallet[7] suggests it continued into the ninth century, and two radiocarbon dates from Templecombe suggest burial continued there as late as the ninth to early tenth centuries.[8] Three dates from the cemetery at Wembdon similarly suggest it continued into the tenth century.[9]

At some time around the ninth and tenth centuries, however, the location of burial shifted away from these late/post-Roman sites to the graveyards associated with parish churches. The date when parish churches were established in our study area is far from clear as very few have archaeological, documentary, or architectural evidence for their existence before the eleventh or twelfth centuries (*see* Chapter 10).[10] The location of these churches shows some marked differences across the regional study area. Turner (2006a, 40–4) has shown that of the twenty early medieval minsters/monasteries in Cornwall, only four were located on hilltops or islands, with eight on hillslopes and valley sides, and eight on valley bottoms or in sand dunes. To the east, in the four counties of western Wessex (Devon, Dorset, Somerset, and Wiltshire) he identifies thirty-two minsters/monasteries of which three or four were hilltop

---

[6] 1220±110 (620–1020 cal. AD), 1130±100 BP (660–1150 cal. AD) and 1130±70 BP (690–1020 cal. AD) (Rahtz et al. 2000, 129).

[7] 722–990 cal. AD (Leach 2001b, 287).

[8] 1190±70 BP (681–974 cal. AD) and 1090±60 BP (892–998 cal. AD) (Newman 1993).

[9] 1300±90 BP (580–970 cal. AD), 1240±70 BP (650–970 cal. AD), and 1060±90 BP (770–1180 cal. AD) (Webster 2008, 183, 187).

[10] East–west oriented inhumations from a site next to the church, but outside the present graveyard, in Langford Budville, are unfortunately undated (Croft 1989).

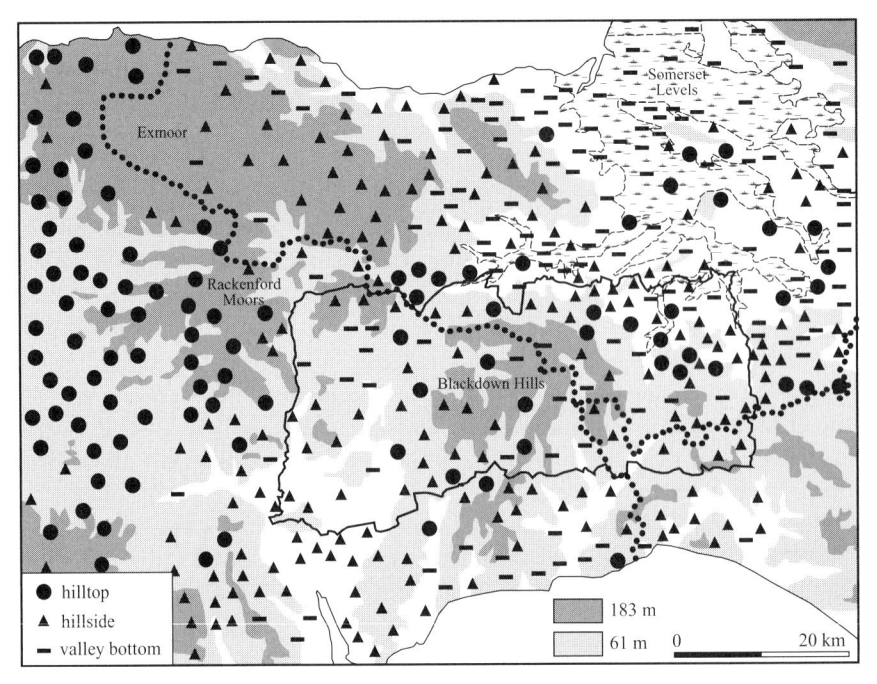

Fig. 4.9. The location of medieval parish churches in relation to their local topography. Note the almost total dominance of hilltop locations in mid and north Devon, as far east as the Rackenford moors. (After Billing 2008.)

(depending on whether Glastonbury is regarded as hilltop or valley side), just one at a valley head, and the rest in valley bottoms or on islands in the marshland. Overall, across the whole of the south-west, early Christian sites show a marked tendency to occur in lowland locations. Once minster churches were replaced by local parish churches, however, we see some very marked regional variation in where they were located (Billing 2008). In Somerset, for example, 39% of parish churches were on valley sides, 47% in valley bottoms, and just 13% on hilltops, while in Devon 44% of parish churches are on hilltops, 41% on hillsides, and just 15% in valley bottoms. On the Culm Measures of northern and western Devon a remarkable 82% of churches were on hilltops, 16% on valley sides, and just 4% were in valley bottoms (Fig. 4.9).

Of these two contrasting traditions of church location, the Somerset pattern is what we would expect to see in the medieval period: lowland positions where the majority of settlements were located, close to water and the best agricultural land. What we see in Devon—and in particular on the Culm Measures—is, however, very different and a difficult pattern to explain. The hilltop churches are certainly far more visible than if they had lain in the relatively steep-sided valleys, and the soils there tend to be slightly better (Agricultural Land Classification 3 as opposed to 4: Ministry of Agriculture, Fisheries and Food 1979). It is interesting to note that the late eighteenth-century Devon topographer, the Reverend John Swete, observed how hilltop locations were inconvenient for worshippers and expensive locations on which to build, and so suggested that these places were chosen because prayers would reach heaven more quickly. A more mundane explanation that he offered is that it reflects a pagan tradition of having shrines in high places (Gray 1997, 107).

PLACE-NAMES IN THE LANDSCAPE

In the discussion so far, attention has focused upon the physical components of the historic landscape, but another very important part of an area's character is the language used to describe it. Sometimes a particular group of place-names contain a common element that defines a particular region. If one was blindfolded and taken to a crossroads in a well-wooded landscape with signposts for Rolvenden, Biddenden, and Tenterden, the dominance of '-den' place-names would suggest that you are in the Weald of Kent, Surrey, and Sussex. If the places on the signposts were Trewithen, Polmassick, and St Ewe, you are likely to be in Cornwall. These examples of place-names forming an important part of landscape character are related to large-scale regional factors in the history of these areas: the survival of extensive wood pasture in the Weald and the lack of Anglo-Saxon influence in Cornwall. There are also far smaller-scale differences in the language of landscape that are related to local dialects, such as the terms used for drainage channels on the wetlands surrounding the Severn Estuary: *reens* in Monmouthshire, *rhynes* in Somerset, and *rhines* in Gloucestershire. Price (2000, map 7) identifies the whole of our study area as lying within the single 'western south-west' division of the 'western' dialect area in England, though with a division between 'East Cornwall and Devon' and 'Dorset and Somerset' dialects running through the Blackdown and Quantock Hills (and *see* Marten 1973 and Barnes 1970). There are also a number of late-medieval and modern linguistic differences either side of the Blackdown Hills (McIntosh *et al.* 1986; Orton *et al.* 1978), and Bonaparte (1876) and Whistler (1908, 33) note how communities living in western Somerset clearly perceived themselves as speaking very differently to their neighbours in the lowlands of central Somerset, describing how, 'it is the tale in Stoke Courcy [Stogursey, at the foot of the Quantock Hills] that a man thence went to work at Puriton beyond the river [Parrett] and returned after a week or two because "they did talk so terribly broad there that he could not rightly zince what they did zay"'. So is this difference in dialect reflected in differences in the place-names of our study area?

In Chapters 8 and 9 we will see how place-names are crucial in reconstructing early medieval territorial arrangements, but first we will look at how they contribute to local variation in landscape character. The analysis is based upon the OS 1st Edn 6" maps of *c*.1880. Certain types of place-name occur widely across the entire study area, such as those which combine a personal name with 'Farm' (e.g. *X*'s Farm: Fig. 4.10). Other place-names, however, are characteristic of different parts of our study area:

>**river names** (Fig. 4.10). That the identity of certain districts is defined by place-names derived from a river is well known (e.g. Hoskins 1952, 302–3; Everitt 1977), and in our local study area, Domesday contains several examples including clusters of manors named after the Clyst, Culm, Lowman, and Otter in Devon, and the Isle in Somerset. The Culm provides a good example. Six Domesday manors were simply called *Colum*, while Cullompton (*Colitone*) and Culmstock (*Culmestoche*) appear to have been the centre (*tūn*) and a peripheral settlement (*stoc*) within an early estate based on the same river. Ashculm in Hemyock is first documented in 1330 (Gover *et al.* 1932, 618), and while other minor settlement names in the area are of less certain antiquity, their continued creation reflects the affinity that local communities had with the river (e.g. East Culme Farm in Cullompton).
>
>**woodland names** (Fig. 4.10). Two names indicative of woodland have noteworthy distributions: the modern place-names *-leigh* and *-ley*, derived from Old English *lēah*, and *-beare/-beer* (Old English *bearu*). The latter means wood, or grove (Gelling and Cole 2000, 221–2), and while the former has traditionally been regarded as indicating woodland, or clearing in a wood (e.g. Rackham 1980, 128; Gelling and Cole 2000, 237), Hooke (1998, 148–54; 2008) has suggested that it may indicate wood pasture. Both *bearu* and *lēah* are present in Domesday in quite large numbers, with many more examples first documented from the late twelfth century. In our study area *lēah* names are found almost exclusively on higher ground being largely absent below 60 m OD. Particular concentrations occur on the hills around Tiverton, on the Blackdown Hills, and the higher ground of southern Somerset and northern Dorset, all areas that had large amounts of woodland in Domesday (Darby and Welldon Finn 1967). That the Blackdown Hills were relatively well-wooded in the early medieval period is also reflected in the charter describing the ten hides in Stockland granted to Milton Abbey as 'land to supply timber', in contrast to Sydling (in Dorset), for example, that was 'land to supply food' (Traskey 1978, 7). The *bearu* names, however, occur in the greatest numbers in lowland areas such as the Culm and Clyst valleys, and here they probably reflect the presence of small areas of woodland that were unusual in what were otherwise largely cleared landscapes.

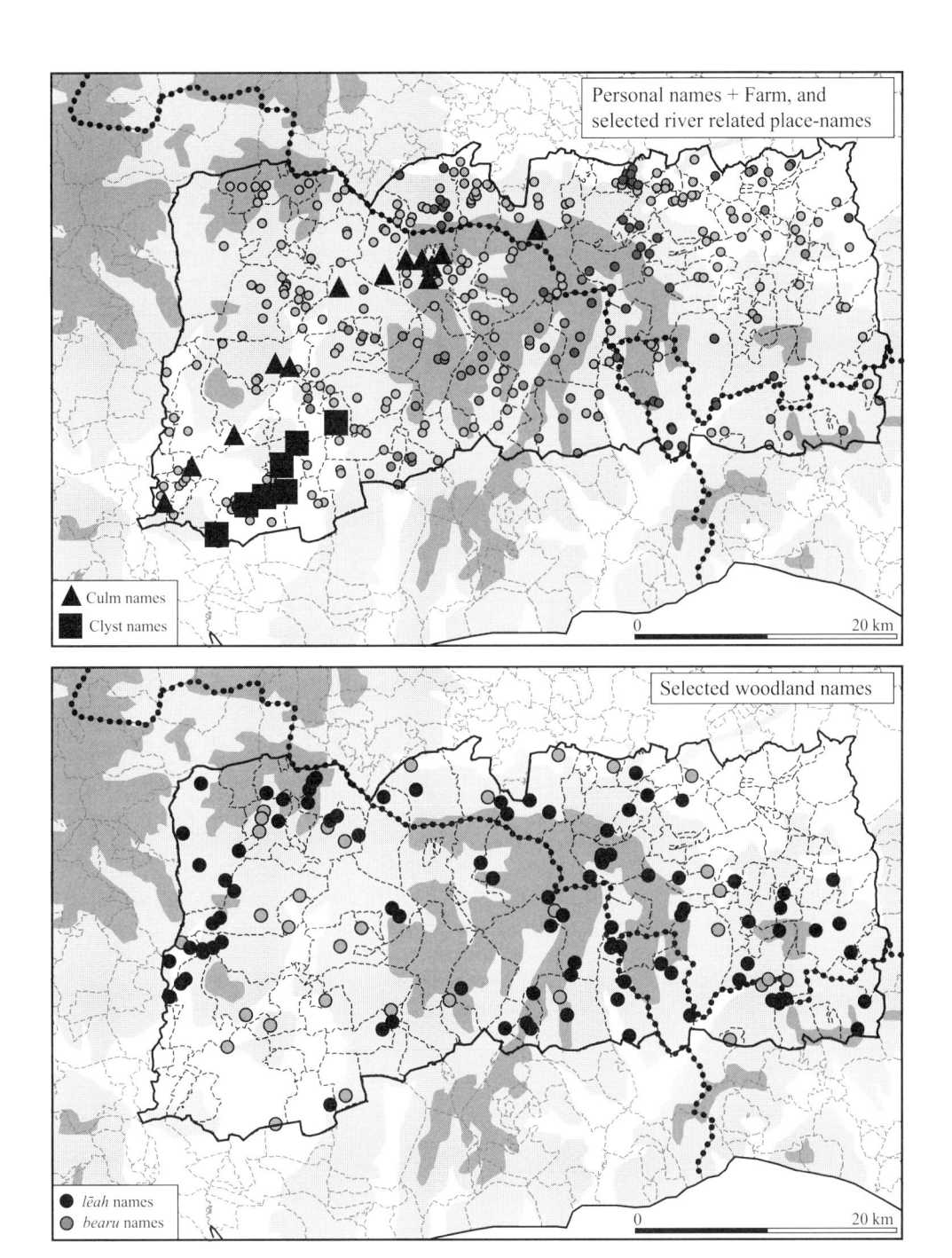

Fig. 4.10. Place-names of the 'personal name + Farm' (e.g. Smith's Farm) are common across the whole study area, whereas other place-name types have more restricted distributions such as river- and woodland-indicative names. *Lēah* is suggestive of clearances within relatively well-wooded landscapes or wood-pasture, while the presence of large numbers of *bearu* names in the lowlands is suggestive of small copses in a largely cleared landscape.

-field (Fig. 4.11). Modern place-names suffixed *-field* may have one of three origins: firstly, from the Old English *feld* (open country) that was in contrast to more wooded areas (Hooke 1998, 149); secondly, from the presence of open fields; and thirdly, enclosed fields in the modern sense (what in the medieval period were often known as 'closes'). There are a small number of Devon and Somerset '-field' place-names in Domesday that may be derived from *feld* (open country) but none within the study area, and here all the examples are minor farm names that would appear to have later origins. There is a marked concentration of '-field' names in the north-east of our study area where the field-boundary pattern shows the distinctive signature of former open field (e.g. Broadfield Farm, Churchfield Lane, and Westfield Lane in Isle Abbots; *see* Chapter 7). There are a smaller number of '-field' place-names to the west of the Blackdown Hills and many of these are associated with the far smaller putative open fields in the lowlands of the Culm and Tale Valleys (e.g. Sandfield Farm in Blackborough, Bradfield in Uffculme, and Turberfield Farm in Sampford Peverell). Other '-field' names are in areas whose historic landscape character provides no evidence for former open field, such as Pitfield Farm in Stockland that is in an area of clearly recent 'Regular Enclosure' (the pit name element presumably relates to marl pits that are also recorded on the OS 1st Edn 6" map).

-ton (Fig. 4.11). The commonest English place-name element is *-ton*, derived from the Old English *tūn*, that originally seems to have meant farmstead, and then manor or estate, and then simply farm (Cameron 1996, 143). In our study area large numbers are found in lowland areas in contrast to higher ground where there are relatively few (as elsewhere in the country the distributions of *tūn* and *lēah* names are largely mutually exclusive: e.g. Gelling and Cole 2000, 237). There are three types of settlement with '-ton' names: firstly, parish names where they refer to the centre of an estate; secondly, hamlets in the peripheral parts of parishes; and thirdly, isolated farms whose names are usually suggestive of an origin as a subsidiary holding of another place. Of the parish names several are of the 'river name + *tūn*-' type indicative of early folk territories and their centres (e.g. Cliston, now Broadclyst, Cullompton, and Tiverton:[11] *see* Chapters 8–9), while others appear to be the centres of smaller estates created through the subdivision of these early territories (e.g. Halberton[12] and Silverton[13]). Feniton is one of a number of parishes that contain hamlets with '-ton' names that are often indicative of subsidiary places such as Higher and Lower Cheriton (*Cherletone*), derived from OE *ceorl* + *tūn*, 'farmstead of the freeman' (Gover *et al.* 1932, 566). The specialized agricultural nature of some of these minor settlements is also reflected in their place-names: Kytton Barton in Holcombe Rogus is 'Kytone' in 1286 ('cow's farm') and Gaddon House in Uffculme is 'Gatton' in 1249 ('goat farm': Gover *et al.* 1932, 535, 539). 'Ton' place-names are scarce on the Blackdown Hills and all are minor places: 'Middleton' in Clayhidon, for example, is a classic directional name for a subsidiary farm ('middle farm': Gover *et al.* 1932, 612).

---

[11] OE *twī-fyrde* + *tūn*: 'settlement at the double ford' (Watts 2004, 620).
[12] OE *haesel* + *bearu* + *tūn*, 'Haligbeorht's farm' (Watts 2004, 270).
[13] OE *sulh* + *ford* + *tūn*, 'settlement at the gully ford' (Watts 2004, 551).

Characterizing the cultural landscape 73

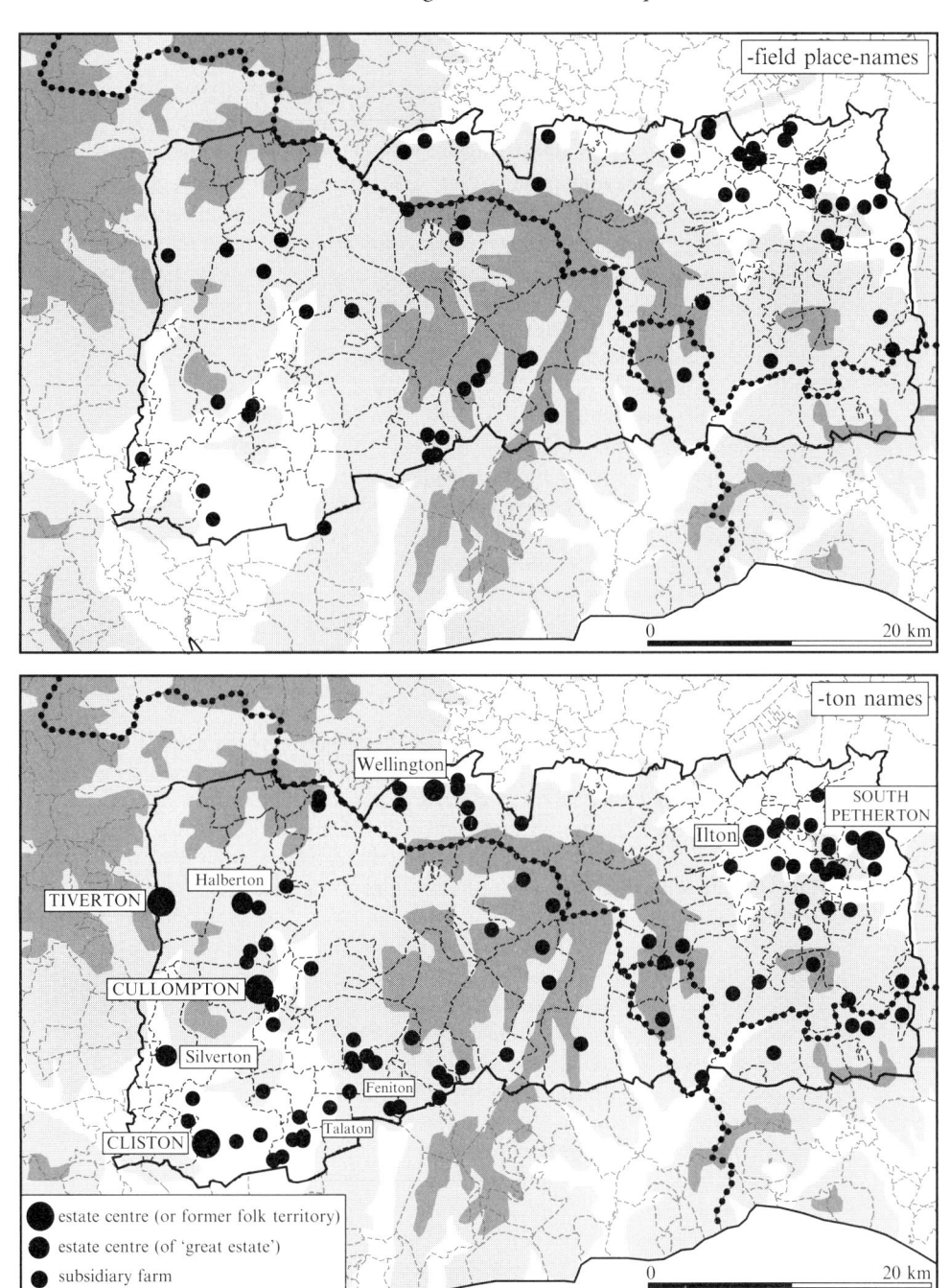

Fig. 4.11. '-field and '-ton' place-names, showing a broadly lowland distribution across both Devon and Somerset.

Our understanding of the '-ton' place-names in Somerset is hampered by the lack of an English Place-Names Society volume that gives the early forms, which means we can only consider the parish names using Watts (2004). In the lowlands of central Somerset there are a significant number of 'personal name + *ingtūn*'-type that are likely to be the manors created through subdividing these larger estates (Chillington, Puckington, and White Lackington: Watts 2004, 134, 484, 356). Seavington, however, is *Seofenempton* around 1025 (OE *seofon* +*hāmtun*: 'village/estate of the people who live at a place called Seven Springs': Watts 2004, 534). The origins of Dillington (in Ilminster parish) and Woolmington Farm (in Ilton) are unclear as these minor names are not included in Watts (2004).

-**cott**/-**cote** (Fig. 4.12). The Old English *cot(e)* (meaning cottage or dwelling) is a common place-name element in north and west Devon (Hoskins 1954, 4; Padel 1999, map 13.5). Like '-ton', it mostly occurs on better agricultural land, though it is also found in more marginal locations. This is borne out in our study area with the largest numbers in the lowlands of eastern Devon (some of which are in Domesday) with some examples on the higher slopes of the Blackdown Hills (none of which are in Domesday): one specific meaning of '-cote' was as a specialist settlement for raising sheep—known as 'Sheepcotes'—as were commonly found on the Gloucestershire Cotswolds (Dyer 1996) and this may account for some of these.[14] The Tithe map field-name 'Netherwick' in Cotleigh may relate to another specialized dairy farm on the Blackdown Hills. There is just a single example in the Somerset part of our study area, Hurcott, which was a detached part of Ilton parish.

-**worthy** (Fig. 4.12). *Worðig* ('worthy', meaning enclosure, or farmstead) is a common place-name element in Devon, particularly in the north and west (Hoskins 1954, 4; Padel 1999, map 13.4; Roberts and Wrathmell 2002, Fig. 7.2). In contrast to the '-ton' names, that concentrate on the better agricultural land, '-worthy' is mostly found in more marginal locations such as the fringes of Dartmoor (Faith 2006) and Exmoor, and on the plateaus of the Culm Measures, suggesting that the main period of its use was somewhat later than '-ton' and '-cott'. This is borne out in our study area with the majority of examples being found on and around the Blackdown Hills, and on higher ground north of Tiverton (e.g. Hockworthy, which is in Domesday). In this sense the '-worthy' place-names could represent the expansion of settlement into physically challenging environments—a classic 'journey to the margins'—or the intensification of land use in what had just been pastoral landscapes, and as such are relatively late. There is, however, a second possible context of our '-worthy' place-names: that they are actually relatively early but have only survived in more 'marginal' landscapes, such as in lowland Somerset where settlement nucleation led to the

---

[14] Edencote Farm in Chardstock (on OS 1st Edn 6" map but not in Gover *et al.* 1932); Newcott in Clayhidon ('Nonicote' in 1242: Gover *et al.* 1932, 611); and Northcott, Southcott, and Westcott in Sheldon ('Northcote' in 1486, 'Suthcot' in 1238 and 'Westcote' in 1509: Gover *et al.* 1932, 569). There is also a Tithe field-name 'Southcott' in Cotleigh.

Characterizing the cultural landscape 75

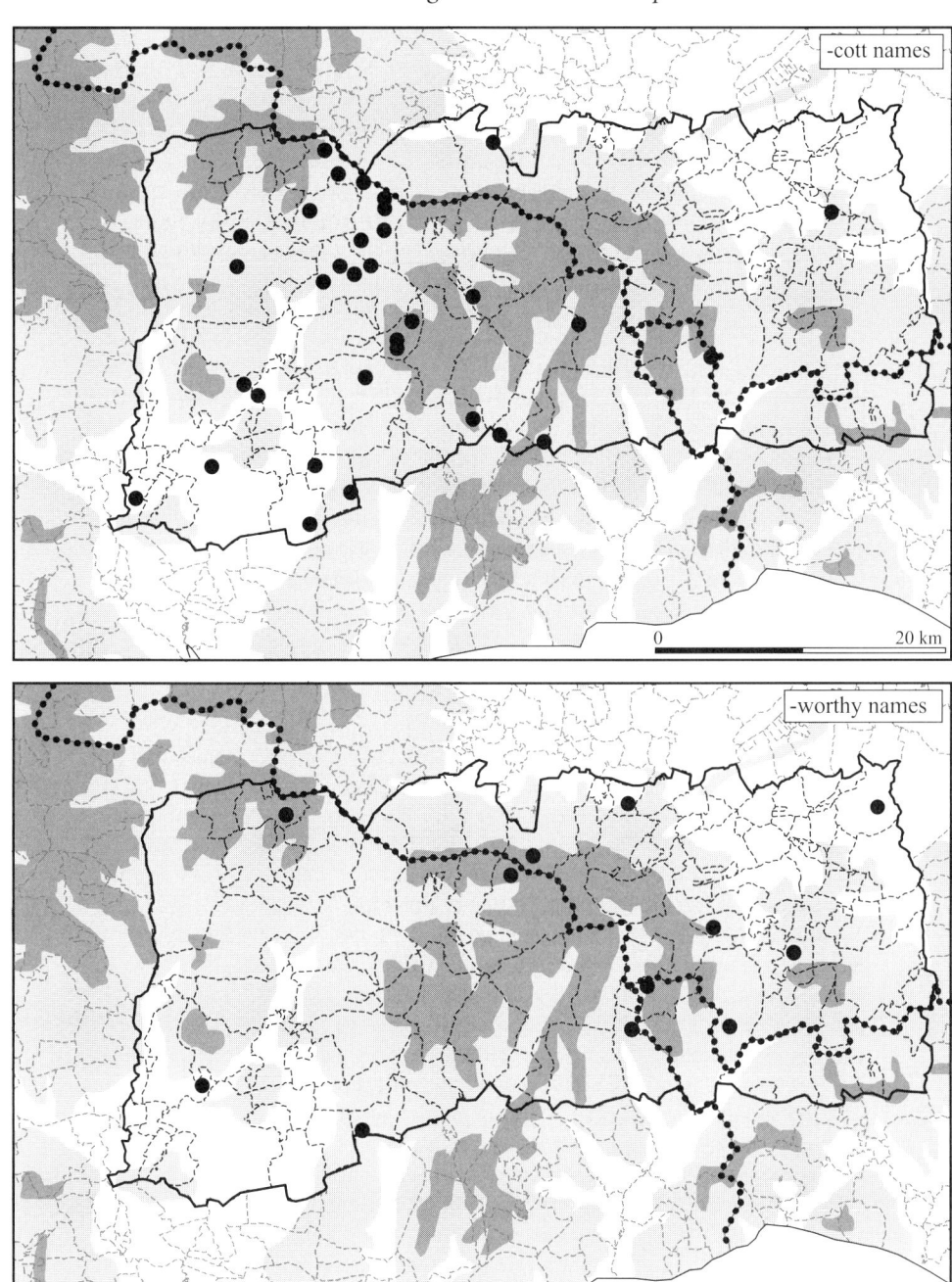

Fig. 4.12. '-cott' and '-worthy' place-names, suggestive of settlements that were subsidiary to '-ton's and/or later colonization. While '-cott' is found in Somerset, it is far more common in Devon.

abandonment of some '-worthy' settlements whose location was recorded in later field-names (Costen 1992b, 81; Faith 2006, 10–12; Faith *et al.* 2007). An examination of a large number of Tithe apportionments in Devon has, however, revealed very few examples (nor indeed many other settlement-indicative field-names).

-hay, -hayes, -haies, and -hayne (Fig. 4.13). '-hayes' (and its derivative '-hayne') is a common place-name element in eastern Devon that forms an important aspect of its landscape character (Hoskins 1954, 4). Possibly derived from the Old English *(ge)haeg*, 'enclosure', it became the Middle English 'hay' (Gover *et al.* 1931, 129). It is hardly represented in Domesday,[15] but is recorded in large numbers from the late twelfth century, mostly compounded with Middle English personal names, when it meant little more than 'farm' or 'holding' (Gover *et al.* 1931, 129; Fox 1972, 89). An example is Bathaies in Bradninch, that is 'Batynheghes' in *c.*1420 and is probably associated with the family of William Batyn (i.e. 'Batyn's Hayes', or 'Batyn's Farm'). Some '-hayes'/'hayne' names are clearly recent: Mosshayne in Broadclyst, for example, was *Clyst Moyes* in 1263, with the '-hayne' element added to 'Moyes' (moss) and the Clyst element dropped, in the post-medieval period (Gover *et al.* 1932, 574). 'New Hayes Farm' in Chard is located within the former Chard Common (enclosed in 1819), while 'Moorhayes Farm' in Burlescombe, and 'Summerhayes' in Upottery, also lie in clearly post-medieval enclosures. That '-hayes'/'-hayne' names were still being created as late as the nineteenth century shows that it was a widely understood term in Devon and on the Blackdown Hills for a farmstead, which makes its scarcity in the lowlands of Somerset particularly interesting. What we do find in lowland Somerset are a small number of '-hay' place-names that are similarly derived from the Old English *(ge)haeg*, 'enclosure', but they appear to relate to the Middle English meaning of 'part of a forest fenced off for hunting' (Cameron 1996, 205). The central Somerset 'hays' are also different from the Devon '-hayes' in lacking personal name suffixes (e.g. Winterhay in Ilminster, and Southay in Isle Brewers, and Kingsbury Episcopi).

Barton (Fig. 4.13). Another distinctive feature in the west of our study area is its Barton place-names, which are found right across Devon. Elsewhere in England one origin for this place-name is the Old English *bere-tūn* (*barley enclosure, barley farm*) which became 'outlying grange, or demesne farm, especially one retained for the lord's use and not let to tenants' (Parsons and Styles 1997, 86). In the South West, from the fourteenth century, it was a place-name used to signify the home farm (i.e. demesne) of a manor, and it has been suggested that a 'barton' was created when the lord of the manor withdrew his strips from an open fields and consolidated his land holding in a series of closes (Finberg 1951, 49; and *see* Fox 1972, 102–4; Parsons and Styles 1997, 86–7). In this sense the 'barton' was a discrete block of closes rather than a specific settlement and while originally it referred to demesne land—many Bartons are indeed attached to the parish name (e.g. Rewe Barton: Fig. 5.3)—over time, the name was increasingly applied to any substantial farmstead and its land. Across

---

[15] *Hertsanhaia* in Cliston Hundred is unlocated (*DB Dev.* 25,27).

Characterizing the cultural landscape 77

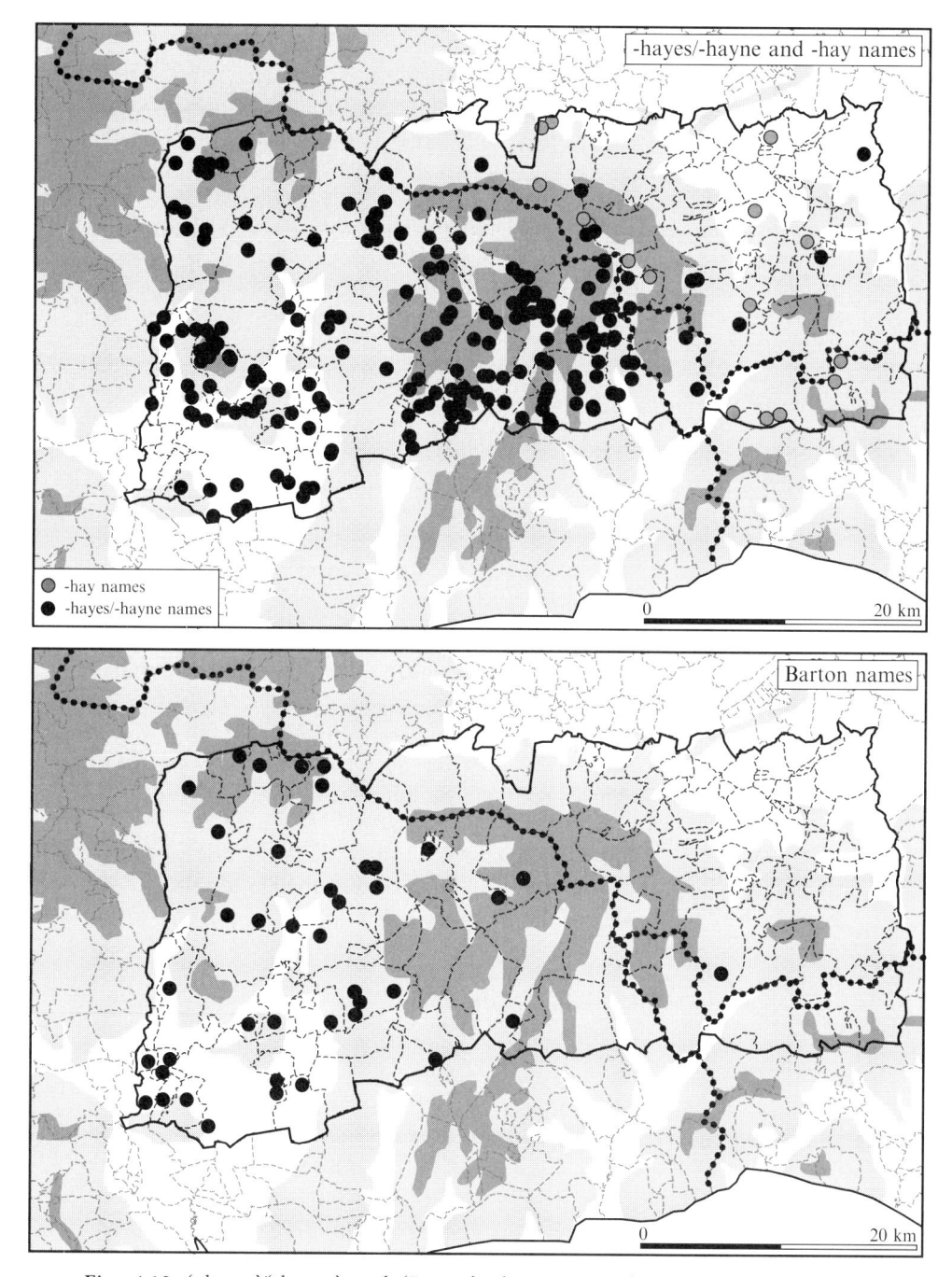

Fig. 4.13. '–hayes'/'-hayne' and 'Barton' place-names, showing their distinctive Devonian distribution.

Devon and Cornwall these 'Barton' farms are often associated with landscapes characterized by relatively large and regularly arranged fields that could represent the enclosure by agreement of former open field, or a reorganization of any fieldscape to facilitate increasingly intensive and mechanized farming in the post-medieval period (Turner 2007, 60–8). This receives some support in our study area, where a number of examples are very clearly associated the enclosed strips of former open field (e.g. Weston Barton in Buckerell, and Woodhayne Barton in Culmstock). Occasionally, 'Barton' place-names are found close to the parish church and may represent the manor houses of absentee landlords, although while this is normal in the far south-west of our study area (Huxham, Nether Exe, Poltimore, Rewe, and Stoke Canon) it is otherwise only found in Holcombe Rogus and Sampford Peverell. Many other 'Barton' place-names are found well away from the parish church, with nothing to distinguish their landscapes from all the other isolated farmsteads in the area, and no evidence for former open field. Here we are probably seeing the adoption of this place-name element as another regionally distinctive place-name element for 'farmstead' (like '-hayes'/'-hayne') with no reference to its original meaning.

In order to compare the character of place-names across our study area we can compare Bradninch on the fringes of the Culm Measures and South Petherton in the central Somerset lowlands (Table 4.2). In Bradninch, around a third of the place-names end in '-haies' (a local variant of '-hayes' that emerged in the post-medieval period), while in South Petherton we see '-ton' names dominating the settlement pattern, and 'Littlefields' reflecting the former open fields. There is a '-hayes' name, but rather than being compounded with a Middle English personal name as is usually the case in Devon, it occurs in a simple form (Hayes End) that may be a corruption of 'hay' in the sense of an enclosure from the open fields.

Overall, it is clear that place-names do add significantly to the character of the landscape across our study area, and add to the growing impression of a clear difference either side of the Blackdown Hills. In Somerset as a whole, 24.8% of the Domesday place-names are '-ton', compared to 6.4% in Devon. In the central Somerset lowlands, the village-based landscape is characterized by its '-ton' names and while Barrington, Chillington, Puckington, and White Lackington are all derived from an OE 'personal name + *ingtūn*', the corruption of the name *Seofenempton* to Seavington reflects the dominance of this '-ington' place-name form in the area. In the same way *Dinnitone* became Dinnington (Watts 2004, 187), and on occasions Lopen has been spelt Lopeton (McDermott and Berry 2011, 258). In eastern Devon, in contrast, the large numbers of –'hayes'/'-hayne' and 'Barton' names, alongside the likes of '-cott', equally reinforce the distinctiveness of a landscape characterized by dispersed settlement. In Devon as a whole, 2.2% of the Domesday place-names are

Table 4.2. The portfolios of place-names in Bradninch and South Petherton (taken from the Ordnance Survey First Edition Six Inch Maps of *c*.1880). The names of farmsteads within larger hamlets and villages are indented.

Bradninch (4,352 acres)	South Petherton (3,111 acres)
On the edge of the Culm Measures in the far west of our study area. Highly dispersed settlement pattern and a fieldscape of predominantly 'Rrregular' and 'Semi-Regular' Enclosure.	In the lowlands of central Somerset. Largely nucleated settlement pattern with a large village surrounded by former open fields, with a small number of hamlets in the peripheral parts of the parish, also surrounded by former open field.
Bagmore	Bridge House
Bathhaies	Compton Durville
Billingmore	Black Rod
Bowhill Farm	Compton House
Bradninch	Harding's Farm
Burnhaies	Manor Farm
Caseberry	New Buildings
Champerhaies	Rydon Farm
Chapelhaies	Drayton
Combe	Littlefields
Cranishaies	Moor Farm
Downhead	Over Stratton
Downs	South Harp Farm
Flesterhaies	South Petherton
Fordishaies	Hart Farm
Gingerland	Hayes End Farm
Halthaies	Hele
Hawkealter	Oaklands
Hele Payne	Pilway
Highdown	West End
Littlebourne	Wigborough
Neleshaies	Pound
Nether Stouthaies	South Harp Farm
New Cott Buildings	The Farm
Pacycombe	Yeabridge
Park	
Peakfield Cross Ways	
Quantishaies	
Rode	
Shevishaies	
Stockwell	
Stokehouse	
Stout	
Tedbridge	
Trinity	
Washbeerhayes	
Waterletown	
Weeke	
Westbear	
Whorridge Farm	
Winham	
Wishay	

'-cott', compared to just 1.7% in Somerset. It is also striking that two names that are so distinctively Devonian, '-hayes'/'-hayne' and 'Barton', are not found in Domesday and appear to have come into use during the high and late medieval period. The variant '-haies', that is so common in Bradninch and which emerged as late as the post-medieval period, also reflects how place-names can add distinctiveness at a very local scale.

LANGUAGE IN THE LANDSCAPE AT THE VERY LOCAL SCALE: FIELD-NAMES

Place-names are just one aspect of the language of landscape, another being what individual fields were called. Minor local place-names, including field-names, have a great degree of intimacy with a place as they were created solely for the use of local people who farmed the land. They are part of a local community's sense of place and belonging and reflect the relationship between people and the land. Although some field-names appear in medieval records of estate management (e.g. Fox 1972), the vast majority are first recorded on the Tithe surveys of *c*.1840. There is a significant difference between field- and place-names; the latter tend to be relatively stable in contrast to the former, and a comparison of Tithe maps/apportionments with earlier estate maps shows some significant change over time. In Misterton, for example, research by Madeline Knibb has shown that 73% of the field-names on an estate map of 1770 were unchanged on the Tithe map, although this was true of only 60% of the field-names in Shepton Beauchamp on an estate map of 1777. While some of these post-medieval field-names may, therefore, be of medieval origin, many will have been created in the eighteenth and nineteenth centuries, and as such in part reflect relatively recent naming traditions.

Across the local study area, the Tithe apportionments were searched for six field-names—breach, eddish, furlong, gratton, park, and close—and their density calculated per 100 acres. Two terms refer to an enclosed field: **gratton** and **park** (*pearroc*, meaning small enclosure: Gover *et al.* 1932, 691; Smith 1970b, 60). These are found almost exclusively to the west of the Blackdown Hills, being almost wholly absent in the lowlands of central Somerset (Fig. 4.14). There are interesting differences between their distributions, with the greatest density of 'park' names found in the lowlands of the Exe and Culm valleys, moderate numbers on the fringes of the Culm Measures, and a few parishes on the Blackdown Hills. Only small numbers of 'park' field-names are found to the north and east of the Blackdown Hills. The largest density of 'gratton' names, in contrast, occurs on the fringes of the Culm Measures, with just a few examples in the lowlands to the east and in the eastern fringes of the Blackdown Hills. Overall, this once again points to the eastern fringes of the Blackdown Hills as marking an important boundary in landscape character, with the distribution of 'park' field-names being remarkably similar to that for '-hayes'/'-hayne' and 'Barton' settlement names (Fig. 4.13).

The terms **arrish**, **eddish**, and **errish**, in contrast, were most common on the Blackdown Hills with a small number found to the west (Fig. 4.15). The Middle English 'eddish' ('aftermath', 'stubble'), derived from the Old English *edisc* ('an enclosure': Williams and Jones 1872, 13; Smith 1970a, 146), and its variants, are particularly common on the Blackdown Hills where it is often found in combination with the name of a crop (e.g. Oat, Peas, and Rye Errish in Membury). Other forms of the 'eddish' name, however, suggest that it was not simply used to refer to current land use but had become the permanent name of a field (e.g. Townhays Errish in Awliscombe, and Higher and Lower Arrish in Payhembury).

Furlong (Fig. 4.15), not surprisingly, is found predominantly in the lowlands of central Somerset where open field is known to have been extensive. The parishes further west where there were significant numbers of 'furlong' field-names (Awliscombe and Burlescombe) also had field-boundary patterns and highly fragmented patterns of land holding that are suggestive of small former open fields (*see* Chapters 6 and 7). It is noteworthy that although most parishes west of the Blackdown Hills contained a very small number of 'furlong' names—usually just one or two in a parish—in some cases these were clearly related to common meadow (e.g. 'Furlong Meadow' in Burlescombe, Halberton, and Wambrook). Fox (1972, 97) has also shown that 'furlong' names in Devon could relate to 'large arable demesne closes containing no intermixed tenant strips'.

'**Breach**', and its variants '**Breech**' and '**Brake**', are field-names derived from the Old English *brēc* meaning 'newly broken land', a common term for newly ploughed land from at least the High Middle Ages (Field 1972, 27; 1993, 80). Across our study area it is mostly found in parishes with higher ground and steeper slopes on the Blackdown Hills and around the fringes of the Culm Measures in the Exe Valley (Fig. 4.16).

The final field-name that has been mapped is '**close**', which refers to an enclosed field. It became particularly common in the post-medieval period (Field 1972, 47; 1993, 21). It is found right across our study area, although the greatest density is on the Blackdown Hills and areas to the west (Fig. 4.16).

82 *Making Sense of An Historic Landscape*

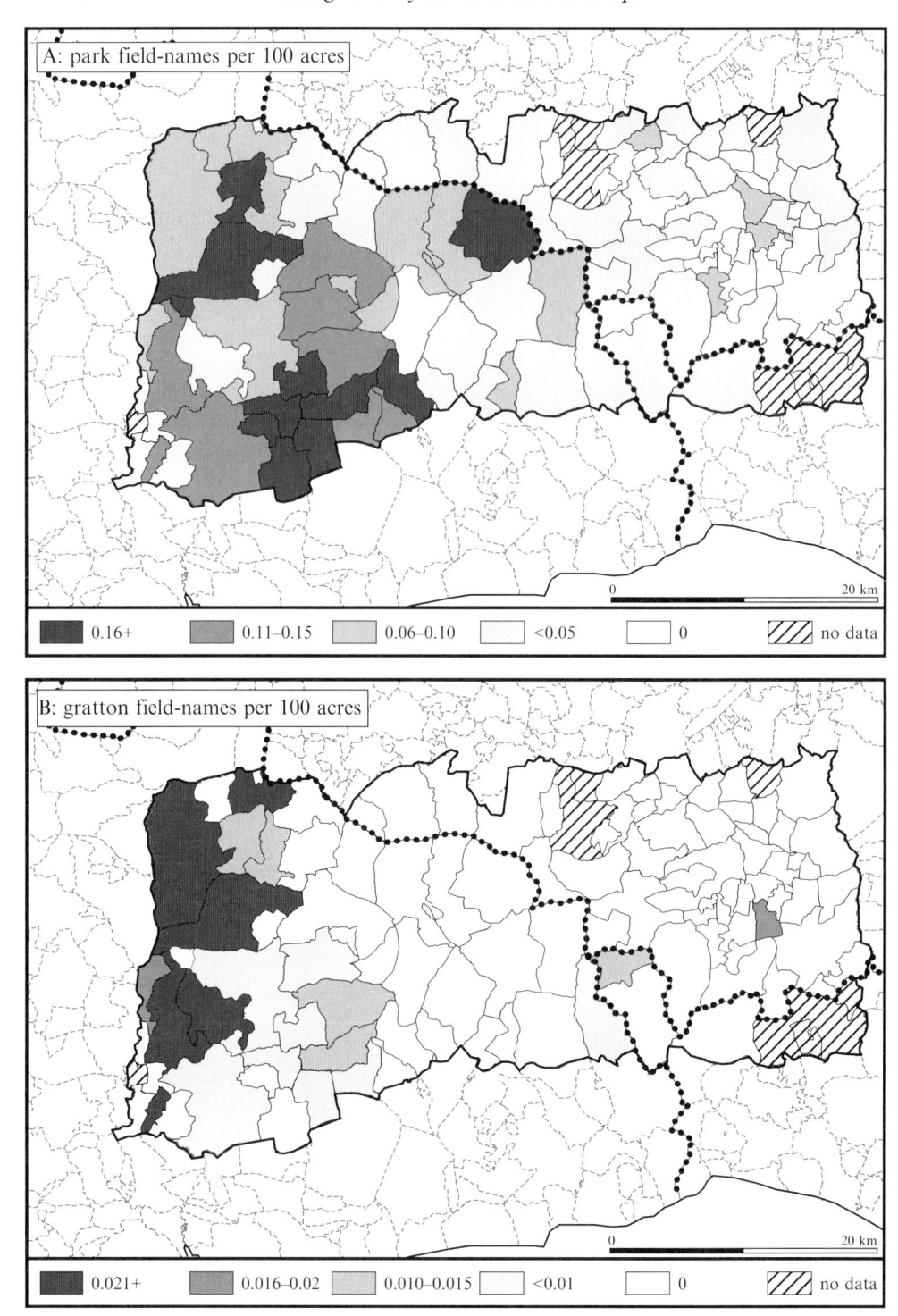

Fig. 4.14. The distribution of (A) 'Park' and (B) 'Gratton' field-names. Both are common in Devon.

A: arrish/errish/edish field-names per 100 acres

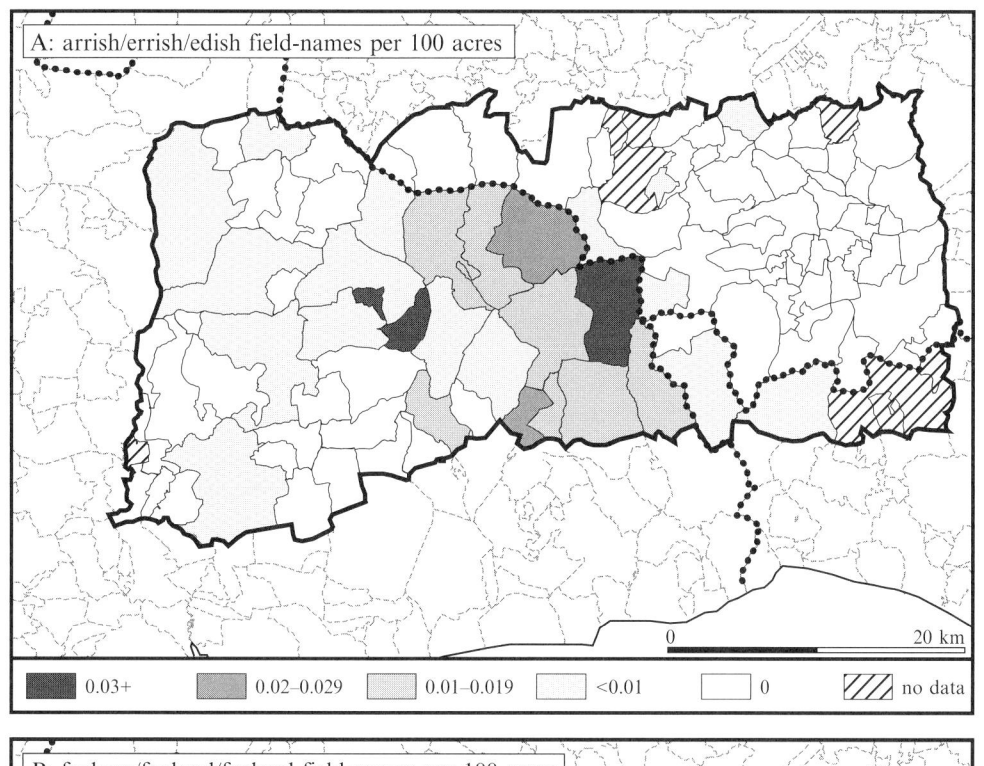

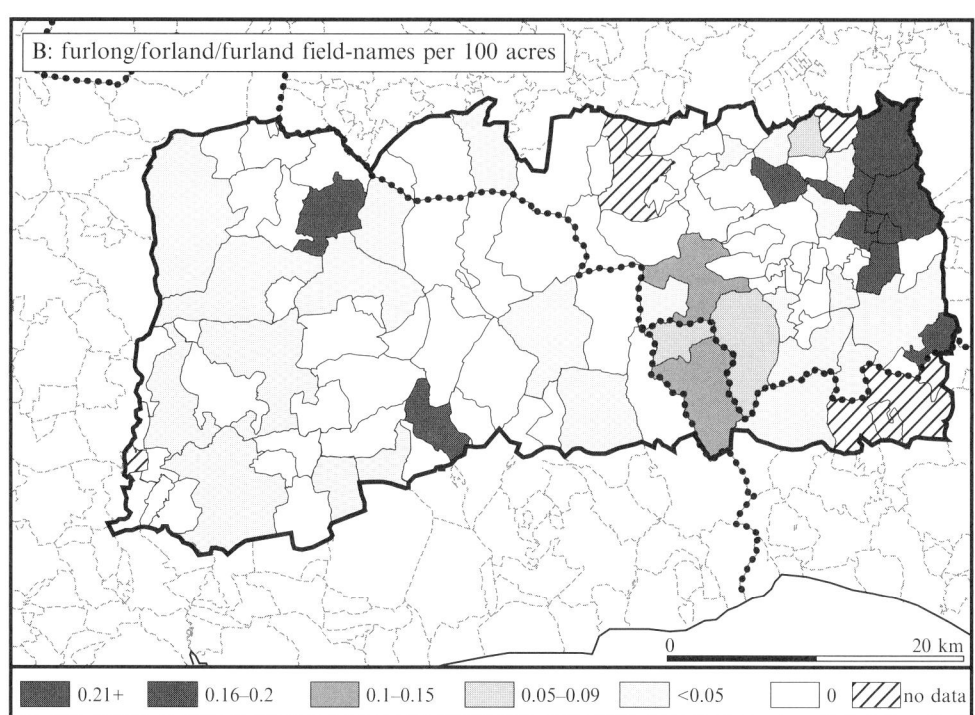

■ 0.03+   ■ 0.02–0.029   ■ 0.01–0.019   □ <0.01   □ 0   ▨ no data

B: furlong/forland/furland field-names per 100 acres

■ 0.21+   ■ 0.16–0.2   ■ 0.1–0.15   □ 0.05–0.09   □ <0.05   □ 0   ▨ no data

Fig. 4.15. The distribution of (A) 'Arrish' and (B) 'Furlong' field-names. 'Arrish' appears to be a name for arable fields that is common on the Blackdown Hills, sparse elsewhere in Devon but extremely rare in Somerset and Dorset. 'Furlong' is mostly found in the areas of former common fields in lowland Somerset, although a small number are found in Devon where they relate to former open fields, common meadows, and 'large arable demesne closes containing no intermixed tenant strips' (Fox 1972, 97).

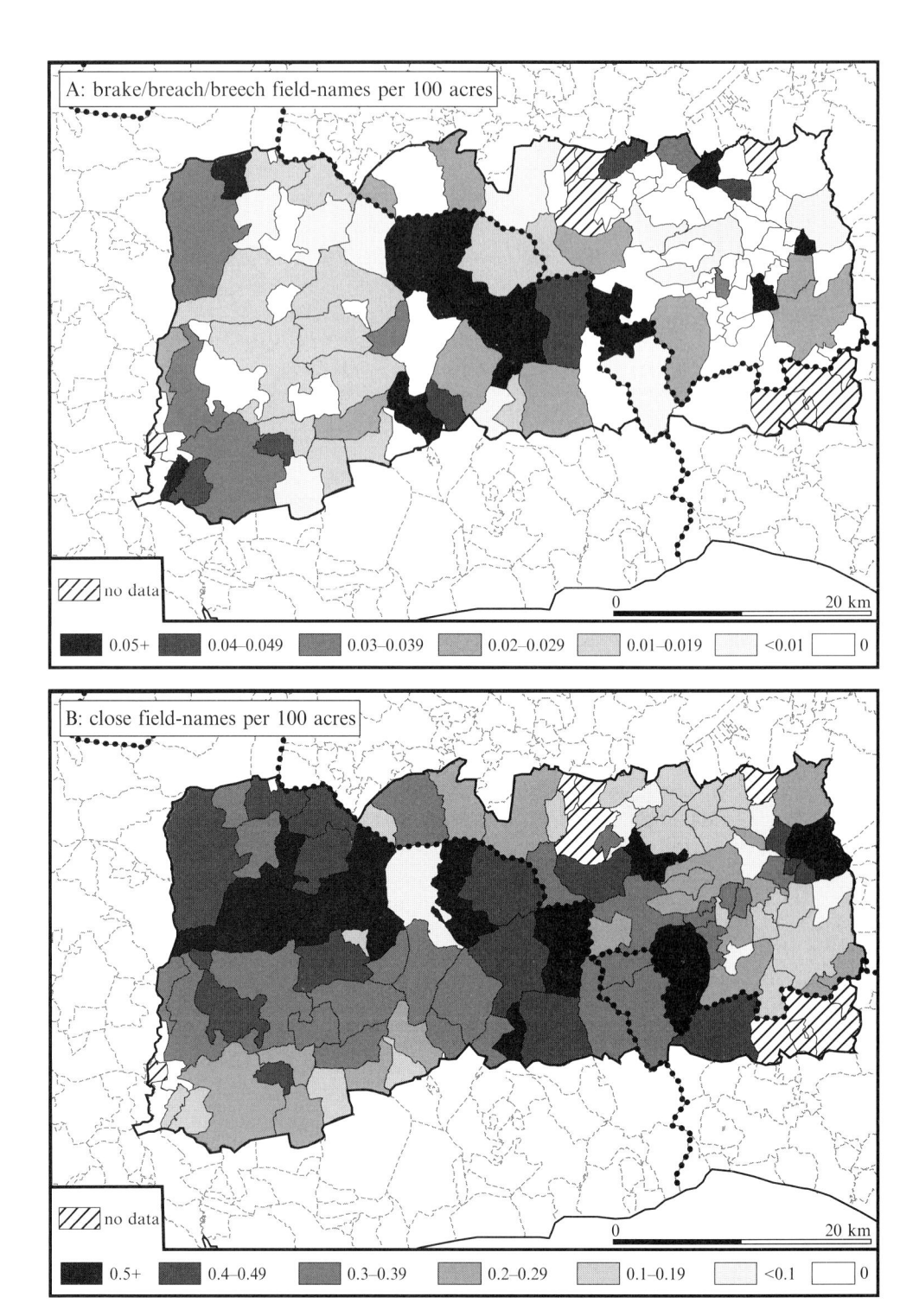

Fig. 4.16. (A) 'Breach' and (B) 'Close' field-names. These are spread more evenly across the study area though both are more common in the more anciently enclosed lands on the Blackdown Hills and areas further west.

DISCUSSION: ADDING DEPTH TO HISTORIC LANDSCAPE CHARACTERIZATION THROUGH THE NATURE OF SETTLEMENT

In this chapter we have started to examine the nature of the cultural landscape that, alongside the physical characteristics outlined in Chapter 2, forms the basis of our study area's distinctive *pays*. Systematically mapping historic landscape character is a relatively new contribution to understanding the history of our countryside, and one that is not without its critics, although the approach adopted here is significantly different to the schemes of Historic Landscape Characterisation developed by English Heritage. The starting point has been the analysis of settlement patterns—a facet of landscape character that did not feature in the HLCs of Devon and Somerset—that across our study area vary from village-dominated landscapes in the lowlands of central Somerset, through a predominance of hamlets in the lowlands of eastern Devon, to highly dispersed patterns on the Blackdown Hills and the fringes of the Culm Measures. There are many other ways that settlement patterns vary across our study area. In Somerset, parish churches—that acted as both physical and social centres for their communities—were predominantly in low-lying locations, while in Devon there is a greater tendency for churches to occur on hilltops, which is particularly clear on the Culm Measures. There are also marked differences in the character of place-names, another facet of landscape character that has been neglected in traditional HLCs. On the Blackdown Hills and in areas to the west, large numbers of farmsteads have place-names ending in '-hayne' or '-hayes', and this term was still being used for newly created farms in the nineteenth century. 'Barton' and '-cott' are also far more common than in Somerset. The village-dominated landscape of central Somerset, in contrast, is characterized by '-ton' and '-ington' names, which probably date back to the late first millennium AD when dispersed settlement patterns were replaced by the present series of nucleated villages. Not surprisingly, regional variation in the language of landscape is also found in the character of field-names, that once again show significant differences either side of the Blackdown Hills, with 'Gratton' and 'Park' amongst the distinctive suite of names found in Devon but not Somerset.

Overall, this work has confirmed the significance of the Blackdown Hills as marking a significant boundary in landscape character in terms of both the physical morphology of settlement patterns and the language of landscape. In Chapter 5 we will turn to another aspect of the settled landscape: regional variation in the character of standing buildings.

5

Houses in the landscape

REGIONAL VARIATION IN ARCHITECTURAL STYLES

Having looked at regional variation in where people lived in the landscape and what they called their settlements, we will now focus on the buildings within these settlements. The dominant building in most rural parishes is the medieval church. It is well known that styles varied from region to region. Somerset, for example, was characterized by its 'noble church towers, unsurpassed elsewhere in England...of cathedral like perfection that they look almost excessively ornate in so rural a setting' (Addison 1982, 60). The great age of church rebuilding in Somerset was the fifteenth century, while in Devon it was the fourteenth, and while there are some striking church towers in Devon, most are modest compared to its eastern neighbour (Addison 1982, 68). Devon also lacks the ornate tracery associated with fourteenth-century building further east, and much of the work was on the scale of alteration as opposed to near complete rebuilding: this was a county where there 'seems to have been extraordinary enthusiasm for the "make do and mend" principle in church restoration' (Addison 1982, 70).

In most areas, however, it is domestic architecture that forms a really distinctive part of landscape character. There have been a number of studies of regional variation in domestic buildings including Atkinson's (1947) *Local Style in English Architecture* and Penoyre and Penoyre's (1978) *Houses in the Landscape: A Regional Study of Vernacular Building Styles in England and Wales* (and *see* Brunskill 1971; Smith 1975; Quinney 1994; Pearson 1998). Such studies have revealed that a wide range of factors influenced local architectural styles including those inherent to a region such as the character of locally available building materials. This focus on building materials is reflected, for example, in Penoyre and Penoyre's (1978) subtitling of chapters; for example 'Devon and Cornwall: Thatch and cob, slate and granite'. The dominance of cob in central Devon and Ham Stone in central Somerset certainly is a major contributor to landscape character in these areas (Figs. 2.4, 2.5, and 5.6). This emphasis on building materials can, however, obscure more important differences in the design and chronology of house building that have rarely been studied at a regional scale and integrated with wider landscape research. Of crucial importance is a range of socio-economic factors, such as levels of wealth (from agriculture, industry, and trade), and the desire to follow, or ignore, fashions developing in neighbouring regions. It is to these that we must now turn.

The particular theme explored here is one aspect of the use of space within houses—where chimney stacks were placed when open halls were enclosed—and the effect that this had on house layout and appearance. Although attempts have been made to map such aspects of design at a broad national scale (e.g. Brunskill 1971), far less work has been carried out on the development of local variation: although many studies of vernacular architecture have been regional in their scope, 'the approach was typological, not topographical' (Pearson 1998, 170). There seems to be a lack of confidence on the part of many specialists when it comes to regional-scale generalizations, without falling back to over-simplifications such as the 'lowland zone' and the 'upland zone' (Mercer 1997; Pearson 1998, 176; Longcroft 2007). Johnson's (1993a, 1997) research in Suffolk, and Pearson's (1994) work in Kent, do advocate a more confident approach, and particularly noteworthy is Johnson's (1993b, 120–1) call for greater attention to be paid to regional variation (as opposed to generalizations at a national scale), a more systematic approach to quantification of data, and consideration of the potential role of factors that are not economic, in shaping how patterns of building/rebuilding developed in different areas. There has also been relatively little integration of research into standing buildings with wider landscape history, a notable exception being Lake and Edwards's (2006a; 2006b) mapping of pre-1750 listed buildings against a background of the Hampshire HLC which shows a strong correlation with areas of early enclosure.

It is hoped that this study will address some of these issues by looking at regional-scale variation in domestic architecture in its wider landscape context. Traditionally, the study of vernacular architecture has been based on detailed measured surveys of individual houses, with particular attention paid to dating evidence provided by plan form, structural elements, and fixtures and fittings. Approaches to studying and publishing vernacular architecture research across the country have, however, varied from county to county. In Devon, for example, two volumes of collected papers (Beacham 1978; 1990) provide excellent overviews, while the *Proceedings of the Devon Archaeological Society* and the *Reports and Transactions of the Devonshire Association* contain a small number of detailed reports on individual buildings (e.g. Alcock 1962; Alcock and Hulland 1972). There has also been a programme of dendrochronological dating which, while broadly confirming the well-established typological dating of vernacular architecture in the county, has shown that some standing structures thought to be late medieval may date back to before the Black Death (Groves 2005). In Somerset, Penoyre

(2005) provides an excellent overview, and the Somerset Vernacular Buildings Research Group (SVBRG) has produced a series of reports on the buildings of selected parishes (SSAVBRG 1982; 1984; 1986; 1988; 1993; 1994; SVBRG 1996; 2001; 2004; 2010), one of which covers Combe St Nicholas within our local study area (SVBRG 2008a). The SVBRG also publishes numerous brief reports on individual buildings in the *Proceedings of the Somerset Archaeological and Natural History Society*, including the results of their own programme of dendrochronological dating (e.g. SVBRG 2008b). Unfortunately, what we lack in both counties are distribution maps of different building types, apart from surviving longhouses that are particularly characteristic of Dartmoor (Beacham 1990, Fig. 3.9).

Surveys of the type carried out by the SVBRG are, however, very time-consuming and it would be impossible to cover the whole of our study area in such detail: it has taken the SVBRG around twenty five years to complete eleven parishes. In order to embrace the study of vernacular architecture in this project, it was therefore necessary to develop some form of rapid assessment that focused on the big regional picture as opposed to the minute detail of individual buildings. This was carried out in two stages (Fig. 5.1):

Stage 1: a rapid assessment
In order to conduct a swift assessment as to whether there were significant variations in vernacular architecture across our local study area, a transect was identified that sampled a series of contrasting *pays*. This transect extended from the eastern fringes of the Culm Measures, across the lowlands of the Culm and Clyst valleys in eastern Devon, up onto the Blackdown Hills, and then across the lowlands of central Somerset. The rapid assessment was undertaken by the author, Jeremy Lake, and Pete Herring. It consisted of driving through selected parishes, with a walk around selected settlements. Advantage was also taken of any vantage points where buildings could be observed at a distance (a particularly useful approach in hillier terrain).

Stage 2: quantification
Having established that there were indeed marked differences in the vernacular architecture across the study area, a quantified analysis of the listed building records was carried out using the *Images of England* website (http://www.imagesofengland.org.uk), where the written descriptions are usually accompanied by a photograph. This analysis of the listed-building records included all domestic houses up until the eighteenth century.

A note of caution should be sounded with regard to the use of listed-building data (Lake and Edwards 2006b, 36–7). The original listing surveys were carried out in the 1950s, and in the re-listing of Somerset in the early 1980s, the written descriptions are still brief as the intention was simply to identify what was of list quality and move on. The re-survey of Devon in the mid-1980s was, however, particularly well-resourced and this resulted in very detailed written descriptions based on both exterior and usually interior inspection. In all areas

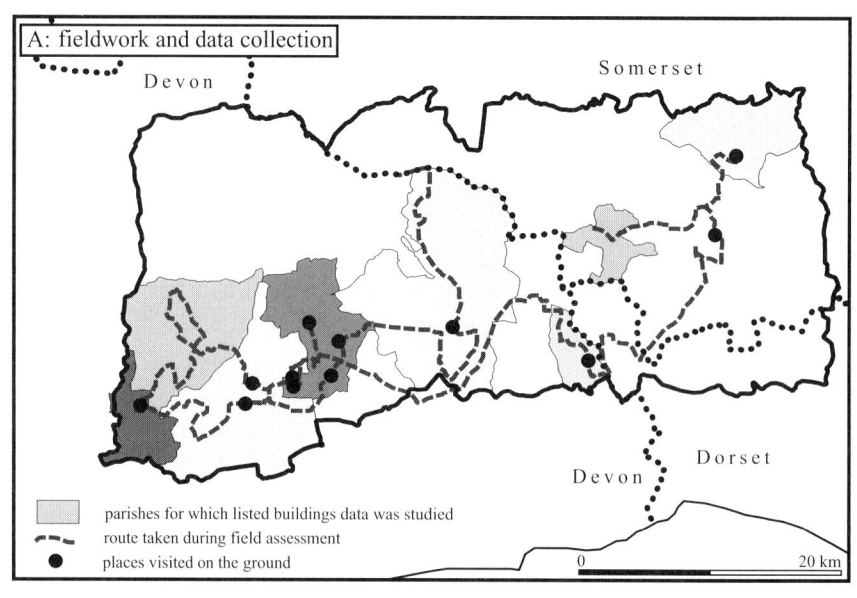

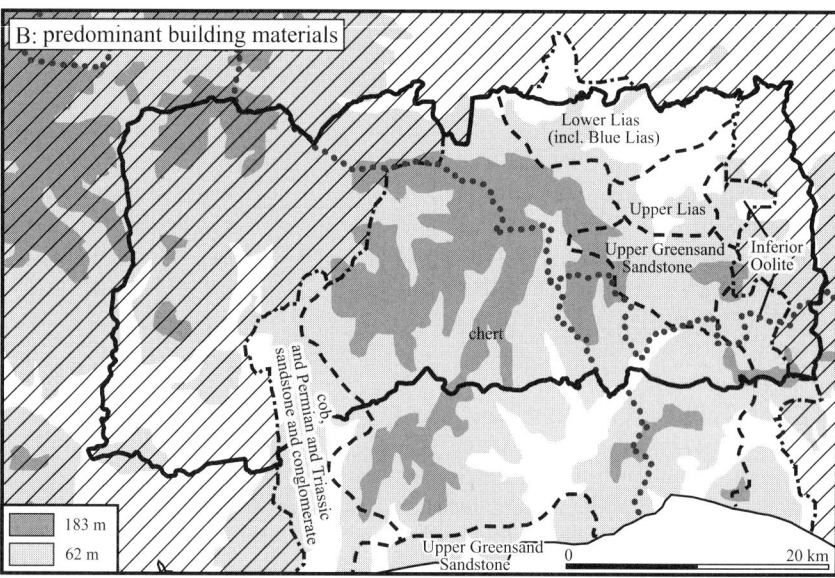

Fig. 5.1. (A) Fieldwork carried out on the vernacular architecture of the local study area; (B) dominant building materials across eastern Devon, southern Somerset, and western Dorset. (After Barr 2006; and *see* Penoyre 2005, fig. 1.7.)

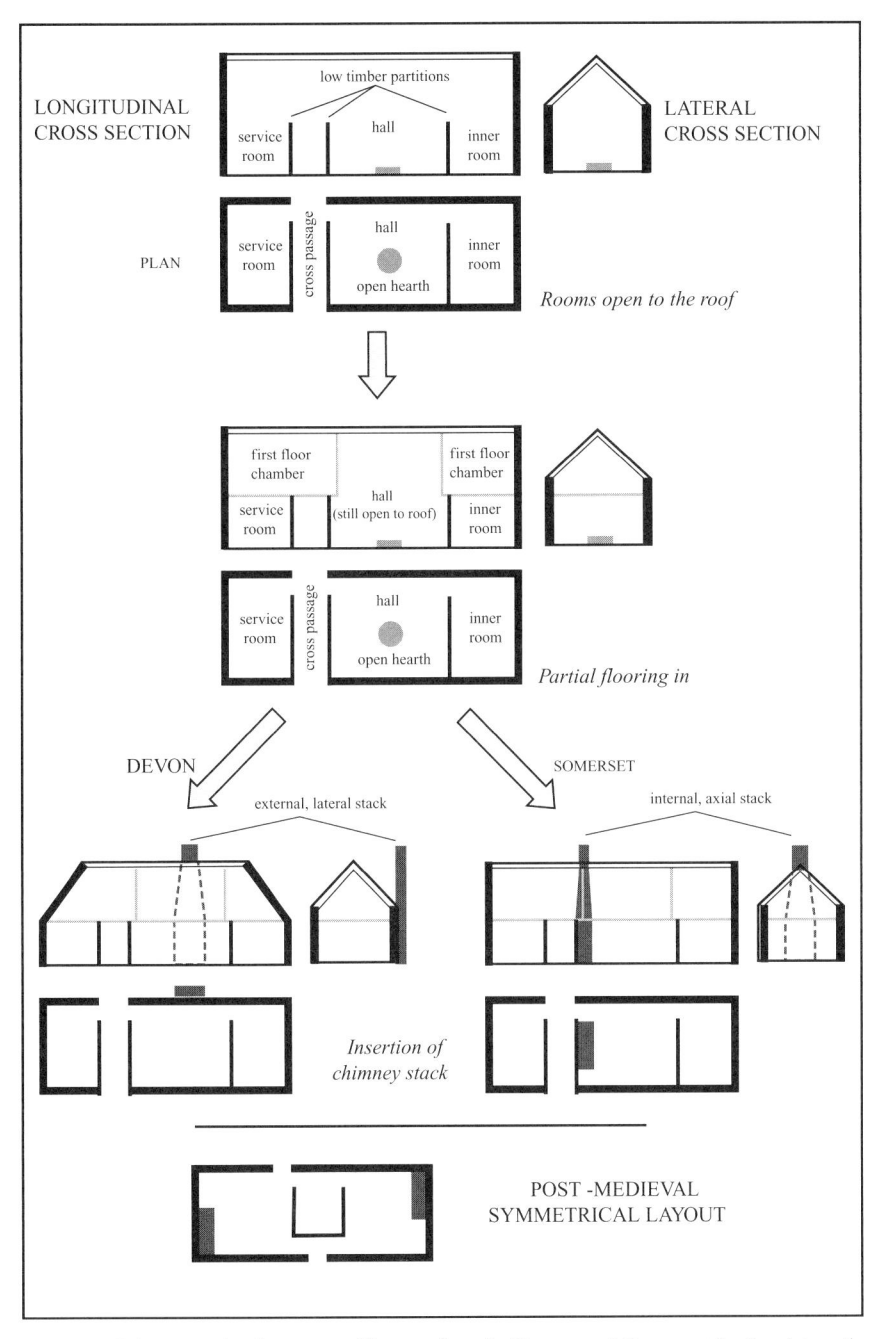

Fig. 5.2. Divergent development of house plans in Devon and Somerset in the sixteenth and seventeenth centuries. In the late medieval period three-roomed cross passage houses were found in both areas, with a central hall open to the roof and an open hearth. When chimney stacks were inserted a regional difference starts to emerge, their being typically located against the cross-passage in Somerset (an axial stack, e.g. Figs. 5.6 and 5.8) but against the front longitudinal wall in Devon (a lateral stack, e.g. Figs. 2.5 and 5.7). More symmetrical layouts came into fashion in Somerset from the seventeenth century at a time when asymmetrical plans remained the norm in Devon.

there will be some eighteenth-century and earlier buildings that have simply not been recognized, and the dating of buildings that have not been viewed from within may not be very accurate. Such issues could be very significant if one was attempting a detailed architectural history of a small area (i.e. with a small sample of buildings), but any problems with the dating of individual buildings will become far less significant when the work carried out is restricted to the plotting of broad trends over a very large area (i.e. with a far larger sample size: 593 listed building records were consulted for this study). Overall, what follows should be seen as a rapid assessment of an easy and accessible source of information on vernacular architecture that is used to identify broad spatial patterning.

CHANGING HOUSE DESIGN IN THE LATE-MEDIEVAL AND POST-MEDIEVAL PERIODS

Until the late-medieval period, lower-status houses across our study area appear to have been of insubstantial build, and very few examples have survived. From around the fifteenth century, however, improved construction techniques meant that large numbers of houses have survived—although these will still be biased towards households of greater means—which represent either new builds or the reconstruction of earlier houses. Across the whole study area the dominant layout of these surviving late-medieval to sixteenth-century houses was the same, with three rooms in a line: a hall and inner room (bedroom) to one side of a passageway, and a 'lower room' to the other (Fig. 5.2). In longhouses on the uplands of Dartmoor, this lower room was a byre for livestock, although in lowland farmhouses it was a kitchen/pantry. Occasionally we see two-roomed cross-passage plans with a hall and service room either side of the passage, and these may be more representative of lower-status houses, which would have been less substantially constructed and so have survived in fewer numbers. In medieval buildings, all these rooms would have been open to the roof and heated by an open fire in the hall, although from the sixteenth century, chimney stacks were inserted and here we do see a significant local variation in style: in Devon and western Somerset (west of the Quantock Hills) the stack was often built onto the outside front wall (a 'lateral stack', Figs. 2.5, 5.2 bottom left, and 5.7), whereas in central, southern, and eastern Somerset the stack was typically placed within the house, usually beside the cross-passage (an 'axial stack', Figs. 5.2 bottom right, 5.6, and 5.8). At around the same time, floors were inserted into first the inner room, and then over the hall and service end. The plan of these late-medieval houses was asymmetrical with a far larger area to one side of the cross-passage (the hall and inner room) than the other (the service end).

When viewed from outside, this asymmetry is readily apparent, with axial stacks protruding through the apex of the roof to one side of the door (reflecting its position against the cross-passage). In the post-medieval period, however, the design of houses started to change in favour of symmetrical layouts with equal-sized rooms on either side of a central passageway, and chimney stacks in the two gable-end walls (e.g. Fig. 5.9).

Another distinctive feature of the vernacular architecture in our study area is the use of 'cob' in both domestic and agricultural buildings (Figs. 2.5 and 5.6). Cob is a mixture of earth, stone, and straw, and while similar earth-built structures can be found across medieval England (Dyer 2008), most of these have been replaced by more durable building materials. The continued use of cob in Devon well into the post-medieval period, and the survival of those buildings to the present day is particularly characteristic of south-western counties.

A CHARACTERIZATION OF THE VERNACULAR ARCHITECTURE ACROSS THE STUDY AREA (TABLE 5.1)

The Exe/Culm confluence

The five small parishes in the southwest corner of the study area—Rewe, Nether Exe, Stoke Canon, Huxham, and Poltimore—extend across the fertile lowlands at the confluence of the Exe and Culm valleys. The density of listed eighteenth-century and earlier houses is close to the average for our study area yet there is not a single mid-sixteenth-century or earlier house, and just a small number that date to the late sixteenth century. The percentage of eighteenth-century and earlier listed houses that are late sixteenth century and earlier (20%) is the lowest in our study area (where the average is 41%). The largest number of listed houses is seventeenth century (59%) with the rest dating to the eighteenth century. This pattern points to a landscape with increasing farm sizes in the post-medieval period, and the emergence of large capital-based estates on which the earlier house stock was replaced. The most distinctive feature of the standing buildings in this area is in fact the large numbers of brick-built mid- to late nineteenth-century farmhouses, cottages, and agricultural buildings, and in particular the large numbers of single-phase regularly laid out courtyard farms. A fine example is at Rewe Barton where a large brick-built model farm lies next to a small farmhouse (presumably for the estate manager), and a row of four semi-detached cottages for the estate workers representing the 'infrastructure of waged labour' (Jeremy Lake pers. comm., Fig. 5.3). It is unclear whether the model farmstead and the adjacent cottages

Fig. 5.3. Rewe Barton Cottages (top) and Rewe Barton Farm (bottom): examples of developments in brick on a nineteenth-century model farm.

replaced a medieval hamlet of the type seen further east in the Culm and Clyst valleys (*see* below), in which each household worked their own tenement.

The Culm Measures

Three large parishes—Bradninch, Cullompton, and Silverton—extend from the eastern fringes of the Culm Measures down into the fertile lowlands of the Permian sandstones in the Culm Valley. All three contain a substantial nucleated settlement at the foot of these hills that in the medieval period was a small market town, although only Cullompton has retained this social and economic status. To the west lie Butterleigh and Bickleigh. The settlement pattern on the fringes of the Culm Measures is highly dispersed, with a few small hamlets and large numbers of isolated farmsteads, although the spacing of these farmsteads about every 500 metres means that they are associated with substantial land holdings that in the medieval period would have been too large for a single household to have managed, a typical medieval tenement in Devon being *c*.15–30 acres in the early fourteenth century and *c*.45–55 acres in the sixteenth century (Fox 1991c, 724). This suggests two possibilities: either there was once a far greater number of farmsteads dotted about the landscape, or what are now isolated farmsteads were once small hamlets (as excavation has established was the case in western Devon: Henderson and Weddell 1994).

Outside the main settlements, the field assessment revealed little about the vernacular architecture as the through-roads tend to follow high ground whereas the farmsteads are located on the valley sides and are accessed by dead-end trackways. The way that the farmsteads are set back from the through-roads gives this landscape a feeling of great privacy, and it is noticeable that there are also very few public footpaths (Fig. 5.4). The relatively few pre-nineteenth-century listed houses are predominantly cob-built on a stone rubble plinth, with a three-room cross-passage layout typical of the region: all are (or were) farmhouses and it is noticeable how few surviving eighteenth-century or earlier cottages there are. Based on this small sample, the dates of building/rebuilding are significantly different to the Exe/Culm confluence group of parishes with relatively little work surviving from the late-medieval period but a major phase of activity in the late sixteenth and seventeenth centuries. Not only are there apparently no houses built in the eighteenth century, but while some of the seventeenth-century and earlier houses saw alterations in the nineteenth century there is no evidence of significant eighteenth-century investment. This points to little growth in the size of land holdings, with any changes in need being accommodated within existing infrastructure. Bickleigh saw more building in the eighteenth century although this is almost wholly in the form of cottages, probably for workers employed in the milling industry.

Fig. 5.4. Road sign for Chapelhaies, Northdown, and Tedbridge in Bradninch. The '-haies' place-name element is a variant of '-hayes' which in this study area is only found in Bradninch. Farmsteads in this area—on the edges of the Culm Measures—are typically set back from the public roads, and the sense of privacy that this creates, along with the scarcity of public footpaths, is a distinctive part of the landscape's character.

The Culm, Clyst, and Tale valleys

South of the hills above Bradninch, Cullompton, and Silverton lie the broad lowland plains of the Culm and Clyst valleys. Most of the pre-nineteenth-century houses are again cob-built, and although all are now whitewashed or rendered, exposed cob is visible in a number of farm buildings whose distinctive red colour reflects that of the local soils. The settlement patterns consist of a small nucleation around the church (the 'churchtown'), several other hamlets in peripheral parts of the parish, and a scatter of isolated farmsteads (potentially former small hamlets) and cottages. The pattern of building/rebuilding, as far as it is reflected in the listed building records, is markedly different to the fringes of the Culm Measures, with very large numbers of late medieval to sixteenth-century houses, many of which saw extensive refurbishment and extension in the seventeenth century. Although there are relatively few seventeenth- and eighteenth-century new builds, these include some notable small country houses such as the brick-built late-seventeenth-century mansion at Great Aunk (Fig. 5.5). Compared to the relative uniformity of the listed rural farmhouses on the Culm Measures—dominated by modest late-sixteenth- and

Fig. 5.5. Great Aunk, Clyst Hydon. This brick-built late-seventeenth-century house is one of several small country mansions in the lowlands of the Culm, Clyst, and Tale valleys that reflect the continued agricultural prosperity of the area.

Fig. 5.6. Town Farm, Clyst St Lawrence. An example of an early to mid-sixteenth-century three-room cross passage house with a chimney stack inserted axially against the side of the cross passage (evident in the way that the chimney stack protrudes through the roof just to one side of the front door in what is an asymmetrical frontage). Note the 'town' place-name, characteristic of these small hamlets in the Culm/Clyst/Tale valleys that were adjacent to parish churches.

seventeenth-century farmhouses that saw relatively little improvement in the eighteenth century—the houses of the Culm and Clyst valleys show a far earlier onset of building/rebuilding, far greater variation in their size, and far greater subsequent remodelling (e.g. Town Farm in Clyst St Lawrence[1]: Fig. 5.6). There are also some noticeable agricultural buildings surviving from the seventeenth and eighteenth centuries. Overall, this was clearly an area of great agricultural wealth with some land holdings being amalgamated to create large farms on which there was capital to invest in buildings. In sharp contrast to the Culm Measures, where the farmsteads are typically set back from the through roads, those in the lowlands normally lie next to the through-roads.

The three parishes to the east of Cullompton and Clyst Hydon—Plymtree, Talaton, and Whimple—all show remarkably similar patterns of building/rebuilding. Compared to the Clyst valley to the west, a smaller proportion of houses appear to have been built/rebuilt in the fifteenth or early sixteenth centuries, although this number is still far greater than on the fringes of the Culm Measures or at the Culm/Exe confluence.[2] After this significant phase of building/rebuilding, there was continued investment that lasted into the seventeenth and eighteenth centuries both in the form of new builds and alternations to existing houses.

Payhembury, Broadhembury, and Kentisbeare are three parishes that extend from the fertile red soils of the Permian sandstone, across the infertile sandy soils of the Triassic Bunter Beds, and across the heavier soils of the Triassic mudstones (Keuper Marls) that form the western foothills of the Blackdown Hills. The houses are once again predominantly cob on stone plinths with thatched roofs, and although all are whitewashed or rendered, the pale brown colour of the cob—in marked contrast to the deep red seen further west in the Culm/Clyst valleys—is visible in a number of unrendered agricultural buildings. The construction of Lower Tale Cottage (in Payhembury) in the mid- to late nineteenth century shows that the use of cob continued remarkably late. The character of the settlement patterns in these parishes is similar to that seen in the Culm/Clyst valleys, with a substantial nucleated settlement around the church, a few smaller hamlets in peripheral parts of the parish, and a scattering of isolated farmsteads. The proportion of houses built up to the sixteenth century in these parishes is typical for our study area as a whole. Most show extensive seventeenth-century and later refurbishment and remodelling, while the proportions of seventeenth- and eighteenth-century new builds is once again typical. Hembercombe, the northerly extension of Broadhembury village, however, consists of three late-seventeenth- and early eighteenth-century and three eighteenth-century houses and would appear to be a post-medieval extension to the medieval village. This is an interesting group that clearly demonstrates that although new symmetrical house plans, with a central passage between two equal-sized rooms, were being adopted from the late

---

[1] <http://www.imagesofengland.org.uk/Details/Default.aspx?id=86809&mode=adv>
[2] For a detailed study of Woodbeer Court in Plymtree, *see* Alcock and Hulland 1972.

seventeenth and early eighteenth century (e.g. Hembercombe Cottage and Woodbine Cottage), traditional asymmetrical layouts were also still being built well into the eighteenth century (e.g. Hembercombe Farm Cottage, Pendeen, and Thatcher's Cottage). Overall, with the exception of Hembercombe, the various settlements in Broadhembury parish show a broadly similar picture to the lowlands further west, with large numbers of late-medieval and sixteenth-century houses, and then significant investment in these existing buildings as well as the building/rebuilding of others during the seventeenth and eighteenth centuries. This impression of a major period of investment in the seventeenth and eighteenth centuries is strengthened by the construction in brick of Leyhill House—a small country mansion in Payhembury—and the building/refacing in brick of a number of other farmhouses.

The Blackdown Hills

Buildings on the Blackdown Hills are typically of chert (a flinty stone) rubble construction, in contrast to the cob-dominated lowlands to the west. All the parishes have dispersed settlement patterns, and while there are significant differences in the patterns of building/rebuilding from parish to parish, the overall picture is of considerable investment in the late medieval period and sixteenth century, with these houses seeing improvement thereafter, but relatively limited new building in the seventeenth and eighteenth centuries.

The central Somerset lowlands

Three parishes in the lowlands of central Somerset were selected for the drive through survey—Stocklinch (and *see* Austin and de Zouche Hall 1972), Puckington, and Barrington (Fig. 2.4)—which revealed a remarkable diversity of vernacular architecture with Stocklinch having a large number of late medieval houses, Puckington having been largely built/rebuilt in the seventeenth and eighteenth centuries, and Barrington showing elements of both periods. Four seventeenth-century houses in Barrington are symmetrical in layout marking the acceptance of a national trend in architectural styles not seen in Devon at this time. Houses in all three villages comprise a mixture of former working farms and smaller cottages, mostly built out of the local Ham Stone which was certainly being used as early as the fifteenth century (e.g. in Brownsells in Barrington). Cob was also used until about 1600 (e.g. Helen's Cottage in Barrington) but apparently no later (but note its continued use in Devon into the eighteenth century, described above). In nearby Stocklinch, The Chantry and Mannings show how in the fifteenth century, stone (used in the front walls) was taking over from cob (used in the rear wall at Mannings and the gable walls at The Chantry).

Fig. 5.7. Fairby, in Tiverton. Sixteenth- or early seventeenth-century three-roomed cross-passage house of cob and rubble construction. The asymmetrical plan, with a lateral stack prominently displayed against the front elevation, is typical of the Devon landscape.

Fig. 5.8. Cottage immediately east of Kingstone church, Somerset, showing the asymmetrical layout and chimney stack located to one side of the cross-passage.

Fig. 5.9. Somerville, in Hinton St George, Somerset. A three-room cross-passage house that was refronted in Ham Stone ashlar during the eighteenth century in the new, fashionable, symmetrical style.

Table 5.1. Summary of the initial date of construction for listed houses in the study area, and from other work in Somerset.

	sample	C16 and earlier	C17	C18	Parishes
This study (based on Listed Buildings surveys)					
Exe/Culm confluence	29	6 (20%)	17 (59%)	6 (21%)	Huxham, Nether Exe, Poltimore, Rewe, Stoke Canon
Culm Measures incl. Bickleigh	42	10 (24%)	20 (48%)	12 (28%)	Bickleigh, Butterleigh, and upland parts of Bradnich, Cullompton, and Silverton
Culm Measures excl. Bickleigh	14	5 (36%)	9 (64%)	0	Butterleigh, and upland parts of Bradnich, Cullompton, and Silverton
Culm/Clyst Valleys	68	40 (59%)	18 (26%)	10 (15%)	Broadclyst, Clyst Hydon, Clyst St Lawrence, and lowland parts of Bradnich, Cullompton, and Silverton

(*continued*)

Table 5.1. Continued

	sample	C16 and earlier	C17	C18	Parishes
Plymtree, Talaton & Whimple	72	22 (31%)	32 (44%)	18 (25%)	Plymtree, Talaton, Whimple
Tale Valley	95	39 (41%)	44 (46%)	12 (13%)	Broadhembury, Kentisbeare, Payhembury
Blackdown Hills	156	77 (49%)	56 (36%)	23 (15%)	Clayhidon, Churchstanton, Combe Raleigh, Cotleigh, Dunkeswell, Luppitt, Membury, Monkton, Sheldon, Upottery
central Somerset lowlands	113	42 (37%)	46 (41%)	25 (22%)	Barrington, Earnshill, Isle Brewers, Isle Abbots, Kingsbury Episcopi, Puckington, Shepton Beauchamp, Stocklinch
totals	575	236 (41%)	46 (41%)	25 (18%)	
SVBRB central Somerset villages					*Source*
Alford and Lovington	24	6 (25%)	14 (58%)	4 (17%)	SSAVBRG 1986, 14
Barton, Winscombe	9	2 (22%)	2 (22%)	5 (56%)	Sue Shaw pers. comm.
Batcombe	29	9 (31%)	12 (41%)	8 (28%)	SSAVARG 1988, 18
Butleigh	54	19 (35%)	22 (41%)	13 (24%)	SVBRG 2001, 15–16
Chiselborough	36	11 (31%)	9 (25%)	16 (44%)	SSAVBRG 1993, 40
Combe St Nicholas	42	10 (24%)	15 (36%)	17 (40%)	SVBRG 2008a
Compton Dundon	43	16 (37%)	15 (35%)	12 (28%)	SVBRG 2004, 20–21
Haselbury Plucknett	39	10 (26%)	18 (46%)	11 (28%)	SSAVBRG 1994, 33
Long Load	27	10 (37%)	10 (37%)	7 (26%)	SSAVBRG 1982, 24–9
Shapwick	26	7 (27%)	9 (35%)	10 (38%)	SVBRG 1996, 44
West and Middle Chinnock	23	9 (39%)	10 (44%)	4 (17%)	SSAVBRG 1984, 30–47
totals	352	109 (31%)	136 (39%)	107 (30%)	
North Somerset Levels	30	14 (47%)	15 (50%)	1 (3%)	Humphreys and Rippon 2006
Northern Somerset					
Newton St Leo	45	0	24* (53%)	21 (47%)	Dallimore 2001
SVBRG western Somerset					
Stogursey village	54	27 (50%)	13 (24%)	14 (26%)	SVBRG 2010
Stogursey hamlets	46	11 (24%)	19 (41%)	16 (35%)	SVBRG 2010
South Gloucestershire	178	87 (49%)	91 (51%)		Hall 1983, 11

* of which 17 were constructed *c.*1690–1700

LOCAL VARIATION IN VERNACULAR ARCHITECTURE ACROSS DEVON AND SOMERSET

Enclosing the open hall

In the late medieval period, surviving house plans were very similar in Devon, Dorset, and Somerset, dominated by three-roomed cross-passage houses (Fig. 5.2), with smaller numbers of two-unit houses also with an asymmetrical layout that once may have been more common. Cruck construction was also found on both sides of the Blackdown Hills (Machin 1978; Alcock 1981, Fig. 32; Roberts and Wrathmell 2002, fig. 1.11). From the sixteenth century, however, differences start to emerge. To the east, in Somerset and Dorset, when stacks were inserted into late-medieval houses they are almost invariably found towards the centre of the house, backing onto the cross-passage, while to the west, in Devon, they are often found on the front-facing outside wall (so-called lateral stacks that are also found across parts of southern Wales: Brunskill 1971; 1992, 136–7, 144–5; Smith 1975, 432; Machin 1977). Although axial and gable-end stacks were inserted into earlier buildings in Devon, this tends to be later than the fashion for axial stacks.

There is no definitive mapping of lateral stacks, but using the Listed Buildings records we can examine their densities across our local study area (Table 5.2; Fig. 5.10). The analysis has been carried out in two ways. Firstly, the density of listed buildings with lateral stacks was mapped as this reflects how one experiences a particular landscape, with this feature of the vernacular architecture being an important part of landscape character in some areas but not others. In the Tale valley, for example, there is a listed building from the eighteenth century or earlier with a lateral stack every 384 acres, compared to one per 13,171 acres in the central Somerset lowlands. The division between communities who favoured lateral stacks and those who did not is remarkably clear, and runs right through the western edge of the Blackdown Hills, being very similar to the distribution of '-hayes'/'-hayne' and 'Barton' place-names (Fig. 4.13), and 'Park' field-names (Fig. 4.14). This analysis reflects the prevalence of lateral stacks in the landscape but could in part also simply reflect where larger numbers of buildings of this period survive. To test this issue, another piece of analysis was carried out that looked at the percentages of stacks in sixteenth-century houses that were located laterally as opposed to axially (gable-end stacks were excluded from this analysis). The parishes in Somerset are often very small, so the numbers of listed buildings are far fewer than in Devon, and in such small samples, some high or low percentages can be achieved through just a small number of buildings. The results, however, reveal a very similar distribution to the overall density, with a very high proportion of stacks positioned laterally in the far west of our study area

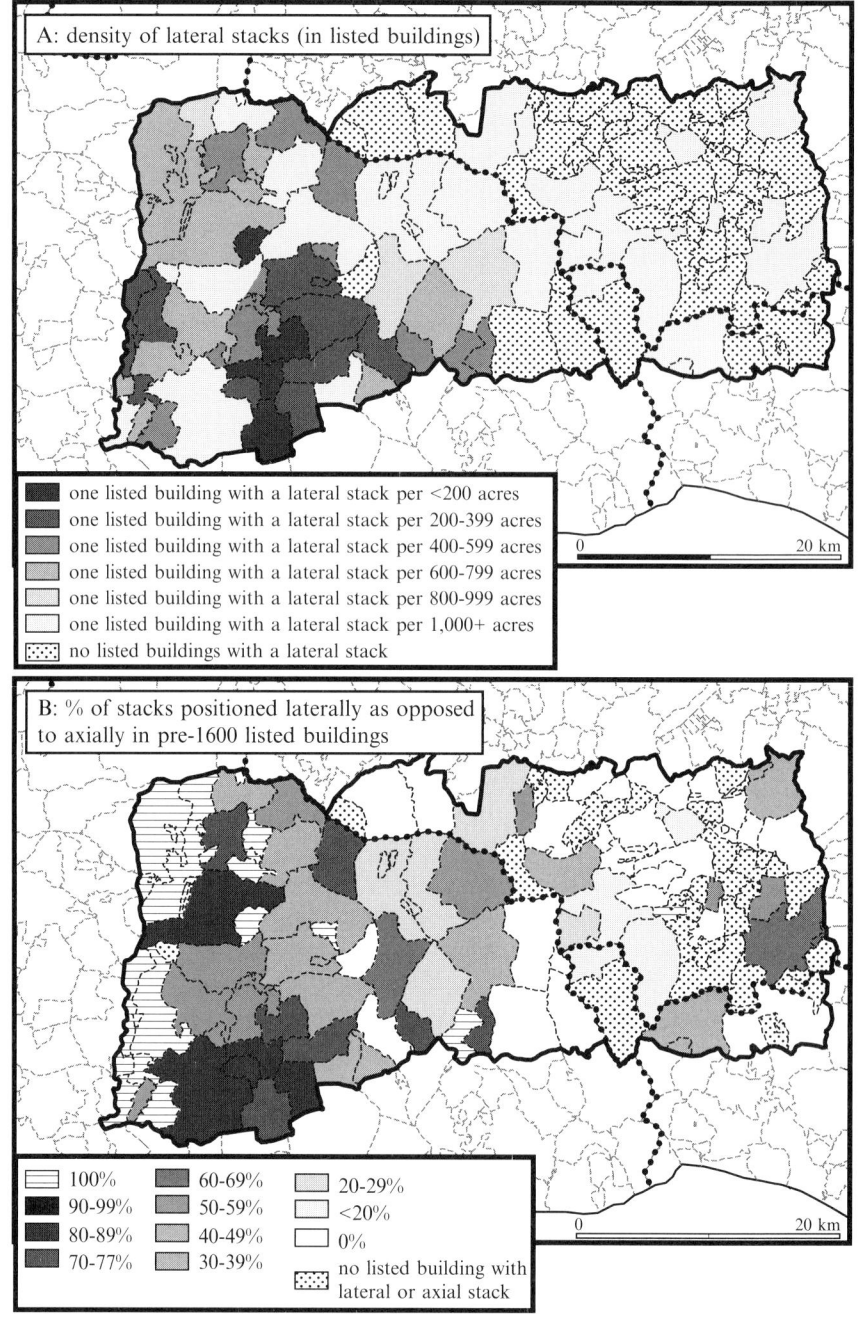

Fig. 5.10. (A) Density of listed buildings with lateral stacks; (B) % of sixteenth-century and earlier listed buildings with lateral as opposed to axial stacks.

Table 5.2. Distribution of lateral stacks.

	acres	lateral stacks	acres per lateral stack	% of C18 and earlier listed buildings with lateral stacks	Parish
Exe/Culm confluence	5,481	11	498 acres	38%	Huxham, Nether Exe, Poltimore, Rewe, Stoke Canon
Culm Measures incl. Bickleigh	10,532	20	527 acres	48%	Bickleigh, Butterleigh, and upland parts of Bradnich, Cullompton, and Silverton
Culm/Clyst Valleys	27,760	68	408 acres	49%	Broadclyst, Clyst Hydon, Clyst St Lawrence, Plymtree, Talaton, Whimple, and lowland parts of Bradnich, Cullompton, and Silverton
Tale Valley	11,124	29	384 acres	31%	Broadhembury, Kentisbeare, Payhembury
Western Blackdown Hills	35,232	32	1,101 acres	21%	Churchstanton, Clayhidon, Combe Raleigh, Cotleigh, Dunkeswell, Luppitt, Monkton, Sheldon and Upottery
Eastern Blackdown Hills	39,754	8 (including one in a school built in 1851)	4,969 acres	3%	Buckland St Mary, Chard, Chardstock, Combe St Nicholas, Membury, Otterford, Stockland, Wambrook, Whitestaunton, Yarcombe
Ilminster area	11,963	1	11,963 acres	<1%	Ashill, Broadway, Donyatt, Ilton, Ilminster, White Lackington
Central Somerset lowlands	13,171	1	13,171 acres	<1%	Barrington, Earnshill, Isle Brewers, Isle Abbots, Kingsbury Episcopi, Puckington, Shepton Beauchamp, Stocklinch

(80–100%), fairly high in the lowlands of eastern Devon and the western fringes of the Blackdown Hills (c.60–80%), and very small proportions further east (typically under 20%).

Choosing a lateral stack, especially if it was on the side of a house facing a road, would have created a visible statement about adopting new technology, but conversely it may also reflect a greater degree of conservatism, because placing the stack externally retains the integrity of the hall as an open space, perhaps reflecting a desire to retain this traditional feature of house design and its associated communality. The way that new styles of symmetrical house design came into fashion in Somerset during the seventeenth century is certainly in sharp contrast to areas west of the Blackdown Hills where old-style asymmetrical plans were still being created as late as the eighteenth century (e.g. Persley Cottage, in Dunkeswell, dated to the late eighteenth and early nineteenth century). Continued adherence to asymmetrical house layouts may once again reflect a desire in the south-west to retain the traditional three-room cross-passage plan (Child 1978; 1990, 40–4).

So why were communities in the South West so conservative in the way that they designed their houses? Although many have argued that the drivers behind patterns of building and rebuilding within a region were primarily economic, such as increasing population, improvements to communication and marketing networks, and the consolidation of small farms into larger, more efficient holdings, Johnson (1993b, 120–1) has suggested that we should not overlook non-economic cultural factors, while Longcroft (2007) has emphasized how buildings form part of a community's sense of place. Austin and Thomas (1990) provide an example of this, illustrating how the arrangement of space within medieval houses on Dartmoor shows a precise repetition of detail suggesting that 'the internal arrangements of these longhouses were carefully constructed to be familiar, not just to the ... inhabitants of the house but also to anybody working and living in that region'. The conservatism of the South West vernacular architecture appears to be another example of this: asymmetrical plans and elevations were the South West's way of building houses.

A 'Great Rebuilding'?

It is clear that across our study area, a significant number of listed buildings were constructed in the late-medieval period, with even more dating to the sixteenth century, and we must now turn to the significance of this. In a pioneering study of vernacular architecture, Hoskins (1953) suggested that there was a 'Great Rebuilding' of rural domestic houses in the period 1570–1640 reflecting both improved construction techniques and a greater desire for privacy. This idea became widely accepted although Machin (1977) argued for a longer chronology and a peak of rebuilding in the late seventeenth century: 'instead of a thesis of a Great Rebuilding at some specific period, we require a theory of building history which will explain ... the medieval preference for impermanent building, the emergence of permanent vernacular building in the 15th century, its extension and successive rebuilding of vernacular houses from the late 16th–early 18th centuries, and the replacement of vernacular by "polite" or "pattern-book" architecture in the mid 18th century' (Machin 1977, 56). One problem with Machin's work, like that of Hoskins, was his reliance on dated inscriptions that relatively few buildings have and which could easily refer to a period of renovation or extension as opposed to initial construction. Recent programmes of dendrochronology have indeed revealed previously unexpected numbers of houses that are pre-sixteenth century (e.g. Penoyre and Penoyre 1999; Groves 2005). This supports the view that rather than a relatively brief 'Great Rebuilding', the transformation of rural housing into more durable structures was a drawn-out process. Currie (1988) added to the debate the concept of 'attrition rates', arguing that factors such as sustained economic prosperity in a region may have led to a high frequency of rebuilding that will have removed perfectly solid houses constructed only a few centuries earlier with the result that if an area today has, for example, mostly eighteenth-century houses, we cannot be sure whether there was an initial phase of building/rebuilding in the late-medieval period.

From the analysis carried out for this study area, using the full range of dating evidence and not just date stones, it seems that the origins of our housing stock does indeed have a far longer time frame than the period 1570–1640 that Hoskins (1953) suggested for the 'Great Rebuilding', or Machin's (1977) late-seventeenth-century peak. There are also, however, clear differences across our *pays* with extensive building/rebuilding seen across most areas in the fifteenth and sixteenth centuries, except around the Exe/Culm confluence and on the Culm Measures whose main period of evident activity was in the seventeenth century. Another significant trend in the seventeenth century is the change of

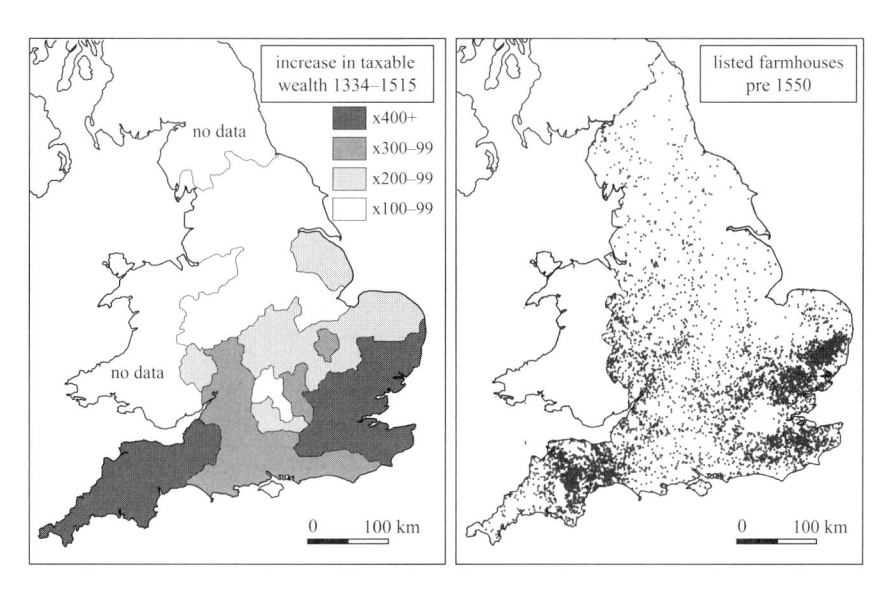

Fig. 5.11. Different rates of growth in lay wealth between 1334 and 1515, and the distribution of pre-1550 listed buildings. (After Butlin 1978, Fig 5.3, and Lake and Edwards 2006a, © Crown Copyright. All rights reserved. English Heritage 100019088.)

house design seen in Somerset, with fashionable new symmetrical layouts replacing the traditional asymmetrical three-room cross-passage houses (Fig. 5.9), a trend that was not followed in Devon until the eighteenth century, and even then, not in all cases. When we take a broader view, we see that the considerable amount of building/rebuilding seen on and to the west of the Blackdown Hills is part of a regional pattern with similar densities of pre-mid-sixteenth-century houses across most of the South West, West Midlands, and south-east of England (Lake and Edwards 2006b, 36–7). It is striking that these areas with relatively dispersed settlement patterns and predominantly enclosed field systems all lie outside England's central zone and are precisely the areas that saw the greatest increase in lay wealth between the early fourteenth and early sixteenth centuries (Fig. 5.11; Butlin 1978, fig. 5.3).

The 'Agricultural Revolution'

The discussion so far has focused on the late medieval period through to the seventeenth century, although in some parts of our study area the standing domestic buildings date predominantly from the eighteenth and nineteenth centuries and the intensification of farming commonly known as the 'Agricultural Revolution'. This had a variable impact on the South West which is reflected in the standing buildings that have survived. Some areas saw agrarian prosperity and investment in the eighteenth century and the greatest densities of eighteenth-century house construction across our study area are in the lowlands of the eastern Devon (e.g. Great Aunk in Clyst Hydon, Fig. 5.5) and central Somerset (e.g. Puckington). Other areas are largely lacking in eighteenth-century house building (or major investment in existing housing stock), a trend that is particularly clear on the Culm Measures (excluding Bickleigh) and Blackdown Hills.

In the nineteenth century, certain parts of our study area saw the development of 'model' farms, with ranges of usually brick-built agricultural buildings laid out around a rectangular courtyard (e.g. Figs. 5.3 and 5.12). Their development reflects three trends in agriculture: first, a growth in the size of landed estates, second, the 'landlord-and-tenant' system of farming whereby the landowner was responsible for the provision and maintenance of buildings which were leased to tenants, and third, agricultural investment and innovations such as mechanization, drainage, new crops, and improved livestock breeds that began in the eighteenth century and culminated during the period of 'High Farming' in the mid-nineteenth century (Barnwell and Giles 1997, xii, 5; Wade Martins 2002; 2004; Williamson 2002; Wakeham 2003). The creation of model farms was seen across most of England although it was not particularly common in the South West which may to a large extent be explained by the small number of very large agricultural estates: in neither

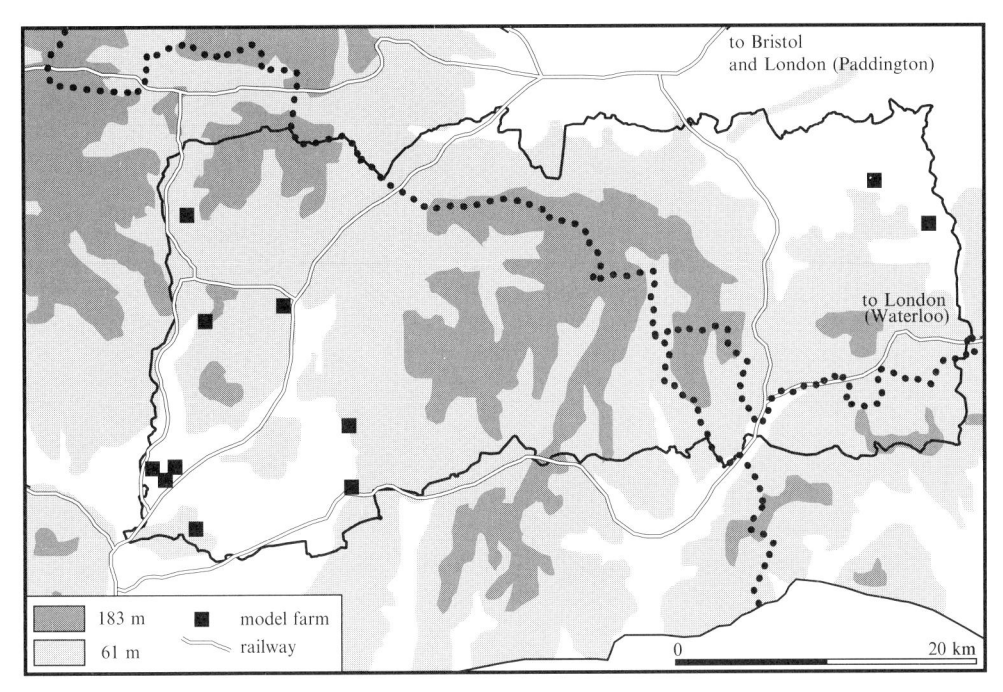

Fig. 5.12. Distribution of model farms in the local study area (after Wade Martins 2004, fig. 8, with additions), showing a fairly close relationship with railways.

Devon nor Somerset were more than 10% of farms over 300 acres, in contrast to Dorset, Wiltshire, and Hampshire where over 20% were of this size (Wade Martins 2002, fig. 6). There were, however, a number of model farms in our study most notably in the Exe/Culm confluence parishes where they were able to take advantage of their proximity to the Exeter to Bristol and London railways (Fig. 5.12).

DISCUSSION

The overall aim of Chapters 4 and 5 was to see whether differences in settlement patterns are also reflected in other facets of landscape character, and this analysis of vernacular architecture has indeed revealed some important trends. Some of the differences we see are determined by the natural environment. Building materials add an important dimension to the character of the built environment, such as the distinctive blue-grey Lias and yellow Ham Stone in central Somerset, chert on the Blackdown Hills, and cob of various colours in Devon. Another difference across our study area emerged in the eighteenth century when pantile roofs started to appear in Somerset (Penoyre and Penoyre 1978, 46). Because of their shape and brittle nature, pantiles lend themselves to simple roof forms. It is difficult, for example, to cut them diagonally as would be required if they were laid on a hipped roof or around dormer windows (common in the one-and-a-half storey houses of the time), and so the move to pantiles was associated with the raising of roofs and creation of gable ends. The relative instability of cob, however, meant that hipped roofs remained the norm in Devon (Fig. 2.5), whereas the good building stone in Somerset meant that gables were far more common (Fig. 5.9).

Whilst these differences in building materials are important, it is the very marked variation in house design that is of greater interest. In the late-medieval period there was a considerable degree of uniformity in house plans across Devon and Somerset, with three-roomed cross-passage houses dominant. From the sixteenth century, however, differences start to emerge. Across all areas fireplaces and chimneystacks were constructed in both existing and new houses, although the position of the stack differed significantly: in Somerset the stacks were usually located within the hall, backing onto the cross-passage, whereas in Devon they were typically attached to the outside of the house. This difference may be explained by a desire in Devon to retain the integrity of the medieval hall, and this is certainly seen in the way that asymmetrical layouts continued to be used for new builds as late as the eighteenth century, at a time when more fashionable symmetrical layouts had become common in Somerset. What we see, therefore, is a paradox. The external lateral stacks seen across Devon, usually located on the prominent front walls of the houses, were a very visible statement that the occupants were 'modern': they were adopting the new technology and the cleaner living environment that chimney stacks afforded. The positioning of these stacks on the exterior of the building, along with an adherence to asymmetrical house plans long after they went out of fashion in Somerset also, however, suggests a degree of conservatism, or at least a continued affinity to the concept of a communal hall. People were doing things differently either side of the Blackdown Hills.

6

The character of the fieldscape

In Chapter 4, a characterization of nineteenth-century settlement patterns across our local study area revealed some marked differences either side of the Blackdown Hills that can be traced back to the medieval period. We will now turn to the nature of the field systems that surrounded these settlements. This chapter presents a characterization of the field-boundary patterns, based on an analysis of the OS 1st Edn 6" maps. Chapter 7 will then add depth to this by looking at patterns of land ownership and land occupancy. It should be said from the start that this chapter was a difficult one to write for two reasons: firstly, its problematic relationship to the somewhat controversial English Heritage-sponsored programme of Historic Landscape Characterisation (HLC), and secondly, a marked difference of opinion that emerged with regard to the extent of open field in Devon. Some form of characterization was essential here in order to give a spatial framework for the wider landscape analysis and to establish whether there were differences in the nature of the field systems either side of the Blackdown Hills. It is fair to say, however, that HLC has provoked much debate within professional archaeology, heritage management, and the academic community, but the formal HLCs conducted do not equate to a complete and definitive historic landscape characterization: there is more than one approach to mapping differences systematically in historic landscape characterization, and the work carried out in this study is somewhat different to HLC. This in itself should not be taken as a criticism of the English Heritage-sponsored programme. While this author does have some issues with a key conclusion of the Devon HLC—the extent of former open field—this debate can only be entered into precisely because that HLC was carried out and published in a thorough and accessible way (both through a published report and through making the data available online).

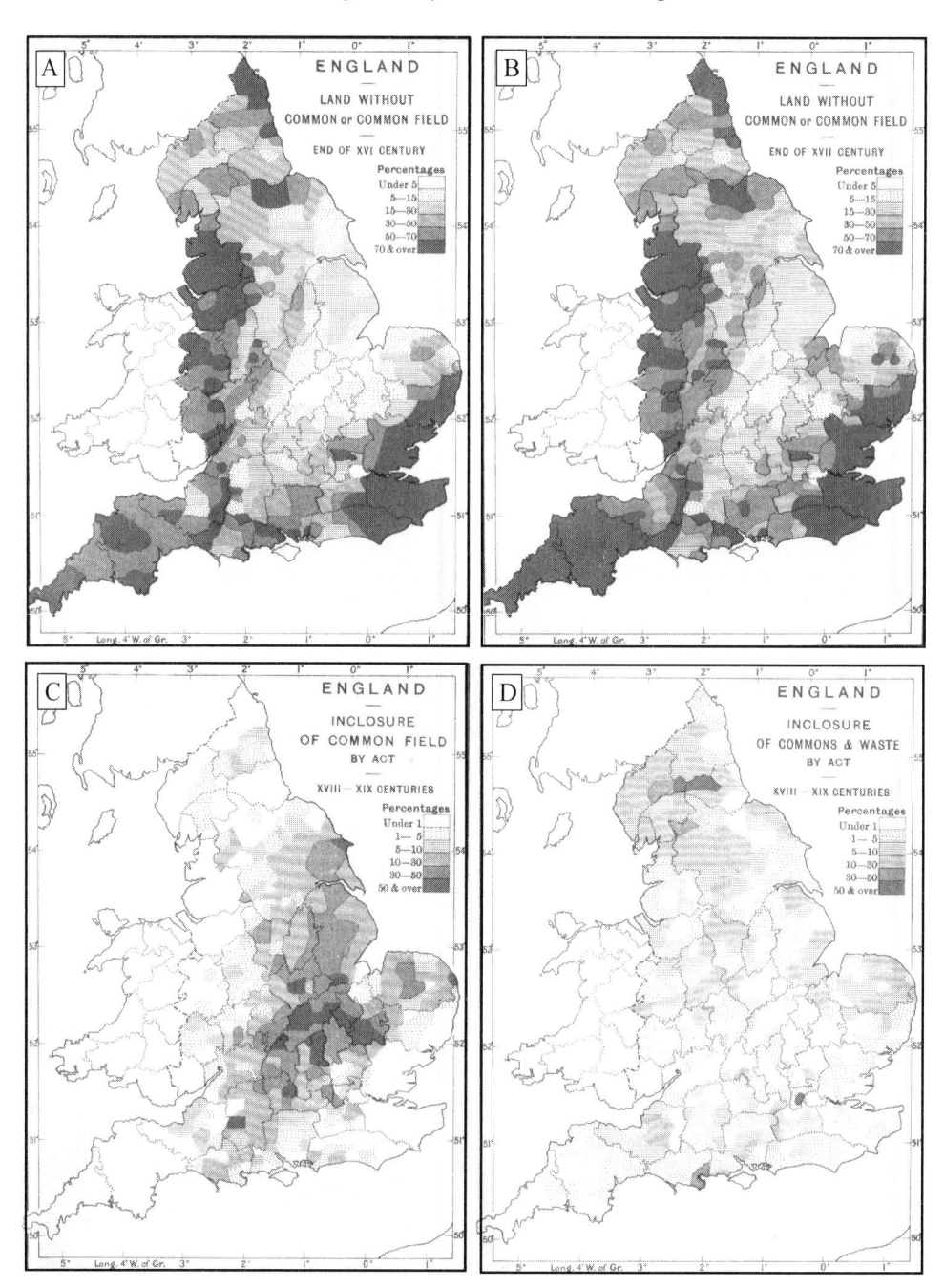

Fig. 6.1. The former extent of former open field as mapped by Gonner (1912, maps A-D). (A) Land without common or common field in the late sixteenth century; (B): Land without common or common field in the late seventeenth century (based on Ogilby's road atlas *Britannia*); (C) Parliamentary Enclosure Acts of common field; (D) Parliamentary Enclosure Acts of commons and waste.

REGIONAL VARIATION IN FIELD SYSTEMS

Across western Europe as a whole, travellers and writers were aware of regional variation in the way that land was managed from at least the thirteenth century, including the extent to which extensive open fields, or 'champion countryside', dominated the landscape in some areas (e.g. Bartholomeus Anglicus's *De proprietatibus rerum*: Cahn 1991). The earliest English writer to describe the landscape was John Leland in the early sixteenth century, and although he never drew a map showing areas of champion countryside, Slater (1907, 47) has plotted those places Leland described in this way, thereby revealing that they were mostly found in a broad swathe of central England stretching from Dorset to Yorkshire (Fig. 3.1). Although the origins of these open fields had been discussed by Seebohm (1890) and Vinogradoff (1892) as early as late in the nineteenth century, the first systematic attempt at accurately mapping their former extent was by Gonner (1912) (Fig. 6.1). Gray (1915) mapped the best-known type of open-field farming, the 'Midland System', whereby the strips of land held by tenants were intermingled with those of the 'demesne' (land managed directly by the lord of the manor) and scattered across two or three extensive open fields, with one field lying fallow each year and being subject to communal grazing (Fig. 6.2). These regularly arranged two- and three-field systems were regulated through local custom, and often survived until the eighteenth and nineteenth centuries when they were enclosed through an Act of Parliament (and *see* Ault 1972; Dodgshon 1980, 47; Kain and Oliver 2004). In contrast to the Midland system, Gray argued that the adjacent regions of East Anglia, Kent, and the Thames basin had their own, less regularly structured system of open-field cultivation, usually with larger numbers of smaller subdivided fields within which only a small number of tenants held strips, and which were therefore more amenable to relatively early enclosure by agreement. Gray argued that the north and west of Britain, in contrast, had a 'celtic' system with small hamlets (typically of less than six farms) associated with relatively small, cultivated 'infields', surrounded by occasionally cultivated 'outfields' and extensive areas of rough grazing. While the cultivated land holdings of each farmstead in these hamlets may have taken the form of intermingled unenclosed strips, these open fields were on a far smaller scale than the vast common fields of the Midlands.

A wide range of terms have been used to describe field systems where an area of land is subdivided without the use of physical barriers such as ditches, hedges, or banks. In one book (Rowley 1981) the terms used in different papers included 'subdivided fields', 'commonfield', 'townfield', 'open field', and the 'Midland system'. The reason for this varied use of terminology is that the authors were often talking about slightly different types of field system, and so it is important here to define the terminology being used. In

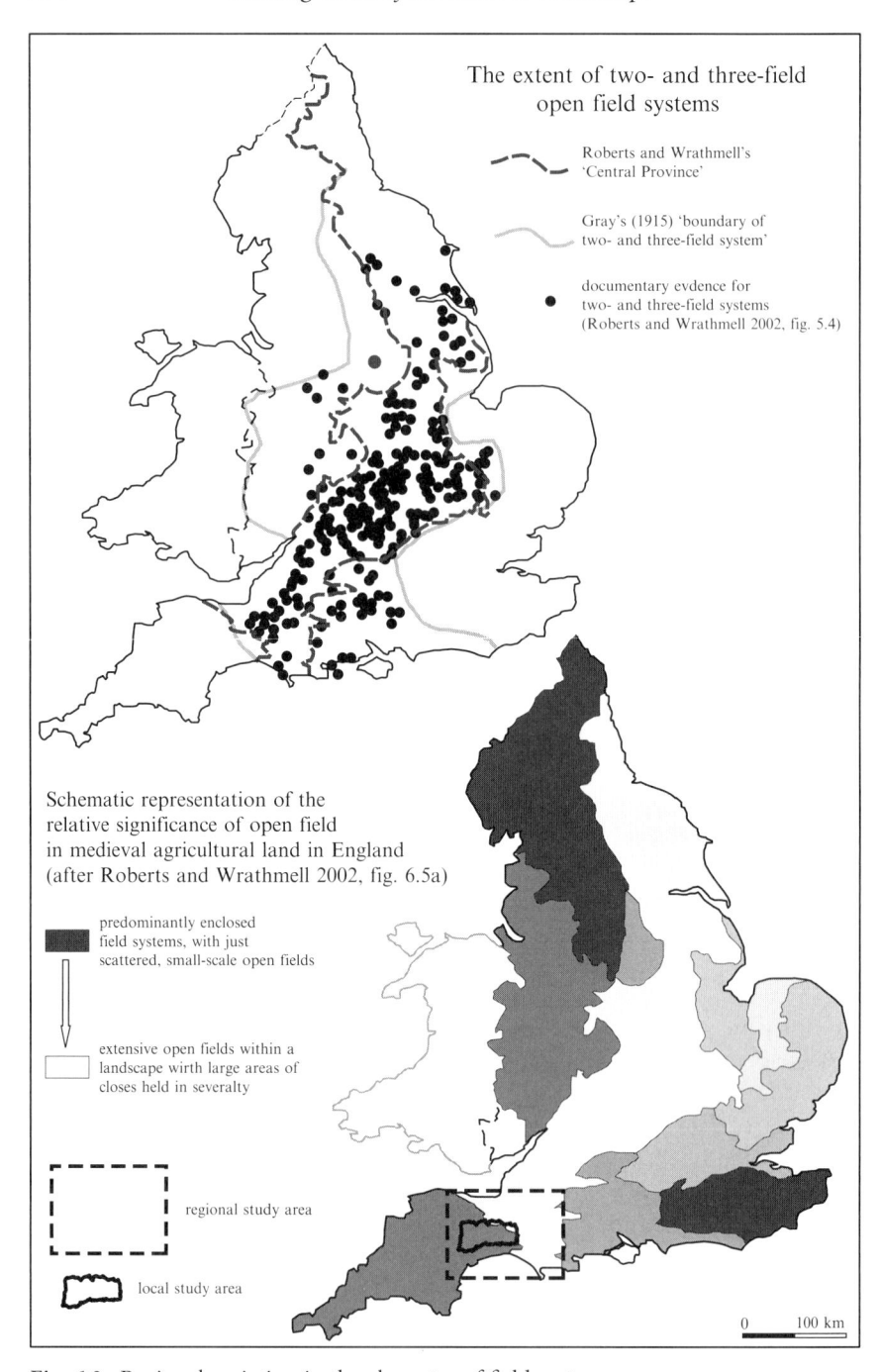

Fig. 6.2. Regional variation in the character of field systems.

this study, 'common field' is used for the regularly arranged Midland-style two- and three-field system, and where we lack the documentary evidence for how a field system was managed, the neutral term 'open field' is used for a field of any scale that was subdivided into strips (following Campbell 1981).

The north-east corner of our study area—in the lowlands of central Somerset—was solidly part of England's central zone, that in the medieval period was dominated by vast open fields that documentary sources show were managed using the Midland-style two- and three-field system (Gray 1915; Roberts and Wrathmell 2000a; 2002). In addition to the earthworks of ridge and furrow, and some seventeenth- and eighteenth-century maps (e.g. Fig. 4.1), evidence for the physical form of these common fields is preserved within the fabric of the today's historic landscape in the form of blocks of long, narrow, often curving fields (i.e. enclosed strips) between long, sinuous boundaries (i.e. the former headlands of furlong blocks). These common fields were on a vast scale, often covering $c.$800–1,600 acres.

In contrast, historians have traditionally argued that there was very little open field in the south-west of England, reflected in Gray's (1915, 258–66) observation that open fields in Devon seem never to have been numerous or, in any parish, extensive, and what open fields there were do not appear to have been managed according to the Midland system. Early agricultural and topographical writers were certainly struck by the almost wholly enclosed nature of Devon's fields, reflected for example in Jeremiah Milles's enquiry into the farming methods of Devonshire in the mid-eighteenth century (Stanes 2008b). Orwin and Orwin (1938, 59) dismissed the evidence for open field in Devon and Cornwall as 'doubtful or non-existent', though interestingly this statement did not appear in the second edition of their book, when instead they commented that 'in Devon, a county lacking any evidence of statutory enclosure of common fields, recent research and work in progress shows conclusively that farming in open fields was practised in various parts where the topography permitted' (Orwin and Orwin 1954, 65). This 'recent work' was that of Finberg (1952) who identified some documentary material that appeared to describe open field, although the mapping of evidence for former open field preserved within modern field-boundary patterns by Rawson (1953) and Shorter *et al.* (1969: fig. 6.3) suggested that it had been extremely limited in extent. More recently, Fox (1972) has argued that open fields were 'unexceptional features' of Devon's landscape, while Herring (2006a, 44) has suggested that in Cornwall 'the bulk of the medieval [fieldscape] is clearly derived from former strip fields', arguing that there has been a failure to appreciate their extent due to 'a romantic certainty that the Cornish "Celtic" character has been built on individualism that saw farming households working their small plots of land separately'. In the Devon HLC, Turner (2007, 48–56) similarly suggests that open fields were far more common than previously thought, arguing that 'medieval enclosures based on strip fields . . . occur in every parish in the county

116 *Making Sense of An Historic Landscape*

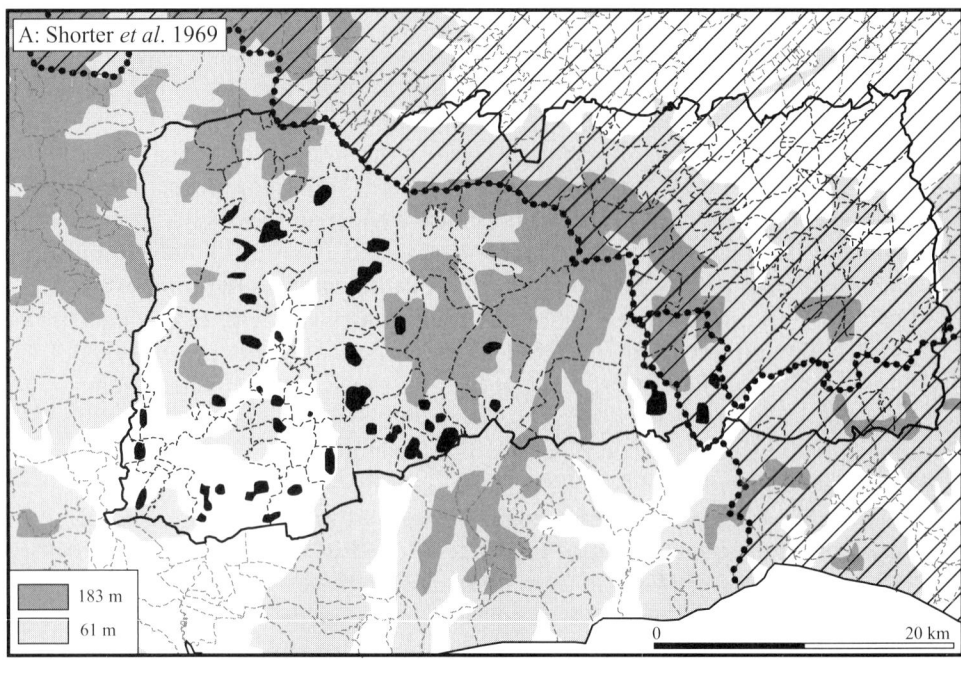

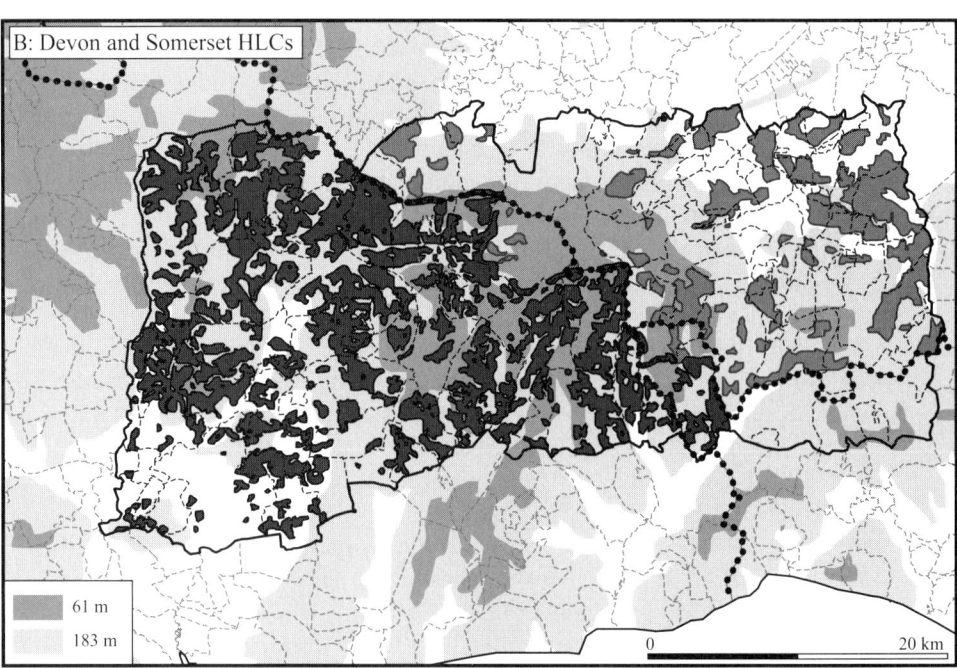

Fig. 6.3. Suggested extents of former open field in the local study area. (A) Shorter *et al.* (1969) that only covers Devon; (B) Somerset and Devon HLCs (Aldred 2001; Turner 2007). Note how the different methodologies used in the two HLCs has resulted in a highly implausible difference in landscape character either side of the county boundary.

[Devon], and in many they still cover by far the greatest proportion of the land' (around 32% of the total land area in 1890). If we exclude the large area that in 1890 was unenclosed moorland ($c.1,157$ km^2), this would mean that 39% of lowland Devon had once been covered in open field. If this was indeed the case, then the difference in the extent of open field on either side of the Blackdown Hills may have been less than was previously thought.

Both Finberg (1952) and Fox (1973; 1975) identified documentary evidence for some open field in the later medieval period, and Fox (1972, fig. 1) even prepared a distribution map of places with such evidence although it gives us no idea of their extent. In this respect Shorter *et al.*'s (1969) mapping of morphological evidence for former strip fields preserved within the physical fabric of the historic landscape is invaluable in showing a scatter of open fields spread right across Devon, although the vast majority were extremely small, especially compared to the Midland-style common fields in central Somerset (an extract of Shorter *et al.*'s map is shown in Fig. 6.3). It is very noticeable, however, that the extent of former open field mapped by Shorter *et al.* is far more limited in extent than that produced by Turner (2007) in the Devon HLC. It is also noticeable that while Turner shows extensive open field right up to the county boundary, the Somerset HLC shows very little open field on its side of the border (Fig. 6.3): the apparent discontinuity in landscape character along the county boundary is such that one of these HLCs is clearly wrong. One of the major questions to be answered in this chapter is, therefore, just what was the extent of open field on and to the west of the Blackdown Hills.

THE HISTORIC LANDSCAPE CHARACTER TYPES

The characterization of the fieldscape in the local study area involved each parcel of land being attributed to one of a series of eleven predetermined historic landscape character types (Plate 2):

- Large Non-Agricultural Settlement
- Woodland
- Ornamental Landscapes
- Floodplains
- Sloping Valley Bottoms
- Unenclosed Land
- Late Enclosures
- Intermediate Enclosures
- Semi-Irregular Enclosures
- Irregular Enclosures
- Enclosed Strip Fields

Scholars of Historic Landscape Characterisation will note that this simple approach is not dissimilar to some of the earliest work carried out in Cornwall. This adoption of such a straightforward methodology is quite deliberate: what is presented here is a simple way of dividing the landscape into a small number of basic types, some of which can then be investigated further (for example, by looking at patterns of land ownership and land occupancy: *see* Chapter 7). The need here was for the big picture which this simple methodology has created, and while far greater sophistication—such as an attribute-led approach now used in English Heritage HLCs—could have been used, that would have gone beyond what was needed for this particular project. In carrying out this work, four basic principles were borne in mind:

- that with an infinite variety of field shapes and sizes, grouping them into types is an inherently subjective process that must be based upon experience and professional judgement: this historic landscape characterization should be regarded as *an* interpretation of the evidence, and not definitive.
- the characterization is based on the oldest surviving cartographic sources that cover the entire study area (the OS 1st Edn 6" maps of *c.*1880) which reflect the landscape before the ravages of modern agricultural intensification: the slightly earlier Tithe maps cannot be used for this purpose as there are several gaps where large areas of parishes such as Dunkeswell did not pay tithes as they were former monastic land (Plate 4). Where available, earlier cartographic sources (e.g. estate maps, eighteenth-century county maps, Parliamentary Enclosure maps, and Tithe maps) and aerial photography (e.g. the RAF vertical coverage of the late-1940s) were, however, consulted to aid the interpretation of the OS 1st Edn 6" maps.
- some historic landscape-character types are more clearly defined than others, and as such, the most effective way of working was to firstly delimit the more straightforward types ('Non-Agricultural Settlements', 'Woodland', 'Floodplains', 'Sloping Valley Bottoms', 'Unenclosed Land' and 'Late Enclosure'), and then spend longer tackling the remaining, more complex areas.
- the identification of morphological types must be a separate process from determining their age and understanding the processes that lay behind their creation: description must be kept separate from interpretation. The latter can only be achieved through 'adding depth' to the characterization, examples of which include examining patterns settlement and place-names (Chapter 4), vernacular architecture (Chapter 5), and land holding (Chapter 7).

The characterization that is presented in Plate 2 (with many of the types illustrated on Figures 6.4–6.8) is actually very cautious in its nature. It is morphological and descriptive, and quite large areas are placed in the 'intermediate' category because it was not possible *at this stage* to determine what their origins are. This characterization is a means to an end, not an end in itself: it is better to be cautious at this early stage than be overly ambitious and make interpretations that the raw data cannot sustain. Having laid this cautious, descriptive foundation, however, we can then add depth to the characterization and add other layers of data. It is therefore important to appreciate that the morphological analysis of field systems presented in Plate 2 is just one layer of data in what is a highly multifaceted study of landscape character which includes the analysis of patterns and land ownership and land occupancy in Chapter 7, the culmination of which is Figure 7.6.

Large Non-Agricultural Settlements

Settlements with a non-agricultural character (i.e. urban or industrial) are the only ones in the study area large enough to warrant description as a separate historic landscape type: agricultural settlements (i.e. villages, hamlets, and isolated farmsteads) form part of the character of other landscapes types.

Woodland

Mixed deciduous woodland cloaks many of the steeper slopes and is also found in smaller areas in the adjacent lowland areas. The heavily wooded scarp of the northern and western Blackdowns is particularly prominent (e.g. Figs. 1.1 and 6.4).

Ornamental Landscapes

Parklands associated with large country houses are scattered across the lower-lying parts of the study area. These landscapes often include areas of woodland maintained partly for aesthetic reasons, and this is included in the 'Ornamental Landscape' type, as opposed to the general Woodland type.

Floodplains

In the middle and lower reaches of the major river valleys, the Floodplains are characteristically wide and flat with areas of lush meadows and pastures, mostly divided into relatively large fields, bounded by hedgerows, along with patches of alder and willow (e.g. Fig. 3.8). Roads typically skirt along the edges of these Floodplains, linking wetland-edge settlements and mills (with their associated leats). A small part of the Yarty Valley was a common meadow, enclosed in the nineteenth century, and documentary sources suggest that some other meadows in Devon were held in common (Fox 1972, 100). East of the Blackdown Hills evidence for common meadows is far clearer. In Lopen, for example, an estate map of 1774 shows unfenced subdivisions in 'Wath Meadow', while the eleven adjacent closes all called 'Broadmead' were held by nine separate tenements and presumably represent the enclosure of what was once another common meadow; another large close was called 'Common Mead' (Fig. 4.1). Worth Mead and Common Mead are documented in 1446 as common meadows (Dunning 1978, 164).

Sloping Valley Bottoms

The higher reaches of rivers and streams on the Blackdown Hills and other high ground have more V-shaped valleys, often with very steep sides. Visitors driving in the region are likely to experience these areas only fleetingly, as the lane they are travelling on dips suddenly into a wooded valley before climbing out again on the opposite side. On the more moderate slopes, fields are typically small or very small with irregular shapes probably derived from the piecemeal assarting of woodland, and wooded areas are still frequent on the steeper slopes. Settlements are rare apart from a number of mills.

Unenclosed Land

By the 1880s unenclosed rough ground was restricted to areas of wet and/or infertile soil on the higher plateaus and steeper slopes of the Blackdown Hills that were the last surviving remnants of what had been extensive upland commons that were enclosed in the eighteenth and early nineteenth centuries (*see* 'Late Enclosure' below). They are marked on the OS 1st Edn 6" maps as 'common' or 'turbary', and were characterized by rough pasture and furze.

Late Enclosure

Landscapes of 'Late Enclosure' are characterized by long straight roads, large rectilinear fields bounded by ruler-straight boundaries, wide skies, and few settlements, creating a sense of solitude: many people travel through this countryside, but few have reasons to stop. It is particularly extensive on the higher plateaus of the Blackdown Hills where it derives from the enclosure of former rough pasture, which is reflected in the large numbers of 'moor' and 'down' place-names. There are some areas of 'Late Enclosure' in the adjacent lowlands and in most cases they replaced former common pasture (e.g. in Kentisbeare where the 'Late Enclosure'-type landscape post-dates a map of *c.*1810: SRO DD/WY/C306/DEV9), although in the lowlands of central Somerset, some of these relate to Parliamentary Enclosure of former open fields. In both cases the outcome of the enclosure was to extinguish common rights and distribute the land, now divided into enclosed fields, amongst those who could prove rights of common and who now held their new allotments in severalty (i.e. the land was their exclusive property). This often resulted in a highly fragmented pattern of land holding reflecting the large numbers of former commoners. The process of enclosure was overseen by Enclosure Commissioners who employed professional surveyors to lay out the allotments, resulting in dead-straight field boundaries and frequent 90° angles.

In many places on the Blackdown Hills, the hedgerows in areas of 'Late Enclosure' are of beech, a popular hedging material in the nineteenth century (also seen on Exmoor where large areas were enclosed at the same time). The few farms located within 'Late Enclosure' landscapes tend to have names descriptive of their location (e.g. Hill Farm, Hemyock), adjacent features (e.g. Beechwood Farm, Dunkeswell), or apparently fanciful names that probably reflect their remoteness (e.g. North Pole Farm on Northdown, Otterford). There was also a small number of public houses or inns that in some cases at least appear to pre-date enclosure, having served travellers and drovers on the old roads crossing these former commons. In some areas of Late Enclosure relatively small, more or less ovoid enclosures associated with farmsteads are embedded amongst the rectilinear fields, which presumably represent earlier encroachments on the former commons, and the possessive place-names of the associated farms (e.g. Cawley's and Hussey's) may commemorate those responsible for the assarting.

Intermediate Enclosure

'Intermediate Enclosure'-type landscape is characterized by long, relatively straight roads (though rarely with exactly parallel sides) which run through blocks of broadly rectilinear fields that lack the dead-straight sides and 90° angles of late enclosure. These landscapes have a markedly more coherent layout than the 'Irregular' and 'Semi-Irregular' types (*see* below), and appear to have been laid out with some degree of planning rather than having evolved piecemeal. A comparison of seventeenth- and eighteenth-century estate maps with the OS 1st Edn 6" maps of the 1880s shows that the character of this landscape type remained largely unchanged: some fields were subdivided and others combined, but this did not alter its overall character (e.g. Figs. 6.4–6.6).

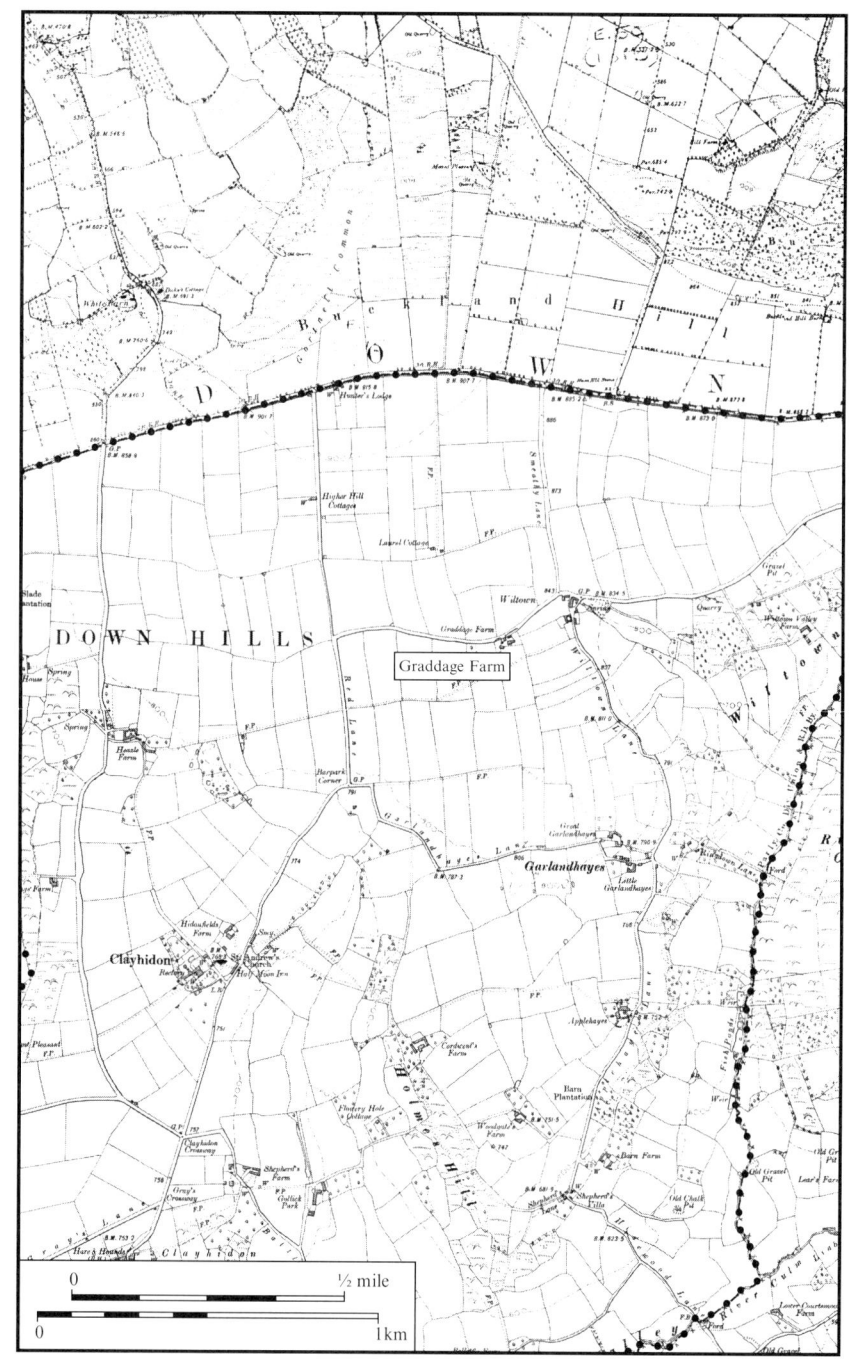

Fig. 6.4. Ordnance Survey First Edition Six Inch map for the northern part of Clayhidon. Graddage was 'Greatediche' in 1566, and was presumably the home of William ate Graddich in 1330 (Gover *et al.* 1932, 611): the 'great ditch' was presumably the boundary between the enclosed land to the south and the open moor beyond (now partly marked by a road). The parish boundary has been highlighted. (Drawing by Mike Rouillard.)

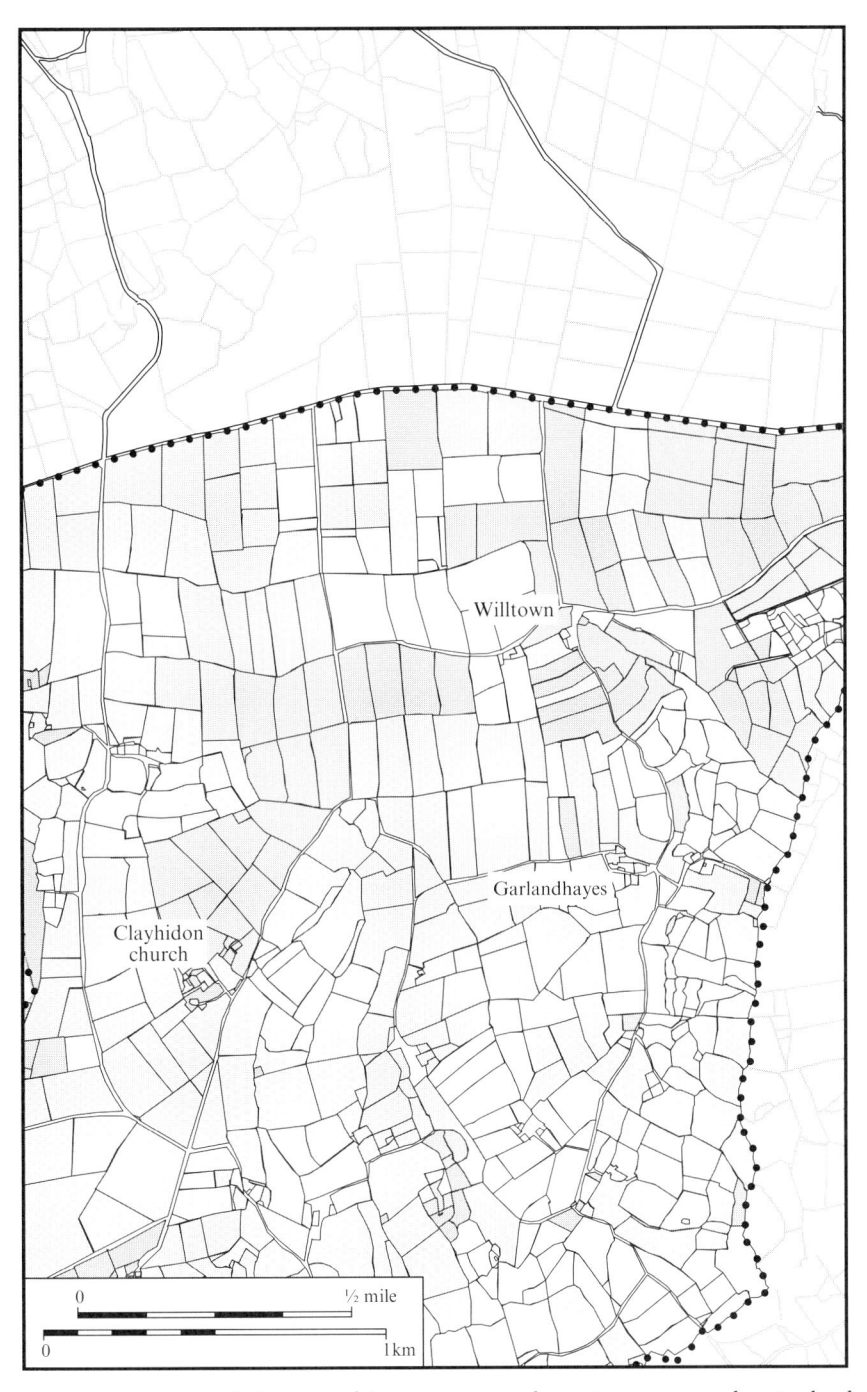

Fig. 6.5. Transcribed Tithe map of the same area as shown in Figure 6.4, showing land occupancy in Clayhidon (drawn by Lucy Ryder; *see* Plate 6 for the whole of the parish). Note the particularly fragmented pattern south of Willtown. (Drawing by Mike Rouillard.)

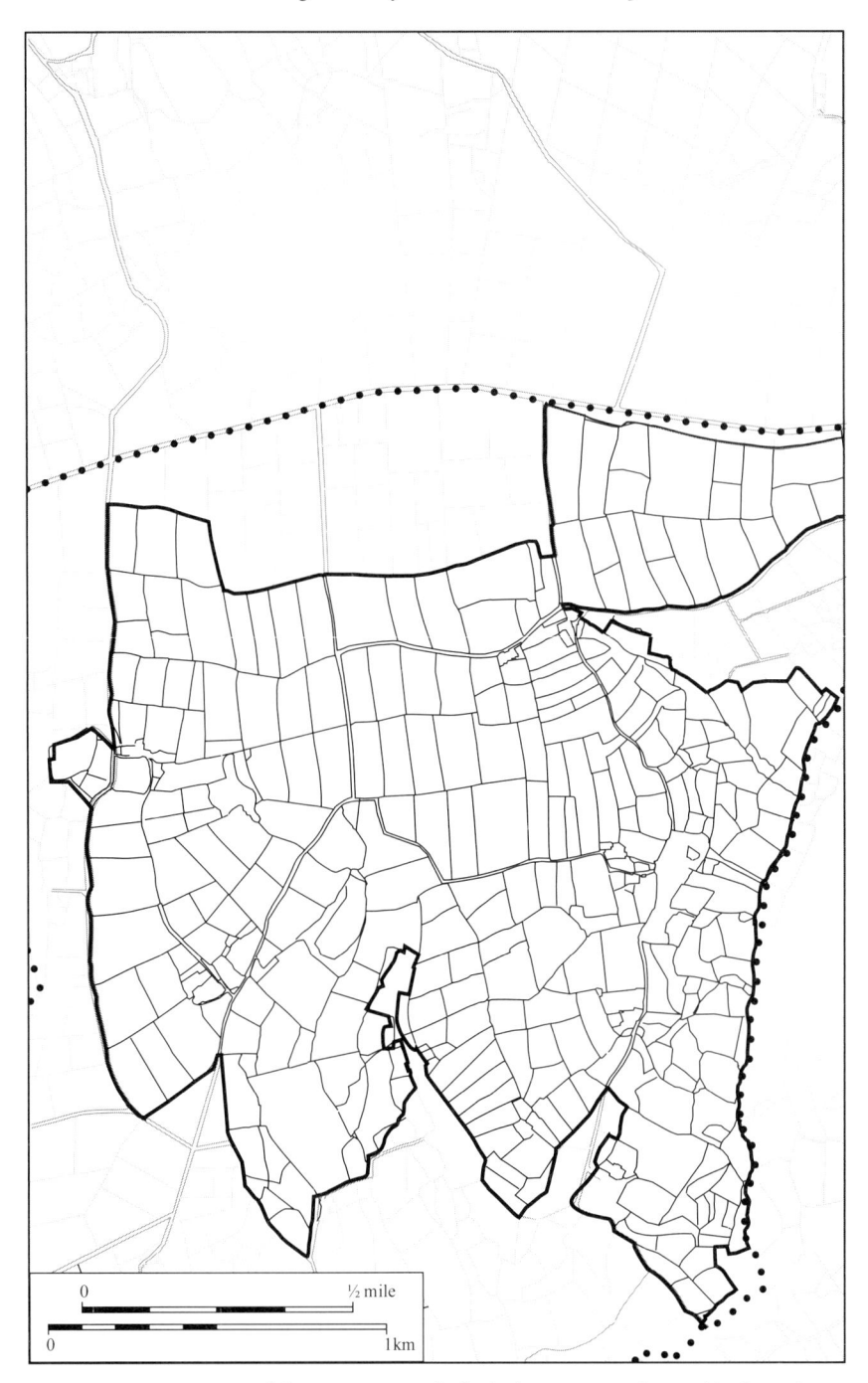

Fig. 6.6. Transcription of the estate map of Clayhidon manor of 1739 (SRO DD/MER 37), in the context of the surrounding landscape as mapped on the Tithe survey; the parish boundary has been added. (Drawing by Mike Rouillard.)

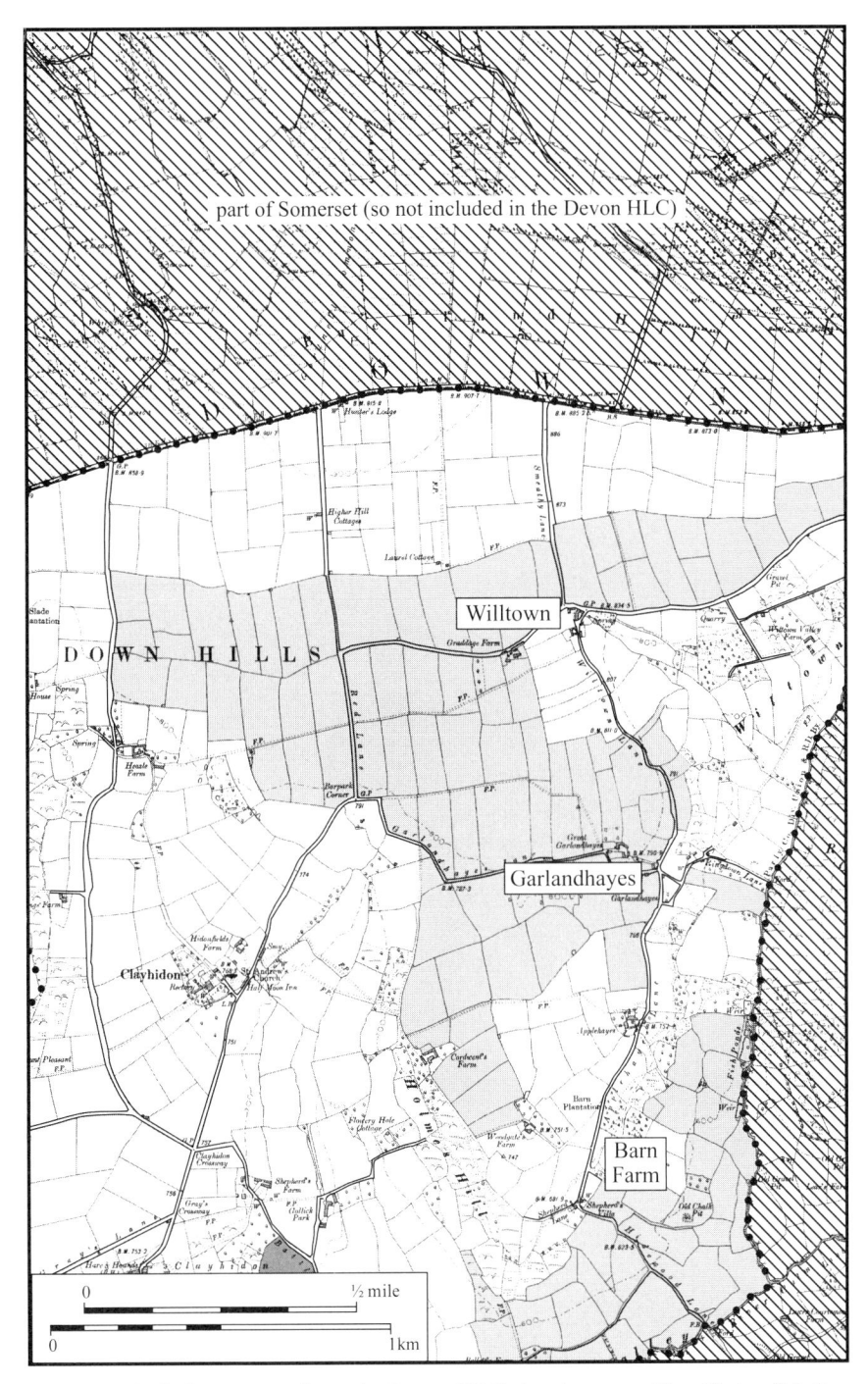

Fig. 6.7. Clayhidon: extract from the Devon HLC showing areas identified as 'Medieval enclosures based on strip fields' (redrawn from http://gis.devon.gov.uk/basedata/viewer.asp?DCCService=hlc). Curiously the clearly former strip fields south of Willtown are not included, while highly irregular shaped fields are Barn Farm are. (Drawing by Mike Rouillard.)

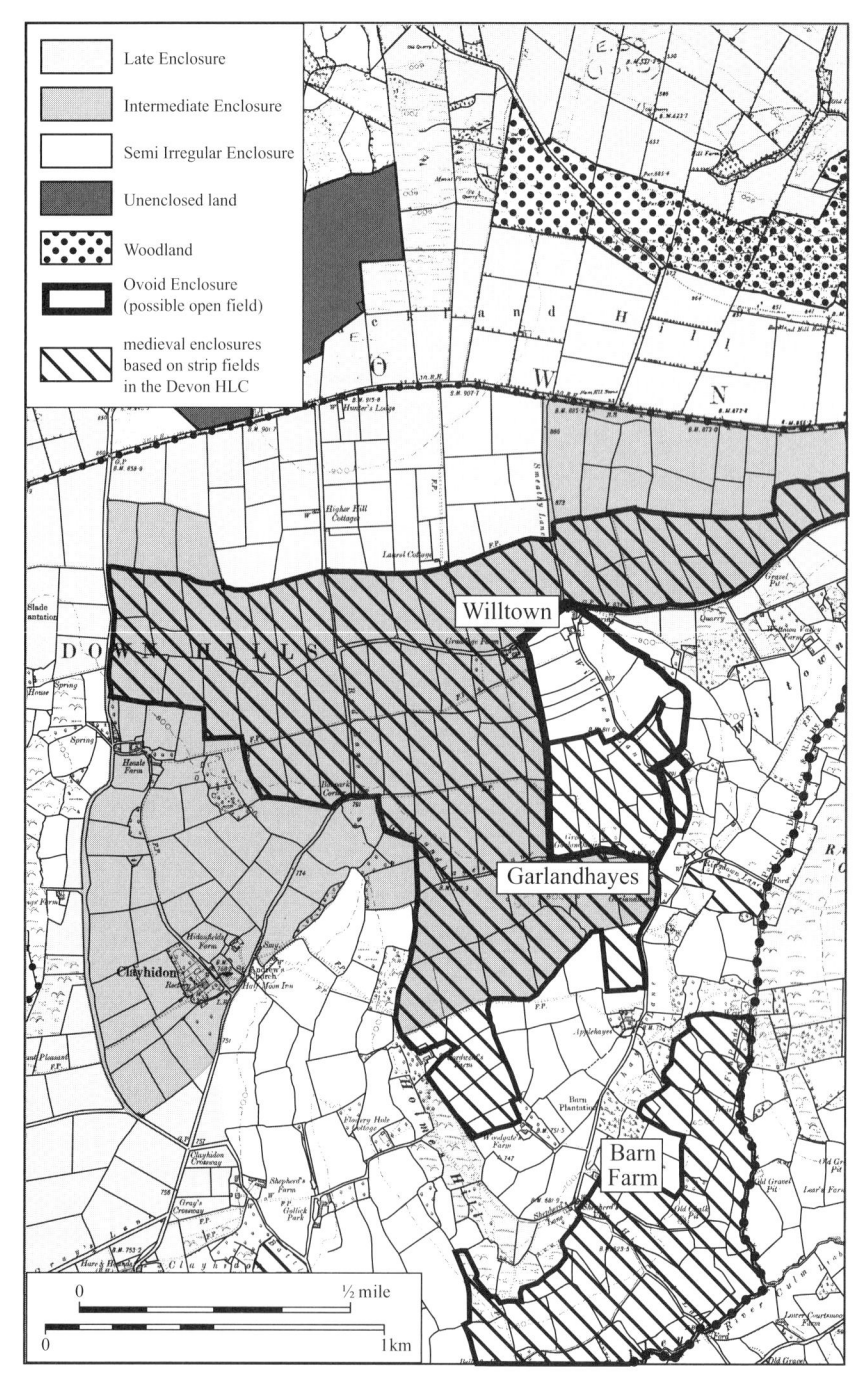

Fig. 6.8. Clayhidon: results of the historic landscape characterization carried out for this project, with the area of 'Medieval enclosures based on strip fields' in the Devon HLC highlighted.

The edge of this landscape type is often very clear, being marked by a long, sinuous boundary such as that at Graddage Farm in Clayhidon (Fig. 6.4). Graddage was 'Greatediche' in 1566, and the home of William ate Graddich in 1330 (Pearse Chope 1911, 269; Gover *et al.* 1932, 611): the 'great ditch' was presumably the boundary between the enclosed land to the south and the open moor beyond.

This historic landscape character type covers 20.7% of the local study area. On the Blackdown Hills, 'Intermediate Enclosure' is found mostly towards the edges of the higher plateaus, in between areas of Late Enclosure on the higher ground, and Irregular and Semi-Irregular Enclosure on the valley sides. In relation to these other types, it is therefore intermediate in terms of its morphology, its position in the landscape, and therefore probably its date. Some areas of Intermediate Enclosure here include small, ovoid-shaped configurations of field boundaries that enclose blocks of long, narrow fields that often had relatively fragmented patterns of land holding at the time of the Tithe survey (discussed further in Chapter 7). The Intermediate Enclosures on the Blackdown Hills may have been used for arable cultivation, although the clay-with-flints substrate of these areas give rise to wet, acidic soils which would have been far from ideal for growing crops and would certainly have benefited from periodic applications of lime or marl (marl is a source of lime which, when applied to the soil, neutralizes acidity and has the effect of stimulating bacterial activity, encouraging the breakdown of organic matter, and releasing essential plant nutrients). These fields are superficially similar to 'cropping unit'-type fields identified in Cornwall that are interpreted as being consolidated strips in a former open field, but such an interpretation can be ruled out on the Blackdown Hills as there are no reversed-S shaped boundaries. The Intermediate Enclosures here are associated with a sparse settlement pattern of what in the nineteenth century at least were isolated farmsteads, some of which are documented from the late twelfth century when we first find significant amounts of documentary evidence for this region. It is not uncommon to find settlements at the down-slope limit of this landscape type, where it typically abuts areas of 'Irregular' or 'Semi-Irregular' Enclosure, and these include several Domesday manors. It is not clear, however, whether the Intermediate Enclosures existed at this time or were open pasture enclosed later (in which case these Domesday manors were strategically located between the open and the enclosed land, as was the case at Graddage in Clayhidon: *see* above).

In predominantly lowland areas, Intermediate Enclosure is sometimes found on high ground or poor soil within the broad swathe of landscape otherwise characterized by Semi-Irregular Enclosure and here it probably represents relatively Late Enclosure of common pasture (especially where it is found in close association with areas of Late Enclosure). Intermediate Enclosure is also found adjacent to Enclosed Strip Fields-type landscape (*see* below) in lower-lying areas and here it might be derived from enclosure by agreement of open fields. In Kentisbeare, for example, an area that on the OS 1st Edn 6" maps of *c.*1880 had a landscape of Intermediate Enclosure-type is shown on a map of *c.*1810 with a greater number of long, narrow fields that would have been characterized as 'Enclosed Strip Fields' (SRO DD/WY/C306/DEV9). That some Intermediate-type landscape in lowland areas may have been derived from the enclosure by agreement of former open field, followed by the amalgamation of long narrow fields into larger closes, is also illustrated in South Petherton where an area of Intermediate Enclosure on the OS 1st Edn 6" maps of *c.*1880 is shown on an estate map of 1773 as 'Enclosed lands' (SRO DD/PE/5). In the lowlands of central Somerset there is also a marked tendency for Enclosed Strip Fields-type landscape to be close to village cores and Intermediate Enclosures to be located towards the edges of parishes, and in such cases the former would appear to be the last areas of open field to be enclosed, while the Intermediate Enclosures represent earlier enclosure by agreement in which some of the long narrow fields that represented individual strips had been amalgamated.

What we appear to have with Intermediate Enclosure is therefore a case of different processes (enclosure from open field and from common pasture) leading to the same end point (fields of this morphology), which is why *at this stage* in the analysis a cautious approach to their interpretation has been adopted and they have been placed in their own category. Only when further layers of data are analysed can this type be subdivided and a greater degree of interpretation added (*see* Chapter 7 and Fig. 7.6).

Semi-Irregular Enclosure

'Semi-Irregular Enclosures' are characterized by a patchwork of fields which are neither highly irregular nor noticeably rectilinear in shape, and are associated with narrow, winding lanes and a predominantly dispersed settlement pattern of isolated farmsteads and small hamlets, some of which are documented in Domesday. This is by far the most common historic landscape character type, covering 41.7% of the local study area. The fields are generally larger than those of the 'Irregular' type (*see* below), with gently sinuous to curving boundaries. This is by far the most common type of landscape, found right across the study area, although there are some very marked patterns in where it is found. On the Blackdown Hills, this type of landscape covers large areas of the gently undulating valley sides, above the Floodplains and steep-sided valley bottoms, and below the steeper upper slopes that are often cloaked in woodland, or covered in Irregular Enclosures. It is not found on the plateau tops. Semi-Irregular-type landscape is found right across the lowlands to the west, north, and east of the Blackdown

Hills. A comparison of seventeenth- and eighteenth-century estate maps and the OS 1st Edn 6" maps of the 1880s shows that the character of this landscape remained largely unchanged: some fields were subdivided and other combined, but in a landscape with no rigid planning this did not alter its overall character.[1]

As Semi-Irregular Enclosures occur across large areas of the lowlands that palaeoenvironmental evidence suggests was extensively cleared of trees by the late prehistoric period (*see* Chapter 11), they are likely to have been enclosed from open pasture/rough ground rather than woodland. The date of this enclosure appears to lie in the early medieval period, as across Devon there is very little evidence for the survival of late prehistoric and Romano-British field systems into the medieval period. A series of excavations along the line of the A30 between Exeter and Honiton, for example, show a historic landscape characterized by Semi-Irregular and Intermediate Enclosures overlying, and on a different orientation to, a series of Bronze Age and Iron Age field systems (Fitzpatrick *et al.* 1999). At Hayes Farm, in Clyst Honiton, Romano-British and early medieval (fifth-century) enclosures are on a different orientation to the Semi-Irregular and Intermediate Enclosures of the historic landscape (Simpson *et al.* 1989), and elsewhere in lowland Devon, historic landscapes of Semi-Irregular type clearly post-date the AD first century enclosure at Rudge, in Morchard Bishop (Todd 1998), the late-Roman enclosure at Newland Mill, North Tawton (Passmore 2005), and a late-Roman field system at Kenn (Weddell 2000).

Irregular Enclosure

Some areas of mostly steeper ground, particularly within the Blackdown Hills, are characterized by a maze of narrow winding lanes between high hedge banks, linking isolated farmsteads and small hamlets, associated with fields of highly irregular shape interspersed with numerous small woods and large numbers of 'leigh' place-names (e.g. Fig. 7.5). This historic landscape character type covers 5.5% of the local study area. The steep slopes and highly irregular shapes of these fields would make ploughing impracticable, implying pastoral use, and are suggestive of gradual piecemeal assarting and encroachments from woodland or former open pasture. Other areas of Irregular Enclosure are found on the steeper slopes around the edges of the Culm Measures and south-west of Crewkerne. This historic landscape type is associated with a small number of Domesday manors (e.g. Bolham in Clayhidon; Greenway and

---

[1] e.g. estate maps of Padbrook in Cullompton (1633: SRO DD/WY/C306/DEV11), Clayhidon (1739: SRO DD/MER 37), and Whitheathfield in Cullompton (1775: SRO DD/HI C/738), Crewkerne (1729: SRO DD/MR 83; 1772: SRO DD/SB/4/5).

Shapcombe in Luppitt), and numerous other settlements documented from the thirteenth century onwards. Cartographic sources show that the field boundary patterns have not significantly changed their character since the eighteenth century (e.g. Clayhidon, 1739: SRO DD/MER 37).

Enclosed Strip Fields (e.g. Plates 2–3 and 9, Fig. 7.1)

Bundles of long, narrow, curving fields (sometimes with reversed-S profiles, and/or dog-legged boundaries), laid out between long, parallel, but sinuous boundaries, are clearly suggestive of former strips and furlong boundaries in an open field that had been enclosed by agreement. This interpretation is strengthened by OS 1st Edn 6" maps that occasionally show unenclosed strips, and Tithe surveys that recorded extremely fragmented patterns of land holding. Numerous estate maps confirm that Enclosed Strip Fields-type landscape was indeed derived from the enclosure of former open field (e.g. Lopen: Fig. 4.1). This historic landscape character type covers 9.6% of the local study area although it is most common in the north-east corner (in the lowlands of central Somerset), where it is associated with a nucleated settlement pattern and '-ton' place-names (Figs. 4.11 and 6.3). There are also smaller areas of Enclosed Strip Fields' on the eastern fringes of the Blackdown Hills in Chard (Fig. 7.1), Combe St Nicholas (Plate 9), Chardstock, and Membury, and in the lowlands of eastern Devon: in both areas they are associated with hamlets/villages within landscapes generally characterized by more dispersed settlement.

These then are the historic landscape character types that have been used in this study. This very straightforward scheme is simply a means to an end, not an end in itself. This characterization of the fieldscape is intended to be used alongside the mapping of many other facets of the landscape including settlement patterns, vernacular architecture, field- and place-names, in order to reconstruct regional variation in landscape character, and it is to several more of these—the patterns of land ownership and land occupancy, and the form of the field boundaries themselves—that we must now turn.

7

Beyond the morphology of fieldscapes

Historic landscape characterization is a good way of classifying field-boundary patterns by their morphology, but in order to understand regional variations in how these fields were managed, we must add depth to this mapping. In this particular study a crucial question is the extent of former open field but unfortunately the South West is not a region that is rich in medieval documentary sources and so other data must be used. The evidence discussed at the start of this chapter relates to patterns of land ownership and land occupancy recorded in the Tithe surveys of *c*.1840, the hypothesis being that areas of former open field that were enclosed by agreement may still have had highly fragmented patterns of land holding which reflect how individual tenements once had strips scattered across several furlongs. There are of course exceptions to this, such as where strips had been consolidated before enclosure, or closes were amalgamated post-enclosure, but fragmented patterns of land holding in conjunction with morphological evidence can at least indicate a minimum possible extent for former open field. Another feature of landscape character that a two-dimensional characterization misses is the nature of the field boundaries themselves, and as a demonstration of this another feature of the landscape in South West England—field boundaries that take the form of a substantial bank topped with a hedge—will be mapped in order to see whether it too extends no further east than the Blackdown Hills.

PATTERNS OF LAND OWNERSHIP AND OCCUPANCY

Scattered patterns of land holding in fieldscapes characterized by long, narrow fields have previously been mapped on a very small scale.[1] Early maps of extant open fields do indeed show that the strips belonging to individual

---

[1] e.g. Pattison's (1999, fig. 26) study of Challacomb, a hamlet in the Dartmoor parish of Manaton based on an estate map of 1787; and *see* Aston 1988b; Herring 2006a; 2006b; and Williamson 2008.

tenements were scattered across many furlongs such as the 1599 map of 'Middle Field' in Tatworth, one of the three open fields surrounding this hamlet in southern Chard (Fig. 7.1, Plate 3). Unfortunately, most parts of our study area do not have pre-nineteenth-century maps and so the only way that we can reconstruct past patterns of land holding is through using the Tithe surveys of *c*.1840. Tithe surveys were carried out on a parish-by-parish basis following the Tithe Commutation Act of 1836. As part of the process of replacing tithes (payments paid to the church 'in kind', i.e. farm produce) with cash payments, a survey was undertaken of each district (parishes in southern England, and townships in the north) in England and Wales between 1836 and 1855, with 90% completed between 1837 and 1845 (Kain 1979, 226). This survey led to the production of three documents: a map on which every parcel of land is numbered; an accompanying 'apportionment' that lists all the parcels of land belonging to each land owner along with its occupier (i.e. the tenant), name, acreage, and land use; and a report (the 'Tithe File') that discusses the acreage and yield of crops, the animal husbandry, and a general description of the local soils and agricultural practices (discussed in Chapter 11; Kain 1979, 227).

For a series of parishes spread across the study area (Table 7.1), the Tithe map was transcribed into a Geographical Information System (GIS). The apportionment was copied into a spreadsheet and by linking this to the GIS, all the parcels of land belonging to a certain land owner or occupier can then be displayed (e.g. Plates 3–8). A total of forty two parishes were transcribed in this way forming a transect running east to west across the Blackdown Hills (Plate 4). The most informative data proved to be land occupancy, because in several parishes very large areas were owned by a small number of individuals, but most of these large estates were subdivided into a series of smaller tenements that were leased out to the 'occupiers' listed in the Tithe apportionment. These data contributed to the interpretation of the landscape not only in the individual parishes for which Tithe data were collected, but through analogy, in parishes with very similar fieldscapes and historic landscape character, and as such contributed to the reconstruction of what the later medieval landscape may have looked like across the whole local study area (Figure 7.6). Selected parishes are illustrated below where they demonstrate particular themes.

In the fertile lowlands of the Culm, Clyst, and Tale valleys there is a consistent picture with small areas around the major hamlets/churchtowns characterized by Enclosed Strip Fields and a highly fragmented pattern of land holding suggestive of small, open fields set within a landscape otherwise dominated by dispersed settlements associated with compact blocks of semi-irregular shaped fields suggestive of closes that have always been held in severalty. Areas of fragmented land-holding in landscapes characterized by Late Enclosures, and their '-moor' and 'Down' names, on higher ground/

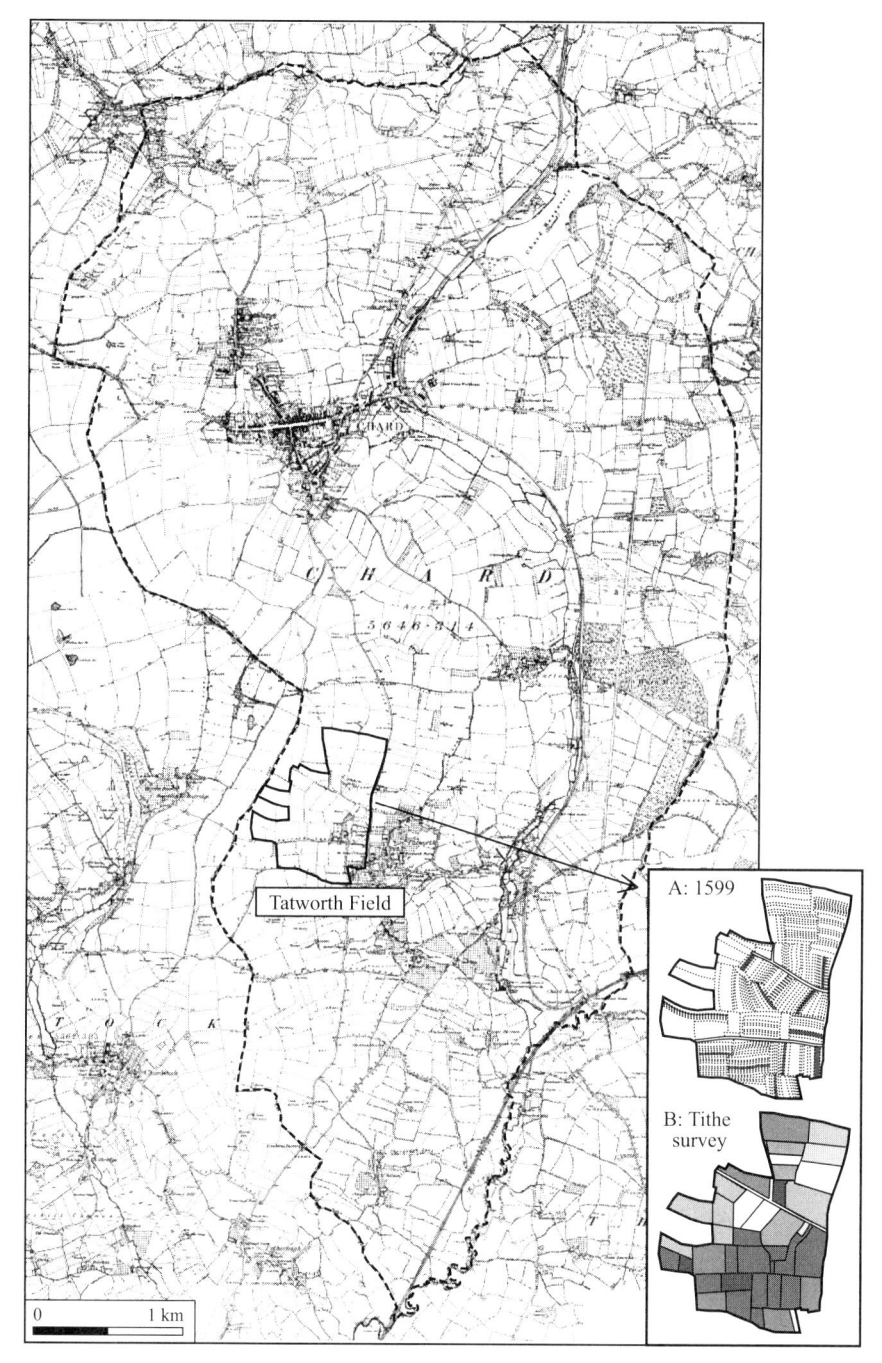

Fig. 7.1. Ordnance Survey First edition Six Inch map of Chard, with the area of the Tatworth Middle Field map of 1599 highlighted. Inset A: transcription of the Tatworth Middle Field in 1599, with the strips of John Warry highlighted. Inset B: land occupancy in the Tithe Survey. (Down and Carter 1989; Carter 2009.)

Table 7.1. Research into patterns of land holding based on the Tithe maps and apportionments of *c*.1840.

Parish	coverage of Tithe survey	work carried out by	context of research	publication and other reports
Awliscombe	complete	Lucy Ryder	Community Landscape Project/PhD	Ryder 2007
Barrington	complete	Phil Knibb	assisting the author	
Blackborough	complete	Richard Sandover	MA Dissertation	
Bradninch	complete	Fiona Reading	MA Dissertation	
Broadclyst	complete	Richard Sandover	PhD	
Broadhembury	complete	Richard Sandover	MA Professional Skills Project	Rippon 2009
Buckerell	complete	Lucy Ryder	Community Landscape Project/PhD	Ryder 2007
Buckland St Mary	complete	Innes McCartney	MA Professional Skills Project	
Burlescombe	complete	Rachael Oakes	MA Professional Skills Project	
Chard	complete	Richard Sandover	MA Dissertation	
Churchstanton	incomplete	Adam Worth	MA Advanced Project	
Clayhidon	complete	Lucy Ryder	Community Landscape Project/PhD	Ryder 2007
Clyst Hydon	complete	Fiona Reading	MA Professional Skills Project	
Clyst St Lawrence	complete	Fiona Reading	MA Professional Skills Project	
Combe Raleigh	complete	Lucy Ryder	Community Landscape Project/PhD	Ryder 2007
Combe St Nicholas	incomplete	Chris Smart & Adam Wainwright	The Living Past Project	Rippon 2007b
Cotleigh	complete	Peter Jameson	MA Professional Skills Project	
Culmstock	complete	Adam Jones	MA Professional Skills Project	
Dunkeswell	incomplete	Lucy Ryder	Community Landscape Project/PhD	Ryder 2007
Hemyock	incomplete	Lucy Ryder	Community Landscape Project/PhD	Ryder 2007
Holcombe Rogus	complete	David Williams	MA Professional Skills Project	
Huxham	complete	Rod Lane	MA Professional Skills Project	
Kentisbeare	complete	Richard Sandover	MA Dissertation	
Lopen	complete	Phil Knibb	MA Professional Skills Project	
Luppitt	complete	Lucy Ryder	Community Landscape Project/PhD	Ryder 2007

Membury	complete	Ruth Steele	MA Professional Skills Project	
Misterton	complete	Phil Knibb	MA Professional Skills Project	
Monkton	complete	Chris Smart & Adam Wainwright	The Living Past Project	Rippon 2007b
Payhembury	complete	Abi Gray	MA Professional Skills Project	
Plymtree	complete	Peter Jameson	MA Professional Skills Project	
Poltimore	complete	Rod Lane	MA Professional Skills Project	
Rewe	complete	Philip Riris	MA Professional Skills Project	
Sheldon	complete	Chris Smart & Adam Wainwright	The Living Past Project	Rippon 2007b
Shepton Beauchamp	complete	Phil Knibb	MA Professional Skills Project	
Silverton	complete	David Williams	MA Dissertation	
Stoke Canon	complete	Philip Riris	MA Professional Skills Project	
Talaton	complete	Martin Oakhurst	MA Professional Skills Project	
Upottery	complete	Richard Sandover	MA Dissertation	
Wambrook	complete	Chris Smart & Adam Wainwright	The Living Past Project	Rippon 2007b
Whimple	complete	Owain Connors	MA Professional Skills Project	
Whitestaunton	Complete	Chris Smart & Adam Wainwright	The Living Past Project	Rippon 2007b
Yarcombe	Incomplete	Jennifer Viner	MA Professional Skills Project	

poorer soils at the edges of parishes, are suggestive of former commons. Burlescombe (Plate 5) provides a good example.

Parishes on the Blackdown Hills are characterized by Semi-Irregular Enclosure and Irregular Enclosure, associated with highly dispersed settlement patterns on valley sides, and Intermediate Enclosures and Late Enclosures on the high flat-topped plateaus. Sheldon (Plate 6), Clayhidon (Plate 7), and Churchstanton (Plate 8) provide examples. On the valley sides, where land ownership within a parish was dominated by a single estate, these were usually divided up into small tenements with compact blocks of fields associated with an isolated farmstead. In parishes with large numbers of land owners the pattern was similarly based on a series of compact land holdings associated with individual farmsteads. There is nothing in this uniform pattern of farmsteads holding compact blocks of fields to suggest there was ever significant open field in this landscape. Some of these land holdings extended up onto the higher ground into areas of Late Enclosure, presumably reflecting the rights they once held in the former commons (the area of enclosed land being in proportion to rights such as the number of livestock that a particular land owner or tenant could graze on the moors). Elsewhere, land holding in the Late Enclosures was sometimes highly fragmented, with enclosed fields having been awarded to tenements that once had grazing rights there. Areas with Intermediate Enclosures generally had one of two patterns of land holding: blocks of closes all in the same occupancy (there being no evidence for open field), and highly fragmented patterns of land holding associated with ovoid-shaped enclosures filled with long, narrow, and sometimes curving closes indicative of former open fields. Good examples are Westcott in Sheldon (Plate 6), Willtown in Clayhidon (Fig. 6.5 and Plate 7) and Southey, in Churchstanton (Plate 8).

On the eastern side of the Blackdowns, the landscape is similarly dominated by Intermediate and Late Enclosure on the higher ground, and Irregular and Semi-Irregular Enclosure on the valley sides, but with some evidence for open field. In Whitestaunton, for example, there is a small area (*c.*75 acres) of enclosed strips by the hamlet of Northay, and while the vast majority of land in the parish was part of a single estate which was divided into a series of tenements made up of compact blocks of fields, the one exception was this putative open field that had a highly fragmented pattern of land holding. Two parishes on the eastern flanks of the Blackdown Hills—Combe St Nicholas (Plate 9) and Chard (Plate 3)—had far larger areas of enclosed strip fields associated with highly fragmented patterns of land holding suggestive of former open fields that were on a similar scale to those of England's central zone (Table 7.2). Parishes in the lowlands of central Somerset, whose fieldscapes were also characterized by Enclosed Strip Fields, similarly had highly fragmented patterns of land occupancy.

Overall, this mapping of land holding provides useful corroboration of hypotheses derived from the morphological analysis of field-boundary patterns. Areas of Enclosed Strip Fields are almost invariably associated with highly fragmented patterns of land holding, supporting the idea that they were derived from the enclosure of open fields. In contrast, areas of Semi-Irregular and Irregular Enclosure are invariably associated with scattered farmsteads located within compact blocks of fields with none of the fragmentation of land holding that is indicative of open field.

Table 7.2. Small ovoid-shaped enclosures with strip-based fields and fragmented land holding in parishes for which Tithe map/apportionment land ownership and land occupancy data have been mapped, and selected open fields in the lowlands of central Somerset for comparison.

Parish	related settlement	settlement first documented (Gover et al. 1932 unless otherwise stated)	length	width	area
Small ovoid enclosures on the Blackdown Hills					
Clayhidon	Garlandhayes	John Garlaund, 1333	c.2,400 ft (731 m)	c.1,000 ft (305 m)	c.44 acres (18 ha)
Combe St Nicholas	Clayhanger	14th century (SVBRG 2008a, 14)	c.2,550 ft (777 m)	c.850 ft (259 m)	c.40 acres (16 ha)
	Wadeford	16th century (SVBRG 2008a, 14)	c.2,850 ft (869 m)	c.1,050 ft (320 m)	c.55 acres (22 ha)
Hemyock	Shuttleton Farm	1566	c.2,200 (671 m)	c.1,100 ft (335 m)	c.36 acres (15 ha)
Luppitt	Calhayes	1620	c.2,200 ft (671 m)	c.900 ft (274 m)	c.36 acres (15 ha)
Membury	Furley	1330	c.2,000 ft (610 m)	c.1,500 ft (457 m)	c.55 acres (22 ha)
Sheldon	Westcott Dairy	1509	c.1,900 ft (579 m)	c.1,000 ft (305 m)	c.35 acres (14 ha)
Wambrook	Dinnett's Farm	[no EPNS volume]	c.2,000 ft (610 m)	c.1,050 ft (320 m)	c.40 acres (16 ha)
Average					**c.42 acres (17 ha)**
Open fields on the eastern flanks of the Blackdown Hills					
Combe St Nicholas	Combe St Nicholas	1086	c.6,500 ft (1,981 m)	c.4,800 ft (1,463 m)	c.573 acres (232 ha)
Chard	Chard	1086	c.7,500 ft (2,286 m)	c.4,100 ft (1,250 m)	c.566 acres (229 ha)
Membury	Membury	1086	c.6,600 ft (2,012 m)	c.2,100 ft (641 m)	c.255 acres (103 ha)
Chard	Ham	[no EPNS volume]	c.2,800 ft (853 m)	c.2,100 ft (640 m)	c.108 acres (44 ha)
Churchstanton	Southey	1525	c.3,000 ft (914 m)	c.1,900 ft (579 m)	c.105 acres (43 ha)
Whitestaunton	Northay	1086	c.3,100 ft (945 m)	c.2,100 ft (640 m)	c.75 acres (30 ha)
Average					**c.280 acres (114 ha)**
Open fields to the west of the Blackdown Hills (in decreasing size order)					
Broadhembury	Luton	1227	c.4,700 ft (1,433 m)	c.3,500 ft (1,067 m)	c.378 acres (153 ha)
Kentisbeare	Kentisbeare	1086	c.6,500 ft (1,981 m)	c.3,100 ft (945 m)	c.370 acres (150 ha)
Broadhembury	Kerswell	1085	c.4,100 ft (1,250 m)	c.3,600 ft (1,097 m)	c.339 acres (137 ha)

(*continued*)

Table 7.2. Continued

Parish	related settlement	settlement first documented (Gover et al. 1932 unless otherwise stated)	length	width	area
Plymtree	Clyst William	1086	c.3,500 ft (1,067 m)	c.3,100 ft (945m)	c.249 acres (101 ha)
Awliscombe	Awliscombe	1086	c.5,200 ft (1,585 m)	c.2,200 ft (671 m)	c.219 acres (85 ha)
Payhembury	Payhembury	1086	c.3,200 ft (975 m)	c.2,500 ft (762 m)	c.184 acres (75 ha)
Awliscombe/Buckerell	Weston	1227	c.3,500 ft (1,067 m)	c.2,800 ft (853 m)	c.180 acres (73 ha)
Payhembury	Lower Cheriton	1086	c.3,500 ft (1,067 m)	c.2,700 ft (823 m)	c.173 acres (70 ha)
Buckerell	Buckerell	1165	c.4,500 ft (1,372 m)	c.1,700 ft (518 m)	c.141 acres (57 ha)
Payhembury	Lower Tale	1086	c.4,200 ft (1,280 m)	c.1,400 ft (427 m)	c.135 acres (55 ha)
Culmstock	Prescott	1238	c.4,100 ft (1,250 m)	c.1,300 ft (396 m)	c.122 acres (49 ha)
Culmstock	Culmstock	938	c.3,600 ft (1,097 m)	c.1,800 ft (549 m)	c.119 acres (48 ha)
Burlescombe	Burlescombe	1086	c.3,300 ft (1,006 m)	c.1,700 ft (518 m)	c.103 acres (42 ha)
Burlescombe	Ayshford	958	c.3,100 ft (945 m)	c.1,800 ft (549 m)	c.103 acres (42 ha)
Plymtree	Plymtree	1086	c.2,700 ft (823 m)	c.1,700 m (518 m)	c.84 acres (34 ha)
Culmstock	Nicholashayne	1305	c.1,800 ft (549 m)	c.1,700 ft (518 m)	c.70 acres (28 ha)
Burlescombe	Westleigh	c.1200	c.2,500 ft (762 m)	c.1,300 ft (396 m)	c.60 acres (24 ha)
Average					**c.176 acres (71 ha)**
common fields in the north east of our study area					
Crewkerne					c.1,660 acres
Merriott					c.1,650 acres
Barrington (open field covers virtually whole parish)					c.1,600 acres
Kingstone					c.900 acres
Shepton Beauchamp (open field covers virtually whole parish)					c.820 acres
Misterton					c.720 acres
Lopen (open field covers virtually whole parish)					c.480 acres
Stocklinch (open field covers virtually whole parish)					c.200 acres

REGIONAL VARIATION IN FIELD BOUNDARIES THEMSELVES: DEVON HEDGEBANKS

A particularly distinctive feature of the landscapes of Devon and Cornwall is its hedgebanks, described by Hooker in 1599 as 'mighty great hedges' (e.g. Plate 10: Stanes 2008a, 4): field boundaries marked by substantial earthen banks topped by a hedge, but without a substantial ditch. Bass and Staines (2008) have published the text of two remarkable eighteenth-century documents that describe the method for making such hedgebanks in Cruwys Morchard, north of Exeter, describing how they should be 6–8 feet[1.8–2.5 metres] wide at the base, 6 feet[1.8 metres] high, and 3–5 feet[0.9–1.5 metres] wide at the top. The document also describes how these hedgebanks served three functions: as stock-proof field boundaries, as a source of timber, and as a means of shelter for livestock. On the Blackdown Hills this tradition of field-boundary construction was still in use as late as the nineteenth century at a time when simple hawthorn hedges were used in Parliamentary Enclosures just a few miles to the east in parishes such as Broadway in the former Neroche Forest. Elsewhere to the east of the Blackdown Hills, field boundaries take the form of a simple hedge or a hedge on top of a small bank whose size is roughly in proportion to an adjacent ditch (i.e. material from the latter was used to construct the former).

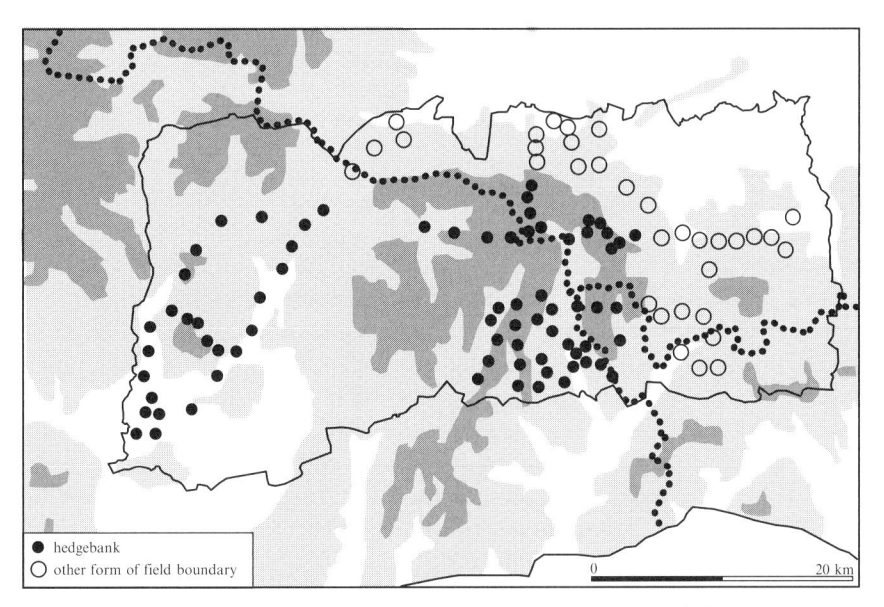

Fig. 7.2. The location of fieldwork to determine the character of field boundaries showing how hedgebanks are restricted to the Blackdown Hills and areas to the west.

In order to map the extent of the hedgebank tradition, a simple programme of fieldwork was carried out. Observations were made across the local study area, with a minimum of three field boundaries observed at a particular location. A series of broadly west-to-east transects was used initially with survey points several kilometres apart, and then more intense work was conducted once the approximate eastward limit of the hedgebank occurrence was determined. The results are shown in Figure 7.2 which reveals that hedgebanks were constructed across eastern Devon and up onto the Blackdown Hills in broadly the same area as '-hayes'/'-hayne' place-names and domestic houses characterized by their lateral stacks. Once again, the Blackdown Hills mark a significant boundary in historic landscape character.

DISCUSSION

In this and the previous chapters we have explored how folklore, settlement patterns, place-names, field-names, standing buildings, patterns of land holding, and the physical form of field boundaries contribute to regional variation in landscape character. This analysis has been carried out along with a simple historic landscape characterization, with a uniform methodology carried out across the entire study area. Having presented these various strands of research, it is now time to move towards a reconstruction of what the medieval landscape might have looked like. It should already be apparent that the major area of debate is over the former extent of open field so this will be discussed first.

The extent of open field

The local study area, straddling the Blackdown Hills and the edge of Roberts and Wrathmell's 'Central Province', was deliberately positioned so that it could inform the debate over the extent of open field in South West England. In the lowlands of central Somerset, the evidence for Midland-style common fields is clear. Various eighteenth-century-estate maps show that they once covered almost entire parishes (e.g. Lopen: Fig. 4.1), and documentary sources from the thirteenth to the fifteenth centuries show that these common fields were managed using two-, three-, or four-field systems (Fig. 7.3.A). Within our study area, those parishes with documentary evidence for common fields all lie in the lowlands of central Somerset (north-east of a line from Misterton to Curry Mallet), which is precisely the area that our historic landscape characterization identified as having large areas of strip-based enclosures. It is also noticeable that those parishes which lack documentary evidence for

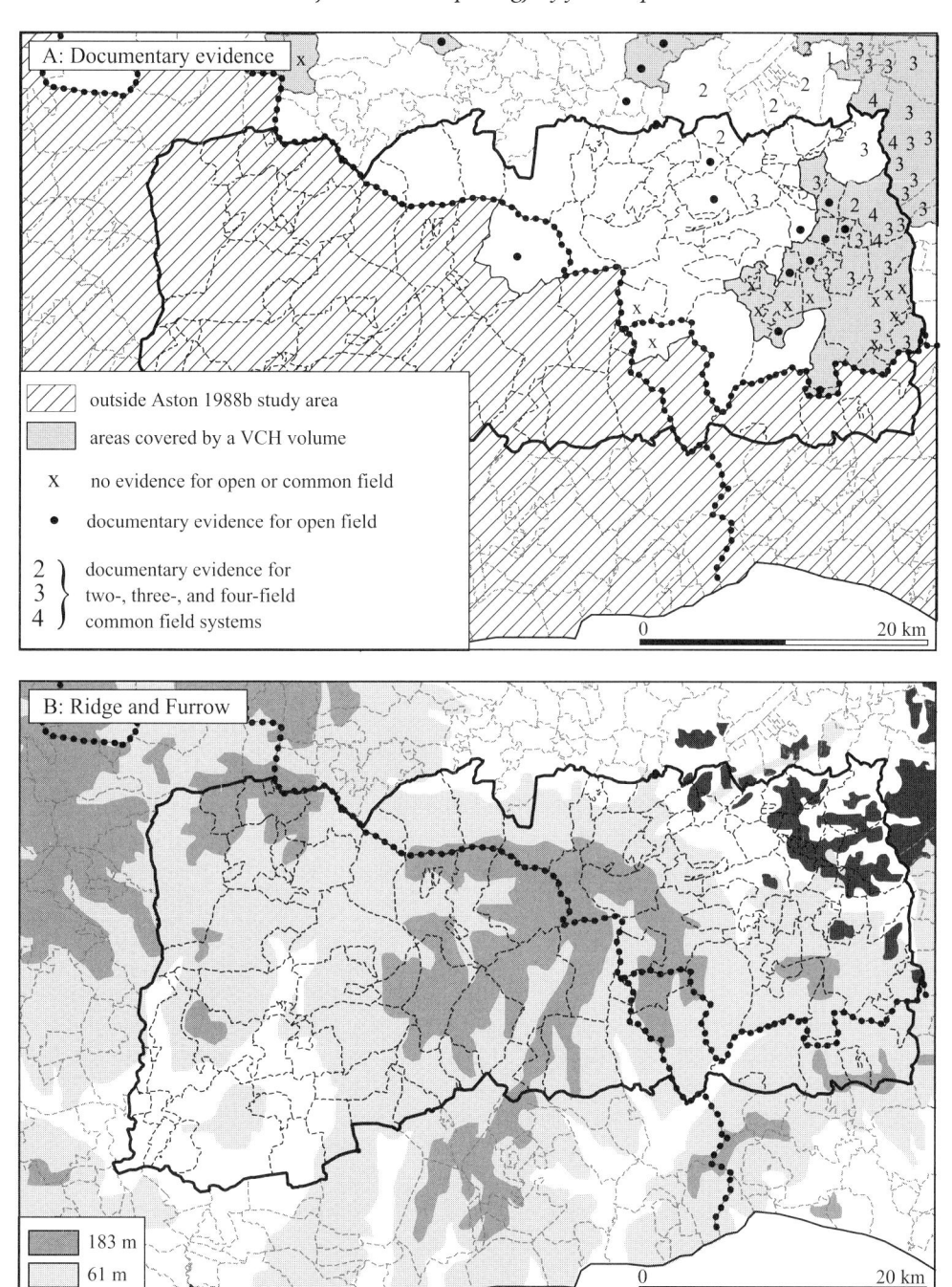

Fig. 7.3. (A) Documentary evidence for common field in Somerset; (B) the extent of ridge and furrow. (After Dunning 1978; Aston 1988b, figs. 5.3 and 5.5.)

common fields all have historic landscapes dominated by Semi-Irregular Enclosures. A further indication of the former extent of common field comes in the form of ridge and furrow, which once again is restricted to a line north-east of Misterton and Curry Mallet (Fig. 7.3.B).

The earliest documentary evidence for open field is in the descriptions of estate boundaries contained within some Anglo-Saxon charters (the so-called 'boundary clauses': e.g. Costen 1988; Hooke 1990; 1994). Using transcriptions produced in *The Language of Landscape (LangScape)* project (http://www.langscape.org.uk/index.html), that are far more reliable than the early work of scholars such as Grundy (1919; 1920), we can search for features diagnostic of different types of field system. Most of the landmarks described relate to land-use types that we would expect around the periphery of an estate (i.e. watercourses, high ground, and wetlands). There are, however, some landmarks indicative of open field (*furlang*: furlong; *(ge)dalland*: shareland; *heafodland*: headland), enclosures (*edisc*, *geard*, *glind*, *haegen*, *lycce*, *loca*, and *teag*), and hedges (*(ge)haeg*, *haga*, *hecg*, *hege*), and when these are mapped some clear regional differences emerge. As the number of charters with boundary clauses varies enormously across the country, looking at absolute numbers of references to open and enclosed fields is fairly meaningless, but the ratio of features indicative of open and enclosed fields is very informative. In Cornwall and Devon there are no references to open field-indicative landmarks, in contrast to 8% in Somerset, 13% in Dorset, 38% in Wiltshire, 46% in Oxfordshire, and 61% in Berkshire. Overall, the analysis of references contained within the boundary clauses of Anglo-Saxon charters suggests relatively extensive open field in the south Midlands, moderate amounts in Dorset and Somerset, and none in Cornwall and Devon.

The detailed characterization of field-boundary patterns presented in Chapter 6, along with the analysis of land holding in this chapter, has proved extremely useful in understanding the different field systems across our study area. In most places where morphology suggests there had once been open field—i.e. strip-based enclosures—the highly fragmented patterns of land occupancy supports this interpretation. The fragmented patterns of land holding have also helped to flag the importance of a series of small ovoid-shaped enclosures, such as Westcott in Sheldon, that are discussed further in Chapter 15. Elsewhere, however, the landscape in all but the lowlands of central Somerset was dominated by Semi-Irregular Enclosure characterized by farmsteads associated with compact blocks of fields suggestive of closes that have always been held in severalty. There is no evidence in the field-boundary pattern or land occupancy for extensive open field across most of the Blackdown Hills and just small areas of open field in the lowlands of eastern Devon that rarely form more than 10% of a parish (compared to the common fields of England's 'central zone' that could cover *c.*90% of a parish). Yes, there were open fields in Devon, and a very small number were on a

Beyond the morphology of fieldscapes 143

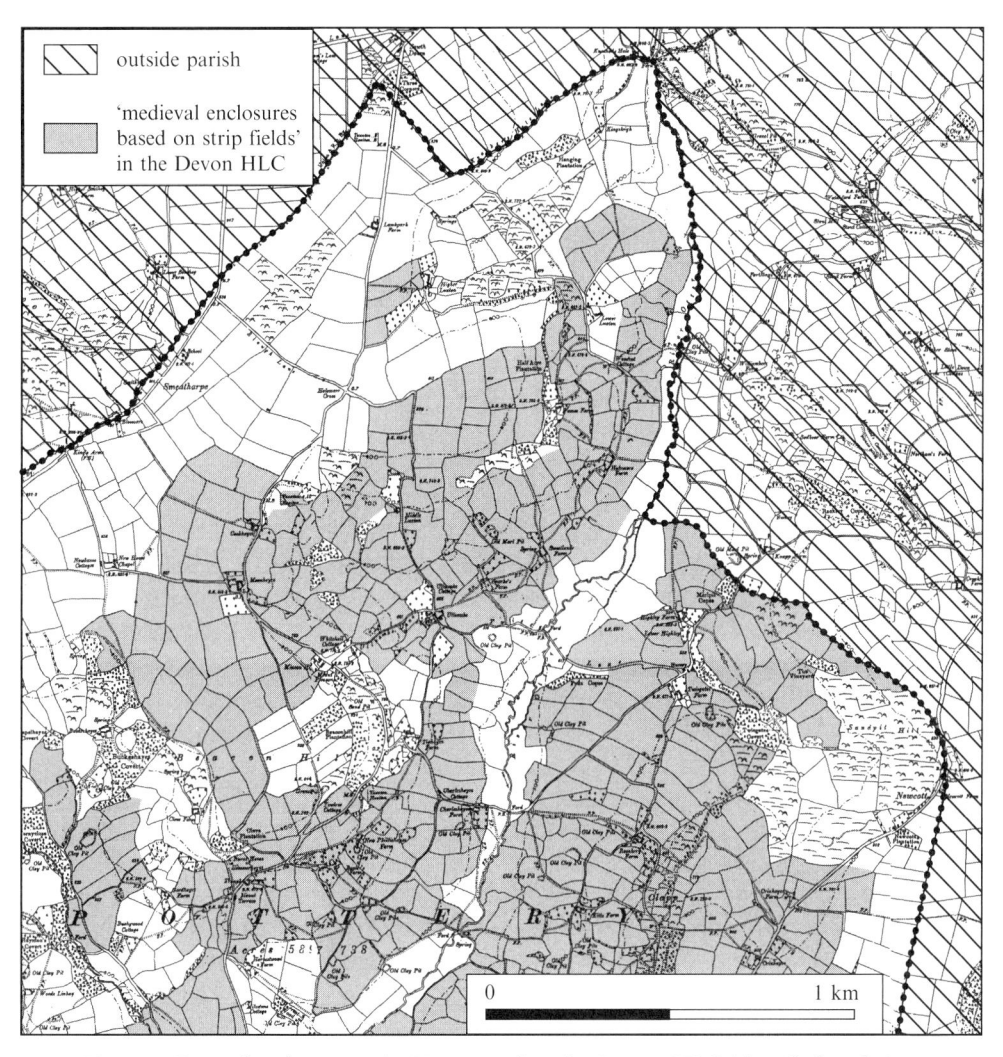

Fig. 7.4. Example of an area in Upottery that the Devon HLC identified as being 'medieval enclosures based on strip fields'. (Redrawn from http://gis.devon.gov.uk/basedata/viewer.asp?DCCService=hlc)

Midland scale but these were very rare (e.g. Braunton: Rippon 2008a, fig. 3.9; Sowton: Alcock 1970; 1973; 1975; Overton 2006, 110–11). Most open fields in Devon appear to have been small, and only ever covered a very small proportion of a parish (e.g. around Exmoor: Gillard 2002; Rippon, Fyfe, and Brown 2006; Chulmleigh: Ebdon 2008; Hartland: Ryder 2007).

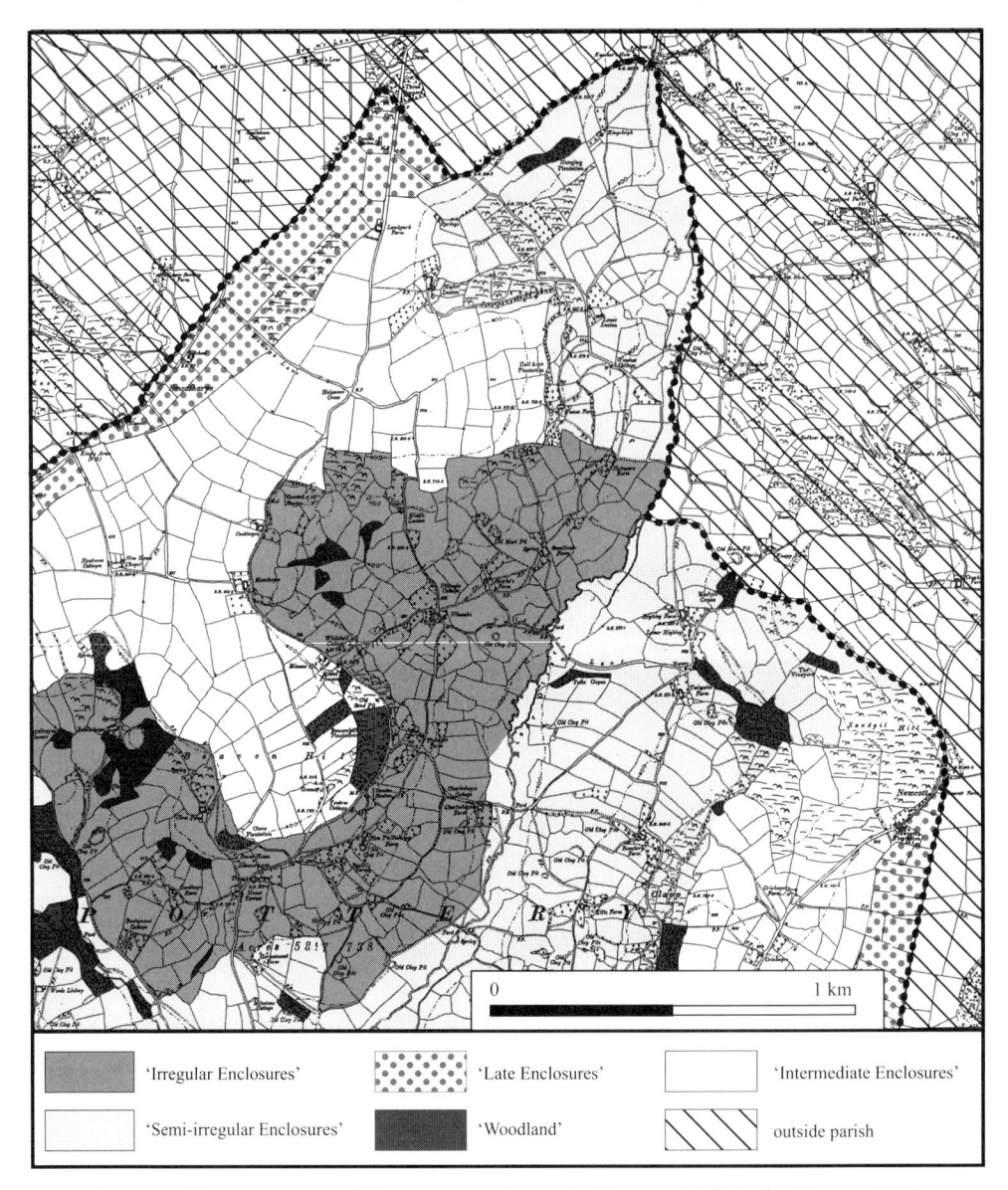

Fig. 7.5. The same area of Upottery as shown in Figure 7.4 that the Devon HLC identified as being 'medieval enclosures based on strip fields', but which the characterization carried out for this study suggests are predominantly Semi-Irregular and Irregular Enclosures.

It is therefore argued here that while there was open field in eastern Devon, its extent was very limited, which is in sharp contrast to the Devon HLC which suggests that *c*.39% of lowland Devon was open field (Turner 2007, 48–56: *see* discussion at start of Chapter 6 above). This difference warrants further discussion. The simple explanation put forward here is that a closer examination of the Devon HLC suggests that the attribution of field systems to its 'medieval enclosures based on strip fields' is mistaken. Figures 7.4–7.5 show an example of what the Devon HLC regards as 'medieval enclosures based on strip fields' in the northern part of Upottery, and it is difficult to see what evidence there is for this area having been former open field. Instead, the fields are irregular or semi-irregular in shape, with extremely sinuous boundaries and barely a right-angle in sight, and slopes that are also so steep that it is difficult to see how many of the fields could even have been ploughed. It would appear, therefore, that the Devon HLC has classified far too many areas as being 'medieval enclosures based on strip fields'. Why this should have been the case is not clear. It is possible that it reflects recent debate in neighbouring Cornwall where Herring (2006a, 44) has suggested that open fields were once extensive. In Cornwall, it is certainly true that the historic landscape contains areas whose morphology is suggestive of former open field, and recent work mapping the highly fragmented patterns of nineteenth-century land holding in these areas supports this (e.g. Herring 2006a, figs. 23, 27–9; Herring *et al.* 2008, fig. 118; Rippon *et al.* 2009, fig. 6.14). Earlier estate maps also show fragmented patterns of land holding and occasionally unenclosed open field (e.g. the Lanhydrock Atlas of 1696: Pounds 1945). That open fields were once present in the landscape does not mean, however, that they were extensive, and the tendency to publish maps of individual open fields associated with small hamlets (e.g. Herring *et al.* 2008, fig. 118) without showing what the landscape character was across the rest of a parish, makes it impossible to determine what proportion of the landscape was once open field. Where this is done (e.g. Rippon 2008a, fig. 4.11 using Herring 2006a, fig. 27), it shows that open field in parts of Cornwall may indeed once have been more extensive than was traditionally thought, but they were still on a far smaller scale than those of England's central zone where up to 90% of the agricultural land in a parish was part of an open-field system (e.g. Foard *et al.* 2009).

Landscapes of enclosure

The fieldscapes characterized by enclosure are more straightforward to explain. These were areas where individual farmers, or groups working collaboratively, divided a landscape into parcels that had permanent boundaries. West of a line running through the eastern fringes of the Blackdown Hills, these field boundaries are marked by substantial earthen banks that are now at least topped by hedges. These banks would not all have been built at the same time, and may have gradually replaced earlier boundaries such as quick-set hedges or fences, but over time the regionally distinctive tradition emerged of fields surrounded by substantial hedgebanks. These were fields that by the Tithe surveys of *c*.1840 belonged to a particular estate or tenement, and which in the medieval period were similarly held 'in severalty': they were not shared, or handed on to a different tenant each year, but stayed part of that tenement for the duration of its term. These were landscapes of the individual, which is also reflected in '-hayes'/'-hayne' place-names which are typically found in combination with Middle English personal names. We can infer little of the land-use history of these closes though most would be suited to both arable cultivation and pasture.

By the nineteenth century, many of these areas are also characterized by highly dispersed settlement patterns with farmsteads associated with compact blocks of closes covering around 100–150 acres. In the medieval period this would have been more than a single household could have exploited, and it is likely that in places, these relatively large farms represent the amalgamation of two or more earlier tenements, although it is possible that use was also made of waged labour. The location of these additional farmsteads is, however, unclear. Across parts of the south-west, archaeological and documentary evidence has shown that what are now isolated farmsteads were sometimes once small hamlets (e.g. Beresford 1964; Fox 1989a; Henderson and Weddell 1994) and this may have been the case in eastern Devon too. Another possibility is that there were once far more isolated farmsteads scattered across the landscape. There is at present, however, very little evidence for settlement shrinkage or desertion within our study area although too much should not be read into this: ploughing in the past could have flattened any shrunken-settlement earthworks, while the predominance of pasture today makes extensive field-walking impossible. One line of enquiry, however, is to explore whether the location of deserted settlements is commemorated by field names, as occurs across parts of Somerset (e.g. Costen 1992b; Gerrard with Aston 2007). An examination of the Tithe maps/apportionments across the local study area, however, reveals almost no settlement-indicative field-names on the Blackdown Hills and in eastern Devon. In the large parish of Broadclyst, for example, there is a single '-bury' field-name (Stanbury), but no examples of 'cott', 'huish', 'ton', 'wick', or 'worthy', while in nearby Broadhembury there is just 'Melhuish' which also appears in Burlescombe where we also find the field-names 'Sutton' and 'Breton' (there being no extant settlements with these names in these or adjacent parishes). Other parishes such as Stockland do not contain any of these settlement-indicative field-names. Overall, there is frustratingly little evidence with regard to whether there were once even more isolated farmsteads scattered across this landscape or some of what are now farmsteads were once small hamlets.

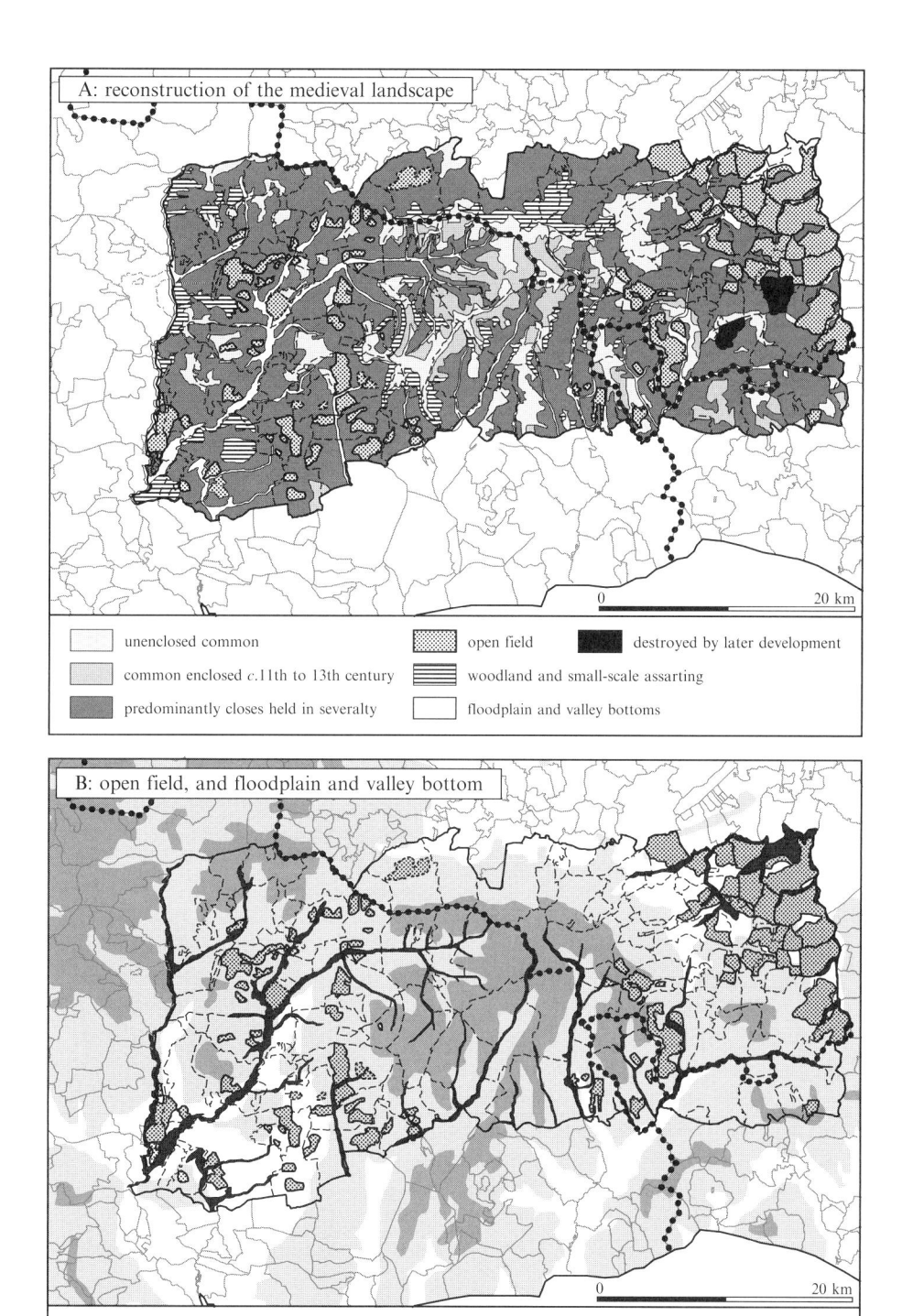

Fig. 7.6. (A) Interpretation of the historic landscape characterization carried out for this project (Plate 2) and additional layers of data such as patterns of land holding (Plate 4); (B) Two selected landscape types (open field, and floodplains and valley bottoms).

Towards a reconstruction of the medieval landscape

Based on a wide range of evidence—an historic landscape characterization, documentary evidence for the presence or absence of common field systems, the former extent of ridge and furrow, and patterns of land holding—we can now move towards a reconstruction of the former extent of open field as part of a wider reconstruction of what the medieval landscape of our local study area may have looked like (a stage of subjective interpretation that should be kept separate from the objective description of historic landscape character types outlined in Chapter 6). Figure 7.6 is therefore an attempt to identify six key landscape types, as they may have existed in *c.*1300:

- Unenclosed commons: based on 'Unenclosed Land' and 'Late Enclosures'.
- Land that was probably enclosed from the commons during the high middle ages: some of the Intermediate Enclosures associated with Unenclosed Land and Late Enclosures.
- Landscapes characterized by a predominance of closes held in severalty: Semi-irregular and Irregular Enclosures.
- Open fields: based on Enclosed Strip Fields, and some Intermediate Enclosures, where there is other evidence to suggest former open fields (e.g. where there are highly fragmented patterns of land holding, or ridge and furrow).
- Woodland: based on woodland shown on the OS 1st Edn 6" maps, and what were clearly relatively recent assarts from it.
- Floodplains and valley bottoms.

With regard to the extent of former open field, the results are broadly in line with what Shorter *et al.* (1969) and Aldred (2001) suggested for Devon and Somerset, respectively, though in each case it is argued here that open fields were slightly more extensive. The Devon HLC, however, has clearly overestimated the extent of former open field. The dividing line in central Somerset between landscapes characterized by villages and open fields to the east, and more dispersed settlement patterns and predominantly enclosed field systems to the west, was remarkably sharp, albeit with several outliers in the eastern foothills of the Blackdown Hills (most notably Chard and Combe St Nicholas). To the east of this line were vast open fields that in typical parishes covered *c.*800–900 acres, and places up to *c.*1,600 acres, and these covered up to 90% of these parishes. Documentary evidence shows that they were managed as Midland-style common fields. In contrast, the smaller open fields of lowland eastern Devon covered *c.*60–380 acres with an average of *c.*175 acres, which covered between *c.*10% (e.g. Burlescombe, Kentisbeare, and Plymtree) and *c.*25% of the parish (e.g. Broadhembury and Payhembury); the limited documentary evidence we have suggests that they lacked the distinctive regular management of the Midland system (Fox 1972; 1973; 1975; 1991a; b). A third form of open field that has been recognized for the first time in this study are the *c.*40 acre small ovoid enclosures on the Blackdown Hills that are clearly on an altogether different scale. The origins of the open-field systems will be discussed further in Chapter 15.

CONCLUSION

Chapters 4 to 7 have sought to explore the physical character of the historic landscape in a transect that straddled the most fundamental division in the British landscape: that between landscapes which in the medieval period were dominated by villages and open fields, and those which had more dispersed settlement patterns and field systems with a large proportion of the land arranged in enclosed fields. Although a morphological analysis of both settlement patterns and field systems has been carried out, and this is supplemented by an analysis of the vernacular architecture, place-names, field-names, and patterns of land holding, no attempt has been made to make this a definitive study of the area's landscape history. This is *an* analysis of the landscape, with a particular purpose in mind—exploring the origins and development of regional variation in landscape character—and it is to be hoped that others will add further depth by looking at other facets of landscape character. A particular focus has been on the distribution of open field, as the Devon HLC has contradicted earlier research in suggesting that much of lowland Devon was once covered by strip fields. This study has indeed found some strong evidence for open field, including the correspondence of highly fragmented patterns of land holding in areas with long, narrow, strip-like fields, but the open fields of which they were once part were extremely small compared to the vast open fields of England's central zone. Indeed, across the Devon landscape far larger areas were covered by more irregular-shaped fields that were held in compact blocks by scattered farmsteads. This study has confirmed, therefore, that the character of the field systems, like the settlement patterns, place-names, field-names, and the nature of the field boundaries themselves, was very different on either side of the Blackdown Hills. In Chapters 8 to 10 we will explore whether differences in landscape character such as this can be explained by the nature of the social and territorial structures within which early medieval society managed the landscape.

8

Reconstructing early medieval territorial arrangements

In the preceding chapters we have looked at some physical components of the landscape, most notably the various settlement patterns and field systems that characterized different parts of the local study area. It is now time to consider the social context within which these landscapes were created and managed, and in particular see whether regional variations in landscape character—as mapped for example in Figure 7.6—can be linked with different territorial structures. Landscape archaeologists and historians have made various attempts at reconstructing what contemporary Middle Saxon writers described as *regiones*, and what modern scholars have variously called 'river estates', 'land units', 'federal' or 'federative' estates, 'archaic hundreds', 'large terrains', and best-known of all, the 'multiple estates' identified by G. R. J. Jones (1979). There are, however, problems with this body of past scholarship. Some, such as Jones, have taken detailed evidence from one specific area to create a model of an early medieval 'estate' and then apply this across the whole country, even to areas with very different cultural histories and physical environments, while others have carried out careful reconstructions of individual estates without much comparison with other places. There has also been a lack of chronological precision, and as Blair (1989, 105) has noted, 'work in this area, including Jones's, has perhaps failed to distinguish adequately between tribal, political and administrative *regiones* on the one hand, and estates as units of exploitation on the other. To neglect this distinction risks conflating two successive stages, for it is often clear that estates were secondary to *regiones*'.

The findings of this study supports Blair's contention that there were 'two successive stages', with a series of what are referred to here as 'early folk territories', that typically covered 250–400 km^2 (the average of the fourteen examples across the regional study area is 330 km^2), and a series of smaller 'great estates' into which these larger districts were divided by around the eighth century, that typically covered 30–200 km^2 (the average of the fifty examples across the regional study area is 91 km^2) (Table 10.1). The larger, earlier districts appear to be equivalent to some of the *regiones* described by

Middle Saxon writers elsewhere in Britain, but this term is not used here as it was also applied to some of the far smaller territorial units that we refer to as 'great estates'. These 'folk territories' were probably kin-based, and while excavations at sites such as the reoccupied hillforts at South Cadbury and Cadbury Congresbury show that there was a degree of stratification within society, it is not clear whether this was based upon land ownership in the Roman or later medieval sense. From around the eighth century these folk territories were divided into a number of what, following Williamson (1993, 92–104) and Dyer (2003, 27), we will call 'great estates' that were centred on a royal vill and were used for a variety of other purposes including the administration of local justice through institutions that in the tenth century became known as hundreds. These great estates may also have corresponded to the large *parochiae* (parishes) of early minster churches that were also established around the eighth century. Over time, successive kings subdivided these great estates in order to create smaller blocks of land that were granted to the church and their major supporters, and it is this process that marks the point where individual people and institutions started to own land in perpetuity. While some of these early subdivisions of the great estates—mostly ecclesiastical—survived into the eleventh century and beyond, most were fragmented even further and became the multiplicity of manors recorded in Domesday Book, just as the large *parochiae* were broken up around the tenth century to create the small parishes with which we are familiar today.

RECONSTRUCTING PAST TERRITORIAL ARRANGEMENTS

This chapter explores how these early medieval territorial arrangements can be reconstructed using a wide range of documentary, place-name, and archaeological evidence including the physical fabric of the historic landscape. Most of the individual sources and techniques have been used in studies elsewhere—examples including Jones's (e.g. 1979) reconstruction of Aberffraw (Anglesey) and Bassett's (1989b, fig. 1.11) study of the 'Rodings' in Essex—but what distinguishes this study from previous work is that rather than simply reconstructing one such territory in isolation from its surroundings, an attempt is made here to map all the early folk territories and great estates across a wide area.[1] This

---

[1] For Devon, Hoskins (1952, 300–8) has discussed the idea that there were large pre-Conquest estates that subsequently fragmented into the manors and parishes of the later medieval period, and although he attempted to map some of them his coverage was far from complete. The relatively small territories he identified, like those reconstructed by Luscombe (2005) in south Devon, are mostly relatively late subdivisions of the great estates identified here.

Reconstructing early medieval territorial arrangements 153

chapter will outline the methodology used, while Chapter 9 presents a series of case studies on and around the Blackdown Hills, and Chapter 10 compares this region to elsewhere in southern Britain.

Territorial centres

Although Blair (2005, 275–85) has cast doubt over whether stable royal estate centres existed in the seventh and eighth centuries (*see* Chapter 10), there are a number of indicators in this region at least that certain locations were meeting places, temporary residences, or permanent settlements where a number of administrative functions were performed. There is a variety of evidence for this:

- Place-names: places of importance in the early medieval period were often associated with simple topographical names. These include Celtic topographical (often river) names (e.g. Curry in Somerset), and 'Celtic river + -ton' names (e.g. Cullompton in Devon). Note that 'Kingston' place-names are not indicative of early estate centres, but simply royal manors that may have been of minor importance and/or in peripheral parts of an estate (Bourne 1986–7; Gelling 1978, 184; Cameron 1996, 133–4; Hooke 1998, 12; Hall 2000).
- Place-names indicative of territories: district, tribal, or folk-group names such as those ending in -*gē* (e.g. *Eastorege*, Eastry in Kent), -*ingas* (e.g. *Rēadingas*; Reading in Berkshire), -*sǣte* (e.g. *Magonsǣte* in the West Midlands: Freeman 2008), and *wara* (e.g. *Meonwara* in southern Hampshire).
- Documented royal manors: *villae regiae* are referred to in a variety of sources including the Anglo-Saxon Chronicle, King Alfred's will, and Anglo-Saxon charters (Sawyer 1983). In Domesday, ancient royal demesne can be identified through the phrase, 'It has never paid tax, nor is it known how many hides[2] there are' (Morland 1990, 97).
- Hundredal centres: in western Wessex, the hundreds that were used for civil administration in the later medieval period evolved from a larger

---

[2] According to Bede, a hide was the 'land of one *familia*': the amount of land required to support a family, probably the extended family of a free man with their slaves and retainers (Faith 1997, 12, 132; Hooke 1998, 50). By the late seventh century, the laws of the West Saxon King Ine reveal that the hide (and in particular ten hide units) was used as the measure of apportioning liability to *feorm* (food render), *gafol* (tax), and various services owed to the king (Attenborough 1922, 59; Whitelock 1955, 364–72; Faith 1997, 38, 105, 107, 128; Dyer 2003, 31). A hide at this time was not a fixed unit of area, the figure of around 120 acres per hide being a post-Conquest notion; instead, a hide was 'the essential unit in assessing, administering and financing service to the king' (Faith 1997, 90, 28).

number of smaller hundreds recorded in various Domesday-related documents. These early hundreds were usually based at royal manors.

- Customary dues: Domesday records that certain places owed dues to royal manors. In the southern Blackdown Hills, for example, Axminster (in Devon) was paid 30d by each of Honiton, Smallridge, Membury, and Rawridge (*DB Dev.* 1,11), and Cricket St Thomas owed South Petherton six sheep with as many lambs, and each freeman paid a bloom of iron (*DB Som.* 1,4).
- Sub-infeudated estates: places associated with large manors of twenty hides or more (documented in pre-Conquest charters or Domesday), that often include unnamed sub-tenancies, are clearly estate centres. Many were royal manors that lay at the centre of earlier great estates, while others lay at the heart of ecclesiastical holdings that were carved out of these earlier territories.
- Minster churches: evidence for early churches includes a few literary references in pre-Conquest documentary sources, 'minster' place-names, and there having been a church recorded in Domesday. Due to the 'innate conservatism of ecclesiastical authority' (Blair 1991, 91) a range of evidence from the later medieval period may also reflect former minster status, such as an unusually large parish, and ecclesiastical relationships such as one place having a chapelry or being owed dues from another church. Archaeological evidence (extremely limited in the

Fig. 8.1. The former minster church at Branscombe in east Devon with its diagnostic crossing tower.

Reconstructing early medieval territorial arrangements 155

South West) includes standing pre-Conquest structures and sculpture, or the cruciform plan or presence of a crossing tower in a post-Conquest structure (e.g. Branscombe: Fig. 8.1).

The extent of territorial structures

A range of evidence can be used to reconstruct the various territorial structures associated with these central places:

- Early hundreds (Fig. 8.2): the extent of the original tenth-century hundreds cannot be reconstructed with certainly, even less so any earlier administrative/judicial territories upon which they may have been based. The earliest record we have for hundreds across most of England is Domesday, which groups the manors held by each landowner in this way, and while this is not the case in the South West we do have the *Inquisitio Gheldi* (geld accounts, or Tax Returns) compiled in *c*.1084–86, and two eleventh-century lists of hundreds that are appended to the

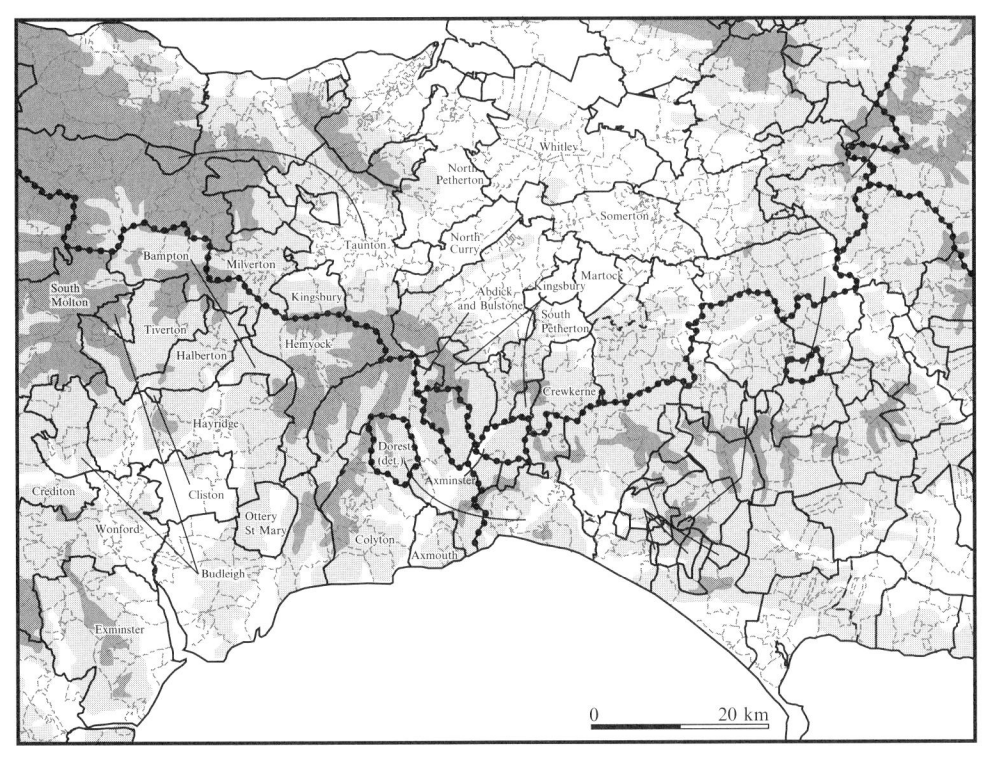

Fig. 8.2. Domesday hundreds across the regional study area. (After Thorn and Thorn 1980; 1983; 1985.)

regional return (the *Liber Exoniensis*, or Exeter Book) used to compile the main exchequer Domesday (Morland 1990). Reconstructing the original tenth-century hundreds is, however, difficult, as even by the eleventh century, 'we can see a gradual change in the hundreds as the ancient, topographically-based land units are broken down, and a more piecemeal collection of units based on ownership take their place' (Hall 2000, 44). This fragmentation, including the creation of 'private' hundreds from the scattered estates of certain great landowners, appears to have been greater in Dorset than Devon or Somerset.

- Ecclesiastical relationships (Figs. 8.3–8.4): early minster *parochiae* are sometimes partially reflected in later ecclesiastical relationships, such as one place being a chapelry of, or owing other dues to, another church. Bassett's (2006) carefully described study of Wootton Wawen in Warwickshire provides a detailed example of how former minster *parochiae* can be reconstructed.

- The relationship between parish boundaries and the historic landscape. Where Youngs (1980; 1991) records that in the sixteenth century somewhere was a chapelry of a church elsewhere, the parish boundary between them, as shown on their Tithe maps, will clearly be later than the sixteenth century (i.e. it will date to when the chapelry became a separate parish in the post-medieval period). In such cases, the physical fabric of the historic landscape—the patterns of roads, fields, and settlements—will largely have been in place, leading to the new parish boundary following existing features resulting in it zigzagging through these existing field systems (e.g. Fig. 8.5). Where one then sees similar cases of a parish boundary being stratigraphically later than the landscape upon which it was imposed, then we can also infer that those parishes were similarly once part of a single, larger, territory. In contrast, where parish boundaries follow long, sinuous features (field boundaries, roads, etc.) that pre-date the historic landscape on either side, the parish boundary could also be relatively early (e.g. Fig. 8.5). The overall shape of a parish can also be informative: some have a very awkward shape that interlocks with adjacent parishes suggesting that they were once a single territory (e.g. Plates 5 and 7).

- Detached parcels: parishes sometimes had one or more 'detached parcels' (small areas that lay within another parish, such as Culm Pyne that was part of Clayhidon: Plate 7). Such a phenomenon could be created in a number of ways, notably where a single large parish was divided into two or more smaller ones, or where former common land, shared between several communities, was enclosed and each of the communities who formerly had rights there received a parcel (Fig. 8.4: West Sedgemoor and Neroche Forest).

- Place-names indicative of territorial relationships: place-names that share a common element may indicate they were once part of the same estate (e.g.

Seavington St Mary and Seavington St Michael). Place-names can indicate settlements that were subsidiary to another (e.g. '-stock' names such as Chard and Chardstock: Hoskins 1952, 303; Everitt 1977; Thorn 2010, 17), and the relative locations of subsidiary settlements, such as Norton (Northton) and Sutton (South-ton). Place-names can also indicate a range of hierarchical relationships such as Charlton ('the *tūn* [farmstead] of the *ceorls*' [free peasant farmers who depended directly on the king]) (Costen 1992a, 90–3). Clusters of place-names of the 'personal name + -ington' type also reflect the fragmentation of larger estates with a series of manors being created and then leased to thanes (e.g. Chillington, Puckington, and White Lackington around South Petherton: Watts 2004, 134, 484, 356).

- Pre-Conquest charters: some charters describe the boundary of an estate, though these tend to be the relatively late products of estate fragmentation rather than the early great estates themselves. A particularly good series of charters exists for the estate of *Pouelt* or *Pouholt*, on the Polden Hills west of Glastonbury, that was progressively broken up during the eighth century (*see* Rippon 2008a, 70–5, and Thorn 2008, that were written independently of each other).

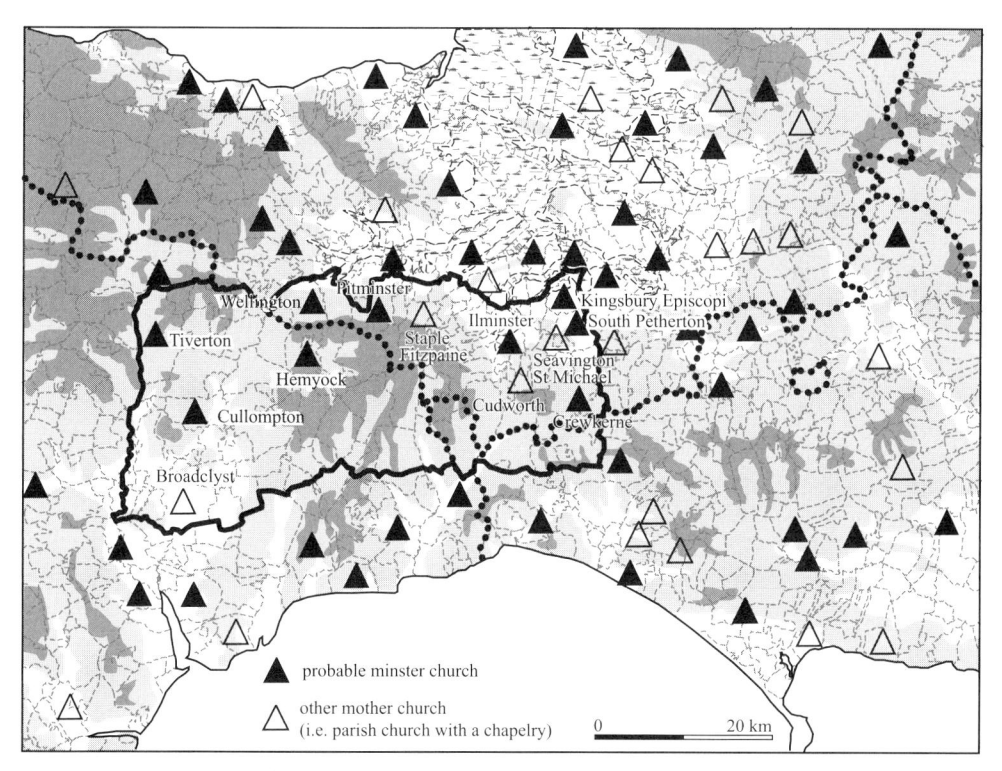

Fig. 8.3. Minster churches across the regional study area. (After Aston 1986; Orme 1991; Costen 1992a, tab. 4.1, Hooke 1999; Hall 2000; Higham 2008.)

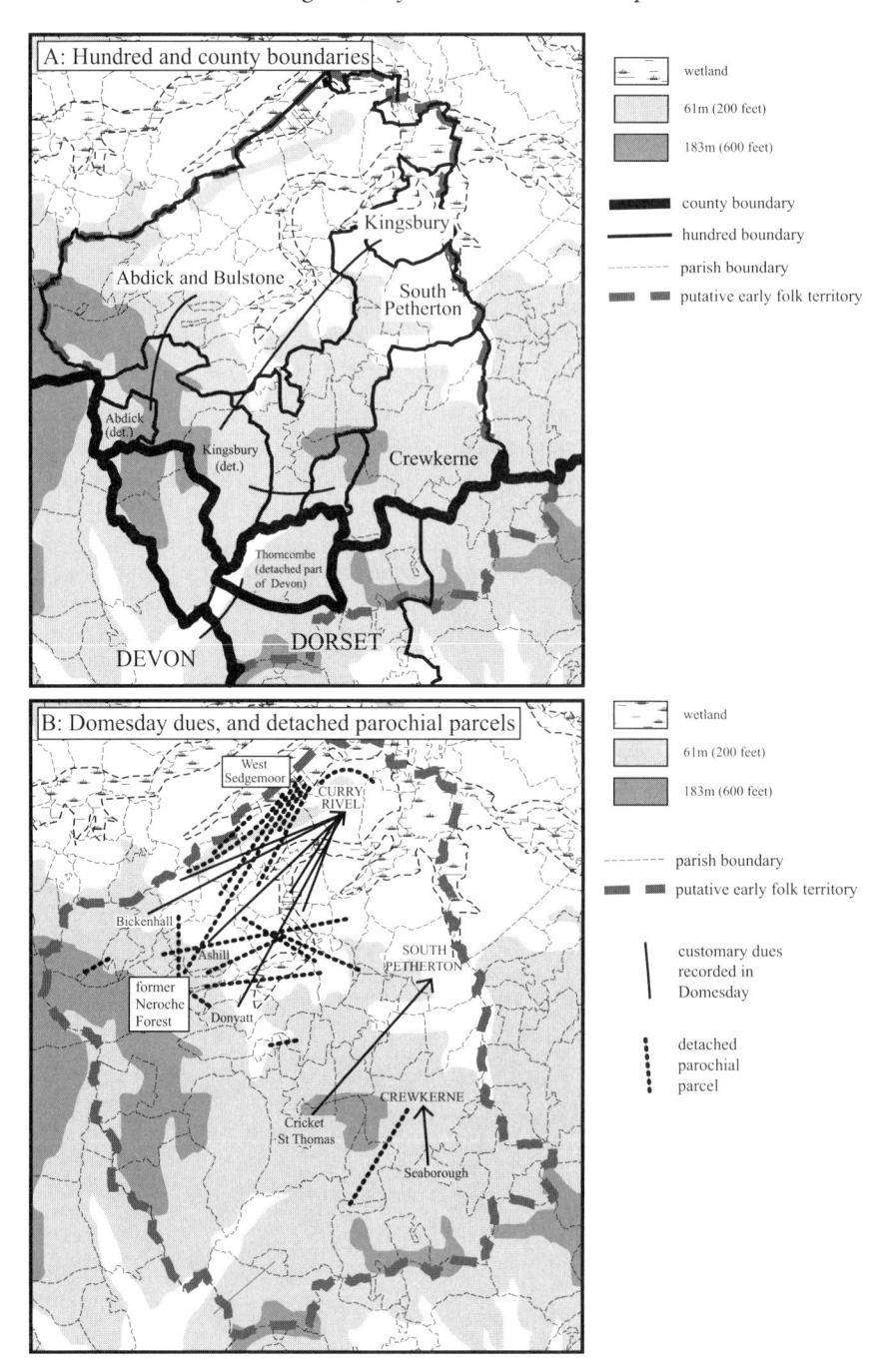

Fig. 8.4. Evidence for part of the Curry/Isle 'early folk territory'. (A) Its relationship to hundred and county boundaries; (B) detached parochial parcels, and customary dues recorded in Domesday. (C) Minster churches and their chapelries; (D) the early folk territory and the 'great estates' into which it fragmented.

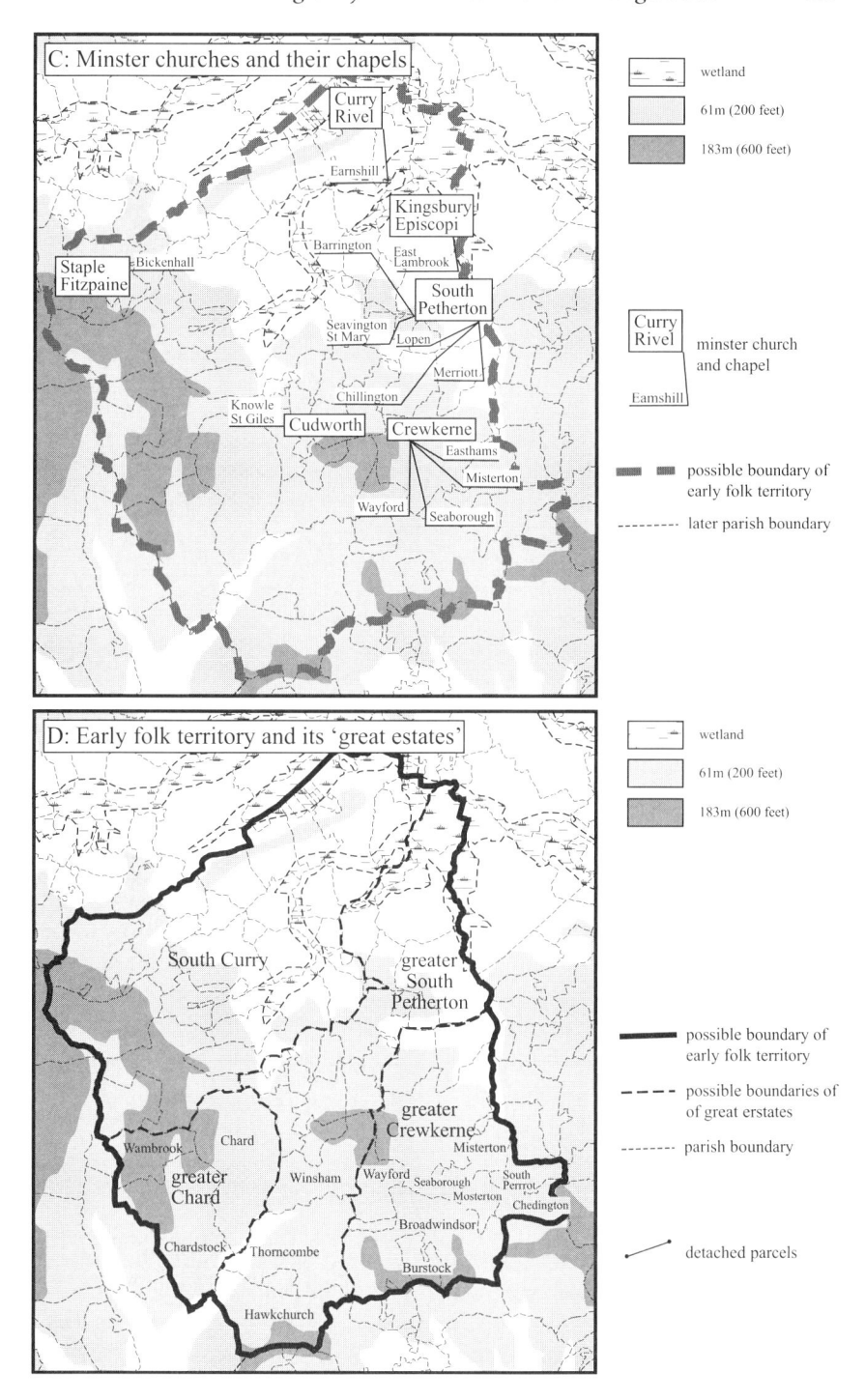

Reconstructing early medieval territorial arrangements 159

FROM THEORY TO PRACTICE: RECONSTRUCTING ESTATES CENTRES AND THEIR TERRITORIES

In order to reconstruct the early territorial arrangements of a particular area, these various categories of evidence need to be mapped out. This can be achieved via a traditional approach of transcribing sets of information onto sheets of tracing-paper laid over a base map, with separate sheets for each category of evidence, but it is best done on a computer using a GIS or graphics package, which also contains a series of layers, albeit digital, onto which data can be transcribed. The following layers need to be compiled:

The base mapping

The starting point is a modern Ordnance Survey base map, which is used to position, and re-scale, copies of the OS 1st Edn 6" map that contain much of the key data used in this analysis.

Ancient ecclesiastical parish boundaries (e.g. Fig. 8.5)

The majority of parish churches date from around the tenth to the twelfth centuries, and while the associated parishes may have been created towards the end of this period, in certain areas at least it appears that the network was 'laid out no later than the tenth century, and that by *c*.1000 it was already in quite an advanced state of development' (Morris 1989, 237; and *see* Blair 2005, 426–504). The earliest maps we have that show all parish boundaries are the Tithe surveys of *c*.1840 (which are available electronically: Kain and Oliver 2001), and the OS 1st Edn 6" maps of *c*.1860–1880. Transcribing these parish boundaries is an excellent way of familiarizing oneself with their relationship to the historic landscape (e.g. if they zigzag through, and so clearly post-date, the historic landscape), and whether there are any detached parcels. (*See* Fig. 8.5.)

Hundred boundaries (Fig. 8.2)

The next layer of data to add is the earliest form of the hundred boundaries. For most counties these are mapped in the Phillimore editions of Domesday, although unfortunately for our south-west counties the later medieval hundreds are used (e.g. Thorn and Thorn 1980; 1983; 1985), and so here the eleventh-century boundaries have been pieced together by determining within

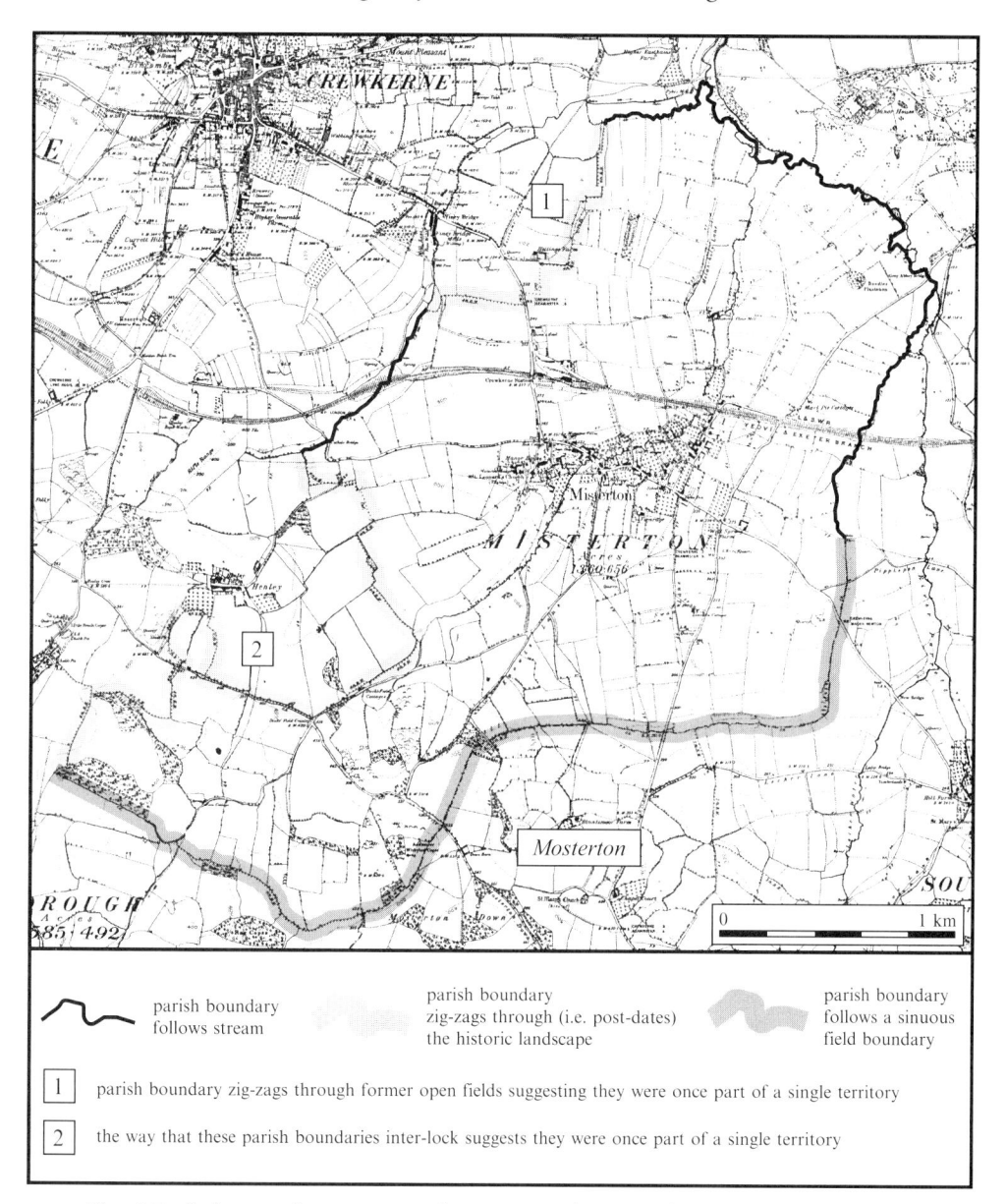

Fig. 8.5. Ordnance Survey First Edition Six Inch map of Misterton. In the later medieval period this was a chapelry of Crewkerne, to the north (Aston 1986, 74), and the parish boundary between the two zig-zags through, and clearly post-dates, the historic landscape. In contrast, the parish boundary between Misterton and Mosterton follows a long, sinuous and clearly ancient field boundary that pre-dates the creation of the historic landscape on either side.

which hundred each vill lay (e.g. Morland 1990). Some hundreds also had detached parcels and the mapping of these is another contribution to the web of territorial links that is building up. (*See* Fig. 8.2.)

Data to be collected parish by parish

Once this basic information is transcribed onto separate layers overlying the base map, there are then a series of sources that should be consulted for each parish in the study area:

- Place-names (indicative of estate centres, minsters, and territorial relationships): Watts 2004 (that replaces Ekwall 1960 and Mills 1991) covers the whole of England but only deals with the names of parishes and major settlements. Many counties have an English Place-Names Society (EPNS) volume that include minor names (i.e. hamlets and farmsteads) that for our region exist for Devon (Gover *et al.* 1931; 1932) and Dorset (Mills 1977; 1980; 1989), but not Somerset—the recent privately published volume by Robinson (1992) is extremely unreliable (Coates 1993–4).

- Domesday contains a wide range of useful information including the relative size of a manor through assessments such as the numbers of hides and plough lands (although the latter is a poorly understood aspect of the Domesday survey: Roffe 2000, 149–65), whether it was an ancient royal estate (in which case there was no hide assessment), and occasionally whether there was a church there or dues were owed to that manor from other places. The most easily accessible sources for Domesday are the Phillimore editions that contain both a translation of the text and a set of notes that often provide invaluable information on place-name identification and the tenurial history of a manor including whether it once lay in a different hundred (e.g. Thorn and Thorn 1980; 1983; 1985).

- Minster churches: Youngs (1980; 1991) provides information on whether somewhere was a parish or a chapelry in 1597, although in some cases parochial status was gained before this date and so more detailed research is required in order to identify earlier chapelries. Archaeological and architectural evidence for pre-Conquest churches is described in Taylor and Taylor (1965) and the *Corpus of Anglo-Saxon Stone Sculpture* (e.g. Cramp 2006). Pevsner's *The Buildings of England* series describes the standing structures of every parish church (e.g. Cherry and Pevsner 1991). For our study area preliminary lists of possible minsters based on documentary sources have been produced by Aston (1986) and Costen (1992a, table 4.1) for Somerset, Orme (1991), Hooke (1999), and Higham (2008) for Devon, and Hall (2000) for Dorset. The size of a parish, and whether it had detached parcels, is recorded in Kain and Oliver (1995; 2001).

- Anglo-Saxon charters survive for a small number of places and are listed in Sawyer (1968) (http://www.trin.cam.ac.uk/chartwww/esawyer.99/esawyer2.html). More detail is given in a series of regional volumes published by the Department of English Local History at the University of Leicester (e.g. Devon and Cornwall: Finberg 1954; Wessex: Finberg 1964). Some later charters contain a description of the estate's boundary (http://www.langscape.org.uk/index.html), and these have been studied and mapped in detail for some regions (e.g. Hooke 1994).

All these different categories of data need to be mapped, with different symbols used for royal manors, hundred centres, and former minster churches (although they often coincide with each other). Lines can then be drawn for the various territorial links: between a parish centre and any detached parcels; between a former minster and its chapelries; royal manors and the places that owed it customary dues in Domesday; and linked place-names (e.g. Fig. 8.4). Another layer of data is the relationship of parish boundaries to the historic landscape, and where the boundary between two parishes zigzags through the historic landscape suggesting it is relatively recent, a line can be drawn between those parishes to show that they were once a single territory (or that boundary can be shown as a dashed line). What emerges is a web of lines representing the various territorial links that will stop short of the boundary of that early territory, which will invariably be a long, sinuous, parish boundary that clearly pre-dates the surrounding historic landscape.

All the evidence described so far is totally objective, but there will be cases where it is unclear whether a particular place fell within one early territory or another. In such cases we must use more subjective judgements that can include evidence such as topography. Within this study area at least, unequivocal early territorial boundaries usually correspond to major physical features such as watersheds, rivers, and wetlands. Having established this phenomenon based on examples where the early territorial boundaries are very straightforward, in those cases where it is not altogether clear whether a parish or group of parishes lay within one territory or another, this clear relationship between early boundaries and topography seen elsewhere can be taken into consideration.

SOME TERMINOLOGY

Where estates are referred to in documentary sources they are normally named after a focal settlement, with the result that the same place-name could be used for an early estate, a Domesday manor, the vill within which that manor lay, and a settlement. In order to avoid confusion, the convention here is to prefix the names of large early medieval estates by 'greater'. There is little evidence what the earlier folk territories were called but as they usually have river valleys at their heart and boundaries that followed watersheds, in this study they are named after these major river systems. The 'Culm/Clyst' early folk territory, for example, embraced the drainage basins of the rivers Culm and Clyst, and was subdivided into two great estates that are referred to here as 'greater Cullompton' and 'greater Cliston'.

9

Early folk territories on and around the Blackdown Hills

Early folk territories, and the great estates into which they fragmented, have been reconstructed across the whole of eastern Devon, western Dorset, and southern Somerset (Fig. 9.1). The four that embraced most of the land within our local study area are discussed below: the Exe/Lowman and Culm/Clyst territories in the lowlands of eastern Devon, the Curry/Isle territory in the lowlands of central Somerset, and the Blackdown Hills territory which occupied the high ground between them (Fig. 9.2). In describing these case studies, it will be shown how the various sources and methods described in Chapter 8 can be woven together.

THE EXE/LOWMAN TERRITORY: 'GREATER TIVERTON' AND 'GREATER HALBERTON' (FIGS. 9.1–9.2 AND 10.2)

A relatively simple early folk territory can be reconstructed in the north-west corner of our local study area that was focused on the two very large parishes of Tiverton and Halberton.

'Greater Tiverton'

Tiverton lies at the junction of the river Exe and one of its major tributaries, the Lowman. It was a royal estate in the will of King Alfred (873 × 88) (Sawyer 1968, No. 1507), a hundredal centre in Domesday, and a very large manor which included thirty-six plough-lands but was assessed as just three and a half hides. As a very large parish staffed (in the thirteenth century at least) by several clergy, it shares the characteristics of other former minster churches (Orme 1991, 9). The zigzagging parish boundaries between Tiverton,

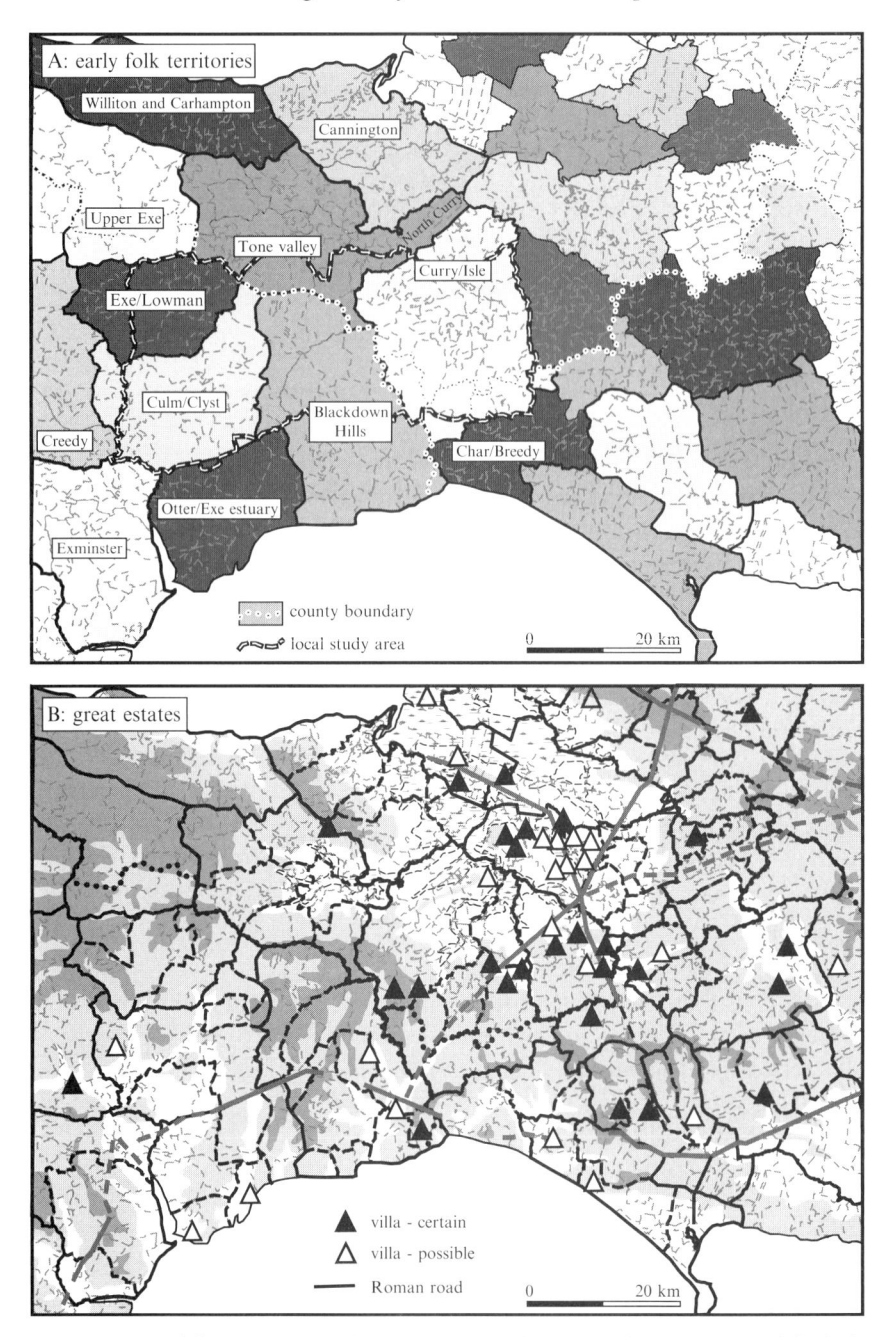

Fig. 9.1. Early folk territories and great estates in the regional study area, and the lack of any relationship to Roman villas. (Roman villas after Ordnance Survey 2001.

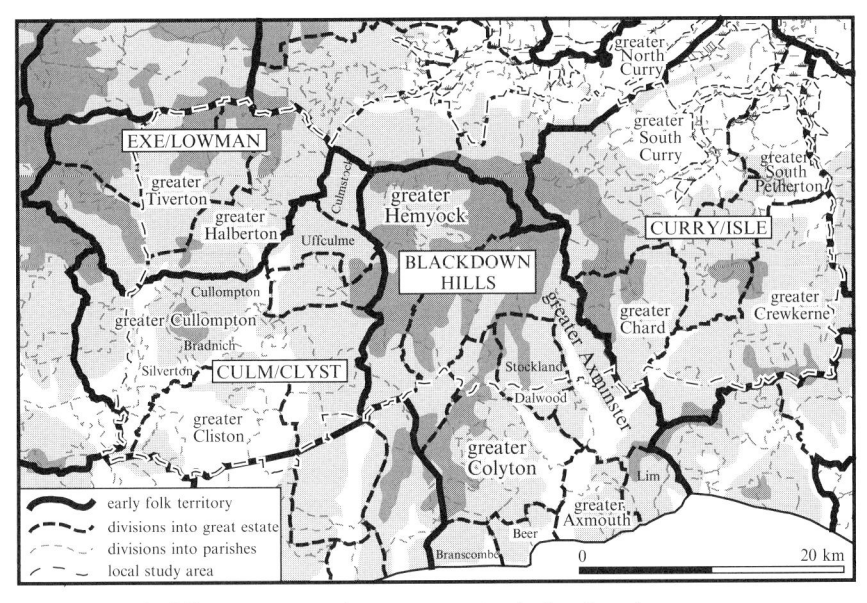

Fig. 9.2. Early folk territories and great estates in the local study area.

Washfield, and Stoodleigh suggest they were also part of this early territory. In contrast, the northern boundary of Stoodleigh follows the Mill Stream (a tributary of the Exe) along its deep steep-sided valley that is a major physical feature in the landscape, while its western boundary, along with that of Templeton, extends across the high unenclosed ground of Witheridge Moor forming a classic watershed boundary. In total this putative estate covers 33,255 acres (135 km^2).

'Greater Halberton'

The eastern edge of Tiverton parish is mostly marked by sinuous boundaries that are clearly relatively ancient, beyond which lay Halberton, another royal manor that was also the centre of a Domesday hundred. Halberton was a large manor (assessed as having land for twenty-eight ploughs, but just five hides) and parish that had various links with Tiverton: some of its land was assessed within Tiverton Hundred in the Tax Returns, and later in the Middle Ages, a detached part of Halberton parish—Chieflowman in the parish of Uplowman—was in Tiverton Hundred. Sampford Peverell also lay in both hundreds, while Combe, Murley, and Kidwell—all later parts of Uplowman parish in Halberton Hundred—were in Tiverton Hundred in 1086 (Thorn and Thorn 1985, notes 1,70; 27,1; Appendix). A long, narrow arm of Halberton parish

168   *Making Sense of An Historic Landscape*

also extended around the south of Tiverton as far as the river Exe in a way that suggests they were once part of the same territory. The parish boundary with Willand cuts through the historic landscape suggesting it was carved out of Halberton, while the configuration of the boundaries between Halberton, Uplowman (including the Halberton's detached parcel of Chieflowman), Sampford Peverell, Burlescombe, Huntsham, Holcombe Rogus, and Hockworthy (which included Huntsham's, a detached parcel of Stallenge) suggests they too were once a single estate. In total this putative estate based at Halberton covers 19,900 acres (81 km^2).

Discussion

The configuration of the parish boundaries, including detached parcels and Halberton's extension south of Tiverton, and the interspersion of Tiverton and Halberton Hundreds, suggests that this was an early folk territory amounting to 53,155 acres (215 km^2). At its core lay an extensive lowland area with rich soils, while to the north, west, and south it extended up onto the poorer soils of the Culm Measures. The northern boundary ran along Bampton Down—the highest ground in the region south of Exmoor—and then into Marcombe Lake, a stream that flows into the river Tone. The southern boundary ran along high ground south of Halberton and then along Fulford Water, the only major stream to flow off this part of the Culm Measures. The early folk territory appears to have been divided into an eastern great estate centred on Halberton and a western one based on Tiverton, before fragmenting further into the various vills and manors recorded in Domesday.

THE CULM/CLYST TERRITORY: 'GREATER CULLOMPTON' AND 'GREATER CLISTON' (FIGS. 9.1 AND 10.2)

To the south of Tiverton and Halberton, another early territory can be identified that included the large parishes of Silverton, Cullompton, and Broadclyst. Although it straddled the steep-sided Exe valley—the major river in Devon—this territory appears to have been focused on the extensive fertile lowlands of the Culm and Clyst valleys. It extended from the edge of the Culm Measures to the west, across the lowlands of eastern Devon, to the edge of the Blackdown Hills in the east.

'Greater Cullompton'

The western area based at Silverton

Silverton was a royal manor in 1066 that had never paid tax, and was head of the Domesday hundred of Silverton (later called Hayridge Hundred). There was land for forty-one ploughs so it was clearly a very substantial estate. In 1066 it included Thorverton (Thorn and Thorn 1985, notes 1,7) which mostly lay on the western side of the Exe apart from its chapelry of Nether Exe that lay to the east of the river (Youngs 1980, 84). Nether Exe was one of four small Domesday manors to the south-west of Silverton, of which two—Rewe and Stoke Canon—were parishes whose boundaries clearly post-date the historic landscape through which they zigzag. The fourth manor—Up Exe—was part of Rewe parish: it was in Wonford Hundred in the post-medieval period but was part of Silverton Hundred in 1086 (Thorn and Thorn 1985, notes 3,70). Nether Exe, Up Exe, and Rewe were all held by Wulfnoth in 1066, while six *perticae* at *Hrocastoc* (Stoke Canon) were granted to the church of St Mary in Exeter by King Æthelstan (925–39) (Finberg 1954, No. 22; Sawyer 1968, No. 389; Hooke 1994, 134–7). Overall, Nether Exe, Up Exe, Rewe, and Stoke Canon appear to have been small manors detached from the south-western corner of the royal manor of Silverton, that were bounded by the Culm to the south and the Exe to the west.

The western boundary of Thorverton (and Cadbury to the north), which corresponds to the western edge of Silverton Hundred, follow a long, sinuous, watershed boundary that clearly pre-dates the historic landscape on either side (Fig. 9.3). To the north, the parishes of Cadeleigh and Bickleigh form the north-eastern part of Silverton/Hayridge Hundred, and their western/northern boundaries are formed by a combination of long, sinuous field boundaries and the rivers Dart and Exe (in sharp contrast to their southern and eastern boundaries—with Silverton and Thorverton—that clearly post-date the historic landscape through which they zigzag). Butterleigh—a detached part of Cliston Hundred—was clearly carved out of the north-east corner of Silverton at a relatively late date. Overall, Silverton, Thorverton, the four manors carved out to the south west (Nether Exe, Up Exe, Rewe, and Stoke Canon), and Cadbury, Cadeleigh, Bickleigh, and Butterleigh to the north-west, appear to have once been a single estate.

The central and eastern area based at Cullompton

To the east of Silverton lay the parish of Bradninch, the boundary between them zigzagging through the historic landscape. Bradninch contained a single manor in Domesday that paid tax for two and a half hides but which contained land for twenty ploughs. To the east lay the large parish of Cullompton, the

note how the north–south boundary pre-dates the east–west boundary

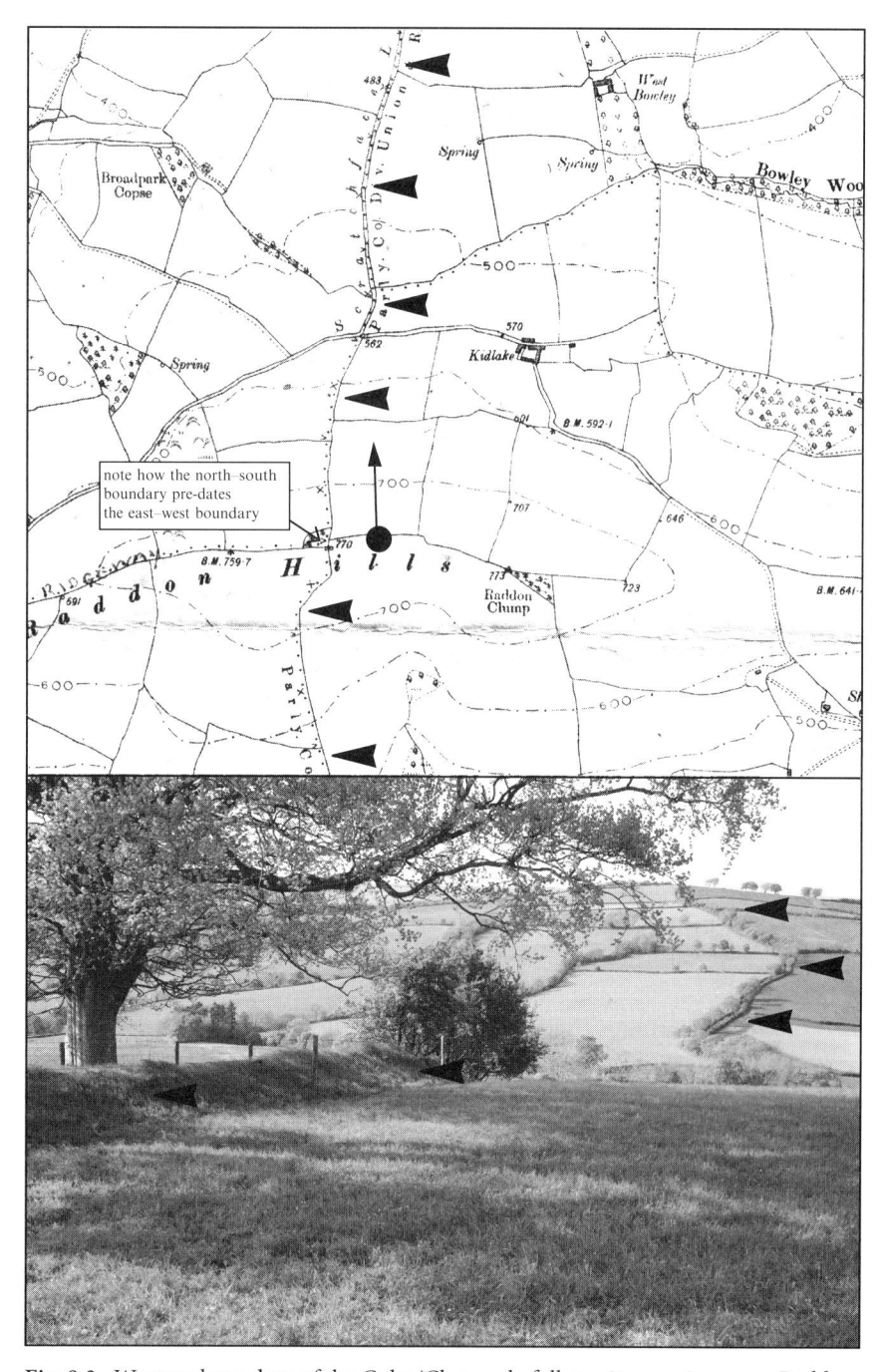

Fig. 9.3. Western boundary of the Culm/Clyst early folk territory as it crosses Raddon Hill, west of Thorverton. This boundary crosses another long, sinuous field boundary that runs east–west along Raddon Hill, and which post-dates an excavated *c.*sixth-century enclosure (Gent and Quinnell 1999a). The Raddon Hill boundary is 2 m high in places and is clearly a relatively early feature in the surrounding historic landscape, but close examination of the OS 1st Edn 6″ map, supported by fieldwork, shows that it is in fact later than the parish boundary pictured above (between Thorverton to the east, and Shobrooke and Stockleigh Pomeroy to the west).

boundary between the two also zigzagging through the landscape, with both parishes straddling the river Culm. A manor of Cullompton is not recorded in Domesday and it was probably included under Silverton (Thorn and Thorn 1985, notes 1,7) as all that is otherwise accounted for are the small manors of Colebrook (half a hide), Hillersdon (half a hide), Ponsford (two manors of half a hide each), and Langford (a single hide and three virgates) in the far east and south of the parish. Domesday also includes reference to a church at Cullompton suggesting there may have been a pre-Conquest minster. The place-name Cullompton is derived from the Celtic river name *cwlwn* ('looped' or 'winding' river) and -ton (Gover *et al.* 1932, 560; Watts 2004, 175), suggestive of an important early estate centre.

The parish boundary between Cullompton and Kentisbeare to the east (the latter including the Domesday manors of Blackborough, Kingsford, Orway, and Pirzwell) clearly post-dates the historic landscape, and that these were once part of a single estate is also suggested by Cullompton having a detached parcel—Hemland Farm—in Kentisbeare. The boundaries between Cullompton, Plymtree, Broadhembury, Payhembury, and Feniton also zigzag through the historic landscape suggesting that they are all divisions of what in the past was a single territory embracing the eastern part of Silverton Hundred. To the east lies Sheldon, up on the Blackdown Hills, whose long, gently curving eastern boundary runs along a watershed that also forms the eastern edge of Silverton/Hayridge Hundred. The southern boundary of Feniton (with Ottery St Mary) follows a field boundary that in various places appears to cut across a number of earlier boundaries. Although this does appear to be the line described in the boundary clause of the Ottery St Mary charter of 1061 (Hooke 1994, 207–12) a more logical southern boundary for Feniton and the early Culm/Clyst territory is along the Roman road from Exeter to Axminster that also marks the southern edge of Talaton, Broadclyst, and part of Whimple in Cliston Hundred (*see* below).

Uffculme and Culmstock

To the north of Kentisbeare and Sheldon lies Uffculme that in Domesday was a separate hundred before becoming a detached part of Bampton (Thorn and Thorn 1985, notes 23,9). The boundary between Uffculme and Kentisbeare/Sheldon is clearly relatively late, zigzagging through existing field systems. On these grounds it would appear that Uffculme might have been detached from the greater Cullompton estate. The boundary between Uffculme and Culmstock is also clearly recent, being a long, straight lane and hedgebank that clearly cuts across an existing field system whose long, narrow parcels are suggestive of a former open field north of the hamlet of Northcott.[1]

---

[1] A number of landmarks in the boundary clause of the *Culmestoche* charter (Sawyer 1968, No. 386) purporting to be of King Æthelstan (925–39) can be identified that correspond with the

A series of charters suggest that Uffculme and Culmstock were a discrete estate as early as the eighth or ninth centuries. In 854, twenty-four hides (possibly a scribal error for fourteen which is the number of hides in Domesday) at Uffculme were granted to Glastonbury Abbey (Finberg 1954, No. 11; Sawyer 1968, No. 1697; Abrams 1996, 235–41); this included one-and-a-half hides at *Colom*, possibly Culmstock. In another charter—probably an eleventh-century reconstruction of an original lost in 1003—King Æthelstan (925–39) granted five hides at *Culmestoche* to the church of Saints Mary and Peter in Exeter (Finberg 1954, No. 12a (p. 32) and No. 23; Sawyer 1968, No. 386; Hooke 1994, 137). Two entries in Glastonbury's *Liber terrarium* also refer to *Culum*: King Cynewulf of Wessex (757–86) granted land at *Culum* to a layman (Sawyer 1968, No. 1687), while Cuthbert (the layman?) gave eleven hides at *Culum* to Sulca who in turn gave it to Glastonbury (Sawyer 1968, No. 1691; Abrams 1996, 101–3, 235–41).

A final strand of evidence that Culmstock was probably part of a larger estate focused on the Culm is its place-name that can be interpreted as 'stoc on the Culm', or 'outlying farm on the Culm' (Gover *et al.* 1932, 612; Watts 2004, 175). Overall, it would appear that Uffculme and Culmstock were once a single estate, and as the most remote part of greater Cullompton was the first piece to be carved up and granted away.

Cullompton: an estate centre?

The final matter to resolve is where any centre of this territory lay. Based on the evidence in Domesday, Silverton is most likely as this was the royal manor and head of the hundred whereas Cullompton is not listed. Silverton lies, however, at the foot of a series of steep-sided hills mid-way between the Culm and Exe valleys, and is far from being an agricultural heartland. Cullompton, on the other hand, lies on the banks of the Culm and extends out across the fertile lowland plain of eastern Devon. The 'Celtic river + -ton' place-name is also indicative of an ancient centre, and unlike Silverton appears to have had a minster church. We can therefore suggest that Cullompton may have been the original centre of an early estate that covered 58,224 acres (236 km^2), but that the administrative centre later moved to Silverton. It had at its heart an extensive area of fertile lowland, and extended westwards up onto the Culm Measures to the west and up onto the Blackdown Hills in the east. In the far north-east, Uffculme and Culmstock may have been one of the earliest parts of

western, northern, and eastern boundaries of Culmstock, including White Ball Hill that marks the northwest corner, and Hackpen Hill to the south-east. The southern boundary, however, is a stream called *craducc* that has given its name to the hamlet of Craddock (Gover *et al.* 1932, 538; Hooke 1994, 137–41). This lies some distance to the south of the present parish boundary.

the estate to be detached and granted to one of the king's followers, eventually coming into the hands of Glastonbury Abbey.

'Greater Cliston' (Broadclyst)

South of Cullompton lay the small Domesday hundred of Cliston which consisted of the parishes of Broadclyst, Clyst Hydon, Clyst St Lawrence, and Whimple (Thorn and Thorn 1985, notes 1,56). Clyst is a Celtic river name (Watts 2004, 146), and so Cliston (the eleventh name for Broadclyst) is a 'river + -ton' place-name suggestive of an early estate centre. Cliston was a royal manor in 1086 and which only paid tax for nine and a half hides despite there being land for thirty-five ploughs. Its interlocking parish boundaries with the far smaller parishes of Clyst Hydon, Clyst St Lawrence, and Whimple to the east clearly post-date the historic landscape, as is the case with Huxham and Poltimore to the west. The very modest church at Huxham lacks a tower, suggesting that it was once a chapelry, presumably of Broadclyst (Nether Exe, the chapelry of Thorverton, and Up Exe, the chapelry of Rewe, also lack towers). Although part of Whimple's southern boundary was marked by the Roman road from Exeter to Axminster it also extended to the south to and included the manor of Strete Raleigh. In Domesday, however, Strete Raleigh was in East Budleigh Hundred (Thorn and Thorn 1985, notes 34,38), suggesting that it was added to Whimple at a later date, and that Whimple's original boundary was along the Roman road. Several strands of evidence suggest that greater Cliston was carved out of the Culm/Clyst early folk territory. Butterleigh, to the north of Silverton, was a detached part of Cliston Hundred, and the parish boundary between Whimple (in Cliston Hundred) and Talaton (in the Silverton/Hayridge Hundred) is clearly relatively recent, cutting diagonally across several fields. In total, the area of this putative greater Cliston estate is 17,465 acres (71 km^2), with an average parish size of 2,911 acres.

Discussion

What emerges from this analysis is an early folk territory covering 75,689 acres (307 km^2) that broadly corresponds with the later Silverton and Cliston hundreds. The original early folk territory was divided into two great estates based at Cullompton/Silverton and Cliston, which in turn were broken up into a series of manors of 118 hides in total in Domesday. The early folk territory stretched from the high ground of the Culm Measures to the west, across the fertile lowlands of the Culm and Clyst valleys, and up onto the Blackdown Hills to the east: it is very noticeable that the web of territorial links that binds this territory together extend up to the western edge of the Blackdown Hills but no further. To the north, the boundary was marked by the River Dart, the hills north of Butterleigh, and Fulford Water (a tributary of the Culm). To the south, the boundary was probably marked by the Roman road from Exeter to Axminster, although Ottery St Mary subsequently expanded north into Feniton, and Whimple was extended south into Rockbeare.

THE BLACKDOWN HILLS: 'GREATER AXMINSTER', 'GREATER COLYTON', AND 'GREATER HEMYOCK'

To the east of the Culm/Clyst territory lay the Blackdown Hills, the majority of which fell within the four Domesday hundreds of Axminster, Axmouth, Colyton, and Hemyock (the other part being Stockland that in Domesday was a detached part of Dorset) (Figs. 9.1–9.2). Rather than being characterized by the predominantly lowland drainage basin of a river system, this early territory was defined by its mostly upland topography of flat topped plateaus dissected by a series of broad valleys.

'Greater Axminster'

In 757 the Anglo-Saxon chronicle records that a prince Cyneheard was buried at Axminster (Swanton 1996, 49), and a church there is referred to again in 1066 and in Domesday (Sawyer 1968, No. 161). Axminster was a large parish of which Kilmington and Membury were chapelries (Youngs 1980, 76), and the present church has a cruciform plan with a crossing tower, and contains some Norman fabric (Cherry and Pevsner 1991, 142). Axminster was a royal manor in Domesday that never paid tax, and it was owed 15d from the manors of Charlton (lost, but probably in Upottery: *DB Dev.* 3,96 notes), Honiton, Smallridge (in Axminster), Membury, and Rawridge (in Upottery) (all in Axminster Hundred; *DB Dev.* 1,11). Not surprisingly, the boundaries between Axminster, Kilmington, and Membury are clearly late, zigzagging through the historic landscape, as is also the case with the boundary between Axminster and Musbury that lies in Axmouth Hundred (*see* below). A detached parcel of Axminster that lies between Axmouth and Uplyme, but which appears to originally have been part of Axmouth, strengthens the network of territorial links that bind these two hundreds together. Further north, the parish boundaries between Honiton, Combe Raleigh, Luppitt, and Yarcombe clearly postdate the historic landscape, as do the boundaries between Honiton and Upottery in Axminster Hundred, and Monkton, Cotleigh, and Offwell in

Colyton Hundred (*see* below). Overall, the Domesday hundred of Axminster appears to have once been a single estate which amounted to 37,346 acres (151 km^2),[2] and that this in turn was once part of a larger territory that included Axmouth and Colyton hundreds.

'Greater Axmouth'

Axmouth was a royal manor that was included in King Alfred's will (Sawyer 1968, No. 1507). In Domesday it was a royal manor that never paid tax, and the centre of a small fourteen-hide hundred that consisted of the later parishes of Axmouth, Rousden, Combpyne, and Musbury whose boundaries with Axmouth zigzag through the historic landscape in a way that suggests they were once all part of a single estate. Although later in Axminster Hundred, in Domesday two hides of Musbury lay in Axmouth Hundred (the other two being in Axminster: *DB Dev.* 16,164 notes), and the parish boundary between Musbury and Axminster parishes zigzags through the historic landscape. It would appear, therefore, that greater Axmouth was an estate of 7,952 acres (32 km^2) carved out of an earlier territory that also included greater Axminster.

'Greater Colyton'

The 'river (derived from the Celtic *cul*, or 'narrow') + -ton' place-name Colyton is first recorded in 946 (Gover *et al.* 1932, 621). The extremely large parish of Colyton, on the western side of the Axe, was a hundredal centre and royal manor in Domesday that paid tax for one hide although there was land for sixteen ploughs. There was also a church—which has a cruciform plan with a Norman crossing tower (Cherry and Pevsner 1991, 279)—with half a virgate of land, and a further indication of its former minster status is that it had chapelries at Monkton (also a sub-manor of Colyton), and at Shute, neither of which have separate entries in Domesday (Youngs 1980, 81; Thorn and Thorn 1985, 1,13 notes). Northleigh and Southleigh were also chapelries of Colyton, which may equate to the three Domesday manors of *Legh* (Hoskins 1952, 305). The boundaries between Colyton, Shute, Widworthy, Farway, Offwell, Northleigh, and Southleigh all zigzag through the historic landscape and along with a series of detached parcels suggest that these were once part of the same estate.

---

[2] The configuration of the parish boundaries, and a series of charters, suggests that this included Lyme Regis (Finberg 1964, Nos. 27 and 562; Sawyer 1968, Nos. 263 and 442; Fox 1970; Hooke 1994, 127–34; Abrams 1996, 156; Barker 2005, 45).

In contrast to this series of strongly interconnected parishes, two coastal parishes covered relatively discrete blocks of land. Branscombe was a royal estate in King Alfred's will (Sawyer 1968, No. 1507) and whose long, sinuous boundaries suggest that it existed as a discrete entity relatively early, as is the case with Seaton and its chapelry of Beer which was a royal manor granted by King Æthelred in 1005 to Eadsige (Sawyer 1968, No. 910). Branscombe church has a cruciform plan, with a Norman crossing tower (Fig. 8.1; Cherry and Pevsner 1991, 204). Based on the configuration of the parish boundaries, Branscombe and Seaton were probably relatively early subdivisions of the larger territory based at Colyton that covered 28,434 acres (115 km^2), and at the time of Domesday was assessed as just over twenty-eight hides.

Stockland

Stockland was a large parish that in Domesday was a ten-hide manor forming a detached parcel of Whitchurch Hundred in Dorset (Fig. 9.2): it was transferred to Devon in 1866, and included the chapelry and later parish of Dalwood to the south (Youngs 1980, 119). It may have been detached from Devon when it was granted to the church at Milton (Abbas) in central Dorset, who held it in Domesday (*DB Dor.* 12,14). To the east and west its boundaries are marked by watercourses (the river Yarty and the Umborne Brook respectively), while its boundary to the north appears to post-date the historic landscape. The southern boundary of Dalwood partly follows the likely course of the Roman road from Axminster to Honiton but otherwise similarly zigzags through the historic landscape. The way that the boundaries of Stockland run between two rivers, rather than across a valley from watershed to watershed as is the norm on the Blackdown Hills, is unusual but is also paralleled at Ottery St Mary, in the lowlands of eastern Devon to the west. In both cases it would appear that these compact estates were created relatively late, being carved out of earlier territories (in the case of Stockland from estates based at Axminster and Colyton). The *stoc* place name implies that it was once a subsidiary holding of another place.

'Greater Hemyock'

Hemyock was a royal estate that in 1066 paid tax for just one virgate of land, although there was land for twelve ploughs. It was also the centre of a hundred at the time of Domesday (Thorn and Thorn 1985, appendix), which along with its royal status make it a likely location for a minster church. The present parish church appears to have originally had a cruciform plan as there are blocked doorways on the northern and southern side of the nave (Cherry and

Pevsner 1991, 478). Other parishes in the hundred were Clayhidon, Churchstanton (transferred to Somerset in 1896), Dunkeswell, Awliscombe, and Buckerell. There is no entry for Buckerell in Domesday and the way that its eastern boundary zigzags through what was clearly an open field associated with the hamlet of Weston between it and Awliscombe suggests that they were once a single territory. The way that the parish boundaries of Clayhidon, Churchstanton, Hemyock, Dunkeswell, and Awliscombe interlock suggest the subdivision of a larger unit, while Clayhidon has two detached parcels within Hemyock (including Culm Pyne: *DB Dev.* 16,122 notes). Churchstanton parish is dominated by high upland plateau and the configuration of its parish boundaries suggests an area of late colonization carved out of Clayhidon, although the Domesday assessment of three hides, land for twenty ploughs, and ten and a half actual ploughs means that this must have happened some time before the Conquest. Overall, greater Hemyock covered 24,797 acres (100 km^2) and in Domesday was assessed as just over twenty-three hides.

Discussion

Based on this analysis, it appears that the hundreds of Axminster, Axmouth, Colyton, and Hemyock, along with Stockland and Lyme Regis, were once a single territory that occupied the vast majority of the Blackdown Hills, covering 106,089 acres (429 km^2). The likely sequence of its fragmentation is that greater Hemyock, greater Axmouth, and greater Colyton were detached first, leaving the rump as greater Axminster, accounting for the curious way that it partly encircles the last two of these. An estate at Stockland then appears to have been carved out of Colyton and Axminster whose original boundary may have run along the high ground of Stockland Hill that runs through the centre of the parish.

THE CURRY/ISLE TERRITORY: GREATER 'SOUTH CURRY', 'GREATER SOUTH PETHERTON', AND 'GREATER CREWKERNE' (FIG. 8.4)

The lowlands east of the Blackdown Hills lay within a series of great estates, each closely related to a minster church and early hundred, that appear to have once formed a large folk territory extending from the river Parrett in the east, the wetlands of West Sedgemoor in the north, the edge of the Blackdown Hills to the west, and the Wessex Ridgeway to the south (Fig. 9.2).

'Greater Crewkerne'

Crewkerne was a Domesday hundredal centre and royal manor which did not pay tax, and from which Easthams had been removed. The two Domesday manors of Seaborough were also part of Crewkerne before 1066, and they paid the king's manor a customary due of twelve sheep with their lambs and one bloom of iron from every freeman. Its simple topographical place-name is also indicative of an early estate. There was a church there at the time of Domesday, and that it was formerly a minster church is indicated by the four adjacent parishes having formerly been chapelries (Easthams, Misterton (*Minstretone* in Domesday, meaning 'minster estate': Watts 2010, 417), Seaborough, and Wayford: Aston 1986, 74). Not surprisingly the boundaries between these later parishes zigzag through the historic landscape, as is the case with Hinton St George and Merriott to the north. Overall, these form a relatively compact area of 12,077 acres which corresponded to the Domesday hundred (Morland 1990, 112) and which is bounded to the north by the Lopen Brook, to the east by the river Parrett, and to the west by a series of sinuous boundaries that are relatively early in the formation of the historic landscape.

The southern boundary of this group of parishes, however, presents a problem as it does not follow the most logical route along the river Axe: Wayford, in Somerset, extends to the south of the river Axe, seemingly taking a large chunk out of Broadwindsor (in Dorset); Crewkerne had a detached parcel—Sandford Orcos—to the south of Wayford; and the boundary between Wayford and Broadwindsor to the east, and Thorncombe to the west, clearly zigzags through the historic landscape. There are other oddities. In Seaborough the southern boundary of Somerset is the Axe, but to the east the county boundary turns an abrupt right-angle heading north around Mosterton, a manor that in Domesday was in Dorset; while most of Mosterton lies to the north of the Axe a long narrow arm of the parish extends south of the river into Broadwindsor. To the east lies South Perrott, a Domesday manor in Dorset, while North Perrott lay in Somerset: the boundary between South Perrott and Chedington to the south zigzags through the historic landscape in a way that suggests they were once a single territory.

Mosterton, South Perrott, and Chedington would, therefore, fit far more comfortably within an early territory that looked north towards Crewkerne, rather than south into modern Dorset. The same is true of Broadwindsor, into which Mosterton, Wayford, and Crewkerne (through its detached parcel) extend. The southern boundary of Broadwindsor, in contrast, is very simple in following the high ground of the Wessex Ridgeway that also marks the limit of the tenurial and ecclesiastical links of Whitchurch Canonicorum, a clearly defined folk territory to the south. West of Broadwindsor (and Wayford/ Sandford Orcos) lay Thorncombe that in Domesday was a detached part of Axminster Hundred in Devon (*DB Dev.* 16,165) when it was held by 'Baldwin the Sherriff' (of Devon). South of Thorncombe lay Hawkchurch, which is not named in Domesday but which may have been included under the entry for Cerne Abbey that held it by the thirteenth century (Thorn and Thorn 1983, 11,1 notes). The southern boundaries of Thorncombe and Hawkchurch also follow the high ground of the Wessex Ridgeway, and we can therefore be confident that they lay within an early territory that looked north rather than south, although the configuration of the parish boundaries suggests that Thorncombe and Hawkchurch may have been part of the greater South Petherton estate (*see* below) rather than greater Crewkerne.

Overall, the evidence suggests that Broadwindsor, Burstock, Mosterton, South Perrott, and Cheddington in north-east Dorset were part of an early estate based at Crewkerne, the total area of which was 22,450 acres (91 km^2), and which in Domesday was assessed as 119 hides.

'Greater South Petherton'

South Petherton was another major royal manor that never paid tax (*DB Som.* 1,4), to which customary dues of six sheep with as many lambs, and one bloom of iron from each free man, were owed from Cricket St Thomas. South Petherton was also the centre of a Domesday hundred (Aston 1986, tab. 73; Thorn and Thorn 1985, 370–2). In Domesday there was a priest in South Petherton, and that it was a former minster church is supported by the later parishes of Barrington, Chillington, Lopen, and Seavington St Mary being former chapelries (Aston 1986, 75). Although Barrington was in Abdick Hundred in Domesday, the way that its boundary with Shepton Beauchamp—in South Petherton Hundred—zigzags through the historic landscape (in contrast to its very sinuous western boundary) suggests that it too was originally part of a greater South Petherton. Although Cricket Malherbie and West Dowlish were in Abdick Hundred in the Geld Inquest (Morland 1990, 101), the way that their boundaries with adjacent parishes—all in South Petherton Hundred—zigzag through the historic landscape, and the way that Cricket Malherbie divides West Dowlish from its detached parcel at Bere Mills Farm to the south, suggests that they all formed part of the greater South Petherton estate.

The Episcopal hundred of Kingsbury, which included the scattered parishes of Kingsbury Episcopi, Winsham, Combe St Nicholas, and Chard, appears to have been carved out of a greater South Petherton, having been formed from a series of estates acquired by the bishops of Wells (*DB Som.* 6,2–4). The place-name of Chardstock, that at the time of Domesday lay in Dorset,[3] suggests that

---

[3] Chardstock was a detached part of Beaminster Hundred and may have been transferred to Dorset after it was granted to the church at Sherborne who held it in 1066 along with Beaminster (*DB Dor.* 3,10; 3,13).

it may have been part of a greater Chard estate that along with Wambrook appears to form a discrete subdivision of this putative greater South Petherton territory amounting to 13,106 acres (53 km^2). The configuration of the parish boundaries of Thorncombe and Hawkchurch, now in Dorset, suggest they were also part of this greater South Petherton estate (*see* above). In total, greater South Petherton covered 30,877 acres (125 km^2), and in Domesday was assessed as one hundred and fifty two and a half hides, of which twenty hides lay in greater Chard.

'South Curry'

Another great estate can be reconstructed to the north of greater South Petherton and which broadly corresponds to the later hundred of Abdick and Bulstone, and which is referred to here as 'South Curry' (to distinguish it from North Curry Hundred). Of the two lists of hundreds attached to the Exeter Domesday the second contains two entries for *Chori* (Curry, which was separate from *Nortchori*), while the first lists *Abedic* and *Couri* that appear to equate to *Abediccha* and *Bolestana* in the Tax Return (which were later combined to form Abdick and Bulstone hundred: Thorn and Thorn 1980, 370–2; Morland 1990, 100–1). The meeting place of Bulstone Hundred lay at a stone south of Curry Rivel (Aston 1986, tab. 7.3), while Abdick Hundred was probably based around Curry Mallet: the intermingled nature of these two post-Conquest hundreds (e.g. Buckland St Mary was a detached part of Bulstone Hundred: Aston 2009, fig. 4), and the territorial links that cut across their boundaries (*see* below) suggests that they represent the subdivision of what was once a single district, parts of which were given to Muchelney Abbey in a series of grants during the late seventh and eighth centuries (Thorn and Thorn 1980, 370–2; Aston 2009).

Curry Rivel was a royal manor in Domesday that also had a church. A further indication of its former status as a minster is its chapelry at Earnshill (Youngs 1980, 424). It lies at the centre of a particularly clear network of territorial links. The Domesday manors of Ashill, Bickenhall, Bradon (in Puckington), Donyatt, and Hatch Beauchamp all owed customary dues to Curry Rivel.[4] The parish boundary between Curry Rivel and Swell, to the west, zigzags through the historic landscape, and in Domesday one virgate of the manor of Swell lay in the King's manor of Curry Rivel; the vill of Moortown,

---

[4] Ashill ought to pay Curry (Rivel) 30 pence (*DB Som.* 19,18), while the two manors of Bradon each paid Curry (Rivel) one sheep and a lamb (*DB Som.* 19,17; 19,23); Bickenhall paid Curry Rivel five sheep and as many lambs, while each freeman owed a bloom of iron (*DB Som.* 19,27). Donyatt owed five sheep and as many lambs (*DB Som.* 19,24). One hide in Hatch (Beauchamp) owed one sheep and a lamb (*DB Som.* 19, 29).

that lay within Swell parish west of Curry Rivel, was a detached part of Drayton parish (east of Curry Rivel) in Domesday but part of Fivehead at the time of the Tithe survey. Drayton also held a detached parcel—Burton—in the west of Curry Rivel, and Curry Rivel's boundary with Drayton clearly post-dates the now-enclosed strips and furlongs through which it passes. The wetlands of West Sedgemoor, to the north-west, were divided between Curry Rivel, Swell, and Fivehead, but also contained detached parcels of six other parishes (Isle Abbots, Fivehead, Curry Mallet, Hatch Beauchamp, Beercrocombe, and Broadway) suggesting that it was formerly an area of common land serving all these communities. Several detached parcels in Broadway parish (belonging to Ilton, Donyatt, and White Lackington) probably reflect former grazing rights on the commons of what was to become Neroche Forest (Rackham 1988, fig. 1.9); Barrington, in Abdick Hundred, also held a detached parcel in Broadway, along with a small parcel in Puckington, but other indications are that it formed part of an estate based at South Petherton (*see* above).

When these various tenurial and ecclesiastical links are mapped a very compact territory emerges whose northern and western boundaries match those of the early *Chori* (Curry) hundred, running from the wetlands of West Sedgemoor up to the top of the well-wooded scarp slope that marks the boundary with North Curry Hundred (*see* below). The one area that makes little sense is to the south-west, where the parish boundary of Combe St Nicholas, which lay in Kingsbury Hundred, zigzags through the historic landscape and so appears to be relatively late, while Whitestaunton to the south-west of Combe was a detached part of Abdick Hundred. The answer appears to be that Kingsbury Hundred was composed of a series of estates that had been acquired by the bishops of Wells to which the addition of *Cumba* (Combe St Nicholas) appears to have occurred shortly before 1086 (its loss being recorded in the Abdick Tax Return: Thorn and Thorn 1980, 373). Whitestaunton, in contrast, remained in Abdick Hundred. Overall, this putative South Curry estate covered 44,413 acres (180 km^2) and was assessed as one hundred and seventy nine hides.

The dilemma of greater North Curry

To the north of this putative South Curry estate lay North Curry that the King held in 1086, as twenty hides. In a previous reconstruction of early folk territories in Somerset it was included with South Curry (Rippon 2008a, fig. 3.13), largely on the basis of the common place-name 'Curry', but further consideration suggest that it was actually part of the Tone Valley territory to the north (Fig. 9.1). That North Curry was formerly a minster is suggested by the presence of a church in 1086, and that the adjacent parishes of Stoke

St Gregory and West Hatch were former chapelries (Youngs 1980, 424). The way in which the parish boundary between North Curry, West Hatch, and Thorn Falcon zigzag through the field-boundary pattern suggests that the latter also once formed part of this early territory. Thurlbear was a chapel of Taunton, but other evidence suggests that it was formerly within the North Curry estate: it lay within the hundred of North Curry, and its boundary with West Hatch zigzags through the historic landscape. Altogether, the later parishes of North Curry, Stoke St Gregory, West Hatch, Thorn Falcon, and Thurlbear—that comprise the whole of North Curry Hundred at the time of Domesday—form a coherent great estate of 12,790 acres. The boundaries are all defined by significant topographical features: the Tone valley to the north, the extensive wetlands of Southlake Moor and West Sedgemoor to the east and south-east, and a steep wooded escarpment to the south-west that is a prominent feature in the landscape of central Somerset. In contrast, the western boundary of this putative greater North Curry estate is marked by the relatively minor Broughton Brook and Thornwater stream, and topographically it very much looks west towards the Tone valley, as opposed to up and over the steep scarp slope to the south of the river Curry.

Discussion

The way that this group of three great estates—greater South Curry, greater South Petherton (from which greater Chard was extracted), and greater Crewkerne—interlock with each other suggests they were once a single folk territory, for which Barrington (in greater South Petherton but having a detached parcel in the former commons of Neroche Forest in South Curry), is a connecting thread of evidence. This territory has a considerable physical coherence, bounded by the Blackdown Hills to the south-west, the high ground of Staple Fitzpaine, Bickenhall, and Curry Mallet to the north, the wetlands of the Somerset Levels to the north-east, and the River Parrett to the east. Rather than the river Axe as its southern boundary, it appears that the early folk territory extended as far south as the high ground of the Wessex Ridgeway. It is very noticeable that the web of territorial links that binds this territory together extend up onto the eastern fringes of the Blackdown Hills but no further. In total, this early folk territory appears to have covered 110,846 acres (449 km^2) and in Domesday was assessed as one hundred and thirty four and a half hides.

REFLECTIONS

The methodology presented in Chapter 8, whose application is illustrated in the case studies above, suggests that in the early medieval period western Wessex and eastern Dumnonia were divided into a series of large early folk territories. By around the eighth century these appear to have been broken down into a series of smaller territories, referred to here as 'great estates', that had at their centre a *villae regalis* and minster church, and also formed the basis of administrative districts that later became known as 'hundreds'. Although documentary sources such as the Anglo-Saxon Chronicle and King Alfred's Will refer to large numbers of *villae regiae* (listed in Sawyer 1983, and mapped in Hooke 1998, fig. 17), Blair (2005, 275–85) rejects the idea that these were stable estate centres, contrasting their undeveloped nature and functional limitations to the major royal palaces found on the continent. Instead, he argues that the Anglo-Saxon *villae regiae* were very varied in their character, with most simply being temporary residential bases and food-render collection points for itinerant kings, and only a few, such as Tamworth, developing into more stable centres in the eighth century during the Mercian dominance. In comparing most *villae regiae* to camp sites, he argues that 'however stable the *regiones* of early England may have been, and however effectively exploited through hidage-based assessment, there is no real reason, except possibly in Kent, to suppose that their central places were stable too' (Blair 2005, 281). Across western Wessex and eastern Dumnonia, however, there is a marked recurrent coincidence of places with 'river + -ton' names, that were royal manors, Domesday hundredal centres, and minster churches. In this region there do appear to have been locations within the landscape that were more important than others over a prolonged period of time. Identifying these provides a useful starting point for reconstructing the territories they administered and from which they received service.

The reconstruction of these territories was done in an objective way, without pre-judging whether all areas of the landscape were ever within an early folk territory or great estate, although the results suggest that here at least they were. It is very noticeable that the vast majority of these territorial units have as their boundaries areas of high ground or wetland, but it seems clear that none of the early folk territories or great estates that were centred in the lowlands to the west, north, or east of the Blackdowns extended very far into the upland area. Instead, the Blackdowns appear to have been occupied by a community of its own, although the name of these people has been lost as no folk-based place-name comparable to *-ingas*, *-sæte*, or *wara* survives (such names are extremely rare right across the South West).

Another key conclusion of this work is that when county boundaries were created, although they sometimes used these existing territorial boundaries, this was not always the case. In the author's earlier work (Rippon 2008a) the reconstruction of early medieval territorial arrangements stopped at the edge of Somerset. Any landscape research has to have a case study area with a boundary, but for this particular type of work the choice of a county boundary was, with hindsight, not a good one. The subsequent work presented here, in contrast, was based upon a study area that cut across three counties and as a result it revealed a number of parishes which have switched from one county to another and examples of early folk territories and great estates that were dissected by a later county boundary. When researching the early medieval landscape, counties are not necessarily the best study areas.

Having reflected on the methodological aspects of this work we must now turn to the results themselves, and Chapter 10 will explore how the early medieval territorial structures identified here compare to those elsewhere in Britain, and what they tell us about the landscape of our study area. The lack of any correlation between these early folk territories and great estates will be discussed further in Chapter 15.

10

People in the landscape: the development of territorial structures in early medieval western Wessex and beyond

In Chapters 8 and 9 we looked at the sources and methods used to reconstruct early territorial arrangements across part of western Wessex and eastern Dumnonia that revealed how the parishes which are familiar to us today were created through the fragmentation of a series of 'great estates', that in turn appear to have been produced through the subdivision of larger 'early folk territories'. In this chapter we will explore how this evidence from our study area compares to elsewhere in early medieval England, and see whether there were any differences either side of the Blackdown Hills.

THE SURVIVAL OF *CIVITATES*?

Later Roman Britain was administered through a series of territories known as *civitates* that some have suggested survived into the early medieval period, such as Dark's (1999, 83–6; 2000, 144) hypothesis that the *civitas* of the Silures in south-east Wales became the early medieval kingdoms of Glywysing and Gwent. In South West Britain, some *civitates* do bear a superficial resemblance to later shires, with Dorset for example roughly corresponding to the southern division of the Durotriges based at Dorchester, Somerset (possibly only as far north as the Somerset Levels or Mendip) perhaps equating to the northern division of the Durotriges based at Ilchester, and Devon and possibly Cornwall occupying a similar area as the *civitas* and early medieval kingdom of Dumnonia (Winterbottom 1978, 28; Yorke 1995, 15; Dark 2000, 151). There is, however, no evidence for the survival of these *civitates* as administrative districts during the politically turbulent years of the fifth to the seventh centuries, and any similarity to later counties in their geographical extent probably reflects their use of a common set of dominant topographical features for both sets of boundaries.

THE CREATION OF SHIRES

From around the late seventh or early eighth century, a series of *scir* (shires) appear to have emerged across Wessex, with the laws of King Ine (688–726), for example, referring to 'shiremen' and describing how a man should pay a fine to his lord if he 'steals into another shire' (Attenborough 1922, 39, 49; Whitelock 1955, 368; Yorke 1989; 1995; Reynolds 1999, 72; Draper 2004; 2006, 59). While the boundaries of these 'shires' are not recorded, it is tempting to see them as the predecessors of Hampshire, Wiltshire, Somerset, Dorset, and Devon whose original borders may have made extensive use of natural features such as the high ground of Selwood Forest (on the Somerset–Wiltshire border) and the Blackdown Hills (the Devon–Somerset and Devon–Dorset boundaries) and man-made structures such as West Wansdyke that runs close to the early boundary between Somerset and Gloucestershire (Yorke 1995, 84–5; Reynolds and Langlands 2006). It is only during the tenth century, however, that a relatively powerful English state started to impose uniform systems of local administration, and we first get clear evidence for the shires that we are familiar with today. Although the relationship of these tenth-century shires to the Middle Saxon *scir* is not clear, in areas such as the South West—that suffered less disruption from the Viking incursions, the creation and dissolution of Danelaw, and the subsequent re-establishment of Saxon authority—it is more likely that the shires were based on existing territorial units.

LARGER *REGIONES* AND THE EARLY 'FOLK TERRITORIES' OF WESTERN WESSEX

Documents from around the eighth century also make reference to various territories that appear to have been autonomous or semi-autonomous districts known as *regiones*, or occasionally *provinciae* (J. Campbell 1979; Bassett 1989b, 17–21; Hooke 1998, 46–54). Where these can be reconstructed they varied considerably in size, with the larger examples being substantial subdivisions of later counties, such as Winchcombeshire in modern Gloucestershire that covered around a thousand square kilometres (Fig. 10.1). Some of these larger *regiones* equate to the smaller tribal areas and kingdoms recorded in the Tribal Hidage, that is traditionally dated to the seventh or eighth century but which only survives as an eleventh-century manuscript that may be a composite of various earlier documents (Blair 1999).

There is, however, a problem with the term *regiones* as it was also used to describe far smaller territories for which archaeologists, historians, and historical geographers have developed a bewildering range of other terms such as

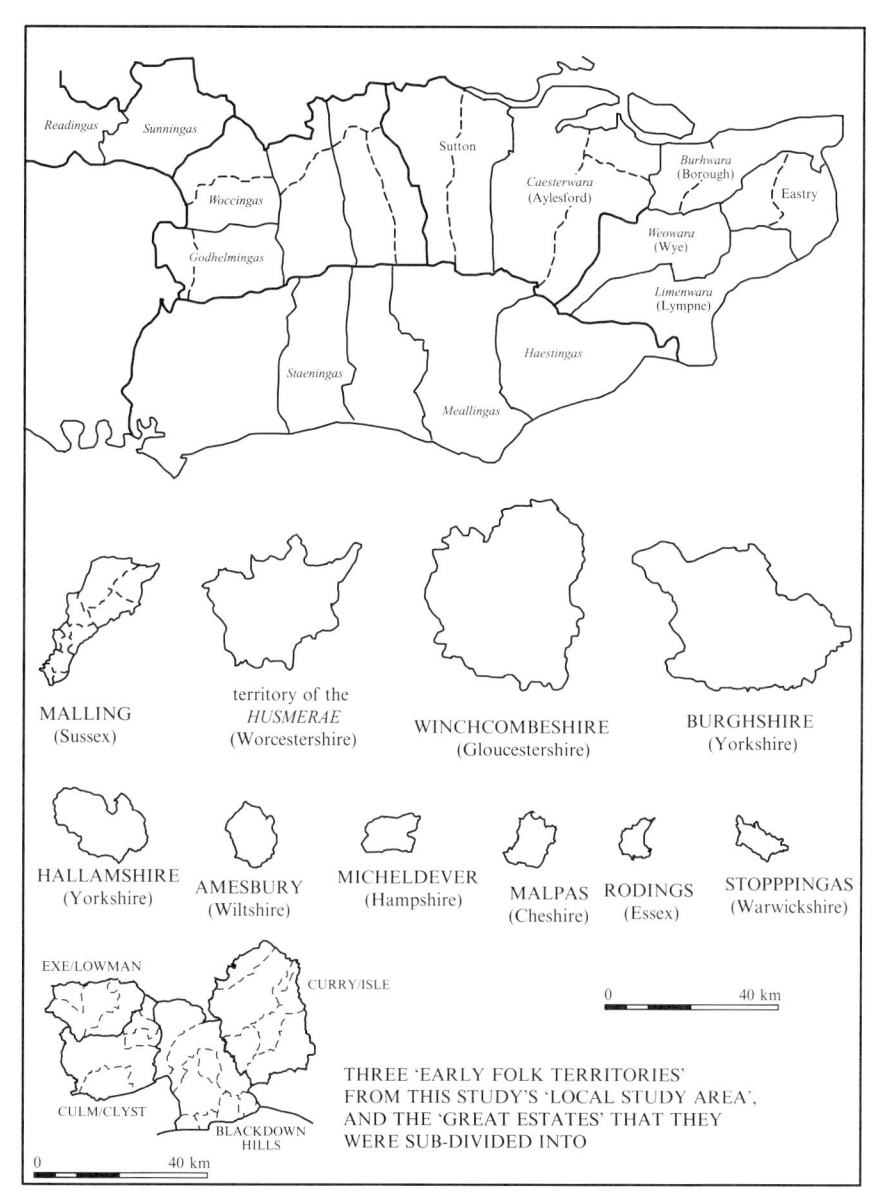

People in the landscape: the development of territorial structures 187

Fig. 10.1. A comparison of early territorial arrangements from across early medieval England with those reconstructed on and around the Blackdown Hills including the lathes, rapes and *regios* of Kent, Sussex, and Surrey (Blair 1989, fig. 4.2), Malling (Jones 1979, fig. 2.3), the *regio* of the *Husmerae* (Hooke 1998, fig. 14), Winchcombeshire (Bassett 1989b, fig. 1.1), Burghshire (Jones 1979, fig. 2.4), Hallamshire (Faith 1997, fig. 1), Amesbury (Hooke 1998, fig. 22), Micheldever (Hooke 1998, fig. 18), Malpas (Faith 1997, fig. 2), the Rodings and *regio* of the *Stoppingas* (Bassett 1989b, figs. 1.10–1.11).

'river estates' (Hoskins 1952, 303–4), 'multiple estates' (G. Jones 1979; 1985), 'land units' and 'federal estates' (Lewis *et al.* 1997, 9, 20, 90), 'federative estates' (Blair 1991, 24), 'archaic hundreds' (Klingelhöfer 1992), 'large terrains' (Fleming 1998b, 51), and 'folk-groups' (Blair 2005, 49). It is the concept of 'multiple estates' that is the mostly widely used but its value has been much debated as the model is based on Welsh law codes written down in the thirteenth century albeit possibly containing material from the early medieval period (Gregson 1986; Faith 2008; Winchester 2008). The main socio-economic principles and federative structures of these Welsh estates are the way that they embraced a range of environments resulting in specialized settlements that had a degree of interdependence, and a hierarchical structure with dues owed to a central place, which as an approach towards managing the landscape that is supported by the evidence both in Wales and elsewhere (including in this study). The problem with the term 'multiple estate', however, is that is has become inextricably linked with the legalistic and highly theoretical concepts of the Welsh law codes that were clearly distant in time and geographically from the rest of fifth- to eighth-century Britain.

There is also a problem with the use of the term 'estate' in the fifth to the seventh centuries, as it implies a concept of private ownership that is probably inappropriate for this period. While there were indeed large blocks of land that from the late seventh century were owned by an individual or institution—most notably kings and the church—this would probably not have been the case in the preceding two or three hundred years. Another problem with recent research into early medieval territorial organization is that it has tended to conflate two somewhat different phenomena: relatively large and informal districts covering many hundreds of square kilometres that may date to the fifth to seventh centuries, and more formal 'great estates' in the order of tens of square kilometres that had emerged by around the seventh to eighth centuries (Blair 1989, 105). This problem is clearly illustrated in the 'multiple estates' illustrated by Jones (1979) that range in size from Aberffraw (on Anglesey in Wales) covering $c.180$ km^2 to Burghshire (Yorkshire) that amounted to $c.900$ km^2 (Fig. 10.1).

Due to the problems with phrases such as *regiones* and 'multiple estates', a different set of terms is used in this study: 'early folk territories' and 'great estates'. The 'early folk territories' would not have been units of land ownership—they were not estates in the later sense of the term—but were territories within which communities had a common sense of identity. They embraced a range of environments and while focused on good agricultural land in lowland areas, they were often bounded with what would have been physically, environmentally, and psychologically 'marginal areas': uplands and wetlands that were sparsely settled and rarely visited. Around the late seventh or early eighth centuries, these early folk territories were subdivided into a number of smaller great estates that appear to have been the territories associated with

People in the landscape: the development of territorial structures 189

Table 10.1. The early folk territories and the 'great estates' into which they fragmented, as mapped in Figure 9.1 (acreages from the Tithe surveys of *c*.1840: Kain and Oliver 1995).

Early folk territory	acreages	km²	Great estate	acreage	km²
Carhampton/Williton	81,199	329 km²	Carhampton	53,379	216 km²
			Williton	27,820	113 km²
east of the Quantocks	86,337	349 km²	Cannington	19,848	80 km²
			Stogursey	18,270	74 km²
			Bridgwater	16,040	65 km²
			North Petherton	32,179	130 km²
Upper Exe	74,593	302 km²		74,593	302 km²
Exe/Lowman	53,155	216 km²	Tiverton	33,255	135 km²
			Halberton	19,900	81 km²
Culm/Clyst	75,689	307 km²	Silverton/Cullompton	49,271	200 km²
			Cliston	17,465	71 km²
			Uffculme and Culmstock	8,953	36 km²
Exeter/Exminster	90,676	367 km²	Exeter	38,821	157 km²
			Exminster	40,981	166 km²
			Teignton	10,874	44 km²
Otter/Exe Estuary	62,846	255 km²	East Budleigh	9,506	39 km²
			Ottery St Mary	12,381	50 km²
			Sudbury	11,501	47 km²
			Woodbury	29,458	119 km²
Blackdown Hills	106,089	429 km²	Axminster (+ Lyme Regis)	37,346	151 km²
			Axmouth	7,952	32 km²
			Colyton	28,434	115 km²
			Stockland	7,560	31 km²
			Hemyock	24,797	100 km²
Tone	99,991	405 km²	Taunton	10,821	44 km²
			Pitminster	9,269	38 km²
			North Curry	12,790	52 km²
			Lydeard	21,341	86 km²
			Wiveliscombe	17,894	72 km²
			Milverton	17,866	72 km²
			Wellington	10,010	41 km²
Curry/Isle	110,846	449 km²	'South Curry'	44,413	180 km²
			South Petherton	30,877	125 km²
			Chard	13,106	53 km²
			Crewkerne	22,450	91 km²
Coastal Dorset	96,798	390 km²	Whitchurch Canonicorum	20,336	82 km²
			Beaminster	14,450	58 km²
			Powerstock	5,980	24 km²
			Burton Bradstock	10,638	43 km²
			Litton Cheney	13,162	53 km²
			Abbotsbury	14,085	57 km²
			Wyke Regis	18,147	73 km²
Frome valley	61,988	252 km²	Dorchester	18,154	74 km²
			Frampton	10,883	44 km²
			Toller	15,479	63 km²
			Sydling St Nicholas	6,711	27 km²
			Charminster/Cerne	10,761	44 km²
Sturminster	68,234	277 km²	Sturminster	59,048	240 km²
			+ bit of Sherborne	9,186	37 km²
Upper Yeo	74,346	301 km²	Martock	37,944	154 km²
			Yetminster	23,122	94 km²
			Sherborne	13,280	54 km²

royal centres, and which in turn were broken up into the vills and manors recorded in Domesday, and it was this process that marked the emergence of a concept whereby individuals and institutions could own land.

Detailed evidence for those examples that fall within our local study area has been described in Chapter 9, and all of the folk territories and great estates that have been mapped across the regional study area (Fig. 9.1) are listed in Table 10.1. There are few discernable differences in their size or structure either side of the Blackdown Hills. The early folk territories identified here covered around 250–400 km^2 and are therefore at the smaller end of the scale for the 'small shires' that have been identified elsewhere in early medieval England such as Hallamshire (Yorkshire, c.250 km^2), Burghshire (Yorkshire, c.900 km^2), and Winchcombeshire (Gloucestershire, c.1,000 km^2) (Fig. 10.1). 'Banburyshire' in Oxfordshire may be another example (Faith 1997, 9; 2008). The early folk territories identified here may also have been equivalent to the 'lathes' of Kent such as Sutton (c.650 km^2) (Brookes 1989, fig. 4.2), folk or tribal groups such as the *Husmeræ* in Worcestershire (c.550 km^2: Hooke 1998, fig. 14), or other small tribal or kin groups that can be identified in areas of Anglo-Saxon settlement through their *-ingas* place-names (e.g. *Rēadingas* (Reading) in Berkshire: Fig. 10.1). Other folk-based place-names relating to similar sized territories include *-gē* (e.g. Eastry in Kent), *-wara* (e.g. the *Meonware*, 'the dwellers of the Meon', of southern Hampshire), and *-sæte* (e.g. *Magonsæte* in the West Midlands) (Everitt 1986; Gelling 1989, 199–201; Pretty 1989; Hooke 1998, 46). The 'rapes' of Sussex,[1] 'sokes' of East Anglia, and the 'small shires' and 'thanages' of northern England and Scotland may all have had similar origins (Brooks 1989, 69–74; Williamson 1993, 94; Blair 2005, 154), as might the *túath* in Ireland and *plebs* in Brittany, both terms meaning 'folk-territories' (Bassett 1989b, 1; Blair 2005, 155).

The term 'folk territory' was adopted in this study specifically to reflect the significance of community and kinship in early medieval society, which is illustrated, for example, in the development of law. In the early medieval period, a body of customary law common to a community—known as *eald riht* (old law, or *folcriht*, 'folkright')—was clarified and added to by royal initiative illustrated, for example, in the law codes of King Ine (688–725) of Wessex (Attenborough 1922, 115–17; Whitelock 1955, 364–72; Loyn 1984, 42, 43, 67; Faith 1997, 89–90). Folkright applied the law of land tenure, and land held according to folkright was known as *folcland* (folkland). In the early tenth century, King Edward the Elder attempted to establish effective royal supervision of folklaw, and at Exeter he laid down a set of decrees that were to be applied to the whole of his kingdom including a stipulation that each local royal official (reeve) was to hold a meeting every four weeks to hear lawsuits

---

[1] the 'rapes' of Sussex as described in Domesday are Norman lordships whose relationship to earlier territorial structures is unclear (Welch 1989, 79).

and to ensure that every man obtained the benefit of public law. These gatherings had authority over defined districts that particularly in Wessex were probably based on existing territories associated with a royal manor and administered by a reeve (Sawyer 1978, 197–200; Loyn 1984, 140).

THE ORIGINS OF THE EARLY FOLK TERRITORIES

At least three scenarios can be envisaged for the emergence of the folk territories: that they were Romano-British (or earlier) in origin, perhaps succeeding the administrative subdivisions of *civitates* known as *pagi*; that they were formed during the fifth to the seventh centuries following the cessation of Roman rule, or that they were created as administrative structures following the West Saxon conquest in the mid-seventh century. One way of providing a dating horizon is to examine their relationship to Roman roads as a number of previous studies have suggested that there is a stratigraphic relationship between dated linear features such as these and parish boundaries (e.g. Bonney 1972; 1979; Williamson 1986; Fowler 2000). One example was Leech's (1982a) analysis of the Fosse Way in Somerset which revealed that to the north and east of the river Parrett most parish boundaries follow the line of the road—that is, they appear to post-date it—whereas to the south they do not and so appear to pre-date it (Fig. 14.4). The reality, however, could be far more complicated as parish boundaries that follow the line of the road may result from the relatively late fragmentation of larger, earlier territories that could have pre-dated the road. On a first viewing of the evidence this does appear to be the case in the lowlands of central Somerset, where the southern boundary of Martock parish, for example, follows the Fosse Way, whereas the boundaries of the great estate and early folk territory within which Martock lay appear to pre-date the road (Aston 2007, fig. 2). A closer examination of the evidence, however, shows that the boundaries of the early folk territories in this area usually followed natural features such as rivers, and so even if the putative greater Martock estate came into existence after the Roman road was created, its boundaries would logically still have followed these natural landscape features.

With so many of the boundaries of great estates and early folk territories following natural features that pre-date the Roman road network, it is therefore difficult to draw any conclusions about their relative dates. To the west of the Blackdown Hills, however, the situation is different (Fig. 10.2). The Roman road from Honiton to Exeter is followed by a series of parish boundaries as well as the postulated boundary between the Culm/Clyst early folk territory to the north and the Exe/Otter territory to the south. There are only two places where

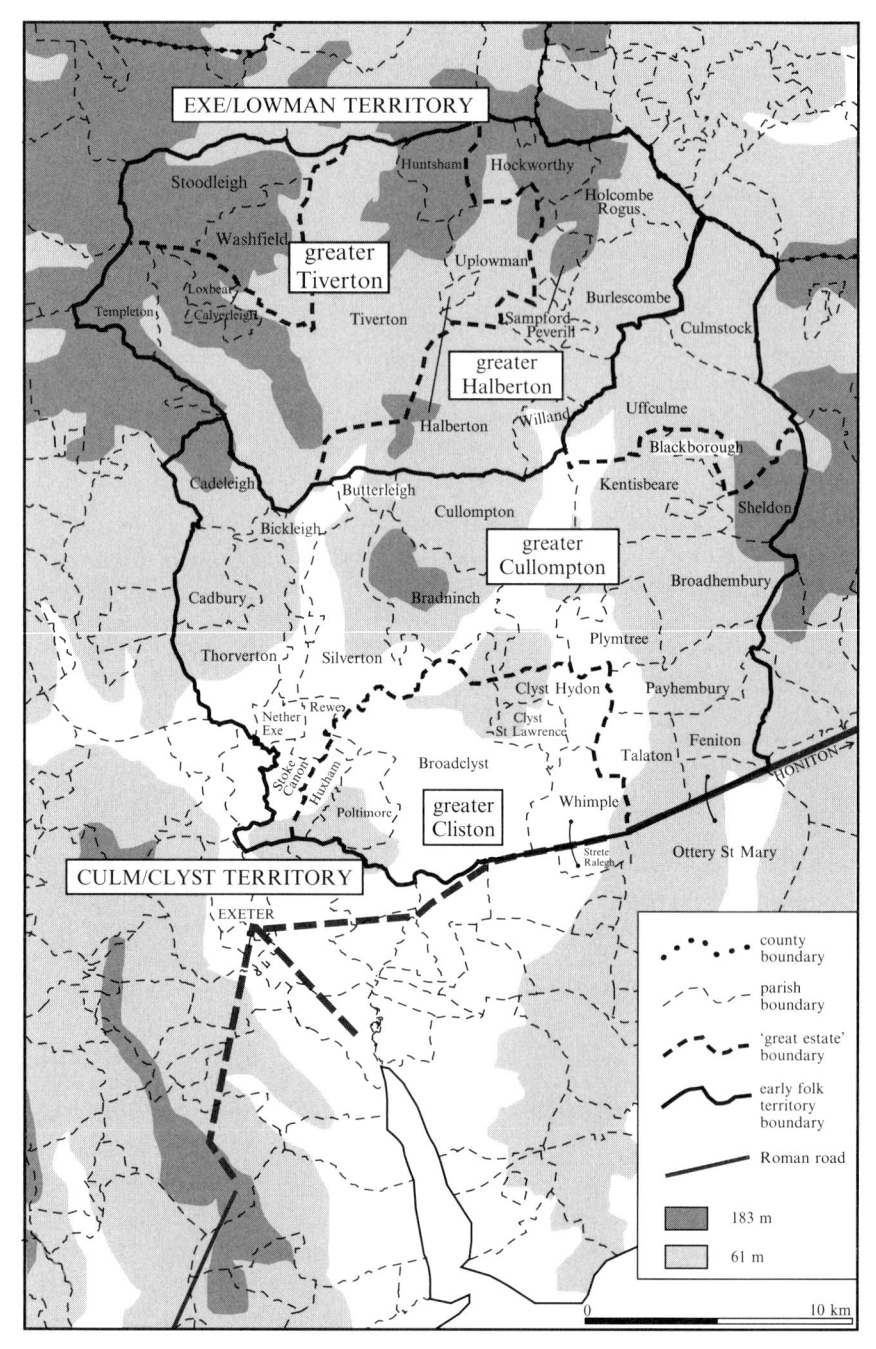

Fig. 10.2. The Exe/Lowman and Culm/Clyst early folk territories. Note how the Roman road from Exeter to Woodbury appears to cut across the parishes of Whimple and Ottery St Mary, but forms the boundary of Broadclyst and Talaton.

short stretches of parish boundary do not follow the road, although in both cases these appear to have been later changes (Feniton/Ottery St Mary and Whimple/ Strete Ralegh: *see* Chapter 9), and the original boundary of Culm/Clyst territory was, therefore, probably the Roman road, suggesting that is early Roman or later in date.

THE RELATIONSHIP OF EARLY FOLK TERRITORIES TO TOPOGRAPHY

Although the southern boundary of the Culm/Clyst territory appears to have run along a Roman road, the majority of early folk territory boundaries appear to have followed major natural features. The geology and topography of our region are extremely varied and it is not surprising, therefore, that the early folk territories embraced a wide variety of environments although in most cases their boundaries followed watersheds: the Culm/Clyst territory, for example, runs from the western edge of the Blackdown Hills, across the lowlands of eastern Devon, and up onto the Culm Measures. To the north, the Tone Valley territory runs from the uplands of the Brendon and Quantock Hills across the lowlands of the Vale of Taunton Deane, and up to the northern edge of the Blackdown Hills. To the east, in central Somerset, it is the Somerset Levels that provide the main physical framework of the landscape, with a series of long narrow wetlands that penetrate deep into the surrounding drylands. The Curry/Isle early folk territory, for example, occupies the dryland between the wetlands of West Sedgemoor and the Parrett valley while to the west it extended up onto the edge of Blackdown Hills. In using natural features such as these, the boundaries of the early territories went through landscapes that were physically challenging to pass through—wetlands and high ground—and were psychologically liminal (as reflected in the discussion of folklore in Chapter 3): stand in the Culm and Clyst valleys, and the well-wooded slopes of the Blackdown Hills and the Culm Measures loom dark and forbidding to the east and the west (e.g. Fig. 1.1).

THE 'GREAT ESTATES'

From the late seventh century, Anglo-Saxon charters start to record territorial divisions within the landscape that can be regarded as true estates in that they were the property of individuals or institutions. These blocks of land were granted by various kings initially to the church and later to leading lay members of society, and represent the breakup of larger territorial units that Williamson (1993, 92–104) and Dyer (2003, 27) call 'great estates'. These great estates were centred on a royal vill, were typically based in fertile agricultural areas, usually river valleys, and extended out into adjacent environments that may have supported specialist settlements in more peripheral areas such as low-lying wetland, upland summer pasture, or woodland. Where they can be reconstructed, their boundaries usually followed natural features such as rivers, or they ran through areas of unenclosed 'waste' on higher ground. In terms of their size, early estates on the Wessex chalklands, such as in the Avon and Test valleys, were around 100 km^2 (Hooke 1998, figs. 18 and 21), while some of the smaller *regiones* such as the *Hrothingas* (Rodings) in Essex (Fig. 10.1), *Stoppingas* in Warwickshire (Fig. 10.1), and Burnham, Cotessey, Hingham, and Wymondham in Norfolk (Williamson 1993, 93, 98) were around 40–60 km^2.

Dyer (2003, 30) suggests that the great estates were royal property and did not cover the entire landscape, as 'relatively small estates lay in the interstices of their larger neighbours' (although as the vast majority of early charters relate to grants by the king, any areas beyond these royal estates are undocumented and as a result, very poorly understood). In this study, in contrast, the systematic mapping of evidence for early territorial structures suggests that initially the whole landscape was divided up between a series of large great estates with a royal manor at their centre, although at this stage they may have been administrative districts and the territories from which dues were paid, rather than being units of land ownership in the modern sense. The size of these great estates varied considerably, although there is no evidence for a significant difference in this either side of the Blackdown Hills. Overall, it would appear that on and around the Blackdown Hills a series of early folk territories of around 250–400 km^2 were broken up into smaller great estates of around 30–200 km^2.

THE FRAGMENTATION OF 'GREAT ESTATES'

From the late seventh to the early eighth centuries, the great estates in turn started to fragment as successive kings granted land in perpetuity to the church (from the 670s) and noble families (from the 770s). These grants were of either *bookland*, which gave them complete security, or *loenland* (leasehold) usually in the form of a grant for three lives whereupon the land theoretically returned to the lord, although in practice the lease was usually renewed (Faith 1997, 159–61; Dyer 2003, 29–30). The estates granted in these charters were often assessed as around fifty or even one hundred hides, and where the estates can be reconstructed they covered tens of square kilometres. To place this figure of fifty to one hundred hides in context, the parishes in our study area contained manors that on average were assessed as 5.73 hides in Domesday, although they ranged from under one to over thirty hides depending on their size.

This process of fragmentation accelerated from around the mid-ninth century, and while some of the estates received by the church survived intact, forming large manors of thirty hides or more, others were progressively subdivided into smaller holdings typically of one to five hides (e.g. for Dorset: Costen 2008, 61; Oxfordshire: Blair 1994, 133; Somerset: Costen 1992a, 113–33; Surrey: Blair 1991, 30–4). The boundaries of these manors—occasionally recorded in charter boundary clauses—are often the same as those of ecclesiastical parishes, although as the fragmentation of estates progressed, many were subdivided into even smaller units in what Blair (1994, 133) describes as 'the creation of the English country gentry: a new class of small resident proprietors for whom manorial fragmentation provided an economic base'. Some of the earliest estates to have been detached may have lain towards the periphery of the great estates, such as Uffculme and Culmstock in the Culm/Clyst territory (Fig. 10.2; Table 10.2), Chard and Chardstock in greater South Petherton, and Hemyock in the Blackdown Hills territory. The tendency for peripheral areas of an estate to be detached first is also seen in the fragmentation of the great estates themselves. In greater Cliston, for example, the large parish of Cliston (Broadclyst) lies at the centre of the great estate with a series of smaller parishes around its periphery that were probably the earliest parts to be detached (Clyst Hydon, Clyst St Lawrence, Whimple, Poltimore, and Huxham). If we examine Domesday, we can see how this fragmentation had progressed even further, with a series of small estates being carved out of the peripheral areas of Broadclyst itself (Ashclyst, Clyst Gerred, Columbjohn, and West Clyst).

It is also noticeable how many of these peripheral estates included places with a '-stock' name (e.g. Chardstock and Culmstock), to which can be added Stoke Canon in the far south-west of the Culm/Clyst territory, and Stocklinch on the very eastern edge of the South Curry estate. There is also a 'Stockham Hill' on the OS 1st Edn 6" map in Branscombe (Gover *et al.*'s (1932, 621) suggestion that it is associated with the Stottcombe family first recorded in 1524 is not convincing). 'Colstock' (Colestock) is recorded in Feniton in 1675 (Gover *et al.* 1932, 563), in the far south-east corner of the Culm/Clyst territory. Stockland, on the Blackdown Hills, may mean 'newly cultivated land at Stoke [OE *stoc*]' (Watts 2004, 576), and within this

Table 10.2. The fragmentation of the Culm/Clyst folk territory (and *see* Fig.10.2).

Great estate	parish	parish acreage	manor	hidage	ploughlands
Cullompton	Silverton	4,714	Silverton	never paid tax [c.13h?]	41
			Combe Sackville	1h	3
			Greenslinch	3v	3
			Yard	1v	0.5
	Silverton or Bradninch		Bernardsmoor	0.5h	3
			Monk Culm (part of Silverton)	1h	4
	Thorverton	4,037	Nether Exe	1h 1v	8
			Raddon	2.5v	3
			Raddon	1v	2
	Cadbury	1,899	Cadbury	3v	5
			Bowley	0.5h	2
	Cadeleigh	2,191	Cadeleigh	1h	7
			Cadeleigh	3v	3
			Dart	1h	6
	Rewe	1,341	Rewe	1h	5
			Up Exe	1v	3
	Stoke Canon	1,217	Stoke Canon	1h	6
	Bickleigh	1,835	Bickleigh	1h	8
			Burn	1v	0.5
			Chitterley	3v	4
	Butterleigh	479	Butterleigh	1v	2
	Cullompton	7,370	(part of Silverton)		
			Cullompton church	1h	1
			Colebrook	0.5h	2
			Hillersdon	0.5h	3
			Langford	1h 3v	6
			Ponsford	0.5h	2
			Ponsford	0.5h	2
	Bradninch	4,351	Bradninch	2.5 (* see below [c.6h?])	20
	Kentisbeare	3,720	Kentisbeare	1v	2
			Kentisbeare	0.5h	4
			Aller	1h	10
			Aller	1v	2
			Blackborough	1h 1v	3
			Blackborough	0.5h	2
			Blackborough	0.5h	2
			Kingsford	0.5v	0.5
			Orway	0.5h	3
			Pirzwell	1h 1v	4
	Sheldon	1,681	Sheldon	1h	6
	Plymtree	2,185	Plymtree	2h 1v	5
			Clyst William	0.5h	0.5

			Woodbeare	1h	4
	Broadhembury	4,703	Broadhembury	4h	14
			Kerswell	2h	8
			Shapcombe	1h	4
	Payhembury	2,698	Payhembury	2h	8
			Payhembury	1h	2
			Cheriton	1h	2
			Tale	1h	4
			Tale	1.5h	3
	Talaton	2,365	Talaton	7h	16
	Feniton	1,822	Feniton	3h	6
			Curscombe	1h	4
sub-total 'greater Cullompton'		48,608		40.125h	155
Uffculme	Uffculme	6,122	Uffculme	14h	30
	Culmstock	3,494	Culmstock	5h	15
sub-total 'greater Uffculme'		9,616		19	45
unlocated (in Silverton Hundred)			*Hewise*	0.5h	1
			Stochelie	1v	2
Cliston	Broadclyst	9,188	Broadclyst	9.5 h	35
			Ashclyst	1h 0.5v	9
			Clyst Gerred	3h 1v	8
			Columbjohn	3v	3
			West Clyst	2.5h	3
	Clyst Hydon	1,725	Clyst Hydon	3h	8
			Aunk	3h	7
	Clyst St Lawrence	1,060	Clyst St Lawrence	4h	7
	Whimple	3,019	Whimple	2h 1v	10
			Whimple (Cobbeton)	1h 0.5v	4
			Larkbeare	0.5h	2
	Poltimore	1,711	Poltimore	0.5h 1f	2
			Poltimore (Cutton)	3h 1v 3f	9
	Huxham	762	Huxham	3.5v	6
Sub-total 'Greater Cliston'		17,465		35.88h	113

* Bradninch: the 2.5 hides equate to an enormous 20 ploughlands suggesting that a large area did not pay tax (and so was not hidated); this was also the case in neighbouring Silverton where Domesday states that this is the case.

parish there is also a 'Haystocke' (now Heathstock) documented in 1606 (Gover *et al.* 1932, 648). Two farms called Stockwell (possibly documented from 1543 as *Stokhill*: Gover *et al.* 1932, 557, 571) are divided by the Bradninch–Silverton parish boundary. There is also a Bystock in the far east of Withycombe Raleigh, up on the poor sandy soils that are still dominated by the unenclosed Woodbury Common ('Boystok' in 1242: Gover *et al.* 1932, 600).

HUNDREDS: THE ADDITION OF SECULAR ADMINISTRATIVE RESPONSIBILITIES

As the Anglo-Saxon kings started to increase their authority, various administrative structures were established including subdivisions of the shires known as hundreds. In areas such as the Midlands, hundreds appear to have been newly created in the mid-tenth century and were close to being one hundred hides, although such regularity is not found south of the Thames: in Wiltshire, for example, the Domesday hundreds varied from 11 to 195 hides (Sawyer 1978, 197). Such irregularity was also seen in Devon, Dorset, and Somerset where it was clearly due in part to changes made to hundred boundaries after they were created, for example, through the construction of small and sometimes sprawling 'private' hundreds such as Kingsbury in Somerset which was made up of the estates of the bishops of Bath and Wells (*see* Chapter 9: Yorke 1995, 126). While the first explicit reference to hundreds is under King Edgar (957–75), when along with the shires they were given more formal administrative and judicial responsibilities, it is likely that in Wessex at least they were created through the 'reshuffling' of existing social and political institutions' (Reynolds 1999, 65). Yorke (1995, 125) suggests that 'it is likely that there was no one point at which hundreds were created in Wessex, rather they were a natural evolution from earlier administrative arrangements whereby estates were grouped together for fiscal and other royal demands and supervised from a king's *tun* or royal vill' (and *see* Faith 1997, 118). Indeed, Reynolds (2009) has shown that from the late seventh or early eighth centuries there is increasing evidence that the location of execution cemeteries show a very strong relationship with later hundred boundaries. In Wessex, at least, other evidence for the mid-tenth-century hundreds having been based on earlier administrative structures include meetings that resemble hundred courts being recorded under Edward the Elder (899–924), and the 'folkmoots' under Alfred (871–899). The Laws of Ine (688–726) even make reference to a judicial territory of one hundred hides: 'If anyone is accused of homicide and he wishes to deny the deed with an oath, there shall be in the 100 hides one entitled to give a king's oath' (Attenborough 1922, 55). The evidence from our study area in Devon and Somerset certainly suggests a strong correlation between the Domesday hundreds and the 'great estates' into which the larger early medieval folk territories were subdivided (Fig. 9.1).

ECCLESIASTICAL ADMINISTRATION: MINSTER *PAROCHIAE*

In addition to assuming secular administrative functions as hundreds, it appears that the 'great estates' within our study area were also used as religious jurisdictions. In recent decades a consensus has developed that from the late seventh to the ninth centuries there emerged a series of 'minster' churches, often located at royal centres (*villae regiae*), whose *parochiae* were coterminous with early territorial structures that were also used in creating hundreds during the tenth century (e.g. in Hampshire: Hase 1988; 1994; Surrey: Blair 1991, 104; Wiltshire: Pitt 2003, 62). When a minster was established at Wootton Wawen, in Warwickshire, for example, the land it was granted lay 'within the boundaries established by the ancient possessors' (Hooke 1998, 70). It is argued that these minsters provided pastoral care for the population of their *parochiae*, and that these large territories then fragmented into the small local parishes with which we are familiar today (e.g. Morris 1989, 93–167; Blair 1992, 227–31; 1994, 61–3; Costen 1992a, 105; Hall 2000, 49; Bassett 2006). In the 1990s, however, doubts started to be expressed about this traditional 'minster model', with disagreement focused on when the minsters gained a pastoral role for their wider region: some have suggested that they had this function from the very start, while others argue that the large *parochiae* were only tenth century in origin, being created by the West Saxon kings as they re-asserted their authority following the Viking incursions (e.g. Cambridge and Rollason 1995; *see* Blair 1995 for a response).

Early medieval documents make frequent reference to early churches using the Latin *monasterium* and the Old English *mynster*, and though it is easy to assume that these refer respectively to 'enclosed and primarily contemplative communities living a clear-cut normative role' (i.e. monasteries in the later medieval sense), and a group of priests who served the pastoral needs of a local community (i.e. a minster), in the early medieval period the words referred simply to any religious establishment with a church (Blair 2005, 3, 80). A key question is the extent to which these religious communities interacted with the wider local population within a framework of 'mutual obligations' that are so familiar in the late- and post-medieval periods in the form of parochial allegiance: pastoral care provided by a priest in return for financial support (tithes) (Blair 2005, 153). When documentary sources become more abundant from the twelfth century, it is clear that there had once been two tiers of parishes: small, local ones that still existed and with which we are still familiar, and what by then was an obsolete layer of older and larger parishes (i.e. the *parochiae*) evidenced by payments and other recurrent obligations from what had been a 'daughter' church (i.e. a chapelry) to a 'mother' church (i.e. the minster) (Morris 1989, 128–9; Blair 2005, 153). Law codes of 1014 and 1020–21 describe this hierarchical structure of churches with 'head minsters' (i.e. cathedrals), 'rather smaller minsters', 'one still smaller where there is little service but there is a graveyard' (presumably representing the numerous thegn's churches that were evolving into the parish churches of today), and a 'field church where there is no graveyard' (i.e. a chapel that was dependent on another church for the administering of the sacraments: Blair 2005, 368). These 'rather smaller minsters' would therefore appear to be the remains of a network of churches with vested rights of parochial allegiance and church dues that existed before the eleventh century, serving communities across large *parochiae* that in the tenth century were in the process of being broken up as local manorial churches acquired their responsibilities and income (Morris 1989, 140; Blair 2005, 160). Blair argues convincingly that these law codes of 1014 describe an ecclesiastical hierarchy that was in a state of change, with the 'rather smaller minsters' being replaced by local churches, and it hardly seems credible that a system of *parochiae* created a few decades before, in the tenth century, disintegrated so quickly. Contrary to the revisionism of the 1990s, it would appear, therefore, that there were indeed a series of minster churches and large *parochiae* in the eighth and ninth centuries.

There are two schools of thought with regard to the extent of these *parochiae*, with some arguing that they only covered part of the landscape (e.g. Hall's (2000) study of Dorset) while others have suggested that every part of the landscape was part of a Parish which meant that the entire rural population was served by a community of priests (e.g. Hase's (1988) work in Hampshire). It is generally the case that the minster territories as far as we can reconstruct them today are generally smaller than the great estates, but the evidence we have varies from county to county with marked differences in, for example, the degree to which churches still had dependent chapels by the sixteenth century (this being far more common in Somerset, for example, than in Devon). This lack of comprehensive evidence for the extent of these early monster *parochiae* means that it is impossible to tell whether they ever covered the entire landscape, although the link with *villae regiae* does seem clear.

ECONOMIC TERRITORIALITY

Another aspect of territoriality within the landscape is that of economic hinterlands, which can be reconstructed from a variety of archaeological and documentary evidence, and through these we can examine the effect that the Blackdown Hills had upon the movement of people and goods. Saint White Down, to the east of the Blackdowns in Cricket St Thomas, for example, was the site of a particularly well-documented fair from the fourteenth century whose hinterland was clearly restricted to the west by the Blackdowns (Fig. 10.3). Kowaleski's (1995, 274–324) study of Exeter in the late fourteenth century shows a similar phenomenon with its links extending far greater distances to the west and south of the city than to the east (Fig. 10.3).

Unfortunately, there is very little material culture from the early medieval period, although it is very noticeable that the distribution of fifth- and sixth-century imports from the Mediterranean is spread across various locations along the coastal seaboard of South West England but not to the east of the Blackdown Hills (material from central Somerset appearing to have come in via the Bristol Channel: *see* Chapter 14). For the later medieval period, Jope's (1963, Fig. 65) work suggested that some artefact types were found both to the east and to the west of the Blackdown Hills, but subsequent work has shown that the products of specific industries had a more limited distribution. One example is the thirteenth- to late fifteenth-century Exeter fabric 40 that was made in the Exe Valley and which was amongst the finest medieval pottery in South West England. It has been found widely across eastern and southern Devon but although it reached Cleeve Abbey and Taunton in western Somerset (Allan 1984, 5–6, fig. 5; 1999, 40), it did not penetrate east of the Parrett estuary or the Blackdown Hills.[2] Similarly, in the early post-medieval period, North Devon wares are significant as far east as the lowlands of eastern Devon (e.g. in Tiverton, Nether Exe and Exeter) but are absent further east, although this could be explained by the presence of competing industries based in southern Somerset. By the sixteenth century nearly all of Exeter's coarsewares came from what has traditionally been referred to as the 'South Somerset' industry (Coleman-Smith and Pearson 1988; Allan 1984, fig. 59; 1994, fig. 1). More recent work, however, has identified other potential kiln sites in and around the Blackdown Hills (Allan 2003), one of which has recently been excavated at Hemyock. Without extensive scientific testing it is impossible to establish whether a 'South Somerset ware' sherd was in fact from Donyatt, to the east of the Blackdown Hills, or Honiton and Hemyock on their western flanks (Allan 1998, 46; 2003). Chert-tempered Exeter fabric 20, a variant of which has been identified as 'Membury-type ware', also appears to have been produced on the Blackdown Hills (Allan and Langman 2002).

---

[2] It is absent from Bickley (Ponsford 2002), Bleadon (Young 2007), Cheddar (Evans and Hancocks 2005), Glastonbury (Woods 1994), Shapwick (Gerrard with Aston 2007), South Brent (Young 2009), and West Wick in Banwell (Powell 2009).

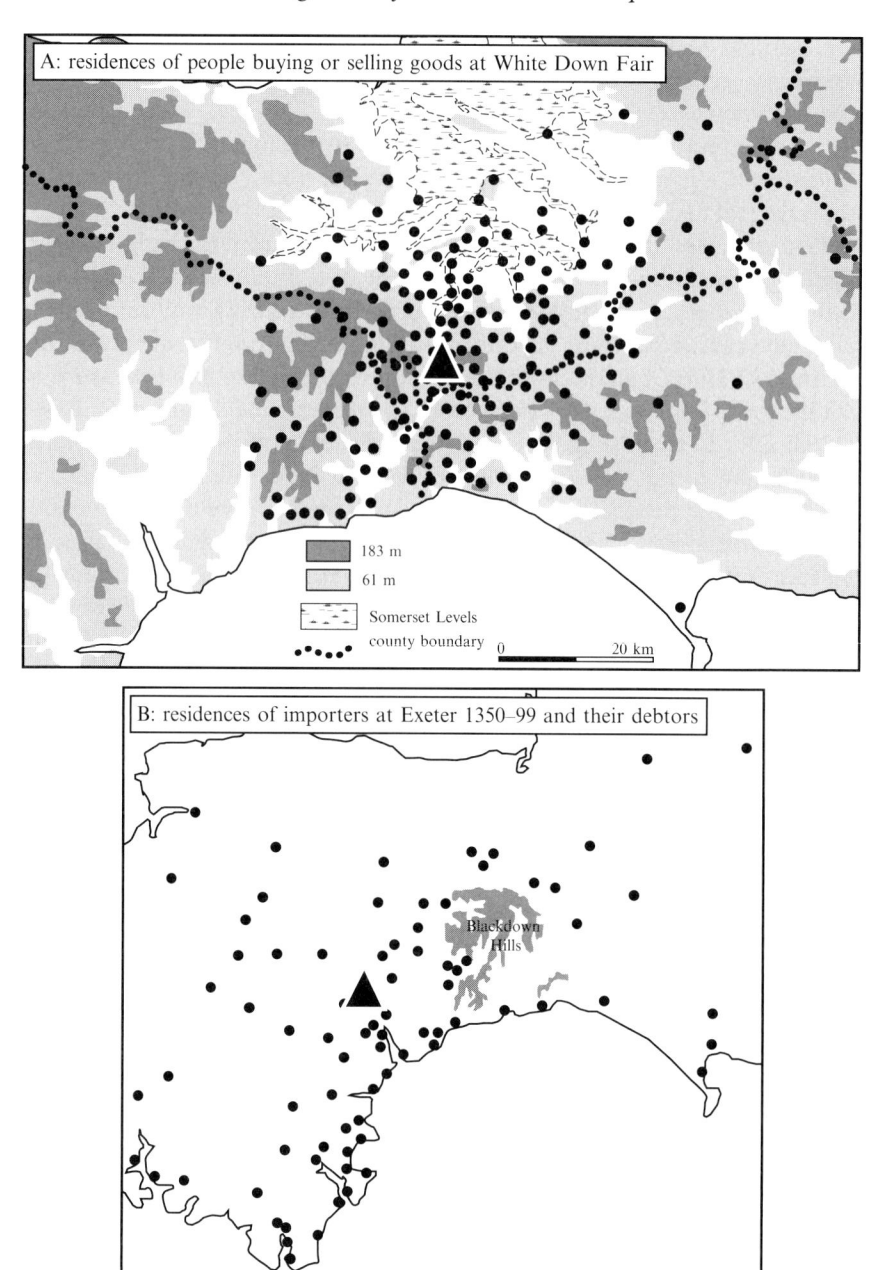

Fig. 10.3. The impact of the Blackdown Hills on the movement of people. (A) The trading influence of Saint White Down fair 1637–49 reflected in the residences of people buying or selling goods (after Hamer 1968, fig. 1); (B) the importers of goods into Exeter 1350–99 and their debtors (Kowaleski 1995, fig. 6.1).

THE MOVEMENT OF PEOPLE WITHIN THE LANDSCAPE

The extent to which members of medieval peasant society moved between regions can be studied through the surnames recorded in records such as the Lay Subsidies for 1327 and 1332 that survive for Devon (Erskine 1969), Dorset (Mills 1971), and Somerset (Dickinson 1889). When looking at the personal names recorded across our local study area it is immediately apparent that of those incorporating recognizable place-names, the vast majority are local: in Yarcombe, for example we find William de Knyghtesheg, Walter ate Mershe, and Walter Wyllingbere, whose names are preserved as Knightshayne Farm, the hamlet of Marsh, and Williambeer Farm (Erskine 1969, 45–6; Gover *et al.* 1932, 651). A number of parishes, however, contain names from further afield and these do suggest that the Blackdown Hills were, to a certain extent, a barrier to population movement as in Somerset parishes the vast majority of place-name-related surnames are from areas to the east of the Blackdowns, while in Devon the names are from areas to the west. A very small number of names do suggest some movement across the hills—such as Johanne de Halberton in Stocklinch and Johanne de Poultymor [Poltimore] in Combe St Nicholas (Dickinson 1889, 189, 195)—but these are rare.

DISCUSSION: TERRITORIALITY AND LANDSCAPE CHARACTER

So what does this tell us about the origins and development of regional variation in landscape character? So far in this study we have seen very clear differences either side of the Blackdown Hills such as medieval villages to the east, and more dispersed settlement patterns to the west. Such differences did not emerge in a vacuum, but rather within the spatial context of socially constructed territories based upon community and lordship. Our study area lies within western Wessex and appears to follow a pattern that is evident elsewhere in early medieval Britain of large territorial units—that we have called early folk territories—being subdivided into great estates, that in turn were broken up into smaller estates that were granted to the church and the king's supporters and which became the manors and vills recorded in Domesday. These great estates appear to have served as units for civil administrations—predecessors to the system of hundreds—and may also have been coterminous with ecclesiastical *parochiae*.

This reconstruction of the early folk territories and great estates was based upon a wide range of documentary, place-name, and cartographic evidence that when combined produced webs of territorial links that bound discrete areas together. When plotted these territories usually had watersheds or extensive wetland areas as their boundaries, exemplified by the Curry/Isle territory that stretched from the Somerset Levels up onto the eastern fringes of the Blackdown Hills, and the Culm/Clyst territory that extended from the fringes of the Culm Measures, down to the lowlands of eastern Devon, and up onto the western fringes of the Blackdown Hills. One aspect of this reconstruction that is of particular interest, however, is that the central area of the Blackdowns appears to have been occupied by a separate early folk territory rather than having been simply the upland areas of otherwise largely lowland territories: in the early medieval period there appears to have been a distinct people of the Blackdown Hills. Also of interest is the relationship—or rather, lack of any relationship—between the early folk territories and the great estates into which they fragmented, and the differences in landscape character described in Chapters 4–7. The Curry/Isle early folk territory, and Greater South Curry, greater South Petherton, and greater Crewkerne estates that were carved out of it, all extended from the lowlands of central Somerset up to the fringes of the Blackdown Hills and the Dorset Ridgeway, but in the later medieval period they all included landscapes characterized by both villages and open fields, and dispersed settlement patterns associated with predominantly enclosed fields. This is also seen to the west of the Blackdown Hills where the distribution of small villages and open fields similarly bears no relationship whatsoever to the reconstructed early folk territories and great estates. This gives rise to three possibilities as to the relationship between these early medieval territorial arrangements and the reorganization of the landscape in order to create villages and open fields. The first is that villages and open fields were laid out before the creation of the early folk territories and great estates and their presence/absence had no effect on where the boundaries of these districts were located; this seems highly implausible as all the evidence we have both from our study area and elsewhere in England is that settlement nucleation and the associated reorganization of field systems happened in the eighth to the tenth centuries. The second possibility is that villages and open fields were created as part of a landscape reorganization that saw the early folk territories broken up into a series of great estates, but this can also be dismissed such is the lack of correlation between the distribution of villages and open fields and the great estates. The third possibility, therefore, is that villages and open fields were created after these great estates had themselves started to fragment into the multiplicity of manors that are recorded through Anglo-Saxon charters and the Domesday survey. This possibility fits the evidence, and will be discussed further in Chapter 15.

11

Patterns of land use: documentary evidence and palaeoenvironmental sequences

So far in this study we have explored how, in the medieval and post-medieval periods, there were very different patterns of settlement and field systems, styles of domestic houses, and suites of place and field-names, either side of the Blackdown Hills, and we have seen that there is no obvious explanation for this in the structure of the early medieval great estates or the early folk territories that appear to have preceded them. In the next three chapters, therefore, we will turn to another facet of landscape character—land use—in order to explore its relationship to the Blackdown Hills. In particular we will consider whether the regional farming systems that historians have identified in the post-medieval period were simply the product of relatively recent changes in the economy and society, or whether they reflect more deeply rooted differences in how local communities exploited their environment.

Today, there are many different patterns of agricultural management across our study area: the plateaus and valleys of the Blackdown Hills, for example, are a largely pastoral landscape with the steeper slopes cloaked in woodland, while to east in the lowlands of central Somerset, arable land is dominant with very little woodland. In the Vale of Taunton Deane and the lowlands of eastern Devon there is a mixed pattern of arable cultivation and pasture, while in marked contrast, the Culm Measures of western Devon are predominantly pasture, and the chalk downlands of Wessex are predominantly arable. The question to be explored here is whether these regions are inherently suited to these farming practices, so providing a degree of stability in historic landscape character, or whether the present patterns of agriculture simply reflect current technology and market conditions. In favour of stability is the fact that some crops grow better on particular soils with barley, for example, preferring lighter soils and wheat producing the best yields on heavier soils. Livestock are suited to certain types of landscape, with sheep ideal for the steep slopes and thin soils of upland areas, and cattle preferring the lush grassland of heavier soils in the lowlands. It is equally clear, however, that patterns of land use have changed significantly over time, for example, sheep farming replacing arable cultivation in some areas during the late medieval period as falling grain prices and the rising value of wool led to a shift from arable land to pasture (Dyer 2003). So did the *pays* of South West Britain have certain inherent properties with regards to their agriculture, or are the regional differences in land use observable in the recent past simply the product of current agrarian technology and market conditions?

STUDYING PAST PATTERNS OF LAND USE AT A *PAYS* LEVEL

From the eleventh century onwards, studying patterns of land use is relatively straightforward as there is a wide range of written sources that provide both quantitative and qualitative information. Other evidence comes from the plant and animal remains preserved on some archaeological sites and in natural deposits such as peat bogs. This archaeological and palaeoenvironmental material is the only source of data we have before the eleventh century. In the past, most archaeological studies of food consumption in the Roman and medieval periods have focused on variations between sites of different status such as towns, rural settlements, and military sites (e.g. Grant 1988; King 1999; Albarella and Davis 1994; Albarella 2005; Van der Veen 2008; Van der Veen *et al.* 2007; 2008), rather than variations in farming practice between different regions. A recent volume, *Food in Medieval England* (Woolgar *et al.* 2006a), provides a good example of this with a series of papers studying how patterns in the consumption of cereals, meat, and other foodstuffs varied on sites of different social status, and how these patterns changed over time, but with only passing references to the possibility that there may have been regional variation. The comment, 'There are some indications of variations in diet on a regional basis, but it is less marked in these studies than might have been expected' (Woolgar *et al.* 2006b, 274) is a reflection of how the data have not been systematically analysed. This study will, therefore, have as its focus a comparison of cereal cultivation and animal husbandry within a series of different *pays*, and in particular will explore whether regional variations in farming practices that are so well documented in the post-medieval period can be traced back into earlier times.

Such is the scarcity of good archaeological assemblages and medieval documentary sources that the regional study area did not contain sufficient data and so the whole of Cornwall, Devon, Dorset, Somerset, and Wiltshire have been included. Whilst this extended study area did produce sufficient data for most *pays*, the scarcity of material in Cornwall and the west of Devon led to this area being treated as one. To summarize, the *pays* are (Fig. 11.1):

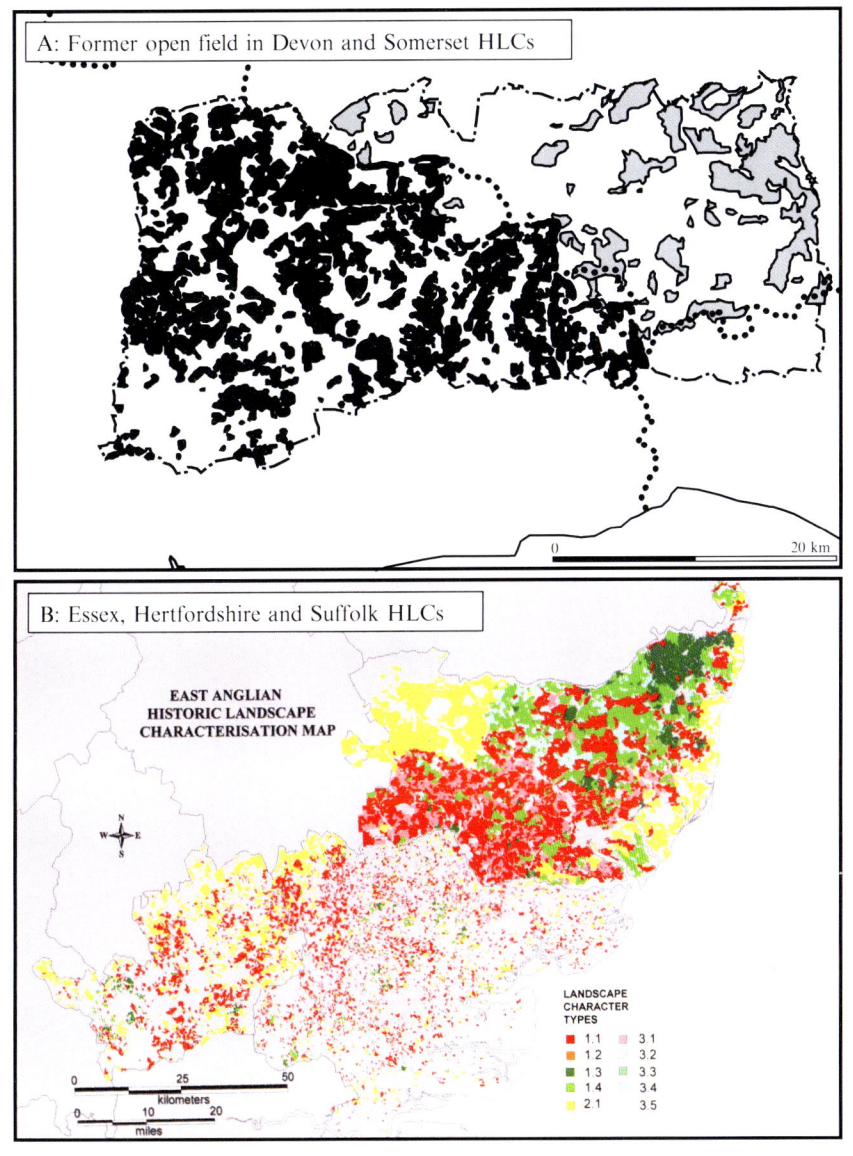

Plate 1. The extent of former open field mapped in the Somerset and Devon HLCs, and HLCs for Hertfordshire, Essex, and Suffolk.

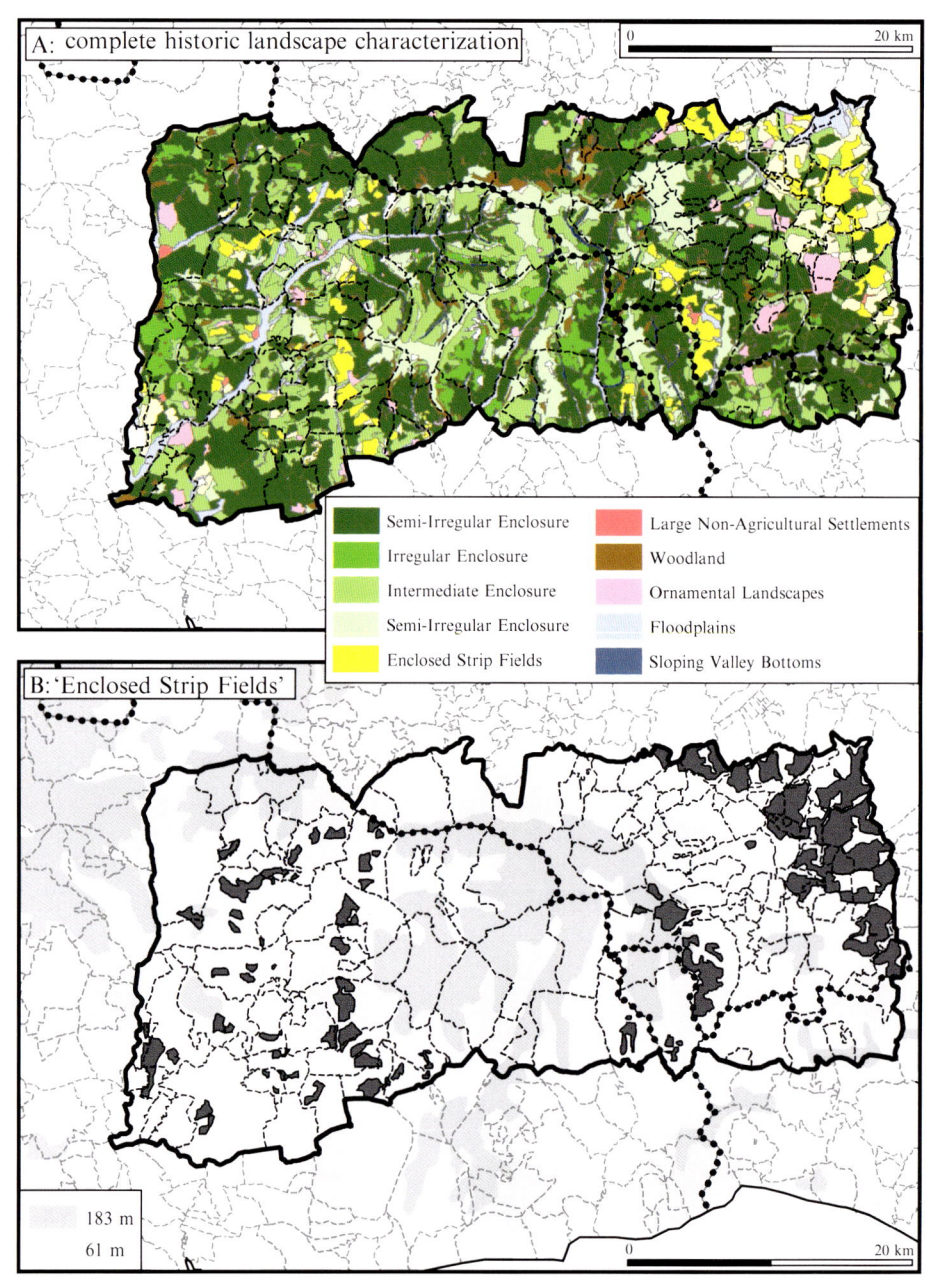

Plate 2. The historic landscape characterization carried out as part of this study, and the historic landscape character type 'enclosed strip fields'.

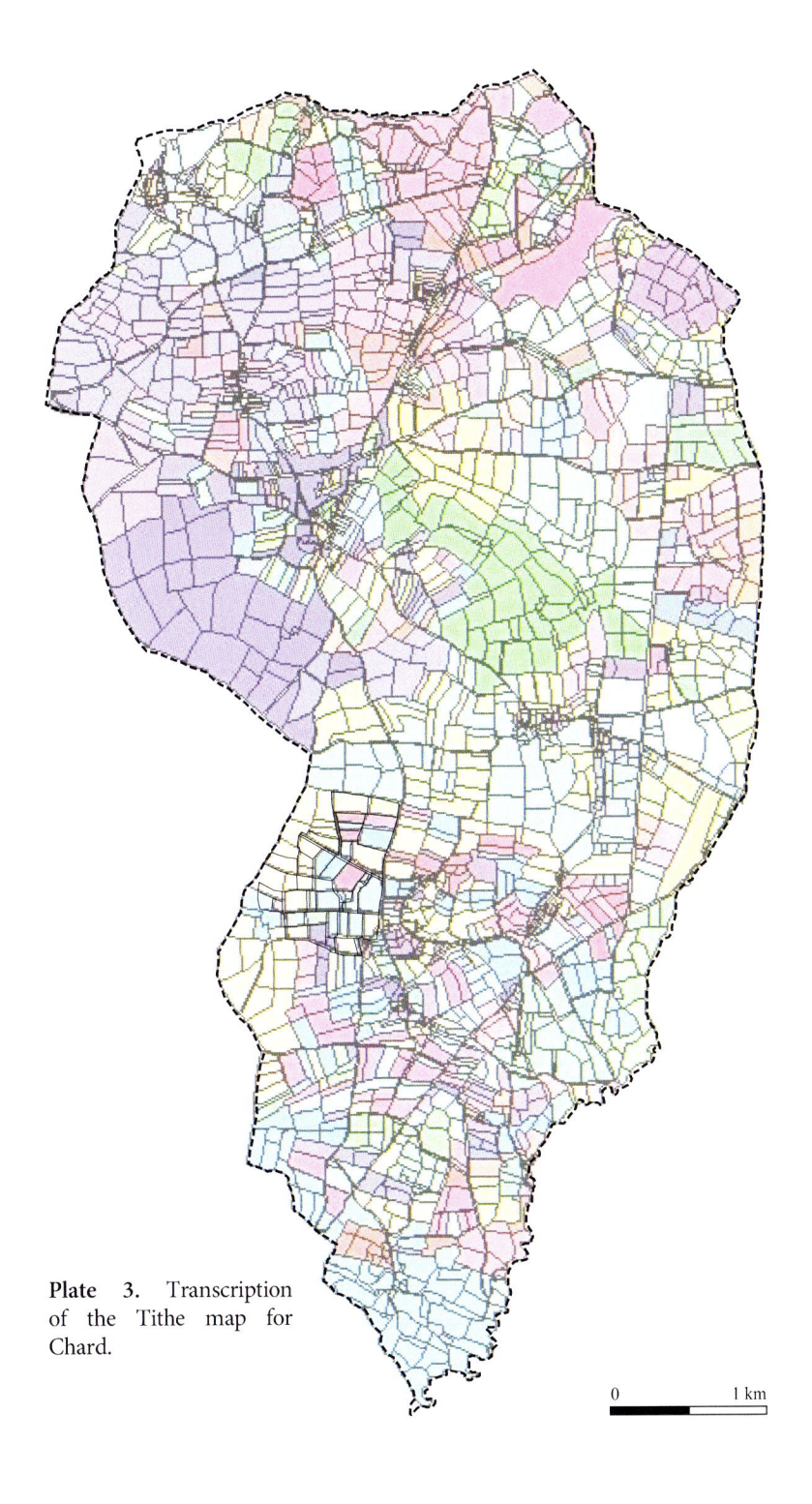

Plate 3. Transcription of the Tithe map for Chard.

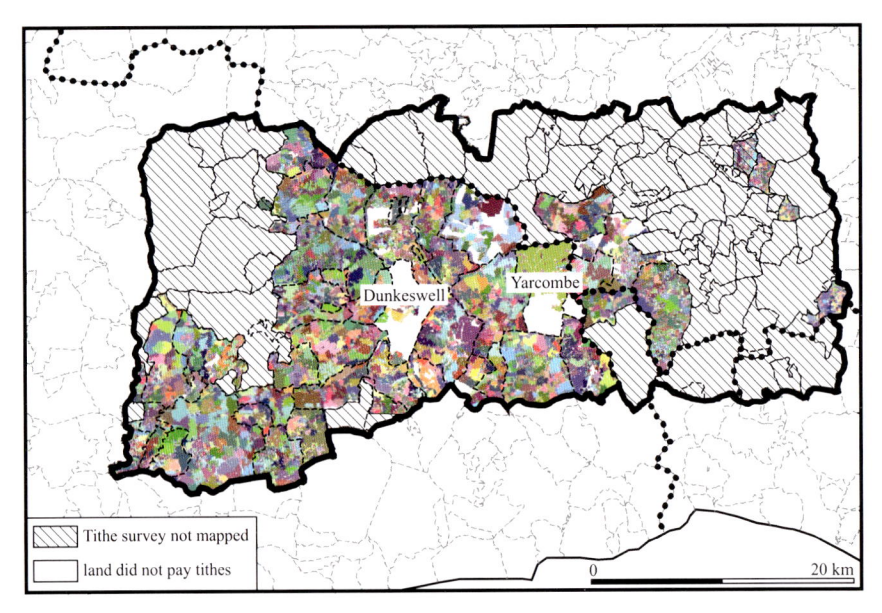

Plate 4. Parishes in the local study area for which data on land ownership and land occupancy have been mapped based on the Tithe surveys of *c*.1840.

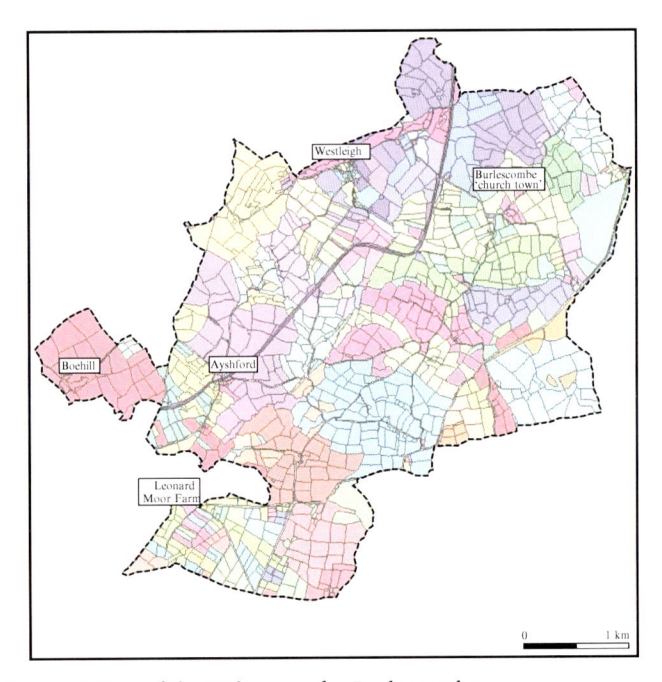

Plate 5. Transcription of the Tithe map for Burlescombe.

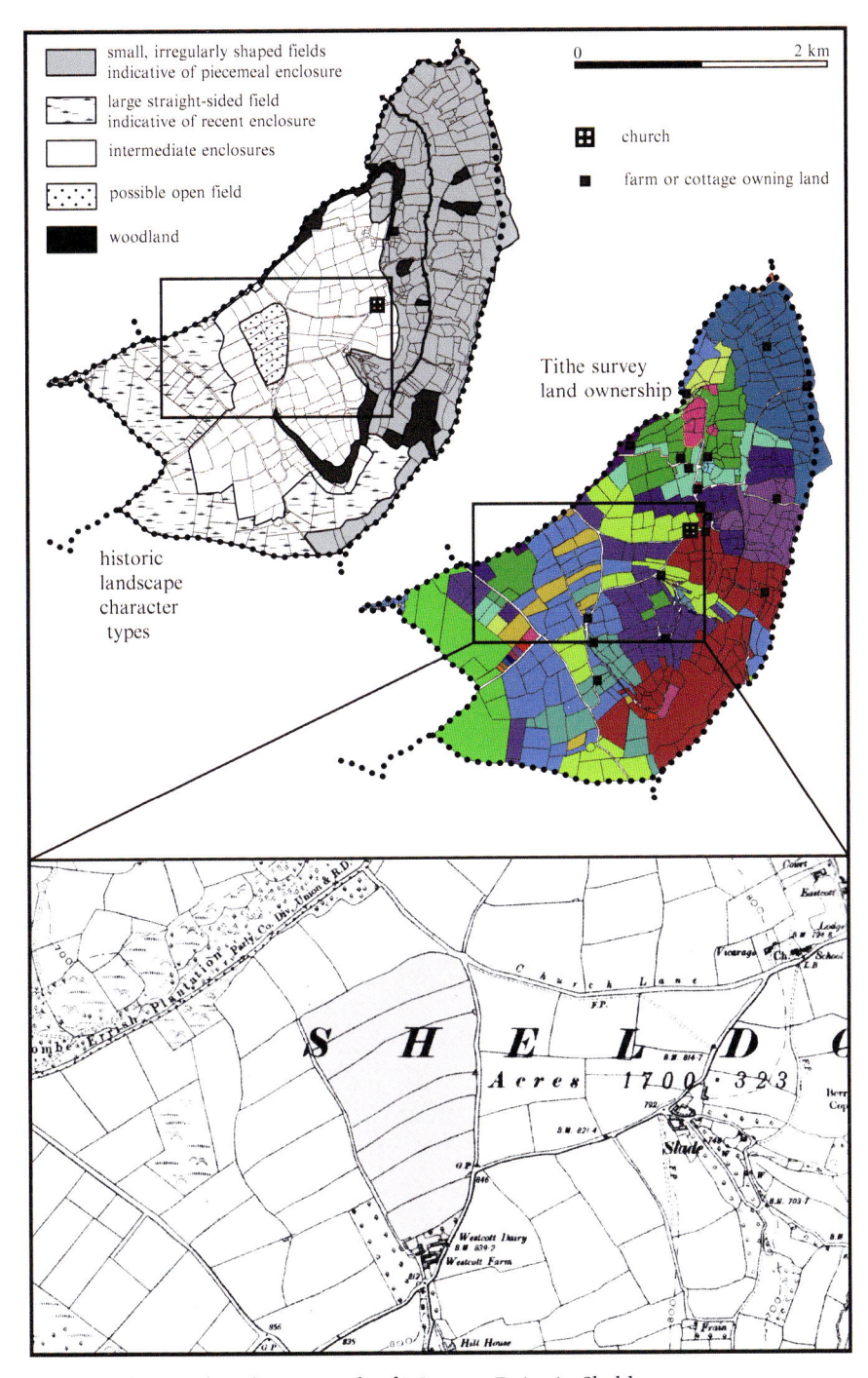

Plate 6. The ovoid enclosure north of Westcott Dairy in Sheldon.

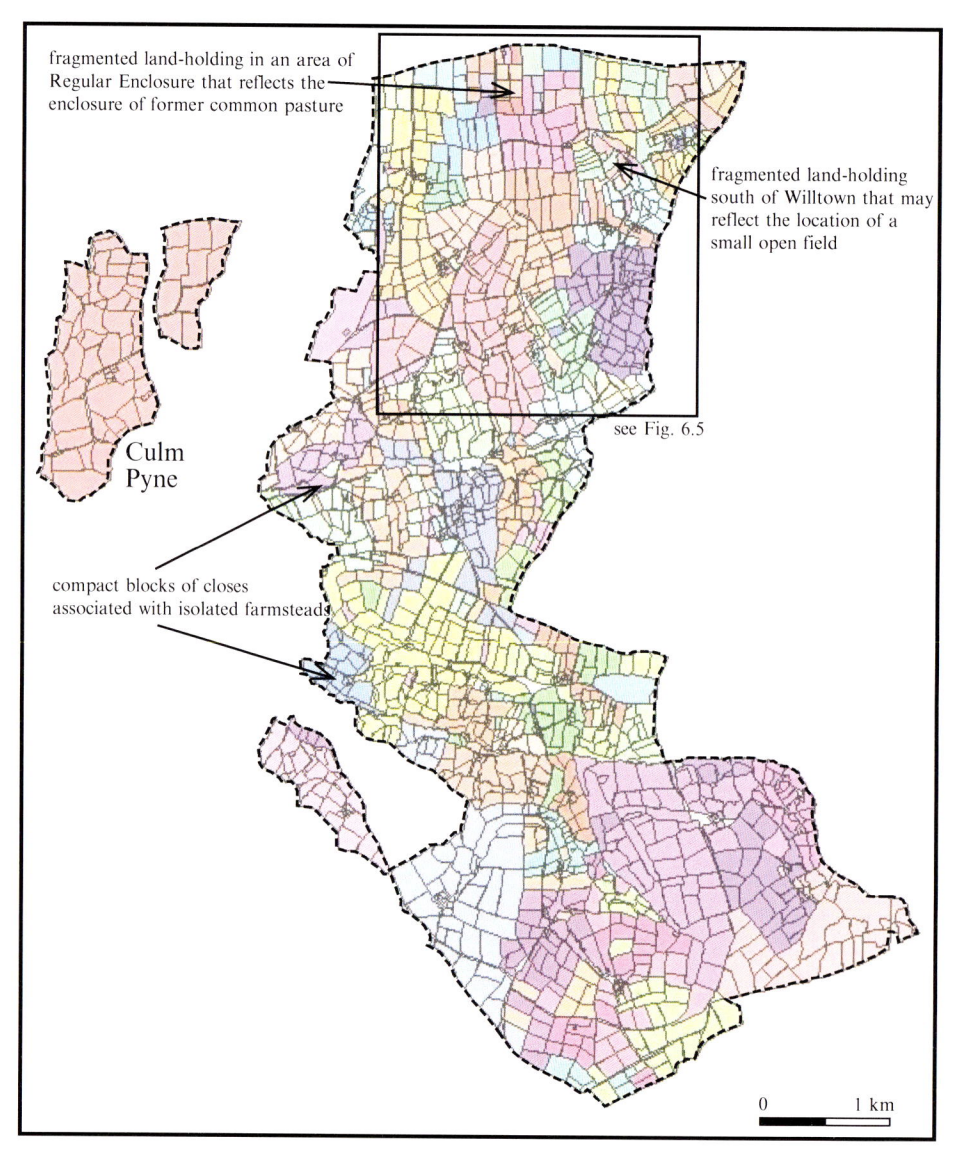

Plate 7. Transcription of the Tithe map for Clayhidon.

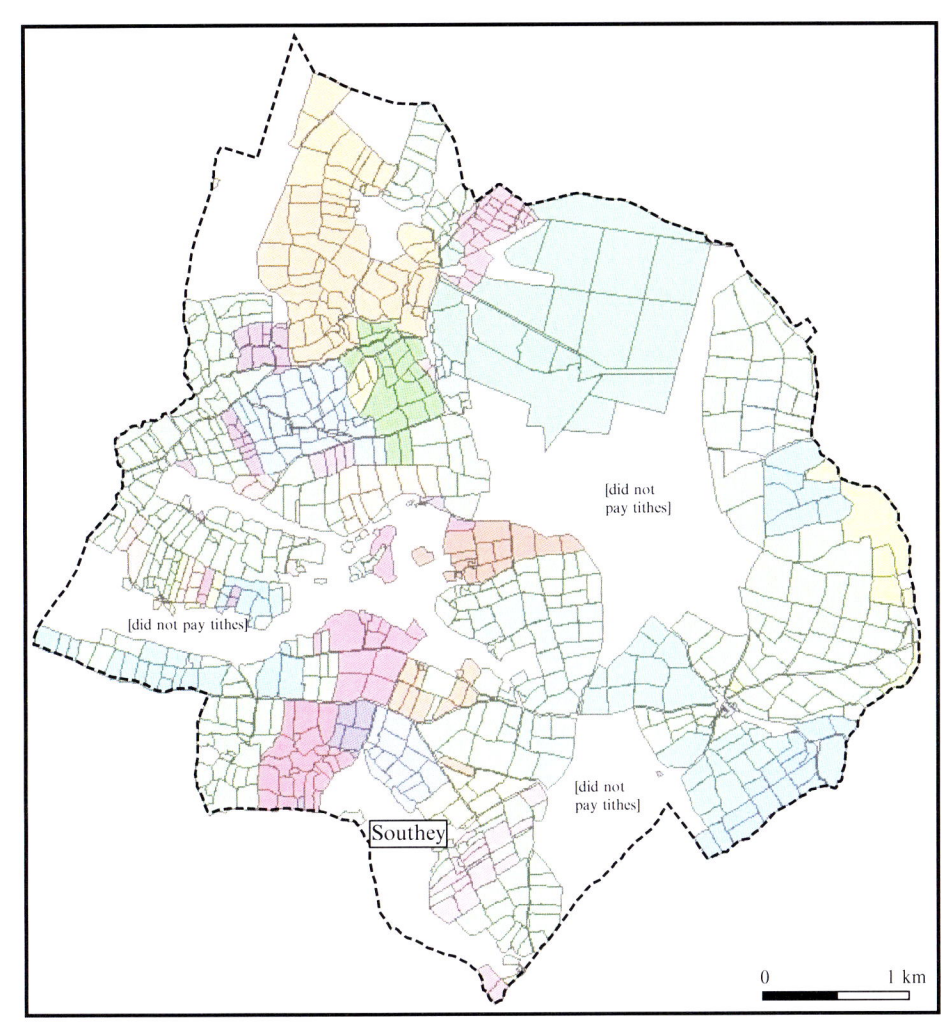

Plate 8. Transcription of the Tithe map for Churchstanton.

Plate 9. Aerial photograph of Combe St Nicholas from the west.

Plate 10. Cross-section through a typical Devon hedgebank at West Raddon in Shobrooke.

western Devon and Cornwall: predominantly acidic soils of the Culm Measures, granite uplands, and their surrounding lowlands (mostly Devonian sandstones).

eastern Devon: fertile soils derived from Permian and Triassic sandstones in the Exe, Creedy, and Culm valleys.

Blackdown Hills: range of flat-topped hills of Cretaceous Upper Greensand, dissected by valleys cut into the underlying Triassic mudstone giving rise to heavy soils.

Vale of Taunton Deane: low-lying plains with moderately heavy soils derived from the Triassic mudstones.

central Somerset lowlands: low-lying plains with moderately heavy soils derived from the Jurassic Lower Lias.

northern Somerset hills and vales: landscape of hills and vales with thin, dry soils on Carboniferous limestone hills separated by broad valleys cut into Triassic mudstone and Jurassic Lower Lias that give rise to heavier soils.

marshland: the wetlands of the Somerset and North Somerset Levels comprising a complex mosaic of environments, of which only the coastal alluvial marshes were settled during the Roman and medieval periods.

Jurassic limestone hills: landscape of complex Jurassic geology dominated by oolitic limestone hills and clayland vales.

Jurassic clay vales: broad, low-lying vales with heavy soils derived from Jurassic clays found between the Jurassic limestone hills of Somerset and Gloucestershire and chalk downland of Dorset and Wiltshire.

chalk downland: thin calcareous soils on high downland stretching from central Dorset north into Wiltshire.

heathland: low-lying areas with acidic soils forming over Tertiary sands in south-east Dorset.

There are many studies of agricultural practices in the Roman (e.g. M. Jones 1989) and later medieval periods (e.g. Campbell 2000; 2008; Campbell and Bartley 2006), and while some embraced both the Roman and the early medieval periods (e.g. Fowler 2002), such are the differences in source material either side of the eleventh century that a longer time frame embracing all of the last two millennia has rarely been taken. Before the eleventh century we must rely almost wholly upon archaeology, for although place-names and charter boundary-clauses provide a little information on land use in the early medieval period, it is only with Domesday and later written sources that we have significant amounts of documentary data. Indeed, it is only in the nineteenth and twentieth centuries that we have the most detailed information in the form of cartographic sources that map land use field by field across

208   *Making Sense of An Historic Landscape*

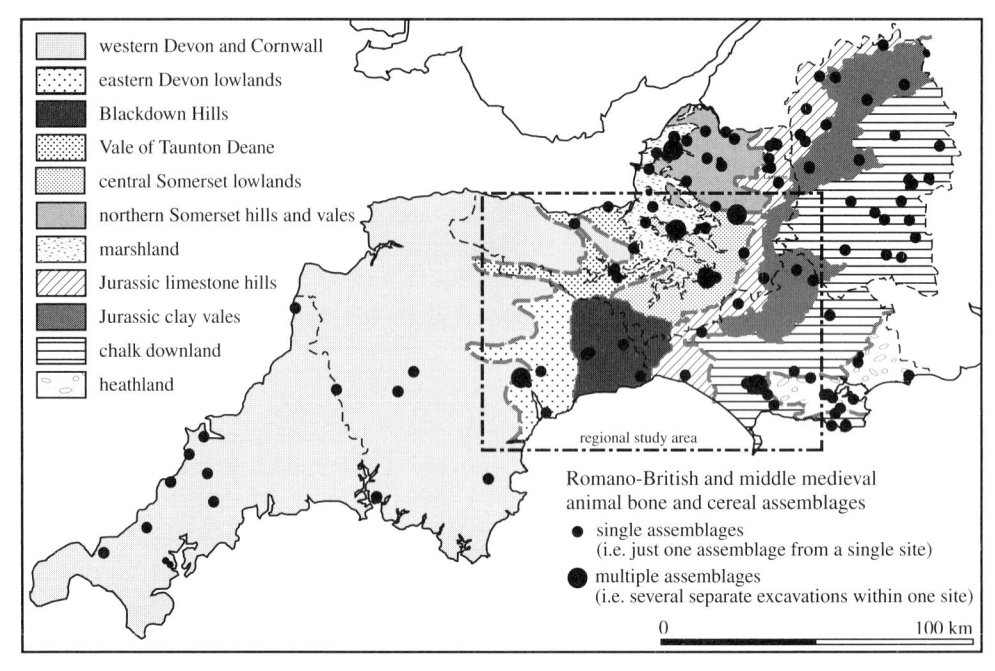

Fig. 11.1. The regions used in the study of palaeoeconomic data (animal bones and charred cereals).

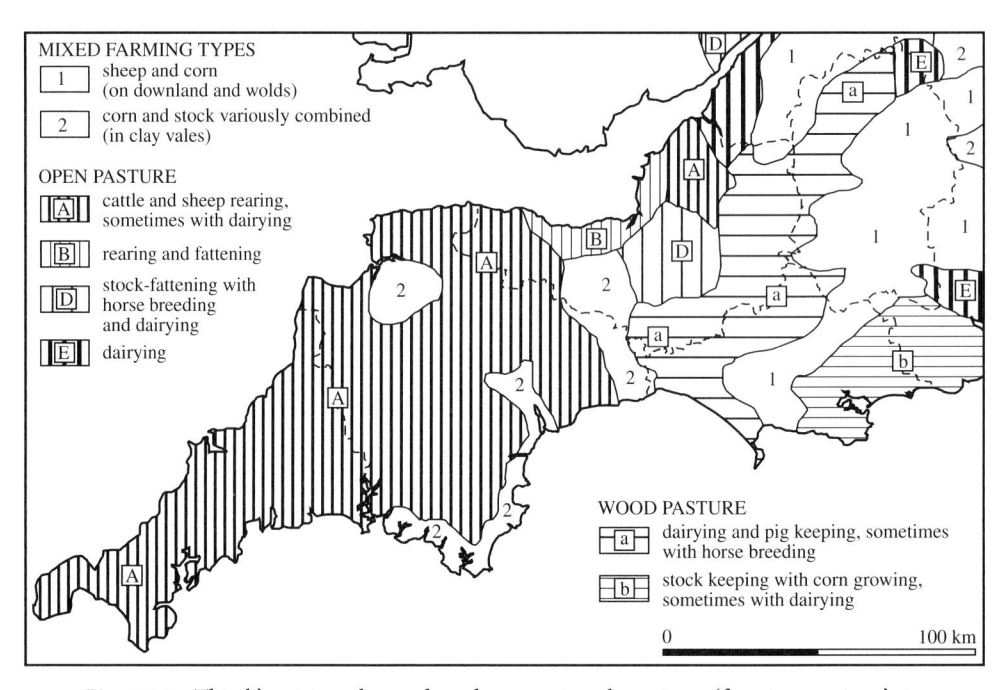

Fig. 11.2. Thirsk's sixteenth- and early seventeenth-century 'farming regions' in South West England. (After Thirsk 1967, fig. 1; 1984.)

Patterns of land use

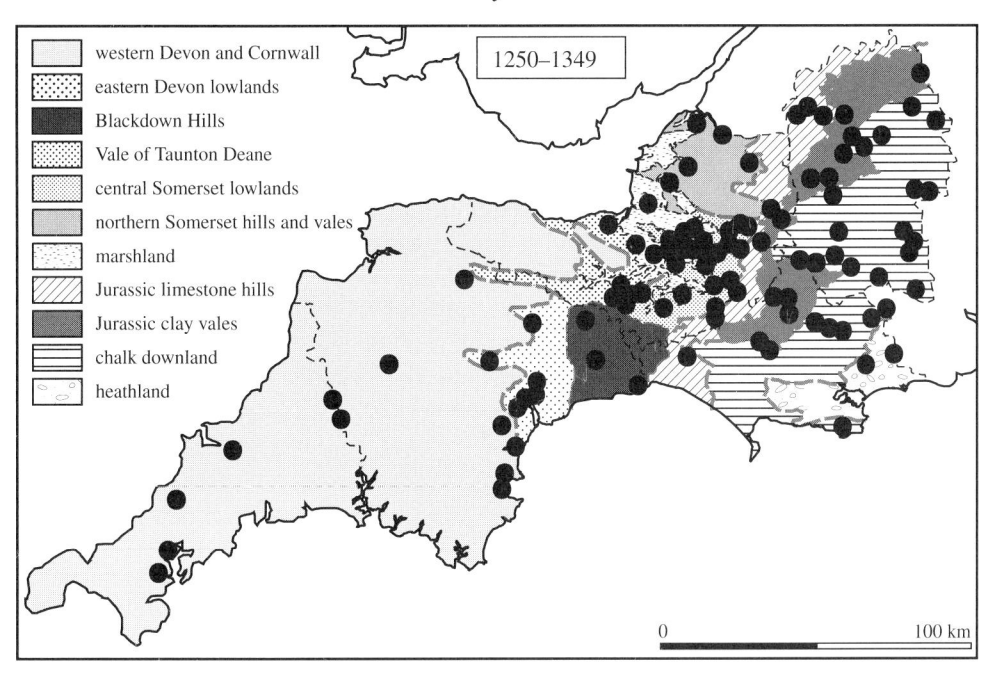

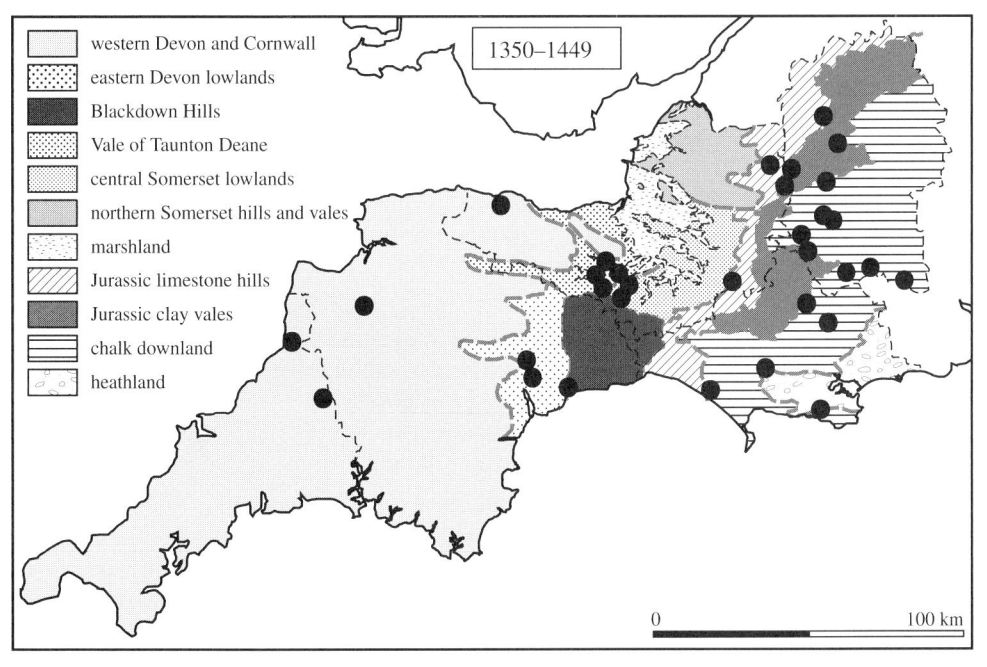

Fig. 11.3. Places with documentary records used by Campbell to study medieval demesne agriculture. (After Campbell 2000, figs. 2.04 and 2.05.)

the whole country. In this study, therefore, an attempt is made to use both archaeological and documentary sources to study changing patterns of land use across the different *pays* of South West England over the past two millennia. It would be relatively straightforward to present this in a traditional chronological way, starting with the Roman period and ending in the twentieth century, telling the story of how land use changed over time, but this was not the way that the research process actually worked. Before embarking upon a time-consuming and potentially fruitless period of data collection and analysis, a *prima facie* case had to be made for there having been regional variation in farming practices in the past: it was possible that differences in land use seen so clearly in the nineteenth and twentieth centuries were a relatively recent phenomenon reflecting the developed market economy of our industrial and urban age. Past historical research has, however, clearly established that there were distinctive 'farming regions' as long ago as the sixteenth century (e.g. Fig. 11.2), while Campbell (2000) has revealed that there were marked differences in farming practice on many of the thirteenth- to fifteenth-century demesne for which records survive (Fig. 11.3). As far back as the late medieval period at least, there were very distinctive farming practices across our various *pays*.

REGIONAL VARIATION IN AGRICULTURE AS RECORDED IN DOMESDAY

Continuing back in time, the late eleventh-century Domesday survey provides a remarkably detailed record of some categories of land use, notably the numbers of plough teams on each manor (from which an estimate of the extent of arable cultivation can be made), along with the areas of woodland, meadow, and pasture (for a recent discussion of Domesday land use, *see* Roffe 2000 and 2007). Domesday is most readily available in a series of county-based translations published by Phillimore (e.g. Thorn and Thorn 1985), and a complete edition edited by Williams and Martin (1992), while much of the data are mapped and discussed county by county in a series of regional studies published by H. C. Darby and his colleagues (e.g. Darby and Welldon Finn 1967). Scholars studying Cornwall, Devon, Dorset, and Somerset, however, are fortunate in having an earlier draft of the Domesday survey—the *Liber Exoniensis*—which includes details that were subsequently omitted from the main Domesday volume, such as demesne livestock numbers. This additional data is included in the Phillimore editions for the south-western counties, but not Williams and Martin (1992).

Table 11.1. Demesne livestock listed in the *Liber Exoniensis* for Devon, Dorset, and Somerset (from Darby and Welldon Finn 1967, 123, 206, 286)

	Devon 6,698 km²	Dorset 2,538 km²	Somerset 4,248 km²	totals
sheep[1]	50,884	22,977	469,813	543,674
per km²	7.6	9.1	11.1	
% of main livestock	73.3%	88.2%	96.7%	93.5%
goats[2]	7,263	780	4,505	12,548
per km²	1.1	0.3	1.1	
% of main livestock	10.5%	3.0%	0.9%	2.2%
cattle[3]	7,539	730	4,865	13,134
per km²	1.1	0.3	1.2	
% of main livestock	10.9%	2.8%	1.0%	2.3%
pigs[4]	3,682	1,567	6,847	12,096
per km²	0.6	0.6	1.6	
% of main livestock	5.3%	6.0%	1.4%	2.1%
Total livestock	69,368	26,054	486,030	581,452

[1] includes sheep (*oves*) and wethers (*berbices*)
[2] *caprae*
[3] includes animals (*animalia*), rounceys (*runcini*), and cows (*vaccae*)
[4] *porci*

The total numbers of sheep, goats, cattle, and pigs on demesnes are calculated for each county in the *Domesday Geography*. Note that goats were generally far more common in medieval England than is often assumed, particularly in the west, although numbers declined rapidly from the eleventh century onwards (Dyer 2004a). Domesday reveals that livestock husbandry in Devon had a stronger emphasis on cattle (10.9% of the productive livestock) compared to Somerset (just 1.0%), and was generally more diverse (10.5% goats and 5.3% pigs, compared to 0.9% goats and 1.4% pigs in Somerset) (Table 11.1). Using this data in *Liber Exoniensis* we can also explore differences in animal husbandry across our local study area in more detail by looking at some of the early medieval districts identified in Chapters 8–10 (Figs. 11.4–11.5 and Tables 11.2–11.4). Of the 15,644 livestock listed 10.4% were cattle, 7.9% pigs, 73.4% sheep, and 8.3% goats. All areas were characterized by mixed animal husbandry, though with some significant differences in the balance between different species. In the Exe/Lowman territory around Tiverton, for example, there were relatively large numbers of cattle (15.2%), pigs (8.4%), and goats (11.5%), but relatively few sheep (64.9%). In the lowlands of the Culm/Clyst valleys to the south the relative proportions of livestock and their stocking densities were generally close to the averages for our local study area, though pigs (4.8%) were under-represented. On the Blackdown Hills cattle (12.7%) were well represented and had a relatively high stocking density; sheep and goats were close to the average, and pigs

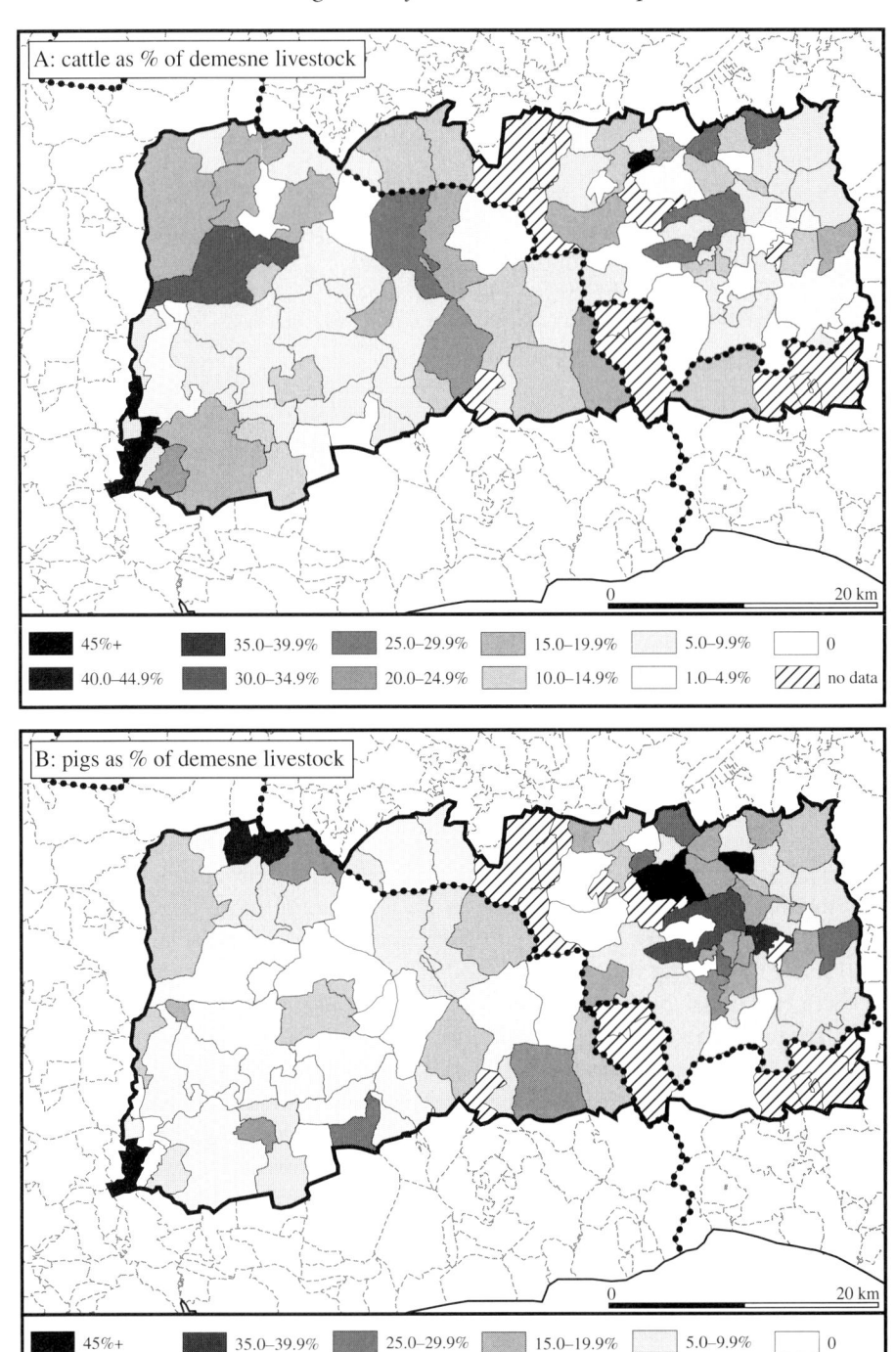

Fig. 11.4. Cattle and pigs as a percentage of the demesne livestock recorded in Domesday across the local study area.

Patterns of land use 213

A: sheep as % of demesne livestock

■ 90%+	■ 80.0–84.9%	▨ 70.0–74.9%	▨ 60.0–64.9%	▨ 50.0–54.9%	□ <45%	
■ 85.0–89.9%	■ 75.0–79.9%	▨ 65.0–69.9%	▨ 55.0–54.9%	▨ 45.0–49.9%	▨ no data	

B: goats as % of demesne livestock

■ 45%+	■ 35.0–39.9%	▨ 25.0–29.9%	▨ 15.0–19.9%	▨ 5.0–9.9%	□ 0	
■ 40.0–44.9%	■ 30.0–34.9%	▨ 20.0–24.9%	▨ 10.0–14.9%	▨ 1.0–4.9%	▨ no data	

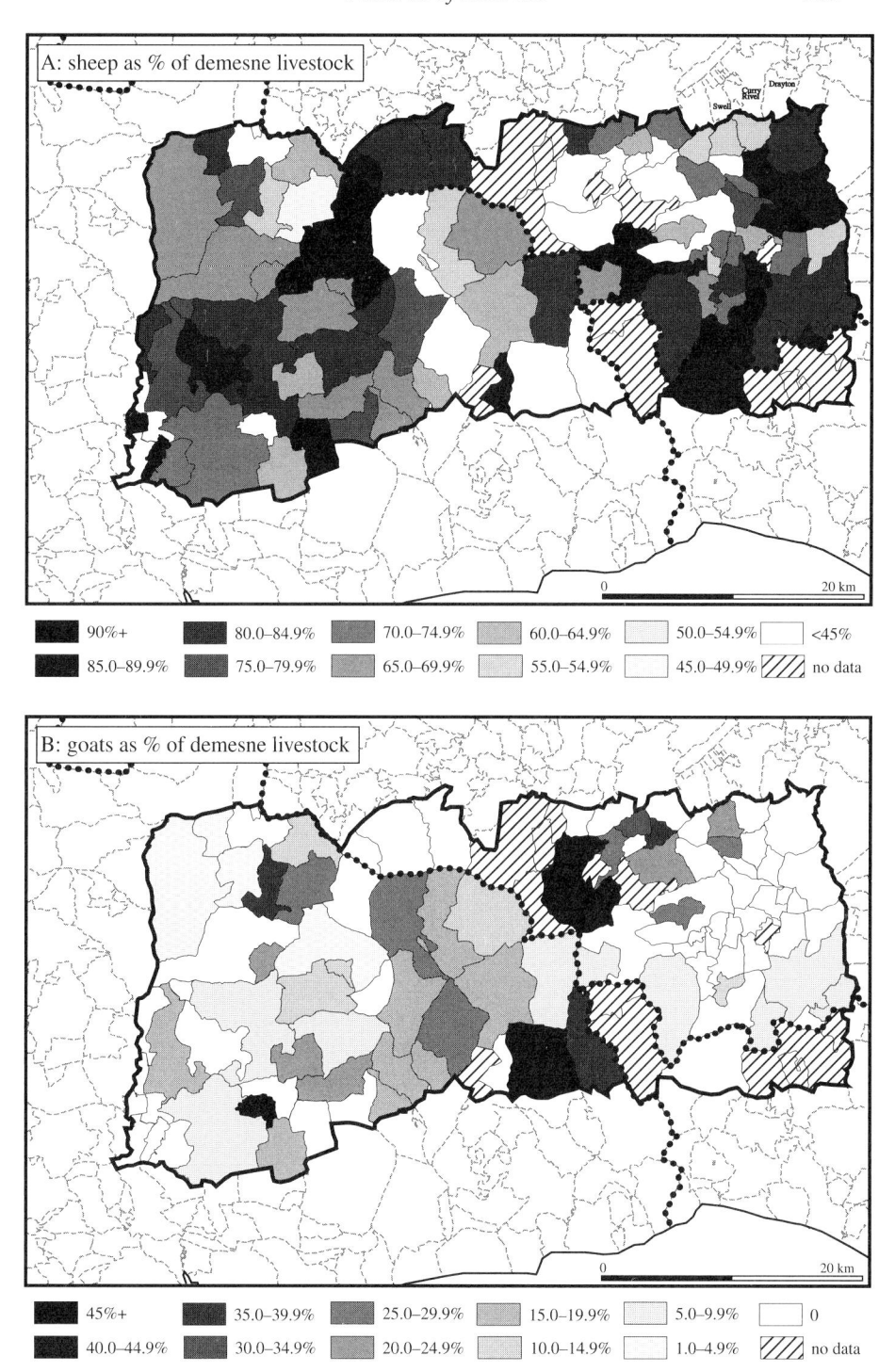

Fig. 11.5. Sheep and goats as a percentage of the demesne livestock recorded in Domesday across the local study area.

Table 11.2. The relative proportions of Domesday demesne livestock in the four early folk territories that embrace most of the Blackdown Hills and adjacent areas.

	acreage	km²	cattle		pigs		sheep		goats		sheep + goats		total
			n	%	n	%	n	%	n	%	n	%	
greater Halberton	18,064	73.1	118	15.0	63	8.0	450	57.3	155	19.7	605	77.0	786
greater Washfield	7,655	31.0	58	15.8	28	7.6	242	65.8	40	10.9	282	76.6	368
greater Tiverton	25,600	103.6	115	15.2	70	9.2	549	72.4	24	3.2	573	75.6	758
Exe/Lowman territory	**51,319**	**207.7**	**291**	**15.2**	**161**	**8.4**	**1,241**	**64.9**	**219**	**11.5**	**1,460**	**76.4**	**1,912**
greater Silverton	17,713	71.7	47	6.4	43	5.8	614	83.4	32	4.3	646	87.8	736
greater Cullompton incl. Sheldon	40,511	163.9	158	8.2	72	3.7	1,529	79.3	168	8.7	1,697	88.1	1,927
greater Cliston	17,465	70.7	127	14.7	55	6.4	593	68.6	89	10.3	682	78.9	864
Culm/Clyst incl. Sheldon	**75,689**	**306.4**	**332**	**9.4**	**170**	**4.8**	**2,736**	**77.6**	**289**	**8.2**	**3,025**	**85.8**	**3,527**
greater Hemyock	24,797	100.4	144	8.8	72	4.4	1,269	77.2	158	9.6	1,427	86.9	1,643
greater Axminster	37,346	151.2	281	20.0	147	10.5	975	69.5		0.0	975	69.5	1,403
Stockland	7,558	30.6	4	12.9	7	22.6	0	0.0	20	64.5	20	64.5	31
greater Axmouth	7,952	32.2	19	5.8	16	4.8	238	72.1	57	17.3	295	89.4	330
greater Colyton	28,434	115.1	117	11.2	25	2.4	810	77.7	90	8.6	900	86.4	1,042
Blackdown Hills territory	**106,087**	**429.4**	**565**	**12.7**	**267**	**6.0**	**3292**	**74.0**	**325**	**7.3**	**3,617**	**81.3**	**4449**
greater Curry Rivel	44,413	179.8	226	10.0	307	13.6	1,367	60.5	360	15.9	1,727	76.4	2,260
greater South Petherton	30,877	125.0	114	5.9	178	9.2	1,621	83.7	24	1.2	1,645	84.9	1,937
greater Crewkerne	22,450	90.9	83	6.9	132	11.0	923	76.8	64	5.3	987	82.1	1,202
greater Chard	13,106	53.1	13	3.6	20	5.6	300	84.0	24	6.7	324	90.8	357
South Curry	**110,846**	**448.7**	**436**	**7.6**	**637**	**11.1**	**4,211**	**73.2**	**472**	**8.2**	**4,683**	**81.4**	**5,756**
TOTALS	343,941	13,92.2	1624	10.4	1,235	7.9	11,480	73.4	1,305	8.3	12,785	81.7	15,644

Table 11.3. Domesday stocking densities of demesne livestock in the four early folk territories that embrace most of the Blackdown Hills and adjacent areas.

	acreage	km²	cattle n	cattle n/km²	pigs n	pigs n/km²	sheep n	sheep n/km²	goats n	goats n/km²	sheep + goats n	sheep + goats n/km²
greater Halberton	18,064	73.1	118	1.6	63	0.9	450	6.2	155	2.1	605	8.3
greater Washfield	7,655	31.0	58	1.9	28	0.9	242	7.8	40	1.3	282	9.1
greater Tiverton	25,600	103.6	115	1.1	70	0.7	549	5.3	24	0.2	573	5.5
Exe/Lowman territory	**51,319**	**207.7**	**291**	**1.4**	**161**	**0.8**	**1,241**	**6.0**	**219**	**1.1**	**1,460**	**7.0**
greater Silverton	17,713	71.7	47	0.7	43	0.6	614	8.6	32	0.4	646	9.0
greater Cullompton	40,511	163.9	158	1.0	72	0.4	1,529	9.3	168	1.0	1,697	10.4
greater Cullompton	38,830	157.1	148	0.9	72	0.5	1,484	9.4	168	1.1	1,652	10.5
greater Cliston	17,465	70.7	127	1.8	55	0.8	593	8.4	89	1.3	682	9.6
Culm/Clyst incl. Sheldon	**75,689**	**306.4**	**332**	**1.1**	**170**	**0.6**	**2,736**	**8.9**	**289**	**0.9**	**3,025**	**9.9**
greater Hemyock	24,797	100.4	144	1.4	72	0.7	1,269	12.6	158	1.6	1,427	14.2
greater Axminster	37,346	151.2	281	1.9	147	1.0	975	6.4		0.0	975	6.4
Stockland	7,558	30.6	4	0.1	7	0.2	0	0.0	20	0.7	20	0.7
greater Axmouth	7,952	32.2	19	0.6	16	0.5	238	7.4	57	1.8	295	9.2
greater Colyton	28,434	115.1	117	1.0	25	0.2	810	7.0	90	0.8	900	7.8
Blackdown Hills territory	**106,087**	**429.4**	**565**	**1.3**	**267**	**0.6**	**3,292**	**7.7**	**325**	**0.8**	**3,617**	**8.4**
greater Curry Rivel	44,413	179.8	226	1.3	307	1.7	1,367	7.6	360	2.0	1,727	9.6
greater South Petherton	30,877	125.0	114	0.9	178	1.4	1,621	13.0	24	0.2	1,645	13.2
greater Crewkerne	22,450	90.9	83	0.9	132	1.5	923	10.2	64	0.7	987	10.9
greater Chard	13,106	53.1	13	0.2	20	0.4	300	5.7	24	0.5	324	6.1
South Curry	**110,846**	**448.7**	**436**	**1.0**	**637**	**1.4**	**4,211**	**9.4**	**472**	**1.1**	**4,683**	**10.4**
TOTALS	**343,941**	**1,392.2**	**1,624**	**1.2**	**1,235**	**0.9**	**11,480**	**8.2**	**1,305**	**0.9**	**12,785**	**9.2**

Table 11.4. Domesday herd/flock sizes of demesne livestock in the four early folk territories that embrace most of the Blackdown Hills and adjacent areas.

	acreage	km²	herd/flocks size			
			cattle	pigs	sheep	goats
greater Halberton	18,064	73.1	9.0	9.0	50.0	25.8
greater Washfield	7,655	31.0	8.2	9.3	40.3	20.0
greater Tiverton	25,600	103.6	8.3	5.4	30.5	6.0
Exe/Lowman territory	**51,319**	**207.7**	**8.6**	**6.0**	**40.0**	**18.3**
greater Silverton	17,713	71.7	5.2	8.6	51.2	10.7
greater Cullompton	40,511	163.9	8.3	5.1	63.7	24.0
greater Cliston	17,465	70.7	10.6	7.9	49.4	29.7
Culm/Clyst territory	**75,689**	**306.4**	**8.3**	**6.5**	**57.0**	**22.3**
greater Hemyock	24,797	100.4	10.4	12.8	61.4	24.8
greater Axminster	37,346	151.2	14.1	11.3	69.6	26.1
Stockland	7,558	30.6	4.0	7.0	0.0	20.0
greater Axmouth	7,952	32.2	9.5	16	47.6	19.0
greater Colyton	28,434	115.1	7.3	6.3	47.7	18.0
Blackdown Hills territory	**106,087**	**429.4**	**10.7**	**10.7**	**68.6**	**10.2**
greater Curry Rivel	44,413	179.8	9.8	12.8	61.3	34.0
greater South Petherton	30,877	125.0	5.7	11.1	73.7	24.0
greater Crewkerne	22,450	90.9	11.9	18.9	131.9	64.0
greater Chard	13,106	53.1	13.0	20.0	300.0	24.0
South Curry territory	**110,846**	**448.7**	**8.5**	**12.2**	**81.0**	**36.3**
TOTALS	**343,941**	**13,92.2**				

(6.0%) under-represented which is somewhat surprising considering the abundant woodland (although the size of the swine herds was large: see below). In the lowlands of central-southern Somerset, in contrast, cattle (7.6%) were under-represented, pigs (11.1%) were relatively abundant, and sheep and goats were close to the case-study average. There are also some interesting differences in the herd and flock sizes. Cattle herds were of similar size across the study area ranging from c.8.5 in most lowland areas to 10.7 on the Blackdown Hills. West of the Blackdowns swine herds numbered c.6.3 but nearly double this on the Blackdown Hills and in central-southern Somerset. The size of sheep flocks varied enormously, averaging just 40 in the Tiverton area, 57 in the Culm/Clyst lowlands, 69 on the Blackdown Hills, and 81 in central-southern Somerset. The size of the goat herds also varied being small to the west of the Blackdown Hills (18.3 in the Exe/Lowman territory, and 22.3 in the Culm/Clyst valleys), very small (10.2) on the Blackdown Hills, and 36.3 in the lowlands of central Somerset.

The density of plough teams is mapped in Figure 15.3 in the context of a broader discussion in Chapter 15 of the potential role of arable intensification in the creation of villages and open fields. In the lowlands of central Somerset there was on average one plough per 177 acres in contrast to the Blackdown Hills where there was on average 319 acres per plough, reflecting the large amounts of pasture, woodland, and unenclosed common land on the upland areas. In the lowlands west of the Blackdowns there was on average one plough per 236 acres.

LAND USE CHANGE OVER THE FIRST MILLENNIUM AD

What emerges from the analysis of Domesday is that there were significant differences in livestock husbandry across different *pays* in the eleventh century, and a comparison with a range of later sources presented in Table 11.5 suggests that certain districts do show a strong degree of consistency in how they have been exploited over the past thousand years. At the heart of our study area, the **Blackdown Hills** have consistently had a relatively low population. Until the twentieth century, agriculture has always been mixed, albeit with an emphasis on pastoralism (sheep and cattle), and arable cultivation—probably at its most extensive in the twelfth and thirteenth centuries—traditionally combined wheat with some oats (Overton 2006, fig. 7.9). The area has always been relatively deficient in meadow due to its topography, with very restricted valley floodplains. In Domesday, the Blackdown Hills are recorded as relatively well-wooded, though much of this probably lay on the steeper slopes (as it does today). The contrast with the **lowlands of eastern Devon** could not be clearer. This area consistently had a relatively high population and a high proportion of arable land. Crop regimes have varied somewhat over time with oats dominant in the twelfth and thirteenth centuries and wheat of secondary importance, shifting to wheat as the major crop in combination with oats and barley in the late medieval period (Overton 2006, fig. 7.9). Livestock husbandry also varied over time, though it was always supported by an abundance of meadow on the broad floodplains. The **Culm Measures**, in contrast, had a consistently low population and predominance of pasture in all but the twelfth and thirteenth centuries when arable cultivation briefly increased. Livestock rearing was the dominant pattern of husbandry which in part reflects the scarcity of meadow. What arable cultivation there was generally saw a restricted cropping regime dominated by oats with some wheat. Taken with the soils and topography of these three areas it seems fair to conclude that the fertile lowlands of eastern Devon were a preferred area for settlement, with the adjacent Blackdown Hills and Culm Measures being less favoured (an impression borne out by the perceptions of early writers: *see* Chapter 3).

In the medieval period, the **Vale of Taunton Deane** consistently had a relatively high population density, though this fell away to average in the post-medieval period. The area always had a mixed farming economy with cropping regimes in the medieval period characterized by wheat and oats (the latter being replaced by barley in the post-medieval period). The large amounts of meadow would have lain in the many valleys that join the more extensive wetlands of the Somerset Levels. The **lowlands of central Somerset** were also a densely settled area. Arable cultivation dominated in the drylands although there was abundant meadow and pasture in the Somerset Levels and their tributary valleys. Cropping regimes were characterized by wheat and oats throughout the medieval period, with a variety of secondary crops being grown in the post-medieval period. Livestock husbandry was characterized by dairying. The **hills and vales of North Somerset** consistently had an average to high population density. In the medieval period there was mixed farming with an average to high density of plough teams in Domesday, although in the post-medieval period there was a significant shift towards pastoralism, perhaps reflecting the proximity of Bristol as a major market centre for dairy produce. The **Somerset Levels** had a particularly distinctive economy. The population densities were fairly average for Somerset as a whole in the medieval period suggesting that following reclamation this was not a physically 'marginal' landscape, and in Domesday the density of plough teams was similarly average for the county. Pasture, and particularly dairying, came to dominate thereafter, with wheat and oats grown in what arable fields there were. In this group of districts, therefore, the Vale of Taunton Deane, central Somerset lowlands, and vales of North Somerset would all appear to have had a strong tradition of mixed farming regimes, in contrast to the adjacent Blackdown Hills and the Somerset Levels that had more specialized pastoral economies.

Further east lay the **Jurassic Hills** that consistently had a high population density, and a mixture of arable land and pasture. In contrast to the lowlands of central Somerset, sheep were dominant in the medieval period being replaced by cattle in the post-medieval period. Wheat and oats once again characterized medieval crop husbandry regimes, with a greater diversity of secondary crops in the post-medieval period. The **Jurassic clay vales** further east also had a relatively high population density although farming regimes appear to have changed significantly over time. In Domesday there was a low density of plough teams, although in the twelfth and thirteenth centuries arable land and pasture were present in roughly equal amounts with wheat, oats, and rye being grown. For most of the post-medieval period the area was dominated by pasture, with dairying the major occupation, and wheat, barley, and oats grown on what arable land there was. The **chalk downland** generally supported average population densities. In Domesday there was some arable land within a predominantly pastoral landscape, although the twelfth and thirteenth centuries saw arable land coming to prominence. Sheep always dominated the livestock husbandry, while wheat was the main crop along with barley and oats. In the post-medieval period arable land and sheep continued to be important, with wheat and barley still the main crops. The final *pays*—the **heathlands** of South East Dorset—also had a distinctive land-use history with consistently low population densities and predominantly pastoral regimes in which cattle dominated (unfortunately there is a lack of documentary data with regard to cropping regimes, though the archaeological evidence points to a particularly distinctive range of crops: *see* below).

THE SEASONAL MOVEMENT OF LIVESTOCK?

The literal reading of the available documentary sources described above suggests some marked spatial variations in the patterns of agriculture, but in reality these differences may have been even greater as the sources we have record livestock on the manors where they were owned, whereas in practice some of the animals could actually have been elsewhere for at least part of the year. The seasonal movement of livestock across the landscape—what is sometimes referred to as 'transhumance'—has not received the attention it deserves, but evidence for the practice in medieval Britain is preserved in a number of ways, including distinctive settlement and building types (e.g. shielings), place-names, droveways leading from lowlands to uplands, territorial links such as parishes having detached parcels in other areas, and direct written evidence in records of estate management (e.g. Everitt 1986; Fox 1996b; Rippon 2000a; Herring 2009). The Blackdown Hills, with their large areas of unenclosed land, is one location where we might expect to see summer grazing although the evidence at present is extremely limited. No lowland parish held detached parcels up on the hills, and no possible shielings have been recognized (although this is not unexpected as even the highest ground has all now been enclosed and agriculturally improved). A small number of '-cote' place-names may be indicative of what were originally seasonal settlements associated with the summer grazing of in particular sheep, lying as they do on the edges of what in the medieval period was largely unenclosed land on the higher hilltops. A number of 'summer' place-names[1] also suggest seasonal grazing, but not necessarily the movement of livestock to these areas from a long distance. There are a small number of possible long-distance droveways that radiate from the Blackdown Hills, such as that from Mutterton, in Cullompton, along the southern

---

[1] e.g. Summerhays in the hamlet of Southey in Churchstanton (Gover *et al.* 1932, 619–20) and Summerhays in Upottery which both lie on high ground ('Somerhayes' in 1713: Gover *et al.* 1932, 651); Summerland Cottage in Combe Raleigh which is not in Gover *et al.* and may not be of great antiquity.

side of Kentismoor in Broadhembury, and hence up to Black Down in Sheldon, but what is more striking is how few they are, with most roads in the lowlands meandering through the landscape without much regard to the adjacent uplands. Overall, there is far less evidence for seasonal grazing and in particular the long-distance movement of livestock than on other upland areas in the South West such as Dartmoor (e.g. Herring 2009; Fox forthcoming).

DISCUSSION

This rapid assessment of some easily accessible documentary sources does, therefore, suggests that there were indeed marked regional variations in agricultural regimes across our study area, with some long-lasting patterns such as the generally mixed farming regimes to the west of the Blackdown Hills, and some more specialized husbandry to the east. Within this big picture of regional variation, there were also very marked local variations between particular *pays* such as dairying in the Somerset lowlands and sheep and corn husbandry on the chalk downland. These sources are, however, only telling us part of the story as they relate specifically to the demesnes held by major land

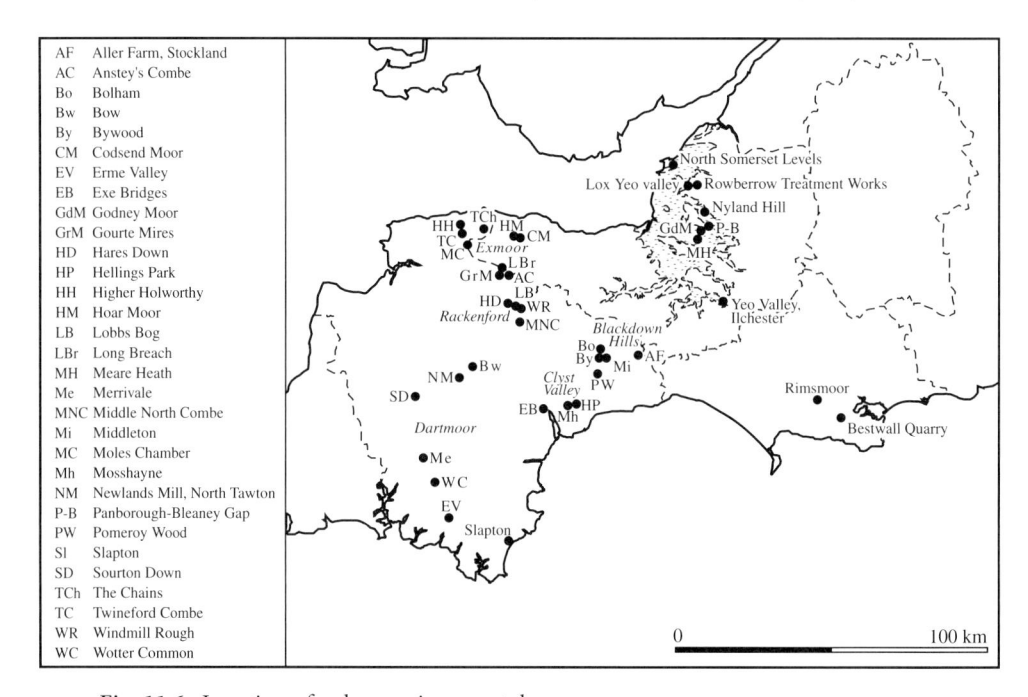

AF	Aller Farm, Stockland
AC	Anstey's Combe
Bo	Bolham
Bw	Bow
By	Bywood
CM	Codsend Moor
EV	Erme Valley
EB	Exe Bridges
GdM	Godney Moor
GrM	Gourte Mires
HD	Hares Down
HP	Hellings Park
HH	Higher Holworthy
HM	Hoar Moor
LB	Lobbs Bog
LBr	Long Breach
MH	Meare Heath
Me	Merrivale
MNC	Middle North Combe
Mi	Middleton
MC	Moles Chamber
Mh	Mosshayne
NM	Newlands Mill, North Tawton
P-B	Panborough-Bleaney Gap
PW	Pomeroy Wood
Sl	Slapton
SD	Sourton Down
TCh	The Chains
TC	Twineford Combe
WR	Windmill Rough
WC	Wotter Common

Fig. 11.6. Location of palaeoenvironmental sequences.

Table 11.5. Changing patterns of population density and predominant land use across the regional study area (*see* Fig. 11.1 for the location of these districts).

district	Domesday	1250–1349 (including population density 1327–32)	1350–1449	16th to early 17th century	mid-17th to mid-18th century	early to mid-19th century	1930s Land Utilisation Survey	present day
Source		*Inquisitions post mortem* and surveys/account rolls that formed part of the records of estate management used in national (Campbell 2000; Campbell and Bartley 2006) and local studies (e.g. Fox 1972; 1999). The Lay Subsidies of 1327, 1332, and 1334 are individually incomplete but can be combined to provide a national coverage (Glasscock 1975, map 1; Campbell and Bartley 2006). The Poll Tax records of 1377–81 record both the number of tax payers and the tax they paid in those areas in which records have survived (Fenwick 1998; 2001; 2005).		Thirsk's (1967; 1984; 1987) farming regions, based on probate inventories Sheail (1972; 1998) has used the Lay Subsidies of 1524–5 to map the distribution of taxable population and wealth, although this has only been mapped at a very small scale.		1801: Crop Returns (Turner 1982a; 1982b; 1982c; 1983a; 1983b; 1984; 1986; Williams 1969)* c.1840: Tithe Files (Kain 1979; 1986)	county reports (e.g. Somerset: Stuart Menteath 1938), and summary map (http://www.visionofbritain.org.uk/maps/index.jsp)	Fieldwork and Google Earth

(*continued*)

Table 11.5. Continued

district	Domesday	1250–1349 (including population density 1327–32)	1350–1449	16th to early 17th century	mid-17th to mid-18th century	early to mid-19th century	1930s Land Utilisation Survey	present day
Culm Measures	low to average population density; low density of plough teams; moderate amounts of pasture, moderate numbers of sheep; deficient in meadow; some extensive areas of woodland	low population density; roughly twice as much arable as pasture in demesnes; oats dominant, with some wheat and rye; cattle and sheep both important; deficient in meadow	no data on cropping or livestock	low population density; pasture dominant: cattle and sheep rearing	pasture dominant: subsistence arable with cattle rearing and sheep keeping	c.1840: pasture dominant but with up to 40% arable (wheat the major crop, with some barley and oats)	predominantly pasture for rearing livestock, with some arable land (dominated by oats), and rough pasture and moorland	predominantly pasture
lowlands of eastern Devon	average to high population density (high in the Exe valley); high density of plough teams (particularly in the Exe Valley);	average to high population density; roughly equal proportions of arable and pasture in	wheat and oats with some barley; sheep with	high population density; mixed farming (corn and stock)	arable land dominant: corn and livestock with special enterprises (e.g. horses, pigs, fruit, vegetables)	c.1840: pasture dominant but with up to 40% arable (wheat and barley the major crops, with some oats)	arable land (predominantly wheat with some oats, barley and potatoes), and pasture (particularly for dairying) in	mixture of arable land and pasture

moderate amounts of pasture, moderate numbers of sheep; abundant meadow; relatively little woodland	demesnes (slightly less arable in Culm valley); oats dominant, with some wheat, rye and barley; cattle dominant amongst livestock; abundant meadow	some cattle			roughly equal proportions, with some heathland		
Blackdown Hills	low to average population density; low density of plough teams (though close to average in the south); abundant pasture, small numbers of sheep; deficient in meadow (except in Culm and Axe valleys); some extensive areas of woodland	low to average population density; roughly equal proportions of arable land and pasture in demesnes; wheat with some oats; cattle and sheep both important; low to average amounts of meadow	no data on cropping or livestock	low population density; pasture dominant: cattle and sheep rearing	arable land dominant: corn and livestock with special enterprises (e.g. horses, pigs, fruit, vegetables)	1801: wheat and oats, with some barley, turnip, rape, peas and beans. c.1840: pasture dominant but with up to 40% arable land (wheat and oats the major crops, with a little barley)	predominantly pasture (mostly for dairying), with some arable land (wheat and oats), and rough pasture and moorland	predominantly pasture with extensive woodland on the steeper slopes

(*continued*)

Table 11.5. Continued

district	Domesday	1250–1349 (including population density 1327–32)	1350–1449	16th to early 17th century	mid-17th to mid-18th century	early to mid-19th century	1930s Land Utilisation Survey	present day
Vale of Taunton Deane	densely populated; average density of plough teams (higher than in central Somerset claylands); moderate amounts of pasture, small numbers of sheep; abundant meadow; relatively little woodland	high population density; roughly equal proportions of arable land and pasture in demesnes; wheat and oats; working animals dominate the livestock; abundant meadow	wheat and oats with some barley; sheep and cattle	average population density; mixed farming: corn and stock variously combined	arable land dominant: corn and cattle with substantial dairying	1801: wheat and barley, with some turnips, rape, peas and beans. c.1840: arable land and pasture in roughly equal amounts (predominantly wheat)	arable land and pasture (particularly dairying) in roughly equal proportions	mixture of arable land and pasture
central Somerset lowlands	densely populated; average density of plough teams; moderate amounts of pasture, small numbers of	high population density; roughly twice as much arable land as pasture in demesnes;	wheat, oats and barley; cattle and sheep	no population data; pasture dominant: cattle (dairying) and pig-keeping	arable land dominant: corn and cattle with substantial dairying	1801: wheat, with barley, turnips, rape, peas and beans. c.1840: arable land and pasture in roughly equal amounts (wheat	arable land and pasture (particularly dairying) in roughly equal proportions	mixture of arable land and pasture

	sheep; abundant meadow; some extensive areas of woodland to the south west	wheat and oats dominant in the hinterland of Glastonbury Abbey); cattle dominant amongst livestock; abundant meadow		and pulses the major crops, with some oats and barley)	
North Somerset hills and valleys	average to high density of population; average to high density of plough teams; average amounts of pasture and abundant meadow, large numbers of sheep; average amounts of woodland	average to high population density; wheat and barley or oats; cattle dominant amongst livestock; average amounts of meadow	no data on cropping or livestock	average population density; pasture dominant: cattle and sheep rearing	pasture dominant: subsistence corn with cattle rearing, dairying and/or grazing	1801: wheat, with oats, barley, potatoes and peas. c.1840: pasture dominant (up to 80%) but with up to 40% arable land (wheat the major crop with some oats)	predominantly pasture with rough grazing on the higher areas	mixture of arable land and pasture
Somerset marshlands (settled coastal claylands)	average population density (on the settled coastal claylands); average density	average to high population density; greater amount of	no data on cropping or livestock	no population data; pasture dominant: stock fattening, with horse-	pasture dominant: subsistence corn, with cattle rearing	1801: wheat, with peas and beans. c.1840: pasture dominant with	almost wholly pasture (for dairying)	predominantly pasture but with some arable land

(*continued*)

Table 11.5. Continued

district	Domesday	1250–1349 (including population density 1327–32)	1350–1449	16th to early 17th century	mid-17th to mid-18th century	early to mid-19th century	1930s Land Utilisation Survey	present day
	of plough teams on the settled coastal claylands; abundant pasture and meadow, small numbers of sheep; no woodland	pasture than arable land in demesnes; wheat and oats with some barley; cattle dominant amongst livestock; abundant meadow		breeding and dairying	and sheep keeping	up to just 20% arable land (wheat the major crop and pulses)		
Jurassic limestone hills	average to high population density; average density of plough teams (higher than in central Somerset lowlands); small amounts of pasture recorded, large numbers of sheep; average amounts of	high population density; roughly twice as much arable land as pasture in demesnes; wheat and oats with some barley; sheep dominant amongst	no data on cropping or livestock	no population data; pasture dominant: cattle (dairying) and pig-keeping	arable land dominant: corn and cattle with substantial dairying	1801: wheat, oats and barley, with some turnips, rape, peas and beans. c.1840: arable land and pasture in roughly equal amounts (wheat the major crop, with some barley)	arable land and pasture in roughly equal proportions	mixture of arable land and pasture

	meadow; relatively little woodland							predominantly pasture but with some arable land
Jurassic clay vales (Blackmoor Vale etc.)	average population density; low density of plough teams; small amounts of pasture (data of livestock not recorded); average amounts of meadow; some extensive areas of woodland	high population density; roughly equal proportions of arable land and pasture in demesnes; wheat with a small amount of oats and rye; cattle dominant amongst livestock; abundant meadow	no data on cropping or livestock	high population density; pasture dominant: cattle (dairying) and pig-keeping	arable land dominant: corn and cattle with substantial dairying	c.1840: predominantly pasture with some arable land (wheat, barley, and oats the major crops)	predominantly pasture (for dairying) with some arable land	predominantly pasture but with some arable land
chalk downland	average population density; low density of plough teams; abundant pasture, large numbers of sheep; average to abundant amounts of meadow;	high population density; roughly equal proportions of arable land and pasture in demesnes; wheat, oats and barley; sheep dominant	wheat and barley, with some oats; cattle and sheep	average population density; mixed farming; sheep and corn	arable land dominant: corn and sheep	c.1840: pasture dominant but with up to 40% arable land (wheat and barley the major crops)	arable land and pasture (for sheep) in roughly equal proportions	predominantly arable land but some areas of pasture

(continued)

Table 11.5. Continued

district	Domesday	1250–1349 (including population density 1327–32)	1350–1449	16th to early 17th century	mid-17th to mid-18th century	early to mid-19th century	1930s Land Utilisation Survey	present day
	relatively little woodland	amongst livestock; deficient in meadow						
South east Dorset heathlands	low population density; low density of plough teams; average amounts of pasture, relatively few sheep; relatively little meadow; relatively little woodland	low to average population density; no data on cropping; cattle dominant amongst livestock; average amounts of meadow	no data on cropping or livestock	low population density; pasture dominant: livestock rearing and fattening	pasture dominant: subsistence corn, with cattle rearing and sheep keeping	c.1840: arable land and pasture in roughly equal amounts, but relatively large amounts of common land (wheat and oats the major crops)	predominantly rough grazing	predominantly heathland and rough pasture, but with some improved pasture and arable land
	population density: low = 2.5–5 persons/mile^2 average = 5–10 persons/mile^2	population density: low = <50 taxpayers/10 mile^2		population density: low = 2.0–3.5 taxpayers/mile^2				

high = 10–15 persons/mile^2 (Darby and Welldon Finn 1967)

Plough team density:
low = 1.0–2.5/mile^2
average = 2.5–3.5/mile^2
high = over 3.5/mile^2
(Darby and Welldon Finn 1967)

average = 50–74 taxpayers/10 mile^2
high = >75 taxpayers/10 mile^2
(Campbell and Bartley 2006, map 18.10)

average = 4.0–5.5 taxpayers/mile^2
high = 6.0–7.5 taxpayers/mile^2
(Sheail 1972)

---

* available electronically (http://ahds.ac.uk/catalogue/collection.htm?uri=hist-5156-1).

owners as opposed to the peasantry. Domesday is also silent on what crops were being grown, and in order to get a more rounded picture of medieval agriculture, we must therefore compare these documentary sources with archaeological evidence. Indeed, before the eleventh century, this archaeological evidence is all we have. In Chapters 12–13 we will examine the archaeological evidence for animal husbandry and arable regimes in the medieval and Roman periods, but first we must examine sequences of preserved environmental material that cover the whole period.

PALAEOENVIRONMENTAL SEQUENCES

There are two types of palaeoenvironmental evidence (i.e. plant and animal remains preserved within natural deposits or on archaeological sites) that shed light on past patterns of land use: assemblages of charred cereals and animal bones from settlement sites ('on-site' assemblages), and material preserved within sequences of natural sediments that have built up over time such as peat bogs and in valley bottoms ('off-site' sequences). Within the on-site evidence we can distinguish 'palaeoeconomic material', that is the remains of domesticates, from the wild plants and animals that were living naturally in the area. Another key piece of terminology is that where plant remains are visible to the eye (e.g. cereal grains and chaff) they are known as 'macrofossils', in contrast to 'microscopic' pollen grains.

Spatial and temporal biases in the available evidence (Fig. 11.6 and Table 11.6)

Within our study area, some of the best palaeoenvironmental evidence comes from Devon (summarized in Rippon, Fyfe, and Brown 2006; Rippon 2008a; Straker 2008a; 2008b; Straker *et al.* 2008). Early work focused on the traditional locations for palynological work—the blanket bogs that cover the high uplands such as Dartmoor and Exmoor (e.g. Moore *et al.* 1984; Francis and Slater 1990; 1992; Straker and Crabtree 1995; Gearey and Charman 1996; Gearey *et al.* 1997; 2000a; 2000b)—but these lay beyond areas that were settled in the Roman and medieval periods. In recent years, however, several projects have investigated small valley mires in lowland areas of eastern Devon and in the Blackdown Hills (Caseldine *et al.* 2000; Hawkins 2005; Rippon, Fyfe, and Brown 2006), along with the major valley floodplains (Fyfe 2000; Fyfe *et al.* 2003; Barnett *et al.* 2007). In Dorset and Wiltshire there has been a very marked temporal and spatial bias in palaeoenvironmental studies towards the prehistoric period and the chalk downland, with little work carried out on sequences extending into later periods or on other geologies (e.g. Woodward 1991; Smith *et al.* 1997; Allen 1998a; 1998b; Allen and Green 1998; French *et al.* 2000; 2003),[2] the exceptions being Rimsmoor and Bestwall Quarry on the edges of the heathlands of south-east Dorset (Waton 1982; Ladle and Woodward 2009). In a number of places, however, a series of excavations in relatively close proximity have produced closely dated on-site assemblages that when taken altogether do allow the reconstruction of changing patterns of land use during the Roman and medieval periods, such as the chalk downland south of Dorchester (Smith *et al.* 1997; Davies *et al.* 2002) and the heathlands of Dorset (Cox and Hearne 1991; Ladle and Woodward 2009).

In Somerset there is a marked bias in the distribution of pollen sequences towards the traditional types of locations for such work: upland blanket bogs on Exmoor and lowland raised mires in the Somerset Levels. On Exmoor the peat sequences sometimes continue to the present day, and while in the Somerset Levels desiccation and peat cutting mean that most sequences are truncated in the late prehistoric period, those at Meare Heath and Godney Moor do extend into the early medieval period (Becket and Hibbert 1979; Housley *et al.* 2007).[3] Various other studies have examined aspects of the alluvial sequence that makes up the Somerset Levels, and although not producing continuous pollen sequences they do shed light on changing sea levels, local conditions in the wetlands, and sometimes wider patterns of land use in the region (e.g. Haslett *et al.* 1998; 2000a; 2000b; Haslett and Davies 2002; Haslett *et al.* 2006). A lack of organic material for radiocarbon dating the upper parts of these sequences has led to a reliance on chemostratigraphic dating, notably equating an increase in lead with the onset of Roman mining in the late 40s AD, from which a date in the second or third century AD is suggested for the reclamation of this area. Studies of alluviation in the Lox Yeo valley, on the southern flanks of Mendip, have also focused on heavy metal analysis as an indication of mining history, and a pollen sequence there is unfortunately undated (although based on the flora types it probably extends from the Mesolithic through to the medieval period: Macklin *et al.* 1985; Macklin and Hunt 1988). A pollen sequence from Rowberrow Hill, in Shipham, on the edge of the Mendip Hills, is also undated although 'a Roman or later date is postulated for the open herbaceous environment which is strongly arable with some pasture' (Wessex Archaeology 1998; Straker *et al.* 2008, 146). A more intensive programme of work on the North Somerset Levels allows the changing patterns of land use to be reconstructed from the Iron Age through

---

[2] In the Upper Allen valley, on Cranborne Chase, coring at St Giles House revealed a shallow peat whose pollen assemblages were characteristic of the post Middle-Late Bronze Age and before the later eighteenth century, but it was not radiocarbon dated (French *et al.* 2003, 225).

[3] A recent assessment of several other peat bogs has revealed a number of sequences that extend into the historic period (Brown *et al.* 2003).

to the medieval period, confirming a third-century date for the reclamation of that area, followed by abandonment in the late Roman/early medieval period, and recolonization from around the tenth century (Rippon 2000b; 2006a). A study of floodplain alluviation in the Yeo Valley around the Roman town of Ilchester has produced interesting results for the Roman and medieval periods, though dating is imprecise (Leach 1987; Thews 1994; Brett *et al.* 2009).[4]

Regional variations in land-use history

In total there are twenty-eight locations that either have an off-site palaeo-environmental sequence covering the Roman and/or medieval periods, or a series of on-site contexts that have produced discrete assemblages of material that cumulatively allow a broad environmental history to be reconstructed. These are summarized in Table 11.6. All the lowland sequences in Devon show a landscape extensively cleared of woodland by the middle of the Iron Age, apart from small patches of alder carr on the wetter low-lying areas, and some oak and hazel woodland presumably restricted to the steeper hillsides. An increase in cereal pollen in the early Roman period is then followed by broad continuity in land use through to the early medieval period. There is no evidence for an extensive or long-lasting woodland regeneration in the post-Roman period, although the possibility of very short-lived episodes that failed to register in the pollen analysis cannot be ruled out. Around the seventh to eighth centuries, however, many of these sequences do show significant changes in the local land use. In the eastern lowlands of Devon near Exeter, for example, a small peat bog at Hellings Park in the Loxbrook Valley (Broadclyst) first saw the appearance of cereals and the weeds of disturbed ground at this time, alongside an increase in grass and herbaceous species. At Burlescombe, the pollen assemblage from the fill of a seventh- or eighth-century well similarly shows a landscape that was extensively cleared of woodland and with some arable cultivation in the vicinity (Best and Gent 2007, 24). This change in agricultural practice around the eighth century AD, that sees a marked increase in cereal pollen, may be accounted for by the development of a new form of agriculture known as convertible husbandry, rather than a simple expansion of cultivation. Throughout most of the medieval and post-medieval period the fields in Devon—both open and enclosed—were managed through this form of rotational cultivation whereby the majority of land within a tenement (closes or parcels of open fields) were subject to alternating grain and grass crops, with a short period of cultivation (about two to three years), followed by a long

---

[4] An episode of increased alluviation at Slapton, in South Devon, is dated to around the eleventh to twelfth centuries (Foster *et al.* 2000).

grass ley (about six to eight years) producing a rotation of around ten years (Finberg 1951; Wood 1963; Hatcher 1970; H. Fox 1972; 1991b; Alcock 1975; H. Fox and Padel 2000, liii–xciv; Stanes 1964; 2005; 2008b; Stanes *et al.* 2008). From around the eighth century until the post-medieval period the pollen sequences in lowland Devon suggest little significant change in agricultural practice, whereafter there is a decline in arable cultivation.

The Blackdown Hills were, not surprisingly, rather more wooded in the Iron Age, although there had already been some clearance at Bywood by the fourth century BC, and limited cultivation in a largely open, pastoral, landscape at Greenway by the later first millennium BC. At Bywood, cereal cultivation appears in the pollen record for the first time around the Late Iron Age to early Roman period in what was largely a pastoral landscape where woodland was probably restricted to the steeper slopes. This woodland would have been an important resource as there was a nearby iron smelting industry throughout the Roman and early medieval periods (Griffith and Weddell 1996; Wieken 2004). Bywood and Greenway both show continuity in land use into the early medieval period, but around the eighth century there is a change evident at a number of sites such as Middleton where the stratigraphy within this valley-side mire changed from an organic clay to herbaceous peat. This may have been the result of erosion caused by local deforestation (reflected in the pollen sequence by a marked decline in woodland) that led to waterlogging of the site and the consequent growth of sedges and mosses; wheat/oats appear soon after. An increase in cereals and a decline in woodland at nearby Greenway may also have occurred at this time, although this date is interpolated from an earlier radiocarbon determination and must be treated with caution. At Aller Farm, on the eastern fringes of the Blackdown Hills, there was an increase in cereals somewhat later, perhaps around the ninth or tenth centuries.

To the east of the Blackdown Hills, the evidence we have suggests once again that the landscape was largely cleared of woodland by the Iron Age. In the Late Iron Age and Roman periods there was an intensification of land use, reflected in the Yeo valley near Ilchester, for example, by increased alluviation. A reduction in the intensity of agriculture in the late Roman/early medieval period is suggested by a decrease in alluviation in the Yeo valley and some increase in scrub and woodland at sites such as Baltmoor Wall, Godney, the Upper Brue Valley, and Rismoor, although there is no evidence for a widespread or long-lasting woodland regeneration. At Bestwall Quarry there is no indication of a decrease in the intensity of landscape exploitation in the early medieval period, mirroring the situation seen in Devon. An increase in the intensity of agriculture in the central Somerset Levels around the eighth century is reflected in greater alluviation in the Upper Brue valley. An increase in cereal pollen at the Baltmoor Wall dates to around the same time, and

Table 11.6. Summary of the results from palaeoenvironmental analyses from off-site sequences and major concentrations of on-site assemblages.

Site	Time span	Summary for Iron Age to present day	Reference
West of the Blackdown-Quantock Hills			
Lowlands of eastern Devon			
Hellings Park	Prehistoric to early medieval?	The first appearance of cereals appears to be in the later 7th/8th century, though the dating of this sequence is problematic.	Hawkins 2005
Mosshayne	Iron Age to medieval	Open, largely pastoral landscape on the Clyst floodplain in the Iron Age with rich meadows and some alder carr woodland. Some clearance of woodland both on the floodplain and the adjacent drylands in the Roman period and the first appearance of cereal cultivation in a predominantly pastoral landscape. Broad continuity thereafter, with no evidence for a post-Roman woodland regeneration.	Hawkins 2005
Culm Measures			
Hares Down, in Knowstone	Middle Iron Age to present day	Open, largely pastoral landscape in the Iron Age with some arable cultivation; woodland restricted to the steeper valley sides. Some woodland clearance in the Middle to Late Iron Age, and possibly again in the late Roman period (at Lobbs Bog). No significant change in land use in the earliest medieval period (5th to 7th centuries). Increased cereal pollen around the 8th century (representing the introduction of 'convertible husbandry'?), and clearance of wet alder woodland (at Hares Down). Continuity thereafter till 16th to 18th centuries with some increase in woodland and bracken suggesting a decline in the intensity of agriculture and grazing.	Fyfe *et al.* 2004
Lobbs Bog, in Rackenford	Middle Iron Age to present day		Fyfe *et al.* 2004
Middle North Combe, in Templeton	Late Bronze Age to present day		Fyfe *et al.* 2004
Windmill Rough, in Rackenford	Late Bronze Age to present day		Fyfe *et al.* 2004
Exmoor: southern flanks			
Ansteys Combe, in Molland	Late Iron Age/early Roman to present day	Open, largely pastoral landscape in the Iron Age with some arable cultivation; woodland restricted to the steeper valley sides. Some woodland clearance in the Middle to Late Iron Age. No significant change in land use in the early medieval period (5th to 9th centuries). Increased cereal pollen in 10th/11th centuries, and clearance of	Fyfe *et al.* 2003
Gourte Mires, in Molland	Late Neolithic to medieval		Fyfe *et al.* 2003
Long Breach, in Molland	Late Mesolithic to present day		Fyfe *et al.* 2003

		woodland. Continuity thereafter till around the 18th century with some increase in woodland and bracken suggesting a decline in the intensity of agriculture and grazing.	
Brightworthy, in Withypool	Mesolithic to present day	Iron Age and later part of sequence not radiocarbon dated, but clearance of woodland from valley sides appears to have occurred around AD 800–1200.	Fyfe 2000
Exmoor: high moorland			
Codsend Moor, in Cutcombe	Middle Iron Age to present	Largely open landscape by the Middle to Late Iron Age. Some further woodland clearance in the Late Iron Age/early Roman period, and possibly again in the late Roman period at Hoar Moor, but expansion of wood and scrub at Codsend Moor, followed by clearance. May have been some cereal cultivation in the late Roman period at Codsend Moor. A decline in grassland and arable cultivation, and increase in heather and woodland in the early medieval period (5th to 9th centuries). Thereafter a return to open grassland with possible evidence for limited arable cultivation. Woodland clearance in 16th/17th centuries, but no evidence for arable cultivation; increase in grassland at expense of heather from 18th century suggesting agricultural improvement.	Francis and Slater 1992
Hoar Moor, in Exford	Late Mesolithic to present day		Francis and Slater 1990
Moles Chamber, modern parish of Exmoor (formerly extra-parochial Exmoor Forest)	Middle Bronze Age to present day	Some open grassland but with extensive woodland, until a clearance event probably in the Late Iron Age that led to a more open pastoral landscape. No evidence of a post-Roman regeneration suggesting continued grazing. This open, pastoral landscape continues until around the 12th century when there is an increase in heather.	Fyfe 2000, 176–210
Blackdown-Quantock Hills			
Aller Farm, Stockland	Mid-Roman to early medieval	Extensive clearance of what was probably secondary woodland (i.e. not wildwood) in the late Roman period, leading to a more open pastoral landscape with some arable cultivation. Clearance of alder woodland, presumably on the valley floor around the 8th century, and an increase in cereal cultivation on the surrounding slopes from around the early 9th century.	Hatton and Caseldine 1991

(*continued*)

Table 11.6. Continued

Site	Time span	Summary for Iron Age to present day	Reference
Bolham	later medieval to post medieval	Peat starts to develop around the 11th/12th century in a predominantly open landscape dominated by pasture and meadow, but with large areas of woodland. A decline in woodland and increase in pasture around the 13th/14th centuries, that was reversed around the 16th century.	Hawkins 2005
Bywood	Iron Age to medieval	Woodland clearance in the Late Iron Age leading to a predominantly open landscape, though with some woodland presumably on nearby steep slopes. Some arable cultivation. Broad continuity in land use thereafter, and no evidence of a post-Roman woodland regeneration.	Hawkins 2005
Middleton	Early to late medieval	A mainly open, pastoral landscape by the 7th/8th century with some woodland (presumably on nearby steep slopes). Further woodland clearance around the 10th/11th centuries and the appearance of small-scale arable cultivation. Arable cultivation ceases around the 14th century when there was a shift to pasture and an increase in woodland.	Hawkins 2005

East of the Blackdown-Quantock Hills

Central Somerset lowlands

Yeo Valley, in Ilchester	Iron Age to medieval	Largely open landscape in the Iron Age, with the emergence of large numbers of villas in the hinterland of the small town of Ilchester. Increased alluvial accretion in the Roman period, followed by its virtual cessation in the early medieval period which may reflect a shift from arable cultivation to pasture within the river's catchment. Renewed alluviation not well dated but may have begun around the 9th century and ceased by the 14th century.	Thew 1994, 169–70

Somerset Levels

Baltmoor Wall, in East Lyng		A largely open, pastoral landscape during the Roman period on the drylands adjacent to this wetland though with a slight increase in woodland and decline in cereals in the late Roman/early medieval period (the dating is not precise and derived from interpolating between radiocarbon dates higher and lower in the sequence). Again	Watts and Scaife 2008

		based on interpolated dates, a slight increase in cereals occurred around the 8th century, and a more significant increase around the 10th century.		
Godney Moor, in Meare	Early Iron Age to c.10th century AD	Woodland clearance during Early to Middle Iron Age leading to an open landscape that continued until the late Roman/early medieval period when there was a slight increase in woodland. Sharp increase in woodland around the 8th/9th centuries, followed by an equally sharp reduction.		Housley et al. 2007
Meare Heath	Bronze Age to around ninth century AD	A largely open landscape during the Iron Age on the drylands and islands surrounding this peat bog, though with some increase in woodland in the later Middle Iron Age on Meare island. This was followed by an expansion of agriculture across the region as a whole, and this open landscape continued throughout the Roman and early medieval periods: no woodland regeneration in the 5th century.		Beckett and Hibbert 1979
Panborough-Bleadney Gap		Change in sedimentation—the onset of fluvial clay replacing freshwater organic channel deposits—in the palaeo-channel of the former river Brue/Sheppey, just south of the Panborough-Bleadney Gap, may have been brought about by a reduction in flow caused by the diversion of the Brue west past Meare (1170+/-60 BP, cal. AD 786–968). The top of the freshwater deposits 2cm below the base of the fluvial clay is dated 1531+/-35 BP, cal. AD 431–601, but this is clearly too old. The date was based on shells and is likely to be 400–500 years too old, suggesting an actual date around the 8th century.		Aalbersberg 1999
Street Causeway	Iron Age and early medieval	In both the Iron Age and c.7th to 9th centuries the local environment was a freshwater fen with areas of sedge and alder/willow carr. The adjacent drylands were extensively cleared of woodland by the Iron Age, with some arable cultivation, but far greater evidence for arable cultivation in the Middle Saxon period.		Brunning 2010
Upper Brue Valley	Iron Age to medieval	Both the floodplain and the adjacent drylands had been extensively cleared of woodland by the Late Iron Age. Some increase in woodland,		Aalbersberg 1999

(*continued*)

Table 11.6. Continued

Site	Time span	Summary for Iron Age to present day	Reference
		including alder/willow carr on the floodplain around the late Roman period. Peatland replaced by alluvial sedimentation around c.7th–9th centuries suggesting increased cultivation, and/or autumn ploughing, and/or the creation of open fields in the Brue's catchment (1247+/−34 BP, cal. AD 679–872).	
Dorset Chalk downland			
Dorchester By-pass and Allington Avenue, Fordington	Mesolithic to present	A largely open landscape that in the Bronze Age was divided up into a number of formalized field systems, although in the Early and Middle Iron Age the landscape was once again largely unenclosed. Increase in settlement and changes in land use in the Late Iron Age with long cultivated areas becoming pasture, ploughing up of new areas, and an increase in the growing of barley. Unusually for Roman towns in the wider region, no cluster of villas developed around Dorchester, although numerous farmsteads were associated with corn-drying ovens and extensive field systems. Late Roman period sees agricultural prosperity and intensification, and an increasing emphasis on cattle. Retreat from chalk downland to the river valleys in the early medieval period, but a continued mixed farming regime with arable cultivation and pasture, and an emphasis on sheep. Restructuring of the landscape, perhaps around the 8th century, with the nucleation of settlement and laying out of open fields.	Sharples 1991; Smith *et al.* 1997; Davies *et al.* 2002
South East Dorset heathlands			
Bestwall Quarry	Late Neolithic to early medieval	Well-wooded landscape in the Late Neolithic to Early Bronze Age with some small-scale clearances. Extensive clearance in the Early Bronze Age creating an initially pastoral landscape, with some arable cultivation appearing in the Middle Bronze Age to Early Iron Age. A decline in arable cultivation in the Middle Iron Age but then no apparent change in land use from the Iron Age through to the Roman	Ladle and Woodward 2009

		period. No indication of an increase in woodland in the early medieval period.	
Rimsmoor, in Bere Regis (Dorset)	Late Mesolithic to present day	Valley mire, 500m from the edge of the chalk. An episode of woodland clearance in the Middle Iron Age leads to a largely open, pastoral landscape with limited evidence for cultivation. Cereals increase in the Roman period, which also sees the appearance of rye. Increase in woodland/scrub in late Roman or early medieval period, followed by clearance.	Waton 1982
Wytch Farm, in Arne, Corfe Castle and Wareham (Dorset)	Mesolithic to present day	The Iron Age to Romano-British landscape was largely cleared of woodland, but with alder carr in the wetter valleys; extensive heathland, whose acidic soils account for the relatively high proportion of rye amongst the cultivated cereals. The post-Roman period may have seen some woodland regeneration as heathland was no longer managed through grazing and periodic burning, though later in the medieval period there was a reduction in woodland.	Cox and Hearne 1991

similar but less well-dated increases in cereal at Panborough and in the Yeo Valley date to around the eighth to the tenth centuries.

DISCUSSION

Palaeoenvironmental sequences such as these provide a valuable insight into long-term changes in land use. They show that the lowland areas of the South West and western Wessex were extensively cleared of trees by the late prehistoric period, although more woodland survived in hilly/upland areas such as the Blackdown Hills. The Roman period saw some intensification both to the east and the west of the Blackdowns, and while there may have seen some reversal of this in the early medieval period particularly in more Romanized areas to the east, there was no extensive woodland regeneration. Agriculture intensified again in the late first millennium AD, as early as the eighth century in the far South West and perhaps a little later to the east. These palaeoenvironmental sequences therefore give us the big picture of long-term, regional trends but unfortunately they tell use little about the crops being grown and nothing about the livestock grazing in the fields. For this we must turn to the animal bones and charred cereals that are preserved on many archaeological sites which are discussed in Chapters 12–13.

12

Arable cultivation and animal husbandry in the medieval period

ARCHAEOLOGICAL EVIDENCE: THE PALAEOECONOMIC DATA

In order to examine farming practices in more detail, and in particular compare the crops and livestock in the different *pays* that comprise our study area, we can now turn to the animal bones and charred cereals that are preserved on many archaeological sites. The collection of this data began with references in previously published national overviews (e.g. Levitan 1987; Albarella and Davis 1994; Sykes 2007), and then searching through the journals of county archaeological societies and published monographs. Further references/reports were identified in various online resources,[1] while numerous local authority Historic Environment Records, field units, and specialists also kindly supplied as yet unpublished reports.

For animal bones, data collection was restricted to the major domesticates—cattle, sheep/goat,[2] and pigs—that formed the mainstay of farming economies and contributed the vast majority of meat in the diet. In the Roman period, for example, other mammals do not appear to have been of great significance, and even on wetland sites in the region it is noteworthy how few fish or bird bones are recovered when midden deposits are extensively sieved (Rippon 2000b; 2006a). While the medieval period saw increased consumption of wild animals

---

[1] *South West Archaeological Research Framework Resource Assessment* (Webster 2008), the *Environmental Archaeology Bibliography* (EAB) (http://ads.ahds.ac.uk/catalogue/specColl/eab_eh_2004/), and reports from the Centre for Applied Archaeological Analyses at the University of Southampton (http://wac.soton.ac.uk/Centres/CAAA/Facilities/sites.htm), Wessex Archaeology (http://www.wessexarch.co.uk/reports), the Ancient Monuments Laboratory (now English Heritage's Centre for Archaeology) (http://www.english-heritage.org.uk/server/show/nav.9596), and other 'grey literature' available through the OASIS project (http://ads.ahds.ac.uk/catalogue/library/greylit/index.cfm).

[2] In most cases the bones of sheep and goats cannot be distinguished and so they are grouped together as sheep/goat in faunal reports.

such as deer, rabbit, and fish, as well as domesticated fowl (e.g. Rippon 2006a), even then the major source of protein came from the main domesticates. To be statistically reliable, animal bone assemblages should ideally contain over five hundred identified specimens, with a minimum of one hundred, but as the emphasis here is to group data from each *pays*, and such is the dearth of well-excavated material from parts of our study area, smaller assemblages are included in the overall totals for each *pays* (although when calculating the average of site averages only assemblages with one hundred or more fragments are included). As the vast majority of animal bone reports only provide a simple fragment count or Number of Identified Specimens (NISP), these are the data used here, although it should be borne in mind that this tends to produce a slight bias towards cattle (as larger animals have larger bones that tend to fragment into more identifiable pieces). In compiling statistics on the percentages of cattle, sheep/goat, and pig bones, it must be stressed that these do not simply equate to the different proportions of animals kept, as pigs, for example, have a larger number of bones than cattle or sheep, and the bones of cattle tend to fragment into more pieces that those of sheep. Another factor is that animals kept for their meat, and which are therefore killed young, will be over-represented compared to livestock that was kept into maturity and for products such as milk and wool (in young animals most bones consists of three parts that eventually fuse together to form a single element). It is to be hoped that if further work is carried out on regional variation in faunal assemblages it will be possible to consider the age-at-death data.

Of the arable crops, wheat, barley, oats, and rye have been studied as these are the most archaeologically visible. Wheat prefers heavier soils, while barley and rye prefer lighter ground. Oats prefer heavier ground and can tolerate greater acidity than other cereals. As with animal bones, certain types will be better represented than others as they undergo different types of processing. Emmer wheat (that prefers light and dry soils) and spelt wheat (that can grow on light or heavy soils) are 'hulled' varieties, which means that their grains are held within tightly adhering 'glumes' (cases). This has the advantage of providing protection against fungal attack and birds, but the disadvantage of the grain being more difficult to extract. In free-threshing wheats (e.g. bread wheat, that prefers heavier soils, and can be autumn sown), however, the grain is more exposed making it easier to extract, but prone to fungal attack and birds. It is also a poor competitor with weeds, and is prone to premature sprouting in the ear during damp weather close to harvest time. As free-threshing wheats do not require heat in order to remove grain from the chaff, they are less likely to be preserved through charring on archaeological sites as threshing is more likely to have occurred away from settlements. In the medieval period this difference in the likelihood of emmer/spelt and bread wheat being preserved is not particularly an issue as virtually all the wheat grown was bread wheat, but it is a problem in the Roman period when emmer, spelt, and bread wheat all appear to have been cultivated (Jones 1982; 1989; 1991). For example, if on one site there were thirty grains of emmer (3.9%), 230 grains of spelt (29.7%), 500 grains (64.5%) identified simply as emmer or spelt, and fifteen grains of bread wheat (1.9%) we can infer that spelt was far more important than emmer, but not that bread wheat was only 1.9% of all the wheat harvested. If, however, we compare this site with another where 3% of the grain was emmer, 47% spelt, 40% emmer or spelt, and 10% bread wheat, then we can say that bread wheat was a more important crop here compared to the first site.

Emmer and spelt are difficult to distinguish based on grain shape, although some reports do attempt this and those data are used here. In many cases, however, most if not all grains are listed as emmer/spelt and we must turn to any preserved chaff in order to establish their relative importance. What chaff cannot tell us, however, is the relative significance of emmer and spelt compared to bread wheat, or oats, barley, and rye, as they all produce different amounts of chaff of varying robustness.[3] Another problem is that it is difficult to determine whether the oats were wild or cultivated as the grains are indistinguishable, although if chaff is preserved this can sometimes distinguish them. Overall, attention here has focused on the grain data, with the analysis of chaff restricted to what it tells us about specific issues such as the relative significance of emmer and spelt, and whether any oats were cultivated.

Another factor in the interpretation of the charred cereal assemblages is the possibility that some may not have been grown locally but were imported from nearby markets, something that may well have been the practice in both the Roman and middle to late medieval periods for which we have most data. The importation of cereals is particularly likely where assemblages of grain have been cleaned of chaff, except for free-threshing wheat that would normally have been processed away from settlements. Even if grain had been imported from a local town, however, it may well still reflect what was being grown in the local area: for the Roman period, for example, barley is 37% of the grain in Dorchester (compared to 45% on rural settlements on the downland), which

---

[3] In hulled wheat (e.g. emmer and spelt), for example, a single grain is held in place by one glume base, with a single rachis segment usually holding two grains, with both glume bases and rachis segments sufficiently robust to have survived in the archaeological record. In free-threshing wheat, in contrast, the glumes are too soft to survive charring, and one rachis node can hold up to six grains, with the result that if equal acreages of emmer, spelt, and bread wheat were harvested, far less bread wheat chaff would survive. Another factor that leads to far less chaff from free-threshing wheat being preserved is that it is more likely to be processed close to where it was harvested (i.e. out in the fields, not in the settlements where excavations take place), whereas hulled wheat is more likely to be stored in spikelet form within granaries in settlements and then processed in the home (and so will be encountered in excavations). Barley rachis segments can also hold up to six grains and the glumes do not survive, while oat and rye chaff is similarly rarely preserved, so that if equal acreages of oats, barley, and spelt wheat were harvested, there would be far less evidence of the barley and oat chaff.

compares to just 2% in Ilchester and Shepton Mallet in the central Somerset lowlands where barley is 5% on rural settlements. The composition of an imported grain assemblage will, therefore, reflect local agricultural regimes if both the site and the town from where the grain came are in the same *pays*.

A final factor to consider when interpreting cereal assemblages is whether they were being grown for human and/or animal consumption as although cereals are more likely to have been charred if they were being threshed and cleaned for human use, small amounts of animal bedding and fodder may also have got burnt. In pre-modern times, all farming regimes had a requirement for livestock, if only for traction, and even in periods with a market economy, most regions would therefore have grown at least some crops and kept some livestock, the latter providing valuable manure for the arable fields. Although barley and oats were the main fodder crops, in the South West at least these were also grown for human consumption (Fox 1991b, 303–4). The extent to which any of the regional variation in the crops that were grown across the study area was due to different animal husbandry is a topic that could be explored further in future work.

In collecting data for this study some temporal and regional patterning also emerged in terms of its recovery from archaeological sites. It was only in the 1970s that the systematic collection of palaeoenvironmental data began, for example, through wet sieving in order to recover charred cereals (e.g. Van der Veen 2008; Van der Veen *et al.* 2007). Delays in publishing old excavations mean that even recent reports can be devoid of charred cereals due to the lack of sampling procedures on the original excavations (e.g. Atworth villa, Wiltshire, excavated in 1970–5 but not published until 2008: Erskine and Ellis 2008). Until the late 1980s it was often only larger-scale developments that were preceded by archaeological work although from the early 1990s implementation of the then *Planning Policy Guidance Note 16: Archaeology and Planning* (PPG16)[4] has ensured that the vast majority of developments that threaten archaeological deposits are subject to proper investigation. This has resulted in far more archaeological work being carried out, with the effect that whereas until recently the South West lacked well-preserved assemblages of plant macrofossils for the Roman and medieval periods (e.g. van der Veen 2008; van der Veen *et al.* 2007), there are now a series of important assemblages (albeit many not yet published). Within the framework provided by PPG16, archaeological investigation is usually carried out in two stages: an evaluation of the archaeological preservation on a proposed development site through small-scale trenching, and if significant remains are discovered, and the development is to precede, a full-scale excavation. As part of the evaluation stage, an assessment of any palaeoenvironmental material recovered should

---

[4] now replaced by *Planning Policy Statement 5: Planning for the Historic Environment*.

be carried out that notes what species are present, although it is only if a full excavation takes place that a detailed report is produced that quantifies the different species present. If the development does not proceed, then the initial assessment of the palaeoenvironmental material is all the data that we have, and such circumstances account for the references below to 'unquantified assessment' of assemblages. One result of the increasing amount of development-led work, however, is that there are major biases in where excavations are occurring which mirrors very closely where the greatest economic growth is (i.e. urban expansion and infrastructure development such as road construction). Another factor that has led to marked regional variation in the amount of palaeoenvironmental data we have is differential preservation of the plant and animal remains. For animal bones the best preservation is to the east of the Blackdown and Quantock Hills, with the generally acidic soils of Devon and Cornwall meaning that most sites do not have faunal assemblages. The exceptions are a number of coastal sites where blown sand contains sufficient shell material to produce neutral or alkali conditions as at Atlantic Road in Newquay, Cornwall (Ingrem forthcoming), and Bantham in Devon (Silvester 1981; Griffith 1986; Griffith and Reed 1996; Reed and Bidwell 2007).

These then are some of the factors that influence the palaeoeconomic material that we have available, and the problems we face in interpreting it. Were the aims of our research to reconstruct the agricultural regimes on individual sites, then a far more detailed set of analyses would have to be carried out. Instead, the aim here is to establish the bigger picture and determine whether there were differences in arable cultivation and animal husbandry in different *pays*.

A LANDSCAPE-BASED CHRONOLOGY

Before reviewing the animal bone and charred cereal assemblages, the chronological framework that is used needs to be explained. The medieval period stretches from the fifth to the fifteenth centuries, and we know from studies at a national scale that agricultural practices changed significantly over this time. The traditional divisions of the medieval period are early medieval (AD 410–1066, also known as the Anglo-Saxon period), the High Middle Ages (AD 1066–1348), and late medieval (AD 1348–c.1500), but this is not really appropriate for such a strongly landscape-focused study such as this. In southern England at least, landscapes of the tenth century appear to have had far more in common with those of the twelfth and thirteenth centuries than those of the sixth and seventh centuries. In recent years a number of authors have argued that there were significant changes in the landscape around the eighth century (e.g. Brown and Foard 1998; Williamson 2003;

Rippon 2008a), and in this study, therefore, the following threefold division of the medieval period has been adopted:

- Fifth to the seventh centuries (earliest medieval period): in western Wessex this essentially reflects the gradual evolution of the Romano-British landscape (indeed, this has times been referred to as the 'sub Roman' or 'late antique' period: e.g. Collins and Gerrard 2004).
- Eighth to the mid-fourteenth century (middle medieval period): starting with a widespread period of landscape restructuring and agricultural intensification, and through centuries of continued growth and expansion that ended with the fourteenth-century plagues. In practice, the vast majority of the palaeoeconomic assemblages are eleventh to thirteenth century.
- Mid-fourteenth to the late fifteenth century (late medieval period): a period that documentary sources suggest saw significant changes in land use following the outbreak of plague and resultant decline in population, including a shift from arable cultivation to pasture in some areas.

MEDIEVAL ANIMAL HUSBANDRY

Earliest medieval (fifth to the seventh century)

There are relatively few assemblages from the earliest medieval period. In Cornwall and Devon the generally acidic soils, particularly in the uplands where most rural settlement excavations have taken place, mean that there are very few animal bone assemblages. The larger of two assemblages has come from the coastal trading settlement at Bantham, in south Devon (Silvester 1981; Reed and Bidwell 2007), where cattle (59%) were dominant with sheep/goat just 21% (although in the far smaller assemblage of fifty eight bones from Tintagel cattle were just 28%: Barrowman *et al.* 2007). In Somerset there are just two significant assemblages: the reoccupied hillfort at Cadbury Congresbury where cattle were 58%, sheep/goat 6%, and pig 36%, and the hilltop site at Glastonbury Tor where there were 'minimum numbers of individuals' of 43% cattle, 42% sheep/goat, and 17% pig (Rahtz *et al.* 1992). The high status of these sites probably accounts for the high proportions of pig. At Brickley Lane in Devizes, in the Jurassic clay vales of Wiltshire, cattle were 81% of a small assemblage of just twenty six bones (Poore *et al.* 2002), while three early medieval lower-status rural settlements on the chalk downlands all show cattle were similarly dominant (Poundbury, 50%: Sparey Green 1987; Wilton, 60%: Grimm 2008b; and Tidworth, 84%: Godden *et al.* 2002). Overall, we appear to be seeing a mix of cattle and sheep/goat in the south-west and a greater emphasis on cattle further east.

Middle medieval (eighth to the mid-fourteenth century)

Western Devon and Cornwall

At Mawgan Porth (Clutton-Brock 1976; Bruce Mitford 1997) and Gwithian (Turk 1969) cattle (*c*.45%) were more significant than is seen nationally on rural sites (cf. Tables 12.1–12.2). In contrast, two castles in the South West, Launceston (Albarella and Davis 1994; Saunders 2006) and Okehampton (Higham *et al.* 1982), have produced remarkably similar assemblages in which cattle were *c*.31% compared to the national average of *c*.36%. In the major urban assemblages cattle are also slightly under-represented and sheep/goat over-represented (Exeter: Maltby 1979; Levitan 1987; Woolster Street and the waterfront in Plymouth: Gaskill Brown 1986), although this is reversed at Lydford on the edge of Dartmoor (Levitan 1987). The South West's animal husbandry in the middle medieval period was therefore characterized by a relatively balanced husbandry of cattle and sheep/goat—continuing a trend seen in the early medieval period—but with pig under-represented.

Central Somerset

In the *pays* of central Somerset, that all lie adjacent to extensive wetlands, cattle dominate the animal bone assemblages. There are no rural assemblages from the Vale of Taunton Deane, although a series of excavations from urban contexts in Taunton show that cattle (49%) were above the regional average for towns of 43% (Leach 1984; Burrow 1988; Hutcheson and Andrews 2002). Cattle were also slightly more significant at Taunton Priory (Leach 1984). This significance of cattle probably reflects the easy access that these farming communities had to the rich pastures and meadows that were available on the nearby Somerset Levels. The central Somerset towns of Glastonbury and Ilchester, whose hinterlands will also have embraced extensive areas of the Somerset Levels, have produced assemblages with cattle (44%) again higher than the regional average.[5] Cattle were very dominant on the five rural sites that have produced animal bone assemblages (51% compared to the regional average for rural sites of 42% and national average of *c*.46%).[6] Unfortunately there are relatively few sites in northern Somerset, and although the

---

[5] **Glastonbury**: Bove Town (Nancy Hollinrake pers. comm.) and Wirral Park (Levitan 1987); **Ilchester**: Kingham (Leach 1982), Limmington Road, Church Street and Manor House (Levitan 1987), and Great Yard (Broomhead 1998); **Taunton**: 5–8 Fore Street (Burrow 1988), Bentham's Garage (Leach 1984) and County Hotel (Hutcheson and Andrews 2002).

[6] Beckery (Rahtz and Hirst 1974); Brent Knoll (Young 2009); Crandon Bridge (Levitan 1987); Little Haven in Edington (Brigers 2006); Shapwick (excluding Church Field: Gerrard with Aston 2007); The Mound, Glastonbury (Carr 1985).

assemblages are all small, there is a slight bias towards cattle, again at the expense of pig.[7]

On the Somerset Levels themselves there are four assemblages, of which only three have been quantified. At the rural settlements of Puxton Home Ground (Rippon 2006a) and West Wick (Powell 2009) cattle bones average 48%, sheep/goat just 27%, and pig 25% (in assemblages totalling just seventy-five fragments), whereas at the probably manorial site of Puxton Church Field cattle were 40%, sheep/goat 27%, and pig 34% in a far larger assemblage of 624 fragments (Rippon 2006a). The small and as yet unquantified assemblage from an eleventh to thirteenth-century farmstead site at St Georges was dominated by cattle (Mary Alexander pers. comm.). This bias in favour of cattle and away from sheep fits with our documentary evidence for communities living on and round wetlands specializing in cattle husbandry.

Specialized animal husbandry in central Wessex

Further east there were a series of *pays* that similarly had specialized animal husbandry regimes. Three sites on the Jurassic limestone hills in Somerset have produced animal bone assemblages showing a marked emphasis on sheep, a pattern that once again follows that seen in the documentary sources. This is seen both on a rural site (Eckweek in Peasedown St John: Davis 1991) where cattle were just 23% and sheep/goat 67%, and urban sites in Bath (Levitan 1987; Davenport 1999; Davenport *et al.* 2007) where cattle were 36% and sheep/goat 50%. In the adjacent Jurassic clay vales there are unfortunately no assemblages from rural settlements but there is material from four towns.[8] On average cattle accounted for 43%, the average for towns across our study area, but sheep (38%) are under-represented at the expense of pig. This low figure for sheep is not surprising as they tend to suffer from ailments such as foot rot and liver fluke on heavy soils, and the documentary sources similarly suggest that cattle were dominant. On the two rural settlements that have been excavated on the chalk downland of Wiltshire cattle were just 35% and sheep/goat 58%.[9] This emphasis on sheep (that are 50% on rural sites across our study area and *c.*46% nationally) confirms the pattern seen in documentary sources. In the chalkland towns the proportions of each species is broadly in line with the averages across our study area.[10] Only one rural

[7] Bickley in Cleeve (Ponsford 2002); Old Show Ground in Cheddar (Evans and Hancocks 2005, 119); manor house in Cheddar (Rahtz 1979); St Cross nunnery in the Chew Valley (Rahtz and Greenfield 1977); the Wells Museum site (Sykes 2007).
[8] Gillingham (Cox 1992; Heaton 1992; Valentin and Robinson 2001), Malmesbury (Currie 1993; Longman 2006), Shaftesbury (Carew 2008) and Trowbridge (Graham and Davies 1993).
[9] Collingbourne Ducis (Pine 2001) and Gomeldon (Musty and Algar 1986).
[10] Amesbury (Powell *et al.* 2009), Ramsbury (Haslam 1980), Salisbury (Allen *et al.* 2000) and Wilton (Andrews *et al.* 2000; Grimm 2008b) in Wiltshire, and Greyhound Yard in Dorchester, Dorset (Woodward *et al.* 1993).

Table 12.1. Statistical analysis of the percentages of cattle, sheep/goat, and pig from different categories of site in medieval Britain.

Site type	cattle	sheep/goat	pig
A. Grant 1988, tab. 8.10 12th/13th centuries			
towns	c.42%	c.42%	c.16%
secular elite	c.42%	c.46%	c.34%
rural	c.33%	c.46%	c.21%
B. Sykes 2009, Fig. 17.1			
towns	c.47%	c.39%	c.14%
secular elite	c.36%	c.33%	c.31%
ecclesiastical elite	c.32%	c.35%	c.33%
rural	c.37%	c.46%	c.17%

settlement in the heathlands of Dorset has been excavated, at Ower Farm, that produced a very small assemblage of twenty-three bones of which 39% were cattle, 57% sheep/goat, and 4% pig (Cox and Hearne 1991). Two towns have produced assemblages dominated by cattle,[11] which corresponds with the documentary evidence.

Discussion

Past studies of palaeoeconomic material from the medieval period have focused on the differences between sites of different social status across medieval England whereas the work here has examined the data both in terms of social status and geographical location (*see* Tables 12.1 and 12.2). Of the 67,161 cattle, sheep/goat, and pig bones the vast majority (49,939 fragments, 74.4%) came from towns. In part, the bones recovered from such sites will reflect the animals raised in the surrounding countryside and brought to market, although dietary preferences for certain meats are liable to have created biases. Of these urban assemblages in Exeter, the Jurassic clay vales, and the chalk downland, cattle are around the overall average for our study area of 43% (which is almost the same as the national average of *c*.42%), though in towns on the Jurassic limestone hills cattle were much less significant (36%) and sheep/goat (50%) are above the regional average (44%). In Taunton (49%) and to a lesser extent the central Somerset lowlands (44%) cattle were particularly important presumably reflecting the extensive wetlands in their hinterland.

---

[11] Christchurch, 1969–1980 (Jarvis 1983) and 1981–3 (Davies 1983), and Wimborne Minster (Woodward 1983).

Table 12.2(A). Summary of middle medieval bones from sites of different social status from each of the *pays* within the study area.

		No. assem. () = assem. >100+	Total frags.	cattle frags	%	ave. of ave.	sheep/goat frags	%	ave. of ave.	pig frags	%	ave. of ave.
Cornwall and Devon	towns	5 (4)	22,670	9,841	43%	45%	10,086	45%	42%	2,743	12%	14%
	monastic	1	1,753	676	39%	39%	879	50%	50%	198	11%	11%
	castle	2	3,857	1,204	31%	31%	1,305	34%	34%	1,348	35%	35%
	manorial	0	0	0	0	0	0	0	0	0	0	0
	rural	2	1,150	521	45%	45%	586	51%	52%	43	4%	3%
Vale of Taunton Deane	towns	4 (2)	4,628	2,246	49%	48%	2,123	46%	43%	259	6	9%
	monastic	1	797	301	38%	38%	435	55%	55%	61	8	8%
	castle		0	0	0	0	0	0	0	0	0	0
	manorial		0	0	0	0	0	0	0	0	0	0
	rural		0	0	0	0	0	0	0	0	0	0
central Somerset lowlands	towns	8 (6)	4,962	2,187	48%	53%	2,203	44%	36%	572	12%	16%
	monastic	1	1,814	604	33%	33%	964	53%	53%	246	14%	14%
	castle	0	0	0	0	0	0	0	0	0	0	0
	manorial	1	1,733	567	33%	33%	789	46%	46%	377	22%	22%
	rural	5 (4)	1,649	817	50%	41%	652	40%	37%	134	8%	22%
North Somerset hills and vales	towns	0	0	0	0	0	0	0	0	0	0	0
	monastic	2 (1)	914	381	42%	41%	198	22%	23%	335	37%	36%
	castle	0	0	0	0	0	0	0	0	0	0	0
	manorial	1	204	124	61%	61%	58	28%	28%	22	11%	11%
	rural	1	140	62	44%	44%	70	50%	50%	8	6%	6%
reclaimed marshland	towns	0	0	0	0	0	0	0	0	0	0	0
	monastic	0	0	0	0	0	0	0	0	0	0	0
	castle	0	0	0	0	0	0	0	0	0	0	0
	manorial	1	624	248	40%	40%	167	27%	27%	209	34%	34%
	rural	2 (0)	75	36	48%	–	20	27%	–	19	25%	–

Region	Type											
Jurassic limestone hills	towns	5 (4)	6,369	2,294	36%	30%	3,200	50%	46%	875	14%	25%
	monastic	0	0	0	0	0	0	0	0	0	0	0
	castle	0	0	0	0	0	0	0	0	0	0	0
	manorial	1	46	15	33%	0	9	20%	0	22	48%	0
	rural	1	500	113	23%	23%	333	67%	67%	54	11%	11%
Jurassic clay vales	towns	8 (6)	4,502	1,936	43%	42%	1,695	38%	41%	871	19%	17%
	monastic	0	0	0	0	0	0	0	0	0	0	0
	castle	1	857	305	36%	36%	339	40%	40%	213	25%	25%
	manorial	0	0	0	0	0	0	0	0	0	0	0
	rural	0	0	0	0	0	0	0	0	0	0	0
chalk downland	towns	7 (6)	6,442	2,706	42%	39%	2,594	40%	41%	1142	18%	19%
	monastic	0	0	0	0	0	0	0	0	0	0	0
	castle	0	0	0	0	0	0	0	0	0	0	0
	manorial	0	0	0	0	0	0	0	0	0	0	0
	rural	2 (2)	1,132	391	35%	25%	657	58%	64%	84	7%	11%
South East Dorset heathlands	towns	3 (2)	366	200	55%	52%	103	28%	28%	63	17%	20%
	monastic	0	0	0	0	0	0	0	0	0	0	0
	castle	0	0	0	0	0	0	0	0	0	0	0
	manorial	0	0	0	0	0	0	0	0	0	0	0
	rural	1	23	9	39%	39%	13	57%	57%	1	4%	4%

Table 12.2(B). Summary of middle medieval bones from each of the *pays* within the study area grouped by sites of different social status.

	No. assem.	Total frags	Cattle			sheep/goat			pig		
	( ) = assem. >100+		frags	%	ave. of ave.	frags	%	ave. of ave.	frags	%	ave. of ave.
TOWNS											
Cornwall and Devon	5 (4)	22,670	9,841	43%	45%	10,086	45%	42%	2,743	12%	14%
Vale of Taunton Deane	4 (2)	4,628	2,246	49%	48%	2,123	46%	43%	259	6%	9%
central Somerset lowlands	8 (6)	4,962	2,187	44%	53%	2,203	44%	36%	572	12%	16%
North Somerset hills and vales	0	0	0	0	0	0	0	0	0	0	0
reclaimed marshland	0	0	0	0	0	0	0	0	0	0	0
Jurassic limestone hills	5 (4)	6,369	2,294	36%	30%	3,200	50%	46%	875	14%	25%
Jurassic clay vales	8 (6)	4,502	1,936	43%	42%	1,695	38%	41%	871	19%	17%
chalk downland	7 (6)	6,442	2,706	42%	39%	2,594	40%	41%	1,142	18%	19%
South East Dorset heathlands	3 (2)	366	200	55%	52%	103	28%	28%	63	17%	20%
total	40 (30)	49,939	21,410	43%	43%	22,004	44%	40%	6,525	13%	18%
MONASTIC SITES											
Cornwall and Devon	1	1,753	676	39%	39%	879	50%	50%	198	11%	11%
Vale of Taunton Deane	1	797	301	38%	38%	435	55%	55%	61	8%	8%
central Somerset lowlands	1	1,814	604	33%	33%	964	53%	53%	246	14%	14%
North Somerset hills and vales	2 (1)	914	381	42%	41%	198	22%	23%	335	37%	36%
reclaimed marshland	0	0	0	0.0	0	0	0.0	0	0	0.0	0
Jurassic limestone hills	0	0	0	0.0	0	0	0.0	0	0	0.0	0
Jurassic clay vales	0	0	0	0.0	0	0	0.0	0	0	0.0	0
chalk downland	0	0	0	0.0	0	0	0.0	0	0	0.0	0
South East Dorset heathlands	0	0	0	0.0	0	0	0.0	0	0	0.0	0
totals	5 (4)	5,278	1,962	37%	38%	2,476	47%	45%	840	16%	17%
CASTLES											
Cornwall and Devon	2	3,857	1,204	31%	33%	1,305	34%	34%	1,348	35%	35%
Vale of Taunton Deane	0	0	0	0.0	0	0	0.0	0	0	0.0	0
central Somerset lowlands	0	0	0	0.0	0	0	0.0		0	0.0	0
North Somerset hills and vales	0	0	0	0.0	0	0	0.0	0	0	0.0	0
reclaimed marshland	0	0	0	0.0	0	0	0.0		0	0.0	0
Jurassic limestone hills	0	0	0	0.0	0	0	0.0		0	0.0	0
Jurassic clay vales	1	857	305	36%	36%	339	40%	40%	213	25%	25%

chalk downland	0	0	0	0.0	0	0	0.0	0	0	0.0	0.0	0	0
South East Dorset heathlands	0	0	0	0.0	0	0	0.0	0	0	0.0	0.0	0	0
totals	3	4,714	1,509	32%	33%	1,644	35%	36%	1,561	33%	32%		

MANORIAL SITES

Cornwall and Devon	0	0	0	0.0	0	0	0.0	0.0	0	0.0	0.0	0	0
Vale of Taunton Deane	0	0	0	0.0	0	0	0.0	0.0	0	0.0	0.0	0	0
central Somerset lowlands	1	1,733	567	33%	33%	789	46%	46%	377	22%	22%		
North Somerset hills and vales	1	204	124	61%	61%	58	28%	28%	22	11%	11%		
reclaimed marshland	1	624	248	40%	40%	167	27%	27%	209	34%	34%		
Jurassic limestone hills	1 (0)	46	15	33%	0	9	20%	0	22	48%	0		
Jurassic clay vales	0	0	0	0.0	0	0	0.0	0	0	0.0	0		
chalk downland	0	0	0	0.0	0	0	0.0	0	0	0.0	0		
South East Dorset heathlands	0	0	0	0.0	0	0	0.0	0	0	0.0	0		
totals	4 (3)	2,607	954	37%	44%	1,023	39%	34%	630	24%	22%		

NON-MANORIAL RURAL SETTLEMENTS

Cornwall and Devon	2	1,150	521	45%	45%	586	51%	52%	43	4%	3%		
Vale of Taunton Deane	0	0	0	0	0	0	0	0	0	0	0		
central Somerset lowlands	6 (4)	1,603	817	51%	41%	652	41%	37%	134	8%	22%		
North Somerset hills and vales	1	140	62	44%	44%	70	50%	50%	8	6%	6%		
reclaimed marshland	2 (0)	75	36	48%	0	20	27%	0	19	25%	0		
Jurassic limestone hills	1	500	113	23%	23%	333	67%	67%	54	11%	11%		
Jurassic clay vales	0	0	0	0	0	0	0	0	0	0	0		
chalk downland	2 (2)	1,132	391	35%	25%	657	58%	64%	84	7%	11%		
South East Dorset heathlands	1	23	9	39%	39%	13	57%	567%	1	4%	4%		
totals	15 (11)	4,623	1,949	42%	37%	2,331	50%	47%	343	7%	12%		

OVERALL TOTALS

towns	49,939	21,410	43%	22,004	44%	6,525	13%
monastic sites	5,278	1,962	37%	2,476	47%	840	16%
castles	4,714	1,509	32%	1,644	35%	1,561	33%
manorial	2,607	954	37%	1,023	39%	630	24%
non-manorial rural settlements	4,623	1,949	42%	2,331	50%	343	7%
totals	67,161	27,784	41%	29,478	44%	9,899	15%

Although non-manorial rural settlements might be expected to more accurately reflect local animal husbandry regimes, it must be remembered that in a period when there was a sophisticated market economy this need not have been the case, with the animals on rural settlements being biased towards those that were not driven to market. The excavated assemblages do, however, show far greater deviation from the regional average than is evident in towns, monastic sites, or castles. The average for cattle on non-manorial rural settlements across our study area is 42% (compared to the national average of 33%), a figure that is exceeded in Cornwall (45%), the North Somerset hills and vales (44%), and in particular the central Somerset lowlands (51%). The significance of the Somerset Levels to the grazing economy is confirmed by the similarly high figure for cattle (48%). Conversely, the figures for cattle bones on the Jurassic limestone hills (23%) and chalk downland (35%) are far lower than the regional average of 42%.

The average across our study area for sheep/goat bones on rural settlements is 50%, and not surprisingly the figures for the Jurassic limestone hills (67%) and chalk downland (58%) are significantly higher, and those for the central Somerset lowlands (41%) and reclaimed marshland far lower (27%). Overall, the results from this analysis confirms the impression gained from the available documentary sources, that there were significant local variations in animal husbandry across the study area in the middle medieval period and that in many places there was a clear correlation between geology/soils and livestock husbandry with heavier soils seeing cattle being favoured over sheep, and the reverse on lighter soils. Areas such as Devon and Cornwall appear to have seen less specialized husbandry.

Late medieval (mid-fourteenth century to the late fifteenth century)

There are, unfortunately, relatively few late medieval animal bone assemblages from our study area, and those we have are mostly high status castles,[12] manor houses,[13] monasteries,[14] or urban sites.[15] As very few of these late medieval

---

[12] Launceston Castle (Albarella and Davis 1994); Okehampton Castle (Higham et al. 1982).

[13] Cheddar (from 1230 the former royal palace was an Episcopal manor: Rahtz 1979); Kingston Lacy (Papworth 1998); Shapwick House (Gerrard with Aston 2007).

[14] Christchurch Priory (Davies 1983); St Katherine's Priory Exeter (Levitan 1987); Glastonbury Abbey Silver Street (Ellis 1982); Taunton Priory Barn (Leach 1984).

[15] Bath (Davenport 1991); Christchurch (Davies 1983; Jarvis 1983); Exeter (Maltby 1979; Levitan 1987); Malmesbury (Currie 1993); Taunton (Hutcheson and Andrews 2000). North Petherton was an ancient royal manor in Domesday with a church, that by the fourteenth century had the right to a market and although never legally a town it was clearly not a wholly agricultural community (Leach 1977).

assemblages fall within the same *pays*, an intra-regional comparison is not possible although compared to the middle medieval period there is a slight increase in cattle.

MEDIEVAL ARABLE CULTIVATION

Earliest medieval period (fifth to the seventh century)

Unfortunately there are very few charred cereal assemblages from our study area dating to the early medieval period. There are three sites in Dumnonia, all of which are coastal, and in all cases oats were dominant (forming 43–91% of the grain assemblages), with barley second in importance (between 27 and 44%) and just small amounts of wheat (Tintagel: Harry and Morris 1997; Barrowman *et al.* 2007; Bantham: Reed and Bidwell 2007; Duckpool in Morwenstow: Ratcliffe 1995).

In the lowlands of central Somerset there are two well-dated and one possible assemblage from this early medieval period. The first well-dated assemblage is at Hayes Barn north of South Petherton, excavated in advance of the laying of the Ilchester to Barrington Pipeline: though currently unquantified, barley dominated with free-threshing wheat and oats also present (Joyce *et al.* 2009). The other well-dated assemblage is from near the Baltmoor Wall where 61% of the seventy-six identified grains were wheat, 33% barley, 4% rye, and 3% oats (Watts and Scaife 2008). The assemblage from Sladwick in Somerset is either late Roman or early medieval: wheat was 94% of this assemblage of 113 grains, the rest being barley (Gerrard with Aston 2007). At Poundbury, on the chalk downland west of Dorchester, wheat declined from 63% in the late Roman period to 48% in the early medieval period, with barley increasing from 25% to 52% and oats from 4–10% (Sparey Green 1987). Overall, the early medieval period appears to have seen relatively diverse crop husbandry though with a marked difference either side of the Blackdown Hills to the west of which oats and barley were far more significant.

Middle medieval period (eighth to the mid-fourteenth century) (Table 12.3)

Western Devon and Cornwall

For the middle medieval period we have a far wider range of charred cereal assemblages, though unfortunately not from Cornwall and Devon as although a series of sites on and around Dartmoor have produced assemblages, none of the data is quantified. In common with the earliest medieval period, it appears that oats were the most important part of a diverse cropping regime. On the Culm Measures immediately north of Dartmoor the unquantified assemblage of charred cereals from the thirteenth to fourteenth-century rural settlement at Sourton Down was 'dominated by oats', with small amounts of barley and rye (Weddell and Reed 1997, 115). Oats and rye were also the 'principal crops' in the extensive deposits of charred grain recovered from the twelfth-century granary at Lydford (Weddell and Reed 1997). Oats were identified amongst the charred plant material at Houndtor (Beresford 1979, 143), and the pollen assemblage from a nearby peat bog contained abundant cereal-type pollen including oats and rye, although the latter will always be over-represented in pollen diagrams as this wind-pollinated plant produces larger amounts of pollen compared to other cereals (Austin and Walker 1985). At Holne Moor rye formed two thirds of the cereal-type pollen, with some wheat but no oats or barley identified (Maguire *et al.* 1983). At Okehampton Park the majority of the cereal pollen was identified as *Hordeum*-type (barley), with significant amounts of rye, and a few grains of oats and wheat (Austin *et al.* 1980): large amounts of barley are, however, very unlikely in upland areas such as this because it cannot tolerate acidic soils, and the *Hordeum*-type pollen was probably mis-identified and is in fact from a wild plant Glyceria that grows in wet places (Rippon, Fyfe, and Brown 2006, 57).

Blackdown Hills

There is a single charred grain assemblage from the Blackdown Hills—the farmstead of Gaffers in Membury—where wheat (78%) dominated, but with some oats (16%), barley (5%), and rye (1%) (Jones 2001a).

Central Somerset

In the Vale of Taunton Deane, Taunton Priory (Leach 1984) and two rural sites (Zinch House in Stogumber: Wessex Archaeology 2003; and Huntworth: Powell *et al.* 2009) have evidence for diverse cropping regimes with significant amounts of oats, barley, and rye in addition to wheat. This is in contrast to the wheat-dominated lowlands of Somerset further east, such as at Shapwick where number of assemblages have been recovered showing that free-threshing wheat was *c.*85% of the preserved grain both on the probable seventh to tenth-century manorial site in Church Field and a variety of eleventh to fourteenth-century contexts in and around the medieval village (Gerrard with Aston 2007). This suggests little difference in agricultural practices on peasant tenements compared to the demesne, which is to be expected in an open field landscape. An unquantified assessment of a charred cereal assemblage from the nearby medieval village of Meare, an island within the Somerset

Levels, also revealed a dominance of free-threshing wheat, with significant amounts of oats, and a single grain of barley (Jones 2002; Whitton and Reed 2002). The farmstead at Whitegate Farm in Bleadon, at the foot of the Mendip hills, produced an assemblage that was 82% free-threshing wheat and the rest barley; a piece of rye chaff was also present (Young 2007). This dominance of wheat is in keeping with what the documentary sources suggest for this area.

Somerset marshlands

On the wetlands of the Somerset Levels, large and well-preserved plant macrofossil assemblages have been recovered from two sites within the still occupied medieval village of Puxton (Rippon 2006a). In Church Field—the probable twelfth-century manorial complex—wheat formed 79% of the cereal grain (none identified to species), with oats 10%, barley 10%, and rye 2%. Of the identified wheat chaff free-threshing wheat was 94%, spelt 1%, and emmer/spelt 5%, and as there is no chance of residuality on this wetland site—the Romano-British landscape is deeply buried by later alluvium—this is clear evidence that the cultivation of spelt continued into the medieval period. In nearby Home Ground, a probable peasant tenement, wheat was just 54%, with barley 29%, and oats 17%: all of the identified wheat chaff was from free-threshing forms. At nearby West Wick, in Banwell, 70% of the grain assemblage was free-threshing wheat, with barley 20% and oats 10% (Powell 2009). Clearly, a greater diversity of crops was grown on the reclaimed marshland compared to the adjacent drylands of central and northern Somerset.

Specialized crop husbandry in central Wessex

On the Jurassic limestone hills the cereal assemblage from the rural settlement at Eckweek in Peasedown St John was dominated by free-threshing wheat (92%) (Carruthers 1995). At Sherborne Old Castle, wheat accounted for 94% of the large cereal assemblage of which all the identifiable grain were of a free-threshing form; of the remaining grain all 6% was barley (Smith 2001). On the heavier soils of the Jurassic Clay Vales there was greater diversity in crop regimes—though not to the extent seen in areas such as Devon and Cornwall—such as at Gillingham (Dorset) where wheat was 80%, barley 18%, and oats 2% (Heaton 1992). At Duke's Break in Latton (Wiltshire) wheat was 88%, oats 7%, and barley 4% (Jones 2001b).

Unfortunately there are very few assemblages from the chalk downland, all of which are small, although it seems clear that barley was more significant here than in any other *pays*. At Tidworth barley was 25% (wheat was 71% and rye 4%: Milward *et al.* 2010), while at Collingbourne Ducis 63% of the sixteen grains were barley, the rest being wheat (Pine 2001). There are other hints that barley may have been relatively more important on the chalk downland than in other areas—which is what the documentary sources suggest—as in the town of Wilton 27% of the eleven grains were barley, the rest being wheat (Andrews *et al.* 2000). In Salisbury, of an assemblage of forty six grains from Ivy Street and Brown Street 17% were barley, 74% wheat, 7% oats, and 2% rye (Allen *et al.* 2000). It must be stressed that none of these small assemblages are statistically valid, but it is noticeable that they all have more barley (average 19%) compared to urban assemblages in the Jurassic clay vales (8%) and the North Somerset Hills and Vales (12%).

Another region that appears to have a distinctive pattern of crop husbandry is the Dorset heathlands. At Ower Farm wheat was just 18%, with rye (49%) and significant amounts of barley and oats (each 17%) (Cox and Hearne 1991). The assemblages from two heathland towns show a similar picture to Ower with significant amounts of barley and rye (Howard's Lane in Wareham: Harding *et al.* 1995; 29 High Street in Wimborne Minster: Coe and Hawkes 1992).

Late medieval period (mid-fourteenth to the late fifteenth century)

Unfortunately there are insufficient charred cereal assemblages dated to the late medieval period for any meaningful discussion.

DISCUSSION

In terms of medieval arable cultivation, a line can be drawn through the Blackdown Hills between areas to the west whose albeit unquantified charred cereal assemblages are characterized by diverse cropping regimes including significant amounts of oats, and those to the east that were more specialized being mostly dominated by wheat, but with barley particularly significant on the chalk downland, and rye on the Dorset heathlands. This division is also seen in the documentary evidence which has been discussed by Fox (1991b, 303) who observed that this emphasis upon the coarse grains of oats and rye in the South West 'was not a backward husbandry constrained simply by soils and by climatic conditions, for in later centuries barley and wheat became as important in Devon and Cornwall as rye and oats were in the middle ages. Lying behind the persistence of oats and rye was preference for the two crops in bread and beer, old and well established already, by the fourteenth century, and very slow to change.' Another factor may be that bread wheat is prone to premature sprouting in the ear during damp weather close to harvest time and so is not ideally suited to western areas, in contrast to oats that are usually

Table 12.3. Summary of the middle medieval cereal grains from sites of different social status from each of the *pays* within the study area.

		No. sites	No. grains	oats		barley		rye		wheat		wheat			
		()= assemblages >100+		%	ave. of ave.	%	ave. of ave.	%	ave. of ave.	%	ave. of ave.	emmer	spelt	emmer/ spelt	bread
Cornwall and Devon		0													
Blackdown Hills	rural settlement	1	2,022	16%	16%	5%	5%	1%	1%	78%	78%	–	–	–	–
Vale of Taunton Deane	rural settlement	2 (0)	117	26%		21%		43%		10%		–	–	–	–
	monastic	1	104	54%	54%	0	0	5%	5%	40%	40%	0	0	0	100%
Central Somerset lowlands	rural settlement	1	2,595	3%	3%	11%	11%	0	0	86%	86%	1%	4%	6%	89%
North Somerset hills and vales	rural settlement	1	1,163	0	0	18%	18%	0	0	82%	82%	0	0	0	100%
	town	1	1,481	23%	23%	12%	12%	0	0	66%	66%	0	0	0	100%
reclaimed marshland	rural settlement	3 (1)	344	9%	10%	23%	10%	0	2%	68%	79%	–	–	–	–
	manorial	1	2,221	10%	10%	10%	10%	2%	2%	79%	79%	–	–	–	–
Jurassic Limestone Hills	rural settlement	1	12,874	3%	3%	5%	5%	0.1%	0.1%	92%	92%	0	0	0	100%
	castle	2 (1)	741	0	0	7%	6%	0	0	93%	94%	0	0	0	100%
	town	2 (1)	279	1%	0	4%	3%	4%	4%	91%	93%	0	0	0	100%
Jurassic clay vales	rural settlement	2	1,373	5%	4%	10%	11%	0.3%	0	85%	85%	0	0	0	100%
	town	1	1,237	8%	8%	8%	8%	0	0	84%	84%	0	0	0	100%
chalk downland	rural settlement	2 (1)	185	0%	0	29%	25%	3%	4%	68%	71%	0	0	0	100%
	towns	2 (0)	57	5%	0	19%	0	2%	0	74%	0	0	0	0	100%
South East Dorset heathlands	rural settlement	2	842	11%	13%	10%	12%	14%	25%	65%	51%	0	0	0	100%
	towns	2	1,776	4%	23%	19%	22%	1%	8%	76%	59%	0	0	0	100%
TOTALS															
towns			4,830	11%		13%		1%		76%					
monastic			94	54%		0		5%		41%					
castles			741	0		7%		0		93%					
manorial			2,221	10%		10%		3%		78%					
rural			21,515	5%		8%		1%		87%					
overall total			29,401	6%		9%		1%		84%				0.1%	99.9%

harvested semi-ripe to prevent grain loss, as the ears shatter on ripening, and are then dried in ovens which is better suited to damper regions (Wendy Carruthers pers. comm.). Fox (1991b, 305–6) also notes the very limited amounts of legumes grown in the South West despite their extensive cultivation just across the Blackdown Hills in Somerset, suggesting that 'farmers had their own old-established means of maintaining soil quality, and early spring grass, a product of mild winters, meant that they were not necessary as livestock feed'. Crop yields in the South West were in fact very high: the yield for oats being 3.2 times greater than the amount sown, compared to an average across England of ×2.7, while rye had a yield of ×6.1 compared to the national average of ×4.5. Wheat yield in the South West was ×4.8 compared to the national average of ×4.6, and only barley at ×3.8 was lower than the average for England of ×4.6 (Fox 1991b, table 3.21). A variety of factors probably account for these high yields that were all key features of the regionally distinctive system of convertible husbandry practised in the South West whereby *c.*25–50% of land was cultivated at any one time (compared to 66% in a three-field system), so maintaining soil fertility. The practice of 'beat burning' (firing the turf lifted before ploughing) would also have maintained fertility, while field management would also have been made easier due to the predominantly enclosed fieldscape as 'by the late fourteenth century...the majority of the demesnes were divided into securely hedged, severally held closes' (Fox 1991b, 312). Overall, agriculture to the west of the Blackdown Hills was different to that further east, because local communities had come up with customary local solutions to the particular challenges of local conditions.

To the east of the Blackdown Hills, the heathlands of Dorset and wetlands of the Somerset Levels also had diverse cropping regimes, probably as a form of risk management on what were environmentally difficult soils (if conditions led to one crop failing, another might survive). The greatest amount of barley was seen on the lighter soils of the chalk downlands, but otherwise arable cultivation east of the Blackdown Hills appears to have been dominated by wheat. As very few monastic, castle, or manorial sites have produced charred cereal assemblages we can say little about different patterns of grain consumption on sites of that status, though towns do appear to reflect patterns of crop husbandry in their hinterland, noticeably the relatively high proportion of barley in the chalk downland, and significance of non-wheat cereals in the heathlands.

Across the study area the medieval assemblages of wheat are dominated by free-threshing bread wheat. Like spelt, that was the dominant form of wheat gown in the Roman period (*see* Chapter 13), free-threshing bread wheat (*Triticum aestivum*) is also frost hardy, prefers heavier soils, and is particularly well-suited to autumn sowing. It is present in the prehistoric and Roman periods, though it achieved dominance quite suddenly in the early medieval period.[16] Nationally, spelt wheat declines sharply in the early medieval period, though in the east of England it was still cultivated in the fifth to the seventh centuries at sites such as West Stow and Mucking (Pelling 1999, 103), to which we can now add Puxton and Shapwick in Somerset (especially as the presence of chaff makes it highly unlikely that the material is residual). It has traditionally been thought that the cultivation of emmer wheat (*Triticum dicoccum*) ceased in the Roman period, with occasional finds in early medieval contexts being regarded as residual, although recent discoveries at sites in the Thames valley, such as Lake End Road in Dorney (where emmer has been radiocarbon dated to the fifth to the seventh centuries) and Yarnton (where it has been radiocarbon dated to the seventh to the ninth centuries) have now proved that its use did continue into the early medieval period (Pelling 1999, 103). We can once again add Shapwick to the list. Pelling (1999, 107) suggests that the sudden dominance of free-threshing wheat was due to cultural factors, such a preference for it on the part of Germanic settlers, and with regard to this specific argument it is frustrating that very little of the early medieval wheat from the far South West—beyond the area of Anglo-Saxon immigration—can be identified to species. The assemblages from the early medieval native British site at Poundbury in Dorset, however, contained 90% bread wheat on non-corn-drier contexts (and 99% in all contexts) (Sparey Green 1987, 134–5), suggesting that its adoption was not associated with Anglo-Saxon immigrants.

---

[16] Grains of the closely related rivet wheat (*Triticum turgidum*) cannot be distinguished from bread wheat although the chaff can, and its earliest recorded presence is in late Saxon contexts (Pelling 1999, 103).

13

Arable cultivation and animal husbandry in the Roman period

The analysis carried out for the medieval period contains few surprises: archaeological evidence has confirmed the existence of regional variation in animal husbandry and crop regimes that the documentary sources for these *pays* had suggested. This was, however, an important exercise in demonstrating that two different types of evidence—archaeological and documentary—come up with the same story. What has clearly emerged is that many of the basic characteristics of the farming regions identified by historians of the post-medieval period can certainly be traced back into the medieval period with, for example, the heavier soils usually supporting above average proportions of cattle and wheat, and light soils leading to a greater significance for sheep and barley. The far South West, beyond the Blackdown Hills, also stands out in lacking the highly specialized farming regimes seen further east, having instead generally mixed animal husbandry and cereal regimes. So does this mean that these different *pays* were inherently more suited to these particular types of farming, or did these differing agricultural practices emerge due to social and economic factors in the medieval period? In order to explore further whether some of our *pays* are inherently more suited to particular types of farming, we therefore need to move further back in time to the Roman period.

ROMANO-BRITISH ANIMAL HUSBANDRY

Previous work on Romano-British animal bone assemblages focused on comparing the proportions of cattle, sheep/goat, and pigs on sites of different status across the province as a whole (e.g. King 1989; 1991; 1999; 2005; Table 13.1). This analysis shows that on highly Romanized sites such as forts and towns, cattle bones are dominant, while this is less marked on rural settlements. That analysis suggests varying dietary preferences on sites of different socio-economic status but does not take into account whether there is any

Table 13.1. A statistical analysis of the percentages of cattle, sheep/goat, and pig from sites of different status in Roman Britain (King 1999, table 3).

Site type	sample size	cattle	sheep/goat	pig
Late Iron Age	10	39.0 ± 14.9	31.3 ± 8.5	29.7 ± 14.5
legionary fortress	16	63.5 ± 16.8	14.9 ± 11.2	21.6 ± 11.0
vici	69	56.3 ± 17.6	31.9 ± 15.5	11.8 ± 7.7
towns	50	53.5 ± 18.5	27.0 ± 14.0	19.5 ± 9.8
villas	58	55.6 ± 15.8	29.8 ± 12.2	14.6 ± 11.7
rural settlements	90	47.1 ± 15.7	41.2 ± 15.7	11.7 ± 9.0

regional variation in livestock husbandry. In this study both rural and urban settlements are included but not military sites, as the Roman army's supply system and the dietary preferences of a garrison that may have been born and bred outside Britain, means that the food consumed within a fort will not reflect animal husbandry in the surrounding region. Romano-Celtic temples have also been excluded due to the bias this lends to the faunal assemblages. Bradley Hill in Somerset—a site traditionally regarded as a farmstead—has therefore been excluded as Smart's (2008) reinterpretation suggests it may have been a temple, of which the high proportion of sheep (66%) is one crucial strand of evidence (Leech 1981; 1986; Watts and Leach 1996; King 2005).

Dumnonia

Due to the mostly acidic soils, there are very few Romano-British animal bones assemblages from the *civitas* of Dumnonia outside its capital at Exeter. At two sites on the west coast of Cornwall, however, burial under calcareous sand, rich in shell, has ensured good survival. At Atlantic Road in Newquay just 18% of the cattle/sheep/goat/pig bones were cattle, while 76% were sheep/goat, and 6% pig (Ingrem forthcoming). At Duckpool in Morwenstow cattle were 50% of a small assemblage, with sheep/goat 23%, and pig 27% (Ratcliffe 1995). When a number of other sites[1] are taken into account, cattle (20%) are well below the regional (31%) and national average (47%) for rural sites, and sheep/goat (73%) significantly higher than the regional (62%) and national averages (41%) (cf. Tables 13.1 and 13.2). In contrast, within fourth-century Exeter (Maltby 1979), cattle were 50% of the bones (compared to a regional average for towns of 42%), sheep/goat 28% (compared to a regional average of 38%), and pig 23% (compared to a regional average of 21%). On the Blackdown Hills, bone was preserved at Membury but the assemblage was too small for

[1] Lellizzick, near Padstow (Wessex Archaeology 2008b) and Kilhallon (Carlyon 1982; Turk 1984).

Table 13.2. Summary of Romano-British animal bones from sites of different social status from each of the *pays* within the study area.

		sample*	No. frags	cattle			sheep/goat			pig		
		( ) = assemblages >100		frags	%	ave. of ave.	frags	%	ave. of ave.	frags	%	ave. of ave.
Cornwall and Devon	rural settlement	3 (2)	1,721	349	20%	21%	1,259	73%	74%	117	7%	5.3%
	town (Exeter C4)	1	7,860	3,892	50%	50%	2,159	28%	28%	1,809	23%	23%
Vale of Taunton Deane	rural settlement	2 (1)	139	82	59%	63%	50	36%	31%	7	5%	6%
Central Somerset lowlands	rural settlement	2	1,459	474	33%	32%	888	61%	61%	97	7%	7%
	villa	2 (1)	269	120	45%	50%	113	42%	35%	36	13%	15%
	towns (Crandon Bridge, Ilchester, and Shepton Mallet)	8	5,295	6,028	54%	53%	2,407	40%	41%	343	6%	6%
North Somerset hills and vales	rural settlement	5 (3)	1,275	633	50%	48%	603	47%	43%	39	3%	9%
	villa	1	169	78	46%	46%	68	40%	40%	23	14%	14%
reclaimed marshland	rural settlement	1	270	146	54%	54%	108	40%	40%	16	6%	6%
unreclaimed marshland	rural settlement	1	74	17	23%	23%	47	64%	64%	10	14%	14%
Jurassic limestone Hills	rural settlement	5 (4)	2,350	682	29%	31%	1,345	57%	57%	323	14%	12%
	villa	3 (2)	3,193	1,675	53%	50%	1,056	33%	34%	462	15%	17%
	town (Bath)	3	2,898	862	30%	25%	1,368	47%	46%	668	23%	27%
Jurassic clay vales	rural settlement	5 (1)	559	225	40%	38%	272	49%	53%	62	11%	9%
	villa	1	3,152	1,424	45%	45%	1,486	47%	47%	242	8%	8%
chalk downs	rural settlement	19 (16)	14,868	4,779	32%	36%	9,193	62%	58%	896	6%	6%
	town (Dorchester)	5	20,096	7,428	37%	36%	8,017	40%	46%	4,651	23%	18%
heathlands	rural settlement	3	3,478	755	22%	25%	2,375	68%	63%	348	10%	12%
TOTALS												
rural settlement		46	26,197	8,142	31%		16,140	62%		1,915	7%	
villas		7	6,783	3,297	52%		2,723	34%		763	14%	
towns		17	36,882	15,460	42%		13,951	38%		7,471	21%	
overall totals		70	69,862	26,899	39%		32,814	47%		10,149	15%	

* number of reported assemblages with fragment counts

any worthwhile conclusions to be drawn (Tingle 2006, 45–6). At Holcombe, near Uplyme, the published report simply states that 'cattle and sheep/goats are represented in fairly equal numbers' (Pollard 1974, 154).

Central Somerset and northern Somerset

There are just two small assemblages with a total of 139 bones from rural sites in the Vale of Taunton Deane, at Bentham's Garage in Taunton (Leach 1984) and Hinkley Point (Cox and Broomhead 1993). Cattle were 59% (well above the regional average of 31%), sheep/goat 36% (well below the regional average of 62%), and pig 5%. Further east, in the lowlands of central Somerset, there are good-sized assemblages from two villas and three rural settlements.[2] On the villas, cattle (45%) were below the regional (52%) average, while sheep/goat (42%) were above the regional average (34%). On the non-villa rural settlements, cattle (33%) were slightly higher than the regional average, and sheep (61%) slightly below. There are also a series of large assemblages from the small towns of Crandon Bridge, Ilchester, and Shepton Mallet, in which cattle (54%) were above the regional average (42%), while sheep/goat (40%) were similar to the regional (38%) and national (41%) average.[3] Northern Somerset presents an interesting contrast as on the four sites with fragment counts cattle are above the regional average and sheep/goat below.[4]

The coastal wetlands of Somerset appear to have been a divided landscape in the Roman period. Extensive fieldwork and palaeoenvironmental sampling has established that on the North Somerset Levels (north of Mendip) the landscape was transformed from intertidal saltmarshes to a freshwater, reclaimed, landscape in the third century AD, while the southern part of the central Somerset Levels appears to have been left unreclaimed and supported an extensive salt production industry (Rippon 1997; 2000a; 2000b; 2006a;

---

[2] Catsgore (both the villa and the adjacent rural settlement: Leech 1982b; Ellis 1984), Shapwick (both the villa and the adjacent rural settlement: Gerrard with Aston 2007), and Yeovilton (Lovell 2006).

[3] Crandon Bridge: Rippon 2008b; Ilchester: Leach 1992; 1994; Broomhead 1998; Shepton Mallet: Albarella and Hammon 1996; Leach 2001b; Birbeck 2002; Higbee 2008.

[4] Butcombe 1966–7 (Fowler 1968), Chew Park villa (excluding the main well with its large dump of cattle bones) and Herriots Bridge in the Chew valley (Rahtz and Greenfield 1977), and Inns Court in Knowle (Jackson 2007). The relatively high figure for cattle is supported by the MNI from Gatcombe of 75% cattle, 16% sheep/goat, and 9% pig (Branigan 1977), although the 1968–9 excavations at Butcombe had MNIs of 33% cattle, 61% sheep/goat, and 6% pig (Fowler 1970).

2008b). There is a single quantified, but small, assemblage from the unreclaimed marsh, at Bleak Bridge in Huntspill where of the seventy-four bones just 23% were cattle, 64% sheep/goat, and 14% pig (Higbee 2003). An as yet unquantified assemblage from the Somerset marshlands before they were reclaimed has been recovered from St Georges (in Banwell, on the North Somerset Levels) in which sheep bones dominate (Mary Alexander pers. comm.). A larger assemblage has been recovered from the late Roman settlement at Kenn Moor which reflects animal husbandry after the Levels had been reclaimed and here cattle accounted for 54%, sheep/goat just 40%, and pig 6% (Rippon 2000b). On the reclaimed wetlands cattle were clearly preferred over sheep/goat, whereas the reverse appears to have been true on unreclaimed saltmarshes.

Specialized animal husbandry in central Wessex

On the Jurassic limestone hills the proportions of the main domesticates on three villa sites[5] and five non-villa sites[6] are very close to the regional averages, although compared to the national figures sheep/goat were far more significant. In the Jurassic clay vales cattle were far more significant than the regional average and sheep/goat less so,[7] the exception being Bucknowle villa (Light and Ellis 2009). The chalk downlands of Wessex have provided the largest number of sites with cattle accounting for just 32%, sheep/goat 62%, and pig 6%.[8] This bias towards sheep/goat is also seen in Dorchester, where cattle form 37% of the assemblages, sheep/goat 40%, and pig 23%, the latter representing a more urban pattern of consumption.[9] The figure of 40% for sheep/goat is

---

[5] Halstock (Lucas 1993), Box (Hurst et al. 1987); Atworth (Erskine and Ellis 2008).

[6] Blacklands (Wessex Archaeology 2007 and Jayne Lawes pers. comm., 2009), Combe Hay (Price and Watts 1980), Showell Farm (Young and Hancocks 2006), and Whitewalls (Wilmott and Shipp 2006).

[7] Compact Farm in Worth Matravers (Clark no date); Gillingham (Cox 1992); Swindon Old Town (Butterworth and Seager Smith 1997), Brickley Lane in Devizes (Poore et al. 2002) and Trowbridge (Graham and Davies 1993).

[8] **Dorset**: Allington Avenue, Dorchester (Davies et al. 2002); Fordington Bottom, Maiden Castle Road and St Georges Road, Dorchester (Smith et al. 1997); Poundbury, Dorchester (Sparey Green 1987); Poxwell (Hurst and Wacher 1986); Tarrant Hinton (Graham 2006); Tolpuddle Ball (Hearne and Birbeck 1999); and Whitcombe (Aitkin and Aitkin 1990).

Wiltshire: A303 Stonehenge Improvement: Grimm 2008a; Butterfield Down, Amesbury (Rawlings and Fitzpatrick 1996); Chapperton Down (Malim and Martin 2007); Chisenbury Warren and Combe Down (Fulford et al. 2006); Figheldean 1991 and 1995 (Graham and Newman 1993; McKinley 1999); Maddington farm, Shrewton (McKinley and Heaton 1996); Overton Down (Fowler 2000); and Wilton (Andrews et al. 2000). Note that the extraordinarily high proportion of pig (66%) at Castle Copse villa has led to its exclusion from this analysis (Hosteller and Noble Howe 1997).

[9] Smith 1993; Woodward et al. 1993; Grimm no date; Ingrem no date.

relatively high, compared to 28% in Exeter, suggesting that the patterns of meat consumption in Dorchester were reflecting livestock husbandry in its hinterland. The relatively high proportion of sheep/goat on the chalk downland is no surprise as the landscape was extensively cleared of woodland and the well-drained chalky soils are free from the host of liver fluke to which sheep are normally very prone (Buckland-Wright 1987, Mf4 D10; Allen 1997, 281–3; Bullock and Allen 1997, 198).

Three sites on the heathlands have produced animal-bone assemblages with cattle just 22%, sheep/goat 68%, and pig 10% (Woodward 1987). Two of the sites—Norden and Ower—lie on the shores of Poole Harbour, and the high figures for sheep may in part reflect their suitability for grazing on intertidal marshes.

Discussion

In many ways, our *pays* to the east of the Blackdown Hills reflect trends in animal husbandry seen across lowland Roman Britain. Over time, for example, there is a general increase in the significance of cattle (Maltby 1981; Grant 1989, 136; King 1991; Fulford *et al.* 2006, 191) and this is seen near Dorchester: at Poundbury, for example, cattle (in terms in the MNI) increased from 21% in the first and second centuries to 39% in the third and fourth centuries, while at Fordington Bottom cattle increased from 22% in the first and second centuries to 43% in the third and fourth centuries. We also see the difference between urban and rural settlements that is evident nationally: in Dorchester, cattle were 37% compared to 32% on rural settlements on the chalk downland, while in the central Somerset small towns cattle are 55%, compared to an average of 35% on rural settlements in the same region. These temporal and social differences in animal husbandry and consumption are well known, but this analysis has also revealed some very marked local variations in animal husbandry. The proportion of cattle bones in Dorchester (37%), for example, is very low compared to the national average for towns of 54%, while the proportion of sheep/goat (40%) is far higher than the national average for towns of 27%. The most obvious explanation for this is that the food consumed within Dorchester reflects local conditions in the hinterland of the town that favoured the raising of sheep on chalk downland. Overall, we can see that all areas had a mixed livestock economy but that sheep/goat were far more significant in Dumnonia, areas with access to unreclaimed marshland, chalk downland, and heathland, while cattle were more important in areas with heavier soils in the lowland clay vales.

ROMANO-BRITISH ARABLE REGIMES

In addition to the general issues concerning the interpretation of charred cereal assemblages, such as the likely under-representation of bread wheat, a factor specific to the Roman period is that large amounts of material comes from specialized structures traditionally known as 'corn driers' that may reflect the processing of the harvest from a specific field, rather than what was cultivated in the locality as a whole. On the County Hall site in Dorchester, for example, the plant remains from one late-Roman corn drier were dominated by barley, whereas those from another were dominated by wheat (Smith 1993, 76). On the A37 Western Link Road, near Dorchester, wheat formed 85% of the assemblage from a corn drier, but just 73% from a nearby midden deposit (Smith *et al.* 1997, 268). The function of corn-drying ovens also appears to have varied (van der Veen 1989): at the A37 Western Link Road site the proportion of grains that had germinated suggests an oven was being used for malting (Smith *et al.* 1997, 268), while the scarcity of sprouted grain at Poxton, also near Dorchester, suggests that the oven there was being used to dry grain (Hurst and Wacher 1986). As the grains selected for malting could be different to those used in baking, individual assemblages such as these may not always be representative of the crops growing in the fields surrounding these settlements, although at Kenn Moor large assemblages from both a corn-drying oven and midden deposits scattered across the rest of the farmstead were actually very similar in their composition (Rippon 2000b). In the following discussion care is therefore taken to separate out any 'corn-drier' assemblages.

Dumnonia

In western Devon and Cornwall four Romano-British sites have significant amounts of material[10] with seven smaller assemblages.[11] Overall, barley (55%) dominates, followed by oats (27%), and wheat (19%) of which emmer, spelt, and bread wheat are all present in significant amounts. Four sites in the eastern Devon lowlands have produced charred cereal assemblages,[12] and

---

[10] Penlee House in Tregony (Carruthers 2007), Atlantic Road in Newquay (Carruthers forthcoming), Penhale Round (Johnson *et al.* 1998–9) and Scarcewater Tip (Jones and Taylor 2010).

[11] Tremough in Penryn (Gossip and Jones 2007), Duckpool in Morwenstow (Ratcliffe 1995), Stencoose (Jones 2000–1), Reawla Round in Gwinwear (Appleton-Fox 1992), Penryn College (Carruthers 2008), Little Quoit (J. Jones forthcoming), and Lellizzick, near Padstow (Wessex Archaeology 2008b).

[12] Parsonage Cross in Littlehempston (Reed and Turton 2005; Julie Jones pers. comm.), Aller Cross in Kingskerswell (Hearne and Seager Smith 1995), Hayes Farm east Exeter (Simpson *et al.* 1989) and Digby Drive near Exeter (Jones 2004).

here wheat (70%) dominates (with emmer more significant than spelt) but with significant amounts of oats (24%) and small amounts of barley (6%). This diversity within Dumnonia may be accounted for in a number of ways. The eastern area was the hinterland of the only major town in the region, Exeter, and as such may reflect a more Romanized style of agriculture that resulted from the region's exposure to the market economy. The scarcity of wheat, and dominance of oats and barley, further west may be a reflection of that area's less Romanized landscape and economy, or may reflect adaptation to local environmental conditions. Barley and oats were commonly grown together, as 'drage', in the medieval period as a way of reducing the risk of adverse weather conditions and crop failure: in wet years the oats will fare better on heavy soils than the oats, whilst barley will perform better in drier conditions (Carruthers 2007).

Blackdown Hills

Assemblages from the roadside agricultural settlement at Pomeroy Wood near Honiton and nearby Gittisham Forge will presumably reflect the crops being grown on the Blackdown Hills and its associated valleys (Fitzpatrick *et al.* 1999). Wheat was dominant in both cases, with spelt once again by far the most significant variety. Barley was 6% at Pomeroy and absent at Gittisham, but oats formed 30% of the grain at both sites. Overall, these Blackdown Hills assemblages continue the trend seen in Dumnonia for wheat, and in particular spelt, to increase in importance from west to east, but for there still to have been a diversity of crops grown.

Central and northern Somerset

There is just a single, small assemblage from the Vale of Taunton Deane, at Hillyfields near Taunton, where of the sixty seven grains, 61% were wheat and 39% barley (Leach 2003).This continues the trend towards relatively diverse cropping regimes seen in this district during the medieval period. In contrast, just a few kilometres to the east, four rural settlements in the lowlands of central Somerset have assemblages dominated by spelt wheat which forms *c*.90% of the grain assemblages.[13] The large assemblages from the two small towns of Ilchester and Shepton Mallet are similarly dominated by wheat (97% of the total grain),[14] although a spread of burnt clay at Tesco's site in Shepton Mallet did produce a large deposit of charred barley (Jones 1998b). In the hills

---

[13] Catsgore (Leech 1982b), Shapwick (Gerrard with Aston 2007), Shapwick villa (Jones n.d.; Abdy *et al.* 2001), and Yeovilton (Lovell 2006).

[14] Leach 1982; 1994; 2001b; J. Jones 1998b; Broomhead 1998; Birbeck 2002.

and clay vales of northern Somerset there are few large well-published assemblages, although at Inns Court in Knowle (Jackson 2007) and at Gatcombe (Branigan 1977, 140), wheat was once again dominant. Excavations at the Roman villa at Star revealed a corn drier associated with a spread of charred barley (Barton 1963–4, 65, 89).

Marshlands

On the reclaimed wetlands of the Somerset Levels[15] we see a distinctive pattern arable cultivation compared to the adjacent drylands with a broad range of crops (53% wheat, 27% oats, and 20% barley). This sort of diversity is consistently seen on wetland sites and the relatively high proportion of barley and oats may reflect their greater tolerance of occasional tidal inundation (Van Zeist 1974; Van Zeist *et al.* 1976; Bottema *et al.* 1980; Behre and Jacomet 1991; Rhoades *et al.* 1992). Indeed, a small assemblage of thirty-seven charred cereal grains recovered from the settlement at Puxton Dolmoors which pre-dated the reclamation of these wetlands (Rippon 2006a, 60–1) was dominated by barley (62%), with oats 22%, wheat just 16%, and a small amount of rye (5%) (Rippon 2006a). A small assemblage from unreclaimed marshland at Bleak Bridge (thirty two grains) had 59% wheat but the scarcity of chaff suggests this was a cleaned crop imported to the area; once again there were significant amounts of barley (38%) and a small amount of oats (3%) (Jones 2003). Overall, the marshlands of the Somerset Levels appear to have seen a distinctive pattern of crop husbandry during the Roman period that was very sensitive to local and changing environmental conditions.

Specialized animal husbandry in central Wessex

On the Jurassic limestone hills, wheat was 86% (all spelt) at Truckle Hill with significant amounts of barley (14%) (Wessex Archaeology 2008a; Andrews 2009), while at Showell Farm, 66% of the grain was wheat and 34% barley (Young and Hancocks 2006). In Somerset, an unquantified assemblage from Blacklands in Laverton, near Frome, was also dominated by spelt wheat but with some barley (Wessex Archaeology 2007). A number of individually small assemblages from the Jurassic clay vales also show wheat (75%) dominating but with significant amounts of barley (15%) and oats (10%).[16]

---

[15] Banwell Moor (Rippon 2000b), Kenn Moor (Rippon 2000b), and Brean (Jones 1998a).
[16] Wiltshire: Farringdon (Smith 2008), Tockenham (Harding and Lewis 1997), and Old Town, Swindon (Butterworth and Seager Smith 1997); Somerset: Horsington (Newman and Morris 1999).

On the chalk downlands of Dorset there is a considerable degree of uniformity in the assemblages not derived from corn driers, with a mix of wheat (46%), barley (45%), and small amounts of oats (8%).[17] The corn-drier assemblages, in contrast, had a greater amount of wheat (62%), but still significant amounts of barley (34%).[18] In the assemblages not derived from corn driers in Wiltshire, wheat was dominant (84%).[19] The greater amount of barley grown on the chalk downland compared to the lowlands further west is also seen in the urban assemblages: 37% barley in Dorchester (Smith 1993; Woodward *et al.* 1993; Stevens no date) compared to just 2% in Ilchester and Shepton Mallet. Only two sites in the heathlands—Bestwall Quarry and Redcliffe—have yielded charred cereal assemblages, and while both are small they are consistent in showing significant amounts of barley (39%) and oats (57%) (Lyne 2002; Carruthers 2006).

Discussion: regional variation in Romano-British cereal cultivation

This analysis has once again revealed remarkable variation in the crops being grown in different *pays*. The detailed analysis carried out here confirms a number of the trends identified nationally by Jones (1981; 1982; 1989; 1991) and van der Veen *et al.* (2008), and regionally by Green (1981; 1996). Romano-British cereal assemblages east of the Blackdown Hills are dominated by spelt wheat, continuing the trend seen in the prehistoric period when emmer (*Triticum dicoccum*) gradually lost its dominant position (Campbell and Straker 2003). Emmer wheat prefers lighter soils, and although it is traditionally thought to have been frost-susceptible and so generally spring-sown, experiments have shown that it can be autumn-sown (Van de Veen and Palmer 1997). Emmer declined in importance during the late prehistoric period, while spelt (*Triticum spelta*), which can grow on both heavier and lighter soils, is frost-hardy and so can be winter-sown, became by far the most important form of wheat in the Roman period. Free-threshing types, notably hexaploid 'bread wheat' (*Triticum aestivum*) and tetraploid 'rivet wheat' (*Triticum turgidum*) are relatively uncommon until the medieval period.

---

[17] Allington Avenue, Maiden Castle Road, and Fordington Bottom all near Dorchester (Smith *et al.* 1997; Davies *et al.* 2002); Figheldean (Graham and Newman 1993); Tolpuddle Ball (Hearne and Birbeck 1999).
[18] Fordington Bottom (Smith *et al.* 1997); Poxwell (Hurst and Wacher 1986); Figheldean (Graham and Newman 1993).
[19] Chisenbury Warren (Fulford *et al.* 2006); Castle Copse in Great Bedwyn (Hosteller and Nobel Howe 1997); Eyewell in Chilmark (Fitzpatrick and Crockett 1998); Maddington Farm in Shrewton (McKinley and Heaton 1996); Wilton (Andrews *et al.* 2000).

Table 13.3. Summary of the Romano-British cereal grains from non-corn-drier contexts on sites of different social status from each of the *pays* within the study area. Figures including corn driers are given in square brackets. See Table 13.4 for the % of emmer, spelt, and bread wheat excluding grains identified simply as 'emmer/spelt'.

		No. sites ( ) = assemblages >100	No. grains	oats %	oats ave. of ave.	barley %	barley ave. of ave.	wheat %	wheat ave. of ave.	emmer	spelt	emmer/spelt	bread
Western Devon and Cornwall	rural settlement	10 (4)	9,967	27%	28%	55%	36%	19%	37%	15%	36%	42%	8%
eastern Devon	rural settlement	3	906	24%	27%	6%	5%	70%	68%	51%	13%	28%	8%
Blackdown Hills	rural settlement	2 (1) [3]	726 [1,426]	30% [17%]	30%	5% [3%]	6%	65% [80%]	64%	34% [9%]	64% [16%]	0 [75%]	2% [1%]
Vale of Taunton Deane	rural settlement	1	67	0	0	39%	39%	61%	61%	–	–	–	–
Central Somerset lowlands	rural settlement	3	1,305	3%	3%	5%	6%	92%	91%	1%	88%	3%	9%
	villa	1	2,130	1%	1%	1%	1%	98%	98%	–	–	–	–
	towns (Ilchester and Shepton Mallet)	6	4,363	1%	4%	2%	6%	97%	90%	0.2%	81%	19%	0.2%
North Somerset hills and vales	rural settlement	1	145	8%	8%	4%	4%	88%	88%	–	–	–	–
reclaimed marshland	rural settlement	4 (3) [4]	1,128 [3,060]	27% [20%]	24%	20% [41%]	31%	53% [39%]	46%	–	–	–	–
unreclaimed marshland	rural settlement	2 (0)	69	13%	12%	51%	50%	36%	38%	–	–	–	–
Jurassic Limestone Hills	rural settlement	2	4,716	0	0	14%	24%	86%	76%	0	0	99.9%	0.1%
Jurassic clay vales	rural settlement	5 (1) [6]	254 [322]	10% [8%]	0	15% [15%]	14%	75% [77%]	86%	40% [36%]	12% [21%]	36% [32%]	12% [11%]
chalk downs: Dorset	rural settlement	7 (4*) [9]	1,246 [2,550]	8% [5%]	8%	45% [34%]	36%	48% [62%]	55%	23% [4%]	47% [62%]	22% [29%]	9% [6%]

(continued)

Table 13.3. Continued

		No. sites	No. grains	oats		barley		wheat		wheat			
		() = assemblages >100		%	ave. of ave.	%	ave. of ave.	%	ave. of ave.	emmer	spelt	emmer/ spelt	bread
	towns (Dorchester)	3 [4]	324 [1,967]	10% [4%]	9%	37% [67%]	34%	53% [29%]	57%	10% [3%]	2% [1%]	69% [68%]	27% [28%]
chalk downs: Wiltshire	rural settlement	4 (2) [6]	810 [981]	0.2% [0.1%]	1%	16% [14%]	16%	84% [86%]	83%	7% [7%]	69% [70%]	10% [13%]	14% [10%]
	villa	1	499	0	0	18%	18%	82%	82%	22%	41%	0	37%
South East Dorset heathlands	rural settlement	2 (0) [3]	67 [113]	57% [43%]	49%	39% [27%]	43%	5% [30%]	8%	– [0]	– [0]	– [96%]	– [4%]
TOTALS (excluding corn driers)			7										
total: towns			4,687	2%		4%		94%					
totals: villas			2,629	1%		4%		95%					
total: non-villa rural settlement			21,406	14%		37%		49%					
overall totals			**28,722**	**10%**		**28%**		**61%**					

* includes Poundbury where the published report only gives the % of grain

What the analysis carried out here has also demonstrated is that these broad trends must be seen in the context of important regional variation in crop husbandry across our study area where cereal cultivation in the Roman period was dominated by wheat (54% of the non-corn-drier grain) and barley (33%), with a small amount of oats (13%), although the significance of these crops varied enormously across different *pays*. The issue of whether the oats recovered from charred cereal assemblages were wild or cultivated is a difficult one to determine as the grains are indistinguishable (*see* above), but what the data collected here suggest is that unless arable fields in some parts of our study area were appreciably more weed-infested than others, there were some areas that saw significant amounts of oats being cultivated. In western Dumnonia, 22% of the identified Romano-British grains are oats, which is very similar to the 24% in eastern Dumnonia and 30% on the Blackdown Hills. High figures for oats are also seen on the marshlands of Somerset (27%) and the heathlands of Dorset (57%). In part, the increased cultivation of oats in the Roman period may have been as a fodder crop, although at least some would probably have been for human consumption as was the case in the medieval period when it was used for oatmeal pottage and beer (Fox 1991b, 303–4). In most cases, areas that appear to have seen significant cultivation of oats also had large areas devoted to barley; in western Dumnonia barley was the dominant crop in terms of preserved cereal grains at 65%, while on reclaimed marshland they were 20%, rising to 51% in the admittedly small assemblage from the unreclaimed marsh. Barley was also a significant crop on the light soils of the Jurassic limestone hills (14%), and the chalk downland of Dorset (45%), and Wiltshire (16%). On the heathlands it was 39%. This extensive cultivation of barley in Dorset is also reflected in the assemblages in Dorchester where it accounted for 37% of the grain assemblages compared to just 2% in the small towns of the central Somerset lowlands: rural settlement in the central Somerset lowlands saw just 3% barley, suggesting that the grain consumed within towns really does reflect what was grown in their immediate hinterland.

The balance between arable cultivation and livestock husbandry across different regions can be difficult to establish from on-site assemblages of cereal and animal bones, although one indication of this is the distribution of specialized structures for the large-scale processing of crops. Although hay production was introduced soon after the Roman Conquest, the main period of agricultural innovation appears to have been the late third and fourth centuries, including the appearance of large numbers of T-shaped corn driers (Rees 1979; Jones 1981; 1982; 1989, 131). The analysis carried out here confirms the picture identified back in the 1970s (Morris 1979), that while relatively abundant in modern Dorset, Somerset (east of the Quantock Hills), and Wiltshire, corn driers are absent from the South West. This could reflect two things: firstly that there was simply less arable cultivation in Dumnonia, or secondly, that there was plenty, but the failure to adopt this distinctive innovation, with the absence of corn-drying ovens being one of many indications that the region failed to Romanize (*see* Chapter 14).

One way of testing this further is to examine in more detail the types of wheat being grown (Table 13.4). In western Dumnonia, emmer was 26% of the wheat grains that could be identified as emmer, spelt, or bread wheat; spelt was 61% and bread wheat 13%. In eastern Dumnonia, emmer (70%) was dominant, though spelt (19%) was of some importance. On the Blackdown Hills, spelt (64%) was also dominant with emmer 34%, while in the lowlands of central Somerset spelt (90%) was by far the most important crop with emmer (1%) of minor importance. While it must be remembered that the distinguishing of emmer and spelt grains is problematic, such marked variations in their proportions such as these must, in part at least, reflect real differences in the extent to which they were cultivated. On the Jurassic limestone hills, the grain could only be identified as emmer or spelt, although over 99% of the chaff was spelt. The figure of 62% for emmer on the Jurassic clay vales should be ignored due to the very small sample size, and spelt forms 99% of the chaff with emmer just 1%. On the chalk downlands, emmer appears to have been slightly more significant in Dorset (29%) than in Wiltshire (8%), and in both areas spelt (60% and 76% respectively) was dominant. On the Dorset heathlands wheat was a minor crop, and there are only a few grains identified to species, though the chaff assemblage comprised 4.5% emmer and 95% spelt. From this analysis it can be seen that spelt was the dominant form of wheat cultivated on the lowlands of central Somerset, on the reclaimed marshlands, in the Jurassic clay

Table 13.4. Percentages of grain identified as emmer, spelt, and bread wheat (*see* Table 13.3 for the percentages including grain identified as emmer or spelt).

area	no. grains	emmer	spelt	bread
western Devon and Cornwall	8,587	26%	61%	13%
eastern Devon	130	70%	19%	12%
Blackdown Hills	218	34%	64%	1%
Vale of Taunton Deane	no data			
central Somerset lowlands	687	1%	90%	9%
Ilchester and Shepton Mallet	2,242	0.3%	99.5%	0.2%
North Somerset hills and vales	no data			
reclaimed marshland	no data (chaff 2% emmer, 97% spelt and 1% bread)			
unreclaimed marshland	no data			
Jurassic limestone hills	no data (chaff 0.1% emmer and 99.9% spelt)			
Jurassic clay vales	Small sample size of grain (42) of which 62% was emmer, 19% spelt, and 19% bread wheat. Of the chaff, spelt forms 99% with emmer just 1%			
chalk downland – Dorset	105	29%	60%	11%
chalk downland – Wiltshire	297	8%	76%	16%
Dorchester	32	25%	6%	69%
South East Dorset heathland	no data (chaff 4.5% emmer, 95% spelt, and 0.5% bread)			

vales and limestone hills, and the heathlands of Dorset. While emmer remained of some significance on the chalk downland, it was only in Dumnonia that it was the dominant form of wheat grown. As emmer actually prefers lighter soils, it is tempting to see its dominance in Dumnonia as yet another indication of its low level of Romanization.

CONCLUSIONS: REGIONAL VARIATION IN FARMING PRACTICES

Chapters 11–13 have examined changing patterns of land use during the Roman, medieval, and post-medieval periods across a study area stretching from the far South West through to central southern England in order to explore whether the regional farming systems that historians have identified in the post-medieval period were simply the product of late-medieval changes in economy and society, or whether they reflect more deeply rooted differences in how local communities exploited their environment. At the heart of this debate is a wider issue of the nature of *pays*: the generic types of landscape—or farming regions—advocated by Thirsk (1987; 2000) and which have certain stable, inherent properties, or unique landscape areas whose characters could change over time. Whilst studying agricultural practices in this way is a well-established approach in agrarian history, it is the first time that the comparison of *pays* has been carried out for the Romano-British and medieval periods using archaeological data.

The approach has been to start with the known and work back into the unknown. For the post-medieval period we have a variety of written sources that paint a detailed picture of variations in agricultural practices across the entire landscape, while for the later medieval period we have useful written sources for a relatively small number of places. Going further back in time, the Domesday Book provides some basic information on the relative extent of arable land, pasture, meadow, and woodland for most of the country, with more detailed data on livestock for certain areas (including the South West counties for which we have the *Liber Exoniensis*). Two important conclusions can be drawn from these various written sources: firstly, that patterns of land use have changed over time, but secondly, that this has happened within some very stable parameters with communities living in certain districts showing a consistent tendency to favour certain types of cereal production and animal husbandry. In areas to the west of the Blackdown Hills, for example, pre-modern farming was dominated by mixed cropping regimes with relatively high proportions of oats and barley, and a mix of cattle and sheep. To the east of the Blackdown Hills, in contrast, we generally see more specialized farming regimes with wheat consistently dominating on the relatively heavy soils of central Somerset and the Jurassic clay vales, and cattle dominated the livestock husbandry. On the light soils of the chalk downland significant amounts of barley were cultivated alongside wheat, while sheep dominated the livestock husbandry.

There are, however, problems with our documentary evidence: the later medieval sources only survive for a small number of places and are particularly sparse for some *pays* (Fig. 11.3); they relate to demesne farming and not what was happening on peasant tenements; later sources tell us little about what crops were grown but Domesday is silent on this; and there is nothing before the eleventh century. We must turn, therefore, to palaeoenvironmental sequences that allow us to chart changing proportions of arable, pasture, and woodland from prehistory through to the present day, and assemblages of animal bones and cereal remains excavated from individual settlements. Our available palaeoenvironmental sequences are not evenly spread across our study area, with relatively large numbers in Devon, the Blackdown Hills and central Somerset, but very few further east, a distribution that is to a certain extent mutually exclusive to our documentary sources (Fig. 11.6). In all cases they show a landscape largely cleared of woodland by the middle of the Iron Age. To the west of the Blackdown Hills there appears to have been a largely pastoral landscape with limited amounts of arable cultivation that shows relatively little change from the late Iron Age through to the early medieval period, while to the east of the Blackdowns there is some evidence for an intensification of agriculture in the Roman period. To the west of the Blackdown Hills there is no evidence for a change in land use at the end of the Roman period, while to the east there appears to have been a decrease in the intensity of farming that is to be expected as the villa-based market economy collapsed, but no widespread or long-lasting woodland regeneration. To the west of the Blackdown Hills there is evidence for a change in farming practices around the eighth century that led to far greater amounts of cereal pollen being deposited in the peat bogs that have been examined, though this may have been due to the introduction of new rotational systems of cultivation as opposed to a simple expansion in the area of arable cultivation. To the east of the Blackdown Hills—in the catchment of the Somerset Levels at least—there is evidence for a change in land-use around the eighth–tenth centuries with increased alluviation possibly resulting from changes in the nature of farming, such as an increase in autumn ploughing and/or the introduction of open fields, or simply an expansion in the area of arable cultivation.

The preserved plant and animal remains from archaeological sites—animal bones and plant macrofossils that can collectively be referred to as 'palaeoeconomic' data—add detail to this picture and show most clearly that there were indeed deeply rooted differences in agricultural practices either side of the Blackdown Hills. For our purposes, the medieval period has been divided into three: the earliest medieval period (the fifth to the seventh century) after the collapse of Roman Britain but before the development of the landscape characterized by surplus production and market exchange; the middle medieval period (eighth to the mid-fourteenth century) when there was an intensification of agriculture and a physical restructuring of settlement patterns and field systems in many areas; and the late medieval period (mid-fourteenth to the late fifteenth century) following the population collapse associated with the Black Death and subsequent outbreaks of plague. Unfortunately there are very few late medieval assemblages, none of them rural, and only a small amount of earliest medieval material, so attention must focus on the eighth to the mid-fourteenth centuries when we can compare relatively abundant archaeological material with the documentary sources for this period. West of the Blackdown Hills we have relatively few assemblages, although they are compatible with the equally sparse documentary sources in suggesting mixed husbandry with both cattle and sheep/goat being significant. In the lowlands of central Somerset a very different picture emerges with animal bone assemblages confirming the data in Domesday that cattle were dominant. In the reclaimed marshlands of the Somerset Levels Domesday suggests relatively low numbers of sheep, and the thirteenth- and fourteenth-century documentary sources confirm that cattle were dominant, which is exactly what the animal bone assemblages tell us. Unfortunately there are few animal bone assemblages from the Jurassic clay vales, though for the chalk downland Domesday, our thirteenth- and fourteenth-century written sources, and the animal bone evidence all agree that sheep were dominant. Evidence for the Dorset heathlands is scarce but once again the archaeological and documentary data are all consistent in suggesting cattle were dominant.

When we turn to arable cultivation very clear differences in farming practice once again emerge. To the west of the Blackdown Hills the archaeological evidence supports the documentary sources in showing that oats were dominant, along with significant amounts of rye in some areas (particularly on poor soils) and, in the lowlands, barley. The Vale of Taunton Deane, between the Blackdown and Quantock Hills, shows a pattern of cereal cultivation that illustrates a transition between the oat-dominated cultivation of the far south-west, and the domination of wheat seen to the east, with the barn at Taunton Priory—whose estates were mostly in the Vale—containing roughly equal amounts of oats and wheat, which is in accordance with the documentary sources. On the Blackdown Hills, the single assemblage from Gaffers, in Membury, shows wheat dominant—though not to the same extent as the lowlands of central Somerset (*see* below)—with significant amounts of oats, and this is similarly what the documentary evidence suggests. Several assemblages of charred cereal from Shapwick come from the heart of Glastonbury Abbey's estates in the lowlands of central Somerset and here we see a different pattern of cereal cultivation with wheat now dominant (*c.*85% of the grains), barley very much secondary (*c.*11%), and oats of minor importance (*c.*3%, which could be largely from weeds). The reclaimed marshlands of Somerset present an interesting example of a *pays* with a distinctive pattern of agriculture as although wheat (77%) was the main crop, barley (12%), oats (10%), and rye (1%) all appear to have been relatively more significant compared to the adjacent drylands. This strategy of growing a diversity of crops may have been a response to the threat of waterlogging and flooding. Moving further east to the Jurassic limestone hills we see again the dominance of wheat, with just a little more diversity in crop husbandry in the Jurassic clay vales. Although we lack rural assemblages from the chalk downland, excavations within the towns have produced relatively large amounts of barley, while both rural and urban settlements in the Dorset heathlands have produced relatively large amounts of oats, barley, and rye making this a region like the reclaimed marshland where a particular range of crops was grown.

Overall, what clearly emerges is that both the archaeological and the documentary sources agree that during the middle medieval period there were very marked regional differences in agricultural practices and that these were remarkably long-lived. The far South West (Devon and Cornwall) in particular had mixed patterns of animal husbandry and cereal cultivation, whereas the lowlands east of the Blackdown Hills generally saw greater specialization with wheat and cattle dominant. There were, however, different emphases in certain *pays*, such as the dominance of sheep on the lighter soils of the limestone hills and chalk downland. All this tallies with what we know about agriculture in the post-medieval period, better documented that it is, and would appear to support the Thirskesque notion of discrete 'farming regions' that, while seeing changes in land use over time, possessed certain inherent properties that favoured particular types of agriculture. If this was indeed the case then we would expect to see the same situation in the Roman period. In Dumnonia, west of the Blackdown Hills, animal husbandry in the Roman period was once again very different to that further to the east, although now it was dominated by sheep not cattle. Barley dominates the cereal assemblages along with significant amounts of oats and some wheat, and the higher proportion of emmer shows a strong degree of continuity with the pre-Roman period. In the east of Dumnonia, for example, wheat was more significant, though still with significant amounts of oats being grown; large amounts of emmer once again show a strong degree of continuity with the pre-Roman period. In the lowlands of central Somerset, however, we see a very different pattern of agriculture as spelt wheat dominated cereal cultivation and sheep dominated livestock husbandry: the former continued into the medieval period, whereas the latter did not, and this could be explained by the more extensive drainage of the Somerset Levels (sheep being ideally suited to saltmarsh as they do not suffer from foot rot and liver fluke). On the reclaimed marshlands cattle were indeed far more important than on the adjacent drylands, while cereal cultivation was noticeably mixed with a balance of wheat, oats, and barley; on settlements in the unreclaimed marshland sheep and barley dominated, both of which cope well with slightly brackish conditions.

Three crucial conclusions emerge from this analysis (Table 13.5). Firstly, in the Roman, middle medieval, and post-medieval periods there were marked regional variations in farming practice across the different *pays* of our study area. The lack of data for the earliest medieval period is particularly frustrating as it is impossible to determine the extent to which there was continuity in land use after the collapse of the Roman economy which we would expect to have had a far greater impact east of the Blackdown Hills compared to Dumnonia. Secondly, it is clear that certain districts have consistently had the same distinctive patterns of agriculture, and this tends to be where the geology leads to soils that impose particular constraints upon agriculture: the thin, dry soils of the chalk downland have consistently seen relatively significant proportions of arable land sown with barley, while the reclaimed marshlands of Somerset and heathlands of Dorset have consistently seen a greater variety of crops grown compared to other areas, perhaps as a way of insuring against extreme weather events in areas with very damp and very dry soils respectively.

The third crucial conclusion, however, is that while some of these distinctive agricultural practices show continuity from the Roman through to the medieval period, others do not. At face value, this implies that *pays* do not possess inherent properties that determine the patterns of agriculture, although in some cases this warrants further investigation. In a number of cases the apparent discontinuity is in the early medieval period whose data must be treated with great caution. In Dumnonia, for example, sheep dominate the animal bone assemblages in both the Roman and the middle medieval periods, while on the one site we have for the early medieval period with good evidence—Bantham—it was cattle. This should not, however, be taken at face value as unlike the Roman and middle medieval sites that were rural settlements, Bantham was a coastal trading site and as such, the people living and working there are likely to have had a higher social status and different dietary preferences. It is noticeable, however, that in all cases where we have early medieval animal-bone assemblages, cattle form a higher percentage than in the Roman and middle medieval periods, and while the number of sites we are dealing with is small, and most are not rural but higher status sites, at Poundbury, cattle similarly rose from 29% in the late-Roman period to 50% in the early medieval period, while sheep fell from 65% to 42%. The number of early medieval cereal assemblages we have are even fewer, though in both Dumnonia and the chalk downland the distinctive patterns of cereal cultivation seen in the Roman and middle medieval periods—the emphasis on barley

Table 13.5. Changing patterns of population density and land use across the regional study area.

District	archaeological evidence			documentary evidence	
	Romano-British	earliest medieval (5th–7th century)	middle medieval (8th to mid-14th century)	Domesday	1250–1349 (including population in 1327/32)
western Devon and Cornwall	very high proportion of sheep compared to cattle; strong emphasis on barley and significant amounts of oats and some wheat	cattle with some sheep; mix of oats and barley with very small amounts of wheat	sheep and cattle bones in roughly equal proportions; no quantified cereal remains though unquantified assemblages and pollen suggests oats, barley, and rye dominate	low to average population density; low density of plough teams; moderate amounts of pasture, moderate numbers of sheep; deficient in meadow; some extensive areas of woodland	low population density; roughly twice as much arable as pasture in demesnes; oats dominant, with some wheat and rye; cattle and sheep both important; deficient in meadow
lowlands of eastern Devon	no animal bone assemblages; wheat dominant but significant amounts of oats and a little barley	no data	no data	average to high population density (high in the Exe valley); high density of plough teams (particularly in the Exe Valley); moderate amounts of pasture, moderate numbers of sheep; abundant meadow; relatively little woodland	average to high population density; roughly equal proportions of arable cultivation and pasture in demesnes (slightly less arable cultivation in Culm valley); oats dominant, with some wheat, rye, and barley; cattle dominant amongst livestock; abundant meadow
Blackdown Hills	no animal bone assemblages; wheat dominant but significant amounts of oats and a little barley	no data	no data	low to average population density; low density of plough teams (though close to average in the south); abundant pasture, small numbers of sheep; deficient in meadow (except in Culm and Axe valleys); some extensive areas of woodland	low to average population density; roughly equal proportions of arable and pasture in demesnes; wheat with some oats; cattle and sheep both important; low to average amounts of meadow

Region				
central Somerset lowlands	relatively high proportion of sheep compared to cattle; wheat overwhelmingly dominant with oats and barley very minor components.	no data	cattle dominant with low numbers of sheep; wheat dominant at Shapwick (85% of grain) with some barley (12%); oats just (3%), but 54% at Taunton Priory further west.	densely populated; average density of plough teams; moderate amounts of pasture, small numbers of sheep; abundant meadow; some extensive areas of woodland to the south west	high population density; roughly twice as much arable as pasture in demesnes; wheat and oats (wheat dominant in the hinterland of Glastonbury Abbey); cattle dominant amongst livestock; abundant meadow
North Somerset hills and valleys	mix of cattle and sheep; wheat overwhelmingly dominant with oats and barley very minor components.	cattle dominant	mix of cattle and sheep; wheat dominant but significant amounts of barley	average to high density of population; average to high density of plough teams; average amounts of pasture and abundant meadow, large numbers of sheep; average amounts of woodland	average to high population density; wheat and barley or oats; cattle dominant amongst livestock; average amounts of meadow
reclaimed Somerset marshlands (settled coastal claylands)	cattle dominant but with some sheep; mixed cereal cultivation with wheat, oats, and barley	no data	cattle dominant with relatively very low numbers of sheep; wheat dominant but significant amounts barley and oats	average population density; average density of plough teams on the settled coastal claylands; abundant pasture and meadow, small numbers of sheep; no woodland	average to high population density; greater amount of pasture than arable in demesnes; wheat and oats with some barley; cattle dominant amongst livestock; abundant meadow
Jurassic limestone hills	cattle dominant and relatively low numbers of sheep; wheat overwhelmingly dominant but with significant amounts of barley	no data	sheep dominant with relatively very low numbers of cattle; wheat overwhelmingly dominant with just small amounts of barley and rye	average to high population density; average density of plough teams (higher than in central Somerset lowlands); small amounts of pasture recorded, large numbers of sheep; average amounts of meadow; relatively little woodland	high population density; roughly twice as much arable as pasture in demesnes; wheat and oats with some barley; sheep dominant amongst livestock; average amounts of meadow
Jurassic clay vales (Blackmoor Vale etc.)	mix of cattle and sheep; wheat dominant but with significant amounts of barley and some oats	cattle dominant (81% of bones) in a very small assemblage of twenty-six bones from Brickley Lane in Devizes	no data for animal bones from rural sites; wheat dominant but small amounts of barley and oats	average population density; low density of plough teams; small amounts of pasture (data of livestock not recorded); average amounts of meadow; some extensive areas of woodland	high population density; roughly equal proportions of arable and pasture in demesnes; wheat with a small amount of oats and rye; cattle dominant amongst livestock; abundant meadow

(*continued*)

Table 13.5. Continued

District	archaeological evidence			documentary evidence	
	Romano-British	earliest medieval (5th–7th century)	middle medieval (8th to mid-14th century)	Domesday	1250–1349 (including population in 1327/32)
chalk downland	sheep dominant and some cattle; mix of wheat and barley in Dorset, though in Wiltshire wheat dominant but still with significant amounts of barley	cattle and sheep; mix of wheat and barley and some oats	sheep dominant with relatively low numbers of cattle; wheat dominant but significant amounts of barley and some rye	average population density; low density of plough teams; abundant pasture, large numbers of sheep; average to abundant amounts of meadow; relatively little woodland	high population density in 1327/1332; roughly equal proportions of arable and pasture in demesnes; wheat, oats, and barley; sheep dominant amongst livestock; deficient in meadow
South east Dorset heathlands	sheep dominant and relatively few cattle; mixed cereal cultivation with oats and barley dominant and just small amounts of wheat	no data	no data for animal bones from rural sites; wheat dominant but significant amounts of rye, oats, and barley	low population density; low density of plough teams; average amounts of pasture, relatively few sheep; relatively little meadow; relatively little woodland population density: low = 2.5–5 persons/mile^2 average = 5–10 persons/mile^2 high = 10–15 persons/mile^2 (Darby and Welldon Finn 1967) Plough team density: low = 1.0–2.5/mile^2 average = 2.5–3.5/mile^2 high = over 3.5/mile^2 (Darby and Welldon Finn 1967)	low to average population density; no data on cropping; cattle dominant amongst livestock; average amounts of meadow population density: low = <50 taxpayers/10 mile^2 average = 50–74 taxpayers/10 mile^2 high = >75 taxpayers/10 mile^2 (Campbell and Bartley 2006, map 18.10)

and oats in the former, and mixture of wheat and barley in the latter—are also seen in the fifth to the seventh centuries.

Overall, it is clear that marked local variations in the patterns of land use were not something new to the post-medieval period as they are clearly evident in both the Roman and medieval periods. Some of the clearest examples are where geology has led to soils that are particularly wet or dry—most obviously the marshlands, chalk downlands, and heathlands—but if we pull back from local detail we see that throughout the Roman and medieval periods there were very different agricultural practices on either side of the Blackdown Hills.

14

Regional variation in landscape character during the late prehistoric and Roman periods

A central theme of this study is the origins and development of regional variation in landscape character, and in particular whether differences in settlement patterns and field systems running through the Blackdown and Quantock Hills, that are so clearly evident in the medieval and post-medieval periods, can be traced back to the Roman period or even earlier. A cursory glance at published maps of Roman Britain suggests that there was indeed a marked difference in landscape character, with large numbers of villas to the east but almost none to the west (Fig. 2.1). The wealth displayed in these villas, and other evidence for extensive investment in agricultural innovation seen during the late Roman period such as corn-drying ovens, suggests that the Roman *civitates* of the Durotriges and the Dobunni were amongst the wealthiest and most innovative in Roman Britain. In contrast, there is just a single Roman town in the whole of the South West (the *civitas* capital of *Isca Dumnoniorum*, modern Exeter: Bidwell 1980), just a handful of very modest villas, and no corn-drying ovens, but while this might give the impression of a sparsely settled landscape, palaeo environmental evidence has shown that it was largely cleared of woodland by the Iron Age and that this remained the case throughout the Roman period (see Chapter 11).

The relative lack of Romanization in the South West has long been recognized, and in his seminal discussion, 'The character and origins of Roman Dumnonia', one of Thomas's themes (1966) was how 'the concept of the Early Iron Age (*sensu stricto*) and the Roman period in the South West [was] a continuous process, scarcely divisible at all, certainly not at any such clear-cut horizon as A.D. 43 (or 49, or 53)'. Since Thomas's overview, increasing numbers of Roman period settlements have been identified, albeit on the basis of radiocarbon dating of just a small amount of pottery, and so it would appear that there were plenty of people living in the South West but that, in contrast to communities further east, they simply chose not to invest

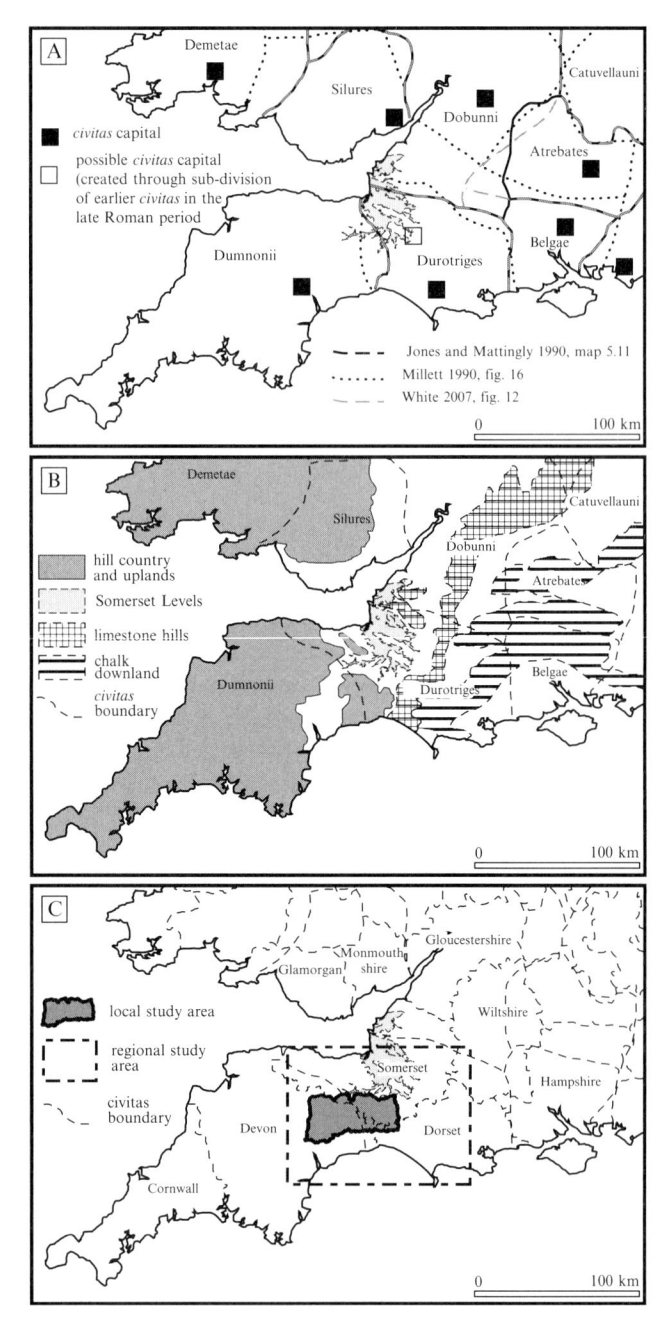

Fig. 14.1. (A) Reconstructions of *civitas* boundaries in the South West of Britain. (B) and (C) suggested *civitas* boundaries mapped against major topographic zones and pre-1974 county boundaries.

their wealth in the trappings of Romanitas. The Blackdown Hills appear to have marked not just a boundary in landscape character but in the nature of society as a whole. In this chapter we will explore that difference in greater detail and see whether it can be traced back into prehistory.

TRIBAL AREAS, *CIVITATES*, AND KINGDOMS: TERRITORIAL DIVISIONS IN SOUTH WEST BRITAIN (FIG. 14.1)

In the mid-second century, the Roman writer Ptolemy tells us that South West Britain was occupied by a people known as the *Damnonii*, with the *Durotriges* to the east (Rivet and Smith 1979, 343, 352; Jones and Mattingly 1990, 16–23). Ptolemy also refers to the *Damnonium* promontory (probably the Lizard in south Cornwall), and in the late fifth or sixth century, Gildas refers to the South West peninsula as *Dumnonia* (Pearce 2004, 23). Traditionally, the whole of the Roman *civitas* of the Dumnonii has been regarded a single region, but in recent years it has become increasingly apparent that there are subtle, but significant, sub-regional differences within it including a distinctive indigenous suite of material culture and settlement forms that are restricted to present-day Cornwall, where there was also a greater amount of Roman pottery and coins in use compared to neighbouring Devon (Quinnell 1993; Rippon 2006b). The Ravenna Cosmography refers to a place called *Durocornavis*, combining the Celtic prefix *Duro-* (fort or stronghold) and *Cornovii* (based on *Corn-* meaning horn or promontory), in referring to a people that were presumably resident in the far South West as the name is perpetuated by the name Cornwall (Todd 1987, 203, 216–17; White 2007, 146; Higham 2008, 16–18). Mattingly (2007, 402–8, fig. 10) even goes so far as to suggest that what is now Cornwall and western Devon may have been an area 'under long-term military, state or external control, perhaps *ager publicus* or imperial property, and so outside the Dumnonian *civitas*'.

Based on analogy with other provinces such as Gaul, the *civitates* in Roman Britain were probably subdivided into smaller rural districts known as *pagi*, of which the *Cornovii* may be an example. While other possible *pagi* have been identified—such as a writing tablet from London that refers to a woodland located in 'the *pagus Dibussu* in the *civitas* of the *Cantiaci* [modern Kent]'— there is insufficient evidence to reconstruct their extent, although another possible example may be the area around Ilchester, that originally fell within the *civitas* of the Durotriges but which became a *civitas* in its own right in the late Roman period (Fulford 2006). At a more local level, the landscape of Roman Britain must have been divided into a series of estates, whose agricultural productivity funded the construction of villas. We have little idea about what these estates looked like, including whether they formed compacted blocks of land or were more sprawling entities comparable to the medieval lordships recorded in Domesday. Various attempts have been made to reconstruct villa estates, including the application of crude spatial models such as Thiessen polygons and suggesting that they have survived as medieval parishes, reflected, for example, in the recurrent proximity of Roman villas and medieval church/manor complexes, the tendency for certain 'early Anglo-Saxon' burials to occur on parish boundaries, and the way that some Roman roads and early medieval linear earthworks appear to post-date their boundaries (Finberg 1955; Fowler 1975; Bonney 1972; 1979; Branigan 1977, 192–7; Leech 1982a; Haslam 1984). Such work has not been without its critics (e.g. Goodier 1984), and in a period of great social upheaval such as the fifth to the seventh centuries, territorial boundaries are features of the landscape that are amongst the least likely to have survived, particularly in eastern England. In South West Britain, however, there is a greater possibility of continuity in the landscape because the Anglo-Saxon conquest was both later in date and likely to have been less disruptive as it did not involve a mass folk migration. That part of Somerset west of Selwood and south of Mendip, for example, was not conquered until 658 when 'Cenwalh [king of the west Saxons] fought at *Peonnum* against the Welsh and drove them in flight as far as the Parrett'; *Peonnum* ('the head of Selwood') is assumed to be Penselwood on the Wiltshire/Somerset border (Swanton 1996, 32–3). Although most of Somerset then became part of the kingdom of Wessex, there is no evidence that this political assimilation involved a mass folk migration with just a handful of possible Germanic burials and no 'Sunken Feature Buildings' (Grubenhäuser) (Fig. 14.5; Eagles 1994; 2004; Tipper 2000). This is one area of Roman Britain where continuity in territorial structures is plausible, but as yet unproven.

THE ROMAN PERIOD

Coinage, manufactured goods, and the market

One of the most distinctive features of Romano-British archaeology in most areas is the abundance of material culture, but this is not the case with the South West. An analysis of recent non-ceramic finds reported through the Portable Antiquities Scheme, the majority of which are coins, reveals some startling patterns with large numbers of findspots in Dorset and Somerset (east of the Quantock Hills), a moderate number in Cornwall, but very few in Devon (Table 14.1). The distribution of coin hoards follows a very similar

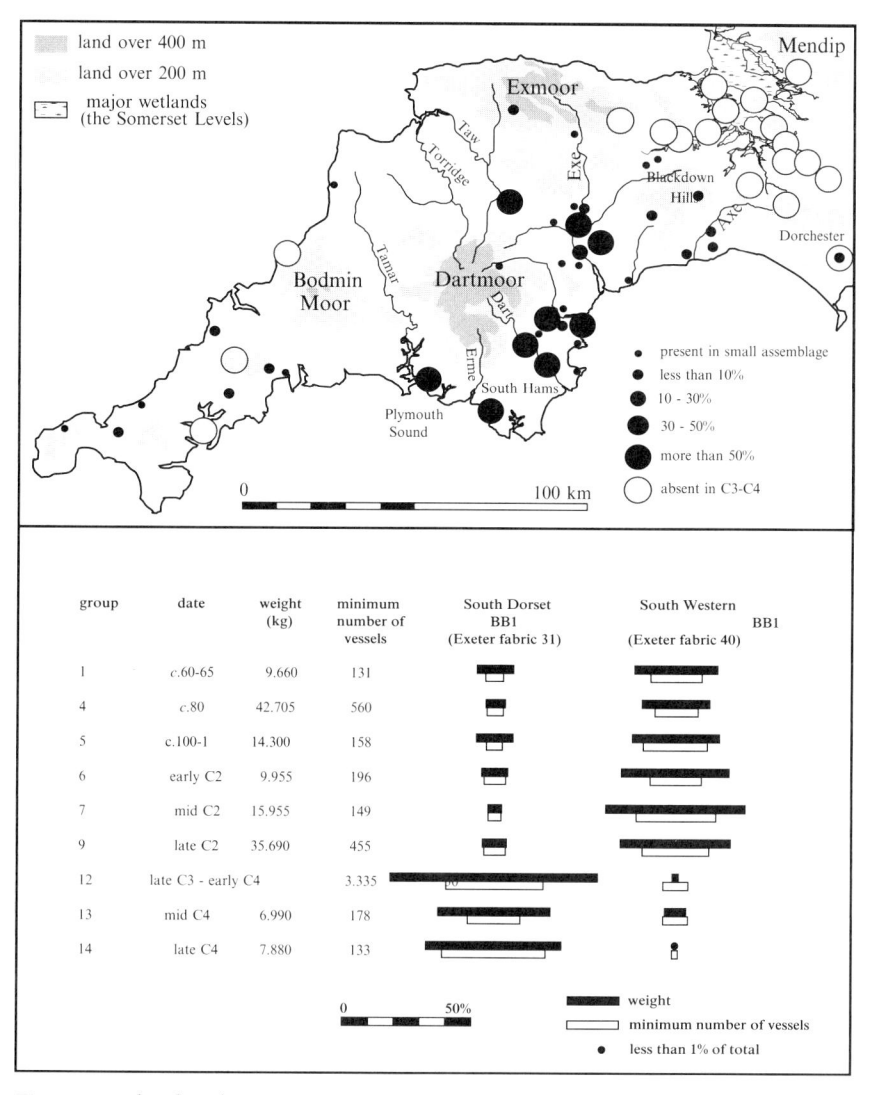

Regional variation in landscape character 291

group	date	weight (kg)	minimum number of vessels	South Dorset BB1 (Exeter fabric 31)	South Western BB1 (Exeter fabric 40)
1	c.60-65	9.660	131		
4	c.80	42.705	560		
5	c.100-1	14.300	158		
6	early C2	9.955	196		
7	mid C2	15.955	149		
9	late C2	35.690	455		
12	late C3 – early C4	3.335	90		
13	mid C4	6.990	178		
14	late C4	7.880	133		

Fig. 14.2. The distribution of South Devon Ware as first mapped by Holbrook and Bidwell (1991, fig. 7), but with additional data that reinforce their initial conclusion that it does not extend east of the Blackdown Hills (Ellis 1989; Lucas 1993; Ratcliffe 1995; Hearne and Seager Smith 1995; Graham and Mills 1996; Griffith and Reed 1998; Johnson 1998–9; Davies *et al.* 2002; Todd 2002; Leach 2003; Valentine 2003; Davey and Cooper 2004; Bray 2006; Evans and Hancocks 2006; Lovell 2006; Tingle 2006; Gerrard with Aston 2007; Powell *et al.* 2009).

Table 14.1. Non-ceramic Romano-British finds reported through the Portable Antiquities Scheme 2003–8 (based on Worrell 2004; 2005; 2006; 2007; 2008; 2009)

County	2003	2004	2005	2006	2007	2008	Total	area	objects/km^2
Somerset	72	155	132	185	305	374	1,223 (50%)	4,171 km^2	0.29
Dorset	43	141	111	79	319	89	782 (32%)	2,653 km^2	0.29
Devon	0	9	28	3	31	69	140 (6%)	6,707 km^2	0.02
Cornwall	10	57	85	50	46	31	279 (12%)	3,563 km^2	0.08

pattern (Robertson 2000).[1] This relative lack of engagement with the market economy of Roman Britain is also seen in the pottery assemblages that, with the exception of Exeter and some coastal settlements, are small in size and predominantly local in origin. In central, southern, and eastern Devon the dominant fabric is South Devon Ware that petrological analysis suggests was produced south of Dartmoor (Bidwell and Silvester 1988, 42–9; Holbrook and Bidwell 1991, 177). The distribution of South Devon Ware is almost wholly restricted to the South West of Britain (Fig. 14.2). There have been isolated findspots in Dorchester (although it has not been recorded in recent excavations), and South Devon possibly London (although this has not been questioned), but South Devon Ware is conspicuously absent from central and southern Somerset (Holbrook and Bidwell 1991, 181, fig. 7; Woodward *et al.* 1993; Davies *et al.* 2002; Tyers 1996, 197).

There was also relatively limited movement of pottery into the South West. A number of industries were based to the east of the Blackdown Hills in southern Somerset and eastern Dorset, such as South-Western Grey Ware whose products only penetrated as far west as Exeter (Holbrook and Bidwell 1991, fig. 69). Products of the major regional industries of Roman Britain are also present in the South West in far smaller amounts than elsewhere. The distribution of some, such as New Forest Ware, is largely restricted to Exeter and a few coastal sites to the east, and while a few examples of Oxfordshire Ware and Severn Valley Ware are found more widely, this is nothing like the amounts seen to the east of the Blackdown Hills (e.g. Allen and Fulford 1996; Tyers 1996). The products of other industries are barely represented in the South West (e.g. South Midlands shell-tempered and Savernake Wares: Tyers 1996).

The distribution of South-East Dorset Black Burnished Ware Category 1 (SEDBB1), produced around Poole Harbour, has been studied in particular detail by Allen and Fulford (1996), and discussed by Gerrard (2004b; 2007; 2008; 2010). Across Dorset and most of Somerset, SEDBB1 makes up at least

---

[1] Robertson (2000) contains finds up until 1992, to which we can add West Bagborough on the Quantock Hills (Burnham *et al.* 2002) and Padstow in Cornwall (Burnham *et al.* 2007, 296).

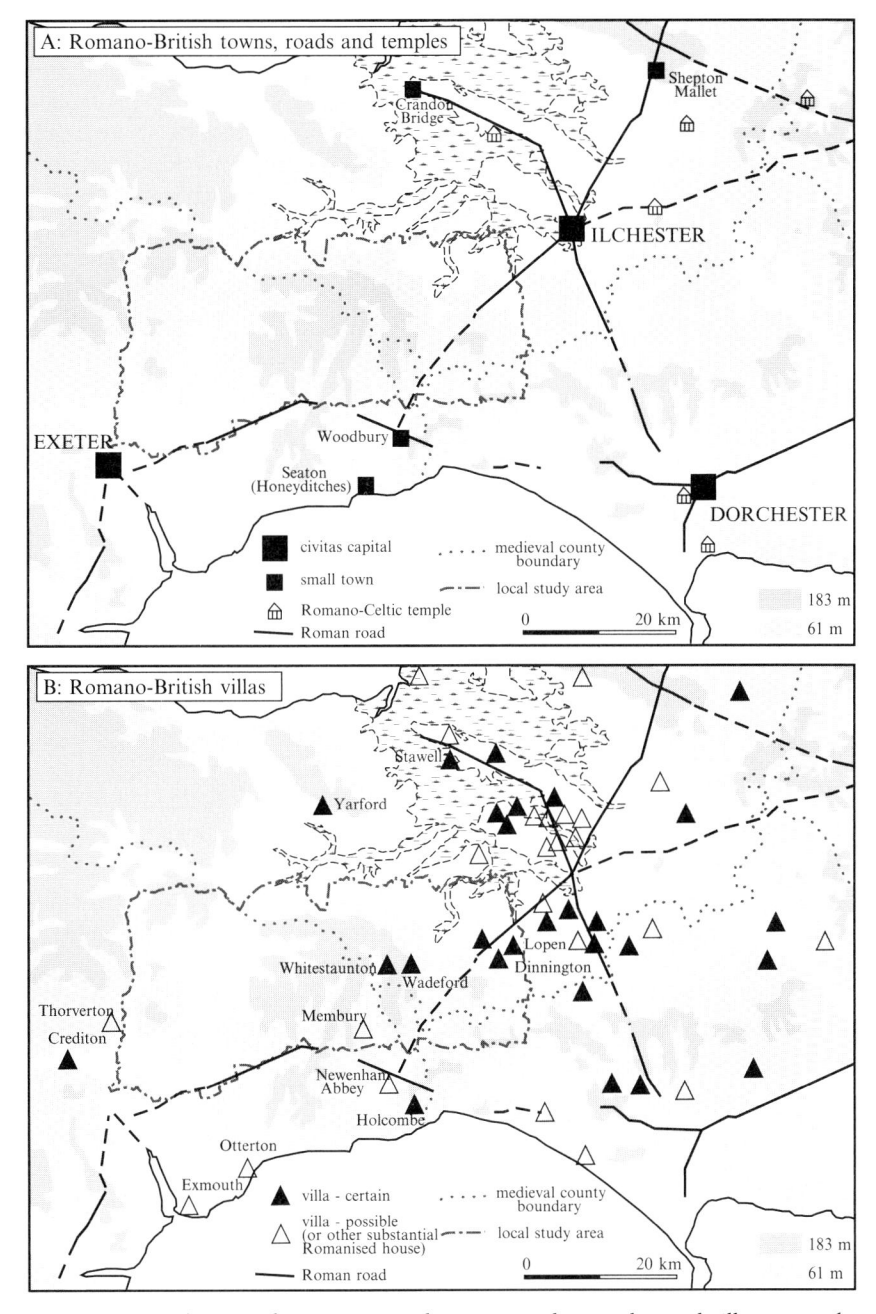

Fig. 14.3. Distribution of Romano-British towns, roads, temples, and villas across the regional study area (after Ordnance Survey 2001).

40% of Romano-British pottery assemblages, in contrast to areas west of the Blackdown Hills where it is mostly under 10%, the exception being in Exeter and a few coastal sites in eastern Devon (Allen and Fulford 1996, fig. 8). Assemblages published since Allen and Fulford's (1996) review support this relatively sharp fall-off in the amount of BB1 from east to west: at Membury (on the Blackdown Hills) it is 56% (Tingle 2006, 40); Pomeroy Wood, near Honiton on the western edge of the Blackdown Hills, 43% (Fitzpatrick *et al.* 1999, 314–15); Aller Cross, in Kingskerswell in south Devon, 25% (Hearne and Seager Smith 1995), while at the nearby Kenn it was just 14% (Weddell 2000, 122–4). There is also clear evidence that the importation of BB1 was a largely late Roman phenomenon, as in Exeter it comprised just 6–8% of the pottery in the first and second centuries when South Devon Ware was dominant, but 40% in the late third to fourth centuries (Fig. 14.2). The same is seen in rural areas: SEDBB1 was absent at Rudge in mid-Devon, which was only occupied in the mid to late first century, whereas at nearby Bury Barton it accounted for 46% of the sherds in a fourth-century pit (Todd 1998; 2002, 51).

Overall, it would appear that in the early Roman period (first to mid-third centuries), locally produced South Devon Ware dominates pottery assemblages in Devon. In part this may reflect the region's geographical isolation, but it also conforms to the lack of other evidence for much engagement with the Roman way of life. The late Roman period does see an increase in the importation of pottery from outside the region, but it remains noticeable that even the hinterland of Exeter did not experience the boom in villa construction seen further east—for example around Ilchester—and it is to the pattern of settlement that we must now turn.

The very different Romano-British settlement patterns (Fig. 14.3)

In the *civitas* of the Durotriges, there was a settlement pattern that was typical of lowland Roman Britain with a series of small towns in addition to the *civitas* capitals at Dorchester (*Durnovaria*) and Ilchester (*Lindinis*) (Burnham and Wacher 1990; Leach 2001a). The extensive spread of occupation at Crandon Bridge has recently been confirmed as a small port town beside the Parrett Estuary (Rippon 2008b), while other substantial settlements that may have been involved in coastal trade can be postulated at all of the major tidal estuaries between there and the river Avon (Rippon 1997, 54, 87; 2008b). There are a number of substantial estate village-like settlements such as Gatcombe, Catsgore, and Congresbury (Branigan 1977; Leech 1982b; Ellis 1984; Rippon 1997, 88–90), an abundance of villas (Leach 2001a), as well as a range of lower-order farmsteads and small hamlets that took the form of clusters of small ditched compounds[2] or more substantial square or rectangular ditched enclosures.[3] The inhabitants of these various rural settlements consumed abundant durable material culture, and the large numbers of coins found on even low-status sites testifies to a flourishing market economy. Extensive wetland reclamation in Somerset, unique in Roman Britain, is another indication of the considerable investment and innovation in agriculture during the late Roman period that is also reflected in the large numbers of corn-drying ovens (Rippon 2006a).

The Blackdown Hills mark the western limit of this Romanized landscape. The only possible small towns to the south-west of Ilchester were at Woodbury and Seaton. The site at Woodbury, near Axminster, covers *c.*12 ha and was located where the Fosse Way, on its way to the coast at Seaton, crossed the Dorchester to Exeter road and the river Yarty. A substantial stone structure occupying the south-eastern quarter of a former fort is suggestive of a mansio, and this substantial roadside settlement may be *Moridunum* recorded in the Antonine Itinerary and other sources (Silvester and Bidwell 1984; Weddell *et al.* 1993; Cole and Linford 1993). Seaton lies at the far end of the Fosse Way at the mouth of the Axe (Maxfield 1986, 4). The remains of a building complex at Honeyditches may be another mansio or some other form of official complex (Holbrook 1987; Todd 1987, 221). Further west, along the Dorchester to Exeter road, another roadside settlement has been partially excavated at Pomeroy Wood near Honiton, though even as late as the second and third centuries the majority of the buildings were roundhouses; although iron smithing was carried out on site, there is nothing to indicate an urban function with the presence of grain driers and four-post granaries suggesting a strong agricultural basis to its economy (Fitzpatrick 1999, 224–404). Seaton and Woodbury are therefore the two most south-westerly possible small towns in Britain, suggesting that the market-based economy and the social structures that such settlements supported did not extend further into modern Devon. The distribution of substantial Roman villas also only extends this far west.[4] Holcombe, on the southern edge of the Blackdown Hills, is the most thoroughly investigated of these frontier villas, and both socially and economically it appears to have looked east not west (Pollard 1974). In the Late Iron Age the

---

[2] e.g. Banwell Moor, Kenn Moor, and Puxton Dolemoors on the North Somerset Levels (Rippon 2000b; 2006a), Englands in Charlton Horethorne (Davey 2005, 48–50), Maidenbrook Farm phase 3 (Ferris and Bevan 1993), Podimore (Griffith and Horner 2000; Leach 2001a, 92), Row of Ashes Farm in Butcombe (Fowler 1968; 1970), RNAS Yeovilton (Lovell 2006), and Shapwick (Gerrard with Aston 2007).

[3] e.g. Chedzoy (Croft and Aston 1993, 48), Maidenbrook Farm phase 2 (Ferris and Bevan 1993), and sites investigated in the University of Winchester's Southern Quantock Hills Archaeological Survey (Webster 2000a; Thorpe 2002; Wilkinson *et al.* 2003; Roffey *et al.* 2003).

[4] Membury Court (Wilkin 1928, 169; Fox 1949, 88; Hoskins 1954, 537, n. 37; Todd 1987, 221), Newenham Abbey (Allan and Silvester 1981; Weddell *et al.* 1993, 79), Wadeford and Whitestaunton (Scott 1993).

pottery assemblage was dominated by Durotrigian ware, and the fourth century saw the construction of a bath house of an unusual octagonal plan, closely paralleled at Lufton in Somerset (Todd 1987, 220). Both structures have recently been re-interpreted as baptistries, with other possible examples being at Keynsham in Somerset, and Chedworth, Great Witcombe, and Stroud, all in Gloucestershire (Todd 2005). Although Henig (2006) rejects this interpretation, suggesting instead that these polygonal structures are simply part of the late Roman architectural repertoire, it would still be the case that the cultural tradition to which the Holcombe structure belongs is firmly part of the Romanized Durotrigian and Dobunnian sphere, as opposed to the less Romanized Dumnonia. Small-scale excavations in nearby Membury revealed a late Roman corn-drying oven which is the most south-westerly occurrence of such a structure (Tingle 2006, 49; Taylor 2007, fig. 7.3).

To the west of the Blackdown Hills there are few substantial Romanized buildings, all in the vicinity of Exeter and the Exe Estuary (Fig. 14.3). The location of two of these sites—Exmouth overlooking the Exe estuary (Scott 1993, 49) and Otterton beside the Otter (Brown and Holbrook 1989)—is similar to Seaton beside the Axe estuary and Holcombe overlooking the Lim, and may have been pleasant locations in which to build a country house, or reflect the significance of coastal and estuarine waters for communication. North-west of Exeter, a small winged corridor villa lies on the rich soils of the Creedy valley near Crediton (Griffith 1988a), while to the north of Exeter, fieldwalking and excavation at Overland, in Thorverton, produced a scatter of second to third century Romano-British pottery, *tegula*, *imbrex*, *pila*, and box-flue tile from a ditched enclosure complex, but no stone structures (Uglow *et al.* 1985; Uglow 2000, 227–34; Bayer in prep.). While there is clear evidence that several of these Dumnonian buildings had hypocaust systems and tiled roofs, the lack of window glass, painted wall plaster, and mosaic floors suggests that even these, the most Romanized buildings in the South West, were in no way comparable to the palatial villas of the Durotrigian *civitas*. As Sargent (2002, 225) has already noted, Wroxeter and Caerwent are parallels for a *civitas* capital not being associated with large numbers of villas, and perhaps the landed elite in these western areas chose to measure and display their wealth in other ways; for example, through the ownership of livestock. Relatively little is known about lower status rural settlement in eastern Dumnonia, although the majority of settlements are square or rectilinear ditched enclosures continuing a tradition seen in the Iron Age.[5] Parsonage Cross near Littlehempston in south Devon, found during

---

[5] A square enclosure at Newland Mill in North Tawton, mid-Devon, has recently been dated to the mid to late Roman period (Passmore 2005), as have incomplete, but rectilinear, enclosures at Aller Cross in Kingskerswell (Hearne and Seager Smith 1995) and Butland Farm in Modbury (Horner 1993). Other rectangular enclosures include Knowle Quarry near Okehampton (Balkwill

the construction of a water main, is an example of an open settlement from this period that have otherwise proved elusive due to their poor visibility (Reed and Turton 2005).

Romano-British field systems

Across all of Somerset to the east of the Blackdown and Quantock Hills rural settlements were associated with ditched field systems of the type found across lowland Roman Britain.[6] Even relatively small-scale excavations often reveal stretches of Romano-British ditch.[7] One of the most extensively examined Romano-British landscapes in Somerset is the North Somerset Levels, where rectilinear fields were laid out around a series of individual settlements with unenclosed areas between them. Fieldwalking has revealed intensively manured 'infields' close to the settlements, less frequently manured 'outfields' further away, and areas devoid of manure scatters beyond that (Rippon 2000b; 2006a). Similar variations in the intensity of manure scatters have also been found in Shapwick (Gerrard with Aston 2007, fig. 3.40).

Another possible indication of the character of Romano-British field systems within the *civitas* of the Durotriges is where they may have survived in use until the present day. Analysis by Turner (2008) reveals that in places, Roman roads in Somerset appear to cut across a series of apparently earlier field boundaries, as has been observed elsewhere in southern Britain (Williamson 1987; 2000; Rippon 1991; Higham 1992, fig. 5.15; Bryant *et al.* 2005; but see Hinton 1997 and Williamson 1998). A particularly clear example is near Lopen where a series of long, sinuous, broadly east–west-oriented field boundaries appear to be cut diagonally by the Fosse Way (Fig. 14.4). A very similar series of coaxial boundaries is found on the Polden Hills, west of Glastonbury, where they clearly pre-date the establishment of both open fields and parish boundaries (Rippon 2008a, figs. 3.3–4), and one of these boundaries—that forming the southern edge of 'Buddle' furlong in Shapwick—has been excavated to reveal how the modern field boundary was preceded by a medieval

---

1976) and Pond Farm near Exminster (Jarvis 1976), as well as the sites at Hayes Farm in Clyst Honiton, Overland in Thorverton, and Rewe Cross and Turnspitt in Rewe, all immediately north of Exeter (Simpson *et al.* 1989; Uglow 2000).

[6] e.g. Ashington and Chilton Cantelo (Rawlings 1992), Brean Down, Butcombe, Lye Hole and Wrington (Fowler 1968; 1970; 1975), Catsgore (Leech 1982b; Ellis 1984), Chedzoy (Croft and Aston 1993, 48), Gatcombe (Branigan 1977), Maidenbrook Farm in Cheddon Fitzpaine near Taunton (Ferris and Bevan 1994), Podimore (Leach 2001a, 92), Princes Pasture south of Ilchester (Crockett 1996, 70), Shapwick (Gerrard with Aston 2007, 183–244), around South Cadbury (Davey 2005), Westland (Leach 1985), Upper Holway near Taunton (Leach 2003), and Yeovilton (Lovell 2006).

[7] e.g. Churchfields in Ansford (Keynes 1985); Church Field in Puxton (Rippon 2000b); Ash near Martock (Graham 2005).

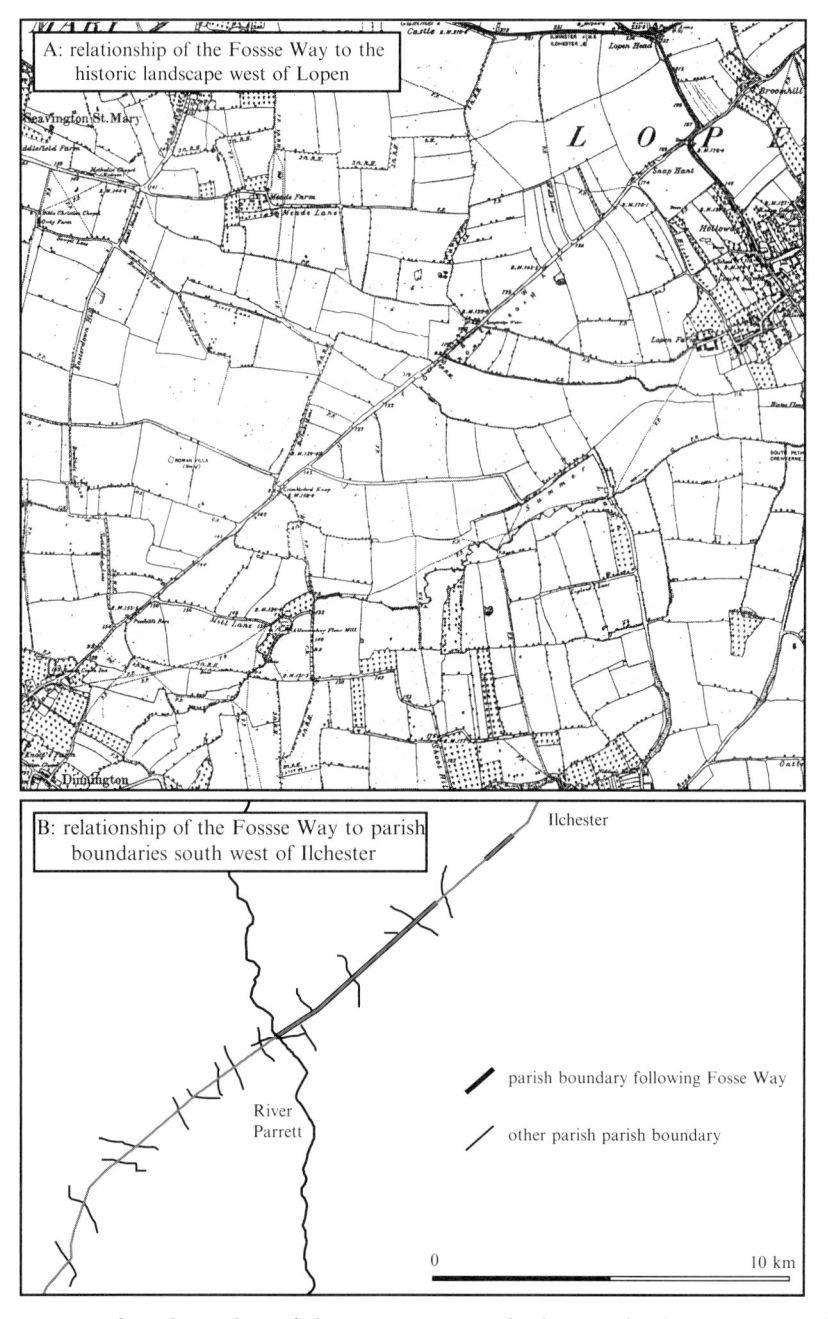

Fig. 14.4. The relationship of the Fosse Way to the historic landscape in central Somerset. (A) between Lopen and Dinnington this NE–SW-aligned Roman road appears to cut across an earlier pattern of roads and fields with a broadly E–W orientation. (B) east of the river Parrett many parish boundaries follow (i.e. post-date) the Fosse Way, whereas to the west they do not. (After Leech 1982a, fig. 10.)

headland, a Romano-British ditch and possible trackway, and an Iron Age ditch (Aston with Gerrard 2007, 372–7). The potential survival of Romano-British field systems in lowland Somerset has also been revealed elsewhere in Somerset. The late Romano-British settlement north of Ashington, for example, is on the same orientation as, and shares individual alignments with the medieval and later landscape (Rawlings 1992, 37–8), while in the hinterland of South Cadbury, geophysical survey and excavation show that a number of Romano-British settlements have elements whose precise alignment is perpetuated by features of the modern landscape (e.g. Charleton Horethorne: Davey 2005, 42–62). Overall, the Romano-British landscape across much of Somerset was parcelled up into field systems, some of which appear to have remained in use into the medieval period.

Given this widespread evidence for Romano-British field systems to the east of the Blackdown Hills, it is very noticeable how little evidence there is to the west, even though palaeoenvironmental sequences show that there was an open landscape that was largely cleared of woodland (see Chapter 11). This scarcity of Romano-British field systems is particularly curious as there is extensive evidence for Middle Bronze Age planned landscapes both in the upland fringes (Fleming 1983; 1988; N. Johnson and Rose 1994; Riley and Wilson-North 2001) and in lowland areas (e.g. Fitzpatrick *et al.* 1999). In contrast, while a small number of Iron Age and Romano-British settlements are associated with very localized field systems,[8] most are not, with the crop marks of ditched enclosures usually lying in splendid isolation.[9] The best preserved Iron Age and Romano-British field systems in Devon are on the limestone hills around Newton Abbot, which consist of small complexes of generally irregularly shaped fields defined by low banks (Phillips 1966, 12–16; Gallant *et al.* 1985; Quinn 1995). The only other possible strand of evidence for Romano-British field systems is a postulated coaxial layout to the present historic landscape around Woodbury that may be cut by the Dorchester-to-Exeter Roman road, and a similar phenomenon on Sourton Down near Okehampton (Weddell *et al.* 1993; Weddell and Reed 1997), but neither is particularly convincing.

So is this lack of evidence for Iron Age and Romano-British field systems west of the Blackdown Hills proof that they never existed? It is possible that although the substantial enclosure ditches around settlements show up as crop marks, smaller field-boundary ditches do not, but an increasing number of excavations are showing a genuine absence of Romano-British ditched fields

---

[8] Jarvis and Maxfield 1975; Jarvis 1976; Fitzpatrick *et al.* 1999; Passmore 2005; Silvester 1980a.
[9] Silvester and Balkwill 1977; Silvester 1978a, b; Silvester 1980b; Griffith 1984; Reed and Manning 2000; Simpson *et al.* 1989; C.A.T. 2000; Weddell 2000; Wilkes 2004; 2006; Riley and Wilson-North 2001, 65–75; Riley 2006, 60–72.

in areas where prehistoric field systems do survive.[10] Another, intriguing, explanation for the scarcity of Romano-British field systems is that rather than being ditched, they consisted of earthen banks such as those surviving on the limestone hills south of Newton Abbot (see above). A characteristic feature of the medieval and later landscape in South West England is its tradition of hedgebanks (see Chapter 7). Were this tradition to have begun in the Roman period then it would be yet another example of landscape evolution west of the Blackdown Hills diverging from that to the east.

Discussion: the Romano-British landscapes of the Dumnonii and the Durotriges

It is clear that the cultural landscapes either side of the Blackdown Hills were very different in the Roman period. Following the Conquest, the area to the east fell within the highly Romanized *civitas* of the Durotriges with a hierarchy of settlement developing including major towns, small towns, and villas. Even lower-status farmsteads saw the use of abundant material culture, and along with the widespread use of coinage this points to a flourishing market economy. Extensive wetland reclamation, the construction of large numbers of corn driers, and possible evidence for woodland clearance from a pollen sequence at Aller Farm, in Stockland, suggest agricultural expansion, prosperity, and innovation in the late Roman period (Hatton and Caseldine 1991).

In contrast, to the west of the Blackdown Hills, in the *civitas* of the Dumnonii, there was just a single town—the *civitas* capital of *Isca Dumnoniorum* (Exeter)—but an otherwise remarkably unstratified settlement pattern with only a handful of sites that show significant signs of Romanization. Indeed, what moves in this direction there may have been were short-lived, as many of the more Romanized buildings that were constructed around Exeter during the third century lack fourth century material (e.g. Otterton and Thorverton), while there was also a decline in the intensity of occupation at the roadside settlement at Pomeroy Wood near Honiton. The relative scarcity of durable material culture, including coinage, certainly suggests a poorly developed market economy and a lack of engagement with the rest of Roman Britain. The lack of evidence for Romano-British field systems is intriguing and may reflect the use of hedgebanks as opposed to ditches, or a more pastoral economy compared to areas further east, and as we have seen in Chapter 13, what arable land there was focused on the cultivation of a far

---

[10] e.g. Hayes Farm near Exeter (Simpson *et al*. 1989; C.A.T. 2000); the A30 Exeter to Honiton road (Fitzpatrick *et al*. 1999), the Kenn to Ashcombe Pipeline (Weddell 2000), Clyst Honiton, St Luke's College at Monkerton, and the former Royal Naval Stores Depot off Topsham Road (Horner 2006; Peter Weddell pers. comm.).

wider range of crops compared to the areas further east. Overall, the Blackdown Hills certainly marked a major boundary in landscape character as far back as the Roman period. Mattingly (2007, 14, 17) has recently discussed the development of just such regionally distinctive societies within Roman Britain, rejecting the term 'Romanization' in favour of 'discrepant experience': 'the co-existence of very different perceptions of history, culture, and relationships between colonizer and colonized'. His emphasis on regional differences is refreshing, as all too often the landscape of Roman Britain has been discussed in terms of a simplistic twofold division between upland and lowland, military and civilian, or native and villa (e.g. Dark and Dark 1997). The experience of communities living either side of the Blackdown Hills in the first century was certainly very different.

THE SUB-ROMAN/EARLIEST MEDIEVAL PERIOD

So what is the relationship between this Romano-British landscape and the medieval and later countryside that has been discussed in the preceding chapters? There has been much discussion about how Roman Britain came to an end with there being two very different schools of thought, the first seeing a period of continuity and gradual evolution, and the other a relatively sudden collapse (*see* Higham 1992; Dark 1999; 2000; Hamerow 2002, Härke 2002; Collins and Gerrard 2004; Pryor 2004). Our study area is an interesting one in which to examine this period, such were the differences in Romanization either side of the Blackdown Hills, although one unifying element was the lack of fifth century Anglo-Saxon immigration. Indeed, there is increasing evidence for a strong degree of continuity right across Devon, western Dorset, and Somerset during the fifth to the mid-seventh centuries, most notably in the palaeoenvironmental record, with the crucial period of change being around the eighth to the tenth centuries.

Civitas of the Durotriges

Considering the degree of late Roman prosperity in the *civitas* of the Durotriges, it might be assumed that the fifth century was a period of profound change, and some have argued that the end of the Roman era here marked a 'complete dislocation of the economy at all levels of society' (Costen 1992a, 54), and a period when most Roman sites were abandoned (Burrow 1981, 14). Along similar lines, and for Roman Britain as a whole, Esmonde Cleary (1989, 173) suggests that 'the fifth century saw a sudden and brutal rupture, and materially a massive discontinuity with what had gone before'. Along similar lines, Faulkner (2001, 175) states that, 'Roman sites simply stop; there is no post-Roman build-up of deposits with timber post-holes, rubbish pits and handmade potsherds to indicate continuing low-grade occupation; there is nothing at all'. Even if Gerrard (2004b; 2010) is correct, and the BB1 pottery industry around Poole Harbour continued for a decade or so into the fifth century suggesting some local exchange networks survived, there is still no evidence for a fully functioning market-based economy after that date. It is certainly true that there are large numbers of late Roman settlements that now lie abandoned, pointing to a discontinuity in the landscape *at some stage*, but the key question is whether these settlements were abandoned in the early fifth century or during the major transformation of the landscape around the eighth to the tenth centuries that led to the creation of villages and open fields. Are generalizations across the whole of Roman Britain, such as Esmonde Cleary's 'sudden and brutal rupture', really useful, or is such a broad-brush approach obscuring significant regional variation in local responses to the ending of Roman authority, the collapse of the market-based economy, and the timing and nature of the Anglo-Saxon conquests?

A series of important excavations in central and eastern Somerset has shed light on what had been a 'Dark Age', including the cemetery at Cannington (Rahtz *et al.* 2000), and hilltop settlements at Cadbury Congresbury (Rahtz *et al.* 1992), South Cadbury (Alcock 1995), and Glastonbury Tor (Rahtz 1970). Such sites appeared to demonstrate some degree of continuity with the Roman period: interments at Cannington, for example, started in the third century (as was also the case at Poundbury near Dorchester)—while the re-occupied hillfort at Cadbury Congresbury may have been the successor to a substantial late Romano-British settlement on the slopes below that included a villa at Woodlands and nearby temple at Henley Wood. There has also been much speculation about possible continuity in the location of estate centres, rural settlements, and even the boundaries of landed estates from the Roman through to the medieval period (Rahtz and Fowler 1972; Fowler 1975; Leech 1982a).

Cannington is one of a growing number of what have been termed 'sub-Roman' cemeteries that are found across the South West that are characterized by east to west-oriented inhumations, with the body in an extended position and accompanied with very few or no grave goods, and in graves sometimes lined with stone (Petts 2004; Webster and Brunning 2004).[11] Even some burial groups that contain Anglo-Saxon objects may include native British people. At

---

[11] Kenn in mid Devon (Weddell 2000), Wembdon and Stoneage Barton Farm in west Somerset (Croft 1988; Webster and Brunning 2004), Portishead, Lamyatt Beacon, West Harptree, Pagans Hill, Brean Down, Henley Wood (Yatton), and Winthill (Banwell) in North Somerset (Rahtz 1977; Rahtz and Watts 1989, 338; Bell 1990; Watts and Leach 1996; Rippon 1997, 139; Webster 2000b), Camerton, Bradley Hill, and Shepton Mallet in central Somerset (Wedlake 1958; Leech 1981; Leach 2001b), and Poundbury and Ulwell in Dorset (Farwell and Molleson 1993).

Hicknoll Slait in Compton Pauncefoot, near South Cadbury, six roughly north to south-oriented inhumations have been excavated, one with an iron knife of Anglo-Saxon type and another with a glass bead necklace; a fragment of shield boss was recovered from the spoil heap. Provisional results from Oxygen- and Strontium-stable isotope analysis suggest, however, that one of the individuals was brought up locally (Taylor 1967; Davey 2005, 112–21; Tabor 2008, 173–4). There is also growing evidence for the continued occupation of Romano-British settlements into the early medieval period. At the Old Showground in Cheddar, for example, Ditch 1 produced a radiocarbon date of 340–570 cal. AD and was recut by Ditch 2 that contained only sherds of a late third to fourth century BB1 jar: had the radiocarbon date not been obtained, the whole sequence would have appeared late Roman whereas it actually points to occupation well into the fifth century. The radiocarbon dating of burnt grain from the latest occupation within the villa at Dinnington suggests that it was similarly still used in the late fifth century.[12] Smart (2008, 282–95) has also examined the extent to which medieval settlements may have had Romano-British predecessors in the Ilchester area. Ninety sites are documented by the fourteenth century, of which thirty-four have seen some form of archaeological investigation and thirteen (38%) of these have produced Romano-British material. Such tentative evidence for continuity on some sites is supported by the palaeoenvironmental sequences which, although suggesting a decrease in the intensity of agriculture in the late Roman/early medieval period, provide no evidence for a widespread or long-lasting woodland regeneration (see Chapter 11). An increase in the intensity of agriculture in central Somerset appears to have occurred from around the eighth century, which is the period that may have seen a more profound transformation of the rural landscape.

In common with Dumnonia (see below), several sites in Somerset have also produced fifth- and sixth-century pottery imported from the Mediterranean and it is noticeable that most of these sites lie on navigable rivers that drain west into the Bristol Channel and Severn Estuary (Fig. 14.5; and *see* Turner and Gerrard 2004). In contrast, along the southern seaboard of the South West Peninsula these Mediterranean imports do not extend beyond eastern Devon, the most easterly site being High Peak near Sidmouth. The lack of fifth-century Mediterranean imports from Dorset is curious, as there is little indication of Anglo-Saxon settlement at that time, the only evidence being two mid-fifth-century brooches and a fifth-century Germanic spearhead from Hod Hill in the north-east of the county (O'Brien 1999; Eagles 2004, 236: Fig. 14.5). In the sixth century there are a number of findspots indicative of Anglo-Saxon influence, including a

---

[12] <http://www.channel4.com/history/microsites/T/timeteam/2006_dinn_found.html>

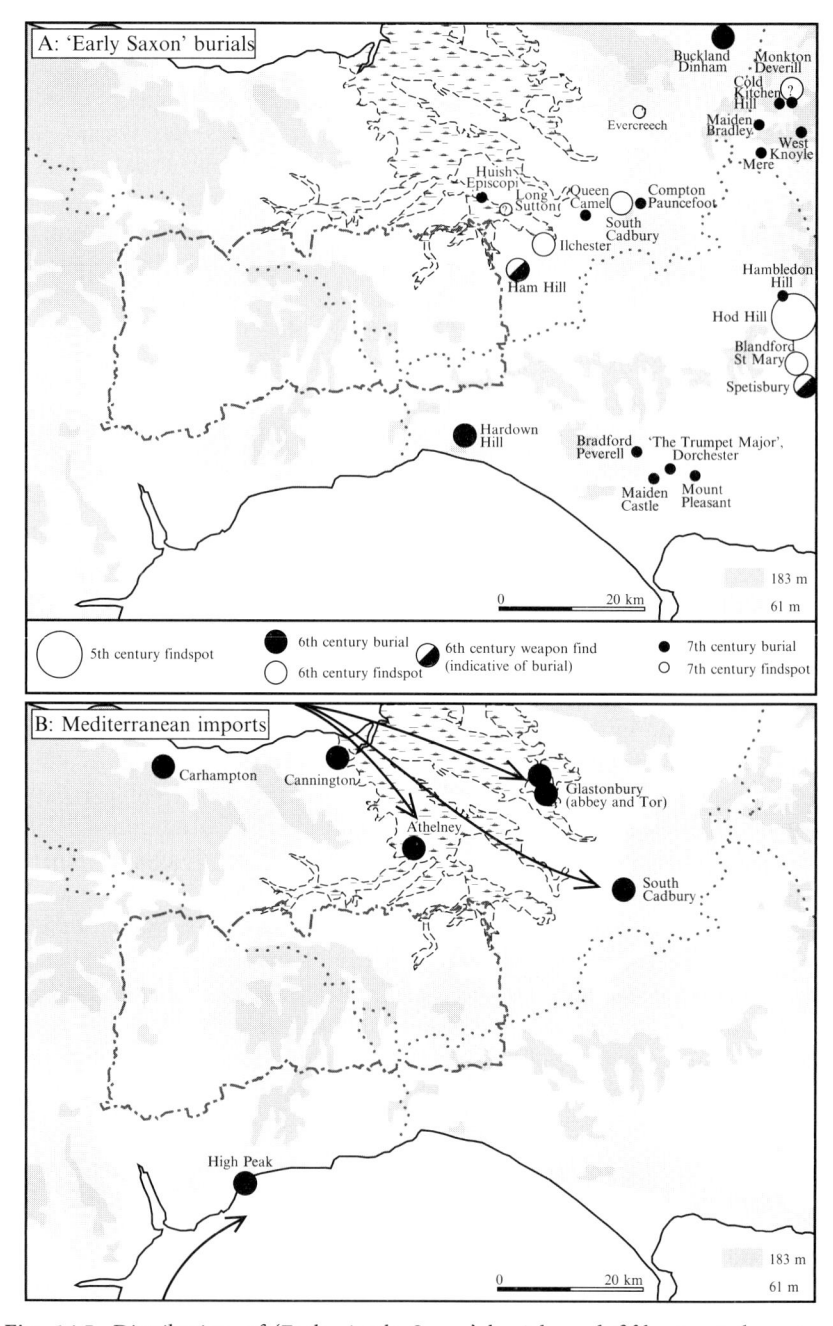

Fig. 14.5. Distribution of 'Early Anglo-Saxon' burials and fifth- to sixth-century Mediterranean imports across the regional study area. (After Meaney 1964; Eagles 1994; 2004; Som. HER 53778; Campbell 2007; Bob Croft pers. comm.; and *see* Allan and Blaylock 2005 for a recent find on Lundy.)

small cemetery at Hardown Hill, in Whitchurch Canonicorum, close to the edge of the Blackdown Hills (Meaney 1964, 81; Evison 1968), but nothing like the density of 'Anglo-Saxon' settlements and cemeteries seen in eastern England. Generally, therefore, the fifth to the mid-seventhth centuries are a likely to have been a period of broad continuity in the landscape of Somerset and western Dorset.

Dumnonia

To the west of the Blackdown Hills, Gildas tells us the *civitas* of the Dumnonii became the kingdom of Dumnonia (Winterbottom 1978, 28). Here we might expect an even stronger degree of continuity from the fourth to the seventh centuries as the relative lack of Romanization meant that the severing of Britain's links to the Roman Empire had less of an impact compared to areas further east. Eastern Dumnonia (broadly speaking modern Devon) was only conquered by the West Saxons in the later seventh century and although some place-name scholars still argue that the scarcity of Brittonic place-names suggests a near complete population replacement, with almost no survival of the native British population (e.g. Padel 2007), it hardly seems credible that as late as the seventh century, tens of thousands of Anglo-Saxons marched into the peninsula and wholly displaced a native population of similar size. Most archaeologists have long stopped using migration as a simple explanation for culture change and it is far more likely that this far west the Anglo-Saxon conquest was a political takeover not a mass folk migration.

A series of palaeoenvironmental sequences in Devon show no significant change in land use between the fourth and the seventh centuries (see Chapter 11). A lack of datable material culture on all but a handful of coastal sites means that settlements of this sub-Roman period are difficult to identify, although the radiocarbon dating of aceramic features is increasing the number of early medieval settlements being recognized with two patterns emerging: firstly, there is a continuation of the late prehistoric/Romano-British tradition of isolated enclosures (e.g. Hayes Farm in Clyst Honiton: Simpson *et al.* 1989), and secondly, that there is some evidence for the re-occupation of hillforts and hilltops as seen in Somerset (Haldon, High Peak, and Raddon: Pollard 1966; 1967; Gent and Quinnell 1999a; 1999b; and see Grant 1995).

Dumnonia appears to have been conquered by the West Saxons in the late seventh century, very soon after the assimilation of modern Somerset. In 658, King Cenwalh defeated the British at *Peonnum* (Penselwood on the Wiltshire/Somerset border) and drove them as far as the Parrett. Immediately west of the river Parrett rise the Blackdown and Quantock Hills that briefly appear to have marked the boundary of the kingdom of Dumnonia. In 682 King Centwine of the West Saxons is said to have 'put the Britons to flight as far as the sea',

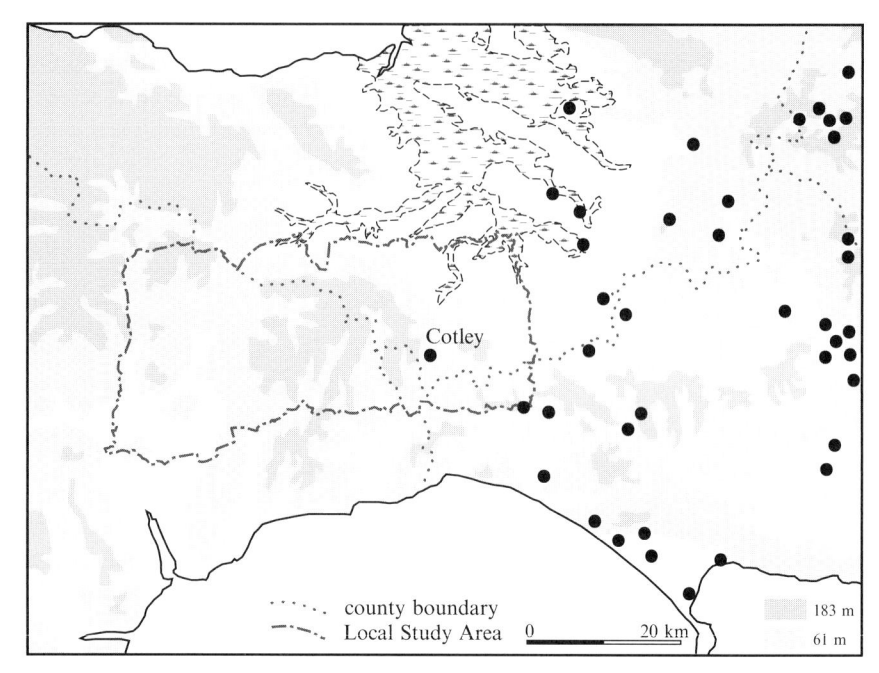

Fig. 14.6. The distribution of Durotrigian coins across the regional study area (Cunliffe 2005, Fig. 8.3; to which a hoard of sixty Durotrigian coins found at Cotley near Chard just to the east of the Blackdown Hills, can be added: Pollard 1974, 65).

although where 'the sea' was remains unclear (Swanton 1996, 38). The West Saxons appear to have controlled Exeter by around 690 when the boy who was to become St Boniface attended an abbey there ruled by a Saxon abbot (Orme 1991, 6), and the earliest[13] record of a West Saxon king granting land in the former kingdom of Dumnonia is Aethelheard's gift of ten hides at *Torric* [Torridge in north-west Devon] to Glastonbury in 729 (Finberg 1954, no. 1; Sawyer 1968, no. 1676; Abrams 1996, 232–4). It would appear, therefore, that most of modern Devon was part of the West Saxon kingdom by the early eighth century. This lateness of the conquest of Dumnonia may account for certain differences in the customary measures used to divide, assess, and administer the landscape. Virgates (one quarter of a carucate, the old Anglo-Saxon measure of land sufficient for one plough team of eight oxen in a year), for example, are not found in Devon and Cornwall, while 'churchscot', a 'legacy of the pre-tithe era paid by freemen to churches of ancient parishes in hens' eggs and grain' and which was characteristic of the Wessex heartlands is found in

---

[13] Although Finberg (1954, no. 73) suggests that the twenty hides King Ine (710 × 20) is said to have granted to Glastonbury Abbey at *Linig* lay between the Tamar and Lynher valleys in eastern Cornwall, they actually lie in the Tone valley in Somerset (Abrams 1996, 231–2).

Dorset and Somerset but only one place in Dumnonia (Exminster in Devon: Campbell and Bartley 2006, 35, 39). Once again, the Blackdown Hills mark a difference in how the landscape was managed.

THE IRON AGE

So far we have seen that it was not just in the medieval period that the Blackdown and Quantock Hills marked a significant boundary in landscape character, but that the same was true during the Roman period. In the final sections of this chapter we must now explore whether this was also the case in prehistory, starting with the Iron Age.

A range of evidence suggests that during the Iron Age, both society and the way that it managed the landscape similarly showed significant differences either side of the Blackdown Hills. The 'cultural poverty' (Thomas 1966, 76) of Dumnonia compared to the rest of southern Britain is one of its distinctive features: the Dumnonii, to the west of the Blackdowns, did not use coins, whereas the Durotriges to the east did, and even though the latter's coins are 'amongst the most widely scattered of all the British coinage' (Boon 1973, 245), with the exception of several examples from around Plymouth Sound, they did not spread further west than the Blackdown Hills (Fig. 14.6). Pottery also shows significant regional differences with a series of Early to Middle Iron Age styles only being found to the east of the Blackdown Hills (Cunliffe 2005, figs. 5.3–5.5). In the Late Iron Age the wheel-turned Durotrigian style developed from the Maiden Castle/Marnhull wares, and once again its distribution is largely restricted to areas east of the Blackdowns. Meanwhile, in the south-west peninsula, what is now called South-Western Decorated Wares (formerly known as 'Glastonbury Ware') developed during the Middle Iron Age, and in Devon continued into the Late Iron Age (Quinnell 1994, 78; Fitzpatrick et al. 1999, 160–212). That the Blackdowns were a boundary in pottery style is seen at Hembury hillfort on their western edge, as Todd (1984, 261) observes that 'decorated La Tene bowls are relatively scarce and their scheme of ornament suggest a local origin, being closer to the vessels from Blackberry Castle [in the southern part of the Blackdown Hills] and Milber Down [south of Exeter] than to the classic Somerset sites at Glastonbury and Meare'. Overall, Iron Age pottery traditions to the west of the Blackdown Hills were significantly different to those further east, and along with the absence of coinage, this suggests that communities either side of them had separate spheres of social and economic interaction.

There is also a marked difference in the character of the Iron Age settlement patterns either side of the Blackdown Hills (Figs. 14.7–14.8). The Durotriges had large 'developed' hillforts, with multiple lines of closely spaced defensive

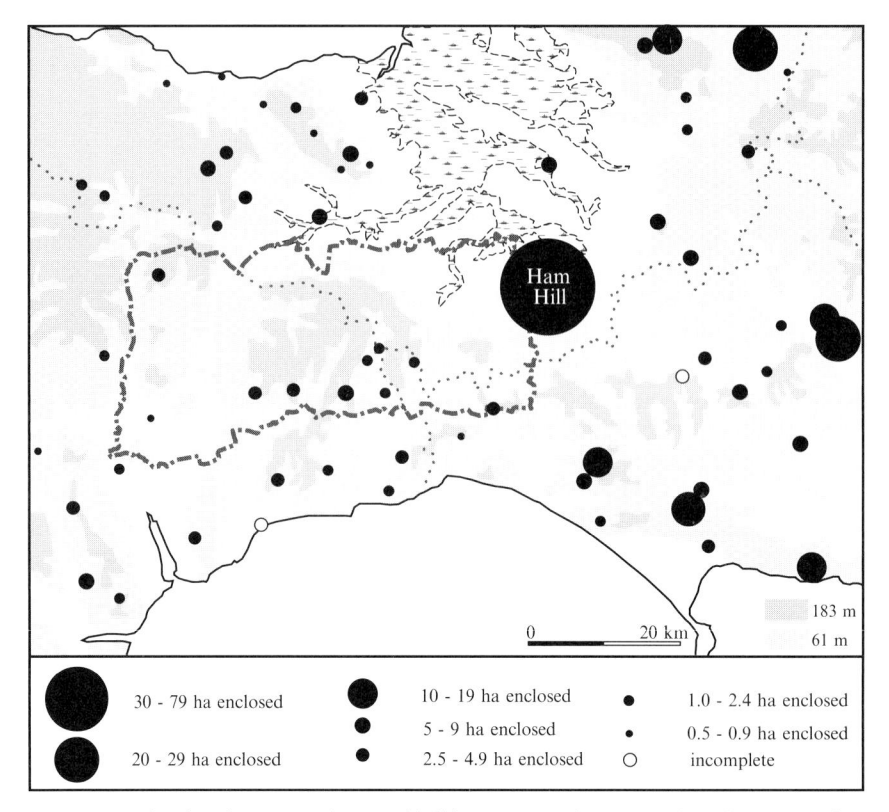

Fig. 14.7. The distribution and size of hillforts across the regional study area. (After RCHME 1970a; 1970b; Burrow 1981; A. Fox 1996, 21–2.)

banks and ditches often enclosing areas in excess of ten hectares, while in Dumnonia most hillforts are univallate and typically cover just two or three hectares (A. Fox 1961; Thomas 1966, 76–7; RCHME 1952; 1970a; 1970b; Burrow 1981; A. Fox 1996, 21–2; Cunliffe 2005, fig. 15.1; Bradley 2007, fig. 5.14). A number of enclosed lower-order settlements in the South West—the so-called hillslope enclosures—do have multiple lines of defence, but it is noticeable that, in contrast to the tightly spaced ramparts of Wessex hillforts, the South West sites have more widely spaced defences that are on a far smaller scale.

Excavations within the Wessex hillforts have shown that they contained both domestic occupation and a large capacity for grain storage in the form of below-ground bell-shaped storage pits and above-ground raised granaries. The distribution of these grain storage pits was first mapped by Thomas (1966, fig. 4), and to the east of the Blackdown Hills more recent excavations

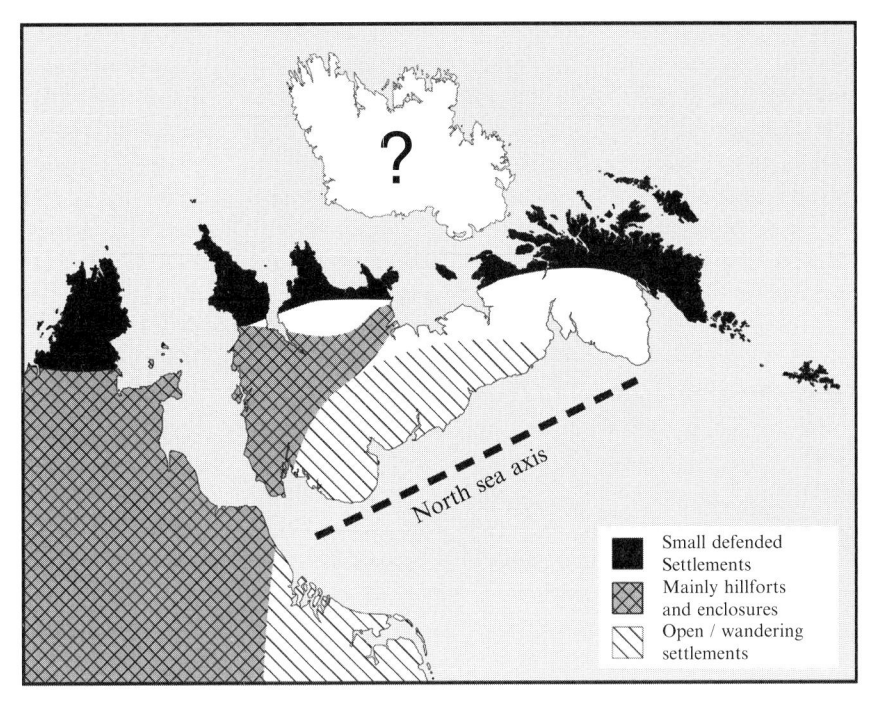

Fig. 14.8. A characterization of Iron Age settlement in Britain and the near continent (Bradley 2007, fig. 5.14, drawn by Aaron Watson).

have confirmed that they are found within major developed hillforts,[14] smaller enclosures,[15] and open settlements.[16] In Dumnonia, however, although clear evidence has emerged for occupation within hillforts grain storage pits are absent,[17] as is the case on non-hillfort rural settlements in Devon.[18] On five Iron Age settlements excavated as part of the University of Winchester's Southern Quantock Hills Archaeological Survey (2000–2005), for example,

---

[14] e.g. Cadbury Congresbury (Rahtz *et al.* 1992), Ham Hill (Leivers *et al.* 2007), South Cadbury (Barrett *et al.* 2000, 160–9), and Worlebury (Dymond and Tomkins 1886).
[15] e.g. Hack Wood in Walton and the banjo enclosure on Walton Common Down (Dymond and Tomkins 1886, 67–8; Phillips 1931), and West Wood near Somerton (Gater *et al.* 1993, 41–7).
[16] e.g. Cannards Grave in Shepton Mallet (Birbeck 2002), Chew Park (Rahtz and Greenfield 1977, 30), Encie Farm in Penselwood (Newman and Morris 1999, 2), Montacute House (Crockett 1995, 84–7), Sigwells in Charlton Horethorne (Tabor 2002, 47–55), Walton Common (Dymond and Tomkins 1886, 67–8, 83–4), Whitegate Farm in Bleadon (Young 2007), and Dibbles Farm in Christon (Morris 1988).
[17] Berry Ball (Manning and Quinnell 2009); Berry Down (Gallant and Silvester 1985); Blackbury Castle (Young and Richardson 1954); Embury (Jeffries 1974); Hembury (Todd 1984); Raddon Hill (Gent and Quinnell 1999a); Woodbury Castle (Miles 1975a).
[18] A30 sites (Fitzpatrick *et al.* 1999, 130–59), Aller Cross near Kingskerswell (Hearne and Seager Smith 1995), Gold Park on Dartmoor (Gibson 1992), Milber Down (Fox *et al.* 1948–52), and Dainton (Silvester 1980a).

none produced grain storage pits, and despite a large-scale programme of wet sieving, charred cereals were only recovered from later, Romano-British, contexts (Webster 2000a; Thorpe 2002; Wilkinson *et al.* 2003; Roffey *et al.* 2004; King *et al.* 2007). Interestingly there were grain storage pits at Holcombe, on Blackdown Hills, but the pottery from this Late Iron Age farmstead included large amounts of Durotrigian Ware suggesting that the social and economic affinities of this community looked east (Pollard 1974, 69). In the past it has been argued that this distribution of grain storage pits reflects the location of free draining geology, but as Todd (1998, 148) has observed 'the traditional objection that the impervious character of the South West bedrock inhibited the use of storage pits in the region may not be valid with the Culm Measures where drainage can be rapid'. Whilst the absence of below-ground grain storage pits may or may not be accounted for by the South West's geology, the scarcity of raised granaries is more telling. Until the 1970s none were known in the region, although as Quinnell (2004) has observed this may in part have been because excavators were not looking for them as they were seen as a feature of the chalk downland. Since then a small number have been recorded, although extensive excavations at Holcome (near Uplyme) and Rudge (near Morchard Bishop), both in Devon, revealed none (Pollard 1974; Todd 1998; Fitzpatrick *et al.* 1999, 167–8; Quinnell 2004).

To the east of the Blackdown Hills there is also a strong tradition of human and animal remains being placed in former grain-storage pits, a practice that is familiar across Iron Age Wessex (Whimster 1981; Hill 1995). Relatively little is known about burial practices in Iron Age Dumnonia, although the pit burials that are so common in Somerset have not been found. The few Iron Age graves that have been recorded in Devon appear to be cist burials, such as a crouched inhumation from Brixham that was surrounded by 'rough drystone walling about two feet and six inches high' and covered with stone slabs (Belleville 1956; and see Whimster 1981, 60–74). The Late Iron Age/early Romano-British cemetery at Mount Batten, whose destruction was recorded in 1863, is of interest as along with ten or so broadly similar inhumation cemeteries in Cornwall and south Devon, 'the rite of careful inhumation in regular cemeteries is virtually unknown over most of the rest of southern Britain at this time, a fact which emphasises the cultural separation of the South West from the rest of the country' (Cunliffe 1988, 98). A single cist burial found in 1961 at Woodleigh, in the South Hams north of Kingsbridge, was associated with second century Romano-British pottery, showing that the tradition continued into the Roman period (Whimster 1981, 285). Overall, Iron Age burial practices, like the circulation of coinage and pottery, and the character of settlements and their capacity for storing grain, suggests that communities either side of the Blackdown Hills developed very different identities.

EARLIER PREHISTORY

During the Mesolithic we would not expect to see regional differences in landscape character as human communities had such a limited impact upon their environment, simply using fire to open up the sedge-dominated peat bogs in the river valleys and woodland clearings on and around the uplands (Caseldine and Hatton 1993; 1996; Straker 1997; Gearey *et al.* 2000a; 2000b; Fyfe *et al.* 2003). The fourth millennium BC, however, saw a profound change in how human communities perceived and exploited the landscape, and it was during the Neolithic that woodland was first cleared on a large scale, followed by the grazing of domestic livestock and cultivation of cereals in the more open landscape. Monuments, many with links to the rituals associated with death, burial, and the 'rites of passage', were constructed while new types of artefact (notably pottery and ground stone axes) reflect the exploitation of a wider range of natural resources (Thomas 1999). During the Early Neolithic, in common with the rest of southern Britain, notable concentrations of domestic activity occur on hilltop sites (e.g. Haldon: Gent and Quinnell 1999b, 101; Hazard Hill: Houlder 1963), some of which are associated with interrupted ditches (Raddon Hill: Gent and Quinnell 1999a; High Peak: Pollard 1966; Hembury: Todd 1984). In Cornwall and west Devon, so-called 'tor enclosures' may represent a regional variation that extends this pattern of causewayed enclosures into the upland fringes (Mercer 1981, 189–93; 1997; Johnson and Rose 1994, 46–8; Darvill 2000, fig. 26; Oswald *et al.* 2001, 85–90; Bradley 2007, 69–71). The communities who used these Neolithic sites were part of exchange networks that extended across the South West and into Wessex, evidenced for example by 'Gabbroic' pottery, made in the Lizard, that is found as far east as Hambledon Hill, Maiden Castle, and Windmill Hill, and a number of igneous rocks in Cornwall were also used to manufacture polished axes that reached beyond the Blackdown Hills (Peacock 1969; 1988).

Within this landscape of semi-mobile communities, there is a range of ritual monuments that could have provided 'monumental permanence' and territorial markers through the burial of the dead and the creation of ancestors. Some of these monuments form part of the suite seen further east in Wessex, such as the South West's single cursus, but there are also more local types, notably 'long cairns/mounds' and 'oblong ditches', which might be the region's equivalent of ditched earthen long barrows (Fitzpatrick *et al.* 1999, 23–6; Griffith and Quinnell 1999; Johnson and Rose 1994, 24–6; Mercer 1986, 54–61; Riley and Wilson-North 2001, 23–31). The recent identification of many of these sites as crop marks in the lowlands helps to balance the distribution of megalithic monuments which concentrate around the peripheries of the granite uplands, and while the extent of monument construction in the South West appears to have been less than in Wessex, it was on a similar scale to the rest of southern

Britain. The South West does not, therefore, appear to have had a particularly distinctive identity at this stage.

In the Late Neolithic more significant differences may have emerged. Pottery of the Grooved Ware and Peterborough Ware traditions has been found on only a handful of sites in the South West, and there are just a few examples of the distinctive monument type—henges—that characterize this period elsewhere in southern Britain (Johnson and Rose 1994, 31–2; Darvill 2000, figs. 33 and 58). Stone circles are, however, common on all the uplands of the South West and while their clear association with Early Bronze Age barrows and cairns shows that they were used during the Early Bronze Age, this does not preclude their having Late Neolithic origins. The same is possibly the case for some stone rows, and there is a desperate need to improve the dating of this relatively common monument type. Local differences in the ways that communities structured themselves such as these, and variations in the character of the resulting cultural landscapes, are to be expected in an area the size of Britain, and they may have provided the roots of the much clearer differences that emerged by the Iron Age.

Although the initial felling of woodland in some parts of the South West occurred at the start of the Neolithic, in many areas it was only during the Early Bronze Age that large-scale, permanent clearances were made and the landscape started to be opened up (Moore *et al.* 1984; Fyfe *et al.* 2003, 11, 17–18). In places this increasingly open landscape was characterized by a suite of ceremonial monuments which show a marked tendency to occur in clusters, often in places of long-lasting importance such as Bow near Crediton (Griffith 1985; Griffith and Quinnell 1999b). Round barrows and cairns, in contrast, occur right across the South West, both in regions that had long been settled and areas such as the Culm Measures that show relatively little sign of earlier occupation (e.g. Pollard and Russell 1969; 1976). Building upon Miles's (1975b; Quinnell 1988) recognition of distinctive Bronze Age burial practice in the South West, including the scarcity of Beaker burials, Jones (2008; 2010; forthcoming) has recently reviewed the 'local character' of the Early Bronze Age in the South West, identifying a series of differences compared to Wessex, including a greater variety of burial practice and barrow form, and a distribution of barrows that is less riverine and more focused on high ground. There is also a far more restricted range of ceramics, with very few food vessels, collared urns, and accessory vessels. Instead, a dominance of locally produced Trevisker Ware and very few metal artefacts suggests that until the very end of the Early Bronze Age people chose not to bury their dead with ostentatious objects. Although there are a small number of well-known high-status objects in South West graves, it is extremely rare for Bronze Age burials to contain such goods and 'given the presumed availability of metal ores, this could indicate that in the South West it was only appropriate to incorporate metal objects into the burial site under certain conditions' (Jones 2008, 155).

While there appears to have been an increase in the area and intensity of landscape exploitation during the Early Bronze Age, there remains little indication of sedentism. The Middle Bronze Age, in contrast, saw the appearance of permanent settlements, often associated with field systems, across the lowlands while the upland fringes of Dartmoor were transformed through the creation of extensive, and sometimes carefully planned, boundaries (the reaves): the everyday practice of agricultural subsistence now comes to dominate the landscape. The same pattern is seen across southern Britain, including the creation of extensive 'celtic' field systems, and there is nothing to suggest that the South West was significantly different in this respect (Fleming 2008). In contrast, the burial traditions and material culture of the South West show a 'localized interpretation of those [i.e. Wessex] traditions' with very little evidence for the construction of barrows, no cremation cemeteries, and very few individuals marked out for special attention (Jones 2008). In these respects, Middle Bronze Age society shows a strong degree of continuity with the Early Bronze Age.

The Late Bronze Age is a difficult period to study as the palaeoenvironmental record is poor and relatively few archaeological sites have been recognized. The Middle Bronze Age burial tradition appears to have ceased, itself indicative of a dislocation within society, and across the South West most settlements occupied in the Middle Bronze Age appear to have been abandoned, sometimes with a process of deliberate 'closing down' (e.g. Trethellen Farm, Cornwall: Nowakowski 2001). Just a handful of Late Bronze Age settlements have been identified, with both open (e.g. Dudley 1941; Jones 1998–9; Silvester 1980a; Willis and Rogers 1951) and enclosed sites represented (e.g. Fitzpatrick *et al.* 1999, 91–129; Griffith 1994, fig. 2), which appear to be closer in character to the Middle Bronze Age than the Iron Age landscape dominated by a hierarchy of more heavily defended sites. In common with elsewhere in Britain, it appears that the South West's uplands were abandoned at this time, a phenomenon that has traditionally been attributed to a climatic deterioration which made farming in these areas increasingly difficult, although this is now questioned (cf. Lamb 1982, 152–3; Burgess 1985; 1989; Silvester 1979; Quinnell 1994, 77–8; Campbell *et al.* 2002; Tipping 2002; Young and Simmonds 1995). Overall, the Late Bronze Age was clearly a period of great change, and as we have seen, the Iron Age societies that emerged thereafter were of significantly different character either side of the Blackdown Hills.

DISCUSSION

This study began with the observation that there was marked regional variation in landscape character either side of the Blackdown Hills, and in Chapters 4 to 7 we saw that settlement patterns, styles of vernacular architecture, place-names, field-names, field systems, and even the form taken by individual field boundaries all reflect this difference as far back as the later medieval period. The discussion of early medieval territorial structures in Chapters 8 to 10 suggested that the Blackdown Hills were settled by a community with a discrete identity, with separate peoples living in the lowlands to the east and to the west, while Chapters 11 to 13 revealed that at least as far back as the Roman period patterns of land use either side of the Blackdown Hills were very different. This chapter has added even greater time depth in revealing how the Blackdown Hills marked the boundary between landscapes of different character not just in the Roman period but in the Iron Age too. Unfortunately we know very little about the Late Bronze Age, a period that appears to have been one of retreat from the uplands and a dislocation in society more generally, but we know a lot more about the Early and Middle Bronze Age and here there once again appear to be differences either side of the Blackdown Hills. What is perhaps most striking is the relative lack of ostentatious display in the burials in the South West, and the modest scale of the enclosed settlements: was society here less stratified than in Wessex? Or was social status displayed in other ways? There are certainly parallels here in the less stratified settlement hierarchies seen in the Iron Age and Roman periods.

15

Discussion and conclusions: communities and their landscapes

RECOGNIZING *PAYS*

The aim of this book was to improve our understanding of the origins and development of long-standing boundaries in landscape character, to which end there were three specific objectives:

- to go beyond the traditional focus of landscape archaeologists and historical geographers on morphological differences in settlement patterns and field systems to explore other facets of landscape character such as how the landscape was perceived in the past, how social identity was expressed through phenomena such as vernacular architecture, the language of landscape (field- and place-names), and patterns of land use;
- to understand the origins and development of local and regional variation in landscape character in the context of the social and territorial structures within which people lived;
- to illustrate the research process, rather than simply presenting the results of all this work as a *fait accompli*.

These aims were to be achieved through a series of nested case study areas that straddle a major boundary in landscape character: the Blackdown Hills. A rapid assessment of the easily accessible data suggested that the Blackdowns marked the difference between countryside dominated by medieval villages, Roman villas, and large Iron Age hillforts to the east, and a dispersed medieval settlement patterns, a lack of Romanization, and far smaller Iron Age enclosed settlements to the west. The analysis of settlements, field systems, and patterns of land use in the preceding chapters have demonstrated the long-standing nature of this division in landscape character, and in Chapter 14 we have seen how these differences are evident from prehistory. We have also seen how the distinctive *pays* that characterize the landscape today, and which we can map in great detail using modern cartographic sources, are clearly not the creation of a modern scholarly mind, but correspond very closely to the landscape as it was perceived by historical travellers and writers. These differences in landscape character are not simply morphological, but are also reflected in the design of buildings, settlements, and the layout of fields, and even in some folklore. The Blackdown Hills were also not just a boundary between landscapes of different character, but they were also a very distinctive *pays* in their own right that in the early medieval period at least appear to have been occupied by a people who had their own identity. Before discussing how these differences in landscape character may have occurred, however, we should first reflect on the research process.

Recent years have seen a series of studies in which mapping different data sets held centre stage, most notably Roberts and Wrathmell's (2000a; 2002) *Atlas of Rural Settlement in England* and *Region and Place*, Lewis, Mitchell-Fox, and Dyer's (1997) *Village, Hamlet and Field*, and Williamson's (2003) *Shaping Medieval Landscapes*. In recent years the most extensive mapping programme has been English Heritage's 'Historic Landscape Characterisation' (HLC), and the related schemes in both Scotland and Wales. Underlying this work is a belief, common to both archaeologists and historical geographers, that we can infer something of the history of a landscape—including the processes that led to its creation—by studying later maps. This was, of course, the underlying premise behind Hoskins's observation that, 'The great Cambridge historian, Maitland, regarded the Ordnance map of England as one of the finest records we have, if only we could learn how to decipher it, and indeed it is. But the landscape itself is an equally revealing document, equally full of significant detail, and difficult to interpret' (Hoskins 1952, 289). His somewhat pithier comment that the landscape is 'the richest historical record we possess' makes the same point (Hoskins 1955, 14). The increased use of morphological analysis in the 1970s and 1980s, reflected for example in Roberts and Glasscock's (1983) *Villages, Fields and Frontiers*, was not without its critics as Austin (1985) suggested in his article 'Doubts about morphogenisis', but as Roberts and Wrathmell's *Atlas* has shown, the appetite for morphological analysis has certainly not diminished.

In this study there are also examples of the analysis of both settlement patterns (Chapter 4) and field systems (Chapter 6), but an attempt has been made to move away from the position whereby morphology is the *only* aspect of historic landscape character that is studied: Historic Landscape Characterisation does not equal historic landscape characterization—indeed, HLC can be regarded as a subset of a broader, more multifaceted historic landscape analysis. In Chapter 2 we began in a fairly traditional way with an examination of different facets of the natural environment (geology, topography, drainage, soils, climate, and current agricultural potential) which led to the identification of a series of discrete and unique districts or *pays*, with a common set of natural character defining features. In Chapter 3 we then looked at the ways that people in the past perceived the landscape and found that there is remarkable consistency in how visitors and local writers alike viewed these districts, with lowlands such as the Exe valley being highly regarded for their fertility, in contrast to the Culm Measures that were invariably seen as barren and inhospitable. These early writers appear to have viewed the Blackdown Hills somewhat indifferently, which may well be because they usually travelled around them rather than through them. Local folklore certainly suggests that these hills were viewed as dangerous places.

In Chapters 4 to 7 we examined the morphology of settlement patterns and field systems, but in contrast to traditional approaches towards landscape characterization, a variety of other data were also analysed including place-names, field-names, vernacular architecture, and the location of churches within the landscape. The extent to which these other facets of landscape character varied across our study area was remarkable, with the Blackdown Hills consistently marking a major division. Settlement patterns to the west were predominantly dispersed with small hamlets and isolated farmsteads being characteristic of most areas, whereas in the lowlands of central Somerset, compact villages predominated in what were mostly relatively small parishes. Churches—forming important focal points within these landscapes—were typically located on high or sloping ground in Devon, and on the Culm Measures virtually every church was on a hilltop. In western Somerset, in contrast, most churches were on hill slopes, while further east the picture is more varied with hilltop, hill slope, and valley bottom locations found in roughly equal proportions. Place-names similarly show significant differences across Devon, Dorset, and Somerset as while elements such as '-ton' are commonly found across all the lowland areas, names such as '-hayes'/'-hayne' and 'Barton' are distinctively Devonian. There are also different field-names on either side of the Blackdowns with 'Gratton' and 'Park' being common in Devon, but extremely rare to the east of the Blackdowns. When we look at vernacular architecture, we see a relatively uniform picture across our study area in the late medieval period, although from the sixteenth century we see a major difference emerging as asymmetrical house layouts continued well into the post-medieval period to the west of the Blackdowns, while to the east they were replaced by more fashionable symmetrical plans in the seventeenth century. The location chosen for the addition of chimney stacks to late medieval houses was also different. They were often positioned on the outside of the front-facing longitudinal wall in Devon houses (the so-called 'lateral stack'), in contrast to the internal position backing onto the cross-passage that was favoured in Somerset (an 'axial stack'). Choosing a lateral stack would have been a visible statement of modernity, that the residents were adopting new technology, but this location also reflects a strong degree of conservatism in retaining the integrity of the hall as an open space. In Somerset, in contrast, there was apparently no such desire to retain this traditional feature of house design.

When considering the character of the field systems that surrounded these settlements, the major matter for debate is the former extent of open fields, and while the English Heritage-sponsored HLC of Somerset is in broad agreement with earlier reconstructions of their extent, this is not true in Devon (e.g. Fig. 6.3 and Plate1). Identifying former open fields simply from later field-boundary patterns will always be problematic, and an additional layer of data that was found to be extremely useful here was the nature of land holding as recorded in the Tithe surveys of *c*.1840. The starting point for this strand of research is the observation that in central Somerset parishes such as Lopen, the highly fragmented patterns of land ownership and land occupancy associated with long, narrow fields (classed here as 'enclosed strip fields') clearly arose from the enclosure by agreement of open fields as there are earlier estate maps that show the unenclosed strips and furlongs. When the same fragmented patterns of land holding are found in other areas with fieldscapes classed morphologically as enclosed strip fields, then it is therefore a reasonable assumption that they are also derived from the enclosure of former open fields. More importantly, where the morphological evidence is inconclusive, a highly fragmented pattern of land holding lends support to a hypothesis that there were once open fields in this locality.

Having characterized the fieldscape as it was depicted on the late nineteenth-century OS 1st Edn 6" maps (Plate 2), and having gathered a variety of other data as outlined above, this evidence was woven together in order to reconstruct what landscape character may have been like in the medieval period, taking *c*.1300 as our benchmark (Fig. 7.6). This revealed seven discrete and unique *pays* (see Fig 15.1):

- the lowlands of central Somerset (the north-east corner of our study area), characterized by villages and open fields;
- the hills and valleys of north-west Dorset, around the eastern slopes of the Blackdown Hills, and into the Vale of Taunton Deane, characterized by dispersed settlement and closes held in severalty, with some unclosed commons on some of the higher ground;
- the eastern foothills of the Blackdown Hills (Chard, Chardstock, Combe St Nicholas, and Membury), characterized by villages and open fields in the centres of the parishes but dispersed settlement and closes held in severalty in the more peripheral areas;
- the Blackdown Hills, characterized by highly dispersed settlement and closes held in severalty in the valleys, extensive unenclosed commons on the hilltops, some of which may have been enclosed around the eleventh to the thirteenth centuries, and extensive woodland on the steeper slopes;
- a relatively narrow north–south zone to the west of the Blackdown Hills, characterized by small villages (churchtowns) and small open fields in the

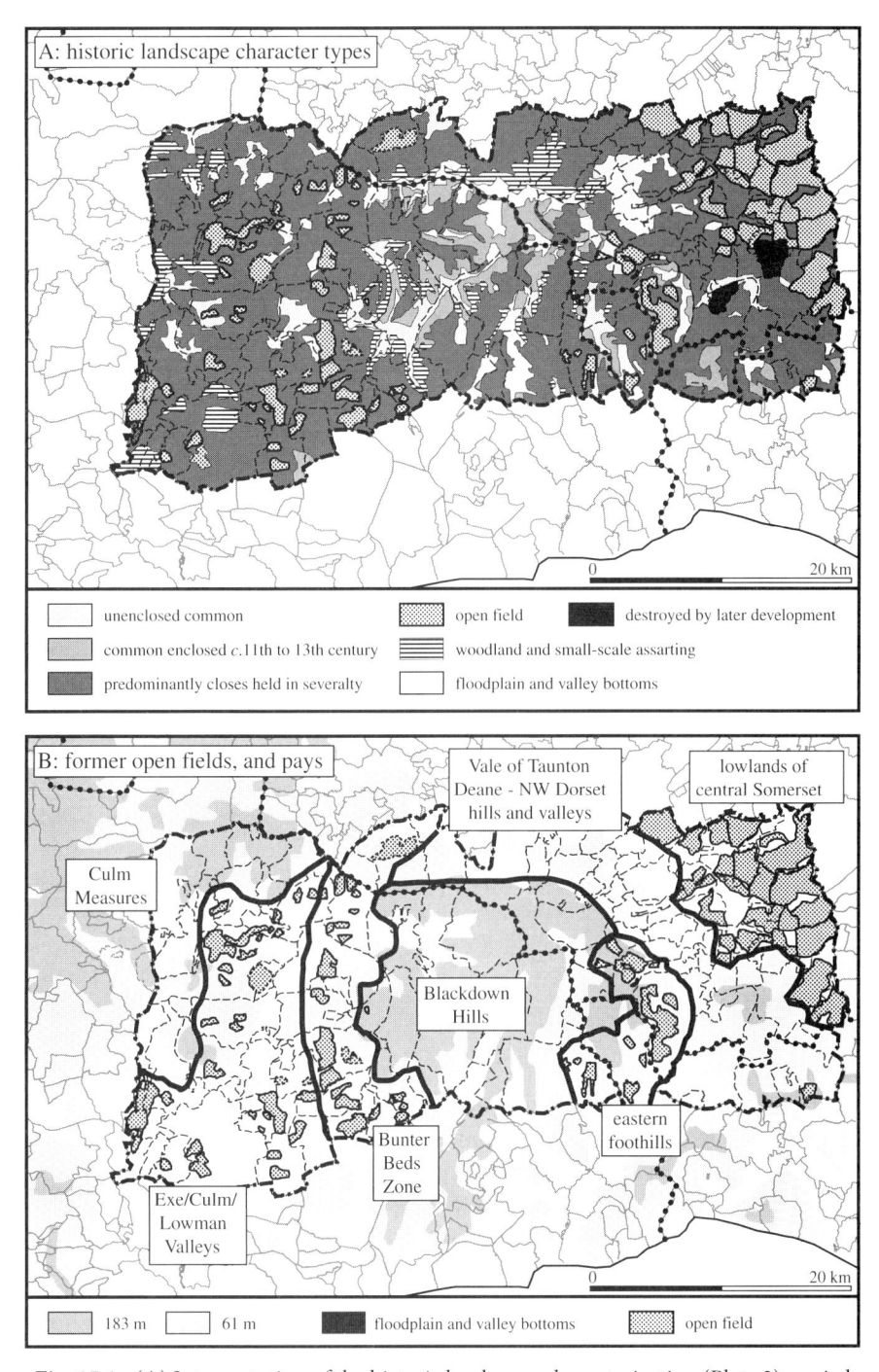

Discussion and conclusions: communities and their landscapes

Fig. 15.1. (A) Interpretation of the historic landscape characterization (Plate 2) carried out for this project and additional layers of data such as patterns of land-holding (Plate 4); (B) the seven *pays* identified from this.

centres of the parishes but dispersed settlement and closes held in severalty in the more peripheral areas (the Bunter Beds zone):
- the remaining lowlands in the Exe, Culm, and Lowman valleys, characterized by a mixed landscape with predominantly dispersed settlement and closes held in severalty, but some hamlets and small open fields, and unenclosed commons and woodland on some of the higher ground;
- the Culm Measures, characterized by highly dispersed settlement and closes held in severalty in the valleys, extensive unenclosed commons on the hilltops, some of which may have been enclosed around the eleventh to the thirteenth centuries, and extensive woodland on the steeper slopes.

In Chapters 4 to 7 we started to trace the origins of these settlement patterns and field systems back into the medieval period, and in Chapters 8 to 10 we saw that those *pays* that were specifically associated with villages and open fields bore no relation to the social and territorial structure of the early medieval period (early folk territories and great estates). Chapters 11 to 13 explored differences in the patterns of land use which add to the emerging picture of long-term regional variation in landscape character. Although there were significant differences between individual *pays*, the big difference was once again across the Blackdown Hills with relatively specialized arable cultivation and animal husbandry to the east, and far more mixed regimes to the west that demonstrate a strong degree of continuity. In Chapter 14 we saw that the Blackdowns marked a very clear division in the Romano-British landscape with areas to the east being amongst the wealthiest and most Romanized in Britain, in contrast to the west that remained highly insular. The relative scarcity of coins and manufactured goods in Dumnonia suggests a poorly developed market economy compared to areas further east, which along with there being just a single town and just a tiny number of villas, suggests either a relatively unstratified society, or one that chose to differentiate itself in non-materialistic ways. This lack of obvious social stratification is also seen in the Iron Age with a marked hierarchy of settlement types to the east, including large numbers of heavily defended hillforts containing large-scale infrastructure for the storage of grain, and a relatively undifferentiated settlement pattern to the west, with large numbers of modest enclosures that where excavated have failed to produce evidence for grain storage pits or raised granaries.

The Late Bronze Age is poorly understood in the South West, though it is clear that it represents a major discontinuity within society and the landscape with the Middle Bronze Age settlement patterns, field systems, and burial traditions all ceasing. It is also striking, however, that during the Early to Middle Bronze Age there were once again differences in the character of society and landscape either side of the Blackdown Hills, including the way in which any social stratification was displayed. In the Early Bronze Age, for example, there are a small number of well-known high-status artefacts from graves, but compared to those found in Wessex, they are very few in number. In a region that was so rich in mineral deposits, perhaps metal artefacts did not have the exotic cachet they did in more remote areas, but there may also be other factors at play, such as a less stratified society or an elite that chose to display its wealth in ways other than durable artefacts and monument types that have survived in the archaeological record. What does seem clear, however, is that these differences in the degree of social stratification—or at least how it was outwardly displayed—persisted into the Iron Age and Roman periods.

UNDERSTANDING THE ORIGINS AND DEVELOPMENT OF *PAYS*: THE LONG-TERM SIGNIFICANCE OF THE BLACKDOWN HILLS

Antecedent landscape character

What has emerged from this review is that the Blackdown Hills marked a major boundary in landscape character that could be some 4,000 years old. Roberts and Wrathmell (2000a; 2000b; 2002) observed a sometimes striking correlation between their 'central province', that once had a landscape characterized by villages, open fields, and areas that by the eleventh century were extensively cleared of woodland. They argue that it was this more intensively cultivated 'antecedent landscape character' that contributed to the creation of villages and common fields in the Midlands. Although less clearly defined than in the Midlands, their mapping does show a greater number of woodland-indicative place-names to the west of the Blackdown Hills than in the lowlands of Somerset (Robert and Wrathmell 2002, 18–24, 72–9): in Devon, for example, 10.5% of the Domesday place-names include *-bearu* or *–lēah*, whereas in Somerset it is just 4.1%. Differences in the early medieval period such as this may therefore be part of the reason why subsequent patterns of development either side of the Blackdown Hills were so different, but this does not explain why those differences in landscape and society developed in the first place.

The fragmentation of earlier estates

It has been suggested that the creation of villages and open fields occurred in the context of the fragmentation of early medieval 'great estates'. Dyer (2003, 29), for example, has suggested that earlier territorial arrangements had not been 'geared towards squeezing the land and its people with any great intensity', with food rents representing just a small fraction of the total produce, although as royal demands and the potential for profit through market exchange increased, there was a growing incentive to exploit estates more efficiently. The result was the gradual fragmentation of the old 'great estates' and the creation of manors, which in turn provided a context for the physical restructuring of the landscape and creation of villages and open fields (e.g. H. Fox 1981, 99–100; Costen 1992a; Dyer 2003, 27, 31; Williamson 2003, 37–46). It is entirely logical that the fragmentation of large estates and the creation of small, self-contained manors provided a context for the physical restructuring of the landscape, but this cannot in itself explain why this happened in some areas but not others. Chapters 8 to 10 have shown that right across our study area, large early folk territories were broken up into a series of 'great estates' which in turn fragmented into smaller manors, yet it was only on a very small number of these manors that villages and open fields were created (notably parts of 'greater South Curry', 'greater South Petherton', and 'greater Crewkerne' estates). Overall, the fragmentation of these early territorial units may have been the context within which settlement patterns and field systems were transformed in certain areas, but it cannot have been a cause.

Ethnicity

Seebohm (1890, 434–6) suggested that many features of medieval society could be traced back to the Roman period or earlier, although the view soon prevailed that villages and common fields were introduced by Anglo-Saxon colonists (e.g. Vinogradoff 1892, 162; Gray 1912, 415; Homans 1941, 83–107; 1969). This view can now be dismissed as fieldwalking, and excavations have consistently shown that the dispersed settlement patterns associated with 'Early and Middle Saxon' pottery are quite unlike those of the later village-based landscapes, and lacked the stability and organization of medieval villages: villages and open fields developed in the eighth to the tenth centuries, not the fifth century, and as such were unrelated to the Anglo-Saxon immigrations. Although explanations for cultural change based on invasion and migration have long since fallen out of favour, Martin and Satchell (2008) recently argued that Scandinavian settlement and/or overlordship may have played a significant role in the tenth-century restructuring of landscapes in northern East Anglia. Within our study area, however, there is no evidence that ethnically different people lived either side of the Blackdown Hills.

Population density

Some have suggested that it was in England's 'central zone' that the landscape was under its greatest pressure, which meant that resources had to be used more efficiently, encouraging the nucleation of settlement and the establishment of communally managed open fields. Thirsk (1964; 1966), along with other historians of her generation, argued that rising population was the prime mover behind landscape change, and instead of seeing common fields as the creation of Anglo-Saxon immigrants, she argued that demographic pressure led to the evolution and expansion of what had been small subdivided fields as land holdings were fragmented through partible inheritance, and a steady conversion of pasture to arable land led to the need for agreed crop rotations, post-harvest grazing, and periods of fallow. Lewis *et al.* (1997, 179–86, 199–200) also argued that rising population led to declining amounts of pasture as more land was ploughed up, and that land holdings became subdivided and intermixed due to inheritance practices and exchange. Their thesis was that villages and common fields were created when a particular set of socio-economic conditions prevailed—their 'village moment'—and that the idea of structuring a landscape around nucleated villages and communally managed common fields then spread by emulation to other areas that similarly saw growing pressure on their agrarian resources. Only where population levels were low, and substantial areas of pasture remained, did dispersed settlement patterns survive. In addition to rising population, the conditions identified by Lewis *et al.* included the growing assertion of royal power over the newly formed kingdom of England from the late ninth century with its associated demands for taxation and military service, and the growth of non-agriculturally productive urban centres which provided the opportunity to gain profit through market-based exchange.

The hypothesis that population was a key factor in determining which areas did, and did not, see the development of villages and open fields can been tested through the mapping of Domesday data. The density of Domesday population has been mapped at a relatively small scale by Darby and his colleagues in the *Domesday Geography* series, and while England's central zone does in general have a relatively high population density, there were other areas with an equally high population that lay outside the champion countryside, for example in East Anglia (Williamson 2003) and the South West (Rippon 2008a; Fig. 15.4). Figure 15.2 presents a detailed analysis for our local study area. Domesday records the population of each manor, the precise extents of which are unknown (particularly where there was more than one manor in a parish). In this analysis therefore, manors are grouped into parishes, the acreages of which are taken from the Tithe surveys of *c.*1840 (Kain and Oliver 1995). There are specific problems with two areas. Firstly, there is just one Domesday manor in the whole of Pitminster, Otterford, Corfe, and Orchard Portman, and although their interlocking parish boundaries suggest they were once part of a single estate, the resources recorded for that single manor are so small that it cannot account for all four parishes: for the purposes of mapping population density here they are therefore regarded

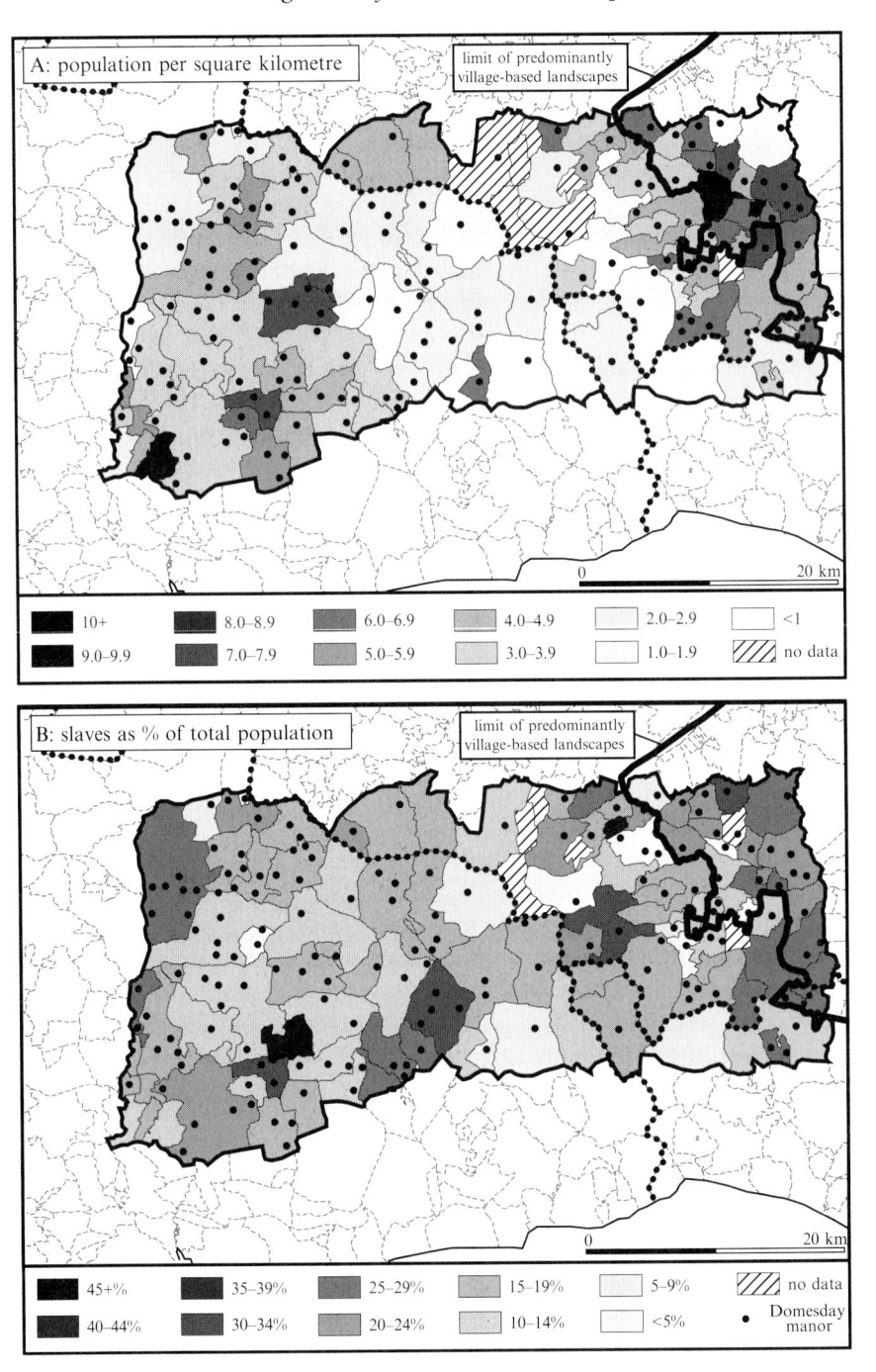

Fig. 15.2. Domesday population density and % slaves.

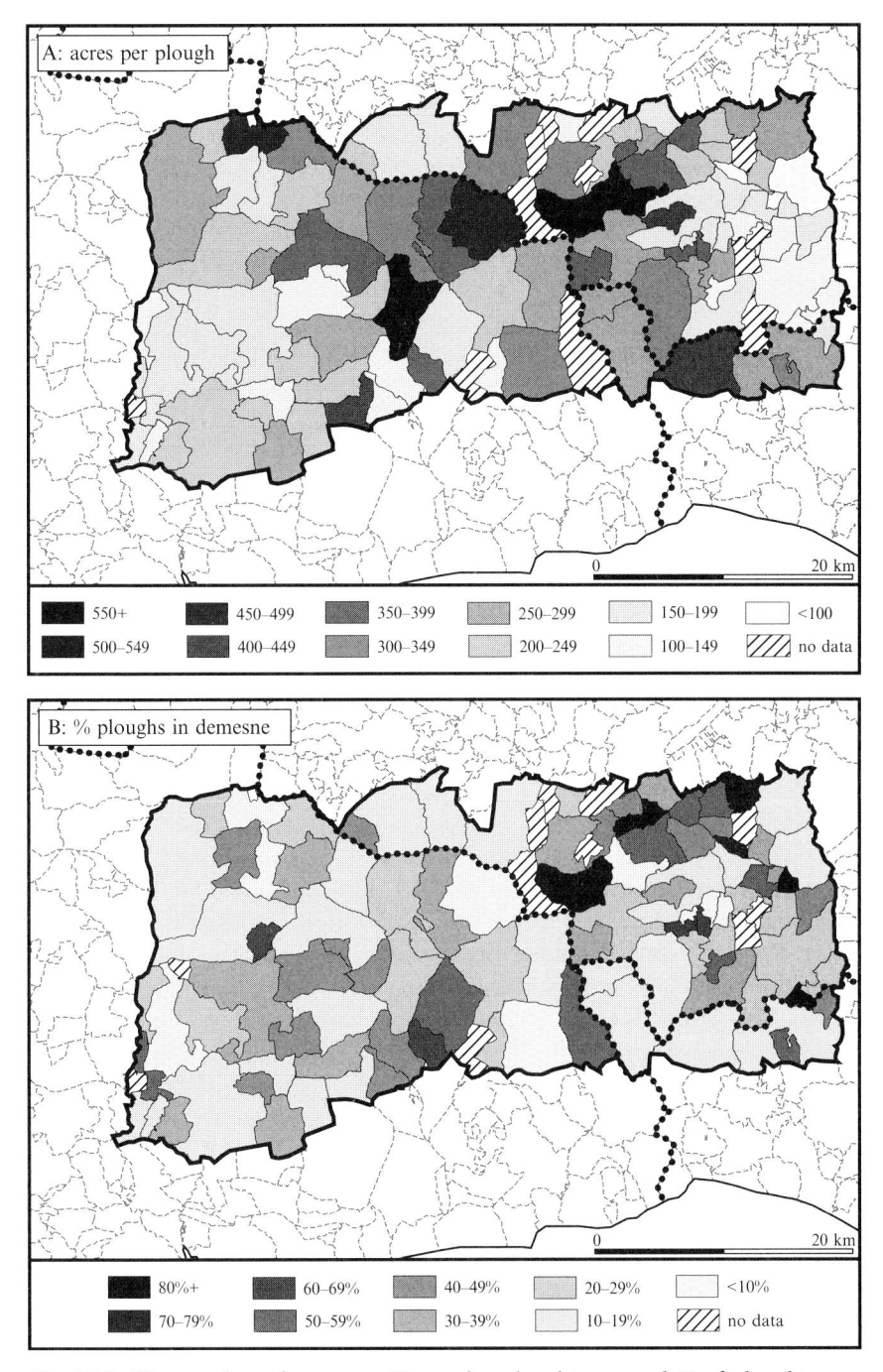

Discussion and conclusions: communities and their landscapes 325

Fig. 15.3. The number of acres per Domesday ploughteam, and % of ploughteams that were on the demesne (where it is specified whether they were on the demesne or belonging to the villagers).

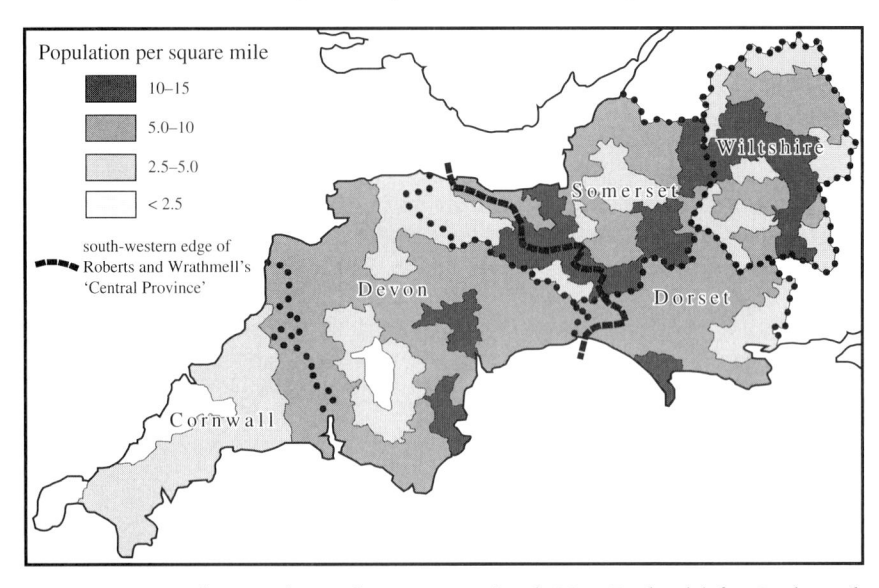

Fig. 15.4. Domesday population density across South West England (after Darby and Welldon Finn 1967, fig. 84) showing no correlation with historic landscape character (reflected here by the south-western edge of Roberts and Wrathmell's 'Central Province'.

as having 'no data'. Secondly, Kingsbury Episcopi and Earnshill also have strangely low population densities.

When mapped across a wide area, however, the data show some very marked trends. The highest population densities are in the lowlands of central Somerset although the correlation with the zone of nucleated settlement and open fields is not precise. The lowlands to the north and west of the Blackdown Hills also had relatively high population densities, while the Hills themselves were less densely settled. In terms of explaining why the lowlands of central Somerset saw the development of villages and open fields, the link with population density is therefore only partial, and it should also be borne in mind that patterns of population density in the eleventh century may in part have been the result of the creation of villages and open fields, rather than the cause. When viewed across the whole of the South West, however, there certainly appears to be no correlation between population density and landscape character (Fig. 15.4).

The balance of arable cultivation and pasture

Another widespread view is that villages and common fields were created in landscapes with large amounts of arable cultivation and a limited area of pasture (and indeed woodland). Lewis *et al.* (1997, 198–200), for example, claim that:

> the areas where the nucleated village was the dominant form of settlement in the middle ages, appear to have had consistently higher proportions of arable land in cultivation in 1086, which is likely to reflect a long standing bias towards cereal cultivation... In other regions, however, this adaptive evolution of field boundaries and settlements was not followed. Where the arable contribution to the economy was less dominant, the pressure on the land never reached the point at which a transformation of the landscape seemed either necessary or desirable. Although the areas of continued dispersed settlement were subject to the same factors, such as increased population or the emergence of markets, nonetheless the availability of additional land for cultivation, their pastoral interests, or opportunities to make a living from the woods and wastes, insulated them from radical change.

There is, however, a problem with this assumption that the champion districts had a long-standing bias towards arable cultivation, as nationally it is once again not borne out by the evidence in Domesday, which shows little relationship between landscapes characterized by villages and open fields and those areas that had a high density of plough teams (Darby 1977, figs. 41–43). The density of Domesday plough teams within our local study area is mapped in Figure 15.3. This shows considerable variation between parishes, though when these are averaged out across each *pays* we find that there was a greater density in the lowlands of central Somerset, and in parishes characterized by villages and open fields there was an average of 177 acres per plough team. This compares to 338 acres per plough team in the remaining lowlands east of the Blackdown Hills, and 319 acres per plough team on the Blackdowns themselves. In the lowlands on eastern Devon to the west—the Culm/Clyst valleys—there were 228 acres per plough team, while on the hills around Tiverton there were 244 acres per plough team.

Although at face value, these figures suggest that the lowlands of central Somerset were the most intensively cultivated area, this high density of plough teams may have been the effect of introducing open fields, rather than the cause.

The role of lordship

While Thirsk saw the creation of common fields as a gradual, evolutionary process, others have argued for a more dramatic replanning of the landscape that was associated with strong lordship. Campbell (1981), for example, argues that lordship was a crucial factor in determining the character of the landscape, suggesting that peasant communities were unlikely to have been capable of restructuring a landscape and that the organized social structures that villages represent were the product of settlement nucleation rather than the cause. Others, however, have rejected the idea that lordly power was a prerequisite for landscape reorganization, citing documentary evidence for the remoteness of land owners from their often scattered estates, and the power and organization that a community could exert locally (e.g. Dyer 1985; P. Harvey 1989; Lewis *et al.* 1997, 172–9; Dyer 2003, 7). We therefore find ourselves in the paradoxical position that 'historians, working on documents, often see the lord of the manor as moving gingerly, pussyfooted even, among the intricacies of his tenants rights and privileges. On the other hand archaeologists and geographers, working in the field, see this same lord sweeping all before him, uprooting entire villages and replanning lands and settlements in an almost arbitrary way' (P. Harvey 1989, 35). While the ability of a community to manage a landscape that already existed is in no doubt, this does not mean that they were also responsible for the initial creation of villages and common fields, as the documentary sources that illustrate the strength of local customary practices date from several centuries after this replanning is thought to have taken place (i.e. the thirteenth and fourteenth centuries). Equally, lords may have exercised 'an intermittent and imperfect control over their subordinates' (Dyer 1985, 27) from the twelfth century onwards, but was this also the case during the eighth to the tenth centuries? As with our discussion of the densities of population and plough teams, the problem with the lordship-versus-community debate is a lack of evidence from the eighth to the tenth centuries when villages and open fields are thought to have been created.

Another problem is that most of these possible causal factors broadly correlate with each other: areas with stronger lordship are thought to have lain in England's central zone, broadly the area that also had an antecedent landscape characterized by its lack of woodland, and relatively high densities of plough teams. In *Beyond the Medieval Village*, this author set about trying to explore specifically the role of lordship and community by choosing landscapes whose soils and antecedent landscape character were entirely uniform, as they were recently reclaimed wetlands. Of particular interest were the North Somerset Levels that were reclaimed from around the tenth century, and where remarkable differences in how settlement patterns and field systems were structured can be observed within the estates of a single land owner, the bishops of Bath and Wells. In this example at least, the land owner clearly did not intervene to manage the landscapes being created following reclamation directly, and their sub-tenants and local communities were left to their own devices (Rippon 2008a). In contrast, on the estates of Glastonbury Abbey, it is very noticeable that villages and open fields were found on its manors even in regions where settlement patterns were otherwise predominantly dispersed and field systems were predominantly enclosed (e.g. Braunton in North

Devon). It would appear, therefore, that in the case of the great ecclesiastical landowners, some were more interventionalist than others.

Although these great ecclesiastical land owners have attracted most attention on the part of historians, due to the survival of a large amount of documentary material, the majority of the landscape was, however, in lay hands, with large areas owned by thanes. Most of these are named in Domesday, so we can reconstruct where their estates lay. In some cases a thane held just one manor, but most held several, and some over twenty. Large lordships such as these consisted of manors that were typically scattered across a wide area, and it was not uncommon for them to be spread across both Devon and Somerset, in areas with and without villages and open fields. Algar, for example, held a series of manors in the lowlands of central Somerset, the hills and vales of North Somerset, and on the Culm Measures, the Blackdown Hills, and the South Hams in Devon (Fig. 15.5). When other thanes' estates are mapped there is similarly no evidence that particular landowners created villages and open fields on all their estates.

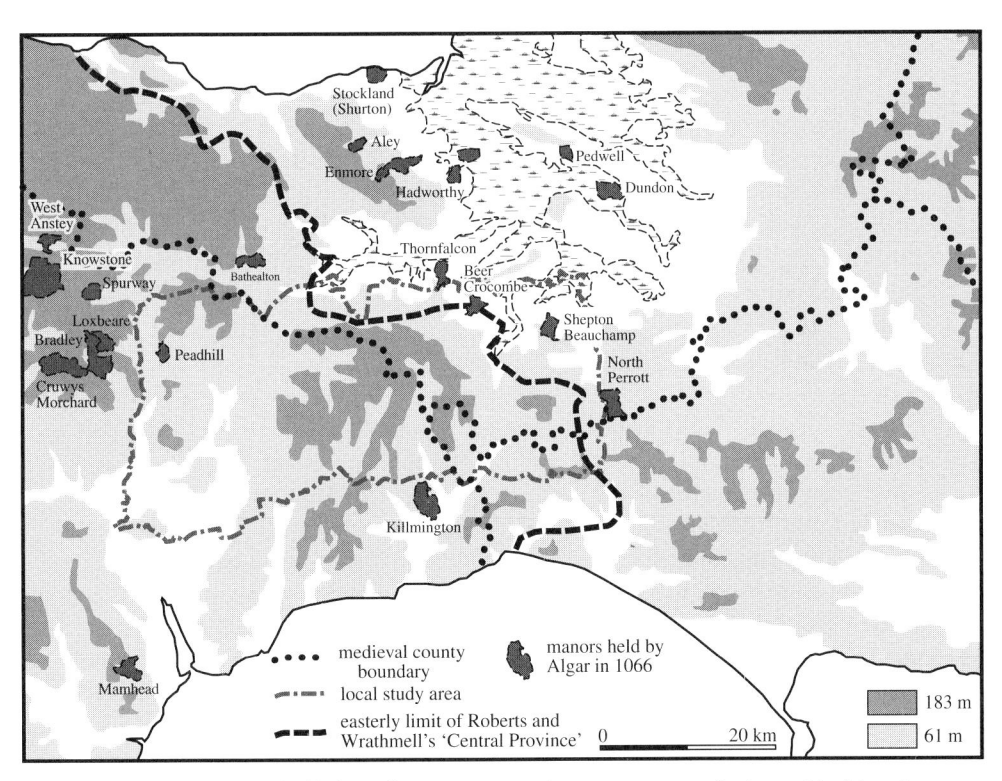

Fig. 15.5. Manors held by Algar in 1066, showing no correlation with historic landscape character (reflected here by the south-western edge of Roberts and Wrathmell's 'Central Province').

A possible indication that there may have been differences in the strength of lordship is the proportion of the population that were slaves, a high proportion indicating strong lordship where we might expect a greater chance of landscape transformation. The percentage of the Domesday population comprising slaves is mapped in Figure 15.2B.[1] Once again, there are hints that the lowlands of central Somerset were different to the rest of our study area as here the vast majority of parishes had Domesday populations that comprised 20–30% slaves, and although some parishes in the lowlands west of the Blackdown Hills had similarly high figures, it was usually somewhat lower (around half the parishes had less than 10% slaves). Another possible indicator of the strength of lordship is the proportions of plough-teams that were on the demesne and held by the peasantry (Fig. 15.3B). While there is considerable variation from parish to parish, when these are averaged out across *pays* there is a remarkable uniformity: in the village and open field landscape of central Somerset, 29% of plough teams were on the demesne, compared to 28% on the remaining lowlands east of the Blackdown Hills. On the Blackdowns themselves 28% of plough teams were on demesnes, compared to 22% in the lowlands of eastern Devon and just 20% on the hills around Tiverton.

Overall, there are hints that by the eleventh century, landscapes characterized by villages and open fields did have stronger lordship, with a slightly higher percentage of the population that were slaves, and a slightly greater proportion of the arable land in the demesne, although the correlation is far from precise. It is also unclear how far this reflects conditions when the countryside of dispersed settlement was transformed around the eighth to the tenth centuries, as opposed to it being the result of this transformation. There also remains the issue why these areas had stronger lordship in the first place.

Soils and the practice of agriculture

Many early scholars explained the development of common fields in terms of agricultural practice, such as the need for a communal pooling of resources when using heavy mouldboard ploughs and the large teams of oxen that they require ('co-aration') (e.g. Seebohm 1890; Orwin and Orwin 1938, 37–44). A rotated scatter of strips across two or three large common fields also shared out the good and bad land in a form of risk management (e.g. Vinogradoff 1892, 235–6; 1905; Gray 1915, 199–202; Thirsk 1964, 11–14; Baker and Butlin 1973, 635–41), but this does not explain why these practices were adopted in some areas but not others (Dodgshon 1980, 29–46).

---

[1] A very small number of manors had 'freed men', which in this analysis are included with the slaves, and a small number of places had 'pigmen' that are grouped here with the small holders.

There has been much discussion of the role of the natural environment in shaping human behaviour and the cultural landscape, with traditional 'environmentally deterministic' ideas having fallen out of favour. There are, however, clear differences in the settlement histories of certain regions that do appear to relate to topography and soils, such as in Northamptonshire where Brown and Foard (1998, 73) suggest that there was an 'intensive but dispersed pattern of [fifth to eighth century] settlement on the permeable geologies' but an 'almost complete loss of settlement from the marginal land, that is, from the claylands on the watersheds between the main river valleys'. A number of other scholars have also recently argued that the significance of the natural environment may have been overlooked in recent years, including Lambourne (2010, 57) who notes that 'environmental factors together with cultural factors produce the mix of components that make up the historic landscape as it evolves over time and through space'. Draper (2006, 112) suggests that the physical landscape is 'fundamental to understanding settlement and society', contrasting the very different patterns of settlement and agriculture in the chalk downland and clay vales of Wiltshire. In his study of Somerset, Corcos (2002, 190) says, 'it must now be clear that a common thread is the importance of ecology and natural environment as important considerations in shaping the nature of medieval settlement, and by extension, the nature of human communities...This is not a "deterministic" conclusion, but one which accepts and indeed celebrates the extraordinary adaptive abilities of pre-industrial societies, and the symbiotic relationship between them and their ecological resource base'.

The relationship between soils and medieval agricultural practices has recently been much debated. Overton (1996, 57) rejects a simple causal link between the nature of soils and farming practice by mapping the distributions of heavy and light soils, and land quality in the 1930s, and showing no correlation with the nature of settlement patterns (Fig. 15.6A–C). In his thought-provoking analysis of East Anglia and the East Midlands, however, Williamson (2003; 2010) suggests that common fields were the response of human communities to some very specific properties of the natural environment and the ways that they affect agricultural practice. He rejects any correlation between common fields and population density or the nature of lordship, and instead stresses the significance of soils, and specifically the need for communal grazing and manuring on areas of particularly light soil, and the problems of ploughing heavy clays that are prone to compaction and 'puddling' (forming a sticky mess which adheres to ploughs, harrows, and other implements, and which then dries to a brick-like hardness). The distribution of soils prone to 'puddling' is broadly similar to that of common fields and Williamson suggests, therefore, that where full advantage had to be taken of the limited times when such soils are suitable for ploughing or harrowing, plough teams needed to be assembled with particular rapidity and this was

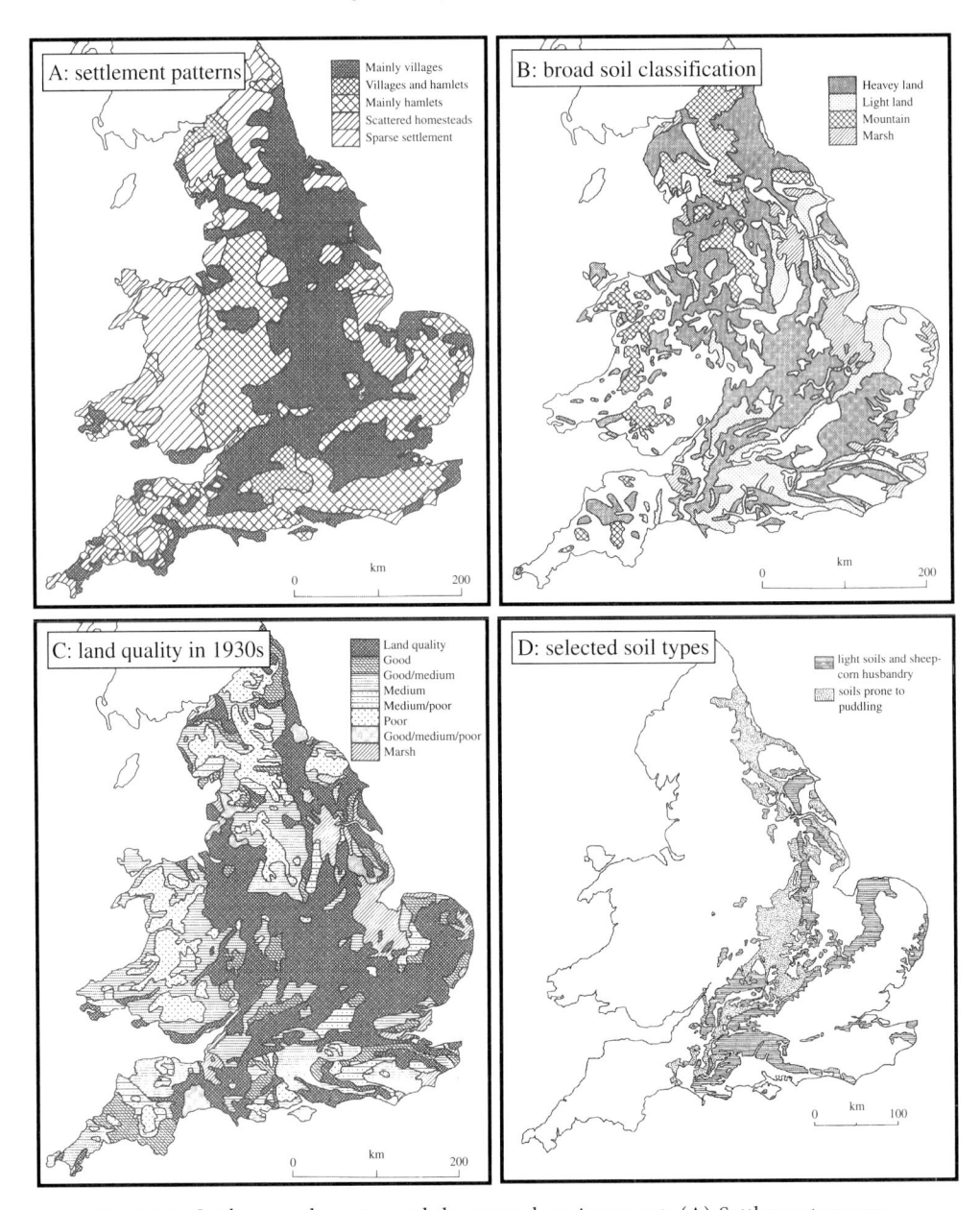

Fig. 15.6. Settlement character and the natural environment. (A) Settlement geography of England and Wales (after Thorpe 1964, fig. 47); (B) major soil types (after Avery *et al.* 1975); (C) land quality in the 1930s (after Dudley Stamp 1948, 383) (source A–C: Overton 1996, figs 2.1, 2.10 and 2.11); (D) light soils supporting sheep and corn husbandry with limited water supplies and soils requiring regular folding, and areas of moderately fertile or fertile clay soil prone to puddling and compaction with restricted opportunities for spring cultivation (principally Denchworth, Ragdale, Dunkeswick, Foggathorpe and Clifton Associations) (Williamson 2007, fig. 28).

much easier where farmsteads and plough teams lay in close proximity, rather than dispersed across the landscape. When the soils had dried out enough to allow them to be worked without adverse effects, but further rain threatened, the time taken to gather together the beasts for the plough team would have been a matter of critical importance (Fig. 15.6D).

The correlation between farming practice and soil type has, however, been questioned (e.g. Dyer 2004b), and the hypothesis that landscape reorganization was essentially driven by agrarian practice—that is the creation of common fields and common meadows—is also at odds with Brown and Foard's (1998) argument that settlement nucleation preceded the creation of common fields by perhaps several centuries. On the reclaimed wetlands such as the Somerset Levels (see above), settlement patterns and field systems of very different character were created on soils that were identical, suggesting that here at least the natural environment was not a determining factor as to whether communities chose to live in nucleated villages or scattered hamlets and farmsteads (Rippon 2006a; 2008a). The soils of our regional study area are mapped in Figure 2.8, where it can be seen that large areas of central Somerset are indeed characterized by the pelo-stagnogleys over clay which are the soils that Williamson identifies as being prone to puddling, and which are also found across much of the southern part of England's 'central province'. When one looks at our study area in detail, however, there are places with the same soils that did not see the development of villages and open fields, such as the area between Corfe, Hatch Beauchamp, and Ilminster. In the lowlands of eastern Devon the small open fields show a very marked concentration on the lighter soils of the Triassic sandstone (Rawson 1953, fig. 1), while in central Somerset they occur on both brown earths and heavier stagnogleys. It is difficult to draw a firm conclusion from this, other than to say soils may have been a contributory factor to landscape reorganization, but they do not appear to have been solely responsible for it.

Access to resources

Williamson (2003) also suggested that another facet of the physical environment which may have encouraged some medieval communities to live together in villages was the extent of meadow. Based on a detailed mapping of medieval agrarian resources by Campbell (2000, 75–6), which showed that meadow was consistently well-represented in the clay vales of England's central zone, Williamson suggests that settlement nucleation was encouraged by the greater efficiency that it affords hay-making as, once again, a community living close together might be more effective at mobilizing the resources needed in a relatively short window of opportunity. We can once again test

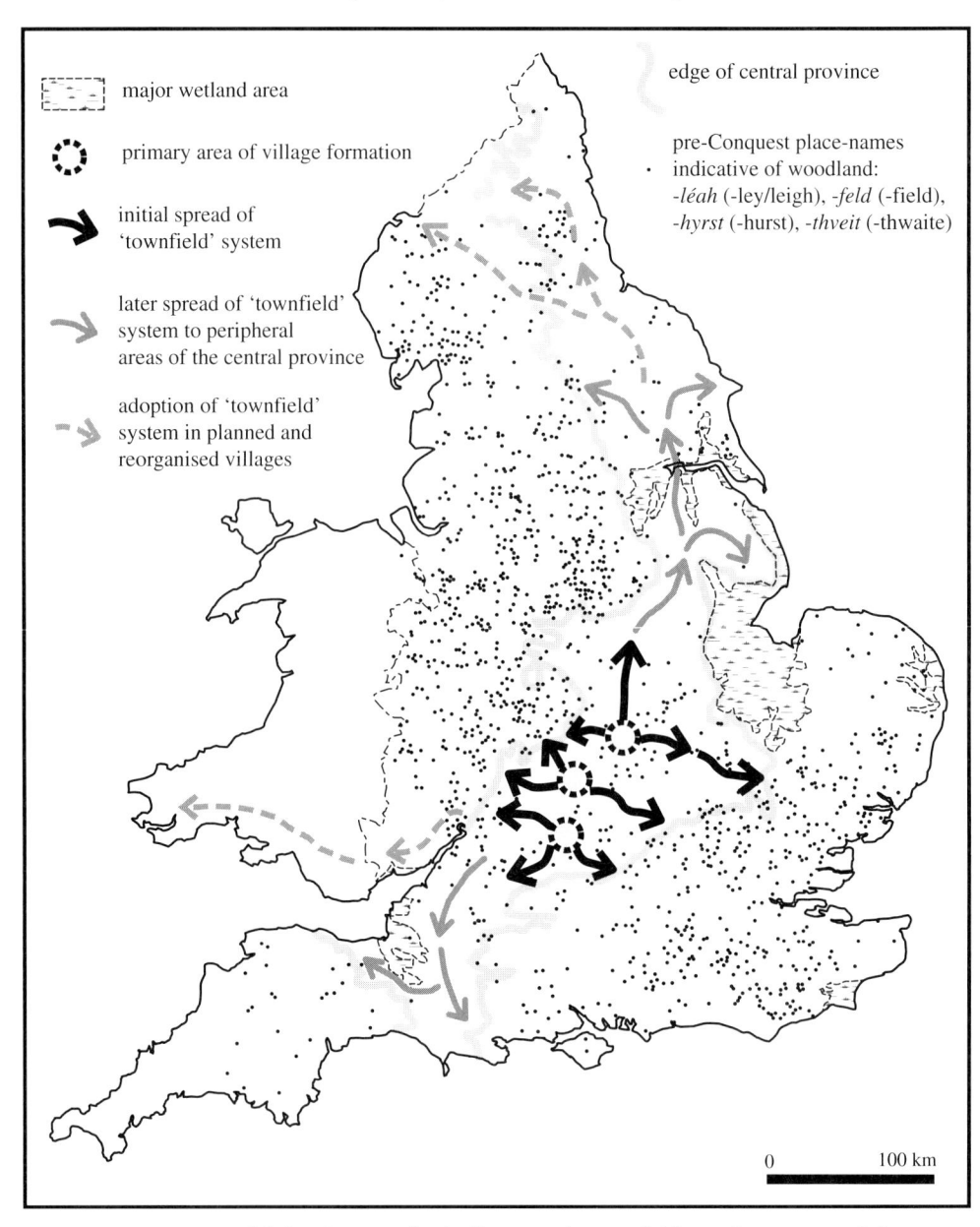

Fig. 15.7. A model for the spread of villages and open fields in the context of the distribution of place-name evidence for the extent of pre-Conquest woodland. (After Roberts and Wrathmell 2002, figs. 1.10 and 5.11.)

this using our study area. It is certainly true that the landscape characterized by villages and open fields in the north-east of our study area does correspond to those parishes on the fringes of the Somerset Levels and the valleys that led into them (Fig. 7.6), but it is also very clear that the broad floodplains of rivers such as the Culm, Clyst, and Tale were just as characteristic of the lowlands west of the Blackdown Hills where open field was less extensive.

The process of emulation

There are hints in some of our data that several of the traditional explanations for the development of villages and open fields—notably a correlation with higher population, stronger lordship, and certain soils—may all have played a part, but none really provides a conclusive answer. In particular, the lack of any differences in the development of early medieval territorial structures across our study area, or the specific ownership of estates, means that we have not yet found the social context within which decisions were made to sweep away dispersed settlement patterns and replace them with nucleated villages. Taylor (2002, 54) has suggested that there was a fashion for villages and common fields that began in the East Midlands and then spread outwards, 'overcoming and overlying the older dispersed pattern', and that the reason why this approach towards structuring the landscape did not cover the whole of Britain was that as the idea spread out from central England, the 'impetus was lost' (Fig. 15.7). Lewis *et al.* (1997, 200) have gone even further, suggesting that 'this adaptation [villages and open fields], once introduced and established, probably spread by emulation: the nucleated settlements and regular open fields in so many communities across the east midlands show so many similarities as to suggest that, as the success of the nucleated open-field village became evident, the idea spread following a standard model'. So how do ideas about the structure and management of a landscape spread through emulation? It is easy to see how the exchange in movable objects facilitates the diffusion of new fashions in material culture, but villages and common fields cannot move in this way. It is well known, however, that in the early medieval period, particularly the 'long eighth century', there was increasing contact between social elites—both secular and ecclesiastical—in western Europe, and maybe this was the means through which knowledge of new agricultural techniques and approaches to shaping settlements spread: by word of mouth and possibly even seeing evidence on the ground. This need not imply that the key force behind landscape change was lordship rather than community, as it is quite possible the concept of villages and common fields could also have spread through simply copying one's neighbours.

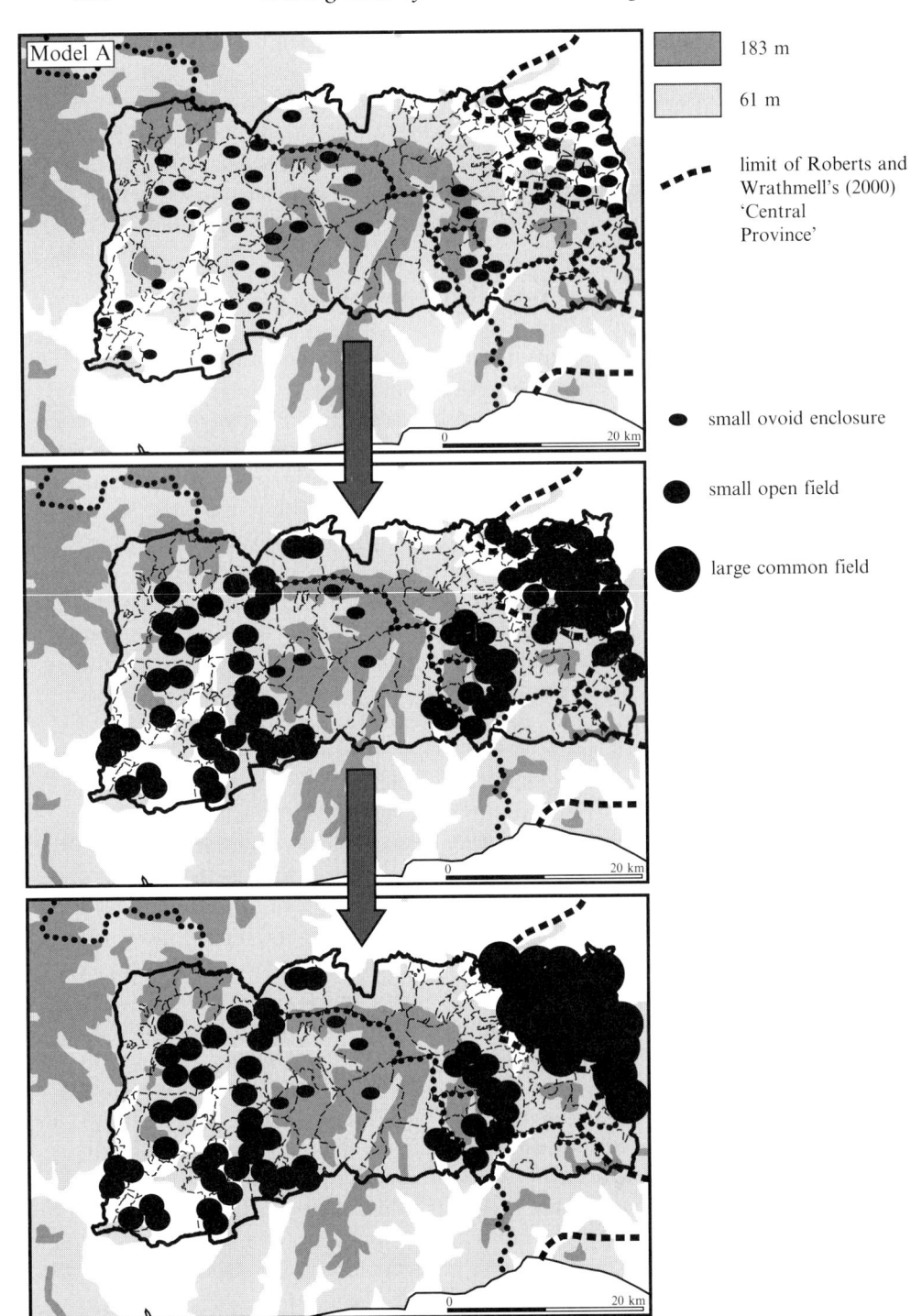

Fig. 15.8. The development of open field, Model A: indigenous development from small ovoid enclosures spread right across the landscape.

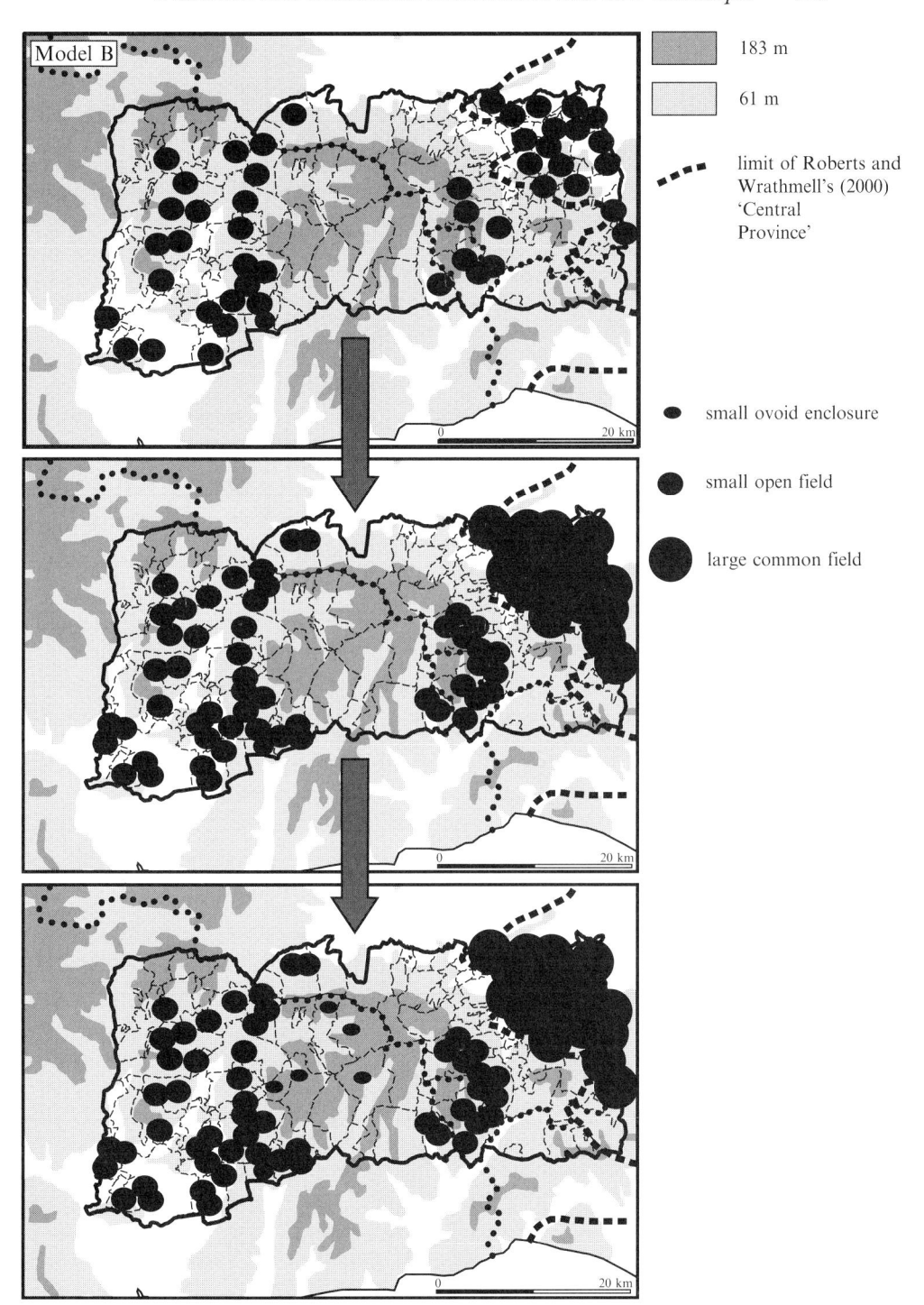

Discussion and conclusions: communities and their landscapes 337

Fig. 15.9. The development of open field, Model B: indigenous development from small open fields in the lowlands, followed by their spread up onto the Blackdown Hills.

338 *Making Sense of An Historic Landscape*

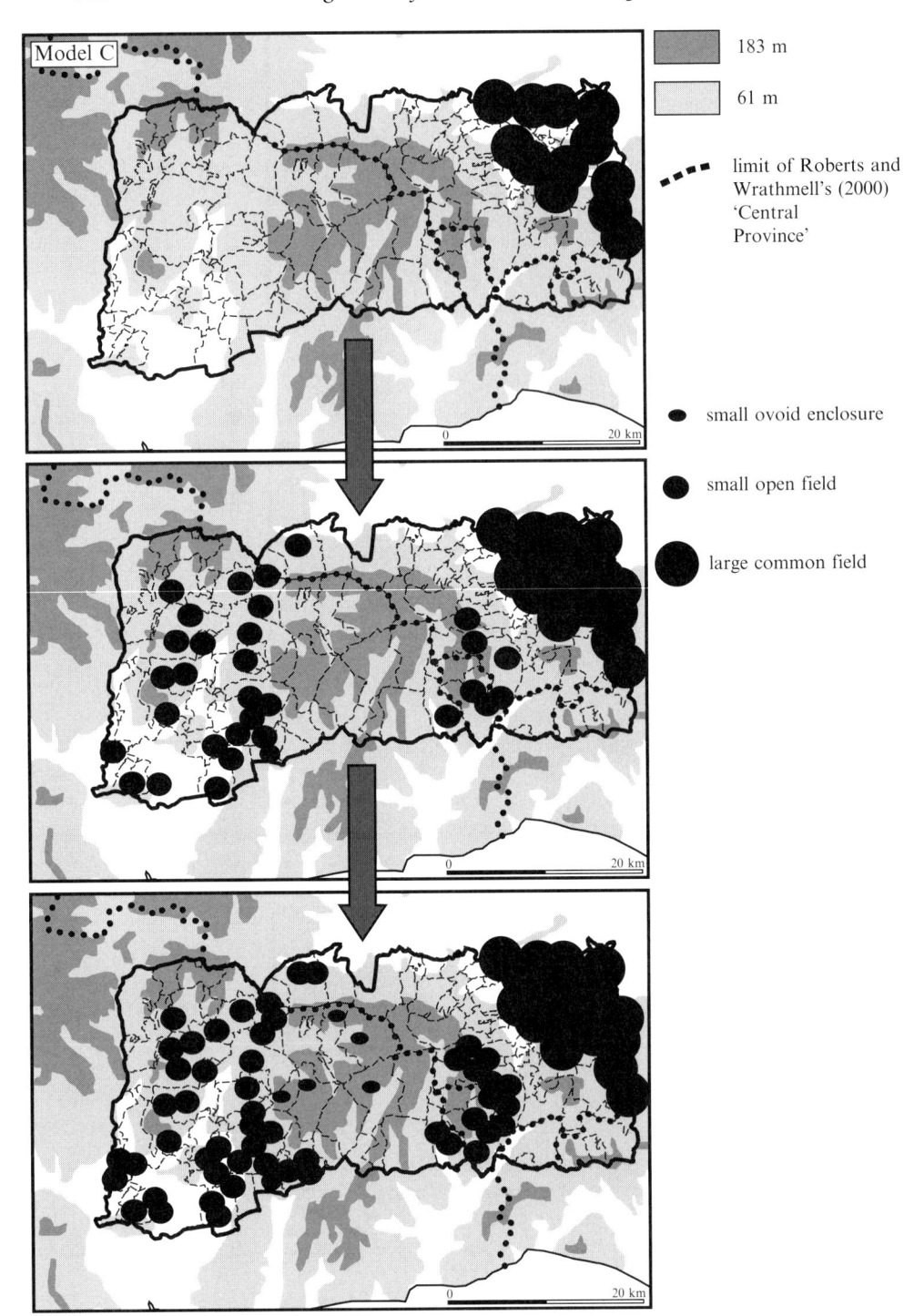

Fig. 15.10. The development of open field, Model C: spread south-westwards from the East Midlands (*see* Fig. 15.7).

Discussion and conclusions: communities and their landscapes 339

THE DEVELOPMENT OF VILLAGES AND OPEN FIELDS IN SOUTH WEST ENGLAND

The dividing line in central Somerset between landscapes characterized by villages and open fields to the east, and more dispersed settlement patterns and predominantly enclosed field systems to the west, was remarkably sharp, albeit with several outliers in the eastern foothills of the Blackdown Hills (most notably Chard and Combe St Nicholas). In fact, there are three clear types of open fields (Table 7.2). Firstly, there were the vast open fields in central Somerset that in typical parishes such as Kingstone and Shepton Beauchamp covered *c.*800–900 acres, and in parishes such as Barrington, Crewkerne, and Merriott spread across *c.*1,600 acres. We know from documentary evidence that these were managed as Midland-style two- and three-field common fields (Fig. 7.3). Secondly, there are the smaller open fields of lowland eastern Devon that covered just *c.*100–350 acres. Thirdly, there are the *c.*40 acre small ovoid enclosures on the Blackdown Hills that are clearly on an altogether different scale (e.g. Westcott in Sheldon (Plate 6)). Based on this study area, we can identify three models for the way that these different open fields may have developed:

Model A (Fig. 15.8). Local development from small ovoid enclosures. In this model, small ovoid enclosures were found across the whole region in the early medieval period, and as such the examples that are found on the Blackdown Hills are survivors of a relatively early landscape form that did not develop further. Dodgshon (1980) has discussed the evidence for 'shareholding' within early medieval field systems, including beyond areas that went on to develop Midland-style two- and three-field common field systems, and these ovoid enclosures could be an example. In areas such the lowlands of eastern Devon and central Somerset these enclosures would then have expanded/amalgamated to create larger open field systems, obliterating evidence for the original enclosure, while some of the small open fields may have been new creations that emulated this form of land management. In lowland eastern Devon these open fields were only ever of modest size, while in central Somerset they continued to evolve into more extensive common fields.

Model B (Fig. 15.9). Local development from small open fields. In this model the small-scale open fields were found in lowland areas both to the east and west of the Blackdown Hills in the early medieval period, but during the tenth century in the lowlands of central Somerset these expanded into larger common fields. Some new, small open fields may have been created in the lowlands of eastern Devon at this time, while the small ovoid enclosures found on the Blackdown Hills are a later development, representing settlement expansion in physically marginal areas.

Model C (Fig. 15.10). Spread by emulation from the east. In this model the concept of open fields originated in areas to the east (e.g. the East Midlands) and spread through the process of emulation south-westwards into the lowlands of central Somerset (see above; Fig. 15.7). The small open fields of Devon represent the relatively late adoption of this form of landscape management, with the ovoid enclosures on the Blackdown Hills being later still.

For models A or B to have been the case, relatively small open fields must have existed before the creation of Midland-style common fields which are generally thought to have developed around the tenth century. There is some documentary evidence to support this. The law code of King Ine (678–726) of Wessex, for example, records that, 'If ceorls have a common meadow or other land divided into shares, and some have fenced their portion and some have not, and [if cattle] eat up their common crops or grass, those who are responsible for the gap are to go, and pay to the others, who have fenced their part, compensation for the damage that has been done there. They are to demand with regard to those cattle such reparation as is proper' (Whitelock 1955, 368–9, clause 42; H. Fox 1981, 86–7). This law code was written in the context of the emergence of stable kingdoms during the late seventh century, at a time when rents, renders, and dues were being imposed and formalized, but there is nothing to suggest that this form of subdivided field was anything new: the law code appears to be stating current practice rather than trying to establishing a new one. There is also evidence for subdivided fields in the early Welsh law codes, which originated in the mid-tenth century (Seebohm 1905, 119–22). These laws describe the communal ploughing of fields that appear to have been divided into strips, since church tithes were assessed by taking every tenth *erw*, the Old Welsh for acre. These *erws* were divided by grass balks, and were subject to the regulated rotation of ownership and co-operative ploughing. These Welsh open fields were, however, on a relatively small scale compared to the vast common fields of England, and were often associated with one family group, or *gwely*, in contrast to the English central zone where the land holdings of all members of a community were included within the two- or three-field system.

It is therefore clear that there was a crucial difference in scale between the early forms of communally managed landed resources found in places such as Wales, and the 'Midland system' as it eventually emerged in the central zone of England. Subdivided fields, and cooperative practices such as communal ploughing and crop rotation can occur at any scale, including the land held by small kin groups or that of a single community living in a hamlet with just a handful of tenements, which was one of many scattered across a parish or township. In the 'Midland system', in contrast, all of the arable land of an entire community was arranged in two or three huge common fields, one of which was put down to common grazing each year, while the other(s) saw a single crop being grown. These common fields were, therefore, on an altogether different scale to open fields in the Welsh landscape both in terms of their physical size, and in the degree of co-operation and communal regulation required. Roberts and Wrathmell (2002, 143) argue that hamlets with small subdivided fields were found right across early medieval Britain, and that what happened in their 'central province' was a expansion of this existing tendency. Over time, they argue, 'the advantages of concentrated tenantry and a system of joint grain production was further stimulated by the inter-state frontier troubles of the eighth century, the Viking incursions of the ninth century and the demands of royal taxation' (ibid.). Overall, there is no reason to assume that small open fields did not exist in early medieval Dumnonia (i.e. west of the Blackdown Hills), though a lack of archaeological or documentary evidence means that we cannot confirm that they did.

In the lowlands of eastern Devon, all three models are therefore plausible as the open fields occur in primary settlement locations on good agricultural land, and in association with church/manor complexes and other Domesday manors. There is no evidence for small ovoid enclosures in this area but their absence may simply be because they have been absorbed within later open fields, and the intensity of farming and landscape change in these core agricultural areas led to all traces of the earliest phases of landscape development being eradicated. Evidence from the Blackdown Hills, however, is a little clearer as it only supports the second and third models. The c.40-acre, small ovoid enclosures occur on high ground in locations that all other evidence points to having been settled after the more hospitable valley sides. None has been found embedded in the Semi-Irregular Enclosures found on the better agricultural land, for example adjacent to a parish church, or associated with a Domesday manor. The closest parallels for these enclosures are in fact assarts and moorland intakes of the high middle ages, such as Holne Moor on Dartmoor where earthwork survey has revealed several small, roughly ovoid-shaped enclosures subdivided into field that contained a series of parallel banks creating the appearance of strip fields (Fleming and Ralph 1982). At Dunnabridge, also on Dartmoor, an account roll of 1304 provides an example of the communal enclosure of waste in order to create a shared open field, when five men each held $19\frac{1}{5}$ acres (a fifth) of a 96-acre assart (Fox 1994, 152). Overall, these small ovoid-shaped enclosures would appear to represent relatively late, and very small-scale, open fields at the spatial and temporal limits of their creation.

As to why common fields did not spread beyond around the Blackdown Hills via the Vale of Taunton Deane and into the lowlands of Devon, it is clear that this was not because the South West was remote and poorly developed, but simply because farming communities there had developed their own very effective ways of managing the land. In discussing the emphasis of oats and rye, for example, Fox (1991b, 303) stressed that arable cultivation in the South West 'was not a backward husbandry constrained simply by soils and by climatic conditions, for in later centuries barley and wheat became as important in Devon and Cornwall as rye and oats were in the middle ages. Lying behind the persistence of oats and rye was preference for the two crops in bread and beer, old and well established already, by the fourteenth century, and very slow to change.' Fox (1991b, 305–6) also notes the very limited areas of legumes grown in the South West despite their extensive cultivation just across the Blackdown Hills in Somerset, noting that 'farmers had their own old-established means of maintaining soil quality, and early spring grass, a product of mild winters, meant that they were not necessary as livestock feed'. Crop yields in the South West were in fact higher than the average for England which was probably due to the regionally distinctive system of convertible husbandry and the predominantly enclosed fieldscape as 'by the late fourteenth century...the majority of the demesnes were divided into securely hedged, severally held closes' (Fox 1991b, 312). Throughout this study we have seen how communities in the South West did things differently—such as using different place-names and field-names, placing chimney stacks in different places within existing houses and retaining traditional layouts in new builds far later than was the case to the east—and the limited extent to which open field farming was adopted is yet another example of this independent thinking.

CONCLUSION

Whether or not there were small open field systems in the lowlands around the Blackdown Hills before the development of common fields in central Somerset around the tenth century, it is clear that this Midland concept of villages and common fields did not spread further west. Whether it be in marking the limit of villages and open fields, a Romanized landscape of towns and villas, or an Iron Age landscape of developed hillforts and the use of coinage, the Blackdown Hills clearly marked a long-standing difference in landscape character which must in turn reflect differences in the nature of society and its interaction with the natural environment. Two themes appear to run through the late prehistoric, Roman, and early medieval periods: firstly, social stratification, or at least the that way that it was displayed through the built environment and material culture and so manifests itself in the archaeological record, and secondly, the degree to which society adopted new ideas. Social stratification is perhaps most clearly identifiable in the hierarchy of settlement during the Roman period with a wide range of farmsteads, villas, and towns to the east of the Blackdown Hills, in contrast to a marked lack of Romanization and relatively little differentiation in the size and status of settlement to the west. This difference in stratification is also seen in material culture with large amounts of coinage and other manufactured goods in use to the east, and relatively little to the west. The decision not to embrace Romanization is suggestive of a degree of conservatism in the South West, as was the continued dominance of emmer wheat, and there are other examples of a slowness to adopt new ideas preserved within the historic landscape of today, such as the unusual positioning of chimney stacks and longevity of asymmetrical house plans, both of which preserved the idea of central hall space within domestic buildings. There were also strong local traditions of what to call settlements, with '-hayes' and '-hayne' names still being coined into the eighteenth and nineteenth centuries.

The central conclusion of this study is therefore that communities living in South West England have a long tradition of doing things differently, of which this study has mapped but a few. This was a county, for example, where there 'seems to have been extraordinary enthusiasm for the "make do and mend" principle in church restoration' which resulted in it missing out on the great era of rebuilding that was seen just to the east, in Somerset, during the fifteenth century (Addison 1982, 70). In the South West, farmers even marked out their fields differently, using substantial banks, in contrast to the simple hedges seen to the east. It is not clear whether society was genuinely less stratified, or that social differentiation was achieved and displayed in ways that have not survived archaeologically. We should certainly resist views that the South West was a somewhat remote and backward region. Indeed, John Aubrey, for example, writing between 1656 and 1684, said, 'The Devonshire men were the earliest improvers. I heard Oliver Cromwell, Protector, at dinner at Hampton Court, in 1657 or 1658, tell the lord Arundell of Wardour and the lord Fitzwilliams that he had been in all the counties of England and the Devonshire husbandry is the best' (Ponting 1969, 103). Devon does have its uplands, but there are also extensive, fertile lowlands that saw the development of small-scale open fields (although not on the scale that the Devon HLC has proposed). That Midland-style villages and open fields did not develop reflects how communities living there chose not to adopt that new form of landscape management, presumably because they were very happy with what they already had.

In the past, when trying to explain the major regional variation in landscape character in medieval England—the extent of nucleated villages and common fields—archaeologists, historians, and historical geographers have tended to seek single-cause explanations such as population density or the nature of the soils. There has also been a very narrow focus on just this one manifestation of regional variation in landscape character. In contrast, the contention here is to show how in order to understand landscape history we need to take a longer and a broader view. If we look at a longer time frame we see that South West England's failure to embrace the concept of villages and common fields developed on the back of a long history of doing things differently, and if we look at the nature of landscape and society beyond settlements and field systems, then we see again that communities had a distinctive and separate identity across many aspects of their environmental management. Throughout this book an attempt has been made to show how historic landscape analysis is at its most powerful when it includes as wide a range of landscape facets as possible, including place-names, vernacular architecture, and patterns of land holding. Any explanation of why the South West never saw the development of Midland-style villages and common fields purely in terms of circumstances in the eighth to the tenth centuries may stumble on the right answer, but there is a good chance that it will not. Both in South West England and in other areas where long-term boundaries in landscape character have been observed, differences in the character of the medieval landscape appear to correspond to far older boundaries such the Gipping–Lark line in Suffolk (Williamson 2006a; Rippon 2007a; Martin and Satchell 2008), and the Felden and Arden in Warwickshire (Robert and Wrathmell 2000b).

It therefore turns out that the concept of 'antecedent landscape character' is an important one, as it reflects how facets of landscape character in one period can affect the nature of the landscape in succeeding periods, and this is exactly what appears to be happening either side of the Blackdown Hills. The differences in landscape character we have seen in South West England go beyond variations in the natural environment, and appear to relate more to deep-rooted differences that gradually emerged within in society that manifested themselves in the extent of visible stratification and the propensity to accept new ideas.

Bibliography

Aalbersberg, G. 1999, 'The Alluvial Fringes of the Somerset Levels', unpublished PhD thesis, University of Exeter.

Abrams, L. 1996, *Anglo-Saxon Glastonbury: Church and Endowment*. Woodbridge: Boydell Press.

Abdy, R., Brunning, R. A., and Webster, C. J. 2001, 'The discovery of a Roman villa at Shapwick and its Severan coin hoard of 9,238 *denarii*', *Journal of Roman Archaeology* 14(i), 358–73.

Addison, W. 1982, *Local Styles of the English Parish Church*. London: Batsford.

Ainsworth, P. and Scott, T. 2000, *Regions and Landscapes*. Oxford: Peter Lang.

Aitkin, G. M. and Aitkin, G. N. 1990, 'Excavations at Whitcombe, 1965–67', *Proceedings of the Dorset Natural History and Archaeological Society* 112, 57–94.

Albarella, U. 2005, 'Meat production and consumption in town and country', in K. Giles and C. Dyer (eds.) *Town and Country in the Middle Ages: Contrasts, Contacts and Interconnections, 1100–1500*, Leeds: Society for Medieval Archaeology monograph 22, 131–47.

—— and Davis, S. J. M. 1994, 'Mammals and birds from Launceston Castle, Cornwall: decline in status and the rise of agriculture', *Circaea, The Journal of the Association for Environmental Archaeology* 12(i), 1–156.

—— and Hammon, A. 1996, 'The animal bone', in *The Roman Small Town at Shepton Mallet, Somerset: The Tesco Excavation 1996*, 85–92. Birmingham University Field Archaeology Unit, unpublished report.

Alcock, L. 1995, *Cadbury Castle, Somerset: the Early Medieval Archaeology*. Cardiff: University of Wales Press.

Alcock, N. W. 1962, 'Houses in an East Devon parish', *Report and Transactions of the Devonshire Association for the Advancement of Science* XCIV, 185–232.

—— 1970, 'An East Devon manor in the later Middle Ages', *Report and Transactions of the Devonshire Association for the Advancement of Science* 102, 141–88.

—— 1973, 'An East Devon manor in the later Middle Ages Part II: leasing the demesne 1423–1525', *Report and Transactions of the Devonshire Association for the Advancement of Science* 105, 141–90.

—— 1975, 'Fields and farms in an East Devon parish', *Report and Transactions of the Devonshire Association for the Advancement of Science* 107, 93–172.

Alcock, N. 1981, *Cruck Construction: An Introduction and Catalogue*. London: Council for British Archaeology Research Report 42.

Alcock, N. W. and Hulland, C. 1972, 'Devonshire farm houses Part IV: some medieval houses in east and north Devon', *Report and Transactions of the Devonshire Association for the Advancement of Science* 104, 35–56.

Aldred, O. 2001, *Somerset and Exmoor National Park Historic Landscape Characterisation Project 1999–2000*. Taunton: Somerset County Council.

Aldred, O. and Fairclough, G. 2003, *Historic Landscape Characterization: Taking Stock of the Method. The National HLC Method Review Carried Out for English Heritage by Somerset County Council*. Taunton: Somerset County Council.

Allan, J. P. 1984, *Medieval and Post Medieval Finds from Exeter, 1971–1980*. Exeter: Exeter City Council and The University of Exeter Press.

—— 1994, 'Medieval pottery and the dating of deserted settlements on Dartmoor', *Proceedings of the Devon Archaeological Society* 52, 141–7.

—— 1999, 'Cleeve Abbey; the pottery', *Proceedings of the Somerset Archaeological and Natural History Society* 142, 41–75.

—— 2003, 'A group of early 13th-century pottery from Sherborne Old Castle and its wider context', *Proceedings of the Dorset Natural History and Archaeological Society* 125, 71–82.

Allan, J. and Blaylock, S. 2005, 'Medieval pottery and other finds from Pigs Paradise, Lundy', *Proceedings of the Devon Archaeological Society* 63, 65–91.

Allan, J. P. and Langman, G. 2002, 'A group of medieval pottery from Haycroft Farm, Membury', *Proceedings of the Devon Archaeological Society* 60, 59–73.

—— and Silvester, R. J. 1981, 'Newenham Abbey, Axminster', *Proceedings of the Devon Archaeological Society* 39, 159–71.

Allen, J. R. L. and Fulford, M. G. 1996, 'The distribution of South-East Dorset Black Burnished Category I pottery in South-West Britain', *Britannia* XXVII, 223–81.

Allen, M. 1997, 'Landscape, land-use and farming', in R. J. C. Smith *et al*. 1997, 277–83.

Allen, M. J. 1998a, 'A note on reconstructing the prehistoric landscape environment in Cranborne Chase: the Allen Valley', *Proceedings of the Dorset Natural History and Archaeological Society* 120, 39–44.

—— 1998b, 'Fontmell Down, Dorset, land-use, landscape and land management; the land snail evidence', *Proceedings of the Dorset Natural History and Archaeological Society* 120, 89–91.

—— and Green, M. 1998, 'The Fir Tree Field shaft: the date and archaeological and palaeo-environmental potential of a chalk swallowhole feature', *Proceedings of the Dorset Natural History and Archaeological Society* 120, 25–38.

——, Chandler, J., Hinton, P., Hamilton-Dyer, S., Loader, E., Mepham, L., and Wyles, S. F. 2000, 'Excavations at Ivy Street and Brown Street, Salisbury, 1994, *Wiltshire Archaeological and Natural History Magazine* 93, 20–62.

Andrews, P. 2009, 'The discovery, excavation and preservation of a detached Roman bath house at Truckle Hill, North Wraxall', *Wiltshire Archaeological and Natural History Magazine* 102, 129–49.

——, Mepham, L., and Seagar Smith, R. 2000, 'Excavations in Wilton, 1995–6: St John's Hospital and South Street', *Wiltshire Archaeological and Natural History Magazine* 93, 181–204.

Appleton-Fox, N. 1992, 'Excavations at a Romano-British round: Reawla, Gwinear, Cornwall', *Cornish Archaeology* 31, 69–123.

ApSimon, A. 1965, 'The Roman Temple on Brean Down, Somerset', *Proceedings of the University of Bristol Spelaeological Society* 10(3), 195–258.

Astill, G. 2009, 'Anglo-Saxon attitudes: how should post-AD700 burials be interpreted', in D. Sayer and H. Williams (eds.) *Mortuary Practices and Social Identities*

in the Middle Ages: Essays in Burial Archaeology in Honour of Heinrich Härke. Exeter: University of Exeter Press, 222–3.
Aston, M. 1986, 'Post Roman central places in Somerset', in E. Grant (ed.) *Central Places, Archaeology and History*, Sheffield: University of Sheffield, 49–77.
—— 1988a, *Aspects of the Medieval Landscape of Somerset*, Taunton: Somerset County Council.
—— 1988b, 'Land-use and field systems', in M. Aston (ed.) 1988a, 82–97.
—— 2007, 'An archipelago in central Somerset: the origins of Muchelney Abbey', *Proceedings of the Somerset Archaeological and Natural History Society* 150, 63–72.
—— 2009, 'An early medieval estate in the Isle valley of south Somerset and the early endowments of Muchelney Abbey', *Proceedings of the Somerset Archaeological and Natural History Society* 152, 83–103.
——, Chapman, J. and Mckinley, J. 2011, 'Banwell Winthill', *SANHS News* (*The Newsletter of the Somerset Archaeological & Natural History Society*) No. 83, 2–3.
Atkinson, T. D. 1947, *Local Style in English Architecture: an Enquiry into its Origin and Development*. London: Batsford.
Attenborough, F. L. 1922, *The Laws of the Earliest English Kings*. Cambridge: Cambridge University Press.
Ault, W. O. 1972, *Open-Field Farming in Medieval England*. London: George Allen and Unwin.
Austin, C. and De Zouche Hall, R. 1972, 'The medieval houses of Stocklinch', *Proceedings of the Somerset Archaeological and Natural History Society* 116, 86–100.
Austin, D. 1985, 'Doubts about morphogenisis', *Journal of Historical Geography* 11(ii), 201–9.
——, Daggett, R. H., and Walker, M. J. C. 1980, 'Farms and fields on Okehampton Park, Devon: the problems of studying medieval landscape, *Landscape History* 2, 39–57.
——, Rippon, S. and Stamper, P. 2007, *Landscapes* 8(ii) Macclesfield: Windgather Press.
—— and Stamper, P. 2006, 'Editorial', *Landscapes* 7(ii), vii–viii.
—— and Thomas, J. 1990, 'The "proper study" of medieval archaeology; a case study', in D. Austin and L. Alcock (eds.) *From the Baltic to the Black Sea: Studies in Medieval Archaeology*. London: Routledge, 43–78.
—— and Walker, M. J. C. 1985, 'A new landscape context for Houndtor, Devon', *Medieval Archaeology* 29, 147–52.
Avery, B. W., Findlay, D. C., and Mackney, D. 1975, *Soil map of England and Wales*, Southampton: Ordnance Survey, for the Soil Survey of England and Wales.
Bailey, M. 1989, *A Marginal Economy? East Anglian Breckland in the Later Middle Ages*, Cambridge: Cambridge University Press.
Baker A. R. H. and Butlin R. A. 1973, 'Conclusions: problems and perspectives' in A. R. H. Baker, and R. A. Butlin (eds.) *Studies of Field Systems in the British Isles*. Cambridge: Cambridge University Press, 619–56.
Bailey, M. 1989, *A Marginal Economy*. Cambridge: Cambridge University Press.
Baillie, M. 2001, 'The AD540 event', *Current Archaeology* 174, 173–9.
—— and Brown, D. M. 2001, 'Dendrochronology and the reconstruction of fine resolution environmental change in the Holocene', in A. Mackay, R. Battarbee,

J. Birks, and E. Oldfield (eds.) *Global Change in the Holocene*. London: Hodder Headline Group, 75–91.

Balkwill, C. J. 1976, 'A Roman site at Okehampton', *Proceedings of the Devon Archaeological Society* 34, 89–92.

Barker, K. 2005, '*Salis ad ripam maris aet Lim*: of salt and the Dorset coast at Lyme', *Proceedings of the Dorset Natural History and Archaeological Society* 127, 43–51.

Barnes, W. 1970, *A Glossary of the Dorset Dialect*. St Peter Port, Guernsey: The Toucan Press.

Barnett, C., Scaife, R., and Cooke, N. 2007, 'Iron Age to Saxon landscape and landuse change in the Taw Valley: evidence from an infilled river channel at Little Pill Farm, Sticklepath Hill, near Barnstaple', *Proceedings of the Devon Archaeological Society* 65, 15–34.

Barnwell, P. S. and Giles, C. 1997, *English Farmsteads, 1750–1914*. Swindon: RCHME.

Barr, M. 2006, 'Building stone in East Devon and adjacent parts of Dorset and Somerset', *Report and Transactions of the Devonshire Association for the Advancement of Science* 138, 185–224.

Barrett, J. C., Freeman, P. W. M., and Woodward, A. 2000, *Cadbury Castle Somerset: The Later Prehistoric and Early Historic Archaeology*. London: English Heritage Archaeological Report 20.

Barrowman, R. C., Batey, C. E., and Morris, C. D. 2007, *Excavations at Tintagel Castle, Cornwall 1990–1999*. London: Reports of the Research Committee of the Society of Antiquaries of London, No. 74.

Bartlett, R. and Mackay, A. 1989, *Medieval Frontier Societies*. Oxford: Clarendon Press.

Barton, K. 1963–4, 'Star Roman villa, Shipham, Somerset', *Proceedings of the Somerset Archaeological and Natural History Society* 106, 45–93.

Bass, R. and Stanes, R. 2008, 'The Devonshire hedgebank', in R. Stanes *et al.* (eds.) 2008, 139–49.

Bassett, S. 1989a, *The Origins of Anglo-Saxon Kingdoms*, Leicester: Leicester University Press.

—— 1989b, 'In search of the origins of the Anglo-Saxon kingdoms', in S. Bassett (ed.) 1989a, 3–27.

—— 2006, 'Boundaries of knowledge: mapping the land units of late Anglo-Saxon and Norman England', in W. Davies, G. Hasall, and A. Reynolds (eds.) *People and Space in the Middle Ages, 300–1300*, Turnhout, Belgium: Brepols, 115–42.

Bayer, O. J., in prep. 'Lithic scatters, landscape and inhabitation in the lower Exe valley, Devon'. PhD thesis, Preston: School of Forensic and Investigative Sciences, University of Central Lancashire.

Beacham, P. (ed.) 1978, *Devon's Traditional Buildings*. Exeter: Devon County Council.

—— 1990, *Devon Building: An Introduction to Local Traditions*. Tiverton: Devon Books/Halsgrove.

Beckett, S. C. and Hibbert, F. A. 1979, 'Vegetational change and the influence of prehistoric man in the Somerset Levels', *New Phytologist*, 83(ii), 577–600.

Behre, K.-E. and Jacomet, S. 1991, 'The ecological interpretation of archaeobotanical data', in W. Van Zeist, K. Wasylikowa, and K.-E. Behre (eds.) *Progress in Old World Palaeoethnobotany*, Rotterdam: Balkema, 81–108.

Belcher, J. 2008, 'Historic Landscape Characterisation: an exploration of the method as a means of understanding enclosure', *Landscapes* 9(ii), 26–44.

Bell, M. 1990, *Brean Down Excavations 1983–1987*. London: English Heritage Archaeological Report No. 15.

Belleville, G. 1956, 'A crouched burial found in King Street, Brixham', *Proceedings of the Devon Archaeological Exploration Society* V(iv), 124.

Beresford, G. 1979, 'Three deserted medieval settlements on Dartmoor: a report on the late E. Marie Minter's excavations', *Medieval Archaeology* 23, 98–158.

Beresford, M. W. 1964, 'Dispersed and grouped settlement in medieval Cornwall', *Agricultural History Review,* 12(i), 13–27.

—— and Finberg, H. P. R. 1973, *English Medieval Boroughs: A Hand-List*. Newton Abbot: David and Charles.

Beresford, M. and Hurst, J. 1990, *The English Heritage Book of Wharram*. London: English Heritage.

Best, J. and Gent, T. 2007, 'Bronze Age burnt mounds and early medieval timber structures at Town Farm Quarry, Burlescombe, Devon', *Archaeological Journal* 164, 1–79.

Bidwell, P. T. 1980, *Roman Exeter: Fortress and Town*. Exeter: Exeter Museum Service.

—— and Silvester, R. J. 1988, 'The Roman pottery', in B. C. Cunliffe (ed.) *Mount Batten Plymouth: A Prehistoric and Roman Fort*, Oxford: Oxford University Committee for Archaeology Monograph 26, 42–9.

Billing, T. R. 2008, 'Variations in landscape: An Archaeological Investigation of the parish Churches of Devon and Somerset'. Unpublished MA dissertation, Department of Archaeology, University of Exeter.

Billingsley, J. 1797, *A General View of the Agriculture of the County of Somerset*. London: Board of Agriculture.

Birbeck, V. 2002, 'Excavations on Iron Age and Romano-British settlement at Cannard's Grave, Shepton Mallet', *Somerset Archaeology and Natural History* 144, 41–116.

Blair, J. 1989, 'Frithuwold's kingdom and the origins of Surrey', in S. Bassett (ed.) 1989a, 97–107.

—— 1991, *Early Medieval Surrey: Landholding, Church and Settlement Before 1300*. Stroud: Alan Sutton.

—— 1992, 'Anglo-Saxon minsters: a topographical review', in J. Blair and R. Sharpe (eds.) *Pastoral Care Before the Parish*, Leicester: Leicester University Press, 226–66.

—— 1994, *Anglo-Saxon Oxfordshire*. Stroud: Alan Sutton Publishing.

—— 1995, 'Debate: ecclesiastical organization and pastoral care in Anglo-Saxon England, *Early Medieval Europe* 4(ii), 193–212.

—— 1999, 'Tribal Hidage', in M. Lapidge, J. Blair, S. Keynes, and D. Scragg (eds.) *The Blackwells Encyclopedia of Anglo-Saxon England*. Oxford: Blackwell, 455–6.

—— 2005, *The Church in Anglo-Saxon Society*, Oxford: Oxford University Press.

Bloemers, J. H. F. 2002, 'Past- and future-oriented archaeology: protecting and developing the archaeological-historical landscape in the Netherlands', in G. Fairclough and S. Rippon (eds.) *Europe's Cultural Landscape: Archaeologists and the Management of Change*. Brussels: Europae Archaeologiae Consilium, 89–96.

Bonaparte, L. L. 1876, 'Observations on the Somerset dialect', *Transactions of the Philosophical Society* 19, 579–81.
Bonney, D. 1972, 'Early boundaries in Wessex', in P. J. Fowler (ed.) *Archaeology and the Landscape*, London: John Baker, 168–86.
—— 1979, 'Early Boundaries and Estates in Southern England', in P. H. Sawyer (ed.) *English Medieval Settlement*. London: Hodder Arnold, 41–51.
Boon, G.C. 1973, 'Two Durotrigian coins from Glamorgan', *Bulletin of the Board of Celtic Studies* 25(ii), 245–6.
Bottema, S., Hoorn, T. C. Van, Woldring, H., and Gremmen, W. H. E. 1980, 'An agricultural experiment in the unprotected saltmarsh part II', *Palaeohistoria* XXII, 127–40.
Bourne, J. 1986–7, 'Kingston place-names: an interim report', *Journal of the English Place-Name Society* 20, 13–37.
Bradley, R. 2007, *The Prehistory of Britain and Ireland*. Cambridge: Cambridge University Press.
Branigan, K. 1977, *Gatcombe Roman Villa*. Oxford: British Archaeological Reports British Series 44, Oxford.
Bray, L. S. 2006, 'The Archaeology of Iron production: Romano-British Evidence from the Exmoor Region'. Unpublished PhD, University of Exeter.
Brett, M., Mudd, A., and Collard, M. 2009, *Ilchester to Barrington Gas Pipeline, Somerset. Post-Excavation Assessment and Updated project Design Issue 4*. Cotswold Archaeology Report 09022.
Brigers, J. 2006, 'Little Haven, Church Road, Edington, Somerset: Report on an Archaeological Investigation'. Unpublished report: Somerset County Council HER PRN 14452.
Brooks, N. 1989, 'The creation and early structure of the kingdom of Kent', in S. Bassett (ed.) 1989a, 55–74.
Broomhead, D. 1998, 'Ilchester, Great Yard excavations 1995', *Proceedings of the Somerset Archaeological and Natural History Society* 142, 139–91.
Brown, S. and Holbrook, N. 1989, 'A Roman site at Otterton Point', *Proceedings of the Devon Archaeological Society* 47, 29–42.
Brown, A. G., Dinnin, M., and Toogood, T. 2003, 'Peat Wastage in the Somerset Levels: A Study Based on Field Evidence'. Unpublished report for Somerset County Council Historic Environment Service by the School of Geography and Archaeology, University of Exeter.
Brown, T. and Foard, G. 1998, 'The Saxon Landscape: a regional perspective', in P. Everson and T. Williamson (ed.) 1998, 67–94.
—— 1961, 'Some examples of post Reformation folklore in Devon', *Folklore* 72, 388–99.
Bruce-Mitford, R. 1997, *Mawgan Porth; A Settlement of the Late Saxon Period on the North Cornish Coast. Excavations 1949–52, 1954, and 1974*. London: English Heritage Archaeological Report 13.
Brunning, R. 2010, 'Taming the floodplain: river canalization and causeway formation in the Middle Anglo-Saxon period at Glastonbury, Somerset', *Medieval Archaeology* 54, 319–29.

Brunskill, R. W. 1971, *Illustrated Handbook of Vernacular Architecture*. London: Faber and Faber.

—— 1992, *Traditional Buildings of Britain*. London: Victor Gollancz.

Bryant, S., Perry, B., and Williamson, T. 2005, 'A "relict landscape" in South-East Hertfordshire; archaeological and topographic investigations in the Wormley area', *Landscape History* 27, 5–16.

Buckland-Wright, J. C. 1987, 'The animal bones', in C. Sparey Green 1987, 129–32.

Bullock, A. E. and Allen, M. J. 1997, 'Animal bones', in R. J. C. Smith *et al.* 1997, 190–9.

Burgess, C. 1985, 'Population, climate and upland settlement', in D. Spratt and C. Burgess (eds.) *Upland Settlement in Britain: The 2nd Millennium BC and After*. Oxford: British Archaeological Reports, British Series, 143, 195–219.

—— 1989, 'Volcanoes, catastrophes and the global crisis of the late second millennium', *Current Archaeology* 10, 325–9.

Burnham, B. C., Hunter, F., Fitzpatrick, A. P., Worrell, S., Hassall, M. W. C., and Tomlin, R. S. O. 2002, 'Roman Britain in 2001', *Britannia* XXXIII, 275–371.

—— ——, Booth, P., Worrell, S., Hassall, M. W. C., and Tomlin, R. S. O. 2007, 'Roman Britain in 2003', *Britannia* XXXVI, 253–349.

—— and Wacher, J. 1990, *The 'Small Towns' of Roman Britain*. London: B. T. Batsford Ltd.

Burrow, I. 1981, *Hillfort and Hill-top Settlement in Somerset in the First to Eighth Centuries A.D.* Oxford: British Archaeological Reports, British Series 91.

—— 1988, 'Excavations at 5–9 Fore Street, Taunton, 1979', *Proceedings of the Somerset Archaeological and Natural History Society* 132, 95–164.

Butlin R. A. 1978, 'The late Middle Ages, *c.*1350–1500', in R. A. Dodgshon and R. A. Butlin, (eds.) *An Historical Geography of England and Wales*. London: Academic Press, 119–50.

Butterworth, C. A. and Seager Smith, R. 1997, 'Excavations at The Hermitage, Old Town, Swindon', *Wiltshire Archaeological and Natural History Magazine* 90, 55–76.

Cadw 1998, *Register of Landscapes of Outstanding Historic Interest in Wales*. Cardiff: Cadw Welsh Historic Monuments.

—— 2001, *Register of Landscapes of Special Historic Interest in Wales*. Cardiff: Cadw Welsh Historic Monuments.

Cahn, W. 1991, 'Medieval landscape and the encyclopedic tradition', *Yale French Studies* 80, 11–24.

Cameron, K. 1996, *English Place-Names*. London: B. T. Batsford.

Campbell, B. M. S. 1981, 'Commonfield origins—the regional dimension', in T. Rowley (ed.) 1981, 112–29.

—— 2000, *English Seigniorial Agriculture, 1250–1450*. Cambridge: Cambridge University Press.

—— 2008, *Field Systems and Farming Systems in Late Medieval England*. Farnham: Ashgate.

—— and Bartley, K. 2006, *England on the Eve of the Black Death: An Atlas of Lay Lordship, Land and Wealth, 1300–49*. Manchester: Manchester University Press.

Campbell, C., Tipping, R., and Cowley, D. 2002, 'Continuity and stability in past upland land uses in the western Cheviot Hills, southern Scotland', *Landscape History* 24, 111–18.

Campbell, E. 2007, *Continental and Mediterranean Imports to Atlantic Britain and Ireland, AD 400–800*. York: Council for British Archaeology Research Report 157.

Campbell, G. and Straker, V. 2003, 'Prehistoric crop husbandry and plant use in southern England: development and regionality', in K. A. Robson Brown (ed.) *Archaeological Sciences 1999: Proceedings of the Archaeological Sciences Conference, University of Bristol, 1999*. Oxford: British Archaeological Reports, International Series, 1111, 14–30.

Campbell, J. 1979, *Bede's* Reges *and* Principes. Durham: University of Durham, Jarrow Lecture.

Cambridge, E. and Rollason, D. 1995, 'The pastoral organisation of the Anglo-Saxon church: a review of the "minster hypothesis"', *Early Medieval Europe* 4, 87–104.

Cameron, K. 1996, *English Place-Names*. London: B. T. Batsford.

Cannell, J. 2005, *The Archaeology of Woodland Exploitation in the Greater Exmoor Area in the Historic Period*. Oxford: British Archaeological Reports, British Series, 398.

Carlyon, P. M. 1982, 'A Romano-British site at Kilhallon, Tywardreath: excavation in 1975', *Cornish Archaeology* 21, 155–70.

Carew, T. 2008, 'An Early Bronze Age timber structure, a Saxon kiln, and Saxon and medieval occupation at Coppice Street, Shaftesbury, Dorset', *Proceedings of the Dorset Natural History and Archaeological Society* 129, 59–96.

Carr, J. 1985, 'Excavations on the Mound, Glastonbury, Somerset, 1971', *Proceedings of the Somerset Archaeological and Natural History Society* 129, 37–62.

Carruthers, W. 1995, 'Charred Plant Remains From the Medieval Farmstead at Eckweek, Avon'. London: Historic Buildings and Monuments Commission, Ancient Monuments Laboratory report 27/95.

——2006, 'Bestwall Quarry, Wareham: The Charred Plant Remains from Iron Age, Romano-British and Later Contexts', Unpublished Report.

——forthcoming, 'Penlee House, Tregony, Cornwall: the charred plant remains', in S. Taylor (ed.) 'Excavations of a Roman and post-Roman site at Penlee House, Tregony: a cremation burial and other burning issues', *Cornish Archaeology*.

——2008, 'Penryn College: The Charred Plant Remains'. Unpublished report.

——forthcoming, 'Plant macrofossils', in A. Reynolds (ed.) 'Excavations at Atlantic Road, Newquay', *Cornish Archaeology*.

Carter, R. W. 2009, 'Former medieval open fields in the eastern Blackdowns', *Proceedings of the Somerset Archaeological and Natural History Society* 152, 153–64.

Caseldine, C. 1999, 'Environmental setting', in R. J. P. Kain and W. Ravenhill (eds.), 25–34.

Caseldine, C. J., Coles, B. J., Griffith, F. M., and Hatton, J. M. 2000, 'Conservation or change? Human influence on the mid-Devon Landscape', in R. A. Nicholson and T. P. O'Connor (eds.) *People as Agents of Environmental Change*, Oxford: Oxbow, 60–9.

—— and Hatton, J. 1993, 'The development of high moorland on Dartmoor: fire and the influence of Mesolithic activity on vegetation change', in F. M. Chambers (ed.) *Climate Change and Human Impact on the Landscape*. London: Chapman and Hall, 119–31.

——— 1996, 'Vegetational History of Dartmoor—Holocene development and the impact of human activity', in D. J. Charman, R. M. Newnham, and D. G. Croot (eds.) *Devon and East Cornwall Field Guide*. London: Quaternary Research Association, 48–62.

C.A.T. 2000, 'Hayes Farm, Clyst Honiton, Nr. Exeter, Devon: Archaeological Evaluation Phase 1 (1999)'. Cotswold Archaeological Trust Report 001127, Cirencester.

Chandler, J. 1993, *John Leland's Itinerary: Travels in Tudor England*, Stroud: Alan Sutton.

Chapman, A. 2010, *West Cotton, Raunds. A Study of Medieval Settlement Dynamics AD 450–1450*. Oxford: Oxbow Books.

Cherry, B. and Pevsner, N. 1991, *Devon*. London: Penguin.

Child, P. 1978, 'Farmhouse building traditions', in P. Beacham (ed.) 1978, 7–17.

—— 1990, 'Farmhouse building traditions', in P. Beacham (ed.) 1990, 33–45.

Clark, K. no date, 'Compact farm, Worth Matravers, Dorset', <http://wac.soton.ac.uk/Centres/CAAA/Facilities/sites/compact%20farm.htm>

Clayden, B. 1971, *Soils of the Exeter District (Sheets 325 and 339)*. Harpenden: Memoirs of the Soil Survey of Great England and Wales.

Clutton-Brock, J. 1976, 'The animal resources', in D. M. Wilson (ed.) *The Archaeology of Anglo-Saxon England*. Cambridge: Cambridge University Press, 373–92.

Coates, R. 1993–4, 'Review: Stephen Robinson, *Somerset Place Names*', *Journal of the English Place-Names Society* 26, 33.

Coe, D. and Hawkes, J. W. 1992, 'Excavations at 29 High Street, Wimborne Minster, Dorset, 1990', *Proceedings of the Dorset Natural History and Archaeological Society* 114, 135–44.

Coleman-Smith, R. and Pearson, T. 1988, *Excavations in the Donyatt Potteries*. Chichester: Phillimore.

Collins, R. and Gerrard, J. (eds) 2004, *Debating Late Antiquity in Britain AD 300–700*, Oxford: British Archaeological Reports British Series 365.

Corbin, A. 1994, *The Lure of the Sea: The Discovery of the Seaside in the Western World 1750–1840* (Translated by Jocelyn Phelps), Oxford: Blackwell.

Corcos, N. 2002, *The Affinities and Antecedents of Medieval Settlement: Topographical Perspectives from Three Somerset Hundreds*. Oxford: British Archaeological Reports, British Series, 337.

Cornwall County Council 1994, *Cornwall Landscape Assessment 1994*. Truro: Cornwall County Council.

Costen, M. 1988, 'The late Saxon landscape: the evidence from charters and place-names', in M. Aston (ed.) 1988a, 32–47.

—— 1992a, *The Origins of Somerset*. Manchester: Manchester University Press.

—— 1992b, 'Huish and worth: Old English survivals in a later landscape', *Anglo-Saxon Studies in Archaeology and History* 5, 65–83.

Costen, M. 2008, 'Anonymous thegns in the landscape of Wessex 900–1066', in M. Costen (ed.) *People and Places: Essays in Honour of Mick Aston*. Oxford: Oxbow Books, 61–75.

Cox, P. W. 1992, 'Excavation at the Waitrose Supermarket Site, Chantry Fields, Gillingham, Dorset, 1991–2', *Proceedings of the Dorset and Natural History and Archaeological Society* 114, 135–44.

—— and Broomhead, R. A. 1993, *The Archaeological Evaluation of the Proposed Accommodation Facilities at Hinkley 'C' Power Station, Somerset*. Unpublished Report, AC Archaeology report 6693/1/10.

—— and Hearne, C. M. 1991, *Redeemed from the Heath: The Archaeology of the Wytch Farm Oilfield (1989–90)*. Dorchester: Dorset Natural History and Archaeological Society Monograph Series 9.

Coxhead, J. R. W. 1954, *Legends of Devon*. Westward Ho!: The Western Press.

Cramp, R. 2006, *Corpus of Anglo-Saxon Stone Sculpture. Vol. 7, South-West England*. Oxford: Published for The British Academy by Oxford University Press.

Crockett, A. 1996, 'Archaeological sites along the Ilchester to Odcombe pipeline', *Somerset Archaeology and Natural History* 139, 59–88.

Croft, R. 1988, 'Bridgwater, Wembdon Hill', *Somerset Archaeology and Natural History* 132, 221.

Croft, R. A. 1989, 'Langford Budville', in J. Bradbury and R. A. Croft, 'Somerset Archaeology 1989', *Somerset Archaeological and Natural History* 133, 172.

Croft, R. and Aston, M. 1993, *Somerset from the Air: An Aerial Guide to the Heritage of the County*. Taunton: Somerset County Council.

Cunliffe, B. 1979, *Excavations in Bath, 1950–75*. Bristol: Committee for Rescue Archaeology in Avon, Gloucestershire and Somerset Excavation Monograph 1.

—— 1988, *Mount Batten Plymouth: A Prehistoric and Roman Port*. Oxford: Oxford University Committee for Archaeology Monograph 26.

—— 2005, *Iron Age Communities in Britain*. Fourth Edition, London: Routledge.

Currie, C. K. 1993, 'Excavations at the Postern Mill site, Malmesbury, 1986–87', *Wiltshire Archaeological and Natural History Magazine* 86, 58–74.

Currie, C. 1988, 'Time and chance: modeling the attrition of old houses', *Vernacular Architecture* 19, 1–9.

Currie, C. R. J. and Lewis, C. P. (eds.) 1994, *A Guide to English County Histories*. Stroud: Alan Sutton Publishing.

Dallimore, J. 2001, *Newton St Loe, N E Somerset: A Study of the Vernacular Building Survey*. Bath: Bath and North East Somerset Council.

Darby, H. C. 1967, 'Dorset', in H. C. Darby and R. Welldon Finn (eds.) 1967, 67–131.

—— 1977, *Domesday England*. Cambridge: Cambridge University Press.

—— and Welldon Finn, R. 1967, *The Domesday Geography of South-West England*, Cambridge: Cambridge University Press.

Dark, K. 1999, *Civitas to Kingdom: British Political Continuity 300–800*. London: Leicester University Press.

—— 2000, *Britain and the End of the Roman Empire*. Stroud: Tempus.

Dark, P. 2000, *The Environment of Britain in the First Millennium A.D.* London: Duckworth.

Dark, K. and Dark, P. 1997, *The Landscape of Roman Britain.* Stroud: Tempus.

Darvill, T. 2000, *Prehistoric Britain.* London: Routledge.

Davenport, P. 1991, *Archaeology in Bath 1976–1985.* Oxford University Committee for Archaeology Monograph 28, Oxford: Oxford University Committee for Archaeology.

—— 1999, *Archaeology in Bath: Excavations 1984–1989.* Oxford: British Archaeological Reports, British Series, 284.

—— Poole, C. and Jordan, D. 2007, *Excavations at the New Royal Baths (the Spa), and Bellott's Hospital 1998-1999.* Oxford: Oxford Archaeology monograph 3.

Davey, J. E. 2005, *The Roman to Medieval Transition in the Region of South Cadbury Castle, Somerset.* Oxford: British Archaeological Reports, British Series, 399.

Davey, J. and Cooper, G. 2004, 'Romano-British sites in the parish of Sandford Orcas, Dorset', *Proceedings of the Dorset Natural History and Archaeological Society* 126, 43–62.

Davies, S. M. 1983, 'Excavations at Christchurch, Dorset, 1981 to 1983', *Proceedings of the Dorset Natural History and Archaeological Society* 105, 21–56.

——, Bellamy, P. S., Heaton, M. J., and Woodward, P. J. 2002, *Excavations at Allington Avenue, Fordington, Dorchester, Dorset, 1984–87.* Dorset Natural History and Archaeological Society Monograph Series No. 15.

—— 1991, 'Faunal Remains from the Late Saxon-Mediaeval Farmstead at Eckweek in Avon, 1988–1989 Excavations'. London: Historic Buildings and Monuments Commission, Ancient Monuments Laboratory report 35/91.

Deacon, B. 2007, *Cornwall: A Concise History.* Cardiff: University of Wales Press.

Defoe, D. 1742a, *A Tour Thro' the Whole Island of Great Britain, Divided into Circuits or Journeys Giving a Particular and Entertaining Account of Whatever is Curious, and Worth Observation*, volume 1, 3rd edn., edited by Samuel Richardson, London: Garland Publishing (1975).

—— 1742b, *A Tour Thro' the Whole Island of Great Britain, Divided into Circuits or Journeys Giving a Particular and Entertaining Account of Whatever is Curious, and Worth Observation*, volume 2, 3rd edn., edited by Samuel Richardson, London: Garland Publishing (1975).

Dickinson, F. H. 1889, *Kirby's Quest for Somerset.* Somerset Records Society 3. Taunton: Somerset Records society.

Dodgshon, R. A. 1980, *The Origins of British Field Systems.* London: Academic Press.

Down, T. and Carter, R. W. 1989, 'Tatworth Middle Field', *Proceedings of the Somerset Archaeological and Natural History Society* 133, 103–24.

Draper, S. 2004, 'Roman estates to English parishes? The legacy of Desmond Bonney reconsidered', in R. Collins and J. Gerrard (eds.), 55–64.

—— 2006, *Landscape, Settlement and Society in Roman and Early Medieval Wiltshire*, Oxford: British Archaeological Reports, British Series, 419.

Dudley, D. 1941, 'A Late Bronze Age Settlement on Trewey Downs, Zennor, Cornwall', *Archaeological Journal* XCVIII, 105–30.

Dudley Stamp, L. 1941, 'Devonshire', in L. Dudley Stamp (ed.) *The Land of Britain: the Report of the Land Utilisation Survey of Britain*, Part 92, London: Geographic Publications, 469–544.

Dudley Stamp, L. 1948, *The Land of Britain: Its Use and Mis-Use*. London: Longmans, Green and Co., in conjunction with Geographical Publications.

Dudridge, M. 1984, *Superstition and Folklore of the West Country: Dorset, Devon and Somerset*. Lyme Regis: Nigel J. Clarke Publications.

Dunning, R. W. 1978, *A History of the County of Somerset, Volume IV: Crewkerne, Martock and South Petherton Hundreds*. London: Institute of Historical Research.

Dyer, C. 1985, 'Power and conflict in the medieval village', in D. Hooke (ed.) *Medieval Villages*, Oxford: Oxford University Committee for Archaeology, 27–32.

——1988, 'Documentary evidence: problems and enquiries', in G. Astill and A. Grant (eds.) *The Countryside of Medieval England*, Oxford: Blackwell, 12–35.

——1996, 'Seasonal settlement in medieval Gloucestershire', in H. S. A. Fox (ed.) 1996a, 25–34.

——2003, *Making a Living in the Middle Ages. The People of Britain 850–1520*. London: Penguin.

——2004a, 'Alternative agriculture: goats in medieval England', in R. W. Hyle (ed.) *People, Landscape and Alternative Agriculture: Essays for Joan Thirsk*. Exeter: British Agricultural History Society, The Agricultural History Review Supplementary series 3, 20–38.

——2004b, Review of *Shaping Medieval Landscapes. Settlement, Society, Environment* by Tom Williamson, in *Landscape History*, 26, 131–2.

——2008, 'Building in earth in late-medieval England', *Vernacular Architecture* 39, 63–70.

Dymond, C. W. and Tomkins, H. G. 1886, *Worlebury: An Ancient Stronghold in the County of Somerset*, Bristol: printed for the authors.

Eagles, B. 1994, 'The archaeological evidence for settlement in the fifth to seventh centuries AD', in M. Aston and C. Lewis (eds.) *The Landscape of Medieval Wessex*, Oxford: Oxbow, 13–32.

——2004, 'Britons and Saxons on the eastern boundary of the Civitas Durotrigum', *Britannia* XXXV, 234–40.

Ebdon, M. 2008, 'The landscape around Chulmleigh in 1711: a reconstruction map', *Report and Transactions of the Devonshire Association for the Advancement of Science* 140, 45–90.

Eddison, J. 2000, *Romney Marsh: Survival on a Frontier*, Stroud: Tempus.

Edwards, R. A. 2000, *The Geology of the Country around Exeter (Explanation of Sheet 325)*, London: Memoirs of the British Geological Survey.

Edmonds, E. A., Mckeown, M. C., and Williams, M. 1975, *British Regional Geology: South-West England*. London, British Geological Survey.

Ekwall, E. 1960. *The Concise Oxford Dictionary of English Place-Names*. Fourth edition. Oxford: Clarendon Press.

Ellis, P. 1982, 'Excavations at Silver Street, Glastonbury, 1978', *Proceedings of the Somerset Archaeological and Natural History Society* 126, 17–31.

——1984, *Catsgore 1979. Further Excavation of the Romano-British Village*. Bristol: Western Archaeological Trust monograph 7.

——1989, 'Norton Fitzwarren hillfort: a report on the excavations by Nancy and Philip Langmaid between 1968 and 1971', *Somerset Archaeology and Natural History* 133, 1–74.

Ellison, A. and Pearson, T. 1981, *The Wincanton Bypass. A Study in the Archaeological Recording of Road Works*. Bristol: Committee for Rescue Archaeology in Avon, Gloucestershire and Somerset, Occasional Papers No. 8.

Erskine, A. M. 1969, *The Devonshire Lay Subsidy of 1332*. Devon and Cornwall Records Society (new series) 14. Exeter: Devon and Cornwall Records Society.

Erskine, J. G. P. and Ellis, P. 2008, 'Excavations at Atworth Roman villa Wiltshire 1970-75', *Wiltshire Archaeological and Natural History Society Magazine* 101, 51-129.

Esmonde-Cleary, S. 1989, *The Ending of Roman Britain*. London: B. T. Batsford.

Evans, D. and Hancocks, A. 2005, 'Romano-British, late Saxon and medieval remains at the Old Showground, Cheddar: excavations in 2001', *Proceedings of the Somerset Archaeological and Natural History Society* 149, 107-22.

Evans, J. and Rouse, A. J. 1991, 'The river valleys of the South Winterbourne and Frome', in N. M. Sharples, *Maiden Castle: Excavations and Field Survey, 1985-6*, London: English Heritage Archaeological Report 19, 15-17.

Everitt, A. 1977, 'River and wold: reflections on the historical origin of regions and *pays*', *Journal of Historical Geography* 3, 1-19.

—— 1979, 'Country, county and town: patterns of regional evolution in England', *Transactions of the Royal Historical Society* (5th Series), 29, 79-108.

—— 1986, *Continuity and Colonization: The Evolution of Kentish Settlement*. Leicester: Leicester University Press.

Everson, P. and Williamson, T. (ed.) 1998, *The Archaeology of Landscape*. Manchester: Manchester University Press.

Evison, V. I. 1968, 'The Anglo-Saxon finds from Hardown Hill', *Proceedings of the Dorset Natural History and Archaeological Society* 90, 232-40.

Esmonde Cleary, S. 1989, *The Ending of Roman Britain*. London: B. T. Batsford.

Faith, R. 1997, *The English Peasantry and the Growth of Lordship*. London: Leicester University Press.

—— 2006, 'Worthys and enclosures', *Medieval Settlement Research Group Annual Report* 21, 9-14.

—— 2008, 'Forms of dominance and the early medieval landscape', *Medieval Settlement Research* (Journal and Annual Report of the Medieval Settlement Research Group) 23, 9-13.

—— Fleming, A. and Kitchen, R. 2007, 'Worthy farms on the edge of Dartmoor: a preliminary report', *Medieval Settlement Research Group Annual Report* 22, 57.

Farwell, D. E. and Molleson, T. I. 1993, *Poundbury Volume 2: The Cemeteries*. Dorchester: Dorset Natural History and Archaeological Society Monograph Series Number 11.

Faulkner, N. 2001, *The Decline and Fall of Roman Britain*. Stroud: Tempus.

Fenwick, C. C. 1998, *The Poll Taxes of 1377, 1379 and 1381. Part 1 Bedfordshire-Leicestershire*. London: British Academy, Records of Social and Economic History, New Series, 27.

—— 2001, *The Poll Taxes of 1377, 1379 and 1381. Part 2 Lincolnshire-Westmorland*. London: British Academy, Records of Social and Economic History, New Series, 29.

Fenwick, C. C. 2005, *The Poll Taxes of 1377, 1379 and 1381. Part 3 Wiltshire–Yorkshire*. London: British Academy, Records of Social and Economic History, New Series, 37.

Ferris, I. M. and Bevan, L. 1994, 'Excavations at Maidenbrook Farm, Cheddon Fitzpaine, in 1990', *Somerset Archaeology and Natural History* 137, 1–40.

Field, J. 1972, *English Field-Names: A Dictionary*. Newton Abbott: David and Charles.

—— 1993, *A History of English Field-Names*. London: Longman.

Finberg, H. P. R. 1951, *Tavistock Abbey: A Study in the Social and Economic History of Devon*. Cambridge: Cambridge University Press.

—— 1952, 'The open field in Devon', in, W. G. Hoskins and H. P. R. Finberg (eds.) *Devonshire Studies*, London: Jonathan Cape, 265–88.

—— 1954, *The Early Charters of Devon and Cornwall*. Leicester: University of Leicester Press.

—— 1955, *Roman and Saxon Withington: a Study in Continuity*. Leicester, University College of Leicester, Department of English Local History, Occasional papers 8.

—— 1964, *The Early Charters of Wessex*. Leicester: University of Leicester Press.

—— 1969, *Tavistock Abbey: A Study in the Social and Economic History of Devon*. Newton Abbot: David and Charles.

Fitzpatrick, A., Butterworth, C. A., and Grove, J. 1999, *Prehistoric & Roman Sites in East Devon: the A30 Honiton to Exeter Improvement DBFO Scheme, 1996–9*, Salisbury: Wessex Archaeology.

—— and Crockett, A. D. 1998, 'A Romano-British settlement and inhumation cemetery at Eyewell Farm, Chilmark', *Wiltshire Archaeological and Natural History Magazine* 91, 11–33.

Fleming, A. 1983, 'The Prehistoric Landscape of Dartmoor Part 2: North and East Dartmoor', *Proceedings of the. Prehistoric Society* 49, 195–241.

—— 1988, *The Dartmoor Reaves*, London: B. T. Batsford.

—— 1998a, *Swaledale: Valley of the Wild River*, Edinburgh: Edinburgh University Press.

—— 1998b, 'Prehistoric landscapes and the quest for territorial pattern', in P. Everson and T. Williamson (eds.) 1998, 42–66.

—— 2005, *St Kilda and the Wider World: Tales of an Iconic Island*, Macclesfield: Windgather Press.

—— 2006, 'Post-processual landscape archaeology: a critique', *Cambridge Archaeological Journal* 16(iii), 267–80.

—— 2007, 'Don't bin your boots', *Landscapes* 8(i), 85–99.

—— 2008, *The Dartmoor Reaves,* Second Edition. Macclesfield: Windgather Press.

—— and Ralph, N. 1982, 'Medieval Settlement and landuse on Holne Moor, Dartmoor: the landscape evidence'. *Medieval Archaeology* 26, 101–37.

Foard, G., Hall, D., and Partida, T. 2005, 'Rockingham Forest, Northamptonshire: the evolution of a landscape'. *Landscapes* 6 (ii), 1–29.

—— —— —— 2009, *Rockingham Forest: An Atlas of the Medieval and Early Modern Landscape*. Northampton Records Society LIV. Northampton: Northampton Records Society.

Foster, I. D. L., Mighall, T. M., Wotton, C., Owens, P. N., and Walling, D. E. 2000, 'Evidence for mediaeval soil erosion in the South Hams region of Devon, UK', *The Holocene* 10(ii), 261–92.

Fowler, P. J. 1964, 'Interim report on an excavation in Combs Ditch, Dorset, 1964', *Proceedings of the Dorset Archaeological and Natural History Society* 86, 112.

—— 1968, 'Excavation of a Romano-British settlement at Row of Ashes Farm, Butcombe, North Somerset. Interim report 1966–67', *Proceedings of the University of Bristol Spelaeological Society* 11(ii), 209–36.

—— 1970, 'Fieldwork and excavation in the Butcombe area, North Somerset', *Proceedings of the University of Bristol Spelaeological Society* 12(ii), 169–94.

—— 1975, 'Continuity in the landscape?: a summary of some local archaeology in the Wiltshire, Somerset and Gloucestershire', in P. J. Fowler (ed.) *Recent Work in Rural Archaeology*, Bradford-on-Avon: Moonraker Press, 121–36.

Fowler, P. 2000, *Landscape Plotted and Pieced. Landscape History and Local Archaeology in Fyfield and Overton, Wiltshire*. London: the Society of Antiquaries of London, Research Report 64.

—— 2002, *Farming in the First Millennium AD: British Agriculture Between Julius Caesar and William the Conquerer*. Cambridge: Cambridge University Press.

Fox, A. 1948–52, 'Report on the excavations at Milber Down, 1937–8', *Proceedings of the Devon Archaeological Exploration Society* IV, 27–78.

—— 1949, 'Sixteenth report on the early history of Devon', *Transactions of the Devonshire Association* LXXXI, 85–8.

—— 1954, 'Excavations at Kestor: an early Iron Age settlement near Chagford, Devon', *Report and Transactions of the Devonshire Association* 86, 21–62.

—— 1961, 'South-western hillfort', in S. Frere (eds.) *Problems of the Iron Age in Southern Britain*, London: University of London, Institute of Archaeology, 35–60.

—— 1996, *Prehistoric Hillforts in Devon*, Tiverton: Devon Books.

—— 2009, *A Lost Frontier Revealed: Regional Separation in the East Midlands*. Hatfield: University of Hertfordshire Press.

Fox, C. 1932, *The Personality of Britain*. Cardiff: The National Museum of Wales.

Fox, H. 1970, 'The boundary of Uplyme', *Report and Transactions of the Devonshire Association* 102, 35–47.

Fox, H. S. A. 1972, 'Field systems in the east and south of Devon', *Transactions of the Devonshire Association* 104, 81–135.

—— 1973, 'Outfield cultivation in Devon and Cornwall: a reinterpretation', in M. Havinden (ed.) *Husbandry and Marketing in the South-West 1500–1800*, Exeter: Exeter University Press, 190–38.

—— 1975, 'The chronology of enclosure and economic development in medieval Devon', *Economic History Review*, 2nd Series 28, 181–202.

—— 1981, 'Approaches to the adoption of the Midland system', in T. Rowley (ed.) 1981, 64–111.

—— 1983, 'Contraction: desertion and dwindling of dispersed settlement in a Devon parish', *Medieval Village Research Group Annual Report* 31, 40–2.

Fox, H. S. A. 1989a, 'Peasant farmers, patterns of settlement and pays: transformations in the landscapes of Devon and Cornwall', in R. A. Higham (ed.), *Landscape and Townscape in the South West*, Exeter: University of Exeter Press, 41–75.

—— 1989b, 'The people of the wolds in English settlement history', in M. Aston, D. Austin, and C. Dyer (eds.) *The Rural Settlements of Medieval England*, Oxford: Blackwell, 77–101.

—— 1991a, 'Occupation of the Land: Devon and Cornwall', in E. Miller (ed.) *The Agrarian History of England and Wales* 3, *1348–1500*, Cambridge: Cambridge University Press, 152–74.

—— 1991b, 'Farming practice and techniques: Devon and Cornwall', in E. Miller (ed.) *The Agrarian History of England and Wales* 3, *1348–1500*, Cambridge: Cambridge University Press, 303–23.

—— 1991c, 'Tenant farming and farmers: Devon and Cornwall', in E. Miller (ed.) *The Agrarian History of England and Wales* 3, *1348–1500*, Cambridge: Cambridge University Press, 722–43.

—— 1994, 'Medieval Dartmoor as seen through its account rolls', *Proceedings of the Devon Archaeological Society* 52, 149–72.

—— 1996a, *Seasonal Settlement*. Vaughan Papers in Adult Education No. 39. Leicester: University of Leicester, Department of Adult Education.

—— 1996b, 'Introduction: transhumance and seasonal settlement', in H. S. A. Fox (ed.), 1–23.

Fox, H. 1999, 'Medieval farming and rural settlement', in R. Kain and W. Ravenhill (eds.), 273–80.

—— 2001, *The Evolution of the Fishing Village: Landscape and Society Along the South Devon Coast, 1086–1550*, Oxford: Leopard's Head Press.

—— 2007, 'Two Devon Estuaries in the Middle Ages: fisheries, ports, fortifications and places or worship', *Landscapes* 8(i), 39–68.

Fox, H. S. A. (edited by Tompkins, M. and Dyer, C.) forthcoming, *Dartmoor's Alluring Uplands: Transhumance and Pastoral Management in the Middle Ages*, Exeter: University of Exeter Press.

—— and Padel, O. 2000, *The Cornish Lands of the Arundells of Lanherne, Fourteenth to Sixteenth Centuries*. Devon and Cornwall Records Society 41. Exeter: Devon and Cornwall Records Society.

Francis, P. D. and Slater, D. S. 1990, 'A Record of Vegetational and Land Use Change from Upland Peat Deposits on Exmoor Part 2: Hoar Moor'. *Proceedings of the Somerset Archaeological and Natural History Society* 134, 1–26.

—— —— 1992, 'A Record of Vegetational and Land Use Change from Upland Peat Deposits on Exmoor Part 3: Codsend Moors', *Proceedings of the Somerset Archaeological and Natural History Society* 136, 9–28.

Franklin, L. 2006, 'Imagined landscapes: archaeology, perception and folklore in the study of medieval Devon', in S. Turner (ed.) 2006b, 144–61.

Freeman, J. 2008, 'The name of the Magonsaete', in O. J. Padel and D. Parsons (eds.) *A Commodity of Good Names: Essays in Honour of Margaret Gelling*, Donington: Shaun Tyas, 101–16.

French, C., Lewis, H., Allen, M., and Scaife, R. 2000, 'Palaeoenvironmental and archaeological investigations on Wyke Down and in the upper Allen Valley,

Cranborne Chase, Dorset, England', *Proceedings of the Dorset Natural History and Archaeological Society* 122, 39–44.

—— —— —— ——and Green, M. 2003, 'Archaeological and palaeoenvironmental investigations of the upper Allen Valley, Cranborne Chase, Dorset (1998–2000): a new model of earlier Holocene landscape development', *Proceedings of the Prehistoric Society* 69, 201–34.

Fulford, M. G. 2006, 'Corvées and *civitates*', in R. J. A. Wilson (ed.) *Romanitas: Essays on Roman Archaeology in Honour of Shepherd Frere on the Occasion of His Ninetieth Birthday*. Oxford: Oxbow, 65–71.

——, Powell, A. B., Entwistle, R., and Raymond, F. 2006, *Iron Age and Romano-British Settlements and Landscapes of Salisbury Plain*, Salisbury: Wessex Archaeology Report 20.

Fyfe, R. M. 2000, 'Palaeochannels of the Exe Catchment: Their Age and an Assessment of their Archaeological and Palaeoenvironmental Potential'. Unpublished PhD, University of Exeter.

——, Brown, A. G., and Rippon, S. J. 2003, 'Mid to Late-Holocene vegetation history of Greater Exmoor, UK: estimating the spatial extent of human-induced vegetation change', *Vegetation History and Archaeobotany* 12, 215–32.

—— —— —— 2004, 'Characterising the late prehistoric, "Romano-British" and medieval landscape, and dating the emergence of a regionally distinct agricultural system in South West Britain', *Journal of Archaeological Science* 31, 1699–1714.

—— ——and Coles, B.J. 2003, 'Mesolithic to Bronze Age vegetation change and human activity in the Exe Valley, Devon, UK', *Proceedings of the Prehistoric. So*c*i*ety 69, 161–81.

——and Rippon, S. J. 2004, 'A landscape in transition? Palaeoenvironmental evidence for the end of the "Romano-British" period in South West England', in R. Collins and J. Gerrard (eds.) 2004, 33–42.

Gallant, L., Luxton, N., and Collman, M. 1985, 'Ancient Fields on the South Devon Limestone Plateau', *Proceedings of the Devon Archaeological Society* 43, 23–37.

——and Silvester, R. J. 1985, 'An excavation on the Iron Age hillfort at Berry Down, Newton Abbot', *Proceedings of the Devon Archaeological Society* 43, 39–49.

Gardiner, J., Allen, M. J., Hamilton-Dyer, S., Laidlaw, M., and Scaife, R.G. 2002, 'Making the most of it: late prehistoric pastoralism in the Avon Levels, Severn Estuary', *Proceedings of the Prehistoric Society* 68, 1–39.

Gaskill Brown, C. 1986, *Plymouth Excavations: The Medieval Waterfront Woolster Street: The Finds*. Plymouth: Plymouth Museum Archaeological Series No. 3.

Gater, J., Leech, R. H., and Riley, H. 1993, 'Later prehistoric and Romano-British settlement sites in South Somerset: some recent work', *Somerset Archaeology and Natural History* 137, 41–58.

Gearey, B. and Charman, D. 1996, 'Rough Tor, Bodmin Moor: testing some archaeological hypotheses with landscape palaeoecology', in D. J. Charman, R. M. Newnham and D. G. Croot (eds.) *Devon and East Cornwall Field Guide*, London: Quaternary Research Association, 101–19.

Gearey, B. R., Charman, D. J., and Kent, M. 2000a, 'Palaeoecological evidence for the prehistoric settlement of Bodmin Moor, Cornwall, Southwest England. Part I: the status of woodland and early human impacts', *Journal of Archaeological Science* 27(5), 423–38.

Gearey, B. R., Charman, D. J., and Kent, M. 2000b, 'Palaeoecological evidence for the prehistoric settlement of Bodmin Moor, Cornwall, Southwest England. Part II: landuse changes from the Neolithic to the present', *Journal of Archaeological Science* 27(6), 423–38.

——, West, S., and Charman, D. J. 1997, 'The landscape context of medieval settlement on the South-Western Moors of England. Recent palaeoenvironmental evidence from Bodmin Moor and Dartmoor', *Medieval Archaeology* XLI, 195–209.

Gelling, M. 1978, *Signposts to the Past*. London: Dent.

—— 1984, *Place-Names in the Landscape*. London: Dent.

—— 1989, 'The early history of western Mercia', in S. Bassett (ed.) 1989a, 184–201.

—— and Cole, A. 2000, *The Landscape of Place-Names*. Stamford: Shaun Tyas.

Gent, T. H. and Quinnell, H. 1999a, 'Excavation of a causewayed enclosure and hillfort on Raddon Hill, Stockleigh Pomeroy', *Proceedings of the Devon Archaeological Society* 57, 1–75.

—— —— 1999b, 'Salvage recording on the Neolithic site at Haldon Belvedere', *Proceedings of the Devon Archaeological Society* 57, 77–104.

Gerrard, C. with Aston, M. 2007, *The Shapwick Project, Somerset: A Rural Landscape Explored*. Leeds: Society for Medieval Archaeology Monograph 25.

Gerrard, J. 2004a, 'Bradley Hill, Somerset, and the end of Roman Britain: A study in continuity', *Somerset Archaeology and Natural History* 148, 1–9.

—— 2004b, 'How late is late? Black Burnished Ware and the fifth century', in R. Collins and J. Gerrard (eds.) 2004, 65–75.

—— 2007, 'Establishing an absolute chronology for the demolition of the temple of *Sulis Minerva* at Bath', *Antiquaries Journal* 87, 148–64.

—— 2008, 'Feeding the army from Dorset: pottery, salt and the Roman state', in S. Stallibrass and R. Thomas (eds.) *Feeding the Roman Army: The Archaeology of Production and Supply in North West Europe*. Oxford: Oxbow Books, 116–27.

—— 2010, 'Finding the fifth century: A late fourth- and early fifth-century pottery fabric from south-east Dorset', *Britannia* 41, 293–312.

Gerrard, S. 1997, *Dartmoor*. London: English Heritage.

—— 2000, *The Early British Tin Industry*. Stroud: Tempus.

Gibson, A. 1992, 'The excavation of an Iron Age settlement at Gold Park, Dartmoor', *Proceedings of the Devon Archaeological Society* 50, 19–46.

Gibson, E. 1695, *Camden's Britannia, Newly Translated into English; with Additions and Improvements*, London (reprinted by Times Newspapers Limited, 1971).

Gillard, M. 2002, 'The Medieval Landscape of the Exmoor Region; enclosure and settlement in an upland fringe'. Unpublished thesis, University of Exeter.

Gingell, C. J. and Gingell, J. H. 1981, 'Excavation of a medieval "highworth circle" at Stratton St Margaret', *Wiltshire Archaeological and Natural History Magazine* 74/75, 61–8.

Glasscock, R. 1975, *The Lay Subsidy of 1334*. London: British Academy, Records of Social and Economic History, New Series II.

Godden, D., Hamilton-Dyer, S., Laidlaw, M., and Mepham, L. 2002, 'Excavations of Saxon pits at Tidworth, 1999', *Wiltshire Archaeological and Natural History Magazine* 95, 240–9.

Gonner, E. C. K. 1912, *Common Land and Enclosure*. London: Macmillan.

Goodier, A. 1984, 'The formation of boundaries in Anglo-Saxon England: a statistical study', *Medieval Archaeology* 28, 1–21.

Gossip, J. and Jones, A. M. 2007, *Archaeological Investigations of a Later Prehistoric and a Romano-British Landscape at Tremough, Penryn, Cornwall*. Oxford: British Archaeological Report 0073, British Series, 443.

Gover, J. E. B., Mawer, A., and Stenton, F. M. 1931, *The Place-Names of Devon, part I*. Cambridge: English Place-Names Society Volume VIII.

—— —— —— 1932, *The Place-Names of Devon, part II*. Cambridge: English Place-Names Society Volume IX.

Graham, A. 2005, 'Evidence for the medieval hamlets of Pykesash and Ash Boulogne: archaeological excavation at Ash', *Somerset Archaeology and Natural History* 148, 11–40.

—— 2006, *The Excavation of Five Beaker Burials, The Iron Age and Romano-British Settlements, and the 4th century Courtyard Villa at Barton Field, Tarrant Hinton, Dorset*. Dorset Natural History and Archaeological Society Monograph Series No. 17. Dorchester: Dorset Natural History and Archaeological Society.

Graham, A. H. and Mills, J. M. 1996, 'A Romano-British building at Crimbleford Knap, Seavington St Mary', *Proceedings of the Somerset Archaeological and Natural History* 139, 119–34.

—— and Davies, S. M. 1993, *Excavations in Trowbridge, Wiltshire, 1977 and 1986–88*, Salisbury: Wessex Archaeology Report No. 2.

—— and Newman, C. 1993, 'Recent excavations of Iron Age and Romano-British enclosures in the Avon Valley, Wiltshire', *Wiltshire Archaeological and Natural History Society Magazine* 86, 8–57.

Grant, A. 1988, 'Animal resources', in G. Astill and A. Grant (eds.) *The Countryside of Medieval England*, Oxford: Basil Blackwell Ltd, 149–87.

—— 1989, 'Animals in Roman Britain', in M. Todd (ed.) *Research on Roman Britain 1960–89*, Britannia Monograph Series 11, 135–46. London: Society for the Promotion of Roman Studies.

Grant, N. 1995, 'The occupation of hillforts in Devon during the late Roman and post Roman period', *Proceedings of the Devon Archaeological Society* 53, 97–108.

Gray, H. L. 1915, *English Field Systems*. Cambridge, Massachusetts: Harvard University Press.

Gray, T. 1997, *Travels in Georgian Devon: the Illustrated Journals of the Reverend John Swete, 1789–1800*, Tiverton: Halsgrove and Devon Books.

Gregson, N. 1986, 'The multiple estate model: some critical questions', *Journal of Historical Geography* 11, 352–63.

Green, F. G. 1981, 'Iron Age, Roman and Saxon crops: the archaeological evidence from Wessex', in M. Jones and G. Dimbleby (eds.) *The Environment of Man: The Iron Age to the Anglo-Saxon Period*, Oxford: British Archaeological Reports, British Series 87, 129–53.

Green, F. G. 1996, 'Cereals and plant food: a reassessment of the Saxon economic evidence from Wessex', in J. Rackham (ed.) *Environment and Economy in Anglo-Saxon England*. York: Council for British Archaeology Research Report 89, 83–8.

Green, J. P. 1979, 'Citizen House', in B. Cunliffe (ed.) *Excavations in Bath 1950–1975*. Bristol: Committee for Rescue Archaeology in Avon, Gloucestershire and Somerset, 4–70.

Griffith, F. M. 1984, 'Roman military sites in Devon: some recent discoveries', *Proceedings of the Devon Archaeological Society* 42, 11–32.

—— 1985, 'Some newly discovered ritual monuments in mid Devon', *Proceedings of the Prehistoric Society* 51, 310–15.

—— 1986, 'Salvage observations at Bantham Ham, Thurlestone, in 1982', *Proceedings of the Devon Archaeological Society* 44, 39–58.

Griffith, F. 1988a, 'A Romano-British villa near Crediton', *Proceedings of the Devon Archaeological Society* 46, 137–42.

—— 1988b, *Devon's Past*. Exeter: Devon Books.

Griffith, F. M. 1994, 'Changing perceptions of the context of prehistoric Dartmoor', *Proceedings of the Devon Archaeological Society* 52, 85–99.

—— and Horner, B. 2000, 'Aerial reconnaissance in Somerset', in C. J. Webster (ed.) 2000b, 7–14.

Griffith, F. and Quinnell, H. 1999, 'Barrows and ceremonial sites in the Neolithic and Bronze Age', in R. Kain and W. Ravenhill (eds.) 1999, 55–61.

Griffith, F. M. and Reed, S. J. 1998, 'Rescue recording at Bantham Ham, South Devon, in 1997', *Proceedings of the Devon Archaeological Society* 56, 109–31.

Griffith, F. and Weddell, P. 1996, 'Ironworking in the Blackdown Hills: results of recent survey', in P. Newman (ed.) *The Archaeology of Mining and Metallurgy in South West Britain*, Matlock: Peak District Mines Historical Society/Historical Metallurgy Society, 27–34.

Grimm, J. 2008a, 'Animal Bone', in M. Leivers and C. Moore, *Archaeology on the A303 Stonehenge Improvement* (Salisbury: Wessex Archaeology, <http://www.wessex-arch.co.uk/projects/wiltshire/A303>)

—— 2008b, 'Wilton: Animal Bone Report'. Unpublished report.

Grimm, J. M. no date, 'Suburban Life in Roman Durnovaria: Additional Specialist report—Environmental Animal Bone'. <http://www.wessexarch.co.uk/files/projects/dorchester_county_hospital/07_Animal_bone.pdf>

—— 2008, 'Poundbury: Animal Bone Report (60024)'. Unpublished report, Wessex Archaeology.

Grove, J. C. 2006, 'Archaeological recording at the Kings of Wessex School playing fields, Cheddar', *Proceedings of the Somerset Archaeological and Natural History Society* 150, 182–6.

Groves, C. 2005, *Dendrochronological Research in Devon Phase 1*. English Heritage, Centre for Archaeology Report 56/2005.

Grundy, G. B. 1919, 'The Saxon Land Charters of Wiltshire', *Archaeological Journal*, 2nd Series, XXVI, 143–301.

—— 1920, 'The Saxon Land Charters of Wiltshire', *Archaeological Journal*, 2nd Series, XXVII, 8–126.

Hall, D. 1981, 'The origins of open field agriculture: the archaeological fieldwork evidence', in T. Rowley (ed.) 1981, 22–38.
Hall, L. J. 1983 *The Rural Houses of North Avon and South Gloucestershire 1400–1720*. Bristol: City of Bristol Museum and Art Gallery Monograph 6.
Hall, T. A. 2000, *Minster Churches in the Dorset Landscape*. Oxford: British Archaeological Reports, British Series 304.
Hamer, J. H. 1968, 'Trading at Saint White Down Fair, 1637–1649', *Proceedings of the Somerset Archaeological and Natural History Society* 112, 61–70.
Hamerow, H. 2002, *Early Medieval Settlement*. Oxford: Oxford University Press.
Hanson, L., and Wickham, C. (eds.) 2000, *The Long Eighth Century: Production, Distribution and Demand*, Leiden: Brill.
Harding, P. A. and Lewis, C. 1997, 'Archaeological excavations at Tockenham, 1994', *Wiltshire Archaeological and Natural History Magazine* 90, 26–41.
——, Mepham, L., and Smith, R. J. C. 1995, 'Excavation of 12th and 13th century deposits at Howard's Lane, Wareham', *Proceedings of the Dorset Natural History and Archaeological Society* 117, 81–90.
Harke, H. 2002, 'Kings and warriors', in P. Slack and R. Ward (eds.) *The Peopling of Britain*. Oxford: Oxford University Press, 145–75.
Harry, R. and Morris, C. D. 1997, 'Excavations on the Lower Terrace, Site C, Tintagel Island 1990–94', *Antiquaries Journal* 77, 1–143.
Harvey, J. H. 1969, *William of Worcester Itineraries*. Oxford: Clarendon Press.
Harvey, P. D. A. 1989, 'Initiative and authority in settlement change', in M. Aston, D. Austin, and C. Dyer (eds.) *The Rural Settlements of Medieval England*, Oxford: Blackwells, 31–43.
Harvey, S. P. J. 1985, 'Taxation and the ploughland' in P. H. Sawyer (ed.) *Domesday Book: a Re-Assessment*. London: Edward Arnold, 86–103.
Hase, P. H. 1988, 'The mother churches of Hampshire', in J. Blair (ed.) *Minsters and Parish Churches: The Local Church in Transition 950–1200*, Oxford: Oxford University Committee for Archaeology, monograph 17, 45–66.
—— 1994, 'The Church in the Wessex Heartlands', in M. Aston and C. Lewis (eds.) *The Medieval Landscape of Wessex*. Oxford: Oxbow Books, 47–81.
Haslam, J. 1980, 'A Middle Saxon iron smelting site at Ramsbury, Wiltshire', *Medieval Archaeology* XXIV, 1–68.
—— 1984, 'The towns in Wiltshire', in J. Haslam (ed.) *Anglo-Saxon Towns in Southern England*, Chichester: Phillimore, 87–147.
Haslett, S. K., Davies, P., Curr, R. H. F., Davies, C. F. C., Kennington, K., King, C. P., and Margetts, A. J. 1998, 'Evaluating late-Holocene relative sea level change in the Somerset levels, southwest England', *The Holocene* 8(ii), 197–207.
—— ——, Davies, C. F. C., Margetts, A. J., Scotney, K. H., Thorpse, D. J., and Williams, H. O. 2000, 'The changing estuarine environment in relation to Holocene sea-level and the archaeological implications', *Archaeology in the Severn Estuary* 11, 35–53.
—— —— 2002, 'Holocene lithostratigraphy and coastal change in the Somerset Levels: evidence from Nyland Hill, Axe Valley, Somerset', *Bath Spa University College Occasional Papers in Geography* 2, 37–43.

Haslett, S. K., Howard, K. L., Margetts, A. J., and Davies, P. 2000, 'Holocene stratigraphy and evolution of the northern coastal plain of the Somerset Levels, UK', *Proceedings of the Cotteswold Naturalists Field Club* XLII(i), 78–88.

——, Davies, P., Eales, C. P., Vowles, E. M., and Williams, H. O. 2006, 'Variability in the Holocene lithostratigraphy of the Somerset Levels, UK', in C. O. Hunt and S. K. Haslett (eds.) *Quaternary of Somerset: Field Guide*, London: Quaternary Research Association, 44–52.

Hatcher, J. 1970, *Rural Economy and Society in the Dutchy of Cornwall 1300–1500*. Cambridge: Cambridge university Press.

Hatton, J. and Caseldine, C. 1991, 'Vegetation change and land use history during the first millennium AD at Aller Farm, East Devon as indicated by pollen analysis', *Proceedings of the Devon Archaeological Society* 49, 115–21.

Hawkins, C. 2005, 'Vegetation History and Land Use Change over the Past 10,000 Years in Three Study Areas of Lowland Devon: the Blackdown Hills, the Clyst Valley and Hartland Peninsula'. Unpublished PhD, University of Exeter.

Hayfield, C. 1987, *An Archaeological Survey of the Parish of Wharram Percy, East Yorkshire 1. The Evolution of the Roman Landscape*. Oxford: British Archaeological reports, British series, 172.

Hearne, C. M. and Birbeck, V. 1999, *A35 Tolpuddle to Puddletown Bypass DBFO, Dorset, 1996–8, Incorporating Excavations at Tolpuddle Ball 1993*. Salisbury: Wessex Archaeology.

——and Seager Smith, R. 1995, 'A Middle Iron Age and Roman site at Aller Cross, Kingskerswell, 1993', *Devon Archaeological Society Proceedings* 53, 109–20.

Heaton, M. J. 1992, 'Two mid-Saxon grain driers and later medieval features at Chantry Fields, Gillingham, Dorset', *Proceedings of the Dorset Natural History and Archaeological Society* 114, 97–126.

Henderson, C. G. and Weddell, P. J. 1994, 'Medieval settlement on Dartmoor and in West Devon: the evidence from excavations', *Proceedings of the Devon Archaeological Society* 52, 119–40.

Henig, M. 2006, 'Neither baths nor baptistries', *Oxford Journal of Archaeology* 25(i), 105–7.

Herring, P. 1998, *Cornwall's Historic Landscape: presenting a method of historic landscape character assessment*. Truro: Cornwall Archaeological Unit.

——1999, 'Cornwall: how the Historic Landscape Characterisation methodology was developed', in G. Fairclough (ed.) *Historic Landscape Characterisation: Papers Presented at an English Heritage Seminar, 11th December 1998*. London: English Heritage, 15–32.

——2006a, 'Cornish strip fields', in S. Turner (ed.) 2006b, 44–77.

——2006b, 'Cornish medieval field, a case-study: Brown Willy', in S. Turner (ed.) 2006b, 78–103.

——2009, 'Early medieval transhumance in Cornwall, Great Britain', in, J. Klápště and P. Sommer (eds.) *Medieval Rural Settlement in Marginal Landscapes*, Ruralia VII, Turnhout: Brepols, 47–56.

——and Hooke, D. 1993, 'Interrogating Anglo-Saxons in St Dennis', *Cornish Archaeology* 32, 67–76.

——, Sharpe, A., Smith, J. R., and Giles, C. 2008, *Bodmin Moor: An Archaeological Survey Volume 2—The Industrial and Post Medieval Landscapes*. Swindon: English Heritage.

Hey, G. 2004, *Yarnton: Saxon and Medieval Settlement and Landscape. Results of Excavations 1990–96*, Oxford: Oxford Archaeology Thames Valley Landscapes Monogr. No. 20.

Higbee, L. 2003, 'An assessment of the Animal Bone from Excavations at Bleak Bridge, Huntspill, Somerset'. Unpublished Report, Somerset County Council Historic Environment Record.

——2008, 'Mendip Avenue, Shepton Mallet: The Animal Bones'. Unpublished Report, supplied by Charles and Nancy Hollinrake.

Higham, N. 1990, 'Settlement, Land Use and Domesday ploughlands', *Landscape History* 12, 33–44.

——1992, *Rome, Britain and the Anglo-Saxons*. London: Seaby.

Higham, R. A., Allan, J. P., and Blaylock, S. R. 1982, 'Excavations at Okehampton Castle, Devon: Part 2: the bailey', *Proceedings of the Devon Archaeological Society* 40, 19–152.

Higham, R. 2008, *Making Anglo-Saxon Devon*. Exeter: The Mint Press.

Hill, D. and Worthington, M. 2003, *Offa's Dyke: History and Guide*. Stroud: Tempus.

Hill, J. D. 1995, *Ritual and Rubbish in the Iron Age of Wessex: A Study on the Formation of a Specific Archaeological Record*. Oxford: British Archaeological Reports, British Series, 242.

Hills, C. 2009, 'Anglo-Saxon DNA', in D. Sayer and H. Williams (eds.) *Mortuary Practices and Social Identities in the Middle Ages: Essays in Burial Archaeology in Honour of Heinrich Härke*. Exeter: University of Exeter Press, 123–40.

Hinton, D. A. 1997, 'The "Scole-Dickleburgh system" examined', *Landscape History* 19, 5–12.

Holbrook, N. 1987, 'Trial excavations at Honeyditches and the nature of the Roman occupation at Seaton', *Proceedings of the Devon Archaeological Society* 59, 149–58.

——2001, 'Coastal trade around the South-West peninsula of Britain in the late Roman period: a summary of the evidence', *Proceedings of the Devon Archaeological Society* 45, 59–74.

——and Bidwell, P. T. 1991, *Roman Finds from Exeter*, Exeter: Exeter Archaeological Reports 4.

Homans, G. C. 1941, *English Villagers of the Thirteenth Century*. Cambridge, Massachusetts: Harvard University Press.

——1969, 'The explanation of English regional differences', *Past and Present* 42, 18–34.

Hooke, D. 1990, *Worcestershire Anglo-Saxon Charter Bounds*. Woodbridge: Boydell.

——1994, *The Pre-Conquest Charter-Bounds of Devon and Cornwall*. Woodbridge: Boydell.

——1998, *The Landscape of Anglo-Saxon England*. London: Leicester University Press.

——1999, 'Saxon conquest and settlement', in R. Kain and W. Ravenhill (eds.), 1999, 95–104.

Hooke, D. 2008, 'Early medieval woodland and the place-name term *lēah*', in O. J. Padel and D. Parsons (eds) *A Commodity of Good Names: Essays in Honour of Margaret Gelling*, Donington: Shaun Tyas, 365–766.

Horner, W. S. 1993, 'A Romano-British enclosure at Butland farm, Modbury', *Proceedings of the Devon Archaeological Society* 51, 210–15.

Horner, W. 2006, 'What's under your school?', *Devon Archaeological Society Newsletter*, 94, 1–2.

Hoskins, W. G. 1952, 'The making of the agrarian landscape', in W.G. Hoskins and H. P. R. Finberg, *Devonshire Studies*, London: Jonathan Cape, 289–334.

—— 1953, 'The rebuilding of rural England, 1570–1640', *Past and Present* 4, 44–59.

—— 1954, *Devon*. London: Collins.

—— 1955, *The Making of the English Landscape*, London: Hodder and Stoughton.

Hosteller, E. and Noble Howe, T. 1997, *The Romano-British Villa at Castle Copse, Great Bedwyn*. Bloomington and Indianapolis [USA]: Indiana University Press.

Houlder, C. H. 1963, 'A Neolithic Settlement on Hazard Hill, Totnes', *Proceedings of the Devon Archaeological Society* 21, 2–30.

Housley, R. A., Straker, V., Chambers, F. M., and Lageard, J. G. A. 2007, 'An Ecological Context for the Post-Roman Archaeology of the Somerset Moors (South West England, UK)', *Journal of Wetland Archaeology* 7, 1–22.

Humphreys, C. and Rippon, S. 2006, 'The vernacular buildings', in S. Rippon 2006, *Landscape Community and Colonisation: The North Somerset Levels during the 1st and 2nd millennia AD*, York: Council for British Archaeology Research Report, 154–81.

Hurst, H. R., Dartnall, D. L., and Fisher, C. 1987, 'Excavations at Box Roman Villa, 1967–8', *Wiltshire Archaeological and Natural History Magazine* 81, 19–51.

Hurst, J. D. and Wacher, J. S. 1986, 'A multi-period site at Poxwell, Dorset', *Proceedings of the Dorset Natural History and Archaeological Society* 108, 63–80.

Hutcheson, A. and Andrews, P. 2002, 'Excavations at the County Hotel, Taunton, 1995–6', *Proceedings of the Somerset Archaeological and Natural History Society* 144, 139–63.

Ingrem, C. no date, 'Dorchester Hospital, Dorchester', <http://wac.soton.ac.uk/Centres/CAAA/Facilities/sites/Dorchester%20Hospital.html>

Ingrem, C. forthcoming, 'The animal bone from Romano-British deposits at Atlantic Road, Newquay, Cornwall', in A, Reynolds. 'Excavations at Atlantic Road, Newquay', *Cornish Archaeology*.

Institute of Geological Sciences 1979, *Geological Map of the United Kingdom South, 3rd Edition Solid*. London: Institute of Geological Sciences.

Jackson, R. 2007, *A Roman Settlement and Medieval Manor House in South Bristol: Excavations at Inns Court, Bristol*, Bristol and Region Archaeological Services.

Jarvis, K. 1976, 'The M5 Motorway and the Peamore/Pocombe Link', *Proceedings of the Devon Archaeological Society* 34, 41–72.

Jarvis, K. S. 1983, *Excavations in Christchurch 1969–1980*. Dorchester: Dorset Natural History and Archaeological Society monograph 5.

Jarvis, K. and Maxfield, V. 1975, 'The excavation of a first century Roman farmstead and a late Neolithic settlement, Topsham, Devon', *Proceedings of the Devon Archaeological Society* 33, 209–65.

Jeffries, J. S. 1974, 'An excavation at the coastal promontory fort on Embury Beacon, Devon', *Proceedings of the Prehistoric Society* 40, 136–56.

Johnson, D. A., Moore, C., and Fasham, P. N. 1998–9, 'Excavations at Penhale Round, Fraddon, Cornwall', *Cornish Archaeology* 37–8, 72–120.

Johnson, M. 1993a, *Housing Culture: Traditional Architecture in an English Landscape*. London: UCL Press.

—— 1993b, 'Rethinking the Great Rebuilding', *Oxford Journal of Archaeology* 12(i), 117–25.

—— 1997, 'Vernacular architecture: the loss of innocence', *Vernacular Architecture* 28, 13–19.

—— 2007, *Ideas of Landscape*, Oxford: Blackwell Publishing.

—— 2010, *English Houses 1300–1800*. Harlow: Pearson Education.

Johnson, N. and Rose, P. 1994, *Bodmin Moor: An Archaeological Survey*, volume 1, London: English Heritage.

Jones, A.M. 1998–9, 'The excavation of a Later Bronze Age structure at Callestick', *Cornish Archaeology* 37–8, 5–55.

—— 2000–1, 'The excavation of a multi-period site at Stencoose, Cornwall', *Cornish Archaeology* 39–40, 45–94.

—— 2008, 'Houses for the dead and cairns for the living: a reconsideration of the Early to Middle Bronze Age transition in south-west England', *Oxford Journal of Archaeology* 27(ii), 153–74.

—— 2010, '"Misplaced monuments?" A review of ceremony and monumentality in first millennium cal. BC Cornwall', *Oxford Journal of Archaeology* 29(i), 203–28.

—— forthcoming, 'Without Wessex: the local character of the Early Bronze Age in the South West', in S. Pearce (ed.) *The Archaeology of South Western Britain: Recent Research Papers in Honour of Henrietta Quinnell*, Oxford: British Archaeological Reports (British Series).

—— and Taylor, S. R., 2010, *Scarcewater, Pennance, Cornwall, archaeological excavation of a Bronze Age and Roman landscape*, Oxford: BAR, Brit Ser 516.

Jones, B. and Mattingly, D. 1990, *An Atlas of Roman Britain*, Oxford: Blackwell.

Jones, G. R. J. 1979, 'Multiple estates and early settlement', in P. H. Sawyer (ed.) *English Medieval Settlement*, London: Edward Arnold, 9–34.

—— 1985, 'Multiple estates perceived', *Journal of Historical Geography* 11(iv), 339–51.

Jones, J. n.d., 'Charred Plant Remains from Shapwick Roman Villa, Somerset'. Unpublished Report.

—— 1998a, 'Waterlogged and Charred Plant Macrofossils from Brean Down'. Unpublished Report.

—— 1998b, 'Charred Plant Macrofossils from Fosse lane, Shepton Mallet, Somerset'. Unpublished Report.

—— 2001a, 'Charred Plant Remains from Gaffers, Membury, Devon'. Unpublished report.

—— 2001b, 'Charred Plant Remains from Dukes Break, Latton, Wiltshire'. Unpublished report.

—— 2002, 'Plant Macrofossil Assessment from "The Laurels", Meare, Somerset'. Unpublished report.

Jones, J. 2003, 'Charred Plant Remains from Bleak Bridge, Somerset'. Unpublished Report.

—— 2004, 'Charred Plant Macrofossil Assessment from Digby Drive, Exeter'. Unpublished Report.

—— forthcoming, 'Charred plant remains', in A. Lawson-Jones, 'Smithing in the round, pipeline excavation at Little Quoit Farm, St Columb Major, Cornwall', *Cornish Archaeology*.

Jones, M. 1981, 'The development of crop husbandry', in M. Jones and G. Dimbleby (eds.) *The Environment of Man: The Iron Age to the Anglo-Saxon Period*, Oxford: British Archaeological Reports, British Series, 87, 95–128.

Jones, M.K. 1982, 'Crop production', in D. Miles (ed.) *The Romano-British Countryside*, Oxford: British Archaeological Reports, British Series, 103, 97–108.

—— 1989, 'Agriculture in Roman Britain: the dynamics', in M. Todd (ed.) *Recent Research on Roman Britain*, London: Society for the Promotion of Roman Studies, Britannia Monograph Series 11, 127–34.

—— 1991, 'Food Production—plants', in R. J. F. Jones (ed.) *Roman Britain: Recent Trends*, Sheffield: Department of Archaeology and Prehistory, University of Sheffield, 15–20.

Jones, R. and Page, M. 2006, *Medieval Villages in an English Landscape*. Macclesfield: Windgather Press.

Jope, E. M. 1963, 'The regional cultures of medieval Britain' in I. L. Foster and L. Alcock (eds.) *Culture and Environment: Essays in Honour of Sir Cyril Fox*, London: Kegan Paul, 327–50.

Joyce, S., Mudd, A., and Collard, M. 2010, *South-West Reinforcement Project. Ottery St Mary to Aylesbeare, Aylesbeare to Kenn, Fishacre to Choakford Gas Pipelines Devon. Post-Excavations Assessment and Updated Project Design Issue 2*. Cotswold Archaeology Report 09106.

Kain, R. J. P. 1979, 'Compiling an Atlas of Agriculture in England and Wales from the Tithe Survey', *The Geographical Journal* 145(2), 225–35.

—— 1986, *An Atlas and Index of the Tithe Files of Mid-Nineteenth Century England and Wales*, Cambridge: Cambridge University Press.

—— and Oliver, R. 1995, *The Tithe Maps of England and Wales: A Cartographic Analysis and County-by-County Catalogue*. Cambridge: Cambridge University Press.

—— —— 2001, *Historic Parishes of England and Wales*, Colchester: History Data Service (available online: <http://www.ahds.ac.uk/history/collections/hpew.htm>)

—— —— 2004, *The Enclosure Maps of England and Wales, 1595–1918*. Cambridge: Cambridge University Press.

Kain, R. and Ravenhill, W. (eds.) 1999, *Historical Atlas of South-West England*, Exeter: Exeter University Press.

Kerridge, E. 1967, *The Agricultural Revolution*. London: George Allen & Unwin Ltd.

Keynes, R. 1985, 'Excavations at Churchfields, Ansford, 1975–78', *Somerset Archaeology and Natural History* 129, 81–7.

King, A. 1989, 'Villas and animal bones', in K. Branigan and D. Miles (eds.) *The Economies of Romano-British Villas*, Sheffield: Department of Archaeology and Prehistory, University of Sheffield, 51–9.

—— 1991, 'Food production and consumption—meat', in R. F. J. Jones (ed.) *Roman Britain: Recent Trends*, Chichester: Wiley, 5–120.
King, A. C. 1999, 'Diet in the Roman world: a regional inter-site comparison of the mammal bones', *Journal of Roman Archaeology* 12, 168–202.
King, A. 2005, 'Animal remains from temples in Roman Britain', *Britannia* XXXVI, 329–70.
King, T., Thorpe, N., and Wilkinson, K. 2007, 'Southern Quantocks Archaeological Survey (Somerset, UK)', University of Winchester. <http://www2.winchester.ac.uk/archaeology/SQAS.htm> (accessed 13th April 2008).
Klápště, J. and Sommer, P. 2009, *Medieval Rural Settlement in Marginal Landscapes*. Turnhout: Brepols.
Klingelhöfer, E. C. 1992, *Manor, Vill and Hundred: The Development of Rural Institutions in Early Medieval Hampshire*. Toronto: Pontifical Institute of Medieval Studies, Studies and Texts 112.
Kowaleski, M. 1995, *Local Markets and Regional Trade in Medieval Exeter*. Cambridge: Cambridge University Press.
Ladle, L. and Woodward, A. 2009, *Excavations at Bestwall Quarry, Wareham 1992–2005*. Dorchester: Dorset Natural History and Archaeological Society Monograph Series No. 19.
Lake, J. and Edwards, B. 2006a, 'Farmsteads and landscape: towards an integrated view', *Landscapes* 7(i), 1–36.
—— —— 2006b, 'Buildings and place: farmsteads and the mapping of change', *Vernacular Architecture* 37, 33–49.
Lamb, H. H. 1982, *Climate, History and the Modern World*. London: Methuen.
Lambourne, A. 2008, 'A Puzzle Indeed. A Study of the Incidence and Origins of Regional Variation within the Historic Landscape of Southern England'. Unpublished PhD, University of Exeter.
—— 2010, *Patterning within the Historic Landscape and its Possible Causes*. Oxford: British Archaeological Reports, British Series 509.
Leach, P. J. 1977, 'Excavations at North Petherton, Somerset, 1975', *Proceedings of the Somerset Archaeological and Natural History Society* 121, 9–39.
—— 1982, *Ilchester Volume 1: Excavations 1974–75*. Bristol: Western Archaeological Trust monograph 3.
—— 1985, 'Westland', *Somerset Archaeology and Natural History* 129, 63–7.
Leach, P. 1984, *The Archaeology of Taunton: Excavations and Fieldwork to 1980*. Bristol: Western Archaeological Trust Monograph 8.
Leach, P. 1987, 'The hinterland of Ilchester: archaeology, alleviation and the environment', in N. D. Balaam, B. Levitan, and V. Straker (eds.) *Studies in Palaeoeconomy and Environment in South West England*, Oxford: British Archaeological Reports, British Series, 181, 115–24.
—— 1994, *Ilchester Volume 2: Archaeology, Excavations and Fieldwork to 1984*. Sheffield: Sheffield Excavation Reports No. 2.
—— 2001a, *Roman Somerset*. Wimborne: The Dovecote Press.
Leach, P. 2001b, *Excavation of a Romano-British Roadside Settlement in Somerset: Fosse Lane Shepton Mallet 1990*. Britannia Monograph Series No. 18. London: Society for the Promotion of Roman Studies.

—— 2003, 'Excavations at Hillyfields, Upper Holway, Taunton', *Somerset Archaeology and Natural History* 145, 57–82.

Leech, R. H. 1981: 'The excavation of a Romano-British farmstead and cemetery on Bradley Hill, Somerton, Somerset', *Britannia* 12, 177–252.

—— 1982a: 'The Roman interlude in the south-west: the dynamics of economic and social change in Romano-British south Somerset and north Dorset', in D. Miles (ed.) *The Romano-British Countryside*, Oxford: British Archaeological Reports, British Series, 103(i), 209–67.

—— 1982b: *Excavations at Catsgore 1970–73. A Romano-British village*, Bristol: Western Archaeological Trust monograph 2.

Leech, R. 1986, 'The excavation of a Romano-celtic temple and a later cemetery on Lamyatt Beacon, Somerset', *Britannia* XVII, 259–328.

Leivers, M., Chisham, C., Knight, S., and Stevens, C. 2007, 'Excavations at Ham Hill Quarry, Hamdon Hill, Montacute, 2002', *Somerset Archaeology and Natural History* 150, 39–62.

Lennard, R. 1932, 'English agriculture under Charles II: the evidence of the Royal Society's "Enquiries"', *Economic History Review* 4(1), 23–45.

Letters, S. 2004, *Online Gazetteer of Markets and Fairs in England and Wales to 1516* <http://www.history.ac.uk/cmh/gaz/gazweb2.html>

Levitan, B. 1987, 'Medieval animal husbandry in South West England: a selective review and suggested approach', in N. D. Balaam, B. Levitan, and V. Straker (eds.) *Studies in Palaeoeconomy and Environment in South West England*, Oxford: British Archaeological Reports, British Series, 181, 51–80.

Lewis, C., Mitchell-Fox, P., and Dyer, C. 1997, *Village, Hamlet and Field*. Manchester: Manchester University Press.

Light, T. and Ellis, P. 2009, *Bucknowle. A Romano-British Villa and its Antecedents: Excavations 1976–1991*. Dorchester: Dorset Natural History and Archaeology Society monograph 18.

Longcroft, A. 2007, 'The importance of place: placing vernacular buildings into a landscape context', in P. S. Barnwell and M. Palmer (eds.) *Post-Medieval Landscapes*. Macclesfield: Windgather Press, 23–38.

Longman, T. 2006, 'Iron Age and later defences at Malmesbury: excavations 1998–2000', *Wiltshire Archaeological and Natural History Magazine* 99, 104–64.

Lovell, J. 2006, 'Excavation of a Romano-British farmstead at RNAS Yeovilton', *Somerset Archaeology and Natural History* 149, 7–70.

Loyn, H. R. 1984, *The Governance of Anglo-Saxon England 500–1087*, London: Edward Arnold.

Lucas, R. N. 1993, *The Romano-British Villa at Halstock, Dorset: Excavations 1967–1985*. Dorset Natural History and Archaeological Society Monograph Series No. 13. Dorchester: Dorset Natural History and Archaeology Society.

Luscombe, P. 2005, 'Charters, place-names and Anglo-Saxon settlement in South Devon', *Report and Transactions of the Devonshire Association for the Advancement of Science* 137, 89–138.

Lyne, M. 2002, 'The Late Iron Age and Romano-British pottery production sites at Redcliff, Arne and Stoborough', *Proceedings of the Dorset Natural History and Archaeological Society* 124, 45–100.

Machin, R. 1977, 'The Great Rebuilding: a re-assessment', *Past and Present* 77, 33–6.

—— 1978, *The Houses of Yetminster*. Bristol: University of Bristol, Department of Extra Mural Studies.

Macklin, M. G., Bradley, S. B., and Hunt, C. O. 1985, 'Early mining in Britain: the stratigraphic implications of heavy metals in alluvial sediments', in N. R. J. Fieller, D. D. Gilbertson, and N. G. A. Ralph (eds.) *Palaeoenvironmental Investigations: Research Design, Methods and Data Analysis*, Oxford: British Archaeological Reports, International Series, 258, 45–54.

—— and Hunt, C. O. 1988, 'Late Quaternary alleviation and valley floor development in the upper Axe Valley, Mendip, South West England', *Proceedings of the Geologist's Association* 99(i), 29–40.

Mackney, D. 1979, *Soil Survey of England and Wales Map of Land Use Capability*. Southampton: Ordnance Survey for the Soil Survey of England and Wales.

——, Hodgson, J. M., Hollis, J. M., and Staines, S. J. 1983, *Legend for the 1:250,000 Soil Map of England and Wales*, Harpenden: Soil Survey of England and Wales.

Maguire, D., Ralph, N., and Fleming, A. 1983, 'Early land use on Dartmoor: palaeobotanical and pedological investigations on Holne Moor', in M. Jones (ed.) *Integrating the Subsistence Economy*, Oxford: British Archaeological Reports, British Series, 181, 57–106.

Malim, C. and Martin, A. 2007, 'A Romano-British roadside settlement on Chapperton Down, Salisbury Plain Training Area', *Wiltshire Archaeological and Natural History Society Magazine* 100, 104–30.

Maltby, M. 1979, *The Animal Bones from Exeter 1971–1975*. Sheffield: Exeter Archaeological Reports 2.

—— 1981, 'Iron Age, Romano-British and Anglo-Saxon animal husbandry: a review of faunal evidence', in M. Jones and G. Dimbleby (eds.) *The Environment of Man: The Iron Age to the Anglo-Saxon Period*, Oxford: British Archaeological Reports, British Series, 87, 155–204.

Manning, P. and Quinnell, H. 2009, 'Excavation and field survey at the Iron Age hillfort of Berry Ball, Crediton Hamlets', *Proceedings of the Devon Archaeological Society* 67, 99–132.

Marshall, W. 1808, *The Review and Abstract of the County Reports to the Board of Agriculture from the Several Agricultural Departments of England in Five Volumes. Volume the First: Northern Department*. London: Longman, Hurst, Rees, Orme and Brown.

—— 1809, *The Review and Abstract of the County Reports to the Board of Agriculture from the Several Agricultural Departments of England in Five Volumes. Volume the Second: Western Department*. London: Longman, Hurst, Rees, Orme and Brown.

—— 1811, *The Review and Abstract of the County Reports to the Board of Agriculture from the Several Agricultural Departments of England in Five Volumes. Volume the Third: Eastern Department*. London: Longman, Hurst, Rees, Orme and Brown.

—— 1815, *The Review and Abstract of the County Reports to the Board of Agriculture from the Several Agricultural Departments of England in Five Volumes. Volume* the Fourth: Midland Department. London: Longman, Hurst, Rees, Orme and Brown.

Marshall, W. 1817, *The Review and Abstract of the County Reports to the Board of Agriculture from the Several Agricultural Departments of England in Five Volumes. Volume the Fifth: Southern and Peninsular Department*. London: Longman, Hurst, Rees, Orme and Brown.

Marten, C. 1973, *The Devonshire Dialect*. Exeter: Clement Marten Publications.

Martin, E. and Satchell, M. 2008, *Wheare most Inclosures be. East Anglian Fields: History, Morphology and Management*. East Anglian Archaeology No. 124.

Mattingly, D. 2007, *An Imperial Possession: Britain in the Roman Empire*, London: Penguin Books.

Maxfield, V.A. 1986, 'Devon and the end of the Fosse Frontier', *Proceedings of the Devon Archaeological Society* 44, 1–9.

Mayes, J. and Wheeler, D. 1997, 'Regional perspectives on climatic variability and change', in D. Wheeler and J. Mayes (eds.) *Regional Climates in the British Isles*, London: Routledge, 279–331.

Mcdermott, M., and Berry, S. (eds.) 2011, *Edmund Rack's Survey of Somerset*. Taunton: Somerset Archaeological and Natural History Society.

Mcintosh, A., Samuels, M. L., and Benskin, M. 1986, *A Linguistic Atlas of Late Mediaeval English*. Aberdeen: Aberdeen University Press.

Mckinley, J. I. 1999, 'Further investigations of an Iron Age and Romano-British enclosed settlement at Figheldean, near Netheravon', *Wiltshire Archaeological and Natural History Society Magazine* 92, 7–32.

—— and Heaton, M. 1996, 'A Romano-British farmstead and associated burials at Maddington Farm, Shrewton', *Wiltshire Archaeological and Natural History Society Magazine* 89, 44–72.

Meaney, A. 1964, *A Gazetteer of Early Anglo-Saxon Burial Sites*. London: George Allen and Unwin Ltd.

Mercer, E. 1997, 'The unfulfilled wider implications of vernacular architecture studies', *Vernacular Architecture* 28, 9–12.

Mercer, R. 1970, 'Stannon Down', *Cornish Archaeology* 9, 17–46.

—— 1986, 'The Neolithic in Cornwall', *Cornish Archaeology* 25, 35–80.

Mercer, R. J. 1981, 'Excavations at Carn Brea, Illogan, Cornwall, 1970–73', *Cornish Archaeology* 20, 1–204.

Miles, H. 1975a, 'Excavations at Woodbury Castle, East Devon, 1971', *Proceedings of the Devon Archaeological Society* 33, 183–208.

—— 1975b, 'Barrows on the St Austell granite, Cornwall', *Cornish Archaeology* 14, 5–81.

Millett, M. 1990, *The Romanization of Britain*. Cambridge: Cambridge University Press.

Mills, A. D. 1971, *The Dorset Lay Subsidy Roll of 1332*. Dorset Records Society 4. Dorchester.

—— 1977, *The Place-Names of Dorset Volume I*. English Place-Name Society LII. Dorchester.

—— 1980, *The Place-Names of Dorset Volume II*. English Place-Name Society LIII. Dorchester.

—— 1989, *The Place-Names of Dorset Volume III*. English Place-Name Society LIX/LX. Dorchester.

—— 1991, *A Dictionary of English Place-Names*. Oxford: Oxford University Press.

Milward, J., Manning, A., Mepham, L., and Stephens, C.J. 2010, 'Medieval remains at Penning Road and St Andrews Road, Tidworth', *Wiltshire Archaeological and Natural History Magazine* 103, 181–5.

Ministry Of Agriculture, Fisheries And Food 1979, *Agricultural Land Classification of England and Wales*. Pinner: Ministry of Agriculture, Fisheries and Food.

Moore, P. D., Merryfield D. L., and Price, M. D. R. 1984, 'The vegetation and development of blanket mires', in P. D. Moore (ed.) *European Mires*, London: Academic Press, 203–35.

Moore, T. 1829, *The History of Devonshire*. London: Robert Jennings.

Morland, S. C. 1990, 'The Somerset hundreds in the Geld Inquest and their Domesday manors', *Somerset Archaeology and Natural History* 134, 95–140.

Morris, C. 1984, *The Illustrated Journeys of Celia Fiennes, c.1682–1712*, London: MacDonald and Co.

Morris, E. 1988, 'The Iron Age occupation at Dibbles Farm, Christon', *Somerset Archaeology and Natural History* 132, 23–81.

Morris, P. A. 1979, *Agricultural Buildings in Roman Britain*, Oxford: British Archaeological Reports, British Series, 70.

Morris, R. 1989, *Churches in the Landscape*, London: J. M. Dent and Sons.

Muir, R. 1999, *Approaches to Landscape*. Basingstoke: Macmillan Press.

Musty, J. and Algar, D. 1986, 'Excavations at the deserted medieval village of Gomeldon, near Salisbury', *Wiltshire Archaeological and Natural History Magazine* 80, 127–69.

Mynard, D. C. 1994, *Excavations on Medieval Sites in Milton Keynes*. Aylesbury: Buckinghamshire Archaeological Society.

Newman, C. 1993, 'A late Saxon cemetery at Templecombe', *Proceedings of the Somerset Archaeological and Natural History Society* 136, 61–72.

—— and Morris, E. L. 1999, 'Iron Age and Romano-British sites along the Bowden Reservoir link pipeline, South-East Somerset', *Somerset Archaeology and Natural History* 143, 1–27.

Nowakowski, J. 2001, 'Leaving home in the Cornish Bronze Age: insights into planned abandonment processes', in J. Brück (ed.) *Bronze Age Landscapes*, Oxford: Oxbow, 139–49.

O'Brien, E. 1999, *Post-Roman Britain to Anglo-Saxon England: Burial Practices Reviewed*. Oxford: British Archaeological Reports, British Series, 289.

Ordnance Survey 1978, *Map of Roman Britain*, 4th edition, Southampton: Ordnance Survey.

Ordnance Survey 2001, *Map of Roman Britain*, 5th edition, Southampton: Ordnance Survey.

Orme, N. 1991, 'From the beginnings to 1050', in N. Orme (ed.) *Unity and Variety: A History of the Church in Devon and Cornwall*, Exeter: University of Exeter Press, Exeter Studies in History No. 29, 1–22.

Orton, H., Sanderson, S., and Widdowson, J. 1978, *The Linguistic Atlas of England*. London: Croom Helm.

Orwin, C. S. and Orwin, C. S. 1938, *The Open Fields*. Oxford: The Clarendon Press.

—— 1954, *The Open Fields*. Second edition. Oxford: The Clarendon Press.

Oswald, A., Dyer, C., and Barber, M. 2001, *The Creation of Monuments: Neolithic Causewayed Enclosures in the British Landscape*. London: English Heritage.

Overton, M. 1996, *Agricultural Revolution in England: The Transformation of the Agrarian Economy 1500–1850*. Cambridge: Cambridge University Press.

—— 2006, 'Farming, fishing and rural settlement', in R. J. P. Kain (ed.) *England's Landscape: The South West*, London: English Heritage, 109–30.

Padel, O. 1999, 'Place-names', in R. Kain and W. Ravenhill (eds.) 1999, 88–94.

—— 2007, 'Place-Names and the Saxon Conquest of Devon and Cornwall', in N. J. Higham (ed.) *Britons in Anglo-Saxon England*. Woodbridge: Boydell, 215–30.

Palmer, K. 1976, *The Folklore of Somerset*. London: B. T. Batsford.

Papworth, M. 1998, 'The medieval manorial buildings of Kingston Lacy: survey and excavation results with an analysis of the medieval account rolls 1295–1462, *Proceedings of the Dorset Natural History and Archaeological Society* 120, 45–62.

Parry, S. 2006, *Raunds Area Survey: An Archaeological Study of the Landscape of Raunds, Northamptonshire 1985–94*. Oxford: Oxbow Books.

Parsons, D. and Styles, T. 1997, *The Vocabulary of English Place-Names (Á–Box)*. Nottingham: Centre for English Place-Names Study.

Passmore, A. J. 2005, 'A Roman Enclosure and probable Roman trackway at Newland Mill, North Tawton', *Proceedings of the Devon Archaeological Society* 63, 33–41.

Pattison, P. 1999, 'Challacomb revisited', in P. Pattison, D. Field, and S. Ainsworth (eds.) *Patterns in the Past: Essays in Landscape Archaeology for Christopher Taylor*, Oxford: Oxbow Books, 61–70.

Peacock, D. P. S. 1969, 'Neolithic pottery production in Cornwall', *Antiquity* 43, 145–9.

—— 1988, 'The gabbroic pottery of Cornwall', *Antiquity* 62, 302–4.

Pearce, S. 2004, *South-Western Britain in the Early Middle Ages*. London: Leicester University Press.

Pearse Chope, R. 1911, 'The Lord Dynham's lands', *Report and Transactions of the Devonshire Association* XLIII, 269–92.

Pearson, S. 1994, *The Medieval Houses of Kent: An Historical Analysis*. London: RCHME/HMSO.

—— 1998, 'Vernacular buildings in the landscape', in P. Everson and T. Williamson (eds.) 1998, 167–82.

Pelling, R. 1999, 'Early Saxon cultivation of Emmer wheat in the Thames valley and its cultural implications', in K. A. Robson Brown (ed.) *Archaeological Sciences 1999: Proceedings of the Archaeological Sciences Conference, University of Bristol, 1999*. Oxford: British Archaeological Reports, International Series, 1111, 103–9.

Penoyre, J. 2005, *Traditional Houses of Somerset*. Tiverton: Halsgrove.

—— and Penoyre, J. 1978, *Houses in the Landscape: A Regional Study of Vernacular Building Styles in England and Wale*. London: Faber and Faber.

—— —— 1999, 'Somerset Dendrochronology Project, Phase 3', *Proceedings of the Somerset Archaeological Natural History Society* 142, 311–15.

Perry, A. 1997, 'South West England and the Channel Islands', in D. Wheeler and J. Mayes (eds.) *Regional Climates in the British Isles*, London: Routledge, 47–66.

Petts, D. 2004, 'Burial in western Britain AD 400–800: late antique or early medieval?', in R. Collins and J. Gerrard (eds.) 2004, 77–87.

Phillips, C. W. 1931, 'Earthworks on Walton Common Down, near Clevedon', *Proceedings of the University of Bristol Spelaeological Society* 4(ii), 34–42.

Phillips, E. N. M. 1966, 'Excavation of a Romano-British site at Lower Well Farm, Soke Gabriel, Devon', *Proceedings of the Devon Archaeological Society* 23, 2–62.

Phythian Adams, C. 1993, 'Introduction: an agenda for English local history', in C. Phythian Adams (ed.) *Societies, Cultures and Kinship*, Leicester: Leicester University Press, 1–23.

—— 1999, 'Environments and identities: landscapes as cultural projection in the English provincial past', in P. Slack (ed.) *Environments and Historical Change: The Linacre Lectures 1998*, Oxford: Oxford University Press, 118–46.

Pine, J. 2001, 'The excavation of a Saxon settlement at Cadley Road, Collingbourne Ducis, Wiltshire', *Wiltshire Archaeological and Natural History Magazine* 94, 88–117.

Pitt, J. 2003, 'Minster churches and minster territories in Wiltshire', *Anglo-Saxon Studies in Archaeology and History* 12, 58–71.

Pollard, S. 1974, 'A late Iron Age settlement and a Romano-British villa at Holcombe, near Uplyme, Devon', *Proceedings of the Devon Archaeological Society* 32, 59–162.

Pollard, S. H. M. 1966, 'Neolithic and Dark Age settlement on High Peak, Sidmouth, Devon', *Proceedings of the Devon Archaeological Society* 23, 35–59.

—— 1967, 'Radiocarbon dating. Neolithic and Dark Age settlement on High Peak, Sidmouth, Devon', *Proceedings of the Devon Archaeological Society* 25, 41.

—— and Russell, P. M. G. 1969, 'Excavation of round barrow 248b, Upton Pyne, Exeter', *Proceedings of the Devon Archaeological Society* 27, 49–78.

—— —— 1976, 'Radiocarbon dating excavation at round barrow 248b, Upton Pyne, Exeter', *Proceedings of the Devon Archaeological Society* 34, 95.

Polwhele, R. 1797, *The History of Devonshire in Three Volumes, Volume 1*, reprinted in 1977, Dorking: Kohler and Coombes.

Ponting, K. G. 1969, *Aubrey's Natural History of Wiltshire; A reprint of The Natural History of Wiltshire by John Aubrey*, Newton Abbot: David and Charles.

Ponsford, M. 2002, 'Excavations at a Saxo-Norman settlement, Bickley, Cleeve, 1982-89', *Proceedings of the Somerset Archaeological and Natural History Society* 146, 46–112.

Poole, C. H. 1878, *The Customs, Superstitions, and Legends of the County of Somerset*. London: Sampson Low, Marston, Searle and Rivington (reprinted in 1970; St Peter Port: The Toucan Press).

Poore, D., Thomason, D., and Brossler, A. 2002, 'Iron Age settlement and Roman activity at Brickley Lane, Devizes, Wiltshire, 1999', *Wiltshire Archaeological and Natural History Magazine* 95, 214–39.

Pounds, N. J. G. 1945, 'Lanhydrock Atlas', *Antiquity* 19, 20–6.

Powell, A. B., Chandler, J., Dodden, D., Mepham, L., Stevens, C., and Knight, S. 2009, 'Late Saxon and medieval occupation near Salisbury Street, Amesbury', *Wiltshire Archaeological and Natural History Magazine* 102, 188–210.

Powell, K, 2009, 'Excavation of a medieval site at West Wick, Weston-super-Mare', *Proceedings of the Somerset Archaeological and Natural History Society* 152, 165–88.

——, Mepham, L. and Stevens, C. J. 2009, 'Investigation of later prehistoric and Romano-British settlement at Huntworth, 2006', *Proceedings of the Somerset Archaeological and natural History Society* 152, 69–81.

Power, D. and Standen, N. 1999, *Frontiers in Question: Eurasian Borderlands 700–1700*. Basingstoke: Macmillan.

Pretty, K. 1989, 'Defining the Magonsæte', in S. Bassett (ed.) 1989a, 171–83.

Price, G. 2000, 'English', in G. Price (ed.) *Languages in Britain and Ireland*, Oxford: Blackwell publishers, 141–58.

Price, R. and Watts, L. 1980, 'Rescue excavations at Combe Hay, Somerset, 1968–1973', *Proceedings of the Somerset Archaeological and Natural History Society* 124, 1–50.

Pryor, F. 2004, *Britain AD*. London: Harper Collins.

Quinn, G. F. 1995, 'A new survey of the prehistoric field system on Kerswell Down and Whilborough Common', *Proceedings of the Devon Archaeological Society* 53, 131–4.

Quinnell, H. 1988, 'The local character of the Devon Bronze Age and its interpretation', *Proceedings of the Devon Archaeological Society* 46, 1–12.

—— 1993, 'A sense of identity: distinctive Cornish stone artefacts in the Roman and post-Roman period', *Cornish Archaeology* 32, 29–46.

—— 1994, 'Becoming marginal? Dartmoor in later prehistory', *Proceedings of the Devon Archaeological Society* 52, 75–83.

—— 2004, *Trethurgy. Excavations at Trethurgy Round, St Austell: Community and Status in Roman and Post-Roman Cornwall*. Truro: Cornwall County Council.

Quinney, A. 1994, 'Medieval and post-medieval vernacular architecture', in B. Vyner (ed.) *Building on the Past: Papers Celebrating 150 years of the Royal Archaeological Institute*, London: Royal Archaeological Institute, 228–43.

Rackham, O. 1980, *Ancient Woodland: Its History, Vegetation and Uses in England*. London: Edward Arnold.

—— 1988, 'Woods, hedges and forests', in M. Aston (ed.) 1988, 12–31.

Rahtz, P. 1970, 'Excavations on Glastonbury Tor', *Archaeological Journal* 127, 1–81.

—— 1977, 'Late Roman cemeteries and beyond', in R. Reece (ed.) *Burial in the Roman World*, London: Council for British Archaeology Research Report 22, 53–64.

—— 1979, *The Saxon and Medieval Palaces at Cheddar*. Oxford: British Archaeological Reports, British Series, 65.

Rahtz, P. and Fowler, P. J. 1972, 'Somerset AD 400–700', in P. J. Fowler (ed.) *Archaeology and the Landscape*. London: John Barber, 187–221.

—— and Hirst, S. 1974, *Beckery Chapel, Glastonbury*. Glastonbury: Glastonbury Antiquarian Society.

———— and Wright, S. M. 2000, *Cannington Cemetery*. Britannia Monograph 17. London: Society for the Promotion of Roman Studies.

—— and Watts, L. 1989, 'Pagans Hill revisited', *Archaeological Journal* 146, 330–71.

——, Woodward, A., Burrow, I., Everton, A., Watts, L., Leach, P., Hirst, S., Fowler, P., and Gardner, K. 1992, *Cadbury Congresbury 1968–73: A late/Post-Roman Hilltop Settlement in Somerset*. Oxford: British Archaeological Reports, British Series, 223.

Rahtz, P. A. and Greenfield, E. 1977, *Excavations at Chew Valley Lake, Somerset*, London: HMSO.

Ratcliffe, J. 1995, 'Duckpool, Morwenstow: a Romano-British and early medieval industrial site and harbour', *Cornish Archaeology* 34, 80–175.

Ravenhill, W. 1992, *Christopher Saxton's 16th Century Maps: The Counties of England and Wales*. Shrewsbury: Chatsworth Library/Airlife Publishing.

Rawlings, M. 1992, 'Romano-British sites observed along the Codford–Ilchester water pipeline', *Somerset Archaeology and Natural History* 136, 29–60.

——and Fitzpatrick, A. 1996, 'Prehistoric sites and Romano-British settlement at Butterfield Down, Amesbury', *Wiltshire Archaeological and Natural History Magazine* 89, 1–43.

Rawson, R. R. 1953, 'The open fields in Flintshire, Devonshire and Cornwall', *The Economic History Review*, New Series, Vol. 6(i), 51–4.

RCHME 1952, *An Inventory of the Historical Monuments in Dorset, Volume 1—West*, London: HMSO.

——1970a, *An Inventory of Historical Monuments in Dorset, Volume Two—South-East*, London: HMSO.

——1970b, *An Inventory of Historical Monuments in Dorset, Volume Three—Central*, London: HMSO.

Reed, S. J. and Bidwell, P. 2007, 'Excavation at Bantham, South Devon and post-Roman trade in south-west England', <http://ads.ahds.ac.uk/catalogue/archive/bantham_ecc_2007/>

——, Juleff, G., and Bayer, O. J. 2006, 'Three late Saxon iron smelting furnaces at Burlescombe, Devon', *Proceedings of the Devon Archaeological Society* 64, 71–122.

——and Manning, P. T. 2000, 'Archaeological recording of a hillslope enclosure at North Hill Cleave, Bittadon, North Devon', *Proceedings of the Devon Archaeological Society* 58, 201–14.

——and Turton, S. D. 2005, 'Romano-British structures at Parsonage Cross near Littlehempston', *Proceedings of the Devon Archaeological Society* 63, 43–53.

Rees, S. 1979, *Agricultural Implements in Prehistoric and Roman Britain*, Oxford: British Archaeological Reports, British Series, 69.

Reynolds, A. 1999, *Later Anglo-Saxon England: Life and Landscape*. Stroud: Tempus.

——2009, *Anglo-Saxon Deviant Burial Customs*. Oxford: Oxford University Press.

——and Langlands, A. 2006, 'Social Identities on the Macro Scale: A Maximum View of Wansdyke', in W. Davies, G. Hassall, and A. Reynolds (eds.) *People and Space in the Early Middle Ages AD300–1300*. Turnhout: Brepols, 13–44.

Rhoades, J. D., Kandiah, A., and Mashali, A. M. 1992, *The Use of Saline Waters for Crop Production*. Rome: Food and Agriculture Organization of the United Nations, Irrigation and Drainage Papers 48.

Richter, M. 1976, *Giraldus Cambrensis: The Growth of the Welsh Nation*. Aberystwyth: National Library of Wales.

Riley, H. 2006, *The Historic Landscape of the Quantock Hills*, London: English Heritage.

——and Wilson-North, R. 2001, *The Field Archaeology of Exmoor*, London: English Heritage.

Riley, M., Harvey, D. C., Brown, T., and Mills, S. 2005, 'Narrating landscape: the potential of oral history for landscape archaeology', *Public Archaeology* 4, 15–26.

Rippon, S. 1991, 'Early planned landscapes in South-East Essex', *Essex Archaeology and History* 22, 46–60.

—— 1996, *The Gwent Levels: The Evolution of a Wetland Landscape*. York: Council for British Archaeology Research Report 105.

—— 1997, *The Severn Estuary: Landscape Evolution and Wetland Reclamation*. London: Leicester University Press.

—— 2000a, *The Transformation of Coastal Wetlands*. London: British Academy.

—— 2000b, 'The Romano-British exploitation of coastal wetlands: survey and excavation on the North Somerset Levels, 1993–7', *Britannia* XXXI, 69–200.

—— 2004, *Historic Landscape Analysis: Deciphering the Palimpsest*, York: Council for British Archaeology.

—— 2006a, *Landscape, Community and Colonisation: the North Somerset Levels During the 1st to 2nd millennia AD*. Council for British Archaeology Research Report 152, York: Council for British Archaeology.

—— 2006b, 'Landscapes of pre-medieval occupation', in R. Kain (ed.), *England's Landscape, Volume 3: The South West*. London: Collins/English Heritage, 41–66.

—— 2007a, 'Focus or frontier? The significance of estuaries in the landscape of southern Britain', *Landscapes* 8(i), 23–38.

—— 2007b, 'Historic Landscape Characterization: its role in contemporary British archaeology and landscape history', *Landscapes* 8(ii), 1–14.

—— 2008a, *Beyond the Medieval Village: The Diversification of Landscape Character in Southern Britain*, Oxford: Oxford University Press.

—— 2008b, 'Coastal trade in Roman Britain: the investigation of Crandon Bridge, Somerset, a Romano-British trans-shipment port beside the Severn Estuary', *Britannia* XXXIX, 85–144.

—— 2009, 'Understanding the medieval landscape', in R. Gilchrist and A. Reynolds (eds.) *Fifty Years of Medieval Archaeology*. Leeds: Society for Medieval Archaeology, 227–54.

—— 2010, 'Landscape change during the "long eighth century" in southern England', in N. J. Higham and M. J. Ryan (eds.) *Landscape Archaeology of Anglo-Saxon England*, Woodbridge: The Boydell Press, 39–64.

—— Fyfe, R. M., and Brown, A. G. 2006, 'Beyond villages and open fields: the origins and development of a historic landscape characterised by dispersed settlement in South West England', *Medieval Archaeology* 50, 31–70.

—— Smart, C. and Wainwright, A. 2006, 'The Living Past: the origins and development of the historic landscape of the Blackdown Hills—Phase 1: archive report', unpublished report for the Blackdown Hills Rural Partnership.

—— Claughton, P., and Smart C. 2009, *Mining in a Medieval Landscape: the Royal Silver Mines of the Tamar Valley*. Exeter: University of Exeter Press.

—— and Turner, R. 1993, 'The Gwent Levels Historic Landscape Study', *Archaeology in the Severn Estuary 1993*, 113–17.

Risdon, T. *c*.1630, *The Chorographical Description or Survey of the County of Devon* (first published in 1811; reprinted Barnstaple: Porcupines, 1970).

Rivet, A. L. F. and Smith, C. 1979, *The Place-Names of Roman Britain*. London: Batsford.
Roberts, B. K. 1987, *The Making of the English Village*. London: Longman.
Roberts, B. and Glasscock, R. E. 1983, *Villages, Fields and Frontiers: Studies in European Rural Settlement in the Medieval and Early Modern Periods*. Oxford: British Archaeological Reports, International Series, 185.
—— and Wrathmell, S. 2000a, *An Atlas of Rural Settlement in England*. London: English Heritage.
—— —— 2000b, 'Peoples of wood and plain: an exploration of national and regional contrasts', in D. Hooke (ed.) *Landscape: The Richest Historical Record*. Birmingham: Society for Landscape Studies, 47–62.
—— —— 2002, *Region and Place*. London: English Heritage.
Robertson, A. S. 2000, *An Inventory of Romano-British Coin Hoards*. London: Royal Numismatic Society Special Publication 20.
Robinson, S. 1992, *Somerset Place Names*. Stanbridge, Wimborne: Dovecote Press.
Roffe, D. 2000, *Domesday: The Inquest and the Book*. Oxford: Oxford University Press.
—— 2007, *Decoding Domesday*. Woodbridge: Boydell.
Roffey, S., Wilkinson, K., and Webster, K. 2004, 'Kingston St Mary, Ivyton Farm', *Somerset Archaeology and Natural History* 148, 107–8.
Rowley, T. (ed.) 1981, *The Origins of Open Field Agriculture*. London, Croom Helm.
Ryder, L. 2006, 'Change and Continuity: A Study in the Historic Landscape of Devon'. Unpublished PhD, University of Exeter.
Sargent, A. 2002, 'The North–South divide revisited: thoughts on the character of Roman Britain', *Britannia* XXXIII, 219–26.
Saunders, A. 2006, *Excavations at Launceston Castle, Cornwall*. Society for Medieval Archaeology monograph 24.
Sawyer, P. H. 1968, *Anglo-Saxon Charters: An Annotated List and Bibliography*, London: Royal Historical Institute.
—— 1978, *From Roman Britain to Norman England*. London: Methuen & Co.
—— 1983, 'The royal Tun in pre-Conquest England', in P. Wormald (ed.) *Ideal and Reality in Frankish and Anglo-Saxon Society*. Oxford: Blackwell, 273–99.
Schürer, K. 2004, 'Surnames and the search for regions', *Local Population Studies* 72, 50–76.
Scott, E. 1993, *A Gazetteer of Roman villas in Britain*. Leicester: University of Leicester.
Seebohm, F. 1890, *The English Village Community*. London: Longmans.
Sharples, N. 1991, *Maiden Castle Excavations and Field Survey 1985-6*. London: English Heritage Archaeological Report 19.
Sheail, J. 1972, 'The distribution of taxable population and wealth in England during the early sixteenth century', *Transactions of the British Institute of Geography* 2, 3–20.
—— 1998, *The Regional Distribution of Wealth in England as Indicated in the 1524/5 Lay Subsidy Volumes 1–2*. London: Lists and Index Society Special Series 28.
Shorter, A. H., Ravenhill, W. L. D., and Gregory, K. J. 1969, *South West England*, London: Thomas Nelson and Sons.

Silvester, R. J. 1978a, 'A hillslope enclosure at Collomoor, Bittadon', *Proceedings of the Devon Archaeological Society* 36, 245–9.

——1978b, 'Cropmark sites at North Tawton and Alverdiscott', *Proceedings of the Devon Archaeological Society* 36, 249–54.

——1979, 'The relationship of first millennium settlement to the upland areas of the south-west', *Proceedings of the Devon Archaeological Society* 37, 176–90.

——1980a, 'The prehistoric open settlement at Dainton, South Devon', *Proceedings of the Devon Archaeological Society* 38, 17–48.

——1980b, 'An enclosure in Staverton Ford Plantation', *Proceedings of the Devon Archaeological Society* 38, 119–21.

——1981, 'An excavation on the post-Roman site at Bantham, South Devon', *Proceedings of the Devon Archaeological Society* 39, 89–118.

——and Balkwill, C. J. 1977, 'Three hillslope enclosures in the Lyd Valley, West Devon', *Proceedings of the Devon Archaeological Society* 35, 81–4.

——and Bidwell, P. T. 1984, 'A Roman site at Woodbury, Axminster', *Proceedings of the Devon Archaeological Society* 42, 33–57.

Simpson, S. J., Griffith, F. M., and Holbrook, N. 1989, 'The prehistoric, Roman and early post-Roman site at Hayes Farm, Clyst Honiton', *Proceedings of the Devon Archaeological Society* 47, 1–27.

Slater, G. 1907, 'The inclosure of common fields considered geographically', *Geographical Journal* 29(i), 35–55.

Slater, T. 1999, 'Medieval town plans', in R. J. P. Kain and W. Ravenhill (eds.) 1999, 408–12.

Smart, C. J. 2008, 'Continuity Over Crisis: The Landscapes of Southern Gloucestershire and South-East Somerset in the Late Roman and Early Medieval Periods', unpublished PhD thesis, University of Exeter.

Smith, A. H. 1970a, *The Place-Name Elements. English Place-Name Society Volume XXVI*. Cambridge: Cambridge University Press.

——1970b, *The Place-Name Elements. English Place-Name Society Volume XXVI*. Cambridge: Cambridge University Press.

Smith, P. 1975, *Houses of the Welsh Countryside*. London: HMSO.

Smith, R. J. C. 1993, *Excavations at County Hall, Dorchester, Dorset, 1988*. Salisbury: Wessex Archaeology Report 4.

——Healy, F., Allen, M. J., Morris, E. L., Barnes, I., and Woodward, P. J. 1997, *Excavations Along the Route of the Dorchester By-Pass, Dorset 1968–8*, Salisbury: Wessex Archaeology Report 11.

Smith, W. 2001, 'The Charred Plant Remains and Charcoal from Sherborne Old Castle, Dorset'. English Heritage Centre for Archaeology Report 70/2001. Portsmouth: English Heritage.

——2008, 'Prehistoric and Roman Charred Plant Remains from the Cotswold Community Project, on the Wiltshire/Gloucestershire Border'. Unpublished report.

Society For Medieval Archaeology 2003, 'Chronological conventions', *Medieval Archaeology* XLVII, 199–200.

Sparey Green, C. 1987, *Excavations at Poundbury Volume 1: the Settlement*. Dorchester: Dorset Natural History and Archaeological Society Monograph 7.

SSAVBRG, 1982, *Long Load and Knowle, Long Sutton: Their Houses, Cottages and Farms, Settlement and People*. Somerton: Somerset and South Avon Vernacular Building Research Group.
—— 1984, *The Vernacular Buildings of West and Middle Chinnock*. Somerton: Somerset and South Avon Vernacular Building Research Group.
—— 1986, *The Vernacular Houses with Farms and Farmsteads of Alford and Lovington*. Somerton: Somerset and South Avon Vernacular Building Research Group.
—— 1988, *The Vernacular Buildings of Batcombe*. Somerton: Somerset and South Avon Vernacular Building Research Group.
—— 1993, *The Houses, Cottages and Farms of Chiselborough*. Somerton: Somerset and South Avon Vernacular Building Research Group.
—— 1994, *Haselbury Plucknett: evolution and change of Land, Society and Buildings*. Somerset: Somerset and South Avon Vernacular Building Research Group.
Stanes, R. G. F. 1964, 'A georgicall account of Devonshire and Cornwalle', *Report and Transactions of the Devonshire Association for the Advancement of Science Literature and Art* XCVI, 269–302.
Stanes, R. 2005. *Old Farming Days, Life on the Land in Devon and Cornwall*, Tiverton: Halsgrove.
—— 2008a, 'The husbandry of Devon and Cornwall', in R. Stanes *et al.* (eds.) 2008, 1–29.
—— 2008b, 'Devon agriculture in the mid-eighteenth century: the evidence of the Milles enquiry', in R. Stanes *et al.* (eds.) 2008, 66–85.
—— Jewell, A., and Bass, R. (eds.) 2008, *The Husbandry of Devon and Cornwall*. Private publication, ISBN 978-09560421-0-1.
Stevens, C. no date, 'Suburban Life in Roman Durnovaria: Additional Specialist report—Environmental Charred Plant Remains'. <http://www.wessexarch.co.uk/files/projects/dorchester_county_hospital/03_Charred_plants.pdf>
Stevenson, J. B. and Dyson Bruce, L. 2002, 'RCAHMS: the Historic Landuse Assessment Project and other Work', in T. C. Smout (ed.) *Understanding the Historical Landscape in its Environmental Setting*. Dalkeith: Scottish Cultural Press, 51–9.
Straker, V. 1997, 'Sourton Down, a study of local vegetation change and human impact on the landscape: pollen analysis of buried soils, sediments and peat', in P. J. Weddell and S. J. Reed, Excavations at Sourton Down Okehampton 1986–91, *Proc. Devon Archaeol. Soc.* 55, 95–128.
—— 2008a, 'Early medieval environmental background', in C. J. Webster (ed.) *The Archaeology of South West England. South West Archaeological Research Framework: Resource Assessment and Research Agenda*. Taunton: Somerset County Council, 163–8.
—— 2008b, 'Post-Conquest medieval environmental background', in C. J. Webster (ed.) *The Archaeology of South West England. South West Archaeological Research Framework: Resource Assessment and Research Agenda*. Taunton: Somerset County Council, 189–94.
—— and Crabtree, K. 1995, 'Palaeoenvironmental studies on Exmoor: past research and future potential', in H. Binding (ed.) *The Changing Face of Exmoor*, Dulverton: Exmoor Books, 43–51.

Straker, V., Brown, A., Fyfe, R. and Jones, J. 2008, 'Romano-British environmental background', in C. J. Webster (ed.) *The Archaeology of South West England. South West Archaeological Research Framework: Resource Assessment and Research Agenda*. Taunton: Somerset County Council, 145-50.

Stuart-Monteath, T. 1938, 'Somerset', in L. Dudley Stamp (ed.) *The Land of Britain: the Report of the Land Utilisation Survey of Britain*, Part 86, London: Geographic Publications, 1-141.

SVBRG, 1996, *The Vernacular Buildings of Shapwick*. Somerset: Somerset and South Avon Vernacular Building Research Group.

—— 2001, *Vernacular Houses and Farms of Butleigh*. Somerset: Somerset Vernacular Building Research Group.

—— 2004, *The Traditional Houses and Farms of Compton Dundon*. Somerset: Somerset Vernacular Building Research Group.

—— 2008a, *Traditional Buildings in the Parish of Combe St Nicholas*. Somerset: Somerset Vernacular Buildings Research Group.

—— 2008b, 'Building recording in 2006', *Proceedings of the Somerset Archaeological and Natural History Society* 151, 189-200.

—— 2010, *Traditional Buildings in the Parish of Stogursey*. Somerset: Somerset Vernacular Buildings Research Group.

Swanton, M. 1996, *The Anglo-Saxon Chronicle*, London: J. M. Dent.

Sykes, N. J. 2007, *The Norman Conquest: A Zooarchaeological Perspective*. Oxford: British Archaeological Reports, International Series 1656.

Sykes, N. 2009, 'Animals, the bones of medieval society', in R. Gilchrist and A. Reynolds (eds.) *Reflections: 50 Years of Medieval Archaeology*, Society for Medieval Archaeology Monograph 30, 346-61.

Tabor, R. 2002, *The South Cadbury Environs Project: Fieldwork Report 2002-03*, Bristol: University of Bristol Centre for the Historic Environment.

—— 2008, *Cadbury Castle: The Hillfort and Landscapes*. Stroud: The History Press.

Tavener, L. E. 1940, 'Dorset', in L. Dudley Stamp (ed.) *The Land of Britain: the Report of the Land Utilisation Survey of Britain*, Part 88, London: Geographic Publications, 242-92.

Taylor, C. C. 2002, 'Nucleated settlement: a view from the frontier', *Landscape History* 24, 53-72.

Taylor, H. M. and Taylor, J. 1965, *Anglo-Saxon Architecture*. Cambridge: Cambridge University Press.

Taylor, J. 2007, *An Atlas of Roman Rural Settlement in England*, York: Council for British Archaeology Research Report 151.

Taylor, R. F. 1967, 'An Anglo-Saxon cemetery at Compton Pauncefoot', *Proceedings of the Somerset Archaeological and Natural History Society* 111, 67-9.

Thews, N. 1994, 'Geology and geoarchaeology in the Yeo Valley at Ilchester', in P. Leach 1994, 157-72.

Thirsk, J. 1964, 'The common fields', *Past and Present* 29, 3-29.

—— 1966, 'The origins of the common fields', *Past and Present* 33, 142-7.

—— 1967, 'The farming regions of England', in J. Thirsk (ed.) *The Agrarian History of England and Wales Volume IV 1500–1640*, Cambridge: Cambridge University Press, 1–112.

—— 1984, 'Introduction', in J. Thirsk (ed.) *The Agrarian History of England and Wales Volume V 1640–1750, I: Regional Farming Systems*, Cambridge: Cambridge University Press, xix–xxxi.

—— 1987, *England's Agricultural Regions and Agrarian History, 1500–1750*. Basingstoke: Macmillan Education.

—— 2000, *The English Rural Landscape*. Oxford: Oxford University Press.

Thomas, C. 1966, 'The character and origins of Roman Dumnonia', in C. Thomas (ed.) *Rural Settlement in Roman Britain*, London: Council for British Archaeology Research Report 7, 74–98.

Thomas, J. 1999, *Understanding the Neolithic*. London: Routledge.

Thorn, F. R. 2008, 'Shapwick, Domesday Book and the "Polden Estate"', *Proceedings of the Somerset Archaeological and Natural History Society* 151, 1–30.

—— 2010, '"That most famous *monasterium* at Bath", its hundred hides and its estates, viewed from South Stroke', *Proceedings of the Somerset Archaeological and Natural History Society* 153, 13–53.

Thorn, F. and Thorn, C. 1980, *Domesday Book: Somerset*. Chichester: Phillimore.

—— —— 1983, *Domesday Book: Dorset*. Chichester: Phillimore.

—— —— 1985, *Domesday Book: Devon*. Chichester: Phillimore.

Thorpe, H. 1964, 'Rural settlement', in J. Wreford Watson and J. B. Sissons (eds.) *The British Isles: A Systematic Geography*, London: Nelson, 358–80.

Thorpe, N. 2002, 'Kingston St Mary, Vollis Hill', *Somerset Archaeology and Natural History* 146, 139.

Tingle, M. 2006, 'Excavations of a possible causewayed enclosure and Roman site at Membury 1986 and 1984–2000', *Proceedings of the Devon Archaeological Society* 64, 1–52.

Tipper, J. 2000, 'Grubenhäuser: Pit Fills and Pitfalls'. Unpublished PhD, Christ's College, Cambridge.

Tipping, R. 2002, 'Climatic variability and "Marginal" Settlement in Upland British Landscapes: A Re-Evaluation', *Landscapes* 3(ii), 10–28.

Todd, M. 1984, 'Excavations at Hembury (Devon), 1980–83: a summary report', *Antiquaries Journal* LXIV(ii), 251–68.

—— 1987, *The South-West to AD 1000*. London: Longmans.

—— 1992, 'The hillfort at Dumpdon', *Proceedings of the Devon Archaeological Society* 50, 47–52.

—— 1998, 'A hillslope enclosure at Rudge, Morchard Bishop', *Proceedings of the Devon Archaeological Society* 56, 133–52.

—— 2002, 'The Roman fort and later Roman site at Burry Barton', *Proceedings of the Devon Archaeological Society* 60, 37–58.

—— 2005, 'Baths or baptistries? Holcombe, Lufton and their analogues', *Oxford Journal of Archaeology* 24(iii), 307–11.

Tongue, R. L. 1965, *Somerset Folklore*. London: The Folklore Society.

Toulmin Smith, L. 1906–10, *The Itinerary in Wales of John Leland in or about the years 1536–1539*. London: George Dent.

Traskey, J. P. 1978, *Milton Abbey: A Dorset Monastery in the Middle Ages*. Tisbury: Compton Press.

Turk, A. 1969, 'Notes on Cornish mammals in prehistoric and historic times 2', *Cornish Archaeology* 8, 100–4.

Turk, F. A. 1984, 'Notae de ossibus in Cornubia inventis: manipulus 2', *Cornish Studies: Journal of the Institute of Cornish Studies* 12, 23–30.

Turner, M. E. (ed.) 1982a, *Home Office Acreage Returns (HO 67): List and Analysis*, London: PRO List and Index Society, Volume 189.

—— 1982b, *Home Office Acreage Returns (HO 67): List and Analysis*, London: PRO List and Index Society, Volume 190.

—— 1982c, 'Agricultural productivity in England in the eighteenth century: evidence from crop yields', *Economic History Review*, 35, pp. 489–510.

—— 1983a, *Home Office Acreage Returns (HO 67): List and Analysis*, London: PRO List and Index Society, Volume 195.

—— 1983b, *Home Office Acreage Returns (HO 67): List and Analysis*, London: PRO List and Index Society, Volume 196.

—— 1984, 'Agricultural productivity in eighteenth century England: further strains of speculation', *Economic History Review*, 37, pp. 252–7.

—— 1986, 'Crop distributions, land productivity and English parliamentary enclosure', *Journal of Economic History*, XLVI, pp. 669–92.

Turner, N. J. 2008, 'Beyond the Leech Hypothesis: An Investigation of Pre-Medieval Field Systems in the Somerset Landscape'. Unpublished MA Dissertation, University of Exeter.

Robinson, S. 1992, *Somerset Place-Names*. Wimborne: Stanbridge.

Turner, S. 2005, *Devon Historic landscape Characterisation*. Exeter: Devon County Council Historic Environment Service <http://www.devon.gov.uk/index/environment/historic_environment/landscapes/landscape-characterisation.htm>

—— 2006a, *Making a Christian Landscape: The Countryside in Early Medieval Cornwall, Devon and Wessex*. Exeter; University of Exeter Press.

—— 2006b, *Medieval Devon and Cornwall: Shaping an Ancient Countryside*. Macclesfield: Windgather Press.

—— 2007, *Ancient Countryside: The Historic Character of Rural Devon*. Exeter: Devon Archaeological Society Occasional paper 20.

—— and Gerrard, J. 2004, 'Imported and local pottery from Mothecombe: some new finds amongst old material in Totnes Museum', *Proceedings of the Devon Archaeological Society* 62, 171–6.

Tyers, P. 1996, *Roman Pottery in Britain*. London: Routledge.

Uglow, J., Brown, A., and Silvester, R. J. 1985, 'The investigation of a cropmark in the Lower Exe Valley', *Proceedings of the Devon Archaeological Society* 43, 115–16.

—— 2000, 'Three Romano-British Sites in the Lower Exe Valley', *Proceedings of the Devon Archaeological Society* 58, 227–47.

Ussher, W. A. E. 1902, *The Geology of the Country around Exeter (Explanation of Sheet 325): with Notes on the Petrology of the Igneous Rocks (Explanation of Sheet 325)*, London: Memoirs of the Geological Survey of England and Wales.

Valentine, J. 2003, 'Manor Farm, Portesham, Dorset: excavation on a multi-period religious and settlement site', *Proceedings of the Dorset Natural History and Archaeological Society* 125, 23–70.

—— and Robinson, S. 2001, 'A medieval site at Gillingham, Dorset: further excavations at Chantry Fields 1999', *Proceedings of the Dorset Natural History and Archaeological Society* 123, 23–51.

Van Der Veen, M. 1989, 'Charred grain assemblages from Roman period corn driers in Britain', *Archaeological Journal* 146, 302–19.

—— 2008, 'Food as embodied material culture: diversity and change in plant consumption in Roman Britain', *Journal of Roman Archaeology* 21, 83–110.

——, Livarda, A., and Hill, A. 2007, 'The archaeobotany of Roman Britain: current state and identifications of research priorities', *Britannia* XXXVIII, 181–210.

—— —— —— 2008, 'New plant foods in Roman Britain—dispersal and social access', *Environmental Archaeology* 13(i), 11–36.

—— and Palmer, C. 1997, 'Environmental factors and the yield potential of ancient wheat crops', *Journal of Archaeological Science* 24, 163–82.

Vancouver, C. 1808, *General View of the Agriculture of the County of Devon*, London: Richard Phillips.

Vinogradoff, P. 1892, *Villeinage in England: Essays in English Mediaeval History*. Oxford: Oxford University Press.

Vinogradoff, P. P. 1905, *The Growth of the Manor*. London: Macmillan.

Wade Martins, S. 2002, *The English Model Farm: Building the Agricultural Ideal, 1700–1914*. Macclesfield: Windgather Press.

—— 2004, *Farmers, Landlords and Landscapes: Rural Britain, 1720–1870*. Macclesfield: Windgather Press.

Wakeham, C. 2003, 'Maristow estate farmhouses 1800–1913: a chronological development', *Report and Transactions of the Devonshire Association for the Advancement of Science* 135, 111–71.

Waton, P. V. 1982, 'Man's impact on the chalklands: some new pollen evidence', in M. Bell and S. Limbrey (eds.) *Archaeological Aspects of Woodland Ecology*, Oxford: British Archaeological Reports, International Series, S.146, 75–91.

Watts, L. and Leach, P. 1996, *Henley Wood, Temples and Cemetery Excavations 1962–69 by the Late Ernest Greenfield and Others*. York: Council for British Archaeology Research Report 99.

Watts, M. and Scaife, R. 2008, 'The archaeology and palaeoenvironment of Baltmoor Wall, Somerset Levels: the Lower Tone Flood Defence Scheme, 1996–2002', *Archaeology in the Severn Estuary* 19, 31–70.

Watts, V. 2004, *The Cambridge Dictionary of English Place-Names*. Cambridge: Cambridge University Press.

Webber, R. 1976, *The Devon and Somerset Blackdowns*. London: Robert Hale & Company.

Webster, C. 2000a, 'South East Quantocks Archaeological Survey', *Proceedings of the Somerset Archaeological and Natural History Society* 144, 225–6.

Webster, C. J. 2000b, 'The Dark Ages', in C. J. Webster (ed.) *Somerset Archaeology: Papers to Mark 150 Years of the Somerset Archaeological and Natural History Society*. Taunton: Somerset County Council, 79–83.

Webster, C. J. 2008, *The Archaeology of South West England: South West Archaeological Research Framework Resource Assessment and Research Agenda*. Taunton: Somerset County Council. <http://www.somerset.gov.uk/somerset/cultureheritage/heritage/swarf/index.cfm>

—— and Brunning, R. 2004, 'A seventh-century AD cemetery at Stoneage Barton Farm, Bishop's Lydeard, Somerset and square-ditched burials in post-Roman Britain', *Archaeological Journal*, 161, 54–81.

Weddell, P. J. 2000, 'The Excavation of a post-Roman cemetery near Kenn, South Devon', *Proceedings of the Devon Archaeological Society* 58, 93–126.

—— and Reed, S. J. 1997, 'Excavations at Sourton Down Okehampton 1986–91' *Proceedings of the Devon Archaeological Society* 55, 95–128.

—— Reed, S. and Simpson, S. J. 1993, 'Excavation of the Exeter–Dorchester Roman road at the river Yarty and the Roman fort ditch and settlement site at Woodbury, Near Axminster', *Proceedings of the Devon Archaeological Society* 51, 33–133.

Wedlake, W. J. 1958, *Excavations at Camerton, Somerset: a record of thirty years' excavation, covering the period from Neolithic to Saxon times, 1925–56*. Bath: Camerton Excavation Club.

Welch, M. 1989, 'The kingdom of the South Saxons: the origins', in S. Bassett (ed.) 1989a, 75–83.

Wessex Archaeology 1998, 'Rowberrow Treatment Works Outfall Drain Shipham, Somerset: Report on the results of the post-construction examination of the route, incorporating a preliminary assessment of pollen recorded in samples recovered during previous archaeological evaluation'. Salisbury: Wessex Archaeology Report 44525.02.

—— 2003, 'Zinch House, Station Road, Stogumber, Somerset: Archaeological Evaluation and Assessment', unpublished report', Wessex Archaeology Report 52568.14, <http://ads.ahds.ac.uk/catalogue/adsdata/oasis_reports/wessexar1/ahds/dissemination/pdf/wessexar1-13102.pdf>

—— 2007, Blacklands, Upper Row Farm, Laverton, Somerset: Assessment and Evaluation Results', unpublished report, Wessex Archaeology Report 62504.01: <http://www.wessexarch.co.uk/reports/62504/blacklands-laverton>.

—— 2008a, 'A detached Roman bath-House at Truckle Hill, North Wraxall, Wiltshire: Assessment Report on an Archaeological Excavation, Recording and Outreach Programme', unpublished report, Wessex Archaeology Report 58521.01: <http://www.wessexarch.co.uk/reports/58521/truckle-hill-north-wraxall>.

—— 2008b, 'Lellizzick, near Padstow, Cornwall: Archaeological Evaluation and Assessment Report', unpublished report, Wessex Archaeology Report 653112.01: <http://www.wessexarch.co.uk/reports/65312/lellizzick-padstow>

Whimster, R. 1981, *Burial practices in Iron Age Britain: A Discussion and Gazetteer of the Evidence c. 700 B.C.-A.D. 43*, Oxford: British Archaeological Reports, British Series, 90.

Whistler, C. W. 1908, 'Local traditions of the Quantocks', *Folklore* 19(i), 31–51.

White, R. 2007, *Britannia Prima. Britain's Last Roman Province*. Stroud: Tempus.

White, W. 1850, *History, Gazetteer and Directory of Devonshire* (reprinted Newton Abbot: David and Charles, 1970).

Whitelock, D. 1955, *English Historical Documents c.500–1042*. London: Eyre and Spottiswode.

Whitlock, R. 1977, *The Folklore of Devon*. London: B. T. Batsford.

Whitton, C. J. M. and Reed, S. J. 2002, 'Archaeological Recording at "The Laurels", 60B St Mary's Road, Meare, Somerset', unpublished report: Exeter Archaeology Report 02.52.

Wickham, C. 2005, *Framing the Early Middle Ages*, Oxford: Oxford University Press.

Wieken, J. 2004, *Iron Working in the Blackdown Hills. A report in Two Slag Mounds (Features 3 and 4) on Bywood Farm*. Unpublished report prepared for the Community Landscapes Project. Copy in Devon HER.

Wilkes, E. 2004, 'Survey and excavation at Mount Folly, Bigbury-on-Sea', *Devon Archaeological Society Newsletter* 87, 5.

—— 2006, 'Mount Folly, Bigbury-on-Sea, 2003–6', *Devon Archaeological Society Newsletter* 93, 14–15.

Wilkin, W. H. 1928, 'Notes on Membury Part III', *Transactions of the Devonshire Association* LX, 161–81.

Wilkinson, K., King, T., Marter, P., Stoodley, N., Turner, N. and Webster, C. 2003, 'Southern Quantocks Archaeological Survey', *Somerset Archaeology and Natural History* 147, 191–2.

Williams, A. and Martin, G. H. 1992, *Domesday Book: A Complete Translation*. London: Alecto Historical Editions.

Williams, M. 1969, 'The 1801 Crop Returns for Somerset', *Proceedings of the Somerset Archaeological and Natural History Society* 113, 69–85.

Williams, W. P. and Jones, W. A. 1872, 'A glossary of provincial words and phrases in use in Somersetshire', *Proceedings of the Somerset Archaeological Society* XVIII, Appendix.

Williamson, T. 1986, 'Parish boundaries and early fields; continuity and discontinuity', *Journal of Historical Geography* 12(iii), 241–8.

—— 1987, 'Early co-axial field systems on the East Anglian boulder clays', *Proceedings of the Prehistoric* 53, 419–31.

—— 1993, *The Origins of Norfolk*. Manchester: Manchester University Press.

—— 1998, 'The "Scole-Dickleborough field system" revisited', *Landscape History* 20, 19–28.

—— 2000, *The Origins of Hertfordshire*. Manchester: Manchester University Press.

—— 2002, *The Transformation of Rural England*. Exeter: University of Exeter Press.

—— 2003, *Shaping Medieval Landscapes*. Macclesfield: Windgather Press.

—— 2006a, *England's Landscape: East Anglia*. London: Harper Collins/English Heritage.

—— 2006b, 'Mapping field patterns: a case-study from eastern England', *Landscapes* 7(i), 55–67.

—— 2007, 'The distribution of medieval "woodland" and "champion" landscapes in medieval England', in M. Gardiner and S. Rippon (eds.) *Medieval Landscapes*, Macclesfield: Windgather Press, 89–104.

—— 2008, *Sutton Hoo and its Landscape: The Context of Monuments*. Oxford: Windgather Press.

Williamson, T. 2010, 'The environmental contexts of Anglo-Saxon settlement', in N. J. Higham and M. J. Ryan (eds) *Landscape Archaeology of Anglo-Saxon England*, Woodbridge: The Boydell Press, 133–56.

Willis, J. and Rogers, E. H. 1951, 'Dainton Earthworks', *Proceedings Devon Archaeological Exploration Society* IV, 79–101.

Wilmot, T. and Shipp, D. 2006, 'A Romano-British roadside settlement of Whitewalls, Easton Grey, Wiltshire: recent fieldwork', *Wiltshire Archaeological and Natural History Society Magazine* 99, 165–89.

Winchester, A. J. L. 2008, 'Early estate structures in Cumbria and Lancashire, *Medieval Settlement Research* (Journal and Annual Report of the Medieval Settlement Research Group) 23, 14–21.

Winterbottom, M. 1978, *Gildas: The Ruin of Britain and Other Works*. Chichester: Phillimore.

Wood, P. D. 1963, 'Open field strips, Forrabury Common, Boscastle', *Cornish Archaeology* 2, 29–33.

Woods, H. 1994, 'Excavations at Glastonbury Anney 1987–1993', *Somerset Archaeology and Natural History* 138, 7–74.

Woodward, P. J. 1983, 'Wimborne Monster, Dorset—excavations in the town centre 1975–80', *Proceedings of the Dorset Natural History and Archaeological Society* 105, 57–74.

—— 1987, *Romano-British Industries in Purbeck: Excavations at Norden, and Excavations at Ower and Rope Lake Hole*. Dorset Natural History and Archaeological Society Monograph Series No. 6. Dorchester: Dorset Natural History and Archaeology Society.

—— 1991, *The South Dorset Ridgeway: Survey and Excavations 1977–84*, Dorchester: Dorset Natural History and Archaeological Society Monograph 8.

——, Davies, S. M. and Graham, A. H. 1993, *Excavations at Greyhound Yard, Dorchester 1981–4*. Dorchester: Dorset Natural History and Archaeological Society Monograph Series 12.

Woolgar, C. M., Serjeantson, D. and Waldron, T. 2006a, *Food in Medieval England*. Oxford: Oxford University Press.

—— —— —— 2006b, 'Conclusion', in Woolgar *et al.* (eds) 2006a, 267–80.

Worrell, S. 2004, 'Finds reported under the portable Antiquities Scheme', *Britannia* XXXV, 317–34.

—— 2005, 'Finds reported under the Portable Antiquities Scheme', *Britannia* XXXVI, 447–72.

—— 2006, 'Finds reported under the Portable Antiquities Scheme', *Britannia* XXXVII, 429–66.

—— 2007, 'Finds reported under the Portable Antiquities Scheme', *Britannia* XXXVIII, 303–44.

—— 2008, 'Finds reported under the Portable Antiquities Scheme', *Britannia* XXXIX, 337–67.

—— 2009, 'Finds reported under the Portable Antiquities Scheme', *Britannia* XL, 281–312.

Wright, T. 1968, *The Historical Works of Giraldus Cambrensis: Containing the Topography of Ireland, and the History of the Conquest of Ireland, and the Itinerary through Wales, and the Description of Wales*. New York: AMS Press.

Yorke, B. 1989, 'The Jutes of Hampshire and Wight and the origins of Wessex', in S. Bassett (ed.) 1989a, 84–96.

—— 1995, *Wessex in the Early Middle Ages*. London: Leicester University Press.

Young, A. and Richardson, K. M. 1954, 'Report on the excavations at Blackbury Castle', *Proceedings of the Devon Archaeological Exploration Society* V(ii), 43–67.

Young, D. 2007, 'Iron Age, medieval and recent activity at Whitegate Farm, Bleadon, North Somerset', *Somerset Archaeology and Natural History* 151, 31–81.

—— 2009, 'Excavation of an early medieval site at Brent Knoll, Somerset', *Somerset Archaeology and Natural History* 152, 105–37.

Young, R. and Hancocks, A. 2006, 'Early Bronze Age ring ditches and Romano-British agriculture at Showell Farm, Chippenham. Excavations in 1999', *Wiltshire Archaeological and Natural History Society Magazine* 99, 10–50.

—— and Simmonds, T. 1995, 'Marginality and the nature of later prehistoric upland settlement in the north of England', *Landscape History* 17, 5–16.

Youngs, F. A. 1980, *Guide to the Administrative Units of England. Volume 1: Southern England*. London: Royal Historical Society.

—— 1991, *Guide to the Administrative Units of England. Volume 2: Northern England*. London: Royal Historical Society.

Zest, W. van 1974, 'Palaeobotanical studies of settlement sites in the coastal area of the Netherlands', *Palaeohistoria* 16, 223–371.

——, Hoorn, T. C. van, Bottema, S., and Woldring, H. 1976, 'An agricultural experiment in the unprotected marsh', *Palaeohistoria* 18, 111–53.

Index

Places without a county lie within the study area in Devon, Dorset and Somerset (*see* Figure 1.3). Numbers in italic refer to illustrations. Numbers in bold refer to plates.

Aberffraw (Anglesey) 152, 188
Abdick Hundred *8.2*, *8.4*, 179–81
Agricultural Land Classification *2.9*, 29–34, 69
'Agricultural Revolution' 108–9
Algar 329, *15.5*
animal husbandry 205–85
antiquarians 35–7
arable farming 205–85, 322–42
Arden (Warwickshire) 1, 344
Ashill *1.3*, *8.4*, 134, 138, 180–1
Aubrey, John 3, 343
Awliscombe *1.3*, 81, 134, 138, 177
Axminster (Devon) 154, 174–7, 189, 215–16, 295
Axmouth (Devon) *8.2*, *9.2*, 174–5, 177, 189, 214, 215, 216

Banburyshire (Oxfordshire) 190
Barrington *1.3*, *2.4*, 78, 99, 102, 105, 134, 138, *8.4*, 179, 181–2, 255, 339
Bartholomeus Anglicus 113
barton farms *4.8*, 72, 76–8, *4.13*, 80, 81, 85, 93, *5.3*, 103, 294, 302n, 317
Beer Crocombe *1.3*, 180–1, *15.5*
Bickenhall *1.3*, *8.4*, 180–2
Bickleigh *1.3*, 95, 168, 169, 196, *10.2*
Billingsley, John 41–2
Blackborough *1.3*, 72, 171, 196, *10.2*, 134
Board of Agriculture 10, 41–2, *3.2*
Bradninch *1.3*, 47, *4.6*, 63, 76, 78–80, 95, 96, *5.4*, 134, 169–71, *10.2*, 196–7
Bradon (in Puckington) 180–1
Branscombe *8.1*, 154–5, *9.2*, 176, 195
Braunton (Devon) 143, 328–9
Brent Knoll (Somerset) 62, 247n
Broadclyst *1.3*, 72, 76, 101, 105, 134, 146, 168–73, 197, *10.2*, 195, 232
Broadhembury *1.3*, *4.4*, 63, *4.8*, 98–9, 137, 146, 149, 171, *10.2*, 220
Broadway *1.3*, 105, 139, 180–1
Broadwindsor *1.3*, 12, 129, 159, 178–9, 231, 233–8, 299
Bronze Age 312–14, 320
Buckerell *1.3*, 78, 134, 138, 177
Buckland St Mary *1.3*, 43, 105, 134, 180–1

Bunter Beds: *see* Triassic Sandstone
Burghshire (Yorkshire) *10.1*, 188, 190
Burlescombe *1.3*, 63, 66, 76, 81, 134, 135, 138, 146, 148, 168, *10.2*, 232, **Pl 5**
Burstock *1.3*, *8.4*, 178–9
Butterleigh *1.3*, 95, 101, 105, 169, 173, 174, *10.2*, 196

Cadbury (Somerset) 169, *10.2*, 196
Cadbury Congresbury (Somerset) 152, 246, 302, 309n
Cadeleigh (Devon) 169, *10.2*, 196
Camden, William 10, 37
Cannington (Somerset) 67, *9.1*, 189, 302, *14.5*
Caplan *1.3*
Chaffcombe *1.3*
Challacomb (Dartmoor, Devon) 131n
Chard *1.3*, 39, 56, 63, 76, 130, 131–2, *7.1*, 105, 136, 137, 148, 157, *8.4*, *9.2*, 179, 182, 195, 213, 215, 216, 306, 318, 339, **Pl 3**
Chardstock *1.3*, 74n, 105, 130, 132, 136, 137, 157, *8.4*, 179–80, 195, 318
charter boundary clauses 142, 157, 163, 171, 171n, 195, 207
Cheddington (Dorset) 178–9
Cheriton (in Payhembury) 72, 136, 197
Cheriton Fitzpaine (Devon) *2.5*, 49
Chieflowman (in Uplowman) 167–8
Chillington *1.3*, 74, 78, 157, *8.4*, 179
church architecture 87
church location 67–9, 317
church towns 63, 96, 132, 318
Churchstanton *1.3*, 43, 102, 105, 134, 135, 136, 137, 177, 219n, **Pl 8**
civitates 12, 14, 15, *2.1*, *2.2*, 18, 185–6, 191, 264, 285, 287–307
Clayhidon *1.1*, *1.3*. *4.5*, 63, 66, *4.8*, 72, 74n, *6.4–6.8*, 102, 105, 127, 129–30, 129n, 134–37, 156, 177, **Pl 7**
climate 10, 27–9, 32, 40–2, 316
Clyst Honiton (Devon) 129, 300n, 305
Clyst Hydon *1.3*, 96, *5.5*, 98, 101, 105, 108, 134, 173, *10.2*, 195, 197
Clyst St Lawrence *1.3*, 63, *5.6*, 98, 101, 105, 134, 162, 173, 195, 197

394 Index

cob construction *2.5*, 23, 48–9, 50, *5.1*, 86, 93, 95, 96, 98–9, 109, 110
Colepresse, Samuel 38
Colyton (Devon) *8.2*, *9.2*, 174–7, 189, 214–16
Combe (in Uplowman) 167
Combe Raleigh *1.3*, 102, 105, 134, 174, 177, 219n
Combe St Nicholas *1.3*, 43, 56, 63, 89, 102, 105, 130, 134, 136, 137, 148, 179, 181, 189, 203, 318, 339, **Pl 9**
common field: *see* open field
Corfe *1.3*, 323, 333
Cornwall 1, 8, *1.3*, 19, 38, 54, 63, 67, 69, 78, 87, 115, 118, 127, 138, 142, 145, 163, 185, 206–7, *11.2*, *11.3*, 210, 245, 246–7, 250, 252, 253–9, 264–5, 269–73, 280, 282, *14.1*, 289–92, 306, 310–13, 341
Cotleigh *1.3*, 74, 74n, 102, 105, 134, 174
Crewkerne *1.3*, 129, 129n, 138, *8.2*, *8.3*, *8.4*, *8.5*, *9.2*, 177–82, 204, 214, 216, 322, 339
Cricket Malherbe *1.3*, 179
Cricket St Thomas *1.3*, 154, *8.4*, 179, 200–1
Cromwell, Oliver 343
Cruwys Morchard (Devon) *3.5*, 129, 139, *15.5*, 310
Cudworth *1.3*, *8.3*, *8.4*
Cullompton *1.3*, 39, 40, 47, 63, 70, 72, 95, 129n, 134, 153, 168–73, *10.2*, 189, 197, 219
Culm (coal) 20
Culm Pyne (in Clayhidon) 156, **Pl 7**, 177
Culmstock *1.3*, 70, 78, 138, *9.2*, 171–2, *10.2*, 195
Curland *1.3*
Curry Mallet *1.3*, 140, 142, 180–2
Curry Rivel *1.3*, 24, 27, *8.4*, 180–1, 214–16

Defoe, Daniel 10, 39–40
Devil's Lapfull 43
dialects 3, 69–70
Illington (in Ilminster) 74
Dinnington *1.3*, 78, *14.3*, 298, 303
Donyatt *1.3*, 105, *8.4*, 180–1, 201
Dowlish Wake *1.3*
Drayton (Somerset) 181, *11.5*
Drayton (in South Petherton) *4.2*, *4.8*, 79
Dunkeswell *1.3*, 33, 102, 105, 106, 118, 121, 134, 177, **Pl 4**
Durotriges 12, 14, *2.1*, 185, 186, 286–301, *14.6*, 307–10

Earnshill (in Curry Rivel) *1.3*, *8.4*, 102, 105, 180–1, 326
East Anglia 2, *2.2*, 18, 55, 113, 190, 322, 323, 331
environmental determinism 3, 331

Essex *2.2*, 18, 152, *10.1*, 194
Exeter (Devon) 1, 37, 41, 190, *10.2*, 201, *10.3*, 247, 249, 254n, 268, 287, *14.2*, 292, *14.3*

Fairy Fair 43
Feldon (Warwickshire) 1, 344
Feniton *1.3*, 72, *4.11*, 171, 174, *10.2*, 193, 195, 197
field-names 80–5, 89–4, 103, 140, 149, 314, 317, 342
Fiennes, Celia 10, 38–9
folklore 7, 10, 42–4, 316–17
folkland/folkright 190
Fosse Way 191, *10.2*, *14.4*, 295, 297–9

Garlandhayes (in Clayhidon) *6.5*, *6.7*, *6.8*, 137
geological sequence 20–3
Gildas 289, 305
Giraldus Cambrensis 36
Glastonbury 68, 157, 172–3, 201n, 234, 246, 247n, 254n, 279, 283, 297, 302, *14.5*, 306, 307, 328
Graddage Farm (in Clayhidon) *6.4*, 127
'Great Rebuilding' 106–8

Halberton *1.3*, 48, 63, 72, *4.11*, 81, *8.2*, 167–8, *10.2*, 203, 214–16
Hallamshire (Yorkshire) *10.1*, 190
Ham Stone 22, *2.4*, 24, 87, 99, *5.9*, 109
Hatch Beauchamp *1.3*, 27, *8.4*, 180–1, 333
hedgebanks 11, 139–40, 145–6, *9.3*, 171, 300, **Pl 10**
Hemyock *1.3*, 70, 121, 134, 137, *8.2*, *8.3*, *9.2*, 174–7, 189, 195, 201, 214–16
Higham Ferrers (Northants) 7
hillforts 7, 12, 52, 246, 302, 305, 307–10, 316, 320
Hinton St George *1.3*, *5.9*, 178–9
hipped roofs *2.5*, 110
Historic Landscape Characterisation 54–6, 85, 88, 111, 115–19, 145, 148, 316, 318, **Pl 1**, **Pl 2**, **Pl 6**
Hockworthy *1.3*, 74, 168, *10.2*
Holcombe Rogus *1.3*, 72, 78, 134, 168, *10.2*
Honiton (Devon) *2.6*, 36, 39, 129, 154, 174, 176, 191, 201, 270, 294–5, 300
Husmerae (Worcestershire) *10.1*, 190
hundreds 151, 153–4, 155–6, 160–2, 165–84, 198
Huntsham *1.3*, 48, 168, 173, *10.2*, 195
Huxham *1.3*, 78, 93, 101, 105, 134, 173, *10.2*, 195, 197

Ilminster *1.3*, 74, 76, 105, *8.3*, 180–1, 333
Ine, King (law code) 306n, 340
Ilton *1.3*, *4.11*, 74, 76, 105, 180–1
Isle Abbots *1.3*, 72, 102, 105, 180–1
Isle Brewers *1.3*, 76, 102, 105, 180–1

Kentisbeare *1.3*, 98, 102, 105, 121, 128, 134, 137, 148, 171, *10.2*, 196
Keuper Marls: *see* Mercian Mudstone Group
Kidwell (in Uplowman) 167
Kingsbury Episcopi *1.3*, 64, 76, 102, 105, *8.3*, *8.4*, 179, 198, 326
Kingstone *1.3*, *5.8*, 138, 339
Knowle St Giles *1.3*, *8.4*

Land Use Capability 19, *2.9*, 29–34
lateral chimneystacks *2.5*, *5.2*, 92–3, *5.7*, 103–6, 110, 140, *5.10*, 317, 343
Leicester School 2
Leland, John 10, 35–7, 113
Little Lopen (in South Petherton) *4.8*
Lopen *1.3*, *4.1*, *6.3*, 78, 120, 130, 134, 138, 140, *8.4*, 178, 179, 297, *14.3*, *14.4*, 318
Luppitt *1.3*, 102, 105, 129–30, 134, 137, 174
Lyme Regis (Dorset) 175n, 177, 189

Maiden Down 39
Malling (Kent) *10.1*
Malpas (Cheshire) *10.1*
Martock (Somerset) *8.2*, 189, 191, 297n
Mediterranean imports 62, 201, 303–5
Membury *1.3*, 81, 102, 105, 130, 135, 137, 154, 174, 201, 256, 264–6, 279, *14.3*, 294, 295n, 296
Mercian Mudstone Group 21, *2.3*, 27, 34
Merriott *1.3*, 138, *8.4*, 178–9, 339
Milles, Jeremiah 115
Milton Abbas (Dorset) 176
Misterton *1.3*, *4.3*, 63, 80, 135–6, 138, 140, 142, *8.4*, *8.5*, 178–9
Micheldever (Hampshire) *10.1*
'model farms' 93, *5.3*, 108–9
Monmouth Rebellion 43
Molland Common (Exmoor) *3.3*, *3.4*, 48, 234
Monkton *1.3*, 102, 105, 135, 174–5
Moore, Thomas 40
Mosterton *1.3*, *8.4*, *8.5*, 178–9
Muchelney Abbey 180
Murley (in Uplowman) 167

Neolithic 234–8, 311–12
Neroche Forest 139, 156, *8.4*, 181–2
Nether Exe (in Thorverton) *1.3*, 78, 93, 101, 105, 169, 173, *10.2*, 196, 201
New Red sandstone 21, *2.3*, 34
Nomansland *3.5*, 49

Norfolk *2.2*, 18, 194
North Curry (Somerset) *8.2*, *9.1*, 180–2, 189
North Perrot (Somerset) 178–9, *15.5*
North Somerset Levels 8, 102, 207, 230, 231, *11.6*, 248, 257, 266–7, 295n, 297, 328
North Tawton (Devon) 129, 230, 296n

Offa's Dyke 5
open field 12, *2.1*, 111–49, 318–20, 322–42, **Pl 1, Pl 2**
Orchard Portman *1.3*, 323
Otterford *1.3*, 105, 121
Ottery St Mary (Devon) *8.2*, 171, 174, 176, 189, *10.2*

Payhembury *1.3*, 81, 98, 99, 102, 105, 135, 138, 149, 171, *10.2*, 197
Penselwood (Somerset) 289, 290, 305, 309n
place-names 47–8, 69–80, 85, 103, 129, 130, 132, 146, 153–63, 172, 173, 195, 305, 317, 321, 343
Polwhele, Richard 40, 63
Plymtree *1.3*, 98, 98n, 102, 105, 135, 138, 148, 171, *10.2*, 196
Pitminster *1.3*, 43, 105, 135, *8.3*, 189, 323
Polden Hills (Somerset) 157, 297
pollen sequences *11.6*, 230–40, 311
Poltimore *1.3*, 78, 93, 101, 105, 135, 173, *10.2*, 195, 197, 203
Portable Antiquities Scheme 9, 290, 292
Puckington *1.3*, 74, 78, 99, 102, 105, 108, 157, 180–1

Raddon Court (Thorverton) *3.7*
Raddon Hills (Devon) cover *3.6*, *3.7*, 47, 49, 169, *9.3*, 309n, 311
Raunds (Northants) 7, 8
Reading (Berkshire) *10.1*, 190
regiones 151–2, 185–204
Rewe *1.3*, *3.8*, 47, 76, 78, 93–5, 101, 105, 135, *5.3*, 169, 173, 196, *10.2*, 297n
Risdon, Tristram 38
Rodings (Essex) *10.1*, 152, 194
Rudge (in Morchard Bishop, Devon) 129, 294, 310
Royal Society 38

St Boniface 306
Saint White Down (Cricket St Thomas) 200–2, *10.3*
Sampford Arundell *1.3*, 72
Sampford Peverell *1.3*, 48, 63, 72, 78, 167–8, *10.2*, *10.2*
Saxon burials 7, 13, *2.2*, 19, 67, 290, 303, *14.5*, 305
Seaborough *1.3*, *8.4*, 178–9

seasonality 26–7, 34, *4.1*, 74, 219–20
Seavington St Mary *1.3*, 74, 78, 157, *8.4*, 179
Seavington St Michael *1.3*, 74, 78, 157, *8.3*, *8.4*
Sedgemoor *2.6*, 25, 156, *8.4*, 177, 181, 182, 193
Shapwick (Somerset) 7, 8, 102, 201n, 247n, 254n, 256, 261, 266n, 270n, 279, 283, 295n, 297, 297n
Sheldon *1.3*, 74n, 102, 105, 135, 136, 137, 142, 171, *10.2*, 196, 220, 214, 215, 230, 239, **Pl 6**
Shepton Beauchamp *1.3*, 80, 102, 105, 135, 138, 179, *15.5*, 339
shires (early history of) 18, 186, 190, 198
Silverton *1.3*, 47, 49, 63, 72, *4.11*, 95, 96, 105, 135, 168–73, 189, *10.2*, 196–7, 214, 216
South Cadbury (Somerset) 152, 297n, 299, 302, 303, *14.5*, 309n
South Perrot (Dorset) 178–9
South Petherton *1.3*, 33, 63, 66, *4.2*, 64, *4.8*, *4.11*, 78–80, 128, 154, 157, *8.2*, *8.3*, *8.4*, *9.2*, 177–82, 189, 195, 204, 214–16, 255, 322
Staple Fitzpaine *1.3*, *8.4*, 182
Stockland *1.3*, 70, 72, 105, 146, *9.2*, 174–7, 189, 195, 214–16, *11.6*, 233, 235, 300
Stockleigh Pomeroy *3.7*, 49
Stocklinch *1.3*, 99, 102, 105, 138, 146, 195, 203
Stoke Canon *1.3*, 47, 78, 93, 101, 105, 135, 169, 195, 196, *10.2*
Stoodleigh (Devon) 167, *10.2*
Stoppingas (Warwickshire) *10.1*, 194
Strete Raleigh (in Whimple) 173, *10.2*
Suffolk 2, *2.2*, 18, 88, 344
Swaledale (Yorkshire) 8
Swell (Somerset) 180–1
Swete, John 69

Talaton *1.3*, *4.11*, 98, 102, 105, 135, 171, 173, 197, *10.2*
Templeton (Devon) 167, *10.2*, 234
Thorncombe *1.3*, *8.4*, 178–80
Thorverton *1.3*, 19n, 47, 169, 173, 196, *10.2*, *14.3*, 296, 297n
Thurlbear *1.3*, 182
tithe survey 8, 19n, *4.4*, 74, 76, 80, 118, *6.5*, 127, 130, 131–8, 146, 156, 160, 181, 189, 199, 221, 318, 323, 340

Tiverton *1.3*, 29, 40, 48, 63, 70, 72, *4.11*, 74, *5.7*, *8.2*, *8.3*, 166–7, *10.2*, 201, 318
transhumance 219–20
Triassic Sandstone *2.3*, 98

Uffculme *1.3*, 72, 167, 171–2, 189, *10.2*, 195, 197
Up Exe (in Rewe) 169, 173, 196
Uplowman *1.3*, 48, 167–8, *10.2*
Upottery *1.3*, 76, *7.4–7.5*, 102, 105, 135, 145, 174, 219n

Vancouver, Charles   10, 41–2, *3.2*, 219n
vernacular buildings *4.8*, 87–110, 317
Vikings 186, 199, 341
villae regiae 152–3, 183, 194, 198–200
'village moment' 5, 7, 323–38
villas 7, 15, *2.1*, 19, 289–97, 316

Wambrook *1.3*, 81, 105, 135, *8.4*, 137, 180
Washfield (Devon) 167, *10.2*, 214–16
Wayford *1.3*, *8.4*, 178–9,
Wellington *1.1*, *1.3*, 39, 43n, 63, *4.11*, *8.3*, 189
West Dowlish *1.3*, 179
West Hatch *1.3*, 24, 182
Wharram Percy (Yorkshire) 7, 8
White Down 40
Whimple *1.3*, 33, 98, 102, 105, 135, 171, 173–4, 193, 197, *10.2*, 195
White Lackington *1.3*, 74, 78, 105, 157, 180–1
Whitestaunton *1.3*, 135–7, 181, *14.3*, 295n
Whittlewood (Bucks/Northants) 7, 8
Willand *1.3*, 168, *10.2*
William of Worcester 36
Willtown (Clayhidon) *6.5*, *6.7*, *6.8*, 136
Winchcombeshire (Gloucestershire) 186, *10.1*, 190
Winsham *1.3*, 8.4, 179
Woodbury (in Axminster, Devon) 295, 299
Wootton Wawen (Warwickshire) 156, 199

Yarcombe *1.3*, 105, 135, 174, 203, **Pl 4**
Yarnton (Oxfordshire) 7, 261